Excel® 2013
Power Programming
with VBA

Excel® 2013
Power Programming
with VBA

by John Walkenbach

WILEY

Excel® 2013 Power Programming with VBA

Published by
John Wiley & Sons, Inc.
111 River Street
Hoboken, NJ 07030-5774

www.wiley.com

For general information on our other products and services, please contact our Customer Care Department within the U.S. at 877-762-2974, outside the U.S. at 317-572-3993, or fax 317-572-4002.

For technical support, please visit www.wiley.com/techsupport.

Wiley also publishes its books in a variety of electronic formats. Some content that appears in print may not be available in electronic books.

Library of Congress Control Number: 2013932111

ISBN 978-1-118-49039-6 (pbk); ISBN 978-1-118-49040-2 (ebk); ISBN 978-1-118-49180-5 (ebk); ISBN 978-1-118-49182-9 (ebk)

Manufactured in the United States of America

10 9 8 7 6

About the Author

John Walkenbach is the author of more than 50 spreadsheet books and lives in southern Arizona. Visit his website: `http://spreadsheetpage.com`.

Publisher's Acknowledgments

We're proud of this book; please send us your comments at http://dummies.custhelp.com. For other comments, please contact our Customer Care Department within the U.S. at 877-762-2974, outside the U.S. at 317-572-3993, or fax 317-572-4002.

Some of the people who helped bring this book to market include the following:

Acquisitions and Editorial

Project Editor: Susan Pink

Acquisitions Editor: Katie Mohr

Technical Editor: Niek Otten

Editorial Manager: Jodi Jensen

Editorial Assistant: Annie Sullivan

Sr. Editorial Assistant: Cherie Case

Composition Services

Project Coordinator: Kristie Rees

Layout and Graphics: Jennifer Henry, Andrea Hornberger, Jennifer Mayberry

Proofreader: Christine Sabooni

Indexer: BIM Indexing & Proofreading Services

Publishing and Editorial for Technology Dummies

Richard Swadley, Vice President and Executive Group Publisher

Andy Cummings, Vice President and Publisher

Mary Bednarek, Executive Acquisitions Director

Mary C. Corder, Editorial Director

Publishing for Consumer Dummies

Diane Graves Steele, Vice President and Publisher

Composition Services

Debbie Stailey, Director of Composition Services

⏵ Contents at a Glance

Part VI: Other Topics

Part VII: Appendixes

▶ Table of Contents

Part I: Some Essential Background

Part II: Understanding Visual Basic for Applications

Chapter 6: VBA Programming Fundamentals 177

Chapter 7: Working with VBA Sub Procedures 227

Part III: Working with UserForms

Part IV: Advanced Programming Techniques

Part V: Developing Applications

Part VI: Other Topics

Part VII: Appendixes

INTRODUCTION

Welcome to *Excel 2013 Power Programming with VBA*. If your job involves developing Excel workbooks that others will use — or if you simply want to get the most out of Excel — you've picked up the right book.

Topics Covered

This book focuses on Visual Basic for Applications (VBA), the programming language built into Excel (and other applications that make up Microsoft Office). More specifically, it will show you how to write programs that automate various tasks in Excel. This book covers everything from recording simple macros through creating sophisticated user-oriented applications and utilities.

This book does *not* cover Microsoft Visual Studio Tools for Office (VSTO), a technology that uses Visual Basic .NET and Microsoft Visual C#. VSTO can also be used to control Excel and other Microsoft Office applications.

As you may know, Excel 2013 is available for other platforms. For example, you can use Microsoft's Excel Web App in your browser, and even run Excel on ARM-based Windows RT devices. These versions do not support VBA. In other words, this book is for the desktop version of Excel 2013 for Windows.

What You Need to Know

This is not a book for beginning Excel users. If you have no experience with Excel, a better choice might be my *Excel 2013 Bible,* which provides comprehensive coverage of all the features of Excel and is meant for users of all levels.

To get the most out of this book, you should be a relatively experienced Excel user. I assume that you know how to

➤ Create workbooks, insert sheets, save files, and so on

➤ Navigate through a workbook

➤ Use the Excel Ribbon user interface

➤ Enter formulas

➤ Use Excel's worksheet functions

➤ Name cells and ranges

➤ Use basic Windows features, such as file management techniques and the Clipboard

If you don't know how to perform the preceding tasks, you could find some of this material over your head, so consider yourself warned. If you're an experienced spreadsheet user who hasn't used Excel 2013, Chapter 1 presents a brief overview of what this product offers.

What You Need to Have

To make the best use of this book, you need a copy of Excel 2013. Although most of the material also applies to Excel 2003 and later versions, I assume that you're using Excel 2013. Excel 2007 and later versions are radically different from their predecessors, but the VBA environment hasn't changed. If you plan to develop applications that will be used in earlier versions of Excel, I strongly suggest that you *don't* use Excel 2013 for your development work. Rather, use the earliest version of Excel that your target audience will be using.

This book isn't intended for any version of Excel for Mac. Any computer system that can run Windows will suffice, but you'll be much better off with a fast machine with plenty of memory. Excel is a large program, and using it on a slower system or a system with minimal memory can be extremely frustrating.

I recommend using a high-resolution monitor because you'll often be working with two windows. For optimal results, try a dual-monitor system and place Excel on one screen and Visual Basic Editor on the other. You'll soon become spoiled.

Conventions in This Book

Take a minute to skim this section and learn some of the typographic conventions used throughout this book.

Excel commands

Beginning with Excel 2007, the product features a menu-less user interface. In place of a menu system, Excel uses a context-sensitive Ribbon system. The words along the top (such as Insert and View) are known as *tabs*. Click a tab, and the Ribbon of icons displays the commands that are most suited to the task at hand. Each icon has a name that is (usually) displayed next to or below the icon. The icons are arranged in groups, and the group name appears below the icons.

The convention I use in this book is to indicate the tab name, followed by the group name, followed by the icon name. So, for example, the command used to toggle word wrap in a cell is indicated as:

Home➜Alignment➜Wrap Text

Clicking the first tab, labeled File, takes you to a new screen called Backstage. The Backstage window has commands along the left side of the window. To indicate Backstage commands, I use the word *File*, followed by the command. For example, the following command displays the Excel Options dialog box:

> File➜Options

Visual Basic Editor commands

Visual Basic Editor is the window in which you work with your VBA code. VB Editor uses the traditional menu-and-toolbar interface. A command like the following means to click the Tools menu and select the References menu item:

> Tools➜References

Keyboard conventions

You need to use the keyboard to enter data. In addition, you can work with menus and dialog boxes directly from the keyboard — a method that you might find easier if your hands are already positioned over the keys.

Input

Input that you are supposed to type from the keyboard appears in boldface — for example, enter **=SUM(B2: B50)** in cell B51.

More lengthy input appears on a separate line in a monospace font. For example, I might instruct you to enter the following formula:

```
=VLOOKUP(StockNumber,PriceList,2)
```

VBA code

This book contains many snippets of VBA code, as well as complete procedure listings. Each listing appears in a monospace font; each line of code occupies a separate line. (I copied these listings directly from the VBA module and pasted them into my word processor.) To make the code easier to read, I often use one or more tabs to create indentations. Indentation is optional, but it does help to delineate statements that go together.

If a line of code doesn't fit on a single line in this book, I use the standard VBA line continuation sequence: At the end of a line, a space followed by an underscore character indicates that the line of code extends to the next line. For example, the following two lines are a single code statement:

```
columnCount = Application.WorksheetFunction. _
      CountA(Range("A:A")) + 1
```

You can enter this code either on two lines, exactly as shown, or on a single line without the space and underscore character.

Functions, filenames, and named ranges

Excel's worksheet functions appear in uppercase font, like so: "Enter a SUM formula in cell C20." For VBA procedure names, properties, methods, and objects, I often use mixed uppercase and lowercase letters to make these names easier to read.

Mouse conventions

I assume that you're well versed in mouse usage. The mouse terminology I use is all standard fare: pointing, clicking, right-clicking, dragging, and so on.

What the Icons Mean

Throughout the book, I use icons to call your attention to points that are particularly important:

New Feature

I use this icon to indicate that the material discussed is new to Excel 2013.

Note

I use Note icons to tell you that something is important — perhaps a concept that could help you master the task at hand or something fundamental for understanding subsequent material.

Tip

Tip icons indicate a more efficient way of doing something or a technique that might not be obvious.

On the Web

These icons indicate that an example file is available on the book's website. See the section "About This Book's Website," later in this Introduction.

Caution

I use Caution icons when the operation that I'm describing can cause problems if you're not careful.

Cross-Ref

I use the Cross Reference icon to refer you to other chapters that have more to say on a subject.

How This Book Is Organized

The chapters of this book are grouped into eight main parts.

Part I: Some Essential Background

In Part I, I set the stage for the rest of the book. Chapter 1 is a conceptual overview of Excel 2013. In Chapter 2, I cover the essentials of formulas, including some clever techniques that might be new to you. Chapter 3 covers the ins and outs of the various files used and generated by Excel. Chapter 4 introduces the concept of application development using Excel.

Part II: Understanding Visual Basic for Applications

Chapters 5 through 9 make up Part II, and these chapters include everything that you need to know to start learning VBA. In this part, I introduce you to VBA, provide programming fundamentals, and detail how to develop VBA subroutines and functions. Chapter 9 contains many useful VBA examples.

Part III: Working with UserForms

The four chapters in Part III cover custom dialog boxes, or *UserForms*. Chapter 10 presents some built-in alternatives to creating custom UserForms. Chapter 11 provides an introduction to UserForms and the various controls that you can use. Chapters 12 and 13 present many examples of custom dialog boxes, ranging from basic to advanced.

Part IV: Advanced Programming Techniques

Part IV covers additional techniques that are often considered advanced. The first three chapters discuss how to develop utilities and how to use VBA to work with pivot tables and charts (including Sparkline graphics). Chapter 17 covers event handling, which enables you to execute procedures automatically when certain events occur. Chapter 18 discusses various techniques that you can use to interact with other applications (such as Word). Chapter 19 concludes Part IV with a hands-on discussion of creating add-ins.

Part V: Developing Applications

The chapters in Part V deal with important elements of creating user-oriented applications. Chapter 20 discusses how to modify the new Ribbon interface. Chapter 21 describes how to modify Excel's shortcut menus. Chapter 22 demonstrates several ways to provide online help for your applications. In Chapter 23, I present some basic information about developing user-oriented applications, and I describe such an application in detail.

Part VI: Other Topics

The six chapters in Part VI cover additional topics. Chapter 24 presents information regarding compatibility. In Chapter 25, I discuss various ways to use VBA to work with files. In Chapter 26, I explain how to use VBA to manipulate Visual Basic components such as UserForms and modules. Chapter 27 covers the topic of class modules. Chapter 28 explains how to work with color in Excel. I finish the part with a useful chapter that answers many common questions about Excel programming.

Part VII: Appendixes

Three appendixes round out the book. Appendix A is a reference guide to all VBA keywords (statements and functions). I explain VBA error codes in Appendix B, and Appendix C describes the files available on the companion website.

About This Book's Website

You can (and should) download many useful examples that I discuss in the text. When I write about computer-related material, I emphasize learning by example. I learn more from a well-thought-out example than from reading a dozen pages in a book, and I assume that this is true for many other people. Consequently, I spent more time developing the examples than I did writing chapters.

The files are at `www.wiley.com/go/Excel2013PowerProgramming`.

Cross-Ref
Refer to Appendix C for a description of each file.

About the Power Utility Pak Offer

Toward the back of the book, you'll find a coupon that you can redeem for a discounted copy of my popular Power Utility Pak add-in software. PUP is an award-winning collection of useful Excel utilities and many new worksheet functions. I developed this package exclusively with VBA.

I think you'll find this product useful in your day-to-day work with Excel. You can also purchase the complete VBA source code for a nominal fee. Studying the code is an excellent way to pick up some useful programming techniques.

You can take Power Utility Pak for a test drive by installing the 30-day trial version available at my website: `http://spreadsheetpage.com`.

How to Use This Book

You can use this book any way that you please. If you choose to read it from cover to cover, be my guest. But because I'm dealing with intermediate-to-advanced subject matter, the chapter order is often immaterial. I suspect that most readers will skip around, picking up useful tidbits here and there. If you're faced with a challenging task, you might try the index first to see whether the book specifically addresses your problem.

Some Essential Background

Excel in a Nutshell

In This Chapter

- Introducing Excel's object orientation

- Gaining a conceptual overview of Excel, including a description of its major features

- Discovering the new features in Excel 2013

- Taking advantage of helpful tips and techniques

About Excel

Excel is, by far, the most commonly used spreadsheet product in the world. Because you're reading this book, you are probably familiar with Excel and have used the product for several years. But even a veteran user sometimes needs a refresher course — especially if your experience is mostly with Excel 2003 or earlier versions.

In this chapter, I provide a quick overview of Excel and introduce the concept of objects — an essential component in mastering VBA programming.

Thinking in Terms of Objects

When you're developing applications with Excel (especially when you're dabbling with Visual Basic for Applications — VBA), it's helpful to think in terms of *objects,* or Excel elements that you can manipulate manually or via a macro. Here are some examples of Excel objects:

- ➤ The Excel application

- ➤ An Excel workbook

- ➤ A worksheet in a workbook

- ➤ A range or a table in a worksheet

- ➤ A ListBox control on a UserForm (a custom dialog box)

➤ A chart embedded in a worksheet

➤ A chart series in a chart

➤ A particular data point in a chart

You may notice that an *object hierarchy* exists here: The Excel object contains workbook objects, which contain worksheet objects, which contain range objects. This hierarchy makes up Excel's *object model*. Excel has more than 200 classes of objects that you can control directly or by using VBA. Other Microsoft Office products have their own object models.

Note

Controlling objects is fundamental to developing applications. Throughout this book, you find out how to automate tasks by controlling Excel's objects, and you do so by using VBA. This concept becomes clearer in subsequent chapters.

Workbooks

The most common Excel object is a *workbook*. Everything that you do in Excel takes place in a workbook, which is stored in a file that, by default, has an XLSX extension. An Excel workbook can hold any number of sheets (limited only by memory). There are four types of sheets:

➤ Worksheets

➤ Chart sheets

➤ Excel 4.0 XLM macro sheets (obsolete, but still supported)

➤ Excel 5.0 dialog sheets (obsolete, but still supported)

You can open or create as many workbooks as you like (each in its own window), but only one workbook is the *active workbook* at any given time. Similarly, only one sheet in a workbook is the *active sheet*. To activate a sheet, click its sheet tab at the bottom of the screen. To change a sheet's name, double-click the tab and enter the new text. Right-clicking a tab brings up a shortcut menu with additional options for the sheet, including changing its tab color and hiding the sheet.

You can also hide the window that contains a workbook by using the View➜Window➜Hide command. A hidden workbook window remains open, but it isn't visible to the user. Use the View➜Window➜Unhide command to make the window visible again.

A single workbook can display in multiple windows (choose View➜Window➜New Window). Each window can display a different sheet or a different area of the same sheet.

Worksheets

The most common type of sheet is a worksheet, which is what people normally think of when they think of a spreadsheet. Worksheets contain cells, and the cells store data and formulas.

How big is a worksheet?

Stop and think about the actual size of a worksheet. Do the arithmetic (16,384 × 1,048,576), and you'll see that a worksheet has 17,179,869,184 cells. Remember that this is in just one worksheet — a single workbook can hold more than one worksheet.

If you're using a 1920 x 1200 video mode with the default row heights and column widths, you can see 29 columns and 47 rows (or 1,363 cells) at a time — which is about .0000079 percent of the entire worksheet. In other words, more than 12.6 million screens of information reside in a single worksheet.

If you entered a single digit into each cell at the relatively rapid clip of one cell per second, it would take you over 500 years, nonstop, to fill up a worksheet. To print the results of your efforts would require more than 36 million sheets of paper — a stack about 12,000 feet high. (That's ten Empire State Buildings stacked on top of each other.)

As you might suspect, filling an entire workbook with values is impossible. Even if you use the 64-bit version of Excel (which accommodates much larger workbooks), you'd soon run out of memory, and Excel would probably crash.

Excel 2013 worksheets have 16,384 columns and 1,048,576 rows. You can hide unneeded rows and columns to keep them out of view, but you can't increase or decrease the number of rows or columns.

Note **Versions prior to Excel 2007 used the XLS binary format, and worksheets had only 65,536 rows and 256 columns. If you open such a file, Excel 2013 automatically enters compatibility mode to work with the smaller worksheet grid. To convert such a file to the new format, save it as an XLSX or XLSM file. Then close the workbook and reopen it.**

The real value of using multiple worksheets in a workbook isn't access to more cells. Rather, multiple worksheets enable you to organize your work better. Back in the old days, when a file comprised a single worksheet, developers wasted a lot of time trying to organize the worksheet to hold their information efficiently. Now you can store information on any number of worksheets and still access it instantly by clicking a sheet tab.

A worksheet cell can hold a constant value — a number, a date, a Boolean value (True or False), or text — or the result of a formula. Every worksheet also has an invisible drawing layer, which enables you to insert graphic objects, such as charts, shapes, SmartArt, UserForm controls, pictures, and other embedded objects.

You control the column widths and row heights — you can even hide rows and columns (as well as entire worksheets). You can specify any font size, and you control the colors. You can display text in a cell vertically (or at an angle) and even wrap it around to occupy multiple lines. In addition, you can merge a group of cells to create a single larger cell.

Note **In the past, Excel was limited to a palette of 56 colors. Beginning with Excel 2007, the number of colors has been virtually unlimited. In addition, Excel 2007 introduced document themes. A single click lets you apply a new theme to a workbook, which can give it an entirely different look.**

Chart sheets

A chart sheet holds a single chart. Many users ignore chart sheets, preferring to store charts on the worksheet's drawing layer. Using chart sheets is optional, but they make it a bit easier to print a chart on a page by itself and are especially useful for presentations. Figure 1-1 shows a pie chart on a chart sheet.

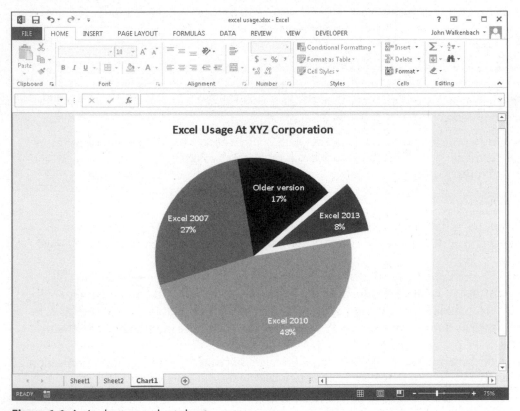

Figure 1-1: A pie chart on a chart sheet.

XLM macro sheets

An XLM macro sheet (also known as an *MS Excel 4 macro sheet*) is essentially a worksheet but with some different defaults. More specifically, an XLM macro sheet displays formulas rather than the results of formulas. In addition, the default column width is larger than in a normal worksheet.

As the name suggests, an XLM macro sheet is designed to hold XLM macros, which were used in Excel 4.0 and earlier. Excel 2013 continues to support XLM macros for compatibility purposes. This book doesn't cover the XLM macro system.

Excel 5 and 95 dialog sheets

In Excel 5 and Excel 95, you created a custom dialog box by inserting a special dialog sheet. Excel 97 and later versions still support these dialog sheets, but a much better alternative is available: UserForms. You work with UserForms in Visual Basic Editor (VBE).

If you open a workbook that contains an Excel 5 or 95 dialog sheet, you can access the dialog sheet by clicking its tab. I don't discuss Excel 5 and Excel 95 dialog sheets in this book.

 # What's new in Excel 2013?

When a new version of Microsoft Office is released, Excel sometimes gets lots of new features and other times gets few new features. In the case of Office 2013, Excel got quite a few new features — but nothing truly earth-shattering.

Here's a quick summary of what's new in Excel 2013, relative to Excel 2010:

- **Cloud storage:** Excel is tightly integrated with Microsoft's Skyview web-based storage.
- **Support for other devices:** Excel is available for other devices, including touch-sensitive Windows RT tablets and Windows phones.
- **New aesthetics:** Excel has new "flat" look and displays an optional graphic in the title bar. Color schemes are limited to white, light gray, and dark gray.
- **Single document interface:** Excel no longer supports the option to display multiple workbooks in a single window. Each workbook has its own top-level Excel window and Ribbon.
- **New types of assistance:** Excel provides recommended pivot tables and recommended charts.
- **Fill Flash:** This feature is a new way to extract (by example) relevant data from text strings. You can also use this feature to combine data in multiple columns.
- **Support for Apps for Office:** You can download or purchase apps that can be embedded in a workbook file.
- **Improved Slicer option:** The Slicer feature, introduced in Excel 2010 for use with pivot tables, has been expanded and now works with tables.
- **Timeline filtering:** Similar to Slicers, a Timeline makes it easy to filter pivot table data by dates.
- **Quick Analysis:** This feature provides single-click access to various data analysis tools.
- **Enhanced chart formatting:** Modifying and fine-tuning charts is significantly easier.
- **Increased use of task panes:** Task panes play a larger role in Excel 2013. For example, every aspect of a chart can be modified using task panes.
- **New worksheet functions:** Excel 2013 supports dozens of new worksheet functions, most of which are esoteric or special-purpose.
- **Restructured Backstage:** The Backstage screen has been reorganized and is easier to use.
- **New add-ins:** Office Professional Plus has three new add-ins: PowerPivot, Power View, and Inquire.

Excel's User Interface

A *user interface* (UI) is the means by which an end user communicates with a computer program. Generally speaking, a UI includes elements such as menus, toolbars, dialog boxes, and keystroke combinations.

The release of Office 2007 signaled the end of traditional menus and toolbars. The UI for Excel consists of the following elements:

➤ Ribbon

➤ Quick Access Toolbar

➤ Right-click shortcut menus

➤ Mini toolbar

➤ Dialog boxes

➤ Keyboard shortcuts

➤ Task pane

Note

Excel 2013 can also be run on touch-enabled devices. This book assumes that the reader has a traditional keyboard and mouse, and it does not cover the touch-related commands.

About the Ribbon

In Office 2007, Microsoft introduced a new UI for its product. Menus and toolbars were replaced with a *tab and Ribbon UI.* Click a tab along the top (that is, a word such as Home, Insert, or Page Layout), and the Ribbon displays the commands for that tab. Office 2007 was the first software in history to use this new interface; a few other companies have incorporated this new UI style in their products.

The appearance of the commands on the Ribbon varies, depending on the width of the Excel window. When the window is too narrow to display everything, some commands may seem to be missing, but they are still available. Figure 1-2 shows the Home tab of the Ribbon as it appears for three different window widths.

On the top Ribbon, all controls are fully visible. The middle Ribbon is when Excel's window is narrower. Note that some descriptive text is gone, but the icons remain. The bottom Ribbon appears when the window is very narrow. Some groups display a single icon; click that icon, and all the group commands become available.

Tip

If you'd like to hide the Ribbon to increase your worksheet view, just double-click any tab. The Ribbon goes away, and you'll be able to see about four additional rows of your worksheet. When you need to use the Ribbon again, just click any tab, and the Ribbon comes back. You can also press Ctrl+F1 to toggle the Ribbon display or use the Ribbon Display Option control, located in the window's title bar.

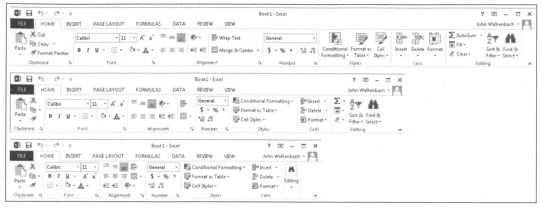

Figure 1-2: The Home tab of the Ribbon, for three window widths.

Contextual tabs

In addition to the standard tabs, Excel includes *contextual tabs*. Whenever an object (such as a chart, a table, a picture, or SmartArt) is selected, tools for working with that specific object are made available on the Ribbon.

Figure 1-3 shows the contextual tabs that appear when an embedded equation is selected. In this case, Excel displays two contextual tabs: Format (for working with object) and Design (for working with the equation). Notice that the contextual tabs contain a description (Drawing Tools and Equation Tools) in Excel's title bar. When contextual tabs are displayed, you can continue to use all the other tabs.

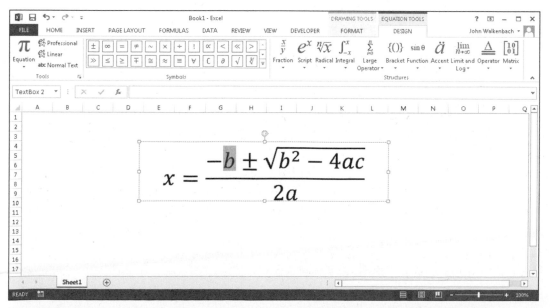

Figure 1-3: When you select an object, contextual tabs contain tools for working with that object.

Types of commands on the Ribbon

For the most part, the commands on the Ribbon work just as you'd expect them to. You'll encounter several different styles of commands on the Ribbon:

➤ **Simple buttons:** Click the button, and it does its thing. An example of a simple button is the Increase Font Size button in the Font group of the Home tab. Some buttons perform the action immediately; others display a dialog box so that you can enter additional information. Button controls may or may not be accompanied by text.

➤ **Toggle buttons:** A toggle button is clickable and also conveys some type of information by the color it displays. An example is the Bold button in the Font group of the Home tab. If the active cell isn't bold, the Bold button displays in its normal color. But if the active cell is already bold, the Bold button displays a different background color. If you click this button, it toggles the Bold attribute for the selection.

➤ **Simple drop-downs:** If the Ribbon command has a small downward-pointing arrow, the command is a drop-down list. An example is the Orientation control in the Alignment group of the Home tab. Click the control and additional commands appear below it.

➤ **Split buttons:** A split button control combines a one-click button with a drop-down. If you click the button part, the command is executed. If you click the drop-down part, you choose from a list of related commands. An example of a split button is the Paste command in the Clipboard group of the Home tab. Clicking the top part of this control pastes the information from the Clipboard. If you click the bottom part of the control, you get a list of paste-related commands (see Figure 1-4).

➤ **Check boxes:** A check box control turns something on or off. An example is the Gridlines control in the Show/Hide group of the View tab. When the Gridlines check box is selected, the sheet displays gridlines. When the control isn't selected, the sheet gridlines aren't displayed.

➤ **Spinners:** An example of a spinner control is in the Scale to Fit group of the Page Layout tab. Click the top part of the spinner to increase the value; click the bottom part of the spinner to decrease the value.

Cross-Ref

Refer to Chapter 20 for information about customizing Excel's Ribbon.

Some Ribbon groups contain a small icon in the lower-right corner, known as a dialog launcher. For example, if you examine the Home➜Alignment group, you'll see this icon (refer to Figure 1-5). Click it, and it displays the Format Cells dialog box, with the Number tab preselected. This dialog box provides options that aren't available on the Ribbon.

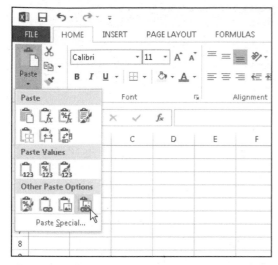

Figure 1-4: The Paste command is a split button control.

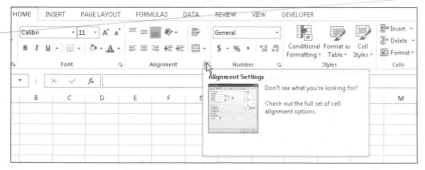

Figure 1-5: This small dialog launcher icon, when clicked, displays a dialog box that has additional options.

The Quick Access toolbar

The Quick Access toolbar is a place to store commonly used commands. The Quick Access toolbar is always visible, regardless of which Ribbon tab you select. Normally, the Quick Access toolbar appears on the left side of the title bar. Alternatively, you can display the Quick Access toolbar below the Ribbon by right-clicking the Quick Access toolbar and choosing Show Quick Access Toolbar Below the Ribbon.

By default, the Quick Access toolbar contains three tools: Save, Undo, and Redo. You can customize the Quick Access toolbar by adding other commands that you use often. To add a command on the Ribbon to your Quick Access toolbar, right-click the command and choose Add To Quick Access toolbar.

Excel has quite a few commands that aren't available on the Ribbon. In most cases, the only way to access these commands is to add them to your Ribbon or Quick Access toolbar. Figure 1-6 shows the Quick Access toolbar section of the Excel Options dialog box. This area is your one-stop shop for Quick Access toolbar customization. A quick way to display this dialog box is to right-click the Quick Access toolbar and choose Customize Quick Access toolbar.

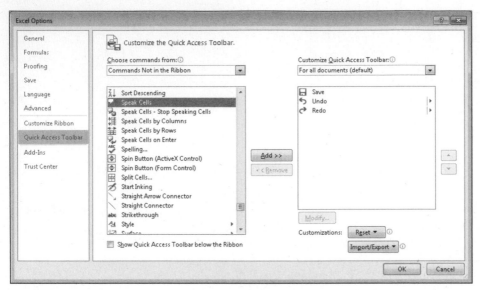

Figure 1-6: Add new icons to your Quick Access toolbar by using the Quick Access toolbar section of the Excel Options dialog box.

Accessing the Ribbon by using your keyboard

At first glance, you may think that the Ribbon is completely mouse-centric. After all, none of the commands has the traditional underlined letter to indicate the Alt+keystrokes. But, in fact, the Ribbon is *very* keyboard friendly. The trick is to press the Alt key to display pop-up *keytips*. Each Ribbon control has a letter (or series of letters) that you type to issue the command.

You don't 'need to hold down the Alt key as you type the keytip letters.

Tip

Figure 1-7 shows how the Ribbon looks after I press the Alt key, followed by M to display keytips in the Formulas tab. If you press one of the keytips, the screen then displays more keytips. For example, to use the keyboard to align the cell contents to the left, press Alt, followed by H (for Home) and then press AL (for Align Left). If you're a keyboard fan (like me), you'll memorize the keystrokes required for common commands after just a few times.

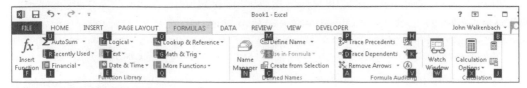

Figure 1-7: The Ribbon, with keytips displayed.

After you press Alt, you can also use the left- and right-arrow keys to scroll through the tabs. When you reach the proper tab, press the down-arrow key to enter the Ribbon. Then use the left- and right-arrow keys to scroll through the Ribbon commands. When you reach the command you need, press Enter to execute it. This method isn't as efficient as using the keytips, but it's a quick way to take a look at the choices on the Ribbon.

Note

Excel 2013 supports the menu-oriented keyboard shortcuts from Excel 2003. This is handy if you've memorized key sequences, such as Alt+ES (to display the Paste Special dialog box).

An excursion into versions

If you plan to develop VBA macros, you should have some understanding of Excel's history. Many different versions of Excel have been released, and quite a few are still commonly used. Because of this, compatibility between versions can be a problem. See Chapter 24 for a discussion of compatibility.

Here are all the major Excel for Windows versions that have been released:

- **Excel 2:** The original version of Excel for Windows was called Version 2 (rather than 1) so that it would correspond to the Macintosh version. Excel 2 first appeared in 1987.

- **Excel 3:** Released in late 1990, this version featured the XLM macro language.

- **Excel 4:** This version was released in early 1992. It also uses the XLM macro language.

- **Excel 5:** This version came out in early 1994. It was the first version to use VBA (but it also supports XLM). It's been years since I've heard from anyone who uses Excel 5.

- **Excel 95:** Technically known as Excel 7 (there is no Excel 6), this version began shipping in the summer of 1995. It's rarely used anymore.

- **Excel 97:** This version (also known as Excel 8) was released in early 1997. It has *many* enhancements and features a new interface for programming VBA macros. Excel 97 also uses a new file format (which previous Excel versions cannot open).

- **Excel 2000:** With this version, the numbering scheme jumped to four digits. Excel 2000 (also known as Excel 9) made its debut in June 1999. It includes only a few enhancements from a programmer's perspective. Excel 2000 is rarely used.

- **Excel 2002:** This version (also known as Excel 10 or Excel XP) appeared in late 2001. Perhaps this version's most significant feature is the capability to recover your work when Excel crashes. Some people still use it.

- **Excel 2003:** Of all the Excel upgrades, Excel 2003 has the fewest new features. In other words, most hard-core Excel users were disappointed with Excel 2003. As I write this, Excel 2003 is still a commonly used version. It's also the last "pre-Ribbon" version of Excel.

- **Excel 2007:** Excel 2007 signaled the beginning of a new era. Excel 2007 replaced the old menu and toolbar interface and introduced the Ribbon. I was disappointed to discover that you can't modify the Ribbon by using VBA. But this version of Excel had enough new features to satisfy me, such as a new file format and support for much larger worksheets — more than a million rows.

continued

continued

- **Excel 2010:** This version includes lots of new features (such as Sparkline graphics) and performs quite a bit better in some areas. And if you need really huge workbooks, you can install the 64-bit version. But again, I was disappointed because you still can't modify the Ribbon using VBA.

- **Excel 2013:** The latest version is the one I used while writing this edition of the book. Excel 2013 is available also in an online version (the Excel web app) and for devices that run on Windows RT ARM-based devices. The Ribbon is still around, but it now has a flat look — and you *still* can't modify it using VBA!

Shortcut menus and the Mini toolbar

Apart from the menus in Visual Basic Editor, the only menus that remain in Excel are shortcut menus. These menus appear when you right-click your mouse. The shortcut menus are context sensitive. In other words, the menu that appears depends on the location of the mouse pointer when you right-click. You can right-click just about anything — a cell, a row or column border, a workbook title bar, an element in a chart, and so on.

Right-clicking some objects displays a Mini toolbar above the shortcut menu. This toolbar provides quick access to commonly used formatting commands. Figure 1-8 shows the Mini toolbar when a cell is right-clicked.

Although you can't customize the Ribbon by using VBA, you can use VBA to customize any of the shortcut menus. You can't, however, modify the Mini toolbar.

Cross-Ref

Refer to Chapter 21 for more information about customizing shortcut menus. Note, however, that the new single document interface in Excel 2013 makes customizing shortcut menus more challenging.

Dialog boxes

Some Ribbon commands display a dialog box, from which you can specify options or issue other commands. You'll find two general classes of dialog boxes in Excel:

➤ **Modal dialog boxes:** When a modal dialog box is displayed, it must be closed to execute the commands. An example is the Format Cells dialog box. None of the options you specify are executed until you click OK. Use the Cancel button to close the dialog box without making any changes.

➤ **Modeless dialog boxes:** These stay-on-top dialog boxes remain visible as you continue to work. An example is the Find and Replace dialog box. Modeless dialog boxes usually have a Close button rather than OK and Cancel buttons.

Some Excel dialog boxes use a notebook tab metaphor, which makes a single dialog box function as several different dialog boxes. An example is the Format Cells dialog box, shown in Figure 1-9.

Figure 1-8: Right-clicking some objects displays a Mini toolbar in addition to a shortcut menu.

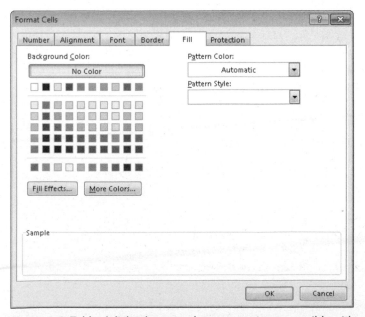

Figure 1-9: Tabbed dialog boxes make many options accessible without overwhelming the user.

Developers can create custom dialog boxes by using the UserForm feature. As you'll see, you can create a wide variety of dialog boxes, including modeless dialog boxes and tabbed dialog boxes.

Cross-Ref

Refer to Part III for information about creating and working with UserForms.

Task pane

Excel 2002 introduced a new UI element known as the *task pane*. This multipurpose user interface element is normally docked on the right side of Excel's window (but you can drag it anywhere). The task pane is used for a variety of purposes, including displaying the Office Clipboard, displaying a pivot table field list, providing research assistance, and mapping eXtensible Markup Language (XML) data.

The task pane plays an enhanced role in Excel 2013. For example, chart formatting and other object formatting is now done in a task pane rather than in a modeless dialog box. Figure 1-10 shows the Format Shape task pane.

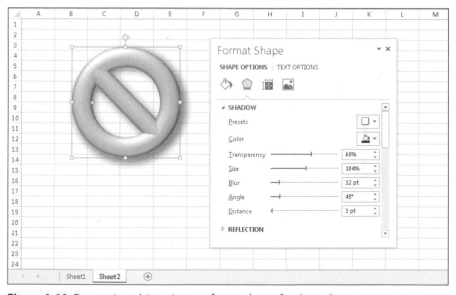

Figure 1-10: Formatting objects is one of several uses for the task pane.

Keyboard shortcuts

Excel has *many* useful keyboard shortcuts. For example, you can press Ctrl+D to copy a cell to selected cells below it. If you're a newcomer to Excel — or you just want to improve your efficiency — I urge you to check out the Help system (search for *keyboard*, and go from there). Learning these shortcuts is key to becoming proficient in Excel. The Help file has tables that summarize useful keyboard commands and shortcuts.

And, as I note previously, you can access the Ribbon commands by using the keyboard.

What's new in Visual Basic Editor?

Nothing.

Most of Excel 2013's updated object model is accessible in your VBA code, but VB Editor hasn't changed in many versions. The Microsoft Office applications have used the Ribbon UI since Office 2007, but VB Editor still uses menus and toolbars and is starting to look old-fashioned. Maybe we'll see an updated UI in the *next* release, but I'm not holding my breath.

Data Entry

Data entry in Excel is straightforward. Excel interprets each cell entry as one of the following:

➤ Numeric value (including date and time values)

➤ Text

➤ Boolean value (True or False)

➤ Formula

Formulas always begin with an equal sign (=). Excel accommodates habitual 1-2-3 users, however, and accepts an at symbol (@), a plus sign (+), or a minus sign (–) as the first character in a formula. Excel automatically adjusts the entry after you press Enter.

Formulas, Functions, and Names

Formulas are what make a spreadsheet a spreadsheet. Excel has some advanced formula-related features that are worth knowing. They enable you to write array formulas, use an intersection operator, include links, and create *megaformulas* (my term for a lengthy and incomprehensible — but very efficient — formula).

 Chapter 2 covers formulas and presents lots of tricks and tips.

Cross-Ref

Excel also has some useful auditing capabilities that help you identify errors or track the logic in an unfamiliar spreadsheet. To access these features, use the commands in the Formulas➜Formula Auditing group.

You may find the Formulas➜Formula Auditing➜Error Checking command useful. This command scans your worksheet and identifies possibly erroneous formulas. In Figure 1-11, for example, Excel identifies a possibly inconsistent formula and provides some options. Excel can also monitor your formulas for potential errors as you work. Error-checking options are available in the Formulas tab of the Excel Options dialog box.

Figure 1-11: Excel can monitor your formulas for possible errors and inconsistencies.

Worksheet functions enable you to perform calculations or operations that would otherwise be impossible. Excel provides a huge number of built-in functions.

The easiest way to locate the function that you need is to use the Insert Function dialog box, as shown in Figure 1-12. Access this dialog box by clicking the Insert Function button on the formula bar (or by pressing Shift+F3). After you select a function, Excel displays its Function Arguments dialog box, which assists with specifying the function's arguments.

Figure 1-12: The Insert Function dialog box is the best way to insert a function into a formula.

Cross-Ref

Excel also lets you create your own worksheet functions by using VBA. For details about this powerful feature, see Chapter 8.

Flash Fill

Flash Fill, a new feature in Excel 2013, uses pattern recognition to extract or combine data from other columns. The user types a few examples, and Excel attempts to complete the column. In some situations, Flash Fill can eliminate the need for formulas.

In the accompanying figure, Flash Fill was used to extract first and last names from column A. It worked reliably but was unable to extract only middle names or initials by using pattern recognition.

The feature works well when the data is consistent. However, users should check the results carefully because Excel does not indicate whether the pattern recognition succeeded in every case.

	A	B	C	D	E	F
1	Mark Russell	Mark	Russell	M.		
2	Tim Colman	Tim	Colman	T.		
3	Sam Daniel Bains	Sam	Bains	D.		
4	Fred James Foster	Fred	Foster	J.		
5	James J. Wehr	James	Wehr	J.		
6	Mitch Nicholls	Mitch	Nicholls	M.		
7	Neal McCaslin	Neal	McCaslin	M.		
8	Ned Poulakis	Ned	Poulakis	N.		
9	Paul T. Wingfield	Paul	Wingfield	T.		
10	Peter Gans	Peter	Gans	P.		
11	Ron. E. Hoffman	Ron	Hoffman	E.		
12	Julia Hayes	Julia	Hayes	J.		
13	Richard P Light	Richard	Light	P.		
14	Ray Walker	Ray	Walker	R.		
15	Robert F. Mahaney	Robert	Mahaney	F.		
16	Robert Fist	Robert	Fist	R.		
17						

Sheet1 **Sheet2** ⊕

A *name* is an identifier that enables you to refer to a cell, range, value, formula, or graphic object. Formulas that use names are much easier to create and to read than formulas that use cell references.

 Cross-Ref   I discuss names in Chapter 2. As you can see there, Excel handles names in some unique ways.

Selecting Objects

Selecting objects in Excel conforms to standard Windows practices. You can select a range of cells by clicking and dragging. (Learning the keyboard shortcuts is more efficient, however.) Clicking an object that has been placed on the drawing layer selects the object. To select multiple objects or noncontiguous cells, press Ctrl while you select the objects or cells.

Note Clicking a chart selects a specific object within the chart. To select the chart object itself, press Ctrl while you click the chart.

If an object has a macro assigned to it, clicking the object executes the macro. To actually select such an object, right-click it and press Esc to hide the shortcut menu. Or press Ctrl while you click the object.

Formatting

Excel provides two types of formatting: numeric formatting and stylistic formatting.

Numeric formatting refers to how a number appears in the cell. In addition to choosing from an extensive list of predefined formats, you can create your own formats (see Figure 1-13). The procedure is thoroughly explained in the Help system.

Excel applies some numeric formatting automatically, based on the entry. For example, if you precede a number with a currency symbol (a dollar sign in the United States), Excel applies Currency number formatting. You can also use the conditional formatting feature to apply number formatting conditionally, based on the magnitude of the number.

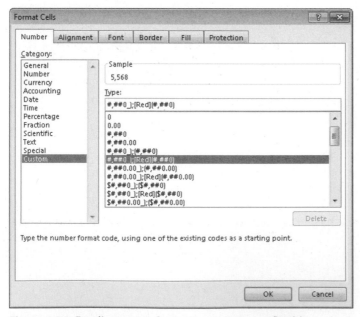

Figure 1-13: Excel's numeric formatting options are flexible.

Stylistic formatting refers to the formatting that you apply to make your work look good. Many Ribbon commands offer direct access to common formatting options, but you'll want to access the object's Format task pane for the full range of formatting options.

The easiest way to get to the correct dialog box and format an object is to select the object and press Ctrl+1. You can also right-click the object and choose Format *xxx* (where *xxx* is the selected object) from the shortcut menu. Either action displays the task pane that holds all the formatting options for the selected object.

Excel does not provide a task pane for formatting cells.

Excel's conditional formatting feature is particularly useful. This feature, accessed by choosing Home➜Styles➜Conditional Formatting, allows you to specify formatting that will be applied only if certain conditions are met. For example, you can make cells that exceed a specified value appear in a different color. The conditional formatting feature also has several data visualization options, including data bars, color scales, and icon sets. Figure 1-14 shows the data bars' conditional formatting option that displays a histogram directly in the cells.

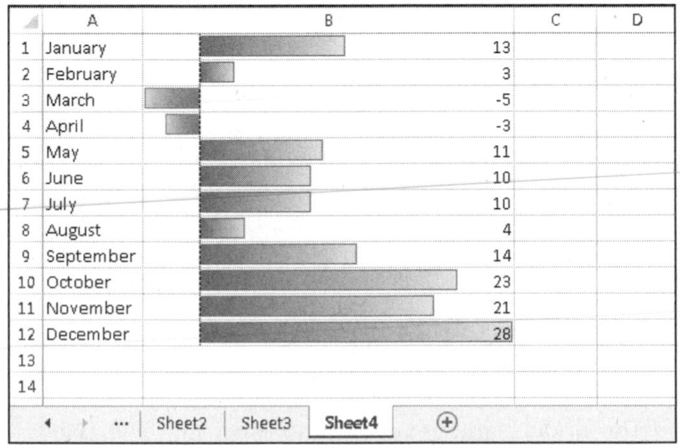

Figure 1-14: The data bars option is one of the conditional formatting features.

Protection Options

Excel offers a number of protection options. For example, you can protect formulas from being overwritten or modified, protect a workbook's structure, password-protect a workbook, and protect your VBA code.

Protecting formulas from being overwritten

In many cases, you might want to protect your formulas from being overwritten or modified. To do so, perform the following steps:

1. Select the cells that *may* be overwritten.

2. Right-click and choose Format Cells from the shortcut menu.

3. In the Format Cells dialog box, click the Protection tab.

4. In the Protection tab, clear the Locked check box.

5. Click OK to close the Format Cells dialog box.

6. Choose Review➔Changes➔Protect Sheet to display the Protect Sheet dialog box, as shown in Figure 1-15.

7. In the Protect Sheet dialog box, select the options that correspond to the actions to allow, specify a password if desired, and then click OK.

Figure 1-15: The Protect Sheet dialog box.

Note

By default, all cells are locked. The locked status of a cell has no effect, however, unless the cells are in a protected worksheet.

You can also hide your formulas so that they won't appear in Excel's formula bar when the cell is activated. To do so, select the formula cells and make sure that the Hidden check box is selected in the Protection tab of the Format Cells dialog box.

Protecting a workbook's structure

When you protect a workbook's structure, you can't add or delete sheets. Choose the Review➔ Changes➔Protect Workbook command to display the Protect Structure and Windows dialog box. Make sure that you select the Structure check box.

If the Windows check box is selected, the user cannot move or resize the workbook's window.

New Feature

In Excel 2013, the Windows check box is disabled. The new single-document interface does not allow fixed-position and nonsizable workbook windows.

Applying password protection to a workbook

In some cases, you may want to limit access to a workbook to only those who know the password.

To save a workbook file with a password, choose File➜Info➜Protect Workbook➜Encrypt with Password to display the Encrypt Document dialog box (see Figure 1-16). In this dialog box, you can specify a password that's required to open the workbook.

Figure 1-16: Use the Encrypt Document dialog box to save a workbook with a password.

Protecting VBA code with a password

If your workbook contains VBA code, you may want to use a password to prevent others from viewing or modifying your macros. To apply a password to the VBA code in a workbook, activate VBE (Alt+F11) and select your project in the Projects window. Then choose Tools➜*xxxx* Properties (where *xxxx* corresponds to your project name) to display the Project Properties dialog box.

In the Project Properties dialog box, click the Protection tab (see Figure 1-17). Select the Lock Project for Viewing check box and enter a password (twice). Click OK and then save your file. When the file is closed and then reopened, a password will be required to view or modify the code.

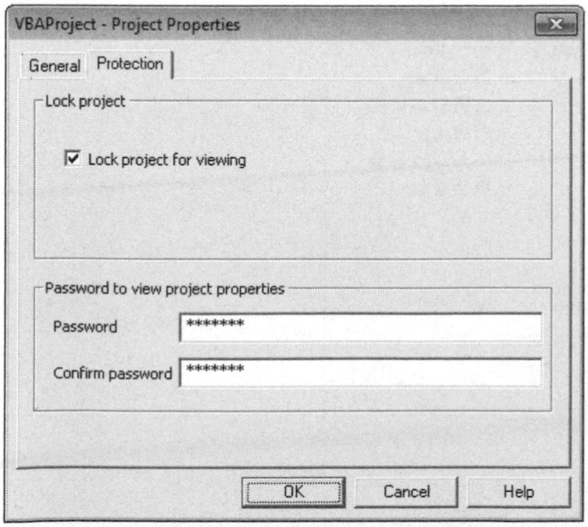

Figure 1-17: Protecting a VBA project with the Project Properties dialog box.

Caution

Keep in mind that Excel isn't a secure application. The protection features, even when used with a password, are intended to prevent casual users from accessing various components of your workbook. Anyone who really wants to defeat your protection can probably do so by using readily available password-cracking utilities (or by knowing a few tricks).

Charts

Excel is perhaps the most commonly used application in the world for creating charts. As I mention earlier in this chapter, you can store charts on a chart sheet or float them on a worksheet. Excel 2013 has some new tools that makes customizing and fine-tuning a chart easier than ever.

You can also create pivot charts. A *pivot chart* is linked to a pivot table, and you can view various graphical summaries of your data by using the same techniques used in a pivot table.

Sparkline graphics, a feature introduced in Excel 2010, consist of small charts that fit inside a cell. This type of chart is separate from Excel's standard chart feature. Figure 1-18 shows a worksheet with Sparkline graphics.

	A	B	C	D	E	F	G	H
1	**Line Sparklines**							
2								
3	**Fund Number**	**Jan**	**Feb**	**Mar**	**Apr**	**May**	**Jun**	**Sparklines**
4	A-13	103.98	98.92	88.12	86.34	75.58	71.2	
5	C-09	212.74	218.7	202.18	198.56	190.12	181.74	
6	K-88	75.74	73.68	69.86	60.34	64.92	59.46	
7	W-91	91.78	95.44	98.1	99.46	98.68	105.86	
8	M-03	324.48	309.14	313.1	287.82	276.24	260.9	
9								
10	**Column Sparklines**							
11								
12	**Fund Number**	**Jan**	**Feb**	**Mar**	**Apr**	**May**	**Jun**	**Sparklines**
13	A-13	103.98	98.92	88.12	86.34	75.58	71.2	
14	C-09	212.74	218.7	202.18	198.56	190.12	181.74	
15	K-88	75.74	73.68	69.86	60.34	64.92	59.46	
16	W-91	91.78	95.44	98.1	99.46	98.68	105.86	
17	M-03	324.48	309.14	313.1	287.82	276.24	260.9	
18								
19	**Win/Loss Sparklines**							
20								
21	**Fund Number**	**Jan**	**Feb**	**Mar**	**Apr**	**May**	**Jun**	**Sparklines**
22	A-13	#N/A	-5.06	-10.8	-1.78	-10.76	-4.38	
23	C-09	#N/A	5.96	-16.52	-3.62	-8.44	-8.38	
24	K-88	#N/A	-2.06	-3.82	-9.52	4.58	-5.46	
25	W-91	#N/A	3.66	2.66	1.36	-0.78	7.18	
26	M-03	#N/A	-15.34	3.96	-25.28	-11.58	-15.34	
27								

Sheet1 | Sheet2 | Sheet3 | Sheet4 | Sheet5 | Sheet6 | Sheet7 | SI ⋯ ⊕

Figure 1-18: Sparkline graphics in a worksheet.

Shapes and SmartArt

As I mention earlier in this chapter, each worksheet has an invisible drawing layer that holds charts, pictures, controls (such as buttons and list boxes), and shapes.

Excel enables you to easily draw a wide variety of geometric shapes directly on your worksheet. To access the Shape gallery, choose Insert➔Illustrations➔Shapes. The shapes are highly customizable, and you can even add text. You can also group objects into a single object, which you can size or position more easily than multiple objects.

A feature introduced in Office 2007 is SmartArt, which you use to create many different customizable diagrams. Figure 1-19 shows an example of a SmartArt diagram on a worksheet.

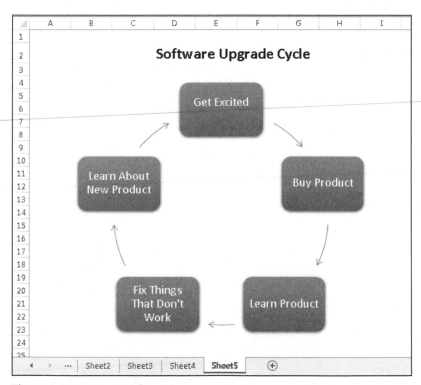

Figure 1-19: A SmartArt diagram.

Database Access

Over the years, most spreadsheets have enabled users to work with simple flat database tables. Excel can work with databases that fall into two categories:

➤ **Worksheet databases:** The entire database is stored in a worksheet.

➤ **External databases:** The database is stored in one or more files and is accessed as needed.

Worksheet databases

Generally, a rectangular range of data that contains column headers can be considered a worksheet database.

Excel 2007 was the first version that enabled you to specifically designate a range as a *table*. Select any cell in your rectangular range of data and choose Insert➔Tables➔Table. Using a table offers many advantages: an automatic summary row at the bottom, easy filtering and sorting, auto-fill formulas in columns, and simplified formatting. In addition, if you create a chart from a table, the chart expands automatically as you add rows to the table.

Tables are particularly useful when working with columns of data. Each column header is actually a drop-down list that contains easy access for filtering or sorting (see Figure 1-20). Table rows that don't meet the filter criteria are temporarily hidden.

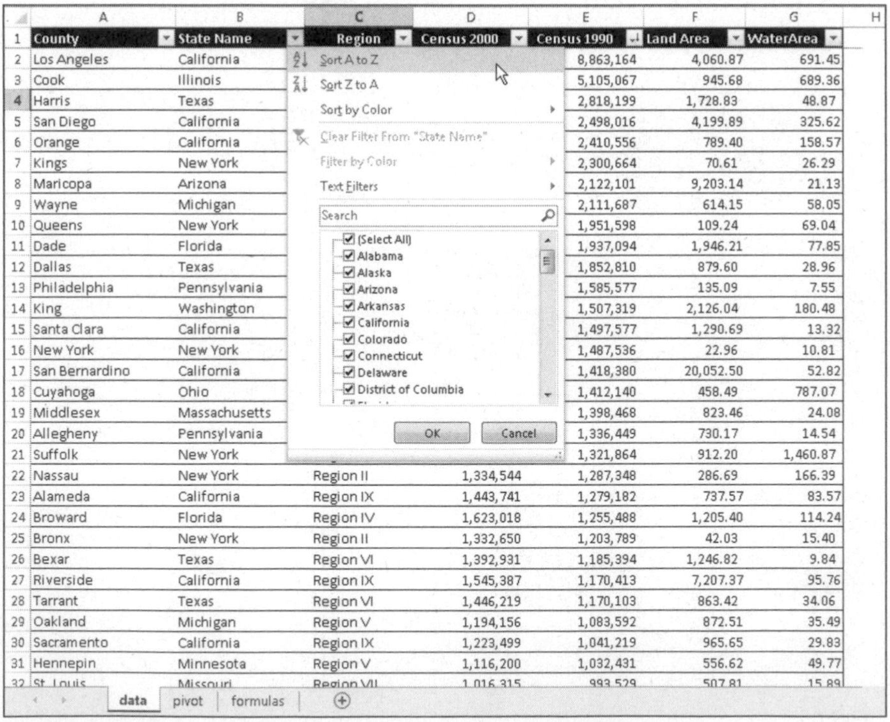

Figure 1-20: Excel's table feature makes it easy to sort and filter rows.

External databases

To work with external database tables, use the commands in the Data➔Get External Data group. Excel 2013 can work with a wide variety of external databases.

Internet Features

Excel includes a number of features that relate to the Internet. For example, you can save a worksheet or an entire workbook in HyperText Markup Language (HTML) format, accessible in a web browser. In addition, you can insert clickable hyperlinks (including e-mail addresses) directly in cells.

Caution

In versions before Excel 2007, HTML was a round-trip file format. In other words, you could save a workbook in HTML format and then reopen it in Excel, and nothing would be lost. That's no longer the case. HTML is now considered an export-only format.

You can also create web queries to bring in data stored in a corporate intranet or on the Internet. Such a query can be refreshed, so the data updates as new information is posted. Figure 1-21 shows an example of a web query.

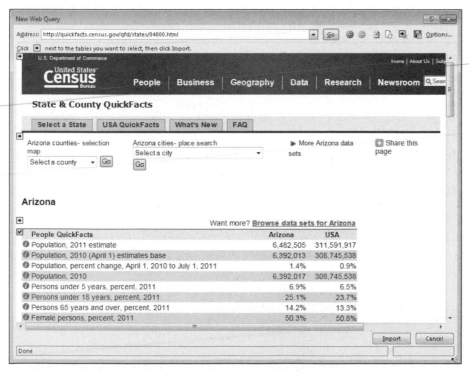

Figure 1-21: Create a web query to import data into a worksheet.

Analysis Tools

Excel is certainly no slouch when it comes to analysis. After all, that's what most people use a spreadsheet for. You can handle most analysis tasks with formulas, but Excel offers many other options:

➤ **Outlines:** A worksheet outline is often an excellent way to work with hierarchical data such as budgets. Excel can create an outline (horizontal, vertical, or both) automatically, or you can do so manually. After you create the outline, you can collapse or expand it to display various levels of detail.

➤ **Analysis ToolPak:** In previous versions of Excel, the Analysis ToolPak add-in provided additional special-purpose analysis tools, primarily statistical in nature. These tools make Excel suitable for casual statistical analysis.

➤ **Pivot tables:** Pivot tables are among Excel's most powerful tools. A pivot table is capable of summarizing data in a handy table, and you can arrange this table in many ways. In addition, you can manipulate a pivot table entirely by VBA. Data for a pivot table comes from a worksheet database or an external database and is stored in a special cache, which enables Excel to recalculate rapidly after a pivot table is altered. Figure 1-22 shows a pivot table formatted as a report.

 See Chapter 15 for information about manipulating pivot tables with VBA.
Cross-Ref

➤ **Solver:** For specialized linear and nonlinear problems, Excel's Solver add-in calculates solutions to what-if scenarios based on adjustable cells, constraint cells, and, optionally, cells that must be maximized or minimized.

Add-Ins

An *add-in* is a program that's attached to an application to give it additional functionality. To attach an Excel add-in, use the Add-Ins tab in the Excel Options dialog box.

In addition to the add-ins that ship with Excel, you can download additional add-ins from Microsoft's website (http://office.microsoft.com), and you can purchase or download many third-party add-ins from online services. You can use the coupon in the back of the book to acquire a discounted copy of the Power Utility Pak add-in. And, as I detail in Chapter 19, creating your own add-ins is *very* easy.

A	B	C	D	E	F	G
		Population Growth by State (1990 - 2000)				
		Census 1990 Population	**Census 2000 Population**	**Pop Change**	**Pct Pop Change**	**Pop/Sq Mile**
Region I		13,206,943	13,922,517	715,574	5.4%	222
	Connecticut	3,287,116	3,405,565	118,449	3.6%	703
	Maine	1,227,928	1,274,923	46,995	3.8%	41
	Massachusetts	6,016,425	6,349,097	332,672	5.5%	810
	New Hampshire	1,109,252	1,235,786	126,534	11.4%	138
	Rhode Island	1,003,464	1,048,319	44,855	4.5%	1,003
	Vermont	562,758	608,827	46,069	8.2%	66
Region II		25,720,643	27,390,807	1,670,164	6.5%	501
	New Jersey	7,730,188	8,414,350	684,162	8.9%	1,134
	New York	17,990,455	18,976,457	986,002	5.5%	402
Region III		25,917,014	27,828,549	1,911,535	7.4%	231
	Delaware	666,168	783,600	117,432	17.6%	401
	District of Columbia	606,900	572,059	(34,841)	-5.7%	9,316
	Maryland	4,781,468	5,296,486	515,018	10.8%	542
	Pennsylvania	11,881,643	12,281,054	399,411	3.4%	274
	Virginia	6,187,358	7,087,006	899,648	14.5%	179
	West Virginia	1,793,477	1,808,344	14,867	0.8%	75
Region IV		46,643,644	55,506,328	8,862,684	19.0%	150
	Alabama	4,040,587	4,447,100	406,513	10.1%	88
	Florida	14,873,804	18,235,740	3,361,936	22.6%	326
	Georgia	6,478,216	8,186,453	1,708,237	26.4%	141
	Kentucky	3,685,296	4,041,769	356,473	9.7%	102

data   **pivot**   formulas   ⊕

Figure 1-22: Excel's pivot table feature can produce attractive reports.

Macros and Programming

Excel has two built-in macro programming languages: XLM and VBA. The original XLM macro language is obsolete and has been replaced by VBA. Excel 2013 can still execute most XLM macros, and you can even create new ones. However, you can't record XLM macros. You'll want to use VBA to develop new macros.

File Format

A key consideration for Excel users and developers is file compatibility. Excel 97 through Excel 2003 all use the same file format, so file compatibility isn't a problem for these versions. Microsoft introduced a new file format with Excel 2007 that is used also in subsequent versions. Microsoft has made a *compatibility pack* available for Excel XP and Excel 2003. This compatibility pack enables these older versions of Excel to read and write the new file format.

It's important to understand the difference between file compatibility and feature compatibility. For example, even though the compatibility pack enables Excel 2003 to open files created by Excel 2007 and later, it can't handle features that were introduced in the later versions.

Cross-Ref

Refer to Chapter 3 for more information about Excel's file format, and read Chapter 24 for more information about compatibility issues for developers.

Excel's Help System

One of Excel's most important features is its Help system (see Figure 1-23). When you get stuck, simply click the question mark below the title bar (or press F1). Excel's Help window appears, and you can search or use the table of contents.

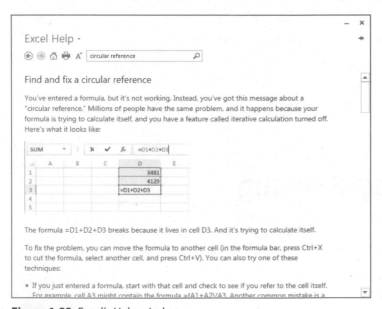

Figure 1-23: Excel's Help window.

Formula Tricks and Techniques

2

In This Chapter

- Getting an overview of Excel formulas
- Differentiating between absolute and relative references in formulas
- Understanding and using names
- Introducing array formulas
- Counting and summing cells
- Working with dates and times
- Creating megaformulas

About Formulas

Virtually every successful spreadsheet application uses formulas. In fact, constructing formulas can certainly be construed as a type of programming. This chapter covers some of the common (and not so common) types of Excel formulas.

Note

For a much more comprehensive treatment of Excel formulas and functions, refer to my Excel 2013 Formulas (Wiley).

Formulas, of course, are what make a spreadsheet a spreadsheet. If it weren't for formulas, your worksheet would be just a static document — something that a word processor that has great support for tables could produce.

Excel has a huge assortment of built-in functions, has excellent support for names, and even supports *array formulas* (a special type of formula that can perform otherwise impossible calculations).

A formula entered into a cell can consist of any of the following elements:

➤ Operators such as + (for addition) and * (for multiplication)

➤ Cell references (including named cells and ranges)

➤ Numbers or text strings

➤ Worksheet functions (such as SUM or AVERAGE)

A formula can consist of up to 8,192 characters. After you enter a formula into a cell, the cell displays the result of the formula. The formula itself appears in the formula bar when the cell is activated. For a better view of a lengthy formula, click and drag the border of the formula bar to expand it vertically. Or click the arrow on the right side of the formula bar.

Calculating Formulas

You've probably noticed that the formulas in your worksheet get calculated immediately. If you change a cell that a formula uses, the formula displays a new result with no effort on your part. This is what happens when the Excel calculation mode is set to Automatic. In this mode (which is the default mode), Excel uses the following rules when calculating your worksheet:

➤ When you make a change — enter or edit data or formulas, for example — Excel immediately calculates those formulas that depend on the new or edited data.

➤ If Excel is in the middle of a lengthy calculation, it temporarily suspends calculation when you need to perform other worksheet tasks; it resumes when you're finished.

➤ Formulas are evaluated in a natural sequence. In other words, if a formula in cell D12 depends on the result of a formula in cell D11, cell D11 is calculated before D12.

Sometimes, however, you might want to control when Excel calculates formulas. For example, if you create a worksheet with thousands of complex formulas, calculation might slow things down. In such a case, you should set Excel's calculation mode to Manual. Use the Calculation Options control in the Formulas➜Calculation group.

When you're working in Manual calculation mode, Excel displays *Calculate* in the status bar when you have any uncalculated formulas. You can press the following shortcut keys to recalculate the formulas:

➤ **F9** calculates the formulas in all open workbooks.

➤ **Shift+F9** calculates the formulas in the active worksheet only. Other worksheets in the same workbook won't be calculated.

➤ **Ctrl+Alt+F9** forces a recalculation of everything in all workbooks. Use it if Excel (for some reason) doesn't seem to be calculating correctly, or if you want to force a recalculation of formulas that use custom functions created with Visual Basic for Applications (VBA).

➤ **Ctrl+Alt+Shift+F9** analyzes all formulas and completely rebuilds (and recalculates) the dependency tree.

Note

Excel's calculation mode isn't specific to a particular workbook. When you change Excel's calculation mode, it affects all open workbooks, not just the active workbook.

Cell and Range References

Most formulas refer to one or more cells. You can make cell references by using the cell or range address or name (if it has one). Cell references come in four styles:

➤ **Relative:** The reference is fully relative. When the formula is copied, the cell reference adjusts to its new location. Example: A1.

➤ **Absolute:** The reference is fully absolute. When the formula is copied, the cell reference doesn't change. Example: $A$1.

➤ **Row Absolute:** The reference is partially absolute. When the formula is copied, the column part adjusts, but the row part doesn't change. Example: A$1.

➤ **Column Absolute:** The reference is partially absolute. When the formula is copied, the row part adjusts, but the column part doesn't change. Example: $A1.

By default, all cell and range references are relative. To change a reference, you must manually add the dollar signs. Or, when editing a cell in the formula bar, move the cursor to a cell address and press F4 repeatedly to cycle through all four types of cell referencing.

Why use references that aren't relative?

If you think about it, you'll realize that the only reason why you would ever need to change a reference is if you plan to copy the formula. Figure 2-1 demonstrates why this is so. The formula in cell C3 is

```
=$B3*C$2
```

This formula calculates the area for various lengths (listed in column B) and widths (listed in row 2). After the formula is entered, you can then copy it down to C9 and across to column I. Because the formula uses absolute references to row 2 and column B and relative references for other rows and columns, each copied formula produces the correct result. If the formula used only relative references, copying the formula would cause all the references to adjust and thus produce incorrect results.

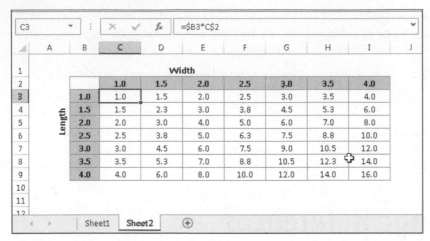

Figure 2-1: An example of using nonrelative references in a formula.

About R1C1 notation

Normally, Excel uses what's known as *A1 notation:* Each cell address consists of a column letter and a row number. However, Excel also supports *R1C1 notation.* In this system, cell A1 is referred to as cell R1C1, cell A2 as R2C1, and so on.

To change to R1C1 notation, access the Formulas tab of the Excel Options dialog box. Place a check mark next to R1C1 Reference Style. After you do so, you'll notice that the column letters all change to numbers. All the cell and range references in your formulas are also adjusted.

Table 2-1 presents some examples of formulas that use standard notation and R1C1 notation. The formula is assumed to be in cell B1 (also known as R1C2).

Table 2-1: Comparing Simple Formulas in Two Notations

Standard	R1C1
=A1+1	=RC[−1]+1
=$A$1+1	=R1C1+1
=$A1+1	=RC1+1
=A$1+1	=R1C[−1]+1
=SUM(A1:A10)	=SUM(RC[−1]:R[9]C[−1])
=SUM($A$1:$A$10)	=SUM(R1C1:R10C1)

If you find R1C1 notation confusing, you're not alone. R1C1 notation isn't too bad when you're dealing with absolute references. But when relative references are involved, the brackets can be confusing.

The numbers in brackets refer to the relative position of the references. For example, R[-5]C[-3] specifies the cell that's five rows above and three columns to the left. On the other hand, R[5]C[3] references the cell that's five rows below and three columns to the right. If the brackets are omitted, the notation specifies the same row or column. For example, R[5]C refers to the cell five rows below in the same column.

You probably won't use R1C1 notation as your standard system. However, if you write VBA code to create worksheet formulas, you might find it easier to create the formulas by using R1C1 notation.

Referencing other sheets or workbooks

When a formula refers to other cells, the references don't need to be on the same sheet as the formula. To refer to a cell in a different worksheet, precede the cell reference with the sheet name followed by an exclamation point. Here's an example of a formula that uses a cell reference in a different worksheet (Sheet2):

```
=Sheet2!A1+1
```

You can also create link formulas that refer to a cell in a different workbook. To do so, precede the cell reference with the workbook name (in square brackets), the worksheet name, and an exclamation point. Here's an example:

```
=[Budget.xlsx]Sheet1!A1
```

If the workbook name in the reference includes one or more spaces, you must enclose it (and the sheet name) in single quotation marks. For example:

```
='[Budget For 2013.xlsx]Sheet1'!A1
```

If the linked workbook is closed, you must add the complete path to the workbook reference. Here's an example:

```
='C:\Budgeting\Excel Files\[Budget For 2013.xlsx]Sheet1'!A1
```

Although you can enter link formulas directly, you can also create the reference by using normal pointing methods, but the source file must be open. When you do so, Excel creates absolute cell references. If you plan to copy the formula to other cells, make the references relative.

Caution

Working with links can be tricky. For example, if you choose the File➡Save As command to make a backup copy of the source workbook, you automatically change the link formulas to refer to the new file (not usually what you want to do). Another way to mess up your links is to rename the source workbook when the dependent workbook is not open.

Referencing Data in a Table

Beginning with Excel 2007, you can designate a range to be a table by using the Insert➜Tables➜ Table command. Tables add a few new twists to formulas.

When you enter a formula into a cell in a table, Excel automatically copies the formula to all the other cells in the column — but only if the column was empty. This is known as a calculated column. If you add a new row to the table, the calculated column formula is entered automatically for the new row. Most of the time, this is exactly what you want. If you don't like the idea of Excel entering formulas for you, use the SmartTag to turn off this feature. The SmartTag appears after Excel enters the calculated column formula.

Excel also supports "structured referencing" for referring to cells within a table. The table in the accompanying figure is named Table1.

	A	B	C	D	E	F
1						
2		**Month** ▼	**State** ▼	**Income** ▼	**Expenses** ▼	
3		Jan	Washington	983	462	
4		Feb	Washington	1,022	549	
5		Mar	Washington	861	503	
6		Jan	Oregon	764	398	
7		Feb	Oregon	993	425	
8		Mar	Oregon	882	387	
9		**Total**		5505	2724	
10						

Sheet1 ⊕

You can create formulas that refer to cells within the table by using the column headers. In some cases, using column headers may make your formulas easier to understand. But the real advantage is that your formulas will continue to be valid if rows are added or removed from the table. For example, these are all valid formulas that use table references:

```
=Table1[[#Totals],[Income]]
=SUM(Table1[Income])
=Table1[[#Totals],[Income]]-Table1[[#Totals],[Expenses]]
=SUM(Table1[Income])-SUM(Table1[Expenses])
=SUMIF(Table1[State],"Oregon",Table1[Income])
=Table1[@Expenses]
```

The last formula uses an at symbol (@), which means "this row." This formula is valid only if it's in a cell in one of the rows occupied by the table.

Using Names

One of the most useful features in Excel is its capability to provide meaningful names for various items. For example, you can name cells, ranges, rows, columns, charts, and other objects. You can even name values or formulas that don't appear in cells in your worksheet. (See the "Naming constants" section, later in this chapter.)

Naming cells and ranges

Excel provides several ways to name a cell or range:

> ➤ Choose Formulas➜Defined Names➜Define Name to display the New Name dialog box.

> ➤ Use the Name Manager dialog box (Formulas➜Defined Names➜Name Manager or press Ctrl+F3). This method isn't the most efficient because it requires clicking the New button in the Name Manager dialog box, which displays the New Name dialog box.

> ➤ Select the cell or range and then type a name in the Name box and press Enter. The Name box is the drop-down control displayed to the left of the formula bar.

> ➤ If your worksheet contains text that you'd like to use for names of adjacent cells or ranges, select the text and the cells to be named and choose Formulas➜Defined Names➜Create from Selection. In Figure 2-2, for example, B3:E3 is named *North,* B4:E4 is named *South,* and so on. Vertically, B3:B6 is named *Qtr_1,* C3:C6 is named *Qtr_2,* and so on. Note that Excel changes the names to make them valid. (A hyphen isn't a valid character in a name.)

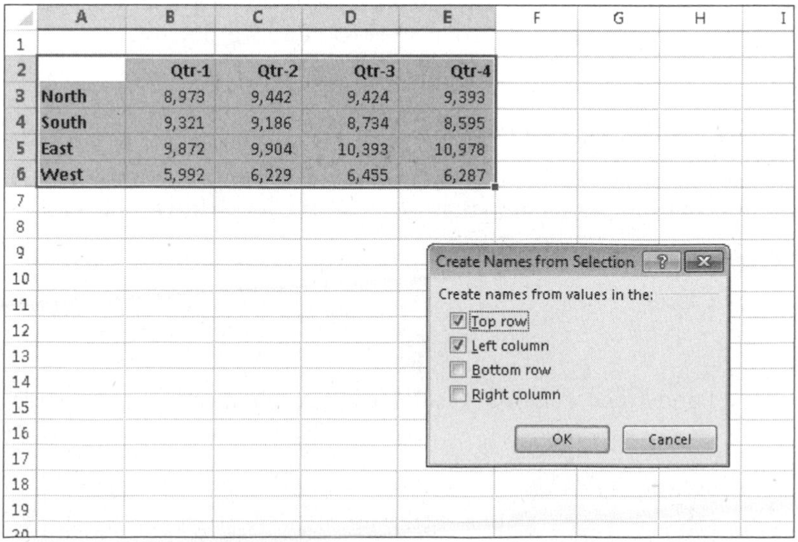

Figure 2-2: Excel makes it easy to create names that use descriptive text in your worksheet.

Hidden names

Some Excel macros and add-ins create *hidden names*. Hidden names exist in a workbook but don't appear in the Name Manager dialog box. For example, the Solver add-in creates a number of hidden names. Normally, you can just ignore these hidden names. However, sometimes these hidden names create a problem. If you copy a sheet to another workbook, the hidden names are also copied, and they might create a link that is very difficult to track down.

You can use the following VBA procedure to delete all hidden names in the workbook:

```
Sub DeleteHiddenNames()
    Dim n As Name
    Dim Count As Integer
    For Each n In ActiveWorkbook.Names
        If Not n.Visible Then
            n.Delete
            Count = Count + 1
        End If
    Next n
    MsgBox Count & " hidden names were deleted."
End Sub
```

Using names is especially important if you write VBA code that uses cell or range references. The reason? VBA does not automatically update its references if you move a cell or range that's referred to in a VBA statement. For example, if your VBA code writes a value to Range("C4"), the data will be written to the wrong cell if the user inserts a new row above or a new column to the left of cell C4. Using a reference to a named cell, such as Range("InterestRate"), avoids these potential problems.

Applying names to existing references

When you create a name for a cell or a range, Excel doesn't automatically use the name in place of existing references in your formulas. For example, assume that you have the following formula in cell F10:

```
=A1-A2
```

If you define the names *Income* for A1 and *Expenses* for A2, Excel doesn't automatically change your formula to

```
=Income-Expenses
```

However, replacing cell or range references with their corresponding names is fairly easy. Start by selecting the range that contains the formulas that you want to modify. Then choose Formulas➜ Defined Names➜Define Name➜Apply Names. In the Apply Names dialog box, select the names that you want to apply and then click OK. Excel replaces the range references with the names in the selected cells.

Note

> Unfortunately, you can't automatically unapply names. In other words, if a formula uses a name, you can't convert the name to an actual cell or range reference. Even worse, if you delete a name that a formula uses, the formula doesn't revert to the cell or range address — it simply returns a #NAME? error.
>
> My Power Utility Pak add-in (available by using the coupon in the back of the book) includes a utility that scans all formulas in a selection and automatically replaces names with their cell addresses.

Intersecting names

Excel has a special operator called the *intersection operator* that comes into play when you're dealing with ranges. This operator is a space character. Using names with the intersection operator makes creating meaningful formulas very easy. For this example, refer to Figure 2-2. If you enter the following formula into a cell

```
=Qtr_2 South
```

the result is 9,186 — the value at the intersection of the *Qtr_2* range and the *South* range.

Naming columns and rows

Excel lets you name complete rows and columns. In Figure 2-2, the name *Qtr_1* is assigned to the range B3:B6. Alternatively, *Qtr_1* could be assigned to all of column B, *Qtr_2* to column C, and so on. You also can do the same horizontally so that *North* refers to row 3, *South* to row 4, and so on.

The intersection operator works exactly as before, but now you can add more regions or quarters without having to change the existing names.

When naming columns and rows, make sure that you don't store any extraneous information in named rows or columns. For example, remember that if you insert a value in cell C7, it is included in the *Qtr_1* range.

Scoping names

A named cell or range normally has a workbook-level *scope*. In other words, you can use the name in any worksheet in the workbook.

Another option is to create names that have a worksheet-level scope. To create a worksheet-level name, define the name by preceding it with the worksheet name followed by an exclamation point: for example, *Sheet1!Sales*. If the name is used on the sheet in which it is designed, you can omit the sheet qualifier when you reference the name. You can, however, reference a worksheet-level name on a different sheet if you precede the name with the sheet qualifier.

The Name Manager dialog box (Formulas➜Defined Names➜Name Manager) makes identifying names by their scope easy (see Figure 2-3). Note that the dialog box is resizable, and you can adjust the column widths. You can also sort and filter the information in this dialog box.

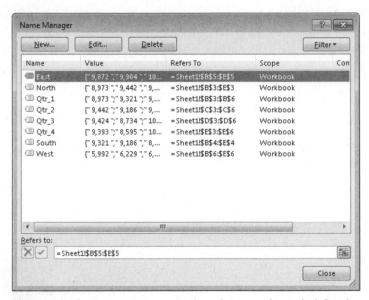

Figure 2-3: The Name Manager displays the scope for each defined name.

Naming constants

Virtually every experienced Excel user knows how to create cell and range names (although not all Excel users actually do so). But most Excel users don't know that you can use names to refer to values that don't appear in your worksheet — that is, *constants*.

Suppose that many formulas in your worksheet need to use a particular interest rate value. One approach is to type the interest rate into a cell and give that cell a name, such as *InterestRate*. After doing so, you can use that name in your formulas, like this:

```
=InterestRate*A3
```

An alternative is to call up the New Name dialog box (Formulas➜Defined Names➜Define Name) and enter the interest rate directly into the Refers To box (see Figure 2-4). Then you can use the name in your formulas just as if the value were stored in a cell. If the interest rate changes, just change the definition for *InterestRate,* and Excel updates all the cells that contain this name.

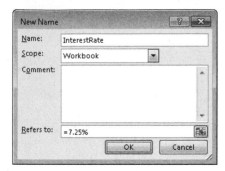

Figure 2-4: Excel lets you name constants that don't appear in worksheet cells.

Tip

This technique also works for text. For example, you can define the name IWC to stand for International Widget Corporation. Then you can enter =IWC into a cell, and the cell displays the full name.

Naming formulas

In addition to naming cells, ranges, and constants, you can also create named formulas. A named formula, as described here, exists only in memory — it does not exist in a cell. To create a named formula, enter a formula directly in the Refers To field in the New Name dialog box.

Note

This point is very important: The formula that you enter uses cell references relative to the active cell at the time that you create the named formula.

Figure 2-5 shows a formula (=A1^B1) entered directly in the Refers To box in the New Name dialog box. In this case, the active cell is C1, so the formula refers to the two cells to its left. (Notice that the cell references are relative.) After this name is defined, entering **=Power** in a cell raises the value two cells to the left to the power represented by the cell directly to the left. For example, if B10 contains 3 and C10 contains 4, entering the following formula in cell D10 returns a value of 81 (3 to the 4th power).

```
=Power
```

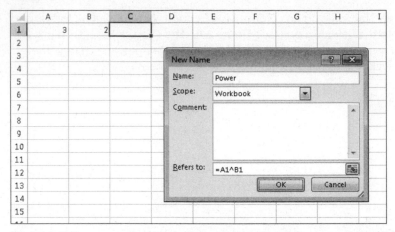

Figure 2-5: You can name a formula that doesn't appear in any worksheet cell.

When you display Name Manager after creating the named formula, the Refers To column displays a formula that is relative to the current active cell. For example, if cell D32 is the active cell, the Refers To column displays

```
=Sheet1!B32^Sheet1!C32
```

Note that Excel qualifies the cell references by adding the worksheet name to the cell references used in your formula. The worksheet name is the sheet that was active when you created the name formula. This, of course, will cause the named formula to produce incorrect results if you use it in a worksheet other than the one in which it was defined. If you'd like to use this named formula in a sheet other than Sheet1, you need to remove the sheet references from the formula (but keep the exclamation points). For example:

```
=!A1^!B1
```

After you understand the concept, you might discover some new uses for named formulas. One distinct advantage is apparent if you need to modify the formula. You can just change the formula one time rather than edit each occurrence of the formula.

On the Web

This book's website contains a workbook with several examples of named formulas. The workbook is called named formulas.xlsx.

Tip

When you're working in the New Name dialog box, the Refers To field is normally in point mode, which makes it easy to enter a range reference by clicking in the worksheet. Press F2 to toggle between point mode and normal editing mode, which allows you to use the arrow keys to edit the formula.

The secret to understanding cell and range names

Excel users often refer to *named ranges* and *named cells*. In fact, I use these terms frequently throughout this chapter. Actually, this terminology isn't quite accurate.

Here's the secret to understanding names: *When you create a name for a cell or a range in Excel, you're actually creating a named formula — a formula that doesn't exist in a cell. Rather, these named formulas exist in Excel's memory.*

When you work with the New Name dialog box, the Refers To field contains the formula, and the Name field contains the formula's name. You'll find that the contents of the Refers To field always begin with an equal sign — which makes it a formula.

This isn't exactly an earthshaking revelation, but keeping this "secret" in mind could help you understand what's going on behind the scenes when you create and use names in your workbooks.

Naming objects

In addition to providing names for cells and ranges, you can give more meaningful names to objects such as pivot tables and shapes. Using meaningful names can make referring to such objects easier, especially when you refer to them in your VBA code.

To change the name of a nonrange object, use the Name box, which is located to the left of the formula bar. Just select the object, type the new name in the Name box, and then press Enter.

Note

If you simply click elsewhere in your workbook after typing the name in the Name box, the name won't stick. You must press Enter.

Object names are different than name ranges and are not included in the Name Manager dialog box.

Formula Errors

Entering a formula and receiving an error in return isn't uncommon. One possibility is that the formula you entered is the cause of the error. Another possibility is that the formula refers to a cell that has an error value. The latter scenario is known as the *ripple effect* — a single error value can make its way to lots of other cells that contain formulas that depend on the cell. The tools in the Formulas➜ Formula Auditing group can help you trace the source of formula errors.

Table 2-2 lists the types of error values that may appear in a cell that has a formula.

Table 2-2: Excel Formula Error Values

Error Value	Explanation
#DIV/0!	The formula is trying to divide by 0 (zero), an operation that's not allowed on this planet. This error also occurs when the formula attempts to divide by a cell that is empty.
#N/A	The formula is referring (directly or indirectly) to a cell that uses the NA worksheet function to signal the fact that data isn't available. A lookup function that can't locate a value also returns #N/A.
#NAME?	The formula uses a name that Excel doesn't recognize. This can happen if you delete a name that's used in the formula, if you have unmatched quotes when using text, if you omit parentheses for a function that uses no arguments, or if you misspell a function or range name. A formula will also display this error if it uses a function defined in an add-in and that add-in isn't installed.
#NULL!	The formula uses an intersection of two ranges that don't intersect. (This concept is described in the section "Intersecting names," earlier in the chapter.)
#NUM!	A function argument has a problem; for example, the SQRT function is attempting to calculate the square root of a negative number. This error also appears if a calculated value is too large or too small. Excel doesn't support nonzero values less than 1E–307 or greater than 1E+308 in absolute value.
#REF!	The formula refers to a cell that isn't valid. This can happen if a cell used in a formula has been deleted from the worksheet.
#VALUE!	The formula includes an argument or operand of the wrong type. An *operand* is a value or cell reference that a formula uses to calculate a result. This error also occurs if your formula uses a custom VBA worksheet function that contains an error.
#####	A cell displays a series of hash marks under two conditions: The column isn't wide enough to display the result, or the formula returns a negative date or time value.

Excel Auditing Tools

Excel includes a number of tools that can help you track down formula errors. This section describes the auditing tools built in to Excel.

Identifying cells of a particular type

The Go to Special dialog box (shown in Figure 2-6) is a handy tool that enables you to locate cells of a particular type. To display this dialog box, choose Home➜Editing ➜Find & Select➜Go to Special.

Note

If you select a multicell range before displaying the Go to Special dialog box, the command operates only within the selected cells. If a single cell is selected, the command operates on the entire worksheet.

Figure 2-6: The Go to Special dialog box.

You can use the Go to Special dialog box to select cells of a certain type, which can often help you identify errors. For example, if you choose the Formulas option, Excel selects all the cells that contain a formula. If you zoom the worksheet out to a small size, you can get a good idea of the worksheet's organization (see Figure 2-7). To zoom a worksheet, use the zoom controls on the right side of the status bar or press Ctrl while you move the scroll wheel on your mouse.

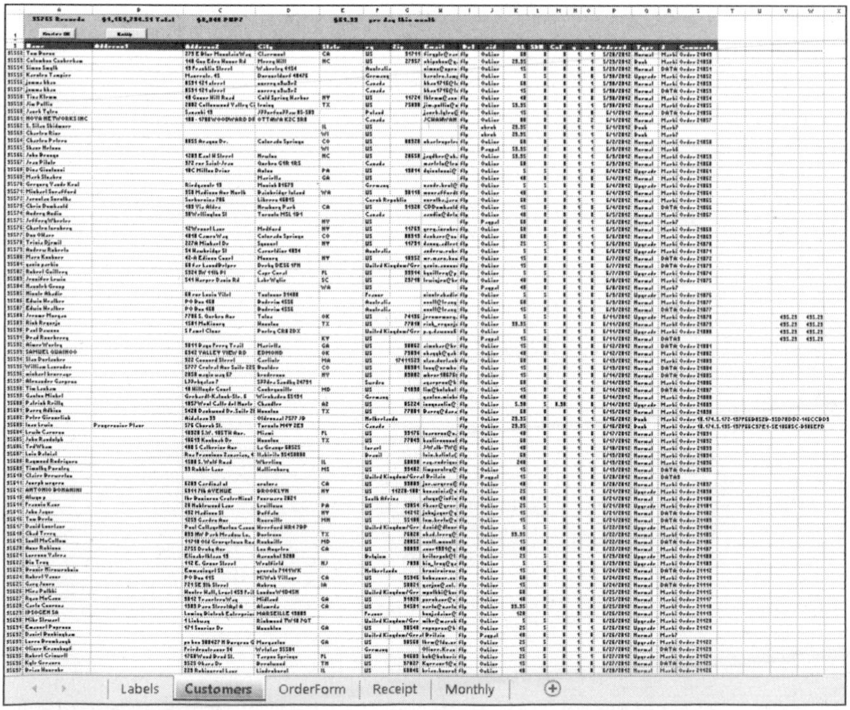

Figure 2-7: Zooming out and selecting all formula cells can give you a good overview of the worksheet's design.

Selecting the formula cells may also help you spot a common error: namely, a formula that has been replaced accidentally with a value. If you find a cell that's not selected amid a group of selected formula cells, chances are good that the cell previously contained a formula that has been replaced by a value.

Tip

Viewing formulas

You can become familiar with an unfamiliar workbook by displaying the formulas rather than the results of the formulas. To toggle the display of formulas, choose Formulas➔Formula Auditing➔ Show Formulas. You may want to create a second window for the workbook before issuing this command. This way, you can see the formulas in one window and the results of the formula in the other window. Choose View➔Window➔New Window to open a new window.

You can also press Ctrl+` (the accent grave key, typically located above the Tab key) to toggle between Formula view and Normal view.

Tip

Figure 2-8 shows an example of a worksheet displayed in two windows. The window on the top shows Normal view (formula results), and the window on the bottom displays the formulas. Choosing View➔Window➔View Side by Side, which allows synchronized scrolling, is also useful for viewing two windows.

	Last Month	This Month	Change	Pct. Change	Met Goal?	Commission
Commission Rate	5.50%	Normal commission rate				
Sales Goal	15%	Improvement from prior month				
Bonus Rate	6.50%	Paid if Sales Goal is attained				
Sales Rep						
Murray	101,233	108,444	7,211	7.1%	TRUE	7,049
Knuckles	120,933	108,434	-12,499	-10.3%	FALSE	5,964
Lefty	139,832	165,901	26,069	18.6%	TRUE	10,784
Lucky	98,323	100,083	1,760	1.8%	FALSE	5,505
Scarface	78,322	79,923	1,601	2.0%	FALSE	4,396
Total	538,643	562,785	24,142	4.5%		33,697
Average Commission Rate:		5.99%				

	Last Month	This Month	Change	Pct. Change	Met Goal?	Commission
Commission Rate	0.055	Normal commission				
Sales Goal	0.15	Improvement from p				
Bonus Rate	0.065	Paid if Sales Goal is a				
Sales Rep						
Murray	101233	108444	=C6-B6	=D6/B6	=E6>=$B$3	=IF(F6,$B$3,$B$1)*C6
Knuckles	120933	108434	=C7-B7	=D7/B7	=E7>=$B$3	=IF(F7,$B$3,$B$1)*C7
Lefty	139832	165901	=C8-B8	=D8/B8	=E8>=$B$3	=IF(F8,$B$3,$B$1)*C8
Lucky	98323	100083	=C9-B9	=D9/B9	=E9>=$B$3	=IF(F9,$B$3,$B$1)*C9
Scarface	78322	79923	=C10-B10	=D10/B10	=E10>=$B$3	=IF(F10,$B$3,$B$1)*C10
Total	=SUM(B6:B10)	=SUM(C6:C10)	=SUM(D6:D10)	=D11/B11		=SUM(G6:G10)
Average Commission Rate:		=G11/C11				

Figure 2-8: Displaying formulas (bottom window) and their results (top window).

New Feature

Using the Inquire Add-in

The Office Professional Plus version of Excel 2013 includes a useful auditing add-in called Inquire. To install Inquire, choose File➔Options to display the Excel Options dialog box. Click the Add-ins tab. At the bottom of the dialog box, choose COM Add-ins from the Manage drop-down list, and click Go.

In the COM Add-Ins dialog box, select the Inquire Add-in option and click OK. The add-in will be loaded automatically when Excel starts. If the Inquire add-in is not listed, your version of Excel does not include the add-in.

Inquire is accessible from the Inquire tab on the Ribbon. You can use this add-in to

- Compare versions of a workbook
- Analyze a workbook for potential problem and inconsistencies
- Display interactive diagnostics (shown here)
- Visualize links between workbook and worksheets
- Clear excess cell formatting
- Manage passwords

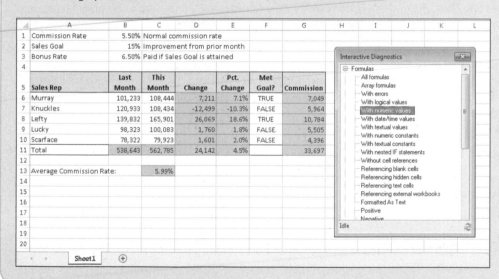

Tracing cell relationships

To understand how to trace cell relationships, you need to familiarize yourself with the following two concepts:

> **Cell precedents:** Applicable only to cells that contain a formula, a formula cell's precedents are all the cells that contribute to the formula's result. A *direct precedent* is a cell that you use directly in the formula. An *indirect precedent* is a cell that isn't used directly in the formula but is used by a cell that you refer to in the formula.

➤ **Cell dependents:** These formula cells depend on a particular cell. A cell's dependents consist of all formula cells that use the cell. Again, the formula cell can be a *direct dependent* or an *indirect dependent.*

For example, consider this simple formula entered into cell A4:

```
=SUM(A1:A3)
```

Cell A4 has three precedent cells (A1, A2, and A3), which are all direct precedents. Cells A1, A2, and A3 each have at least one dependent cell (cell A4), and they're all direct dependents.

Identifying cell precedents for a formula cell often sheds light on why the formula isn't working correctly. Conversely, knowing which formula cells depend on a particular cell is also helpful. For example, if you're about to delete a formula, you may want to check whether it has any dependents.

Identifying precedents

You can identify cells used by a formula in the active cell in a number of ways:

➤ **Press F2.** The cells that are used directly by the formula are outlined in color, and the color corresponds to the cell reference in the formula. This technique is limited to identifying cells in the same sheet as the formula.

➤ **Display the Go to Special dialog box.** (Choose Home➜Editing➜Find & Select➜Go to Special.) Select the Precedents option and then select either Direct Only (for direct precedents only) or All Levels (for direct and indirect precedents). Click OK, and Excel selects the precedent cells for the formula. This technique is limited to identifying cells in the same sheet as the formula.

➤ **Press Ctrl+[.** This keystroke selects all direct precedent cells on the active sheet.

➤ **Press Ctrl+Shift+{.** This keystroke selects all precedent cells (direct and indirect) on the active sheet.

➤ **Choose Formulas➜Formula Auditing➜Trace Precedents.** Excel will draw arrows to indicate the cell's precedents. Click the Trace Precedents button multiple times to see additional levels of precedents. Choose Formulas➜Formula Auditing➜Remove Arrows to hide the arrows. Figure 2-9 shows a worksheet with precedent arrows drawn to indicate the precedents for the formula in cell C13.

	A	B	C	D	E	F	G	H
1	Commission Rate	5.50%	Normal commission rate					
2	Sales Goal	15%	Improvement from prior month					
3	Bonus Rate	6.50%	Paid if Sales Goal is attained					
4								
5	Sales Rep	Last Month	This Month	Change	Pct. Change	Met Goal?	Commission	
6	Murray	101,233	108,444	7,211	7.1%	TRUE	7,049	
7	Knuckles	120,933	108,434	-12,499	-10.3%	FALSE	5,964	
8	Lefty	139,832	165,901	26,069	18.6%	TRUE	10,784	
9	Lucky	98,323	100,083	1,760	1.8%	FALSE	5,505	
10	Scarface	78,322	79,923	1,601	2.0%	FALSE	4,396	
11	Total	538,643	562,785	24,142	4.5%		33,697	
12								
13	Average Commission Rate:		5.99%					
14								

Sheet1 ⊕

Figure 2-9: This worksheet displays arrows that indicate cell precedents for the formula in cell C13.

Identifying dependents

You can identify formula cells that use a particular cell in a number of ways:

➤ **Display the Go to Special dialog box.** Select the Dependents option and then select either Direct Only (for direct dependents only) or All Levels (for direct and indirect dependents). Click OK. Excel selects the cells that depend on the active cell. This technique is limited to identifying cells in the active sheet only.

➤ **Press Ctrl+].** This keystroke selects all direct dependent cells on the active sheet.

➤ **Press Ctrl+Shift+}.** This keystroke selects all dependent cells (direct and indirect) on the active sheet.

➤ **Choose Formulas➜Formula Auditing➜Trace Dependents.** Excel will draw arrows to indicate the cell's dependents. Click the Trace Dependents button multiple times to see additional levels of dependents. Choose Formulas➜Formula Auditing➜Remove Arrows to hide the arrows.

Tracing error values

If a formula displays an error value, Excel can help you identify the cell that is causing that error value. An error in one cell is often the result of an error in a precedent cell. Activate a cell that contains an error value and then choose Formulas➜Formula Auditing➜Error Checking➜Trace Error. Excel draws arrows to indicate the error source.

Fixing circular reference errors

If you accidentally create a circular reference formula, Excel displays a warning message — Circular Reference — with the cell address, in the status bar, and also draws arrows on the worksheet to help you identify the problem. If you can't figure out the source of the problem, choose Formulas→Formula Auditing→Error Checking→Circular References. This command displays a list of all cells that are involved in the circular references. Start by selecting the first cell listed and then work your way down the list until you figure out the problem.

Using the background error-checking feature

Some people may find it helpful to take advantage of the Excel automatic error-checking feature. This feature is enabled or disabled by using the Enable Background Error Checking check box, found on the Formulas tab of the Excel Options dialog box (shown in Figure 2-10). In addition, you can use the check boxes in the Error Checking Rules section to specify which types of errors to check.

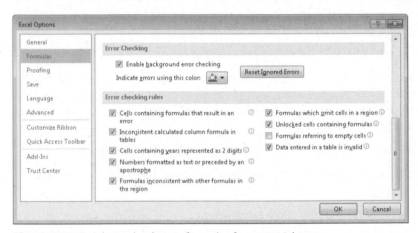

Figure 2-10: Excel can check your formulas for potential errors.

When error checking is turned on, Excel continually evaluates the formulas in your worksheet. If a potential error is identified, Excel places a small triangle in the upper-left corner of the cell. When the cell is activated, a drop-down control appears. Clicking this control provides you with options that vary depending on the type of error. Figure 2-11, for example, shows the options that appear when you click the control in a cell that contains a #DIV/0! error.

	A	B	C	D	E
1	Telemarketing Results				
2					
3	Day	Calls Made	Sales	Percentage	
4	1	3,598	74	2.1%	
5	2	3,032	78	2.6%	
6	3	2,987	68	2.3%	
7	4	3,100	59	1.9%	
8	5	3,523	43	1.2%	
9	6			#DIV/0!	
10	7			#DIV/0!	
11	8		◇ ▾	#DIV/0!	
12	9		Divide by Zero Error		
13	10				
14	11		Help on this error		
15	12		Show Calculation Steps...		
16					
17			Ignore Error		
18			Edit in Formula Bar		
19			Error Checking Options...		
20					
21					

Sheet1 | Sheet2 | Sheet3 | Sheet4 | ... | ⊕

Figure 2-11: When you select a cell that contains an error (or a potential error), a drop-down control gives you a list of options.

In many cases, you will choose to ignore an error by selecting the Ignore Error option. Selecting this option eliminates the cell from subsequent error checks. However, all previously ignored errors can be reset so that they appear again. (Use the Reset Ignored Errors button in the Formulas tab of the Excel Options dialog box.)

You can choose Formulas➜Formula Auditing➜Error Checking to display a dialog box that describes each potential error cell in sequence, much like using a spell-checking command. This command is available even if you disable background error checking. Figure 2-12 shows the Error Checking dialog box. This dialog box is *modeless:* that is, you can still access your worksheet when the Error Checking dialog box is displayed.

Caution

The error-checking feature isn't perfect. In fact, it's not even close to perfect. In other words, you can't assume that you have an error-free worksheet simply because Excel doesn't identify any potential errors! Also, be aware that the error-checking feature won't catch the common error of overwriting a formula cell with a value.

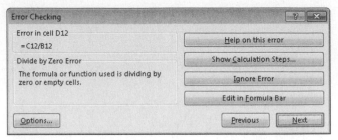

Figure 2-12: Use the Error Checking dialog box to cycle through potential errors identified by Excel.

Using Excel's Formula Evaluator

Formula Evaluator lets you see the various parts of a nested formula evaluated in the order that the formula is calculated. To use Formula Evaluator, select the cell that contains the formula and then choose Formula→Formula Auditing→Evaluate Formula to display the Evaluate Formula dialog box (see Figure 2-13).

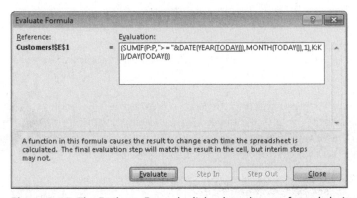

Figure 2-13: The Evaluate Formula dialog box shows a formula being calculated one step at a time.

Click the Evaluate button to show the result of calculating the expressions within the formula. Each button click performs another calculation. This feature may seem a bit complicated at first, but you'll understand how it works and see its value if you spend some time working with it.

Excel provides another way to evaluate a part of a formula:

1. **Select the cell that contains the formula.**

2. **Press F2 to switch to cell edit mode.**

3. **Highlight the portion of the formula you want to evaluate.**

   To highlight, use your mouse or press Shift and use the navigation keys.

4. **Press F9.**

The highlighted portion of the formula displays the calculated result. You can evaluate other parts of the formula or press Esc to cancel and return your formula to its previous state.

Caution

Be careful when using this technique because if you press Enter (rather than Esc), the formula will be modified to use the calculated values.

Array Formulas

In Excel terminology, an *array* is a collection of cells or values that is operated on as a group. An *array formula* is a special type of formula that works with arrays. An array formula can produce a single result, or it can produce multiple results — with each result displayed in a separate cell.

For example, when you multiply a 1 x 5 array by another 1 x 5 array, the result is a third 1 x 5 array. In other words, the result of this kind of operation occupies five cells; each element in the first array is multiplied by each corresponding element in the second array to create five new values, each getting its own cell. The array formula that follows multiplies the values in A1:A5 by the corresponding values in B1:B5. This array formula is entered into five cells simultaneously:

```
{=A1:A5*B1:B5}
```

Note

You enter an array formula by pressing Ctrl+Shift+Enter (not just Enter). To remind you that a formula is an array formula, Excel surrounds it with curly braces in the formula bar. When I present an array formula in this book, I enclose it in curly braces to distinguish it from a normal formula. Don't enter the braces yourself.

An array formula example

An array formula enables you to perform individual operations on each cell in a range in much the same way that a programming language's looping feature enables you to work with elements of an array. If you've never used array formulas before, this section will get your feet wet with a hands-on example.

Figure 2-14 shows a worksheet with text in A1:A5. The goal of this exercise is to create a *single formula* that returns the sum of the total number of characters in the range. Without the *single formula* requirement, you'd write a formula with the LEN function, copy it down the column, and then use the SUM function to add the results of the intermediate formulas.

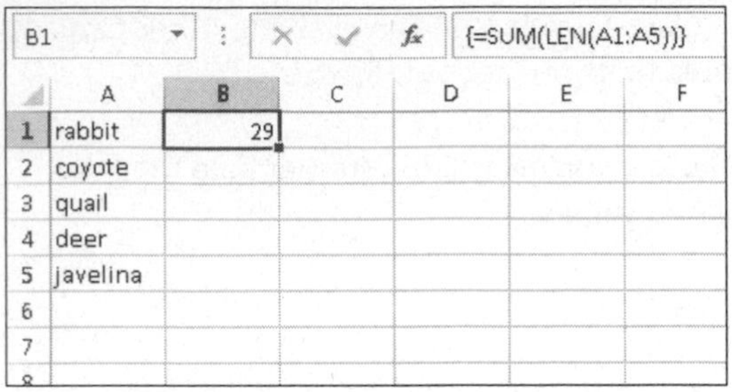

Figure 2-14: Cell B1 contains an array formula that returns the total number of characters contained in range A1:A5. Note the brackets in the formula bar.

To demonstrate how an array formula can occupy more than one cell, create the worksheet shown in the figure and then try these steps:

1. Select the range B1:B5.

2. Type the following formula:

   ```
   =LEN(A1:A5)
   ```

3. Press Ctrl+Shift+Enter.

The preceding steps enter a single array formula into five cells. Enter a SUM formula that adds the values in B1:B5, and you'll see that the total number of characters in A1:A5 is 29.

Here's the key point: It's not necessary to actually *display* those five array elements. Rather, Excel can store the array in memory. Knowing this, you can type the following single array formula in any blank cell (*remember:* don't type the curly brackets and make sure that you enter the array formula by pressing Ctrl+Shift+Enter):

```
{=SUM(LEN(A1:A5))}
```

This formula essentially creates a five-element array (in memory) that consists of the length of each string in A1:A5. The SUM function uses this array as its argument, and the formula returns 29.

An array formula calendar

Figure 2-15 shows a worksheet set up to display a calendar for any month. (Change the month, and the calendar is updated.) Believe it or not, the calendar is created with a single array formula that occupies 42 cells.

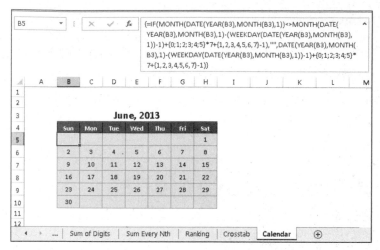

Figure 2-15: A single multicell array formula is all it takes to make a calendar for any month in any year.

The array formula, entered in the range B5:H10, is

```
{=IF(MONTH(DATE(YEAR(B3),MONTH(B3),1))<>MONTH(DATE(YEAR(B3),
MONTH(B3),1)-(WEEKDAY(DATE(YEAR(B3),MONTH(B3),1))-1)
+{0;1;2;3;4;5}*7+{1,2,3,4,5,6,7}-1),"",
DATE(YEAR(B3),MONTH(B3),1)-(WEEKDAY(DATE(YEAR(B3),
MONTH(B3),1))-1)+{0;1;2;3;4;5}*7+{1,2,3,4,5,6,7}-1)}
```

The formula returns date serial numbers, and you need to format the cells to display the day number only by using a custom number format ("d").

On the Web   The book's website contains a workbook with the calendar example, as well as several additional array formula examples. The file is named array formula examples.xlsx. In addition, you'll find a workbook named yearly calendar.xlsx that uses array formulas to display a calendar for a complete year.

Array formula pros and cons

The advantages of using array formulas rather than single-cell formulas include the following:

➤ They can sometimes use less memory.

➤ They can make your work much more efficient.

➤ They can eliminate the need for intermediate formulas.

➤ They can enable you to do things that would be difficult or impossible otherwise.

A few disadvantages of using array formulas are the following:

➤ Using many complex array formulas can sometimes slow your spreadsheet recalculation time.

➤ They can make your worksheet more difficult for others to understand.

➤ You must remember to enter an array formula with a special key sequence (by pressing Ctrl+Shift+Enter).

Counting and Summing Techniques

A common task in Excel is conditional counting or summing. This section contains a number of formula examples that deal with counting various items on a worksheet, based on single or multiple criteria. You can adapt these formulas to your own needs.

Note

Excel 2007 introduced two new counting and summing functions that aren't available in previous versions (COUNTIFS and SUMIFS). Therefore, I present two versions of some formulas: an Excel 2007 and later version and an array formula that works with all versions of Excel.

Figure 2-16 shows a simple worksheet to demonstrate the formulas that follow. The following range names are defined:

➤ **Month:** A2:A10

➤ **Region:** B2:B10

➤ **Sales:** C2:C10

	A	B	C	D	E	F	G	H
1	Month	Region	Sales			XL 2007+	All versions	Description
2	Jan	North	100				3	Count of Region
3	Jan	South	200				2	Count of Sales where Sales=300
4	Jan	West	300				2	Count of Sales where Sales>300
5	Feb	North	150				8	Count of Sales where Sales <> 100
6	Feb	South	250				6	Count of Regions with five letters
7	Feb	West	350				6	Count of Regions that contain the letter "h"
8	Mar	North	200			1	1	Count of Sales where Month ="Jan" and Sales >200
9	Mar	South	300			1	1	Count of Sales where Month="Jan" AND Region="North"
10	Mar	West	400			2	2	Count of Sales where Month = "Jan" AND Region="North" or "South"
11						4	4	Count of Sales between 300 and 400
12								
13								
14						XL 2007	All versions	Description
15							1,600	Sum of Sales greater than 200
16							600	Sum of Sales where Month = "Jan"
17							1,350	Sum of Sales where Month = "Jan" or "Feb"
18						100	100	Sum of Sales where Month="Jan" AND Region="North"
19						500	500	Sum of Sales where Month<>"Jan" AND Region<>"North"
20						500	500	Sum of Sales where Month="Jan" and Sales>= 200
21						1,350	1,350	Sum of Sales between 300 and 400
22								

Sheet1 ⊕

Figure 2-16: This worksheet demonstrates some useful formulas for counting and summing.

Counting formula examples

Table 2-3 contains formulas that demonstrate a variety of counting techniques.

Table 2-3: Counting Formula Examples

Formula	Description
=COUNTIF(Region,"North")	Counts the number of rows in which Region = "North"
=COUNTIF(Sales,300)	Counts the number of rows in which Sales = 300
=COUNTIF(Sales,">300")	Counts the number of rows in which Sales > 300
=COUNTIF(Sales,"<>100")	Counts the number of rows in which Sales <> 100
=COUNTIF(Region,"?????")	Counts the number of rows in which Region contains five letters
=COUNTIF(Region,"*h*")	Counts the number of rows in which Region contains the letter H (not case-sensitive)
=COUNTIFS(Month,"Jan",Sales,">200")	Counts the number of rows in which Month = "Jan" and Sales > 200 (Excel 2007 and later)
{=SUM((Month="Jan")*(Sales>200))}	An array formula that counts the number of rows in which Month = "Jan" and Sales > 200
=COUNTIFS(Month,"Jan",Region,"North")	Counts the number of rows in which Month = "Jan" and Region = "North" (Excel 2007 and later)
{=SUM((Month="Jan")*(Region="North"))}	An array formula that counts the number of rows in which Month = "Jan" and Region = "North"
=COUNTIFS(Month,"Jan",Region,"North")+COUNTIFS (Month,"Jan",Region,"South")	Counts the number of rows in which Month = "Jan" and Region = "North" or "South" (Excel 2007 and later)
{=SUM((Month="Jan")*((Region="North")+(Region=" South")))}	An array formula that counts the number of rows in which Month = "Jan" and Region = "North" or "South"
=COUNTIFS(Sales,">=300",Sales,"<=400")	Counts the number of rows in which Sales is between 300 and 400 (Excel 2007 and later)
{=SUM((Sales>=300)*(Sales<=400))}	An array formula that counts the number of rows in which Sales is between 300 and 400

Summing formula examples

Table 2-4 shows a number of formula examples that demonstrate a variety of summing techniques.

Table 2-4: Summing Formula Examples

Formula	Description
=SUMIF(Sales,">200")	Sum of all Sales over 200
=SUMIF(Month,"Jan",Sales)	Sum of Sales in which Month = "Jan"
=SUMIF(Month,"Jan",Sales)+SUMIF(Month,"Feb", Sales)	Sum of Sales in which Month = "Jan" or "Feb"
{=SUM((Month="Jan")*(Region="North")*Sales)}	Sum of Sales in which Month = "Jan" and Region = "North"
=SUMIFS(Sales,Month,"Jan",Region,"North")	Sum of Sales in which Month = "Jan" and Region = "North" (Excel 2007 and later)
{=SUM((Month="Jan")*(Region="North")*Sales)}	An array formula that returns the sum of Sales in which Month = "Jan" and Region = "North"
=SUMIFS(Sales,Month,"Jan",Region,"<>North")	Sum of Sales in which Month = "Jan" and Region <> "North" (Excel 2007 and later)
{=SUM((Month="Jan")*(Region<>"North")*Sales)}	An array formula that returns the sum of Sales in which Month = "Jan" and Region <> "North"
=SUMIFS(Sales,Month,"Jan",Sales,">=200")	Sum of Sales in which Month = "Jan" and Sales >= 200 (Excel 2007 and later)
{=SUM((Month="Jan")*(Sales>=200)*(Sales))}	An array formula that returns the sum of Sales in which Month = "Jan" and Sales >= 200
=SUMIFS(Sales,Sales,">=300",Sales,"<=400")	Sum of Sales between 300 and 400 (Excel 2007 and later)
{=SUM((Sales>=300)*(Sales<=400)*(Sales))}	An array formula that returns the sum of Sales between 300 and 400

Other counting tools

Other ways to count or sum cells that meet certain criteria are

> ➤ Filtering (using a table)
> ➤ Advanced filtering
> ➤ The DCOUNT and DSUM functions
> ➤ Pivot tables

For more information, consult the Help system.

Lookup Formulas

A common type of Excel formula looks up a value in a table and returns a corresponding value. A common telephone directory (remember those?) provides a good analogy. If you want to find a person's telephone number, you first locate the name (look it up) and then retrieve the corresponding number.

Several Excel functions are useful when writing formulas to look up information in a table. Table 2-5 lists and describes these functions.

Table 2-5: Functions Used in Lookup Formulas

Function	Description
CHOOSE	Returns a specific value from a list of values supplied as arguments.
HLOOKUP	Horizontal lookup. Searches for a value in the top row of a table and returns a value in the same column from a row you specify in the table.
IF	Returns one value if a condition you specify is TRUE, and returns another value if the condition is FALSE.
IFERROR*	If the first argument returns an error, the second argument is evaluated and returned. If the first argument does not return an error, it is evaluated and returned.
INDEX	Returns a value (or the reference to a value) from a table or range.
LOOKUP	Returns a value either from a one-row or one-column range. Another form of the LOOKUP function works like VLOOKUP but is restricted to returning a value from the last column of a range.
MATCH	Returns the relative position of an item in a range that matches a specified value.
OFFSET	Returns a reference to a range that is a specified number of rows and columns from a cell or range of cells.
VLOOKUP	Vertical lookup. Searches for a value in the first column of a table and returns a value in the same row from a column you specify in the table.

You can use the Excel basic lookup functions to search a column or row for a lookup value to return another value as a result. Excel provides three basic lookup functions: HLOOKUP, VLOOKUP, and LOOKUP. In addition, the MATCH and INDEX functions are often used together to return a cell or relative cell reference for a lookup value.

The VLOOKUP function looks up the value in the first column of the lookup table and returns the corresponding value in a specified table column. The lookup table is arranged vertically (which explains the V in the function's name). The syntax for the VLOOKUP function is

```
VLOOKUP(lookup_value,table_array,col_index_num,range_lookup)
```

The VLOOKUP function's arguments are as follows:

➤ *lookup_value*: Required. The value to be looked up in the first column of the lookup table.

➤ *table_array*: Required. The range that contains the lookup table.

➤ *col_index_num*: Required. The column number within the table from which the matching value is returned.

➤ *range_lookup*: Optional. If TRUE or omitted, an approximate match is returned. (If an exact match is not found, the next largest value that is less than *lookup_value* is returned.) If FALSE, VLOOKUP will search for an exact match. If VLOOKUP can't find an exact match, the function returns #N/A.

Note

If the *range_lookup* **argument is TRUE or omitted, the first column of the lookup table must be in ascending order. If** *lookup_value* **is smaller than the smallest value in the first column of** *table_array***, VLOOKUP returns #N/A. If the** *range_lookup* **argument is FALSE, the first column of the lookup table need not be in ascending order. If an exact match is not found, the function returns #N/A.**

A common use for a lookup formula involves an income tax rate schedule (see Figure 2-17). The tax rate schedule shows the income tax rates for various income levels. The following formula (in cell B3) returns the tax rate for the income in cell B2:

```
=VLOOKUP(B2,D2:F7,3)
```

	A	B	C	D	E	F
1				Income is Greater Than or Equal To...	But Less Than or Equal To...	Tax Rate
2	Enter Income:	$32,650		$0	$2,650	15.00%
3	The Tax Rate is:	31.00%		$2,651	$27,300	28.00%
4				$27,301	$58,500	31.00%
5				$58,501	$131,800	36.00%
6				$131,801	$284,700	39.60%
7				$284,701		45.25%
8						
9						
10						
11						

intro example | **vlookup** | hlookup | lookup | match & index

Figure 2-17: Using the VLOOKUP function to look up a tax rate.

The lookup table resides in a range that consists of three columns (D2:F7). Because the last argument for the VLOOKUP function is 3, the formula returns the corresponding value in the third column of the lookup table.

Note that an exact match is not required. If an exact match is not found in the first column of the lookup table, the VLOOKUP function uses the next largest value that is less than the lookup value. In other words, the function uses the row in which the value you want to look up is greater than or equal to the row value but less than the value in the next row. In the case of a tax table, this is exactly what you want to happen.

On the Web

The example in this section is available on this book's website in a file named basic lookup examples.xlsx. The website contains another workbook with additional examples, specialized lookup examples.xlsx.

Working with Dates and Times

Excel uses a serial number system to store dates. The earliest date that Excel can understand is January 1, 1900. This date has a serial number of 1. January 2, 1900, has a serial number of 2, and so on.

Most of the time, you don't have to be concerned with Excel's serial number date system. You simply enter a date in a familiar date format, and Excel takes care of the details behind the scenes. For example, if you need to enter August 15, 2013, you can simply enter the date by typing **August 15, 2013** (or use any of a number of different date formats). Excel interprets your entry and stores the value 41501, which is the serial number for that date.

Note

> In this chapter, I assume the U.S. date system. If your computer uses a different date system, you'll need to adjust accordingly. For example, you might need to enter 15 August 2013.

Entering dates and times

When working with times, you simply enter the time in a cell in a recognized format. Excel's system for representing dates as individual values is extended to include decimals that represent portions or fractions of days. In other words, Excel perceives all time with the same system whether that time is a particular day, a certain hour, or a specific second. For example, the date serial number for August 15, 2013, is 41501. Noon (halfway through the day) is represented internally as 41501.5. Again, you normally don't have to be concerned with these fractional serial numbers.

Because dates and times are stored as serial numbers, it stands to reason that you can add and subtract dates and times. For example, you can enter a formula to calculate the number of days between two dates. If cells A1 and A2 both contain dates, the following formula returns the number of intervening days:

```
=A2-A1
```

Tip

> When performing calculations with time, things get a bit trickier. When you enter a time without an associated date, the date is assumed to be January 0, 1900 (date serial number 0). This is not a problem — unless your calculation produces a negative time value. When this happens, Excel displays an error (displayed as ########). The solution? Switch to the 1904 date system. Display the Excel Options dialog box, click the Advanced tab, and then enable the Use 1904 Date System check box. Be aware that switching to the 1904 date system can cause problems with dates already entered in your file or dates in workbooks that are linked to your file.

Tip

In some cases, you may need to use time values to represent duration, rather than a point in time. For example, you may need to sum the number of hours worked in a week. When you add time values, you can't display more than 24 hours. For each 24-hour period, Excel simply adds another day to the total. The solution is to change the number formatting to use square brackets around the hour part of the format. The following number format, for example, displays more than 24 hours:

```
[hh]:mm
```

Using pre-1900 dates

The world, of course, didn't begin on January 1, 1900. People who work with historical information when using Excel often need to work with dates before January 1, 1900. Unfortunately, the only way to work with pre-1900 dates is to enter the date into a cell as text. For example, you can enter the following into a cell, and Excel won't complain:

```
July 4, 1776
```

You can't, however, perform any manipulation on dates that are actually text. For example, you can't change its formatting, you can't determine which day of the week this date occurred on, and you can't calculate the date that occurs seven days later.

VBA, however, supports a much wider range of dates. I created a number of VBA worksheet functions that allow you to work with pre-1900 dates. Figure 2-18 shows these functions used in a worksheet. It's also an excellent example of how VBA can extend the features in Excel.

	A	B	C	D	E	F	G	H
4	Examples: President Birthdays							
5								
6	President	Year	Month	Day	XDATE	XDATEDIF	XDATEYEARDIF	XDATEDOW
7	George Washington	1732	2	22	February 22, 1732	102,468	280	Friday
8	John Adams	1735	10	30	October 30, 1735	101,122	276	Sunday
9	Thomas Jefferson	1743	4	13	April 13, 1743	98,400	269	Saturday
10	James Madison	1751	3	16	March 16, 1751	95,506	261	Tuesday
11	James Monroe	1758	4	28	April 28, 1758	92,906	254	Friday
12	John Quincy Adams	1767	7	11	July 11, 1767	89,545	245	Saturday
13	Andrew Jackson	1767	3	15	March 15, 1767	89,663	245	Sunday
14	Martin Van Buren	1782	12	5	December 5, 1782	83,919	229	Thursday
15	William Henry Harrison	1773	2	9	February 9, 1773	87,505	239	Tuesday
16	John Tyler	1790	3	29	March 29, 1790	81,248	222	Monday
17	James K. Polk	1795	11	2	November 2, 1795	79,204	216	Monday
18	Zachary Taylor	1784	11	24	November 24, 1784	83,199	227	Wednesday
19	Millard Fillmore	1800	1	7	January 7, 1800	77,677	212	Tuesday
20	Franklin Pierce	1804	11	23	November 23, 1804	75,896	207	Friday
21	James Buchanan	1791	4	23	April 23, 1791	80,858	221	Saturday
22	Abraham Lincoln	1809	2	12	February 12, 1809	74,354	203	Sunday
23	Andrew Johnson	1808	12	29	December 29, 1808	74,399	203	Thursday
24	Ulysses S. Grant	1822	4	27	April 27, 1822	69,532	190	Saturday
25	Rutherford B. Hayes	1822	10	4	October 4, 1822	69,372	189	Friday
26	James A. Garfield	1831	11	19	November 19, 1831	66,039	180	Saturday
27	Chester A. Arthur	1829	10	5	October 5, 1829	66,814	182	Monday
28	Grover Cleveland	1837	3	18	March 18, 1837	64,093	175	Saturday

Sheet1 Sheet2 ⊕

Figure 2-18: The Extended Date Functions add-in lets you work with pre-1900 dates.

Cross-Ref

See Chapter 8 for more information about the Extended Date functions.

Creating Megaformulas

Often, a formula requires intermediate formulas to produce a desired result. In other words, a formula may depend on other formulas, which in turn depend on other formulas. After you get all these formulas working correctly, you can often eliminate the intermediate formulas and use what I refer to as a single *megaformula* instead. The advantages? You use fewer cells (less clutter), the file size is smaller, and recalculation may even be a bit faster. The main disadvantage is that the formula may be impossible to decipher or modify.

Here's an example: Imagine a worksheet that has a column with thousands of people's names. And suppose that you've been asked to remove all the middle names and middle initials from the names — but not all the names have a middle name or initial. Editing the cells manually would take hours, and even Excel's Data➔Data Tools➔Text To Columns command isn't much help. So you opt for a formula-based solution. Although this task isn't difficult, it normally involves several intermediate formulas.

New Feature

The Flash Fill feature in Excel 2013 provides another way to accomplish this task.

Figure 2-19 shows the results of the more conventional solution, which requires six intermediate formulas shown in Table 2-6. The names are in column A; the end result goes in column H. Columns B through G hold the intermediate formulas.

	A	B	C	D	E	F	G	H
1	Name	Formula-1	Formula-2	Formula-3	Formula-4	Formula-5	Formula-6	Result
2	Bob Smith	Bob Smith	4	#VALUE!	4	Bob	Smith	Bob Smith
3	Mike A. Jones	Mike A. Jones	5	8	8	Mike	Jones	Mike Jones
4	Jim Ray Johnson	Jim Ray Johnson	4	8	8	Jim	Johnson	Jim Johnson
5	Tom Alvin Jacobs	Tom Alvin Jacobs	4	10	10	Tom	Jacobs	Tom Jacobs
6	John Q. Public	John Q. Public	5	8	8	John	Public	John Public
7	R.J Smith	R.J Smith	4	#VALUE!	4	R.J	Smith	R.J Smith
8	R. Jay Smith	R. Jay Smith	3	7	7	R.	Smith	R. Smith
9	Tim Jones	Tim Jones	4	#VALUE!	4	Tim	Jones	Tim Jones
10								
11								

Sheet1   +

Figure 2-19: Removing the middle names and initials requires intermediate formulas.

Table 2-6: Intermediate Formulas Written in Row 2 in Figure 2-10

Column	Intermediate Formula	What It Does
B	=TRIM(A2)	Removes excess spaces.
C	=FIND(" ",B2,1)	Locates the first space.
D	=FIND(" ",B2,C2+1)	Locates the second space. Returns #VALUE! if no second space exists.

continued

Table 2-6: Intermediate Formulas Written in Row 2 in Figure 2-10 *(continued)*

Column	Intermediate Formula	What It Does
E	=IF(ISERROR(D2),C2,D2)	Uses the first space if no second space exists.
F	=LEFT(B2,C2)	Extracts the first name.
G	=RIGHT(B2,LEN(B2)-E2)	Extracts the last name.
H	=F2&G2	Concatenates the two names.

You can eliminate the intermediate formulas by creating a megaformula. You do so by creating all the intermediate formulas and then going back into the final result formula and replacing each cell reference with a copy of the formula in the cell referred to (without the equal sign). Fortunately, you can use the Clipboard to copy and paste. Keep repeating this process until cell H2 contains nothing but references to cell A2. You end up with the following megaformula in one cell:

```
=LEFT(TRIM(A2),FIND
(" ",TRIM(A2),1))&RIGHT(TRIM(A2),LEN(TRIM(A2))-
IF(ISERROR(FIND(" ",TRIM(A2),FIND(" ",TRIM(A2),1)+1)),
FIND(" ",TRIM(A2),1),FIND(" ",TRIM(A2),FIND
(" ",TRIM(A2),1)+1)))
```

When you're satisfied that the megaformula is working, you can delete the columns that hold the intermediate formulas because they're no longer used.

The megaformula performs exactly the same tasks as all the intermediate formulas — although it's virtually impossible for anyone to figure out, even the author. If you decide to use megaformulas, make sure that the intermediate formulas are performing correctly before you start building a mega-formula. Even better, keep a single copy of the intermediate formulas somewhere in case you discover an error or need to make a change.

Another way to approach this problem is to create a custom worksheet function in VBA. Then you could replace the megaformula with a simple formula, such as

```
=NOMIDDLE(A1)
```

In fact, I wrote such a function to compare it with intermediate formulas and megaformulas. The listing follows:

```
Function NOMIDDLE(n) As String
    Dim FirstName As String, LastName As String
    n = Application.WorksheetFunction.Trim(n)
    FirstName = Left(n, InStr(1, n, " "))
    LastName = Right(n, Len(n) - InStrRev(n, " "))
    NOMIDDLE = FirstName & LastName
End Function
```

On the Web

A workbook that contains the intermediate formulas, the megaformula, and the NOMIDDLE VBA function is available on the book's website. The workbook is named megaformula.xlsm.

Because a megaformula is so complex, you may think that using one slows down recalculation. Actually, that's not the case. As a test, I created a workbook that used the megaformula 175,000 times. Then I created another workbook that used six intermediate formulas to compute the 175,000 results. In the following, you can see the results in terms of calculation time and file size:

➤ Intermediate formulas: Recalculation time of 5.8 seconds; 12.60MB file size

➤ Megaformula: Recalculation time of 3.9 seconds; 2.95MB file size

The actual results will vary significantly, depending on system speed, amount of memory installed, and the actual formula.

The VBA function was much slower — I abandoned the timed test after five minutes. Slower performance is fairly typical of VBA functions; they are always slower than built-in Excel functions.

Understanding Excel Files

3

In This Chapter

- Starting Excel
- Opening and saving different types of files in Excel
- Understanding the Excel file formats
- Figuring out how Excel uses the Windows Registry

Starting Excel

You can start Excel in various ways, depending on how it's installed. You can double-click an icon on the desktop, click an icon in the taskbar, use the Windows Start button, or double-click a file associated with the Excel application. All methods ultimately launch the excel.exe executable file.

When Excel 2013 starts, it performs many actions, including the following:

➤ It reads its settings stored in the Windows Registry.

➤ It reads and applies any Quick Access toolbar or Ribbon customizations defined in the Excel.officeUI file.

➤ It opens the *.xlb menu/toolbar customization file if it exists.

➤ It opens the AutoCorrect list (and *.ACL file) if it exists.

➤ It opens all add-ins that are installed (that is, those that are checked in the Add-Ins dialog box).

➤ It opens any workbooks in the XLStart directory.

➤ It opens the Personal Macro Workbook (personal.xlsb) if it exists.

➤ It opens any workbooks that are in the alternate start-up directory (specified on the Advanced tab of the Excel Options dialog box).

➤ It determines whether Excel ended with a crash the last time it was used. If so, it displays a list of autorecovered workbooks.

➤ It displays an empty workbook — unless the user specified a workbook to open or one or more files were found in the XLStart or an alternate start-up directory.

You can install Excel in any location. But in most cases, the Excel executable file is located in the default installation directory:

```
C:\Program Files (x86)\Microsoft Office\Office15\EXCEL.EXE
```

or

```
C:\Program Files\Microsoft Office\Office15\EXCEL.EXE
```

To determine where Excel is installed, execute this VBA statement:

```
MsgBox Application.Path
```

Unlike previous versions, Excel 2013 has a single-document interface. In other words, every workbook has its own window and its own Ribbon and is treated as a separate task. In previous versions, multiple workbooks opened in a single Excel window (a multidocument interface).

For VBA developers, the single document interface affects modeless UserForms and custom shortcut menus. These topics are covered later in this book.

Tip

If you press the Ctrl key when you start Excel, the program opens in safe mode. This mode is primarily used for troubleshooting when Excel crashes when it's started.

File Types

Although the Excel 2013 default file format is an XLSX workbook file, the program can also open and save a wide variety of other file formats. This section provides an overview of the file types that Excel 2013 can handle.

Note

Beginning with Excel 2007, Microsoft removed support for Lotus and Quattro Pro spreadsheet file formats.

Excel file formats

Excel 2007 introduced a new default file format, and that format is also used in Excel 2010 and Excel 2013. However, these recent versions can still read and write older Excel file formats.

Tip

To change the default file save setting, choose File➔Options and click the Save tab in the Excel Options dialog box. You'll find a drop-down list that lets you select the default file format.

Table 3-1 lists the Excel file types that Excel 2013 supports. Keep in mind that an Excel workbook or add-in file can have any extension that you like. In other words, these files don't need to be stored with the standard extensions shown in the table. However, Excel may display a warning if you try to open a file in which the content does not match the extension.

Table 3-1: Excel File Types

File Type	Extension	Read/Write	Notes
Excel Workbook	xlsx	Yes/Yes	The default file format. It can't store VBA or XLM macro code. Compatible with Excel 2007 and later.
Excel Macro-Enabled Workbook	xlsm	Yes/Yes	The file format for workbooks that contain macros. Compatible with Excel 2007 and later.
Excel Binary Workbook	xlsb	Yes/Yes	A binary file format. It's an updated version of the previous XLS format. Compatible with Excel 2007 and later.
Template	xltx	Yes/Yes	The file format for a template. It can't store VBA or XLM macro code. Compatible with Excel 2007 and later.
Macro-Enabled Template	xltm	Yes/Yes	The file format for a template that contains macros. Compatible with Excel 2007 and later.
Excel Add-In	xlam	Yes/Yes	The file format for an add-in. It can store VBA and XLM macros. Compatible with Excel 2007 and later.
Excel 97–Excel 2003 Workbook	xls	Yes/Yes	The Excel binary format (BIFF8) that's compatible with Excel 97 and later.
Excel 97–Excel 2003 Template	xlt	Yes/Yes	The Excel binary template format (BIFF8) that's compatible with Excel 97 and later.
Excel 97–Excel 2003 Add-In	xla	Yes/Yes	The Excel binary format (BIFF8) for add-ins that's compatible with Excel 97 and later.
Microsoft Excel 5.0/95 Workbook	xls	Yes/Yes	The Excel binary format (BIFF5) that's compatible with Excel 5.0 and later.
XML Spreadsheet 2003	xml	Yes/Yes	Microsoft's XML Spreadsheet 2003 file format (XMLSS).

Note

Microsoft Office XP and Office 2003 users can install the Microsoft Office Compatibility Pack, which allows them to open and save documents in Office 2007 (and later) file formats. The Compatibility Pack is available at `http://office.microsoft.com`.

Text file formats

When you attempt to load a text file into Excel, the Text Import Wizard might kick in to help you specify how you want the file retrieved.

Tip

To bypass the Text Import Wizard, press the Shift key when you click Open in the Open dialog box.

Table 3-2 lists the text file types supported by Excel 2013. All text file formats are limited to a single worksheet.

Table 3-2: Text File Types

File Type	Extension	Read/Write	Notes
CSV (comma separated values)	csv	Yes/Yes	Columns are delimited with a comma, and rows are delimited with a carriage return. Excel supports subtypes for Macintosh and MS-DOS.
Formatted Text	prn	Yes/Yes	Columns are delimited with a space character, and rows are delimited with a carriage return.
Text	txt	Yes/Yes	Columns are delimited with a tab, and rows are delimited with a carriage return. Excel supports subtypes for Macintosh, MS-DOS, and Unicode.
Data Interchange Format (DIF)	dif	Yes/Yes	The file format originally used by VisiCalc.
Symbolic Link (SYLK)	slk	Yes/Yes	The file format originally used by Multiplan.

 # When Excel can't open a file

If Excel doesn't support a particular file form, don't be too quick to give up. It's likely that others have had the same problem as you. Try searching the web for the file extension, plus the word *excel*. A file converter may be available, or perhaps someone has figured out how to use an intermediary program to open the file and export it into a format that Excel recognizes.

Database file formats

Table 3-3 lists the database file types supported by Excel 2013. All database file formats are limited to a single worksheet.

Table 3-3: Database File Types

File Type	Extension	Read/Write	Notes
Access	mdb, mde, accdb, accde	Yes/No	You can open one table from the database.
dBASE	dbf	Yes/No	The file format originally created by Ashton-Tate.
Others	Various	Yes/No	By using the commands in the Data➜Get External Data group, you can import data from various data sources that have connections or queries defined on your system.

Other file formats

Table 3-4 lists the other file types supported by Excel 2010.

Table 3-4: Other File Types

File Type	Extension	Read/Write	Notes
HyperText Markup Language (HTML)	htm, html	Yes/Yes	Beginning with Excel 2007, this file format no longer supports "round-tripping." If you save a file and then reopen it, you may lose information.
Single File Web Page	mht, mhtml	Yes/Yes	Also known as Archived Web Page. The only browsers that can display these files are Microsoft Internet Explorer and Opera.
OpenDocument Spreadsheet	ods	Yes/Yes	A file format developed by Sun Microsystems and OASIS. Readable by open-source spreadsheets, such as OpenOffice.
Portable Document Format (PDF)	pdf	No/Yes	The file format originated by Adobe.
XML Paper Specification	xps	No/Yes	Microsoft's alternative to Adobe's PDF.

Workspace files

A *workspace file* is a special file that contains information about an Excel workspace. For example, if you have a project that uses two workbooks and you like to have the workbook windows arranged in a particular way, you can save an XLW file to save this window configuration. Then, whenever you open the XLW file, Excel restores the desired workspace.

To save a workspace, choose View➜Window➜Save Workspace and provide a name when prompted.

To open a workspace file, use File➜Open and select Workspaces (*.xlw) from the Files of Type drop-down list.

It's important to understand that a workspace file does *not* include the workbooks — only the configuration information that makes those workbooks visible in your Excel workspace. So if you need to distribute a workspace to someone else, make sure that you include the workbook files as well as the XLW file.

Excel File Compatibility

It's important to understand the limitations regarding version compatibility. Even though a colleague may be able to open your file, there is no guarantee that everything will function correctly or look the same.

If you save your workbook to an older file format (such as XLS, for versions prior to Excel 2007), Excel automatically runs Compatibility Checker. The Compatibility Checker identifies the elements of your workbook that will result in loss of functionality or fidelity (cosmetics).

Figure 3-1 shows the Compatibility Checker dialog box. Use the Select Versions to Show button to limit the compatibility checking to a specific version of Excel.

The bottom part of Compatibility Checker lists potential compatibility problems. To display the results in a more readable format, click the Copy to New Sheet button.

Keep in mind that compatibility problems can occur with Excel 2007 and Excel 2010 even though these versions use the same file format as Excel 2013. You can't expect features that are new to Excel 2013 to work in earlier versions. For example, if you add Slicers (a new feature in Excel 2013) to a table and send it to a colleague who uses Excel 2010, Slicers won't be displayed. In addition, formulas that use any of the new worksheet functions will return an error. Compatibility Checker identifies these types of problems.

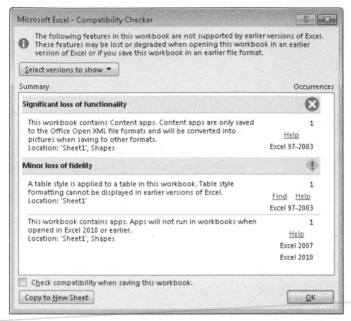

Figure 3-1: The Compatibility Checker is a useful tool for those who share workbooks with others.

Protected View

Excel 2010 introduced a security feature known as *Protected view*. Although it might seem as though Excel is trying to keep you from opening your own files, Protected view is all about protecting you from malware. *Malware* refers to something that can harm your system. Hackers have figured out how to manipulate Excel files such that harmful code can be executed. Protected view essentially prevents these types of attacks by opening a file in a protected environment (a "sandbox").

If you open an Excel workbook that you downloaded from the web, you'll see a colorful message above the formula bar. In addition, the Excel title bar displays [Protected View]. Choose File➜Info to find out why Excel opened the file in Protected view.

If you are certain that the file is safe, click Enable Editing. If you don't enable editing, you will be able to view the contents of the workbook, but you won't be able to make any changes to it.

If the workbook contains macros, you'll see another message after you enable editing: Security Warning. Macros have been disabled. If you are sure that the macros are harmless, click Enable Content.

By default, Protected view is enabled for the following:

➤ Files downloaded from the Internet

➤ Attachments opened from Outlook

➤ Files opened from potentially unsafe locations, such as your Temporary Internet Files folder

➤ File that are blocked by File Block Policy (a Windows feature that allows administrators to define potentially dangerous files)

➤ Files that were digitally signed, but the signature has expired

In some situations, you don't care about working with the document. You just want to print it. In that case, choose File➜Print, and then click the Enable Printing button.

Also, note that you can copy a range of cells from a workbook in Protected view, and paste it into a different workbook.

You have some control over the types of files that trigger Protected View. To change the settings, choose File➜Options, and click Trust Center. Then click the Trust Center Settings button and click the Protected View tab in the Trust Center dialog box.

Using AutoRecover

If you've used computers for any length of time, you've probably lost some work. You forgot to save a file, or maybe the power went out and your unsaved work was lost. Or maybe you were working on something and didn't think it was important, so you closed it without saving — and later realized that it *was* important. A feature introduced in Excel 2010 called AutoRecover might make these types of "D'oh!" moments less frequent.

As you work in Excel, your work is periodically saved, automatically, in the background — you don't even know that it's happening. Excel even saves workbooks that you never explicitly saved.

The AutoRecover feature consists of two components:

➤ Versions of a workbook are saved automatically, and you can view them.

➤ Workbooks that you closed without saving are saved as draft versions.

Recovering versions of the current workbook

To see whether any previous versions of the active workbook are available, choose File➜Info. The Versions section lists the available old versions (if any) of the current workbook. In some cases, more than one autosaved version will be listed. In other cases, no autosaved versions will be available.

You can open an autosaved version by clicking its name. Remember that opening an autosaved version *won't* automatically replace the current version of your workbook. Therefore, you can decide whether the autosaved version is preferable to the current version. Or you can just copy some information that may have been accidentally deleted, and paste it to your current workbook.

When you close the workbook, the autosaved versions are deleted.

Recovering unsaved work

When you close a workbook without saving your changes, Excel asks whether you're sure. If that unsaved workbook has an autosaved version, the "Are you sure?" dialog box informs you of that fact.

To recover a workbook that you closed without saving, choose File→Info→Manage Versions→ Recover Unsaved Workbooks. You'll see a list of all draft versions of your workbooks. You can open them and (if you're lucky) recover something that you needed. Note that the unsaved workbooks are stored in the XLSB file format.

Draft versions are deleted after four days or until you edit the file, whichever comes first.

Configuring AutoRecover

Normally, AutoRecover files are saved every 10 minutes. You can specify a save interval between 1 and 120 minutes in the Save tab of the Excel Options dialog box.

If you work with sensitive documents, you might prefer that previous version don't get saved automatically on your computer. The Save tab of the Excel Options dialog box lets you disable this feature completely or only for a specific workbook.

Working with Template Files

A *template* is essentially a model that serves as the basis for something else. An Excel template is a workbook that's used to create other workbooks. You can save any workbook as a template file (XLTX extension). Doing so is useful if you tend to create similar files on a regular basis. For example, you might need to generate a monthly sales report. You can save some time by creating a template that holds the necessary formulas and charts for your report. When you start new files based on the template, you simply plug in the values.

Viewing templates

Excel gives you access to many templates. To explore the Excel templates, choose File→New, and then enter a search term.

Note

> The location of the Templates folder varies, depending on the version of Excel. To find the location of your Templates folder, execute the following VBA statement:

```
MsgBox Application.TemplatesPath
```

Creating templates

Excel supports three types of templates:

➤ **The default workbook template:** Used as the basis for new workbooks. This file is named book.xltx.

➤ **The default worksheet template:** Used as the basis for new worksheets inserted into a workbook. This file is named sheet.xltx.

➤ **Custom workbook templates:** Usually, ready-to-run workbooks that include formulas. Custom workbook templates can be as simple or as complex as you like. Typically, these templates are set up so that a user can simply plug in values and get immediate results.

Using the workbook template to change workbook defaults

Every new workbook that you create starts out with some default settings. For example, the worksheets have gridlines, text appears in Calibri 11-point font, and columns are 8.43 units wide. If you're not happy with any of the default workbook settings, you can change them.

Making changes to Excel's default workbook is fairly easy and can save you lots of time in the long run. Here's how you change Excel's workbook defaults:

1. Open a new workbook.

2. Add or delete sheets to give the workbook the number of worksheets that you want.

3. Make any other changes, such as changing the column widths, named styles, page setup options, and many of the settings available in the two Display Options sections in the Advanced tab of the Excel Options dialog box.

   To change the default formatting for cells, choose Home➔Styles➔Cell Styles and then modify the settings for the Normal style. For example, you can change the default font, size, or number format.

4. When your workbook is set up to your liking, choose File➔Save As.

5. In the Save As dialog box, select Template (*.xltx) from the box labeled Save As Type.

6. Enter **book.xltx** for the filename.

7. Save the file in your \XLStart folder (*not* in your Templates folder).

8. Close the file.

Tip

To determine the location of \XLStart, execute this VBA statement:

```
MsgBox Application.StartupPath
```

After you perform the preceding steps, the new default workbook that appears when Excel is started is based on the book.xltx workbook template. You can also press Ctrl+N to create a workbook based on this template. If you ever want to revert to the standard default workbook, just delete or rename the book.xltx file.

Note

If you choose File➜New and select Blank Workbook, the workbook will not be based on the book.xltx template. I don't know whether that's a bug or by design. In any case, this command sequence provides a way to override the custom book.xltx template if you need to.

Using the worksheet template to change worksheet defaults

When you insert a new worksheet into a workbook, Excel uses its built-in worksheet defaults for the worksheet. These defaults include items such as column width and row height. If you don't like the default settings for a new worksheet, you can change them by following these steps:

1. Start with a new workbook and delete all the sheets except one.

2. Make your changes, such as changing the column widths, named styles, page setup options, and many of the settings in the Excel Options dialog box.

3. When your workbook is set up to your liking, choose File➜Save As.

4. In the Save As dialog box, select Template (*.xltx) from the Save As Type box.

5. Enter **sheet.xltx** for the filename.

6. Save the file in your \XLStart folder (*not* in your Templates folder).

7. Close the file.

8. Close and restart Excel.

After performing this procedure, all new sheets that you insert by clicking the Insert Worksheet button (which is next to the last sheet tab) will be formatted like your sheet.xltx template. You can also press Shift+F11 to insert a new worksheet.

Creating workbook templates

The book.xltx and sheet.xltx templates discussed in the preceding section are two special types of templates that determine default settings for new workbooks and new worksheets. This section discusses other types of templates, referred to as *workbook templates,* which are simply workbooks that you set up as the basis for new workbooks or worksheets.

Why use a workbook template? The simple answer is that it saves you from repeating work. Assume that you create a monthly sales report that consists of your company's sales by region, plus several summary calculations and charts. You can create a template file that consists of everything except the input values. Then, when it's time to create your report, you can open a workbook based on the template, fill in the blanks, and be finished.

Note

You could, of course, just use the previous month's workbook and save it with a different name. This approach is prone to errors, however, because you easily can forget to use the Save As command and accidentally overwrite the previous month's file. Another option is to right-click a filename and choose Open a Copy. This step creates a new workbook from an existing one, but gives a different name to ensure that the old file is not overwritten.

To create a workbook based on a template you created, choose File➜New, and click Personal (located below the search box).

When you create a workbook that is based on a template, the default workbook name is the template name with a number appended. For example, if you create a new workbook based on a template named Sales Report.xltx, the workbook's default name is Sales Report1.xlsx. The first time that you save a workbook that is created from a template, Excel displays its Save As dialog box so that you can give the template a new name if you want to.

A *custom template* is essentially a normal workbook, and it can use any Excel feature, such as charts, formulas, and macros. Usually, a template is set up so that the user can enter values and get immediate results. In other words, most templates include everything but the data, which is entered by the user.

Note

If your template contains macros, it must be saved as an Excel Macro-Enabled Template, with an XLTM extension.

Inside an Excel File

Excel 2007 and later versions uses an XML format for workbooks, templates, and add-ins. These files are actually Zip compressed files. As such, they can be "unzipped" and examined.

Versions prior to Excel 2007 used a binary file format. Although the binary file format specifications are known, working with binary files is not easy. The Excel XML file format, on the other hand, is an *open format*. As such, these files can be created and manipulated using other software.

Dissecting a file

In this section, I describe the various parts of a typical Excel XLSM (macro-enabled) workbook file. The workbook, named sample.xlsm, is shown in Figure 3-2. It has one worksheet, one chart sheet, and a simple VBA macro. The worksheet contains a table, a button (from the Forms controls), a SmartArt diagram, and a photo.

On the Web   The sample.xlsm workbook is available at this book's website.

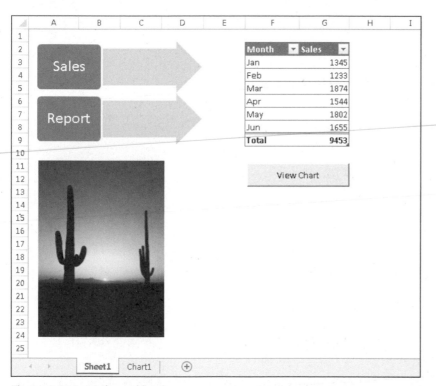

Figure 3-2: A simple workbook.

To view the innards of an Excel XLSX (or XLSM) file, you need to open an Explorer window and add a ZIP extension to the filename. So the sample.xlsm file is renamed to sample.xlsm.zip. You can then open the file by using any unzipping program. I use the Zip feature built into Windows 7.

Note   If your system is set up to hide file extensions, I suggest that you turn off that option. In a Windows Explorer window, choose Tools➜Folder Options and click the View tab. In the File and Folders section, remove the check mark from Hide Extensions for Known File Types.

Tip

You may prefer to extract the zipped files into an uncompressed directory. Doing so makes it easier to view the files. In Windows, right-click the filename and choose Extract All.

The first thing that you notice is that the file contains a directory structure. The left panel of Figure 3-3 shows the fully expanded directory structure for the workbook file. The actual directories will vary with the workbook.

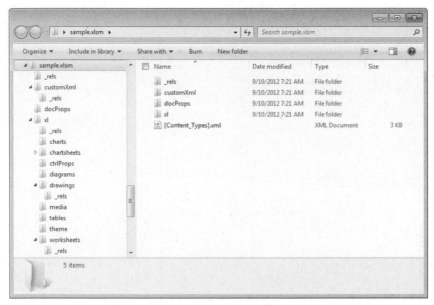

Figure 3-3: The directory structure of the workbook file.

With a few exceptions, all the files are text files. More specifically, they are XML files. You can view them in a text file editor, an XML editor, a web browser, or even Excel. Figure 3-4 shows one of these files viewed in the Chrome browser. The non-XML files include graphic images and VBA projects (these are stored in binary format).

This XML file has four root-level folders, and some of these have subfolders. Many of the folders contain a _rels folder. These _rels folders contain XML files that define the relationships to other parts within the package.

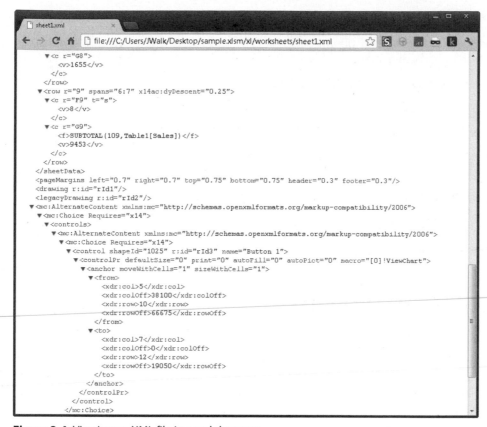

Figure 3-4: Viewing an XML file in a web browser.

Following is a list of the folders in the sample.xlsm workbook:

➤ **_rels:** Contains information about the package relationships.

➤ **customXml:** Contains information about Ribbon enhancements stored in the workbook.

➤ **docProps:** Contains XML files that describe the file properties and application settings.

➤ **xl:** Holds the meat of the file. The folder name varies with the Office document type (xl, ppt, word, and so on). You'll find several XML files that contain settings for the workbook. And if your workbook contains VBA code, it will be in a binary file with a BIN extension. The xl folder has several subfolders. (Some workbooks may have more or fewer subfolders, depending on the content.)

  ● **charts:** Contains an XML file for each chart. This file contains the chart settings.

  ● **chartsheets:** Contains an XML file with data for each chart sheet in the workbook.

- **diagrams:** Contains XML files that describe the diagrams (SmartArt) in the workbook.

- **drawings:** Contains an XML file with data for each *drawing*. Drawings include items such as buttons, charts, and images.

- **media:** Contains embedded media, such GIF and JPG files.

- **tables:** Contains an XML file with data for each table.

- **theme:** Contains an XML file with data about the workbook's theme.

- **worksheets:** Contains an XML file for each worksheet in the workbook.

Tip

If you add a ZIP extension to an Excel file, you can still open it in Excel — although you'll get a warning message first. Also, you can save a workbook with a ZIP extension. In the Save As dialog box, add a ZIP extension and then place double quotation marks around the entire filename — for example, "Myworkbook.xlsx.zip".

Why is the file format important?

The "open" XML file formats introduced in Microsoft Office 2007 represent a significant step for the computing community. For the first time, it was relatively easy to read and write Excel workbooks using software other than Excel. For example, you can write a program to modify thousands of Excel workbook files without even opening Excel. Such a program could insert a new worksheet into every file. The programmer, of course, would need to have excellent knowledge of the XML file structures, but such a task is definitely doable.

Importantly, the new file formats are somewhat less prone to corruption (compared to the old binary formats). I saved a workbook file and then deleted one of the worksheet XML files. When I tried to reopen it in Excel, I got the message shown in Figure 3-5. Excel was able to tell that the file was damaged by comparing the information in the *._rels files with what's actually in the file. In this case, Excel was able to repair the file and open it. The deleted worksheet was reinserted, but it was empty.

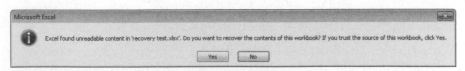

Figure 3-5: Excel can often repair a damaged workbook file.

In addition, the zipped XML files are usually smaller than comparable binary files. And, finally, the structured nature of the files makes extracting individual elements (for example, all graphic images) possible.

The typical Excel user won't need to examine or modify the XML components of a workbook file. But as a developer, you may want to write code that changes Excel's Ribbon user interface. If that's the case, you *will* need to be at least somewhat familiar with the structure of a workbook XML file.

Cross-Ref   **Refer to Chapter 20 for more information about modifying Excel's Ribbon.**

The OfficeUI File

A file named Excel.officeUI stores changes made to the Quick Access toolbar and Ribbon. This XML file is located here:

```
C:\Users\<username>\AppData\Local\Microsoft\Office
```

Whenever a change is made to the Quick Access toolbar or to the Ribbon, the XML file is updated immediately, not when Excel is closed. The file doesn't exist unless you've made at least one change to the user interface.

You can view Excel.officeUI using an XML editor, a web browser, or Excel. To view this file in Excel, follow these steps:

1. Make a copy of the Excel.officeUI file.

2. Add an XML extension to the copy of the file so that the name is Excel.officeUI.XML.

3. Choose File➡Open to open the file or just drag it into Excel's window.

4. You'll see a dialog box with some options; choose As an XML Table.

Figure 3-6 shows an imported Excel.officeUI file (the file is displayed as a table). In this case, five commands are enabled on the Quick Access toolbar (indicated as TRUE in column B), and I added a new group to the View tab, with five commands (rows 16 through 20 in the table).

You can share an Excel.officeUI file with other users. For example, you may have customized your Quick Access toolbar with some handy tools, and added a new Ribbon tab with lots of useful commands, nicely organized. If your colleagues are impressed, just give them a copy of your Excel.officeUI file and tell them where to put it. Keep in mind that replacing an existing Excel.officeUI-file will overwrite any changes your colleagues have made. There is no way to merge multiple Excel.officeUI files.

	A	B	C	D	E	F	G	H	I
1	idQ	visible	idQ2	id	label	insertBeforeQ	autoScale	idQ3	visible4
2	mso:FileNewDefault	FALSE							
3	mso:FileOpen	FALSE							
4	mso:FileSave	TRUE							
5	mso:FileSendAsAttachment	FALSE							
6	mso:FilePrintQuick	FALSE							
7	mso:PrintPreviewAndPrint	FALSE							
8	mso:Spelling	FALSE							
9	mso:Undo	TRUE							
10	mso:Redo	TRUE							
11	mso:SortAscendingExcel	FALSE							
12	mso:SortDescendingExcel	FALSE							
13	mso:FileOpenRecentFile	FALSE							
14	mso:PlayMacro	TRUE							
15	mso:ChartElementSelector	TRUE							
16			mso:TabView	mso_c2.398F93C4	Text To Speech	mso:GroupWindow	TRUE	mso:SpeakCells	TRUE
17			mso:TabView	mso_c2.398F93C4	Text To Speech	mso:GroupWindow	TRUE	mso:SpeakStop	TRUE
18			mso:TabView	mso_c2.398F93C4	Text To Speech	mso:GroupWindow	TRUE	mso:SpeakByColumns	TRUE
19			mso:TabView	mso_c2.398F93C4	Text To Speech	mso:GroupWindow	TRUE	mso:SpeakByRows	TRUE
20			mso:TabView	mso_c2.398F93C4	Text To Speech	mso:GroupWindow	TRUE	mso:SpeakOnEnter	TRUE
21									

Sheet1

Figure 3-6: Viewing an Excel.officeUI data file in Excel.

Don't attempt to modify the Excel.officeUI file unless you know what you're doing. But feel free to experiment. If Excel reports an error in the Excel.officeUI file at startup, you can just delete the file, and Excel will create a new one. Better yet, keep a backup copy of the original.

The XLB File

Excel stores customized toolbar and menu bar configurations in an XLB file. Even though Excel 2013 doesn't officially support custom toolbars and menus in the way that it did in previous versions, it still uses an XLB file if you use any applications that create toolbars or custom menus. If you can't find an XLB file, it means that Excel isn't storing any custom toolbar or menu configurations.

When you exit Excel, the current toolbar configuration is saved in a file named Excel15.xlb. This file is (most likely) located here:

```
C:\Users\<username>\AppData\Roaming\Microsoft\Excel
```

This binary file contains information regarding the position and visibility of all custom toolbars and custom menu bars, plus modifications that you've made to built-in toolbars or menu bars.

Add-In Files

An *add-in* is essentially an Excel workbook file with a few important differences:

➤ The workbook's IsAddin property is True — which means that it can be loaded and unloaded by using the Add-Ins dialog box.

➤ The workbook is hidden and cannot be unhidden by the user. Consequently, an add-in is never the active workbook.

➤ When using VBA, the add-in workbook is not part of the Workbooks collection.

Tip

Access the Add-Ins dialog box by choosing File➔Options. Click the Add-Ins tab, select Excel Add-Ins from the Manage list, and click Go. If you've set up Excel to display the Developer tab, you can also use Developer➔Add-Ins➔Addins. Or (easiest of all), just press Alt+TI, a handy key combination leftover from Excel 2003.

Many add-ins provide new features or functions to Excel. You can access these new features as if they were built into the product.

You can create your own add-ins from workbook files. In fact, creating add-ins is the preferred method of distributing some types of Excel applications. Excel 2007 (and later) add-ins have an XLAM extension by default.

Note

Besides XLAM add-ins, Excel supports XLL add-ins and COM add-ins. These types of add-ins are created using software other than Excel. This book discusses only XLAM add-ins.

Cross-Ref

Chapter 19 covers the topic of add-ins in detail.

Excel Settings in the Registry

The Excel Options dialog box has dozens of user-specified options. Excel uses the Windows Registry to store these settings and retrieve them when Excel is started. In this section, I provide some background information about the Windows Registry and discuss how Excel uses the Registry to store its settings.

About the Registry

The *Windows Registry* is essentially a central hierarchical database that is used by the operating system and by application software. The Registry first appeared in Windows 95 and replaces the old INI files that stored Windows and application settings.

Cross-Ref

Your VBA macros can also read and write information to the Registry. Refer to Chapter 9 for details.

You can use the Registry Editor program (included with Windows) to browse the Registry — and even to edit its contents if you know what you're doing. The Registry Editor is named regedit.exe. Before beginning your explorations, take a minute to read the sidebar "Before you edit the Registry." Figure 3-7 shows what the Registry Editor looks like.

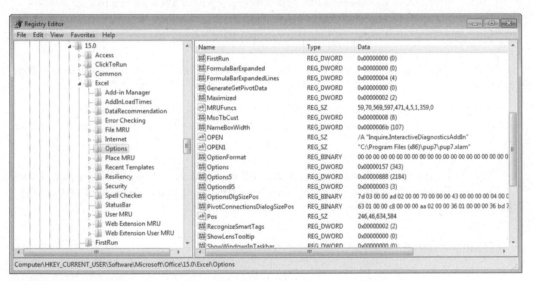

Figure 3-7: Registry Editor lets you browse and make changes to the Registry.

The Registry consists of keys and values, arranged in a hierarchy. The top-level keys are

- ➤ HKEY_CLASSES_ROOT
- ➤ HKEY_CURRENT_USER
- ➤ HKEY_LOCAL_MACHINE
- ➤ HKEY_USERS
- ➤ HKEY_CURRENT_CONFIG

Before you edit the Registry

You can use the regedit.exe program to change anything in the Registry, including information that is critical to your system's operation. In other words, if you change the wrong piece of information, Windows may no longer work properly.

Get into the habit of choosing the File➔Export command in Registry Editor. This command enables you to save an ASCII version of the entire Registry or just a specific branch of the Registry. If you find that you messed up something, you can always import the ASCII file to restore the Registry to its previous condition (choose the File➔Import command). Refer to the Help file for Regedit for details.

Excel's settings

Information used by Excel 2013 is stored in this Registry section:

```
HKEY_CURRENT_USER\Software\Microsoft\Office\15.0\Excel
```

In this section of the Registry, you'll find a number of keys that contain specific values that determine how Excel operates.

The Registry settings are updated automatically by Excel when Excel closes.

Note

It's important to understand that Excel reads the Windows Registry only once — when it starts up. In addition, Excel updates the Registry settings only when Excel closes normally. If Excel crashes (unfortunately, not an uncommon occurrence), the Registry information is not updated. For example, if you change one of Excel's settings, such as the visibility of the formula bar, this setting is not written to the Registry until Excel closes by normal means.

Table 3-5 lists some of the Registry sections that are relevant to Excel 2013. You may not find all these sections in your Registry database, and you may find some others.

Table 3-5: Excel Configuration Information in the Registry

Section	Description
Add-In Manager	Lists add-ins that appear in the Add-Ins dialog box. Add-ins that are included with Excel do not appear in this list. If you have an add-in entry in this list box that you no longer use, you can remove it by using the Registry Editor.
Converters	Lists additional (external) file converters that are not built into Excel.
Error Checking	Holds the settings for formula error checking.

continued

Table 3-5: Excel Configuration Information in the Registry *(continued)*

Section	Description
File MRU	Holds information about the most recently used files (which appears in the Recent Documents list when you choose File→Recent).
Options	A catch-all section; holds a wide variety of settings.
Place MRU	Holds information about the mostly used places (directories and other storage locations).
Recent Templates	Stores the names of templates you've used recently.
Resiliency	Information used for recovering documents.
Security	Specifies the security options for opening files that contain macros.
Spell Checker	Stores information about your spell checker options.
StatusBar	Stores the user choices for what appears in the status bar.
UserInfo	Stores information about the user.

If you have trouble starting Excel, the Registry keys may have become corrupt. You can try using the Registry Editor to delete the entire Excel section:

```
HKEY_CURRENT_USER\Software\Microsoft\Office\15.0\Excel
```

The next time Excel starts, it will rebuild the Registry keys. You will, however, lose all the customization information that was stored there.

Essentials of Spreadsheet Application Development

4

In This Chapter

- Discovering the basic steps involved in spreadsheet application development
- Determining end users' needs
- Planning applications to meet users' needs
- Developing and testing your applications
- Documenting your development efforts and writing user documentation

What Is a Spreadsheet Application?

For the purposes of this book, a *spreadsheet application* is a spreadsheet file (or group of related files) that is designed so that someone other than the developer can perform useful work without extensive training. According to this definition, most of the spreadsheet files that you've developed probably don't qualify as spreadsheet applications. You may have dozens or hundreds of spreadsheet files on your hard drive, but it's a safe bet that most of them aren't designed for others to use.

A good spreadsheet application

- ➤ Enables the end user to perform a task that he or she probably would not be able to do otherwise.
- ➤ Provides the appropriate solution to the problem. (A spreadsheet environment isn't always the optimal approach.)
- ➤ Accomplishes what it is supposed to do. This prerequisite may be obvious, but it's not at all uncommon for applications to fail this test.
- ➤ Produces accurate results and is free of bugs.

➤ Uses appropriate and efficient methods and algorithms to accomplish its job.

➤ Traps errors before the user is forced to deal with them.

➤ Does not allow the user to delete or modify important components accidentally (or intentionally).

➤ Has a clear and consistent user interface so that the user always knows how to proceed.

➤ Has well-documented formulas, macros, and user interface elements that allow for subsequent changes, if necessary.

➤ Is designed so that it can be modified in simple ways without making major changes. A basic fact is that a user's needs change over time.

➤ Has an easily accessible help system that provides useful information on at least the major procedures.

➤ Is designed to be portable and to run on any system that has the proper software (in this case, a copy of the appropriate version of Excel).

It should come as no surprise that it is possible to create spreadsheet applications for many different usage levels, ranging from a simple fill-in-the-blank template to an extremely complex application that uses a custom interface and may not even look like a spreadsheet.

Steps for Application Development

There is no simple, surefire recipe for developing an effective spreadsheet application. Everyone has his or her own style for creating such applications, and I haven't discovered one best way that works for everyone. In addition, every project is different and, therefore, requires its own approach. Finally, the demands and technical expertise of the people you work with (or for) also play a role in how the development process proceeds.

Spreadsheet developers typically perform the following activities:

➤ Determine the needs of the user(s)

➤ Plan an application that meets these needs

➤ Determine the most appropriate user interface

➤ Create the spreadsheet, formulas, macros, and user interface

➤ Test and debug the application

➤ Attempt to make the application bulletproof

➤ Make the application aesthetically appealing and intuitive

➤ Document the development effort

➤ Develop user documentation and Help systems

➤ Distribute the application to the user

➤ Update the application when necessary

Not all these steps are required for each application, and the order in which these activities are performed varies from project to project. I describe each of these activities in the pages that follow. For most of these items, I cover the technical details in subsequent chapters.

Determining User Needs

When you undertake a new Excel project, one of your first steps is to identify exactly what the end users require. Failure to thoroughly assess the end users' needs early on often results in additional work later when you have to adjust the application so that it does what it was supposed to do in the first place.

In some cases, you'll be intimately familiar with the end users — you may even be an end user yourself. In other cases (for example, if you're a consultant developing a project for a new client), you may know little or nothing about the users or their situations.

How do you determine the needs of the user? If you've been asked to develop a spreadsheet application, it's a good idea to meet with the end users and ask specific questions. Better yet, get everything in writing, create flow diagrams, pay attention to minor details, and do anything else to ensure that the product you deliver is the product that is needed.

Here are some guidelines that may help make this phase easier:

➤ Don't assume that you know what the user needs. Second-guessing at this stage almost always causes problems later.

➤ If possible, talk directly to the end users of the application, not just their supervisor or manager.

➤ Learn what, if anything, is currently being done to meet the users' needs. You might be able to save some work by simply adapting an existing application. At the very least, looking at current solutions will familiarize you with the operation.

➤ Identify the resources available at the users' site. For example, try to determine whether you must work around any hardware or software limitations.

➤ If possible, determine the specific hardware systems that will be used. If your application will be used on slow systems, you need to take that into account.

➤ Identify which versions of Excel are in use. Although Microsoft does everything in its power to urge users to upgrade to the latest version of the software, the majority of Excel users don't.

➤ Understand the skill levels of the end users. This information will help you design the application appropriately.

➤ Determine how long the application will be used and whether any changes are anticipated during the lifetime of the project. Knowing this information may influence the amount of effort that you put into the project and help you plan for changes.

And finally, don't be surprised if the project specifications change before you complete the application. This occurrence is common, and you're in a better position if you expect changes rather than being surprised by them. Just make sure that your contract (if you have one) addresses the issue of changing specifications.

Planning an Application That Meets User Needs

After you determine the end users' needs, it's tempting to jump right in and start fiddling around in Excel. Take it from someone who suffers from this problem: Try to restrain yourself. Builders don't construct a house without a set of blueprints, and you shouldn't build a spreadsheet application without some type of plan. The formality of your plan depends on the scope of the project and your general style of working, but you should spend at least *some* time thinking about what you're going to do and coming up with a plan of action.

Before rolling up your sleeves and settling down at your keyboard, you'll benefit by taking some time to consider the various ways you can approach the problem. This planning period is where a thorough knowledge of Excel pays off. Avoiding blind alleys rather than stumbling into them is always a good idea.

If you ask a dozen Excel experts to design an application based on precise specifications, chances are you'll get a dozen different implementations of the project that meet those specifications. Of those solutions, some will be better than the others because Excel often provides several options to accomplish a task. If you know Excel inside and out, you'll have a good idea of the potential methods at your disposal, and you can choose the one most appropriate for the project at hand. Often, a bit of creative thinking yields an unusual approach that's vastly superior to other methods.

So at the beginning stage of this planning period, consider some general options, such as these:

➤ **File structure:** Think about whether you want to use one workbook with multiple sheets, several single-sheet workbooks, or a template file.

➤ **Data structure:** You should always consider how your data will be structured and also determine whether you will be using external database files or storing everything in worksheets.

➤ **Add-in or workbook file:** In some cases, an add-in may be the best choice for your final product. Or perhaps you might use an add-in with a standard workbook.

➤ **Version of Excel:** Will your Excel application be used with Excel 2013 only? With Excel 2007 and later? What about Excel 2003 and earlier versions? Will your application also be run on a Macintosh? These considerations are important because each new version of Excel adds features that aren't available in previous versions. The Ribbon interface introduced in Excel 2007 makes it more challenging than ever to create an application that works with older versions.

➤ **Error handling:** Error handling is a major issue with applications. You need to determine how your application will detect and deal with errors. For example, if your application applies formatting to the active worksheet, you need to be able to handle a case in which a chart sheet is active.

➤ **Use of special features:** If your application needs to summarize a lot of data, you may want to consider using Excel's pivot table feature. Or you may want to use Excel's data validation feature as a check for valid data entry.

➤ **Performance issues:** The time to start thinking about increasing the speed and efficiency of your application is at the development stage, not when the application is completed and users are complaining.

➤ **Level of security:** As you may know, Excel provides several protection options to restrict access to particular elements of a workbook. For example, you can lock cells so that formulas cannot be changed, and you can assign a password to prevent unauthorized users from viewing or accessing specific files. Determining up front exactly what you need to protect — and what level of protection is necessary — will make your job easier.

Note

Be aware that Excel's protection features aren't 100 percent effective — far from it. If you desire complete and absolute security for your application, Excel probably isn't the best platform.

You'll probably have to deal with many other project-specific considerations in this phase. Consider all options and don't settle on the first solution that comes to mind.

Another design consideration is remembering to plan for change. You'll do yourself a favor if you make your application as generic as possible. For example, don't write a procedure that works with only a specific range of cells. Rather, write a procedure that accepts any range as an argument. When the inevitable changes are requested, such a design makes it easier for you to carry out the revisions. Also, you may find that the work that you do for one project is similar to the work that you do for another. Keep reusability in mind when you are planning a project.

One thing that I've learned from experience is to avoid letting the end user completely guide your approach to a problem. For example, suppose that you meet with a manager who tells you that the department needs an application to write text files that will be imported into another application. Don't confuse the user's need with the solution. The user's real need is to share data. Using an intermediate text file to do it is just one possible solution; better ways to approach the problem may exist. In other words, don't let the users define their problem by stating it in terms of a solution approach. Determining the best approach is *your* job.

Determining the Most Appropriate User Interface

When you develop spreadsheets that others will use, you need to pay special attention to the user interface. By *user interface,* I mean the method by which the user interacts with the application and executes your VBA macros.

Since the introduction of Excel 2007, some of these user interface decisions are irrelevant. Custom menus and toolbars are, for all intents and purposes, obsolete. Consequently, developers must learn how to work with the Ribbon.

Excel provides several features that are relevant to user interface design:

- ➤ Ribbon customization
- ➤ Shortcut menu customization
- ➤ Shortcut keys
- ➤ Custom dialog boxes (UserForms)
- ➤ Controls (such as a ListBox or a CommandButton) placed directly on a worksheet

I discuss these features briefly in the following sections and cover them more thoroughly in later chapters.

Customizing the Ribbon

The Ribbon UI introduced in Excel 2007 is a dramatic shift in user interface design. Fortunately, the developer has a fair amount of control over the Ribbon. Although Excel 2013 allows the end user to modify the Ribbon, making UI changes via code isn't a simple task.

Cross-Ref   **See Chapter 20 for information about working with the Ribbon.**

Customizing shortcut menus

Excel 2013 still allows the VBA developer to customize the right-click shortcut menus. Figure 4-1 shows a customized shortcut menu that appears when you right-click a row number. Notice that this shortcut menu has several menu items that aren't normally available (those with a "P" icon).

Cross-Ref   **Chapter 21 describes how to work with shortcut menus using VBA, including some new limitations due to the single document interface in Excel 2013.**

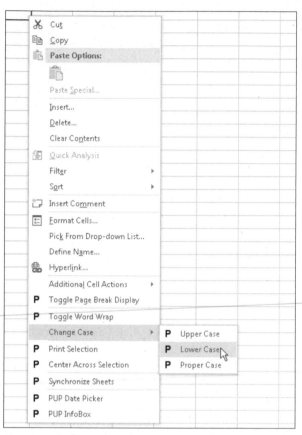

Figure 4-1: A customized shortcut menu.

Creating shortcut keys

Another user interface option at your disposal is a custom shortcut key. Excel lets you assign a Ctrl key (or Shift+Ctrl key) combination to a macro. When the user presses the key combination, the macro executes.

Be aware, however, of two caveats. First, make it clear to the user which keys are active and what they do. Second, do not assign a key combination that's already used for something else. A key combination that you assign to a macro takes precedence over the built-in shortcut keys. For example, Ctrl+S is a built-in Excel shortcut key used to save the current file. If you assign this key combination to a macro, you lose the capability to save the file with Ctrl+S. Remember that shortcut keys are case sensitive, so you can use a combination such as Ctrl+Shift+S.

Creating custom dialog boxes

Anyone who has used a personal computer for any length of time is undoubtedly familiar with dialog boxes. Consequently, custom Excel dialog boxes can play a major role in the user interfaces that you design for your applications. Figure 4-2 shows an example of a custom dialog box.

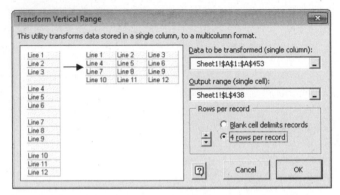

Figure 4-2: A dialog box created with Excel's UserForm feature.

A custom dialog box is known as a *UserForm*. A UserForm can solicit user input, get a user's options or preferences, and direct the flow of your entire application. You create and edit UserForms in VBE. The elements that make up a UserForm (buttons, drop-down lists, check boxes, and so on) are called *controls* — more specifically, *ActiveX controls*. Excel provides a standard assortment of ActiveX controls, and you can also incorporate third-party controls.

After adding a control to a dialog box, you can link it to a worksheet cell so that it doesn't require any macros (except a simple macro to display the dialog box). Linking a control to a cell is easy, but it's not always the best way to get user input from a dialog box. Most of the time, you want to develop VBA macros that work with your custom dialog boxes.

 I cover UserForms in detail in Part III.

Cross-Ref

Using ActiveX controls on a worksheet

Excel also lets you add UserForm ActiveX controls to a worksheet's *drawing layer* (an invisible layer on top of a sheet that holds pictures, charts, and other objects). Figure 4-3 shows a simple worksheet model with several UserForm controls inserted directly in the worksheet. This sheet contains the following ActiveX controls: a CheckBox, a ScrollBar, and two sets of OptionButtons. This workbook uses no macros. Rather, the controls are linked to worksheet cells.

 This workbook is available at this book's website. The file is named worksheet controls.xlsx.

On the Web

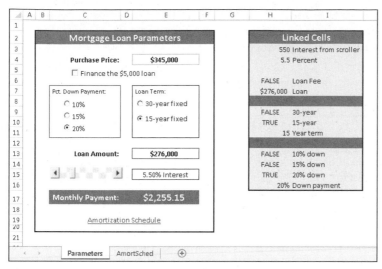

Figure 4-3: You can add UserForm controls to worksheets and link them to cells.

Perhaps the most common control is a CommandButton. By itself, a CommandButton doesn't do anything, so you need to attach a macro to each CommandButton.

Using dialog box controls directly in a worksheet often eliminates the need for custom dialog boxes. You can often greatly simplify the operation of a spreadsheet by adding a few ActiveX controls (or Form controls) to a worksheet. These ActiveX controls let the user make choices by operating familiar controls rather than making entries in cells.

Access these controls by using the Developer→Controls→Insert command (see Figure 4-4). If the Developer tab isn't on the Ribbon, add it by using the Customize Ribbon tab of the Excel Options dialog box.

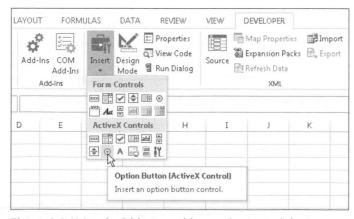

Figure 4-4: Using the Ribbon to add controls to a worksheet.

The controls come in two types: Form controls and ActiveX controls. Both sets of controls have their advantages and disadvantages. Generally, Form controls are easier to use, but ActiveX controls are a bit more flexible. Table 4-1 summarizes these two classes of controls.

Table 4-1: ActiveX Controls versus Form Controls

	ActiveX Controls	Form Controls
Excel versions	97, 2000, 2002, 2003, 2007, 2010, 2013	5, 95, 97, 2000, 2002, 2003, 2007, 2010, 2013
Controls available	CheckBox, TextBox, CommandButton, OptionButton, ListBox, ComboBox, ToggleButton, SpinButton, ScrollBar, Label, Image (and others can be added)	GroupBox, Button, CheckBox, OptionButton, ListBox, DropDown (ComboBox), ScrollBar, Spinner
Macro code storage	In the code module for the sheet	In any standard VBA module
Macro name	Corresponds to the control name (for example, CommandButton1_Click)	Any name you specify
Correspond to	UserForm controls	Pre–Excel 97 dialog sheet controls
Customization	Extensive, using the Properties box	Minimal
Respond to events	Yes	Click or Change events only

Executing the development effort

After you identify user needs, determine the approach that you'll take to meet those needs, and decide on the components that you'll use for the user interface, it's time to get down to the nitty-gritty and start creating the application. This step, of course, comprises a great deal of the total time that you spend on a particular project.

How you go about developing the application depends on your personal style and the nature of the application. Except for simple fill-in-the-blanks template workbooks, your application will probably use macros. Creating macros in Excel is easy, but creating *good* macros is difficult.

Concerning Yourself with the End User

In this section, I discuss the important development issues that surface as your application becomes more and more workable and as the time to package and distribute your work grows nearer.

Testing the application

How many times have you used a commercial software application, only to have it bomb out on you at a crucial moment? Most likely, the problem was caused by insufficient testing that didn't catch all the bugs. All nontrivial software has bugs, but in the best software, the bugs are simply more obscure. As you'll see, you sometimes must work around the bugs in Excel to get your application to perform properly.

After you create your application, you need to test it. Testing is one of the most crucial steps; it's not uncommon to spend as much time testing and debugging an application as you did creating the application. Actually, you should be doing a great deal of testing during the development phase. After all, whether you're writing a VBA routine or creating formulas in a worksheet, you want to make sure that the application is working the way it's supposed to work.

Like standard compiled applications, spreadsheet applications that you develop are prone to bugs. A *bug* can be defined as (1) something that does happen but shouldn't happen while a program (or application) is running, or (2) something that doesn't happen when it should happen. Both species of bugs are equally nasty, and you should plan on devoting a good portion of your development time to testing the application under all reasonable conditions and fixing any problems that you find. In some cases, unfortunately, the problems aren't entirely your fault. Excel, too, has its problems (see the "Bugs? In Excel?" sidebar).

 ## Bugs? In Excel?

You may think that a product such as Excel, which is used by millions of people throughout the world, would be relatively free of bugs. Think again. Excel is such a complex piece of software that it is only natural to expect some problems with it. And Excel *does* have some problems.

Getting a product such as Excel out the door isn't easy, even for Microsoft and its seemingly unlimited resources. Releasing a software product involves compromises and trade-offs. It's commonly known that most major software vendors release their products with full knowledge that they contain bugs. Most bugs are considered insignificant enough to ignore. Software companies could postpone their releases by a few months and fix many of them, but software, like everything else, is ruled by economics. The benefits of delaying a product's release often don't exceed the costs involved. Although Excel definitely has its share of bugs, my guess is that the majority of Excel users never encounter one.

In this book, I point out the problems with Excel that I know about. You'll surely discover some more on your own. Some problems occur only with a particular version of Excel — and under a specific configuration involving hardware or software or both. These bugs are the worst ones because they aren't easily reproducible.

So what's a developer to do? The solution is called a *workaround*. If something that you try to do doesn't work — and all indications say that it *should* work — it's time to move on to Plan B. Frustrating? Sure. A waste of your time? Absolutely. It's all part of being a developer.

What about beta testing?

Software manufacturers typically have a rigorous testing cycle for new products. After extensive internal testing, the pre-release product is usually sent to a group of interested users for *beta testing*. This phase often uncovers additional problems that are usually corrected before the product's final release.

If you're developing an Excel application that more than a few people will use, you may want to consider a beta test. This test enables your intended users to use your application in its intended setting on different hardware (usually).

The beta period should begin after you've completed all your own testing and you feel that the application is ready to distribute. You'll need to identify a group of users to help you. The process works best if you distribute everything that will ultimately be included in your application: user documentation, the installation program, help, and so on. You can evaluate the beta test in a number of ways, including face-to-face discussions, e-mail, questionnaires, and phone calls.

You almost always become aware of problems that you need to correct or improvements that you need to make before you undertake a widespread distribution of the application. Of course, a beta-testing phase takes additional time, and not all projects can afford that luxury.

I probably don't need to tell you to thoroughly test any spreadsheet application that you develop for others. And depending on its eventual audience, you may want to make your application bulletproof. In other words, try to anticipate all the errors and screw-ups that could possibly occur and make concerted efforts to avoid them — or, at least, to handle them gracefully. This foresight not only helps the end user but also makes it easier on you and protects your reputation. Also consider using beta testing; your end users are likely candidates because they're the ones who will be using your product. (See the upcoming sidebar "What about beta testing?")

Although you can't conceivably test for all possibilities, your macros should be able to handle common types of errors. For example, what if the user enters a text string instead of a numeric value? What if the user tries to run your macro when a workbook isn't open? What if he cancels a dialog box without making any selections? What happens if the user presses Ctrl+F6 and jumps to the next window? When you gain experience, these types of issues become very familiar, and you account for them without even thinking.

Making the application bulletproof

If you think about it, destroying a spreadsheet is fairly easy. Erasing one critical formula or value can cause errors throughout the entire worksheet — and perhaps even other dependent worksheets. Even worse, if the damaged workbook is saved, it replaces the good copy on disk. Unless a backup procedure is in place, the user of your application may be in trouble, and *you'll* probably be blamed for it.

Obviously, you can easily see why you need to add some protection when users — especially novices — will be using your worksheets. Excel provides several techniques for protecting worksheets and parts of worksheets:

> ➤ **Lock specific cells:** You can lock specific cells (by using the Protection tab in the Format Cells dialog box) so that users can't change them. Locking takes effect only when the document is protected with the Review➔Changes➔Protect Sheet command. The Protect Sheet dialog box has options that allow you to specify which actions users can perform on a protected sheet (see Figure 4-5).

Figure 4-5: Using the Protect Sheet dialog box to specify what users can and can't do.

> ➤ **Hide the formulas in specific cells:** You can hide the formulas in specific cells (by using the Protection tab in the Format Cells dialog box) so that others can't see them. Again, hiding takes effect only when the document is protected by choosing the Review➔Changes➔ Protect Sheet command.

> ➤ **Protect an entire workbook:** You can protect an entire workbook — the structure of the workbook, the window position and size, or both. Use the Review➔Changes➔Protect Workbook command for this purpose.

➤ **Lock objects on the worksheet:** Use the Properties section in the task pane to lock objects (such as shapes) and prevent them from being moved or changed. To access this section of the task pane, right-click the object and choose Size and Properties. Locking objects takes effect only when the document is protected using the Review➔Changes➔Protect Sheet command. By default, all objects are locked.

➤ **Hide rows, columns, sheets, and documents:** You can hide rows, columns, sheets, and entire workbooks. Doing so helps prevent the worksheet from looking cluttered and also provides some modest protection against prying eyes.

➤ **Designate an Excel workbook as read-only recommended:** You can designate an Excel workbook as read-only recommended (and use a password) to ensure that the file can't be overwritten with any changes. You make this designation in the General Options dialog box. Display this dialog box by choosing File➔Save As, clicking the Tools button, and then choosing General Options.

➤ **Assign a password:** You can assign a password to prevent unauthorized users from opening your file. Choose File➔Info➔Protect Workbook➔Encrypt with Password.

➤ **Use a password-protected add-in:** You can use a password-protected add-in, which doesn't allow the user to change *anything* on its worksheets.

Making the application aesthetically appealing and intuitive

If you've used many different software packages, you've undoubtedly seen examples of poorly designed user interfaces, difficult-to-use programs, and just plain ugly screens. If you're developing spreadsheets for other people, you should pay particular attention to how the application looks.

 How secure are Excel's passwords?

As far as I know, Microsoft has never advertised Excel as a secure program. And for good reason: Circumventing Excel's password system is easy. Several commercial programs are available that can break passwords. Excel 2007 and later versions seem to have stronger security than previous versions, but a determined user can still crack them. Bottom line? Don't think of password protection as foolproof. Sure, it will be effective for the casual user. But if someone *really* wants to break your password, he or she probably can.

How a computer program looks can make all the difference in the world to users, and the same is true with the applications that you develop with Excel. Beauty, however, is in the eye of the beholder. If your skills lean more in the analytical direction, consider enlisting the assistance of someone with a more aesthetic sensibility to provide help with design.

The good news is that features found in Excel 2007 and later make creating better-looking spreadsheets a relatively easy task. If you stick with predesigned cell styles, your work stands a good chance of looking good. And, with the click of a mouse, you can apply a new theme that transforms the look of the workbook — and still looks good.

End users appreciate a good-looking user interface, and your applications will have a much more polished and professional look if you devote additional time to design and aesthetic considerations. An application that looks good demonstrates that its developer cared enough about the product to invest extra time and effort. Take the following suggestions into account:

> **Strive for consistency.** When designing dialog boxes, for example, try to emulate the look and feel of Excel's dialog boxes whenever possible. Be consistent with formatting, fonts, text size, and colors.

> **Keep it simple.** A common mistake that developers make is trying to cram too much information into a single screen or dialog box. A good rule is to present only one or two chunks of information at a time.

> **Break down input screens.** If you use an input screen to solicit information from the user, consider breaking it up into several, less-crowded screens. If you use a complex dialog box, you may want to break it up by using a MultiPage control, which lets you create a familiar tabbed dialog box.

> **Don't overdo color.** Use color sparingly. It's very easy to overdo color and make the screen look gaudy.

> **Monitor typography and graphics.** Pay attention to numeric formats and use consistent typefaces, font sizes, and borders.

Evaluating aesthetic qualities is subjective. When in doubt, strive for simplicity and clarity.

Creating a user Help system

With regard to user documentation, you basically have two options: paper-based documentation or electronic documentation. Providing electronic help is standard fare in Windows applications. Fortunately, your Excel applications can also provide help — even context-sensitive help. Developing help text takes quite a bit of additional effort, but for a large project, it may be worth it. Figure 4-6 shows an example of a custom Help system in compiled HTML format.

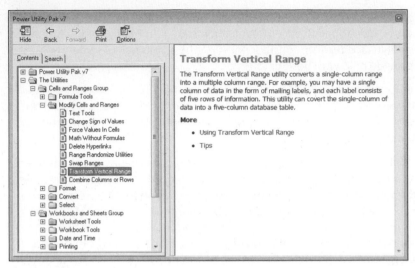

Figure 4-6: An example of a custom help file for an Excel add-in.

Another point to consider is support for your application. In other words, who gets the phone call if the user encounters a problem? If you aren't prepared to handle routine questions, you need to identify someone who is. In some cases, you want to arrange it so that only highly technical or bug-related issues escalate to the developer.

Cross-Ref

In Chapter 22, I discuss several alternatives for providing help for your applications.

Documenting the development effort

Putting a spreadsheet application together is one thing. Making it understandable for other people is another. As with traditional programming, it's important that you thoroughly document your work. Such documentation helps you if you need to go back to it (and you will), and it helps anyone else whom you might pass it on to.

How do you document a workbook application? You can either store the information in a worksheet or use another file. You can even use a paper document, if you prefer. Perhaps the easiest way is to use a separate worksheet to store your comments and key information for the project. For VBA code, use comments liberally. (VBA text preceded with an apostrophe is ignored because that text is designated as a comment.) Although an elegant piece of VBA code can seem perfectly obvious to you today, when you come back to it in a few months, your reasoning may be completely obscured unless you use the VBA comment feature.

Distributing the application to the user

You've completed your project, and you're ready to release it to the end users. How do you go about distributing it? You can choose from many ways to distribute your application, and the method that you choose depends on many factors.

You could just hand over a CD-ROM or thumb drive, scribble a few instructions, and be on your way. Or you may want to install the application yourself — but this approach isn't always feasible. Another option is to develop an official setup program that performs the task automatically. You can write such a program in a traditional programming language, purchase a generic setup program, or write your own in VBA.

Excel incorporates technology to enable developers to digitally sign their applications. This process is designed to help end users identify the author of an application, to ensure that the project has not been altered, and to help prevent the spread of macro viruses or other potentially destructive code. To digitally sign a project, you first apply for a digital certificate from a formal certificate authority (or you can self-sign your project by creating your own digital certificate). Refer to the Help system or the Microsoft website for additional information.

Updating the application when necessary

After you distribute your application, you're finished with it, right? You can sit back, enjoy yourself, and try to forget about the problems that you encountered (and solved) during development. In rare cases, yes, you may be finished. More often, however, the users of your application won't be completely satisfied. Sure, your application adheres to all the *original* specifications, but things change. Seeing an application working often causes the user to think of other things that the application could be doing. I'm talking *updates*.

When you need to update or revise your application, you'll appreciate that you designed it well in the first place and that you fully documented your efforts. If not, well . . . we learn from our experiences.

Other Development Issues

You need to keep several other issues in mind when developing an application — especially if you don't know exactly who will be using the application. If you're developing an application that will have widespread use (a shareware application, for example), you have no way of knowing how the application will be used, what type of system it will run on, or what other software will be running concurrently.

The user's installed version of Excel

With every new release of Excel, the issue of compatibility rears its head. As I write this book, Excel 2013 has just been released — yet many large corporations are still using Excel 2003 and some use even earlier versions.

Unfortunately, there is no guarantee that an application developed for, say, Excel 2003 will work perfectly with later versions of Excel. If you need your application to work with a variety of Excel versions, the best approach is to work with the lowest version — and then test it thoroughly with all other versions.

Things get even more complicated when you consider Excel's subversions. Microsoft distributes service releases (SRs), service packs (SPs), and security updates to correct problems. In some cases, your Excel application won't work correctly unless the user has installed a particular update.

Cross-Ref

I discuss compatibility issues in Chapter 24.

Language issues

Consider yourself fortunate if all your end users have the English language version of Excel. Non-English versions of Excel aren't always 100 percent compatible, so that means additional testing on your part. In addition, keep in mind that two users can both be using the English language version of Excel yet use different Windows regional settings. In some cases, you may need to be aware of potential problems.

Cross-Ref

I briefly discuss language issues in Chapter 24.

System speed

You're probably a fairly advanced computer user and tend to keep your hardware reasonably up to date. In other words, you have a fairly powerful system that is probably better than the average user's system. In some cases, you'll know exactly what hardware the end users of your applications are using. If so, testing your application on that system is vital. A procedure that executes almost instantaneously on your system may take several seconds on another system. In the world of computers, several seconds may be unacceptable.

Tip

When you gain more experience with VBA, you'll discover that there are ways to get the job done, and there are ways to get the job done fast. It's a good idea to get into the habit of coding for speed. Other chapters in this book can certainly help you out in this area.

Video modes

As you probably know, users' video displays vary widely. Currently, the most commonly used video resolution is 1280 x 1024, followed closed by 1024 x 768. Systems with a resolution of 800 x 600 are becoming much less common, but quite a few are still in use. Higher resolution displays and even dual displays are becoming increasingly common. Just because you have a super-high-resolution monitor, you can't assume that everyone else does.

Video resolution can be a problem if your application relies on specific information being displayed on a single screen. For example, if you develop an input screen that fills the screen in 1280 x 1024 mode, users with a 1024 x 768 display won't be able to see the whole input screen without scrolling or zooming.

Also, it's important to realize that a *restored* (that is, not maximized or minimized) workbook is displayed at its previous window size and position. In the extreme case, it's possible that a window saved by using a high-resolution display may be completely off the screen when opened on a system running in a lower resolution.

Unfortunately, you can't automatically scale things so that they look the same regardless of the display resolution. In some cases, you can zoom the worksheet (using the Zoom control in the status bar), but doing so reliably may be difficult. Unless you're certain of the video resolution that the users of your application will use, you should probably design your application so it works with the lowest common denominator — 800 x 600 or 1024 x 768 mode.

As you discover later in the book (see Chapter 8), you can determine the user's video resolution by using Windows API calls from VBA. In some cases, you may want to programmatically adjust things, depending on the user's video resolution.

Understanding Visual Basic for Applications

5

Introducing Visual Basic for Applications

In This Chapter

- Introducing VBA — the programming language built into Excel

- Discovering how VBA differs from traditional spreadsheet macro languages and the Visual Basic language

- Using Visual Basic Editor (VBE)

- Working in the code windows in VBE and customizing the VBE environment

- Using Excel's macro recorder

- Getting an overview of objects, collections, properties, and methods

- Reviewing a case study of the Comment object

- Looking at specific information and examples of working with Range objects

- Accessing a lot of information about Excel objects, properties, and methods

Getting Some BASIC Background

Many hard-core programmers scoff at the idea of programming in BASIC. The name itself (an acronym for Beginner's All-purpose Symbolic Instruction Code) suggests that BASIC isn't a professional language. In fact, BASIC was first developed in the early 1960s as a way to teach programming techniques to college students. BASIC caught on quickly and is available in hundreds of dialects for many types of computers.

BASIC has evolved and improved over the years. For example, in many early implementations, BASIC was an *interpreted* language. Each line was interpreted before it was executed, causing slow performance. Most modern dialects of BASIC allow the code to be *compiled* — converted to machine code — which results in faster and more efficient execution.

BASIC gained quite a bit of respectability in 1991 when Microsoft released Visual Basic for Windows. This product made it easy for the masses to develop stand-alone applications for Windows. Visual Basic has very little in common with early versions of BASIC, but Visual Basic is the foundation on which VBA was built.

Delving into VBA

Excel 5, released in 1994, was the first application on the market to feature Visual Basic for Applications (VBA). VBA is best thought of as Microsoft's common application scripting language, and it's included with most Office 2013 applications and even in applications from other vendors. Therefore, if you master VBA by using Excel, you'll be able to jump right in and write macros for other Microsoft (and some non-Microsoft) products. Even better, you'll be able to create complete solutions that use features across various applications.

Object models

The secret to using VBA with other applications lies in understanding the *object model* for each application. VBA, after all, simply manipulates objects, and each product (Excel, Word, Access, PowerPoint, and so on) has its own unique object model. You can program an application by using the objects that the application exposes.

Excel's object model, for example, exposes several powerful data analysis objects, such as worksheets, charts, pivot tables, and numerous mathematical, financial, engineering, and general business functions. With VBA, you can work with these objects and develop automated procedures. While you work with VBA in Excel, you gradually build an understanding of the object model. *Warning:* The object model will be confusing at first. Eventually, however, the pieces come together — and all of a sudden, you realize that you've mastered it!

VBA versus XLM

Before version 5, Excel used a powerful (but cryptic) macro language called *XLM*. Later versions of Excel (including Excel 2013) still execute XLM macros, but the capability to record macros in XLM was removed beginning with Excel 97. As a developer, you should be aware of XLM (in case you ever encounter macros written in that system), but you should use VBA for your development work.

Note

Don't confuse the XLM macro language with eXtensible Markup Language (XML). Although these terms share the same letters, they have nothing in common. XML is a storage format for structured data. The Office 2013 applications use XML as their default file format.

Is VBA becoming obsolete?

For the past few years, I've heard rumors that Microsoft is going to remove VBA from the Office applications and replace it with .NET (or something else). My understanding is that these rumors are unfounded. Sure, Microsoft has developed another way to automate Office applications, but VBA will be around for quite a while — at least in Excel for Windows. Microsoft did remove VBA from Excel for Mac, but then they put it back in!

Why will VBA survive? Because millions of VBA-based solutions are in use and VBA is much easier to learn and use than the alternatives.

Covering the Basics of VBA

I suggest that you read the material in this section to get a broad overview of the topics I cover in the remainder of this chapter.

Following is a quick-and-dirty summary of what VBA is all about:

➤ **Code:** You perform actions in VBA by executing VBA code. You write (or record) VBA code, which is stored in a VBA module.

➤ **Module:** VBA modules are stored in an Excel workbook file, but you view or edit a module by using Visual Basic Editor (VBE). A VBA module consists of procedures.

➤ **Procedures:** A procedure is basically a unit of computer code that performs some action. VBA supports two types of procedures: Sub procedures and Function procedures.

- Sub: A Sub procedure consists of a series of statements and can be executed in a number of ways. Here's an example of a simple Sub procedure called Test: This procedure calculates a simple sum and then displays the result in a message box.

```
Sub Test()
    Sum = 1 + 1
    MsgBox "The answer is " & Sum
End Sub
```

- Function: A Function procedure returns a single value (or possibly an array). A Function can be called from another VBA procedure or used in a worksheet formula. Here's an example of a Function named AddTwo:

```
Function AddTwo(arg1, arg2)
    AddTwo = arg1 + arg2
End Function
```

➤ **Objects:** VBA manipulates objects contained in its host application. (In this case, Excel is the host application.) Excel provides you with more than 100 classes of objects to manipulate. Examples of objects include a workbook, a worksheet, a range on a worksheet, a chart, and a shape. Many more objects are at your disposal, and you can use VBA code to manipulate them. Object classes are arranged in a hierarchy.

Objects also can act as containers for other objects. For example, Excel is an object called Application, and it contains other objects, such as Workbook objects. The Workbook object contains other objects, such as Worksheet objects and Chart objects. A Worksheet object contains objects such as Range objects, PivotTable objects, and so on. The arrangement of these objects is referred to as Excel's *object model*.

➤ **Collections:** Like objects form a *collection*. For example, the Worksheets collection consists of all the worksheets in a particular workbook. Collections are objects in themselves.

➤ **Object hierarchy:** When you refer to an object, you specify its position in the object hierarchy by using a period (also known as a *dot*) as a separator between the container and the member. For example, you can refer to a workbook named Book1.xlsx as

```
Application.Workbooks("Book1.xlsx")
```

This code refers to the Book1.xlsx workbook in the Workbooks collection. The Workbooks collection is contained in the Excel Application object. Extending this type of referencing to another level, you can refer to Sheet1 in Book1 as

```
Application.Workbooks("Book1.xlsx").Worksheets("Sheet1")
```

You can take it to still another level and refer to a specific cell as follows:

```
Application.Workbooks("Book1.xlsx").Worksheets("Sheet1").Range("A1")
```

➤ **Active objects:** If you omit a specific reference to an object, Excel uses the active objects. If Book1 is the active workbook, the preceding reference can be simplified as

```
Worksheets("Sheet1").Range("A1")
```

If you know that Sheet1 is the active sheet, you can simplify the reference even more:

```
Range("A1")
```

➤ **Objects properties:** Objects have *properties*. A property can be thought of as a *setting* for an object. For example, a range object has properties such as Value and Address. A chart object has properties such as HasTitle and Type. You can use VBA to determine object properties and also to change them. Some properties are read-only properties and can't be changed by using VBA.

You refer to properties by combining the object with the property, separated by a period. For example, you can refer to the value in cell A1 on Sheet1 as

```
Worksheets("Sheet1").Range("A1").Value
```

▶ An analogy

If you like analogies, here's one for you that may help you understand the relationships between objects, properties, and methods in VBA. In this analogy, I compare Excel with a fast-food restaurant chain.

The basic unit of Excel is a Workbook object. In a fast-food chain, the basic unit is an individual restaurant. With Excel, you can add workbooks and close workbooks, and the set of all the open workbooks is known as Workbooks (a collection of Workbook objects). Similarly, the management of a fast-food chain can add restaurants and close restaurants — and all the restaurants in the chain can be viewed as the Restaurants collection — a collection of Restaurant objects.

An Excel workbook is an object, but it also contains other objects, such as worksheets, charts, VBA modules, and so on. Furthermore, each object in a workbook can contain its own objects. For example, a Worksheet object can contain Range objects, PivotTable objects, Shape objects, and so on.

Continuing with the analogy, a fast-food restaurant (like a workbook) contains objects, such as the Kitchen, DiningArea, and Tables (a collection). Furthermore, management can add or remove objects from the Restaurant object. For example, management can add more tables to the Tables collection. Each of these objects can contain other objects. For example, the Kitchen object has a Stove object, a VentilationFan object, a Chef object, a Sink object, and so on.

So far, so good. This analogy seems to work. Let's see whether I can take it further.

Excel objects have properties. For example, a Range object has properties such as Value and Name, and a Shape object has properties such as Width and Height. Not surprisingly, objects in a fast-food restaurant also have properties. The Stove object, for example, has properties such as Temperature and NumberofBurners. The VentilationFan object has its own set of properties (TurnedOn, RPM, and so on).

Besides properties, Excel's objects also have methods, which perform operations on objects. For example, the ClearContents method erases the contents of a Range object. An object in a fast-food restaurant also has methods. You can easily envision a ChangeThermostat method for a Stove object, or a SwitchOn method for a VentilationFan object.

With Excel, methods sometimes change an object's properties. The ClearContents method for a Range object changes the Range Value property. Similarly, the ChangeThermostat method on a Stove object affects its Temperature property.

With VBA, you can write procedures to manipulate Excel's objects. In a fast-food restaurant, the management can give orders to manipulate the objects in the restaurants. ("Turn on the stove and switch the ventilation fan to high.") Now is it clear?

➤ **VBA variables:** You can assign values to VBA variables. Think of a variable as a name that you can use to store a particular value. To assign the value in cell A1 on Sheet1 to a variable called Interest, use the following VBA statement:

```
Interest = Worksheets("Sheet1").Range("A1").Value
```

➤ **Object methods:** Objects have methods. A *method* is an action that is performed with the object. For example, one of the methods for a Range object is ClearContents. This method clears the contents of the range. You specify methods by combining the object with the method, separated by a period. For example, to clear the contents of cell A1 on the active worksheet, use

```
Range("A1").ClearContents
```

➤ **Standard programming constructs:** VBA also includes many constructs found in modern programming languages, including arrays, conditional statements, and loops.

➤ **Events:** Some objects recognize specific events, and you can write VBA code that is executed when the event occurs. For example, opening a workbook triggers a Workbook_Open event. Changing a cell in a worksheet triggers a Worksheet_Change event.

Believe it or not, the preceding section pretty much summarizes what VBA is all about and how it works with Excel. Now you just need to learn the details.

Introducing Visual Basic Editor

You do all your VBA work in Visual Basic Editor (VBE). VBE is a separate application that works seamlessly with Excel. By *seamlessly,* I mean that Excel takes care of the details of opening VBE when you need it. You can't run VBE separately; Excel must be running for VBE to run.

Note

VBA modules are stored in workbook files. However, the VBA modules aren't visible unless you activate VBE.

Displaying Excel's Developer tab

The Excel Ribbon doesn't display the Developer tab by default. If you're going to be working with VBA, it's essential that you turn on the Developer tab:

1. Right-click anywhere on the Ribbon and choose Customize the Ribbon.

   Excel displays the Customize Ribbon tab of the Excel Options dialog box.

2. In the list box on the right, place a check mark next to Developer.

3. Click OK.

After you perform these steps, Excel displays a new tab, as shown in Figure 5-1.

Figure 5-1: By default, the Developer tab is not displayed.

Activating VBE

When you're working in Excel, you can switch to VBE by using either of the following techniques:

➤ Press Alt+F11.

➤ Choose Developer➜Code➜Visual Basic.

Figure 5-2 shows the VBE window, but your window probably will look different. This window is highly customizable — you can hide windows, change their sizes, dock them, rearrange them, and more.

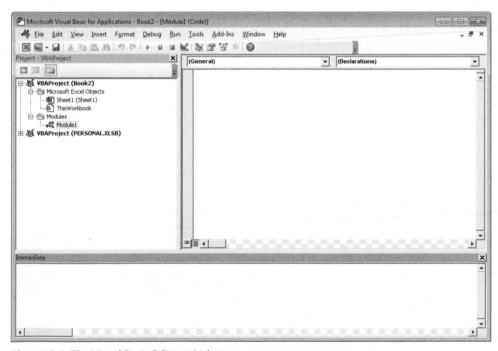

Figure 5-2: The Visual Basic Editor window.

VBE windows

VBE has a number of parts. I briefly describe some of the key components in the following list:

➤ **VBE menu bar:** Although Excel uses a fancy new Ribbon interface, VBE is still stuck in the menu bar and toolbar world. The VBE menu bar works like every other menu bar that you've encountered. It contains commands that you use to work with the various components in VBE. Also, you'll find that shortcut keys are associated with many menu commands. For example, the View➞Immediate Window command has a shortcut key of Ctrl+G.

Tip

VBE also features shortcut menus. As you'll discover, you can right-click virtually anything in a VBE window to get a shortcut menu of common commands.

➤ **VBE toolbars:** The Standard toolbar, which is directly under the menu bar by default, is one of six VBE toolbars. You can customize toolbars, move them around, display other toolbars, and so on. Choose View➞Toolbars to display or hide VBE toolbars.

➤ **Project Explorer window:** The Project Explorer window displays a tree diagram that consists of every workbook that is currently open in Excel (including add-ins and hidden workbooks). Each workbook is known as a *project.* I discuss the Project Explorer window in more detail in the next section ("Working with Project Explorer").

If the Project Explorer window isn't visible, press Ctrl+R. To hide the Project Explorer window, click the Close button in its title bar or right-click anywhere in the Project Explorer window and select Hide from the shortcut menu.

➤ **Code window:** A code window (sometimes known as a module window) contains VBA code. Every item in a project's tree has an associated code window. To view a code window for an object, double-click the object in the Project Explorer window. For example, to view the code window for the Sheet1 object, double-click Sheet1 in the Project Explorer window. Unless you've added some VBA code, the code window is empty.

Another way to view the code window for an object is to select the object in the Project Explorer window and then click the View Code button in the toolbar at the top of the Project Explorer window.

I discuss code windows later in this chapter (see the section "Working with Code Windows").

➤ **Immediate window:** The Immediate window is most useful for executing VBA statements directly, testing statements, and debugging your code. This window may or may not be visible. If the Immediate window isn't visible, press Ctrl+G. To close the Immediate window, click the Close button in its title bar (or right-click anywhere in the Immediate window and select Hide from the shortcut menu).

Working with Project Explorer

When you're working in VBE, each Excel workbook and add-in that's currently open is considered a project. You can think of a *project* as a collection of objects arranged as an expandable tree. You can expand a project by clicking the plus sign (+) at the left of the project's name in the Project Explorer window. You contract a project by clicking the minus sign (–) to the left of a project's name. If you try to expand a project that's protected with a password, you're prompted to enter the password.

Note The top of the Project Explorer window contains three icons. The third icon, named **Toggle Folders,** controls whether the objects in a project are displayed in a hierarchy or are shown in a single nonhierarchical list.

Figure 5-3 shows a Project Explorer window with four projects listed (two XLAM add-ins and two workbooks).

Figure 5-3: A Project Explorer window with four projects listed.

Caution When you activate VBE, you can't assume that the code module that's displayed corresponds to the highlighted object in the Project Explorer window. To make sure that you're working in the correct code module, always double-click the object in the Project Explorer window.

If you have many workbooks and add-ins loaded, the Project Explorer window can be a bit over-whelming. Unfortunately, you can't hide projects in the Project Explorer window. However, you prob-ably want to keep the project outlines contracted if you're not working on them.

When viewing the Project Explorer in Folder view, every project expands to show at least one node called Microsoft Excel Objects. This node expands to show an item for each worksheet and chart sheet in the workbook (each sheet is considered an object) and another object called ThisWorkbook (which represents the Workbook object). If the project has any VBA modules, the project listing also shows a Modules node, and the modules are listed there. A project can also contain a node called Forms that contains UserForm objects (also known as custom dialog boxes). If your project has any class modules, it displays another node called Class Modules. Similarly, if your project has any refer-ences, you see another node called References. The References node is a bit misleading because ref-erences can't contain any VBA code.

Adding a new VBA module

To add a new VBA module to a project, select the project's name in the Project Explorer window and choose Insert➡Module. Or you can just right-click the project's name and choose Insert➡Module from the shortcut menu.

When you record a macro, Excel automatically inserts a VBA module to hold the recorded code.

Removing a VBA module

If you need to remove a VBA module, a class module, or a UserForm from a project, select the mod-ule's name in the Project Explorer window and choose File➡Remove *xxx* (where *xxx* is the name of the module). Or you can right-click the module's name and choose Remove *xxx* from the shortcut menu. You're asked whether you want to export the module before removing it. (See the next sec-tion for details.)

You can't remove code modules associated with the workbook (the ThisWorkbook code module) or with a sheet (for example, the Sheet1 code module).

Exporting and importing objects

Except for those objects listed under the References node, you can save every object in a project to a separate file. Saving an individual object in a project is called *exporting*. It stands to reason that you can also *import* objects into a project. Exporting and importing objects might be useful if you want to use a particular object (such as a VBA module or a UserForm) in a different project or share some code with a colleague.

To export an object, select it in the Project Explorer window and choose File➡Export File. You get a dialog box that asks for a filename. Note that the object remains in the project. (Only a copy of it is exported.) If you export a UserForm object, any code associated with the UserForm is also exported.

To import a file into a project, select the project's name in the Project Explorer window and choose File➤Import File. You get a dialog box that asks for a file. You can import only a file that has been exported by choosing the File➤Export File command.

The exported files have an extension that corresponds to the type of object. Exporting a UserForm generates two files.

Tip

If you want to copy a module or UserForm to another project, you don't need to export and then import the object. Make sure that both projects are open; then simply activate Project Explorer and drag the object from one project to the other. The original module or UserForm remains, and a copy is added to the other project.

Working with Code Windows

When you become proficient with VBA, you'll be spending *lots* of time working in code windows. Each object in a project has an associated code window. To summarize, these objects can be

➤ The workbook itself (ThisWorkbook in the Project Explorer window)

➤ A worksheet or chart sheet in a workbook (for example, Sheet1 or Chart1 in the Project Explorer window)

➤ A VBA module

➤ A *class module* (a special type of module that lets you create new object classes)

➤ A UserForm

Minimizing and maximizing windows

Depending on how many workbooks and add-ins are open, VBE can have many code windows, and things can get a bit confusing. Most people find it most efficient to maximize the code window that they're working in. Doing so enables you to see more code and keeps you from getting distracted. To maximize a code window, click the maximize button in its title bar or just double-click its title bar. To restore a code window (make it nonmaximized), click the Restore button (below the Application title bar).

Sometimes, you may want to have two or more code windows visible. For example, you might want to compare the code in two modules or perhaps copy code from one module to another. To view two or more code windows at once, make sure that the active code window isn't maximized. Then drag and resize the windows that you want to view.

Minimizing a code window gets it out of the way. You can also click the Close button in a code window's title bar to close the window completely. To open it again, just double-click the appropriate object in the Project Explorer window.

You can save a workbook from VBE. Select the workbook in the Project window and chose File➜Save, press Ctrl+S, or click the Save icon in the Standard toolbar.

VBE doesn't have a menu command to close a workbook. You must reactivate Excel and close it from there. You can, however, use the Immediate window to close a workbook or an add-in. Just activate the Immediate window (press Ctrl+G if it's not visible), type a VBA statement like the one that follows, and press Enter:

```
Workbooks("myaddin.xlam").Close
```

As you'll see, this statement executes the Close method of the Workbook object, which closes a workbook. In this case, the workbook happens to be an add-in.

Storing VBA code

In general, a code window can hold four types of code:

> **Sub procedures:** A *procedure* is a set of instructions that performs some action.

> **Function procedures:** A *function* is a set of instructions that returns a single value or an array (similar in concept to a worksheet function, such as SUM).

> **Declarations:** A *declaration* is information about a variable that you provide to VBA. For example, you can declare the data type for variables you plan to use.

> **Property procedures:** These are special procedures used in class modules.

A single VBA module can store any number of Sub procedures, Function procedures, and declarations. How you organize a VBA module is up to you. Some people prefer to keep all their VBA code for an application in a single VBA module; others like to split up the code into several modules.

Note

Although you have lots of flexibility regarding where to store your VBA code, there are some restrictions. Event-handler procedures must be located in the code window for the object that responds to the event. For example, if you write a procedure that executes when the workbook is opened, that procedure must be located in the code window for the ThisWorkbook object, and the procedure must have a special name. This concept will become clearer when I discuss events (Chapter 17) and UserForms (Part III).

Entering VBA code

Before you can do anything meaningful, you must have some VBA code in a code window. This VBA code must be within a procedure. A procedure consists of VBA statements. For now, I focus on one type of code window: a VBA module.

Pause for a terminology break

Throughout this book, I use the terms *routine*, *procedure*, and *macro*. Programming people typically use the word *procedure* to describe an automated task. In Excel, a procedure is also known as a *macro*. Technically, a procedure can be a Sub procedure or a Function procedure, both of which are sometimes called *routines*. I use all these terms pretty much interchangeably. There is, however, an important difference between Sub procedures and Function procedures. This distinction becomes apparent in Chapters 7 and 8.

You can add code to a VBA module in three ways:

➤ **Enter the code manually.** Use your keyboard to type your code.

➤ **Copy and paste.** Copy the code from another module (or from a website) and paste it into the module that you're working in.

➤ **Use the macro-recorder feature.** Use Excel's macro-recorder feature to record your actions and convert them into VBA code.

Entering code manually

Sometimes, the most direct route is the best one. Entering code directly involves . . . well, entering the code directly. In other words, you type the code by using your keyboard. You can use the Tab key to indent the lines that logically belong together — for example, the conditional statements between the If and End If statements. Indenting isn't necessary, but it makes the code easier to read, so it's a good habit to acquire.

Entering and editing text in a VBA module works just as you would expect. You can select text, copy it or cut it, and then paste it to another location.

A single instruction in VBA can be as long as you need it to be. For readability's sake, however, you may want to break a lengthy instruction into two or more lines. To do so, end the line with a space followed by an underscore character and then press Enter and continue the instruction on the following line. The following code, for example, is a single VBA statement split over four lines:

```
MsgBox "Can't find " & UCase(SHORTCUTMENUFILE) _
    & vbCrLf & vbCrLf & "The file should be located in " _
    & ThisWorkbook.Path & vbCrLf & vbCrLf _
    & "You may need to reinstall BudgetMan", vbCritical, APPNAME
```

Notice that I indented the last three lines of this statement. Doing so is optional, but it helps clarify the fact that these four lines are, in fact, a single statement.

Tip

Like Excel, VBE has multiple levels of undo and redo. Therefore, if you find that you deleted an instruction that you shouldn't have, you can click the Undo button (or press Ctrl+Z) repeatedly until the instruction comes back. After undoing, you can click the Redo button (or press Ctrl+Y) to redo changes that were previously undone. This feature can be a lifesaver, so I recommend that you play around with it until you understand how it works.

To get a feel for entering a VBA procedure, try this: Insert a VBA module into a project and then enter the following procedure in the code window of the module:

```
Sub SayHello()
    Msg = "Is your name " & Application.UserName & "?"
    Ans = MsgBox(Msg, vbYesNo)
    If Ans = vbNo Then
        MsgBox "Oh, never mind."
    Else
        MsgBox "I must be clairvoyant!"
    End If
End Sub
```

Figure 5-4 shows how this code looks in a VBA module.

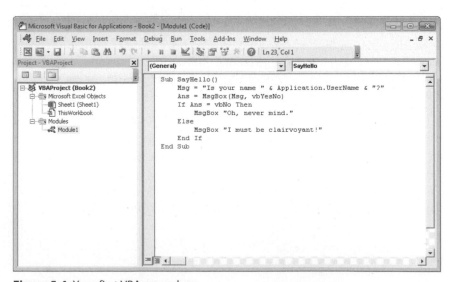

Figure 5-4: Your first VBA procedure.

Note

While you enter the code, note that VBE makes some adjustments to your text. For example, if you omit the space before or after an equal sign (=), VBE inserts the space for you. Also, the color of some of the text is changed. These adjustments are all perfectly normal, and you'll appreciate them later.

To execute the SayHello procedure, make sure that the cursor is located anywhere within the text that you typed. Then do any of the following:

> ➤ Press F5.

> ➤ Choose Run➜Run Sub/UserForm.

> ➤ Click the Run Sub/UserForm button on the Standard toolbar.

If you entered the code correctly, the procedure executes, and you can respond to a simple dialog box (see Figure 5-5) that displays the username, as listed in the Excel Options dialog box. Notice that Excel is activated when the macro executes. At this point, it's not important that you understand how the code works; that becomes clear later in this chapter and in subsequent chapters.

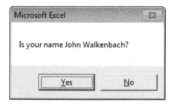

Figure 5-5: The result of running the procedure in Figure 5-4.

Note   **Most of the time, you'll be executing your macros from Excel. However, it's often more efficient to test your macro by running it directly from VBE.**

What you did in this exercise was write a VBA Sub procedure (also known as a *macro*). When you issued the command to execute the macro, VBE quickly compiled the code and executed it. In other words, each instruction was evaluated, and Excel simply did what it was told to do. You can execute this macro any number of times (although it tends to lose its appeal after a while).

For the record, this simple procedure uses the following concepts (all of which I cover later in the book):

> ➤ Declaring a procedure (the first line)

> ➤ Assigning a value to variables (Msg and Ans)

> ➤ Concatenating strings (using the & operator)

> ➤ Using a built-in VBA function (MsgBox)

> ➤ Using built-in VBA constants (vbYesNo and vbNo)

> ➤ Using an If-Then-Else construct

> ➤ Ending a procedure (the last line)

Not bad for a first effort, eh?

Copying VBA code

Another method of getting code into a VBA module is to copy it from another module. For example, you may have written a procedure for one project that would also be useful in your current project. Rather than reenter the code, you can simply open the workbook, activate the module, and use the Clipboard copy-and-paste procedures to copy the code into your current VBA module. After you've finished pasting, you can modify the code as necessary.

Tip

As I note previously in this chapter, you can also import an entire module that has been exported.

And don't forget about the Internet. You'll find thousands of VBA code examples at websites, forums, and blogs. Copying code from a browser and pasting it into a VBA module is simple.

Sometimes, the code copied from a web page includes smart quotes rather than quotation mark characters. Smart quotes will cause an error, so you must replace them with quotation mark characters.

Using the macro recorder

Another way to get code into a VBA module is to record your actions by using the Excel macro recorder.

No matter how hard you try, there is absolutely no way to record the SayHello procedure shown in the previous section. As you'll see, recording macros is useful but has limitations. In fact, when you record a macro, you almost always need to make adjustments or enter some code manually.

This next example shows how to record a macro that simply changes the page setup to landscape orientation. If you want to try any of these examples, start with a blank workbook:

1. Activate a worksheet in the workbook (any worksheet will do).

2. Choose Developer➜Code➜Record Macro.

   Excel displays its Record Macro dialog box.

3. Click OK to accept the default setting for the macro.

   Excel automatically inserts a new VBA module into the workbook's VBA project. From this point on, Excel converts your actions into VBA code. Note that Excel's status bar displays a gray square. You can click that control to stop recording.

4. Choose Page Layout➜Page Setup➜Orientation➜Landscape.

5. Select Developer➜Code➜Stop Recording (or click the gray square in the status bar).

   Excel stops recording your actions.

To view the macro, activate VBE (pressing Alt+F11 is the easiest way) and locate the project in the Project Explorer window. Double-click the Modules node to expand it. Then double-click the Module1 item to display the code window. (If the project already had a Module1, the new macro will be in Module2.) The code generated by this single Excel command is shown in Figure 5-6.

```
Book2 - Module1 (Code)
(General)                                                Macro1

Sub Macro1()
'
' Macro1 Macro
'
    Application.PrintCommunication = False
    With ActiveSheet.PageSetup
        .PrintTitleRows = ""
        .PrintTitleColumns = ""
    End With
    Application.PrintCommunication = True
    ActiveSheet.PageSetup.PrintArea = ""
    Application.PrintCommunication = False
    With ActiveSheet.PageSetup
        .LeftHeader = ""
        .CenterHeader = ""
        .RightHeader = ""
        .LeftFooter = ""
        .CenterFooter = ""
        .RightFooter = ""
        .LeftMargin = Application.InchesToPoints(0.7)
        .RightMargin = Application.InchesToPoints(0.7)
        .TopMargin = Application.InchesToPoints(0.75)
        .BottomMargin = Application.InchesToPoints(0.75)
        .HeaderMargin = Application.InchesToPoints(0.3)
        .FooterMargin = Application.InchesToPoints(0.3)
        .PrintHeadings = False
        .PrintGridlines = False
        .PrintComments = xlPrintNoComments
        .PrintQuality = 600
        .CenterHorizontally = False
        .CenterVertically = False
        .Orientation = xlLandscape
        .Draft = False
        .PaperSize = xlPaperLetter
        .FirstPageNumber = xlAutomatic
        .Order = xlDownThenOver
        .BlackAndWhite = False
        .Zoom = 100
        .PrintErrors = xlPrintErrorsDisplayed
        .OddAndEvenPagesHeaderFooter = False
        .DifferentFirstPageHeaderFooter = False
        .ScaleWithDocHeaderFooter = True
        .AlignMarginsHeaderFooter = True
        .EvenPage.LeftHeader.Text = ""
        .EvenPage.CenterHeader.Text = ""
        .EvenPage.RightHeader.Text = ""
        .EvenPage.LeftFooter.Text = ""
        .EvenPage.CenterFooter.Text = ""
        .EvenPage.RightFooter.Text = ""
        .FirstPage.LeftHeader.Text = ""
        .FirstPage.CenterHeader.Text = ""
        .FirstPage.RightHeader.Text = ""
        .FirstPage.LeftFooter.Text = ""
        .FirstPage.CenterFooter.Text = ""
        .FirstPage.RightFooter.Text = ""
    End With
    Application.PrintCommunication = True
End Sub
```

Figure 5-6: An excessive amount of code generated by Excel's macro recorder.

You may be surprised by the amount of code generated by this single command. (I know I was the first time I tried something like this.) Although you changed only one simple setting in the Page Setup tab, Excel generates more than 50 lines of code that affects dozens of print settings.

This code listing illustrates an important concept. The Excel macro recorder is not the most efficient way to generate VBA code. Often, the code produced when you record a macro is overkill. Consider the recorded macro that switches to landscape mode. Practically every statement in that macro is extraneous. You can simplify this macro considerably by deleting the extraneous code, which makes the macro easier to read and faster to run. In fact, you can simplify this recorded macro to the following:

```
Sub Macro1()
    With ActiveSheet.PageSetup
        .Orientation = xlLandscape
    End With
End Sub
```

I deleted all the code except for the line that sets the Orientation property. Actually, you can simplify this macro even more because the With-End With construct isn't necessary when you're changing only one property:

```
Sub Macro1()
    ActiveSheet.PageSetup.Orientation = xlLandscape
End Sub
```

In this example, the macro changes the Orientation property of the PageSetup object on the active sheet. By the way, xlLandscape is a built-in constant that's provided to make things easier for you. The variable xlLandscape has a value of 2, and xlPortrait has a value of 1. The following macro works the same as the preceding Macro1:

```
Sub Macro1a()
    ActiveSheet.PageSetup.Orientation = 2
End Sub
```

Most would agree that it's easier to remember the name of the constant than the arbitrary numbers. You can use the Help system to learn the relevant constants for a particular command.

You could have entered this procedure directly into a VBA module. To do so, you would have to know which objects, properties, and methods to use. Obviously, recording the macro is much faster, and this example has a built-in bonus: You also learned that the PageSetup object has an Orientation property.

Note

A point that I make clear throughout this book is that recording your actions is perhaps the best way to learn VBA. When in doubt, try recording. Although the result may not be exactly what you want, chances are that it will steer you in the right direction. You can use the Help system to check out the objects, properties, and methods that appear in the recorded code.

Cross-Ref

I discuss the macro recorder in more detail later in this chapter. See the section "The Macro Recorder."

Customizing the VBE Environment

If you're serious about becoming an Excel programmer, you'll be spending a lot of time with the VBE window. To help make things as comfortable as possible, VBE provides quite a few customization options.

When VBE is active, choose Tools➔Options. You see a dialog box with four tabs: Editor, Editor Format, General, and Docking. I discuss some of the most useful options on these tabs in the sections that follow. By the way, don't confuse this Options dialog box with the Excel Options dialog box, which you bring up by choosing File➔Options in Excel.

Using the Editor tab

Figure 5-7 shows the options that you access by clicking the Editor tab of the Options dialog box.

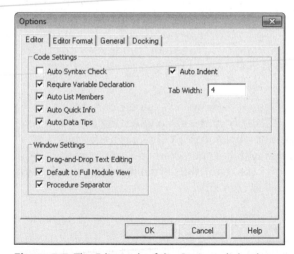

Figure 5-7: The Editor tab of the Options dialog box.

Auto Syntax Check option

The Auto Syntax Check setting determines whether VBE pops up a dialog box if it discovers a syntax error while you're entering your VBA code. The dialog box tells you roughly what the problem is. If you don't choose this setting, VBE flags syntax errors by displaying them in a different color from the rest of the code, and you don't have to deal with any dialog boxes popping up on your screen.

I keep this setting turned off because I find the dialog boxes annoying, and I can usually figure out what's wrong with an instruction. But if you're new to VBA, you might find the Auto Syntax Check assistance helpful.

Require Variable Declaration option

If the Require Variable Declaration option is set, VBE inserts the following statement at the beginning of each new VBA module that you insert:

```
Option Explicit
```

If this statement appears in your module, you must explicitly define each variable that you use. Variable declaration is an excellent habit to get into, although it does require additional effort on your part. If you don't declare your variables, they will all be of the Variant data type, which is flexible but not efficient in terms of storage or speed. I discuss variable declaration in more depth in Chapter 6.

Note

Changing the Require Variable Declaration option affects only new modules, not existing modules.

Auto List Members option

If the Auto List Members option is set, VBE provides help when you're entering your VBA code by displaying a list of member items for an object. These items include methods and properties for the object that you typed.

This option is helpful, and I always keep it turned on. Figure 5-8 shows an example of Auto List Members (which will make a lot more sense when you actually start writing VBA code). In this example, VBE is displaying a list of members for the Application object. The list changes as you type additional characters, showing only the members that begin with the characters you type. You can just select an item from the list and press Tab (or double-click the item), thus avoiding typing it. Using the Auto List Members list also ensures that the item is spelled correctly.

Auto Quick Info option

If the Auto Quick Info option is set, VBE displays information about the arguments available for functions, properties, and methods while you type. This information can be helpful, and I always leave this setting on. Figure 5-9 shows this feature in action, displaying the syntax for the Cells property.

Figure 5-8: An example of Auto List Members.

Figure 5-9: An example of Auto Quick Info offering help about the Cells property.

Auto Data Tips option

If the Auto Data Tips option is set, you can hover your mouse pointer over a variable, and VBE displays the value of the variable. This technique works only when the procedure is paused while debugging. When you enter the wonderful world of debugging, you'll definitely appreciate this option. I always keep this option turned on.

Auto Indent option

The Auto Indent setting determines whether VBE automatically indents each new line of code by the same amount as the previous line. I'm a big fan of using indentations in my code, so I keep this option on. You can also specify the number of characters to indent; the default is four.

Tip

Use the Tab key, not the spacebar, to indent your code. Using the Tab key results in more consistent spacing. In addition, you can use Shift+Tab to unindent a line of code. These keys also work if you select more than one line of code.

Drag-and-Drop Text Editing option

The Drag-and-Drop Text Editing option, when enabled, lets you copy and move text by dragging and dropping. I keep this option turned on, but I never use drag-and-drop editing. I prefer to use keyboard shortcuts for copying and pasting.

Default to Full Module View option

The Default to Full Module View option specifies how procedures are viewed. If this option is set, procedures in the code window appear as a single scrollable window. If this option is turned off, you can see only one procedure at a time. I keep this setting turned on.

Procedure Separator option

When the Procedure Separator option is turned on, VBE displays separator bars between procedures in a code window (assuming that the Default to Full Module View option is also selected). I like the visual cues that show where my procedures end, so I keep this option turned on.

Using the Editor Format tab

Figure 5-10 shows the Editor Format tab of the Options dialog box. The options on this tab control the appearance of VBE itself.

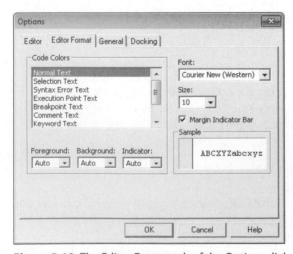

Figure 5-10: The Editor Format tab of the Options dialog box.

➤ **Code Colors option:** The Code Colors option lets you set the text color (foreground and background) and the indicator color displayed for various elements of VBA code. Choosing these colors is largely a matter of individual preference. I find the default colors to be just fine. But for a change of scenery, I occasionally play around with these settings.

➤ **Font option:** The Font option lets you select the font that's used in your VBA modules. For best results, stick with a fixed-width font (monofont) such as Courier New. In a *fixed-width font,* all characters are exactly the same width. Using fixed-width characters makes your code much more readable because the characters are nicely aligned vertically and you can easily distinguish multiple spaces.

➤ **Size setting:** The Size setting specifies the size of the font in the VBA modules. This setting is a matter of personal preference determined by your video display resolution and your eyesight. The default size of 10 (points) works for me.

➤ **Margin Indicator Bar option:** The Margin Indicator Bar option controls the display of the vertical margin indicator bar in your modules. You should keep this turned on; otherwise, you won't be able to see the helpful graphical indicators when you're debugging your code.

Using the General tab

Figure 5-11 shows the following options available under the General tab in the Options dialog box:

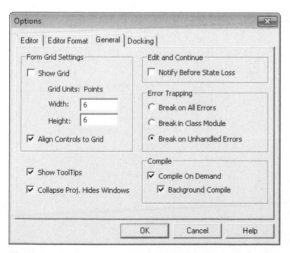

Figure 5-11: The General tab of the Options dialog box.

➤ **Form Grid Settings:** The options in this section let you specify a grid to help align controls on a UserForm (custom dialog box). When you have some experience designing UserForms, you can determine whether a grid display is helpful or not.

➤ **Show ToolTips check box:** This check box refers to toolbar buttons. There's no reason to turn off the tooltips display.

➤ **Collapse Proj. Hides Windows option:** If checked, this setting closes windows automatically when you collapse a project in the project window. I keep this setting turned on.

➤ **Edit and Continue section:** This area contains one option, which may be useful for debugging. When checked, VBA displays a message if your variables are about to lose their values because of a problem.

Cross-Ref

➤ **Error Trapping settings:** These settings determine what happens when an error is encountered. If you write any error-handling code, make sure that the Break on Unhandled Errors option is set. If the Break on All Errors option is set, error-handling code is ignored (which is hardly ever what you want). I discuss error-handling techniques in Chapter 7.

➤ **Compile settings:** The two Compile settings deal with compiling your code. I keep both of these options turned on. Compiling code is virtually instantaneous unless the project is extremely large.

Using the Docking tab

Figure 5-12 shows the Docking tab of the Options dialog box. These options determine how the various windows in VBE behave. When a window is docked, it's fixed in place along one of the edges of the VBE window. Docking windows makes it much easier to identify and locate a particular window. If you turn off all docking, you have a confusing mess of windows. Generally, you'll find that the default settings work fine.

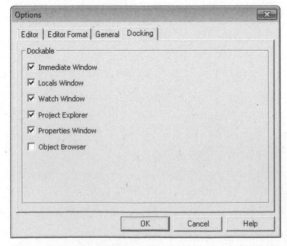

Figure 5-12: The Docking tab of the Options dialog box.

To dock a window, just drag it to the desired location. For example, you might want to dock the Project Explorer window to the left side of the screen. Just drag its title bar to the left, and you see an outline that shows it docked. Release the mouse, and the window is docked.

Note

Docking windows in VBE has always been a bit problematic. Often, you find that some windows simply refuse to be docked. I've found that if you persist long enough, the procedure will eventually work. Unfortunately, I don't have any secret window-docking techniques.

The Macro Recorder

Earlier in this chapter, I discuss the *macro recorder,* which is a tool that converts your Excel actions into VBA code. This section covers the macro recorder in more detail.

Note

Make sure that Excel displays the Developer tab on the Ribbon. If you don't see this tab, refer to the section "Displaying Excel's Developer tab," earlier in this chapter.

The macro recorder is an *extremely* useful tool, but remember the following points:

➤ The macro recorder is appropriate only for simple macros or for recording a small part of a more complex macro.

➤ Not all the actions you make in Excel get recorded.

➤ The macro recorder can't generate code that performs *looping* (that is, repeating statements), assigns variables, executes statements conditionally, displays dialog boxes, and so on.

➤ The macro recorder always creates Sub procedures. You can't create a Function procedure by using the macro recorder.

➤ The code that is generated sometimes depends on certain settings that you specify.

➤ You'll often want to clean up the recorded code to remove extraneous commands.

What the macro recorder actually records

The Excel macro recorder translates your mouse and keyboard actions into VBA code. I could probably write several pages describing how this translation occurs, but the best way to show you is by example. Follow these steps:

1. Start with a blank workbook.

2. Make sure that the Excel window isn't maximized.

   You don't want it to fill the entire screen.

3. Press Alt+F11 to activate the VBE window.

   Note: Make sure that this window isn't maximized. Otherwise, you won't be able to see the VBE window and Excel's window at the same time.

4. Resize and arrange Excel's window and the VBE window so that both are visible. (For best results, minimize any other applications that are running.)

5. Activate Excel, choose Developer➜Code➜Record Macro, and then click OK to start the macro recorder.

6. Activate the VBE window.

7. In the Project Explorer window, double-click Module1 to display that module in the code window.

8. Close the Project Explorer window in VBE to maximize the view of the code window.

Your screen layout should look something like the example in Figure 5-13. The size of the windows depends on your video resolution. If you happen to have a dual-display system, just put the VBA window on one display and the Excel window on the other display.

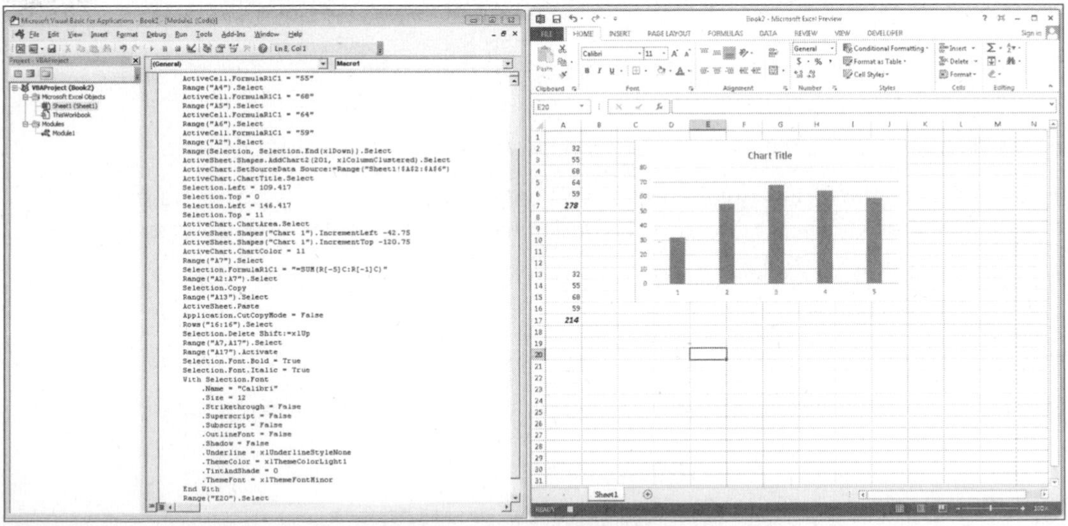

Figure 5-13: A convenient window arrangement for watching the macro recorder do its thing.

Now move around in the worksheet and select various Excel commands. Watch while the code is generated in the window that displays the VBA module. Select cells, enter data, format cells, use the Ribbon commands, create a chart, manipulate graphic objects, and so on. I guarantee that you'll be enlightened while you watch the code being spit out before your very eyes.

Relative or absolute recording?

When recording your actions, Excel normally records *absolute references* to cells. In other words, when you select a cell, it will remember that exact cell (not the cell relative to the current active cell). To demonstrate how absolute references work, perform these steps and examine the code:

1. Activate a worksheet and start the macro recorder.

2. Activate cell B1.

3. Enter **Jan** into cell B1.

4. Move to cell C1 and enter **Feb**.

5. Continue this process until you've entered the first six months of the year in B1:G1.

6. Click cell B1 to activate it again.

7. Stop the macro recorder and examine the new code in VBE.

Excel generates the following code:

```
Sub Macro1()
    Range("B1").Select
    ActiveCell.FormulaR1C1 = "Jan"
    Range("C1").Select
    ActiveCell.FormulaR1C1 = "Feb"
    Range("D1").Select
    ActiveCell.FormulaR1C1 = "Mar"
    Range("E1").Select
    ActiveCell.FormulaR1C1 = "Apr"
    Range("F1").Select
    ActiveCell.FormulaR1C1 = "May"
    Range("G1").Select
    ActiveCell.FormulaR1C1 = "Jun"
    Range("B1").Select
End Sub
```

To execute this macro from Excel, choose Developer➜Code➜Macros (or press Alt+F8) and select Macro1 (or whatever the macro is named) and click the Run button.

The macro, when executed, re-creates the actions that you performed when you recorded it. These same actions occur regardless of which cell is active when you execute the macro. Recording a macro using absolute references always produces the same results.

In some cases, however, you want your recorded macro to work with cell locations in a *relative* manner. For example, you'd probably want such a macro to start entering the month names in the active cell. In such a case, you want to use relative recording to record the macro.

You control how references are recorded by using the Use Relative References button, in the Code group of the Developer tab. This button is a toggle. When the button appears in a different color, the macro recorder records relative references. When the button appears in the standard color, the macro recorder records absolute references. You can change the recording method at any time, even in the middle of recording.

To see how relative referencing is recorded, erase the cells in B1:G1 and then perform the following steps:

1. Activate cell B1.

2. Choose Developer➜Code➜Record Macro.

3. Click OK to begin recording.

4. Click the Use Relative References button to change the recording mode to relative.

   After you click this button, it appears in a different color.

5. Enter the first six months' names in B1:G1, as in the previous example.

6. Select cell B1.

7. Stop the macro recorder.

With the recording mode set to relative, the code that Excel generates is quite different:

```
Sub Macro2()
    ActiveCell.FormulaR1C1 = "Jan"
    ActiveCell.Offset(0, 1).Range("A1").Select
    ActiveCell.FormulaR1C1 = "Feb"
    ActiveCell.Offset(0, 1).Range("A1").Select
    ActiveCell.FormulaR1C1 = "Mar"
    ActiveCell.Offset(0, 1).Range("A1").Select
    ActiveCell.FormulaR1C1 = "Apr"
    ActiveCell.Offset(0, 1).Range("A1").Select
    ActiveCell.FormulaR1C1 = "May"
    ActiveCell.Offset(0, 1).Range("A1").Select
    ActiveCell.FormulaR1C1 = "Jun"
    ActiveCell.Offset(0, -5).Range("A1").Select
End Sub
```

To test this macro, start by activating a cell other than cell B1. Then choose the Developer➜ Code➜Macros command. Select the macro name and then click the Run button. The month names are entered beginning at the active cell.

Notice that I varied the recording procedure slightly in this example: I activated the beginning cell *before* I started recording. This step is important when you record macros that use the active cell as a base.

Although this macro looks complicated, it is fairly simple. The first statement enters Jan into the active cell. (The statement uses the active cell because it's not preceded by a statement that selects a cell.) The next statement uses the Select method (along with the Offset property) to move the selection one cell to the right. The next statement inserts more text, and so on. Finally, the original cell is selected by calculating a relative offset rather than an absolute cell. Unlike the preceding macro, this one always starts entering text in the active cell.

Note

> **You'll notice that this macro generates code that appears to reference cell A1 — which may seem strange because cell A1 wasn't even involved in the macro. This code is simply a by-product of how the macro recorder works. (I discuss the Offset property later in this chapter.) At this point, all you need to know is that the macro works as it should.**

The point here is that the recorder has two distinct modes, and you need to be aware of the mode in which you're recording. Otherwise, the result may not be what you expected.

By the way, the code generated by Excel is more complex than it needs to be, and it's not even the most efficient way to code the operation. The macro that follows, which I entered manually, is a simpler and faster way to perform this same operation. This example demonstrates that VBA doesn't have to select a cell before it puts information into it — an important concept that can speed things up considerably.

```
Sub Macro3()
    ActiveCell.Offset(0, 0) = "Jan"
    ActiveCell.Offset(0, 1) = "Feb"
    ActiveCell.Offset(0, 2) = "Mar"
    ActiveCell.Offset(0, 3) = "Apr"
    ActiveCell.Offset(0, 4) = "May"
    ActiveCell.Offset(0, 5) = "Jun"
End Sub
```

In fact, this macro can be made even more efficient by using the With-End With construct:

```
Sub Macro4()
    With ActiveCell
        .Offset(0, 0) = "Jan"
        .Offset(0, 1) = "Feb"
        .Offset(0, 2) = "Mar"
        .Offset(0, 3) = "Apr"
        .Offset(0, 4) = "May"
        .Offset(0, 5) = "Jun"
    End With
End Sub
```

Or, if you're a VBA guru, you can impress your colleagues by using a single statement:

```
Sub Macro5()
    ActiveCell.Resize(,6)=Array("Jan","Feb","Mar","Apr","May","Jun")
End Sub
```

Recording options

When you record your actions to create VBA code, you have several options in the Record Macro dialog box. The following list describes your options:

➤ **Macro name:** You can enter a name for the procedure that you're recording. By default, Excel uses the names Macro1, Macro2, and so on for each macro that you record. I usually just accept the default name and change the name of the procedure later. You, however, might prefer to name the macro before you record it.

➤ **Shortcut key:** The Shortcut key option lets you execute the macro by pressing a shortcut key combination. For example, if you enter **w** (lowercase), you can execute the macro by pressing Ctrl+W. If you enter **W** (uppercase), the macro comes alive when you press Ctrl+Shift+W. Keep in mind that a shortcut key assigned to a macro overrides a built-in shortcut key (if one exists). For example, if you assign Ctrl+B to a macro, you won't be able to use the key combination to toggle the bold attribute in cells.

You can always add or change a shortcut key at any time, so you don't need to set this option while recording a macro.

➤ **Store Macro In:** The Store Macro In option tells Excel where to store the macro that it records. By default, Excel puts the recorded macro in a module in the active workbook. If you prefer, you can record it in a new workbook (Excel opens a blank workbook) or in your Personal Macro Workbook. (Read more about this in the sidebar, "The Personal Macro Workbook.")

Note

Excel remembers your choice, so the next time you record a macro, it defaults to the same location you used previously.

➤ **Description:** If you like, you can enter a description for your macro in the Description box. Text you enter here appears at the beginning of your macro as a comment.

The Personal Macro Workbook

When you record a macro, one of your options is to record it in your Personal Macro Workbook. If you create some VBA macros that you find particularly useful, you may want to store these routines in your Personal Macro Workbook. This workbook is named Personal.xlsb and is stored in your XLStart directory. Whenever you start Excel, this workbook is loaded, and you have access to the macros stored in the workbook. Personal.xlsb is a hidden workbook, so it's out of your way when you're working in Excel.

The Personal.xlsb file doesn't exist until you record a macro to it.

Cleaning up recorded macros

Earlier in this chapter, you see how recording your actions while you issue a single command (the Page Layout➜Page Setup➜Orientation command) produces an enormous amount of VBA code. This example shows how, in many cases, the recorded code includes extraneous commands that you can delete.

The macro recorder doesn't always generate the most efficient code. If you examine the generated code, you see that Excel generally records what is selected (that is, an object) and then uses the Selection object in subsequent statements. For example, here's what is recorded if you select a range of cells and then use some buttons on the Home tab to change the numeric formatting and apply bold and italic:

```
Range("A1:C5").Select
Selection.Style = "Comma"
Selection.Font.Bold = True
Selection.Font.Italic = True
```

The recorded VBA code works, but it's just one way to perform these actions. You can also use the more efficient With-End With construct, as follows:

```
Range("A1:C5").Select
With Selection
      .Style = "Comma"
      .Font.Bold = True
      .Font.Italic = True
End With
```

Or you can avoid the Select method altogether and write the code even more efficiently:

```
With Range("A1:C5")
    .Style = "Comma"
    .Font.Bold = True
    .Font.Italic = True
End With
```

If speed is essential in your application, you always want to examine any recorded VBA code closely to make sure that it's as efficient as possible.

You need to understand VBA thoroughly before you start cleaning up your recorded macros. But for now, just be aware that recorded VBA code isn't always the best, most efficient code.

 ## About the code examples

Throughout this book, I present many small snippets of VBA code to make a point or to provide an example. In some cases, this code consists of a single statement or only an *expression,* which isn't a valid instruction by itself.

For example, the following is an expression:

```
Range("A1").Value
```

To test an expression, you must evaluate it. The MsgBox function is a handy tool for this:

```
MsgBox Range("A1").Value
```

To try out these examples, put the statement in a procedure in a VBA module, like this:

```
Sub Test()
' statement goes here
End Sub
```

Then put the cursor anywhere in the procedure and press F5 to execute it. Also, make sure that the code is being executed in the proper context. For example, if a statement refers to Sheet1, make sure that the active workbook has a sheet named Sheet1.

If the code is just a single statement, you can use the VBE Immediate window. The Immediate window is useful for executing a statement immediately — without having to create a procedure. If the Immediate window isn't displayed, press Ctrl+G in VBE.

Just type the VBA statement in the Immediate window and press Enter. To evaluate an expression in the Immediate window, precede the expression with a question mark (?), which is a shortcut for Print. For example, you can type the following in the Immediate window:

```
? Range("A1").Value
```

The result of this expression is displayed in the next line of the Immediate window.

About Objects and Collections

If you've worked through the first part of this chapter, you have an overview of VBA, and you know the basics of working with VBA modules in VBE. You've also seen some VBA code and were exposed to concepts such as objects and properties. This section gives you additional details about objects and collections of objects.

When you work with VBA, you must understand the concept of objects and Excel's object model. It helps to think of objects in terms of a *hierarchy*. At the top of this model is the Application object — in this case, Excel itself. But if you're programming in VBA with Microsoft Word, the Application object is Word.

The object hierarchy

The Application object (that is, Excel) contains other objects. Here are a few examples of objects contained in the Application object:

- ➤ Workbooks (a collection of all Workbook objects)
- ➤ Windows (a collection of all Window objects)
- ➤ AddIns (a collection of all AddIn objects)

Some objects can contain other objects. For example, the Workbooks collection consists of all open Workbook objects, and a Workbook object contains other objects, a few of which are as follows:

- ➤ Worksheets (a collection of Worksheet objects)
- ➤ Charts (a collection of Chart objects)
- ➤ Names (a collection of Name objects)

Each of these objects, in turn, can contain other objects. The Worksheets collection consists of all Worksheet objects in a Workbook. A Worksheet object contains many other objects, which include the following:

- ➤ ChartObjects (a collection of ChartObject objects)
- ➤ Range
- ➤ PageSetup
- ➤ PivotTables (a collection of PivotTable objects)

If this seems confusing, trust me, it *will* make sense, and you'll eventually realize that this object hierarchy setup is logical and well structured.

About collections

A key concept in VBA programming is collections. A *collection* is a group of objects of the same class, and a collection is itself an object. As I note earlier, Workbooks is a collection of all Workbook objects currently open. Worksheets is a collection of all Worksheet objects in a particular Workbook object. You can work with an entire collection of objects or with an individual object in a collection. To reference a single object from a collection, you put the object's name or index number in parentheses after the name of the collection, like this:

```
Worksheets("Sheet1")
```

If Sheet1 is the first worksheet in the collection, you could also use the following reference:

```
Worksheets(1)
```

You refer to the second worksheet in a Workbook as Worksheets(2), and so on.

There is also a collection called Sheets, which is made up of all sheets in a workbook, whether they're worksheets or chart sheets. If Sheet1 is the first sheet in the workbook, you can reference it as follows:

```
Sheets(1)
```

Referring to objects

When you refer to an object using VBA, you often must qualify the object by connecting object names with a period (also known as a *dot operator*). What if you had two workbooks open and they both had a worksheet named Sheet1? The solution is to qualify the reference by adding the object's container, like this:

```
Workbooks("Book1").Worksheets("Sheet1")
```

Without the workbook qualifier, VBA would look for Sheet1 in the active workbook.

To refer to a specific range (such as cell A1) on a worksheet named Sheet1 in a workbook named Book1, you can use the following expression:

```
Workbooks("Book1").Worksheets("Sheet1").Range("A1")
```

The fully qualified reference for the preceding example also includes the Application object, as follows:

```
Application.Workbooks("Book1").Worksheets("Sheet1").Range("A1")
```

Most of the time, however, you can omit the Application object in your references because it is assumed. If the Book1 object is the active workbook, you can even omit that object reference and use this:

```
Worksheets("Sheet1").Range("A1")
```

And — I think you know where I'm going with this — if Sheet1 is the active worksheet, you can use an even simpler expression:

```
Range("A1")
```

Note

Contrary to what you might expect, Excel doesn't have an object that refers to an individual cell that is called Cell. A single cell is simply a Range object that happens to consist of just one element.

Simply referring to objects (as in these examples) doesn't do anything. To perform anything meaningful, you must read or modify an object's properties or specify a method to be used with an object.

Properties and Methods

It's easy to be overwhelmed with properties and methods; literally thousands are available. In this section, I describe how to access properties and methods of objects.

Object properties

Every object has properties. For example, a Range object has a property called Value. You can write VBA code to display the Value property or write VBA code to set the Value property to a specific value. Here's a procedure that uses the VBA MsgBox function to pop up a box that displays the value in cell A1 on Sheet1 of the active workbook:

```
Sub ShowValue()
    Msgbox Worksheets("Sheet1").Range("A1").Value
End Sub
```

Note

The VBA MsgBox function provides an easy way to display results while your VBA code is executing. I use it extensively throughout this book.

The code in the preceding example displays the current setting of the Value property of a specific cell: cell A1 on a worksheet named Sheet1 in the active workbook. Note that if the active workbook doesn't have a sheet named Sheet1, the macro generates an error.

What if you want to change the Value property? The following procedure changes the value displayed in cell A1 by changing the cell's Value property:

```
Sub ChangeValue()
    Worksheets("Sheet1").Range("A1").Value = 123.45
End Sub
```

After executing this routine, cell A1 on Sheet1 has the value 123.45.

You may want to enter these procedures in a module and experiment with them.

Keep in mind that you can read the Value property only for a single-cell Range object. However, your code can *write* to the Value property for a multicell Range object. In the following statements, the first one is valid, and the second one is not:

```
Range("A1:C12").Value = 99
MsgBox Range("A1:C12").Value
```

Note

Most objects have a default property. For a Range object, the default property is Value. Therefore, you can omit the .Value part from the preceding code, and it has the same effect. However, it's usually considered good programming practice to include the property in your code, even if it is the default property.

The statement that follows accesses the HasFormula and the Formula properties of a Range object:

```
If Range("A1").HasFormula Then MsgBox Range("A1").Formula
```

I use an If-Then construct to display a message box conditionally: If the cell has a formula, then display the formula by accessing the Formula property. If cell A1 doesn't have a formula, nothing happens.

The Formula property is a read-write property for only single-cell Range objects. For multicell Range objects, it's write-only. The following statement enters a formula into a range of cells:

```
Range("A1:D12").Formula = "=RAND()*100"
```

Specifying arguments for methods and properties

An issue that often leads to confusion among new VBA programmers concerns arguments for methods and properties. Some methods use arguments to further clarify the action to be taken, and some properties use arguments to further specify the property value. In some cases, one or more of the arguments are optional.

If a method uses arguments, place the arguments after the name of the method, separated by commas. If the method uses optional arguments, you can insert blank placeholders for the optional arguments. Later in this sidebar, I show you how to insert these placeholders.

Consider the Protect method for a workbook object. Check the Help system, and you'll find that the Protect method takes three arguments: password, structure, and windows. These arguments correspond to the options in the Protect Structure and Windows dialog box.

If you want to protect a workbook named MyBook.xlsx, for example, you might use a statement like this:

```
Workbooks("MyBook.xlsx").Protect "xyzzy", True, False
```

In this case, the workbook is protected with a password (argument 1). Its structure is protected (argument 2) but not its windows (argument 3).

If you don't want to assign a password, you can use a statement like this:

```
Workbooks("MyBook.xlsx").Protect , True, False
```

Note that the first argument is omitted and that I specified the placeholder by using a comma.

Another approach, which makes your code more readable, is to use named arguments. Here's an example of how you use named arguments for the preceding example:

```
Workbooks("MyBook.xlsx").Protect Structure:=True, Windows:=False
```

Using named arguments is a good idea, especially for methods that have many optional arguments and also when you need to use only a few of them. When you use named arguments, you don't need to use a placeholder for missing arguments.

For properties (and methods) that return a value, you must use parentheses around the arguments. For example, the Address property of a Range object takes five optional arguments. Because the Address property returns a value, the following statement isn't valid because the parentheses are omitted:

```
MsgBox Range("A1").Address False    ' invalid
```

The proper syntax for such a statement requires parentheses, as follows:

```
MsgBox Range("A1").Address(False)
```

You can also write the statement using a named argument:

```
MsgBox Range("A1").Address(rowAbsolute:=False)
```

These nuances will become clearer as you gain more experience with VBA.

Object methods

In addition to properties, objects also have methods. A *method* is an action that you perform with an object. Here's a simple example that uses the Clear method on a Range object. After you execute this procedure, A1:C3 on Sheet1 is empty and all cell formatting is removed.

```
Sub ZapRange()
    Worksheets("Sheet1").Range("A1:C3").Clear
End Sub
```

If you'd like to delete the values in a range but keep the formatting, use the ClearContents method of the Range object.

Most methods also take arguments to define the action further. Here's an example that copies cell A1 to cell B1 on the active sheet by using the Copy method of the Range object. In this example, the Copy method has one argument (the destination of the copy).

```
Sub CopyOne()
    Range("A1").Copy Range("B1")
End Sub
```

The Comment Object: A Case Study

To help you better understand the properties and methods available for an object, I focus on a particular object: the Comment object. In Excel, you create a Comment object when you choose the Review➤Comments➤New Comment command to enter a cell comment. In the sections that follow, you get a feel for working with objects. I chose this object because it doesn't have an overwhelming number of properties and methods.

The point of this section is not so much to teach you about the Comment object but rather to demonstrate how to work with objects in general. Eventually, you will be able to adapt the concepts presented here when you work with other objects.

Viewing Help for the Comment object

One way to learn about a particular object is to look it up in the Help system. Figure 5-14 shows the Help topics for the Comment object. Note that the Help screen has links on the left so you can view the properties and methods for this object.

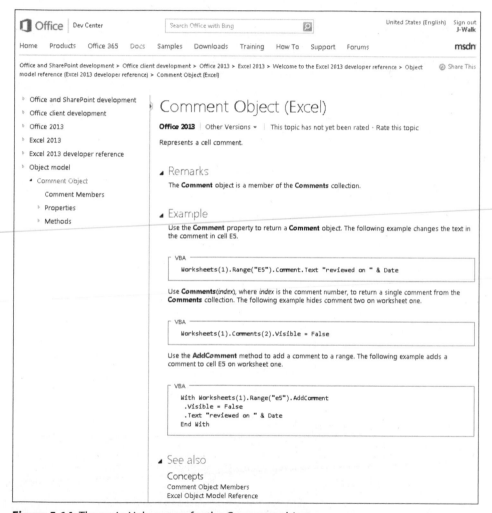

Figure 5-14: The main Help screen for the Comment object.

New Feature

In Excel 2013, Help topics are displayed in your default web browser, and you must be connected to the Internet.

Using the Help system

The easiest way to get specific help about a particular object, property, or method is to type the word in a code window and press F1. If there is any ambiguity about the word you typed, you get a dialog box like the one shown in the following figure.

Unfortunately, the items listed in the dialog box aren't always clear, so locating the correct help topic may require some trial and error. The dialog box in the figure appears when you type **Comment** and then press F1. In this case, although Comment is an object, it's also the name of a property for the Scenario object. Clicking the first item displays the help topic for the Comment object; clicking the second item displays the help topic for the Comment property of the Scenario object.

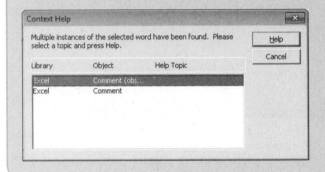

Properties of a Comment object

The Comment object has six properties. Table 5-1 contains a list of these properties, along with a brief description of each. If a property is *read-only,* your VBA code can read the property but can't change it.

Table 5-1: Properties of a Comment Object

Property	Read-Only	Description
Application	Yes	Returns an object that represents the application that created the comment (that is, Excel)
Author	Yes	Returns the name of the person who created the comment
Creator	Yes	Returns an integer that indicates the application in which the object was created
Parent	Yes	Returns the parent object, which is always a Range object, for the comment
Shape	Yes	Returns a Shape object that represents the shape attached to the comment
Visible	No	Is True if the comment is visible

Methods of a Comment object

Table 5-2 shows the methods that you can use with a Comment object. Again, these methods perform common operations that you may have performed manually with a comment at some point . . . but you probably never thought of these operations as methods.

Table 5-2: Methods of a Comment Object

Method	Description
Delete	Deletes a comment
Next	Returns a Comment object that represents the next comment in the worksheet
Previous	Returns a Comment object that represents the previous comment in the worksheet
Text	Returns or sets the text in a comment (takes three arguments)

Note

You may be surprised to see that Text is a method rather than a property, which leads to an important point: The distinction between properties and methods isn't always clear-cut, and the object model isn't perfectly consistent. In fact, as long as you get the syntax correct, it doesn't matter whether a word in your code is a property or a method.

The Comments collection

Recall that a collection is a group of like objects. Every worksheet has a Comments collection, which consists of all Comment objects on the worksheet. If the worksheet has no comments, this collection is empty. Comments appear in the collection based on their position in the worksheet: left-to-right and then top-to-bottom.

For example, the following code refers to the first comment on Sheet1 of the active workbook:

```
Worksheets("Sheet1").Comments(1)
```

The following statement displays the text in the first comment on Sheet1:

```
MsgBox Worksheets("Sheet1").Comments(1).Text
```

Unlike most objects, a Comment object doesn't have a Name property. Therefore, to refer to a specific comment, you must either use an index number or (more frequently) use the Comment property of a Range object to return a specific comment.

The Comments collection is also an object and has its own set of properties and methods. For example, the Comments collection has a Count property that stores the number of items in the collection — which is the number of Comment objects in the active worksheet. The following statement displays the total number of comments on the active worksheet:

```
MsgBox ActiveSheet.Comments.Count
```

The next example shows the address of the cell that has the first comment:

```
MsgBox ActiveSheet.Comments(1).Parent.Address
```

Here, Comments(1) returns the first Comment object in the Comments collection. The Parent property of the Comment object returns its container, which is a Range object. The message box displays the Address property of the Range object. The net effect is that the statement displays the address of the cell that contains the first comment.

You can also loop through all the comments on a sheet by using the For Each-Next construct. (Looping is explained in Chapter 6.) Here's an example that displays a separate message box for each comment on the active worksheet:

```
For Each cmt in ActiveSheet.Comments
    MsgBox cmt.Text
Next cmt
```

If you'd rather not deal with a series of message boxes, use this procedure to print the comments to the Immediate window in VBE:

```
For Each cmt in ActiveSheet.Comments
    Debug.Print cmt.Text
Next cmt
```

About the Comment property

In this section, I've been discussing the Comment object. If you dig through the Help system, you'll find that a Range object has a property named Comment. If the cell contains a comment, the Comment *property* returns a Comment *object*. For example, the following code refers to the Comment object in cell A1:

```
Range("A1").Comment
```

If this comment were the first one on the sheet, you could refer to the same Comment object as follows:

```
ActiveSheet.Comments(1)
```

To display the comment in cell A1 in a message box, use a statement like this:

```
MsgBox Range("A1").Comment.Text
```

If cell A1 doesn't contain a comment, this statement generates an error.

Note

The fact that a property can return an object is an important concept — a difficult one to grasp, perhaps, but critical to mastering VBA.

Objects contained in a Comment object

Working with properties is confusing at first because some properties actually return objects. Suppose that you want to determine the background color of a particular comment on Sheet1. If you look through the list of properties for a Comment object, you won't find anything that relates to color. Rather, you must do these steps:

1. Use the Comment object's Shape property to return the Shape object that's contained in the comment.
2. Use the Shape object's Fill property to return a FillFormat object.
3. Use the FillFormat object's ForeColor property to return a ColorFormat object.
4. Use the ColorFormat object's RGB property to get the color value.

Put another way, getting at the interior color for a Comment object involves accessing other objects contained in the Comment object. Here's a look at the object hierarchy that's involved:

Application (Excel)

Workbook object

Worksheet object

Comment object

Shape object

FillFormat object

ColorFormat object

I'll be the first to admit it: This process can get confusing! But, as an example of the elegance of VBA, you can write a single statement to change the color of a comment. The following statement changes the background color of the first comment on the active sheet:

```
ActiveSheet.Comments(1).Shape.Fill.ForeColor.RGB = RGB(0, 255, 0)
```

This type of referencing is not intuitive at first, but it will eventually make sense. Fortunately, recording your actions in Excel almost always yields some insights regarding the hierarchy of the objects involved.

By the way, to change the color of the text in a comment, you need to access the Comment object's TextFrame object, which contains the Characters object, which contains the Font object. Then you have access to the Font object's Color or ColorIndex properties. Here's an example that sets the ColorIndex property to 5:

```
ActiveSheet.Comments(1).Shape.TextFrame.Characters.Font.ColorIndex = 5
```

Refer to Chapter 28 for more information on colors.

Cross-Ref

Determining whether a cell has a comment

The following statement displays the comment in cell A1 of the active sheet:

```
MsgBox Range("A1").Comment.Text
```

If cell A1 doesn't have a comment, executing this statement generates a cryptic error message: Object variable or With block variable not set.

To determine whether a particular cell has a comment, you can write code to check whether the Comment object is Nothing. (Yes, Nothing is a valid keyword.) The following statement displays True if cell A1 doesn't have a comment:

```
MsgBox Range("A1").Comment Is Nothing
```

Note that I use the Is keyword and not an equal sign.

You can take this one step further and write a statement that displays the cell comment only if the cell actually has a comment (and does not generate an error if the cell lacks a comment). The statement that follows accomplishes this task:

```
If Not Range("A1").Comment Is Nothing Then MsgBox Range("A1").Comment.Text
```

Note that I used the Not keyword, which negates the True value that's returned if the cell has no comment. The statement, in essence, uses a double-negative to test a condition: If the comment isn't nothing, then display it. If this statement is confusing, think about it for a while, and it will make sense.

Adding a new Comment object

You may have noticed that the list of methods for the Comment object (or the Comments collection) doesn't include a method to add a new comment. This is because the AddComment method belongs to the Range object. The following statement adds a comment (an empty comment) to cell A1 on the active worksheet:

```
Range("A1").AddComment
```

If you consult the Help system, you discover that the AddComment method takes an argument that represents the text for the comment. Therefore, you can add a comment and then add text to the comment with a single statement:

```
Range("A1").AddComment "Formula developed by JW."
```

Note

The AddComment method generates an error if the cell already contains a comment. To avoid the error, your code can check whether the cell has a comment before adding one.

On the Web

If you'd like to see these Comment object properties and methods in action, check out the example workbook on this book's website. This workbook, named comment object. xlsm, contains several examples that manipulate Comment objects with VBA code. You probably won't understand all the code at this point, but you will get a feel for how you can use VBA to manipulate an object.

Some Useful Application Properties

When you're working with Excel, only one workbook at a time can be active. In that workbook, only one sheet can be active. And if the sheet is a worksheet, one cell is the active cell (even if a multicell range is selected). VBA knows about active workbooks, worksheets, and cells and lets you refer to these active objects in a simplified manner.

This method of referring to objects is often useful because you won't always know the exact workbook, worksheet, or range on which you want to operate. VBA makes object referencing easy by providing properties of the Application object. For example, the Application object has an ActiveCell property that returns a reference to the active cell. The following instruction assigns the value 1 to the active cell:

```
ActiveCell.Value = 1
```

Note that in the preceding example, I omitted the reference to the Application object and to the active worksheet because both are assumed. This instruction will fail if the active sheet isn't a worksheet. For example, if VBA executes this statement when a chart sheet is active, the procedure halts, and you get an error message.

If a range is selected in a worksheet, the active cell is a cell within the selected range. In other words, the active cell is always a single cell (never a multicell range).

The Application object also has a Selection property that returns a reference to whatever is selected, which may be a single cell (the active cell), a range of cells, or an object such as ChartObject, TextBox, or Shape.

Table 5-3 lists the other Application properties that are useful when working with cells and ranges.

Table 5-3: Some Useful Properties of the Application Object

Property	Object Returned
ActiveCell	The active cell.
ActiveChart	The active chart sheet or chart contained in a ChartObject on a worksheet. This property is Nothing if a chart isn't active.
ActiveSheet	The active sheet (worksheet or chart sheet).
ActiveWindow	The active window.
ActiveWorkbook	The active workbook.
Selection	The object selected. It could be a Range object, Shape, ChartObject, and so on.
ThisWorkbook	The workbook that contains the VBA procedure being executed. This object may or may not be the same as the ActiveWorkbook object.

The advantage of using these properties to return an object is that you don't need to know which cell, worksheet, or workbook is active, and you don't need to provide a specific reference to it. This allows you to write VBA code that isn't specific to a particular workbook, sheet, or range. For example, the following instruction clears the contents of the active cell, even though the address of the active cell isn't known:

```
ActiveCell.ClearContents
```

The example that follows displays a message that tells you the name of the active sheet:

```
MsgBox ActiveSheet.Name
```

If you want to know the name and directory path of the active workbook, use a statement like this:

```
MsgBox ActiveWorkbook.FullName
```

If a range on a worksheet is selected, you can fill the entire range with a value by executing a single statement. In the following example, the Selection property of the Application object returns a Range object that corresponds to the selected cells. The instruction simply modifies the Value property of this Range object, and the result is a range filled with a single value:

```
Selection.Value = 12
```

Note that if something other than a range is selected (such as a ChartObject or a Shape), the preceding statement generates an error because ChartObject and Shape objects don't have a Value property.

The following statement, however, enters a value of 12 into the Range object that was selected before a non-Range object was selected. If you look up the RangeSelection property in the Help system, you find that this property applies only to a Window object.

```
ActiveWindow.RangeSelection.Value = 12
```

To find out how many cells are selected in the active window, access the Count property. Here's an example:

```
MsgBox ActiveWindow.RangeSelection.Count
```

Working with Range Objects

Much of the work that you will do in VBA involves cells and ranges in worksheets. The earlier discussion on relative versus absolute macro recording (see the section "Relative or absolute recording?") exposes you to working with cells in VBA, but you need to know a lot more.

A Range object is contained in a Worksheet object and consists of a single cell or range of cells on a single worksheet. In the sections that follow, I discuss three ways of referring to Range objects in your VBA code:

➤ The Range property of a Worksheet or Range class object

➤ The Cells property of a Worksheet object

➤ The Offset property of a Range object

The Range property

The Range property returns a Range object. If you consult the Help system for the Range property, you learn that this property has two syntaxes:

```
object.Range(cell1)
object.Range(cell1, cell2)
```

The Range property applies to two types of objects: a Worksheet object or a Range object. Here, cell1 and cell2 refer to placeholders for terms that Excel recognizes as identifying the range (in the first instance) and delineating the range (in the second instance). Following are a few examples of using the Range property.

You've already seen examples like the following one earlier in the chapter. The instruction that follows simply enters a value into the specified cell. In this case, it puts the value 12.3 into cell A1 on Sheet1 of the active workbook:

```
Worksheets("Sheet1").Range("A1").Value = 12.3
```

The Range property also recognizes defined names in workbooks. Therefore, if a cell is named Input, you can use the following statement to enter a value into that named cell:

```
Worksheets("Sheet1").Range("Input").Value = 100
```

The example that follows enters the same value in a range of 20 cells on the active sheet. If the active sheet isn't a worksheet, the statement causes an error message:

```
ActiveSheet.Range("A1:B10").Value = 2
```

The next example produces exactly the same result as the preceding example:

```
Range("A1", "B10") = 2
```

The sheet reference is omitted, however, so the active sheet is assumed. Also, the value property is omitted, so the default property (which is Value for a Range object) is assumed. This example also uses the second syntax of the Range property. With this syntax, the first argument is the cell at the top left of the range, and the second argument is the cell at the lower right of the range.

The following example uses the Excel range intersection operator (a space) to return the intersection of two ranges. In this case, the intersection is a single cell, C6. Therefore, this statement enters 3 in cell C6:

```
Range("C1:C10 A6:E6") = 3
```

And finally, this next example enters the value 4 in five cells: that is, a noncontiguous range. The comma serves as the union operator. Note that the commas are within the quote marks.

```
Range("A1,A3,A5,A7,A9") = 4
```

So far, all the examples have used the Range property on a Worksheet object. As I mentioned, you can also use the Range property on a Range object. This concept can be rather confusing, but bear with me.

Following is an example of using the Range property on a Range object. (In this case, the Range object is the active cell.) This example treats the Range object as if it were the upper-left cell in the worksheet, and then it enters a value of 5 in the cell that *would be* B2. In other words, the reference returned is relative to the upper-left corner of the Range object. Therefore, the statement that follows enters a value of 5 into the cell directly to the right and one row below the active cell:

```
ActiveCell.Range("B2") = 5
```

I *said* this is confusing. Fortunately, you can access a cell relative to a range in a much clearer way: the Offset property. I discuss this property after the next section.

Working with merged cells

Working with merged cells can be tricky. If a range contains merged cells, you may need to take some special action with the macros. For example, if cells A1:D1 are merged, the statement that follows selects columns A through D (not just column B, as you might expect):

```
Columns("B:B").Select
```

I don't know if this unexpected behavior is intentional or a bug. However, it can cause your macro to behave in a manner that you didn't expect. Merged cells can also cause problems with sorting.

To determine whether a particular range contains any merged cells, you can use the following VBA function. The function returns True if any cell in the argument range is a merged cell. (Refer to Chapter 8 for more information about Function procedures.)

```
Function ContainsMergedCells(rng As Range)
    Dim cell As Range
    For Each cell In rng
        If cell.MergeCells Then
            ContainsMergedCells = True
            Exit Function
        End If
    Next cell
    ContainsMergedCells = False
End Function
```

To refer to merged cells, you can reference the entire merged range or just the upper-left cell within the merged range. For example, if a worksheet contains four cells merged into one (A1, B1, A2, and B1), reference the merged cells using either of the following expressions:

```
Range("A1:B2")
Range("A1")
```

If you attempt to assign a value to a cell in a merged range that's not the upper-left cell, VBA ignores the instruction and doesn't generate an error. For example, the following statement has no effect if A1:B2 is merged:

```
Range("B2").Value = 43
```

Some operations cause Excel to display a confirmation message. For example, if A1:B2 is merged, the following statement generates a message:
This operation will cause some merged cells to unmerge. Do you wish to continue?

```
Range("B2").Delete
```

Bottom line? Be careful with merged cells. Some have suggested that this feature wasn't very well thought-out before it was implemented. I tend to agree.

The Cells property

Another way to reference a range is to use the Cells property. You can use the Cells property, like the Range property, on Worksheet objects and Range objects. Check the Help system, and you see that the Cells property has three syntaxes:

```
object.Cells(rowIndex, columnIndex)
object.Cells(rowIndex)
object.Cells
```

Some examples demonstrate how to use the Cells property. The first example enters the value 9 in cell A1 on Sheet1. In this case, I'm using the first syntax, which accepts the index number of the row (from 1 to 1048576) and the index number of the column (from 1 to 16384):

```
Worksheets("Sheet1").Cells(1, 1) = 9
```

Here's an example that enters the value 7 in cell D3 (that is, row 3, column 4) in the active worksheet:

```
ActiveSheet.Cells(3, 4) = 7
```

You can also use the Cells property on a Range object. When you do so, the Range object returned by the Cells property is relative to the upper-left cell of the referenced Range. Confusing? Probably. An example may help clear up any confusion. The following instruction enters the value 5 in the active cell. Remember, in this case, the active cell is treated as if it were cell A1 in the worksheet:

```
ActiveCell.Cells(1, 1) = 5
```

 Note   The real advantage of this type of cell referencing will be apparent when I discuss variables and looping (see Chapter 6). In most cases, you don't use actual values for the arguments; rather, you use variables.

To enter a value of 5 in the cell directly below the active cell, you can use the following instruction:

```
ActiveCell.Cells(2, 1) = 5
```

Think of the preceding example as though it said this: "Start with the active cell and consider this cell as cell A1. Place 5 in the cell in the second row and the first column."

The second syntax of the Cells property uses a single argument that can range from 1 to 17,179,869,184. This number is equal to the number of cells in an Excel 2010 worksheet. The cells are numbered starting from A1 and continuing right and then down to the next row. The 16,384th cell is XFD1; the 16,385th is A2.

The next example enters the value 2 into cell SZ1 (which is the 520th cell in the worksheet) of the active worksheet:

```
ActiveSheet.Cells(520) = 2
```

To display the value in the last cell in a worksheet (XFD1048576), use this statement:

```
MsgBox ActiveSheet.Cells(17179869184)
```

You can also use this syntax with a Range object. In this case, the cell returned is relative to the Range object referenced. For example, if the Range object is A1:D10 (40 cells), the Cells property can have an argument from 1 to 40 and can return one of the cells in the Range object. In the following example, a value of 2000 is entered in cell A2 because A2 is the fifth cell (counting from the top, to the right, and then down) in the referenced range:

```
Range("A1:D10").Cells(5) = 2000
```

Note

In the preceding example, the argument for the Cells property isn't limited to values between 1 and 40. If the argument exceeds the number of cells in the range, the counting continues as if the range were taller than it actually is. Therefore, a statement like the preceding one could change the value in a cell that's outside the range A1:D10. The statement that follows, for example, changes the value in cell A11:

```
Range("A1:D10").Cells(41) = 2000
```

The third syntax for the Cells property simply returns all cells on the referenced worksheet. Unlike the other two syntaxes, in this one, the return data isn't a single cell. This example uses the ClearContents method on the range returned by using the Cells property on the active worksheet. The result is that the content of every cell on the worksheet is cleared:

```
ActiveSheet.Cells.ClearContents
```

Getting information from a cell

If you need to get the contents of a cell, VBA provides several properties. Following are the most commonly used properties:

- The Formula property returns the formula in a single cell, if the cell has one. If the cell doesn't contain a formula, it returns the value in the cell. The Formula property is a read/write property. Variations on this property include FormulaR1C1, FormulaLocal, and FormulaArray. (Consult the Help system for details.)

- The Value property returns the raw, unformatted value in the cell. This property is a read/write property.

- The Text property returns the text that is displayed in the cell. If the cell contains a numeric value, this property includes all the formatting, such as commas and currency symbols. The Text property is a read-only property.

- The Value2 property is just like the Value property, except that it doesn't use the Date and Currency data types. Rather, this property converts Date and Currency data types to Variants containing Doubles. If a cell contains the date 3/16/2013, the Value property returns it as a Date, while the Value2 property returns it as a double (for example, 41349).

The Offset property

The Offset property, like the Range and Cells properties, also returns a Range object. But unlike the other two methods that I discussed, the Offset property applies only to a Range object and no other class. Its syntax is as follows:

```
object.Offset(rowOffset, columnOffset)
```

The Offset property takes two arguments that correspond to the relative position from the upper-left cell of the specified Range object. The arguments can be positive (down or to the right), negative (up or to the left), or 0. The example that follows enters a value of 12 into the cell directly below the active cell:

```
ActiveCell.Offset(1,0).Value = 12
```

The next example enters a value of 15 in the cell directly above the active cell:

```
ActiveCell.Offset(-1,0).Value = 15
```

If the active cell is in row 1, the Offset property in the preceding example generates an error because it can't return a Range object that doesn't exist.

The Offset property is useful, especially when you use variables in looping procedures. I discuss these topics in the next chapter.

When you record a macro using the relative reference mode, Excel uses the Offset property to reference cells relative to the starting position (that is, the active cell when macro recording begins). For example, I used the macro recorder to generate the following code. I started with the cell pointer in cell B1, entered values into B1:B3, and then returned to B1.

```
Sub Macro1()
    ActiveCell.FormulaR1C1 = "1"
    ActiveCell.Offset(1, 0).Range("A1").Select
    ActiveCell.FormulaR1C1 = "2"
    ActiveCell.Offset(1, 0).Range("A1").Select
    ActiveCell.FormulaR1C1 = "3"
    ActiveCell.Offset(-2, 0).Range("A1").Select
End Sub
```

Note that the macro recorder uses the FormulaR1C1 property. Normally, you want to use the Value property to enter a value in a cell. However, using FormulaR1C1 or even Formula produces the same result.

Also note that the generated code references cell A1 — a cell that wasn't even involved in the macro. This notation is a quirk in the macro recording procedure that makes the code more complex than necessary. You can delete all references to Range("A1"), and the macro still works perfectly:

```
Sub Modified_Macro1()
    ActiveCell.FormulaR1C1 = "1"
    ActiveCell.Offset(1, 0).Select
    ActiveCell.FormulaR1C1 = "2"
    ActiveCell.Offset(1, 0).Select
    ActiveCell.FormulaR1C1 = "3"
    ActiveCell.Offset(-2, 0).Select
End Sub
```

In fact, here's a much more efficient version of the macro (which I wrote myself) that doesn't do any selecting:

```
Sub Macro1()
    ActiveCell = 1
    ActiveCell.Offset(1, 0) = 2
    ActiveCell.Offset(2, 0) = 3
End Sub
```

Things to Know about Objects

The preceding sections introduced you to objects (including collections), properties, and methods. But I've barely scratched the surface.

Essential concepts to remember

In this section, I note some additional essential concepts for would-be VBA gurus. These concepts will become clearer when you work with VBA and read subsequent chapters:

➤ **Objects have unique properties and methods.** Each object has its own set of properties and methods. Some objects, however, share some properties (for example, Name) and some methods (such as Delete).

➤ **You can manipulate objects without selecting them.** This idea may be contrary to how you normally think about manipulating objects in Excel. The fact is that it's usually more efficient to perform actions on objects without selecting them first. When you record a macro, Excel generally selects the object first, an unnecessary step that may make your macro run more slowly.

➤ **It's important that you understand the concept of collections.** Most of the time, you refer to an object indirectly by referring to the collection that it's in. For example, to access a Workbook object named Myfile, reference the Workbooks collection as follows:

```
Workbooks("Myfile.xlsx")
```

This reference returns an object, which is the workbook with which you're concerned.

➤ **Properties can return a reference to another object.** For example, in the following statement, the Font property returns a Font object contained in a Range object. Bold is a property of the Font object, not the Range object.

```
Range("A1").Font.Bold = True
```

➤ **You can refer to the same object in many different ways.** Assume that you have a workbook named Sales, and it's the only workbook open. Then assume that this workbook has one worksheet, named Summary. You can refer to the sheet in any of the following ways:

```
Workbooks("Sales.xlsx").Worksheets("Summary")
Workbooks(1).Worksheets(1)
Workbooks(1).Sheets(1)
Application.ActiveWorkbook.ActiveSheet
ActiveWorkbook.ActiveSheet
ActiveSheet
```

The method that you use is usually determined by how much you know about the workspace. For example, if more than one workbook is open, the second and third methods aren't reliable. If you want to work with the active sheet (whatever it may be), any of the last three methods would work. To be absolutely sure that you're referring to a specific sheet on a specific workbook, the first method is your best choice.

Learning more about objects and properties

If this is your first exposure to VBA, you're probably a bit overwhelmed by objects, properties, and methods. I don't blame you. If you try to access a property that an object doesn't have, you get a run-time error and your VBA code grinds to a screeching halt until you correct the problem.

Fortunately, you can learn about objects, properties, and methods in several ways.

Read the rest of the book

Don't forget, the name of this chapter is "Introducing Visual Basic for Applications." The remainder of this book covers many additional details and provides many useful and informative examples.

Record your actions

The absolute best way to become familiar with VBA, without question, is to simply turn on the macro recorder and record some actions that you perform in Excel. This approach is a quick way to learn the relevant objects, properties, and methods for a task. It's even better if the VBA module in which the code is being recorded is visible while you're recording.

Use the Help system

The main source of detailed information about Excel's objects, methods, and procedures is the Help system. Many people forget about this resource.

Use Object Browser

Object Browser is a handy tool that lists every property and method available for every object. When VBE is active, you can bring up Object Browser in any of the following three ways:

- ➤ Press F2.
- ➤ Choose the View→Object Browser command from the menu.
- ➤ Click the Object Browser tool on the Standard toolbar.

Object Browser is shown in Figure 5-15.

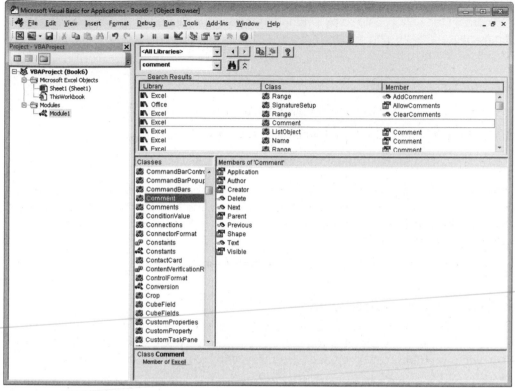

Figure 5-15: Object Browser is a great reference source.

The drop-down list in the upper-left corner of Object Browser includes a list of all object libraries that you have access to:

➤ Excel itself

➤ MSForms (used to create custom dialog boxes)

➤ Office (objects common to all Microsoft Office applications)

➤ Stdole (OLE automation objects)

➤ VBA

➤ The current project (the project that's selected in Project Explorer) and any workbooks referenced by that project

Your selection in this upper-left drop-down list determines what is displayed in the Classes window, and your selection in the Classes window determines what is visible in the Members Of panel.

After you select a library, you can search for a particular text string to get a list of properties and methods that contain the text. You do so by entering the text in the second drop-down list and then clicking the binoculars (Search) icon. For example, assume that you're working on a project that manipulates cell comments:

1. Select the library of interest.

    If you're not sure which object library is appropriate, you can select <All Libraries>.

2. Enter **Comment** in the drop-down list below the library list.

3. Click the binoculars icon to begin the text search.

The Search Results window displays the matching text. Select an object to display its classes in the Classes window. Select a class to display its members (properties, methods, and constants). Pay attention to the bottom pane, which shows more information about the object. You can press F1 to go directly to the appropriate help topic.

Object Browser may seem complex at first, but its usefulness to you will increase over time.

Experiment with the Immediate window

As I describe in the sidebar earlier in this chapter ("About the code examples"), the Immediate window of VBE is useful for testing statements and trying out various VBA expressions. I generally keep the Immediate window visible at all times, and I use it frequently to test various expressions and to help in debugging code.

VBA Programming Fundamentals

VBA Language Elements: An Overview

If you've used other programming languages, much of the information in this chapter may sound familiar. However, VBA has a few unique wrinkles, so even experienced programmers may find some new information.

In Chapter 5, I present an overview of objects, properties, and methods, but I don't tell you much about how to manipulate objects so that they do meaningful things. This chapter gently nudges you in that direction by exploring the VBA *language elements,* which are the keywords and control structures that you use to write VBA routines.

To get the ball rolling, I start by presenting a simple VBA Sub procedure. The following code, which is stored in a VBA module, calculates the sum of the first 100 positive integers. When the code finishes executing, the procedure displays a message with the result.

```
Sub VBA_Demo()
'   This is a simple VBA Example
    Dim Total As Long, i As Long
    Total = 0
    For i = 1 To 100
        Total = Total + i
    Next i
    MsgBox Total
End Sub
```

This procedure uses some common VBA language elements, including:

➤ A comment (the line that begins with an apostrophe)

➤ A variable declaration statement (the line that begins with Dim)

➤ Two variables (Total and i)

➤ Two assignment statements (Total = 0 and Total = Total + i)

➤ A looping structure (For-Next)

➤ A VBA function (MsgBox)

I discuss all these language elements in subsequent sections of this chapter.

Note

VBA procedures need not manipulate any objects. The preceding procedure, for example, doesn't do anything with objects. It simply works with numbers.

 Entering VBA code

VBA code, which resides in a VBA module, consists of instructions. The accepted practice is to use one instruction per line. This standard isn't a requirement, however; you can use a colon to separate multiple instructions on a single line. The following example combines four instructions on one line:

```
Sub OneLine()
    x= 1: y= 2: z= 3: MsgBox x + y + z
End Sub
```

Most programmers agree that code is easier to read if you use one instruction per line:

```
Sub MultipleLines()
    x = 1
    y = 2
    z = 3
    MsgBox x + y + z
End Sub
```

Each line can be as long as you like; the VBA module window scrolls to the left when you reach the right side. For lengthy lines, you may want to use VBA's line continuation sequence: a space followed by an underscore (_). For example:

```
Sub LongLine()
    SummedValue = _
      Worksheets("Sheet1").Range("A1").Value + _
      Worksheets("Sheet2").Range("A1").Value
End Sub
```

When you record macros, Excel often uses the line continuation sequence to break a long statement into multiple lines.

After you enter an instruction, VBA performs the following actions to improve readability:

- **It inserts spaces between operators.** If you enter Ans=1+2 (without spaces), for example, VBA converts it to

    ```
    Ans = 1 + 2
    ```

- **It adjusts the case of the letters for keywords, properties, and methods.** If you enter the following text: Result=activesheet.range("a1").value=12

    VBA converts it to

    ```
    Result = ActiveSheet.Range("a1").Value = 12
    ```

    Notice that text within quotation marks (in this case, "a1") isn't changed.

- **Because VBA variable names aren't case-sensitive, VBE by default adjusts the names of all variables with the same letters so that their case matches the case of letters that you most recently typed.** For example, if you first specify a variable as myvalue (all lowercase) and then enter the variable as MyValue (mixed case), VBA changes all other occurrences of the variable to MyValue. An exception occurs if you declare the variable with Dim or a similar statement; in this case, the variable name always appears as it was declared.

- **VBA scans the instruction for syntax errors.** If VBA finds an error, it changes the color of the line and might display a message describing the problem. Choose the Visual Basic Editor Tools→Options command to display the Options dialog box, where you control the error color (use the Editor Format tab) and whether the error message is displayed (use the Auto Syntax Check option in the Editor tab).

Comments

A *comment* is descriptive text embedded in your code and ignored by VBA. It's a good idea to use comments liberally to describe what you're doing because an instruction's purpose isn't always obvious.

You can use a complete line for your comment, or you can insert a comment *after* an instruction on the same line. A comment is indicated by an apostrophe. VBA ignores any text that follows an apostrophe — except when the apostrophe is contained within quotation marks — up until the end of the line. For example, the following statement doesn't contain a comment, even though it has an apostrophe:

```
Msg = "Can't continue"
```

The following example shows a VBA procedure with three comments:

```
Sub CommentDemo()
'    This procedure does nothing of value
     x = 0    'x represents nothingness
'    Display the result
     MsgBox x
End Sub
```

Although the apostrophe is the preferred comment indicator, you can also use the Rem keyword to mark a line as a comment. For example:

```
Rem -- The next statement prompts the user for a filename
```

The Rem keyword (short for *Remark*) is essentially a holdover from older versions of BASIC and is included in VBA for the sake of compatibility. Unlike the apostrophe, Rem can be written only at the beginning of a line, not on the same line as another instruction.

Following are a few general tips on making the best use of comments:

➤ Use comments to describe briefly the purpose of each procedure that you write.

➤ Use comments to describe changes that you make to a procedure.

➤ Use comments to indicate that you're using functions or constructs in an unusual or a non-standard manner.

➤ Use comments to describe the purpose of variables so that you and other people can decipher otherwise cryptic names.

➤ Use comments to describe workarounds that you develop to overcome Excel bugs or limitations.

➤ Write comments *while* you code rather than after.

Tip

In some cases, you may want to test a procedure without including a particular instruction or group of instructions. Instead of deleting the instruction, convert it to a comment by inserting an apostrophe at the beginning. VBA then ignores the instruction when the routine is executed. To convert the comment back to an instruction, just delete the apostrophe.

The Visual Basic Editor (VBE) Edit toolbar contains two useful buttons. (The Edit toolbar isn't displayed by default. To display this toolbar, choose View➜Toolbars➜Edit.) Select a group of instructions and then click the Comment Block button to convert the instructions to comments. The Uncomment Block button converts a group of comments back to instructions.

Variables, Data Types, and Constants

VBA's main purpose is to manipulate data. Some data resides in objects, such as worksheet ranges. Other data is stored in variables that you create.

You can think of a *variable* as a named storage location in your computer's memory. Variables can accommodate a wide variety of *data types* — from simple Boolean values (True or False) to large, double-precision values (see the following section). You assign a value to a variable by using the equal sign operator (more about this process in the upcoming section, "Assignment Statements").

You make your life easier if you get into the habit of making your variable names as descriptive as possible. VBA does, however, have a few rules regarding variable names:

➤ You can use alphabetic characters, numbers, and some punctuation characters, but the first character must be alphabetic.

➤ VBA doesn't distinguish between case. To make variable names more readable, programmers often use mixed case (for example, InterestRate rather than interestrate).

➤ You can't use spaces or periods. To make variable names more readable, programmers often use the underscore character (Interest_Rate).

➤ You can't embed special type declaration characters (#, $, %, &, or !) in a variable name.

➤ Variable names can be as long as 254 characters — but using such long variable names isn't recommended.

The following list contains some examples of assignment expressions that use various types of variables. The variable names are to the left of the equal sign. Each statement assigns the value to the right of the equal sign to the variable on the left.

```
x = 1
InterestRate = 0.075
LoanPayoffAmount = 243089.87
DataEntered = False
x = x + 1
MyNum = YourNum * 1.25
UserName = "Bob Johnson"
DateStarted = #12/14/2012#
```

VBA has many *reserved words,* which are words that you can't use for variable or procedure names. If you attempt to use one of these words, you get an error message. For example, although the reserved word Next might make a very descriptive variable name, the following instruction generates a syntax error:

```
Next = 132
```

Unfortunately, syntax error messages aren't always descriptive. If the Auto Syntax Check option is turned on, you get the error Compile error: Expected: variable. If Auto Syntax Check is turned off, attempting to execute this statement results in Compile error: Syntax error. It would be more helpful if the error message were something like Reserved word used as a variable. So if an instruction produces a strange error message, check the VBA Help system to ensure that your variable name doesn't have a special use in VBA.

Defining data types

VBA makes life easy for programmers because it can automatically handle all the details involved in dealing with data. Some programming languages, however, are *strictly typed,* which means that the programmer must explicitly define the data type for every variable used.

Data type refers to how data is stored in memory — as integers, real numbers, strings, and so on. Although VBA can take care of data typing automatically, it does so at a cost: slower execution and less efficient use of memory. As a result, letting VBA handle data typing may present problems when you're running large or complex applications. Another advantage of explicitly declaring your variables as a particular data type is that VBA can perform some additional error checking at the compile stage. These errors might otherwise be difficult to locate.

Table 6-1 lists VBA's assortment of built-in data types. (Note that you can also define custom data types, which I describe later in this chapter in the section "User-Defined Data Types.")

Table 6-1: VBA Built-In Data Types

Data Type	Bytes Used	Range of Values
Byte	1 byte	0 to 255
Boolean	2 bytes	True or False
Integer	2 bytes	−32,768 to 32,767
Long	4 bytes	−2,147,483,648 to 2,147,483,647
Single	4 bytes	−3.402823E38 to −1.401298E-45 (for negative values); 1.401298E-45 to 3.402823E38 (for positive values)
Double	8 bytes	−1.79769313486232E308 to −4.94065645841247E-324 (negative values); 4.94065645841247E-324 to 1.79769313486232E308 (for positive values)
Currency	8 bytes	−922,337,203,685,477.5808 to 922,337,203,685,477.5807
Decimal	12 bytes	+/−79,228,162,514,264,337,593,543,950,335 with no decimal point; +/−7.9228162514264337593543950335 with 28 places to the right of the decimal
Date	8 bytes	January 1, 0100 to December 31, 9999
Object	4 bytes	Any object reference
String (variable length)	10 bytes + string length	0 to approximately 2 billion characters
String (fixed length)	Length of string	1 to approximately 65,400 characters
Variant (with numbers)	16 bytes	Any numeric value up to the range of a double data type. It can also hold special values, such as Empty, Error, Nothing, and Null.
Variant (with characters)	22 bytes + string length	0 to approximately 2 billion
User-defined	Varies	Varies by element

Note The Decimal data type is unusual because you can't declare it. In fact, it is a subtype of a variant. You need to use the VBA CDec function to convert a variant to the Decimal data type.

Generally, it's best to use the data type that uses the smallest number of bytes yet still can handle all the data that will be assigned to it. When VBA works with data, execution speed is partially a function of the number of bytes that VBA has at its disposal. In other words, the fewer bytes used by data, the faster VBA can access and manipulate the data.

For worksheet calculation, Excel uses the Double data type, so that's a good choice for processing numbers in VBA when you don't want to lose any precision. For integer calculations, you can use the Integer type (which is limited to values less than or equal to 32,767). Otherwise, use the Long data type. In fact, using the Long data type even for values less than 32,767 is recommended because this data type may be a bit faster than using the Integer type. When dealing with Excel worksheet row numbers, you want to use the Long data type because the number of rows in a worksheet exceeds the maximum value for the Integer data type.

 # Benchmarking variant data types

To test whether data typing is important, I developed the following routine, which performs more than 300 million meaningless calculations in a loop and then displays the procedure's total execution time:

```
Sub TimeTest()
    Dim x As Long, y As Long
    Dim A As Double, B As Double, C As Double
    Dim i As Long, j As Long
    Dim StartTime As Date, EndTime As Date
'   Store the starting time
    StartTime = Timer
'   Perform some calculations
    x = 0
    y = 0
    For i = 1 To 10000
        x = x + 1
        y = x + 1
        For j = 1 To 10000
            A = x + y + i
            B = y - x - i
            C = x / y * i
        Next j
    Next i
'   Get ending time
    EndTime = Timer
'   Display total time in seconds
    MsgBox Format(EndTime - StartTime, "0.0")
End Sub
```

On my system, this routine took 6.8 seconds to run. (The time will vary, depending on your system's processor speed.) I then turned the Dim statements, which declare the data types, into comments by adding an apostrophe at the beginning of the lines. As a result, VBA used the default data type, Variant. I ran the procedure again. It took 22.1 seconds, more than three times as long as before.

The moral is simple: If you want your VBA applications to run as fast as possible, declare your variables!

A workbook that contains this code is available on the companion website in a file named timing text.xlsm.

Declaring variables

If you don't declare the data type for a variable that you use in a VBA routine, VBA uses the default data type, Variant. Data stored as a Variant acts like a chameleon: It changes type, depending on what you do with it.

The following procedure demonstrates how a variable can assume different data types:

```
Sub VariantDemo()
    MyVar = True
    MyVar = MyVar * 100
    MyVar = MyVar / 4
    MyVar = "Answer: " & MyVar
    MsgBox MyVar
End Sub
```

In the VariantDemo procedure, MyVar starts out as a Boolean. The multiplication operation converts it to an Integer. The division operation converts it to a Double. And finally, it's concatenated with text to make it a String. The MsgBox statement displays the final string: Answer: -25.

To further demonstrate the potential problems in dealing with Variant data types, try executing this procedure:

```
Sub VariantDemo2()
    MyVar = "123"
    MyVar = MyVar + MyVar
    MyVar = "Answer: " & MyVar
    MsgBox MyVar
End Sub
```

The message box displays Answer: 123123. This is probably *not* what you wanted. When dealing with variants that contain text strings, the + operator performs string concatenation.

Determining a data type

You can use the VBA TypeName function to determine the data type of a variable. Here's a modified version of the VariantDemo procedure. This version displays the data type of MyVar at each step.

```
Sub VariantDemo3()
    MyVar = True
    MsgBox TypeName(MyVar)
    MyVar = MyVar * 100
    MsgBox TypeName(MyVar)
    MyVar = MyVar / 4
    MsgBox TypeName(MyVar)
    MyVar = "Answer: " & MyVar
    MsgBox TypeName(MyVar)
    MsgBox MyVar
End Sub
```

Thanks to VBA, the data type conversion of undeclared variables is automatic. This process may seem like an easy way out, but remember that you sacrifice speed and memory — and you run the risk of errors that you may not even know about.

Declaring each variable in a procedure before you use it is an excellent habit. Declaring a variable tells VBA its name and data type. Declaring variables provides two main benefits:

> ➤ **Your programs run faster and use memory more efficiently.** The default data type, Variant, causes VBA to repeatedly perform time-consuming checks and reserve more memory than necessary. If VBA knows the data type, it doesn't have to investigate, and it can reserve just enough memory to store the data.

> ➤ **You avoid problems involving misspelled variable names.** This benefit assumes that you use Option Explicit to force yourself to declare all variables (see the next section). Say that you use an undeclared variable named CurrentRate. At some point in your routine, however, you insert the statement CurentRate = .075. This misspelled variable name, which is very difficult to spot, will likely cause your routine to give incorrect results.

Forcing yourself to declare all variables

To force yourself to declare all the variables that you use, include the following as the first instruction in your VBA module:

```
Option Explicit
```

When this statement is present, VBA won't even execute a procedure if it contains an undeclared variable name. VBA issues the error message shown in Figure 6-1, and you must declare the variable before you can proceed.

 ## A note about the examples in this chapter

This chapter contains many examples of VBA code, usually presented in the form of simple procedures. These examples demonstrate various concepts as simply as possible. Most of these examples don't perform any particularly useful task; in fact, the task can often be performed in a different (perhaps more efficient) way. In other words, don't use these examples in your own work. Subsequent chapters provide many more code examples that *are* useful.

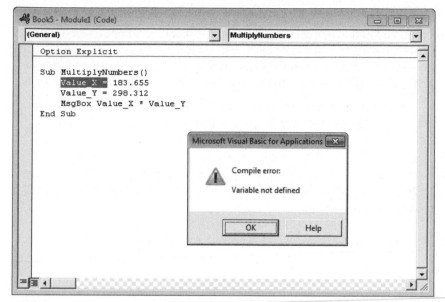

Figure 6-1: VBA's way of telling you that your procedure contains an undeclared variable.

Tip

To ensure that the Option Explicit statement is inserted automatically whenever you insert a new VBA module, enable the Require Variable Declaration option in the Editor tab of the VBE Options dialog box (choose Tools➞Options). I highly recommend doing so. Be aware, however, that this option doesn't affect existing modules.

Scoping variables

A variable's *scope* determines in which modules and procedures you can use the variable. Table 6-2 lists the three ways in which a variable can be scoped.

Table 6-2: Variable Scope

Scope	To Declare a Variable with This Scope
Single procedure	Include a Dim or Static statement within the procedure.
Single module	Include a Dim or Private statement before the first procedure in a module.
All modules	Include a Public statement before the first procedure in a module.

I discuss each scope further in the following sections.

Local variables

A *local variable* is a variable declared within a procedure. You can use local variables only in the procedure in which they're declared. When the procedure ends, the variable no longer exists, and Excel frees up the memory that the variable used. If you need the variable to retain its value when the procedure ends, declare it as a Static variable. (See the section "Static variables," later in this chapter.)

The most common way to declare a local variable is to place a Dim statement between a Sub statement and an End Sub statement. Dim statements usually are placed right after the Sub statement, before the procedure's code.

Note

Dim is a shortened form of Dimension. In old versions of BASIC, this statement was used exclusively to declare the dimensions for an array. In VBA, the Dim keyword is used to declare any variable, not just arrays.

The following procedure uses six local variables declared by using Dim statements:

```
Sub MySub()
    Dim x As Integer
    Dim First As Long
    Dim InterestRate As Single
    Dim TodaysDate As Date
    Dim UserName As String
    Dim MyValue
'   - [The procedure's code goes here] -
End Sub
```

Notice that the last Dim statement in the preceding example doesn't declare a data type; it simply names the variable. As a result, that variable becomes a variant.

You also can declare several variables with a single Dim statement. For example:

```
Dim x As Integer, y As Integer, z As Integer
Dim First As Long, Last As Double
```

Caution

Unlike some languages, VBA doesn't let you declare a group of variables to be a particular data type by separating the variables with commas. For example, the following statement, although valid, does not declare all the variables as integers:

```
Dim i, j, k As Integer
```

In VBA, only k is declared to be an integer; the other variables are declared variants. To declare i, j, and k as integers, use this statement:

```
Dim i As Integer, j As Integer, k As Integer
```

Another way of data-typing variables

Like most other dialects of BASIC, VBA lets you append a character to a variable's name to indicate the data type. For example, you can declare the MyVar variable as an integer by tacking % onto the name:

```
Dim MyVar%
```

Type-declaration characters exist for most VBA data types. Data types not listed in the following table don't have type-declaration characters.

Data Type	Type-Declaration Character
Integer	%
Long	&
Single	!
Double	#
Currency	@
String	$

This method of data typing is essentially a holdover from BASIC; it's better to declare your variables by using the other techniques described in this chapter. I list these type-declaration characters here just in case you encounter them in an older program.

If a variable is declared with a local scope, other procedures in the same module can use the same variable name, but each instance of the variable is unique to its own procedure.

In general, local variables are the most efficient because VBA frees up the memory that they use when the procedure ends.

Module-wide variables

Sometimes, you want a variable to be available to all procedures in a module. If so, just declare the variable *before* the module's first procedure (outside of any procedures or functions).

In the following example, the Dim statement is the first instruction in the module. Both Procedure1 and Procedure2 have access to the CurrentValue variable.

```
Dim CurrentValue as Long

Sub Procedure1()
'    - [Code goes here] -
End Sub

Sub Procedure2()
'    - [Code goes here] -
End Sub
```

The value of a module-wide variable retains its value when a procedure ends normally (that is, when it reaches the End Sub or End Function statement). An exception is if the procedure is halted with an End statement. When VBA encounters an End statement, all module-wide variables in all modules lose their values.

Public variables

To make a variable available to all the procedures in all the VBA modules in a project, declare the variable at the module level (before the first procedure declaration) by using the Public keyword rather than Dim. Here's an example:

```
Public CurrentRate as Long
```

The Public keyword makes the CurrentRate variable available to any procedure in the VBA project, even those in other modules in the project. You must insert this statement before the first procedure in a module (any module). This type of declaration must appear in a standard VBA module, not in a code module for a sheet or a UserForm.

Static variables

Static variables are a special case. They're declared at the procedure level, and they retain their value when the procedure ends normally. However, if the procedure is halted by an End statement, static variables *do* lose their values. Note that an End statement is not the same as an End Sub statement.

You declare static variables by using the Static keyword:

```
Sub MySub()
    Static Counter as Long
    '- [Code goes here] -
End Sub
```

Working with constants

A variable's value may change while a procedure is executing (that's why it's called a *variable*). Sometimes, you need to refer to a named value or string that never changes: a *constant*.

Using constants throughout your code in place of hard-coded values or strings is an excellent programming practice. For example, if your procedure needs to refer to a specific value (such as an interest rate) several times, it's better to declare the value as a constant and use the constant's name rather than its value in your expressions. This technique not only makes your code more readable, it also makes it easier to change should the need arise — you have to change only one instruction rather than several.

Variable naming conventions

Some programmers name variables so that users can identify their data types by just looking at their names. Personally, I don't use this technique very often because I think it makes the code more difficult to read, but you might find it helpful.

The naming convention involves using a standard lowercase prefix for the variable's name. For example, if you have a Boolean variable that tracks whether a workbook has been saved, you might name the variable bWasSaved. That way, it's clear that the variable is a Boolean variable. The following table lists some standard prefixes for data types:

Data Type	Prefix
Boolean	b
Integer	i
Long	l
Single	s
Double	d
Currency	c
Date/Time	dt
String	str
Object	obj
Variant	v
User-defined	u

Declaring constants

You declare constants with the Const statement. Here are some examples:

```
Const NumQuarters as Integer = 4
Const Rate = .0725, Period = 12
Const ModName as String = "Budget Macros"
Public Const AppName as String = "Budget Application"
```

The second example doesn't declare a data type. Consequently, VBA determines the data type from the value. The Rate variable is a Double, and the Period variable is an Integer. Because a constant never changes its value, you normally want to declare your constants as a specific data type.

Like variables, constants also have a scope. If you want a constant to be available within a single procedure only, declare it after the Sub or Function statement to make it a local constant. To make a constant available to all procedures in a module, declare it before the first procedure in the module. To make a constant available to all modules in the workbook, use the Public keyword and declare the constant before the first procedure in a module. For example:

```
Public Const InterestRate As Double = 0.0725
```

Note

If your VBA code attempts to change the value of a constant, you get an error (Assignment to constant not permitted). This message is what you would expect. A constant is a constant, not a variable.

Using predefined constants

Excel and VBA make available many predefined constants, which you can use without declaring. In fact, you don't even need to know the value of these constants to use them. The macro recorder generally uses constants rather than actual values. The following procedure uses a built-in constant (xlLandscape) to set the page orientation to landscape for the active sheet:

```
Sub SetToLandscape()
    ActiveSheet.PageSetup.Orientation = xlLandscape
End Sub
```

I discovered the xlLandscape constant by recording a macro. I also could have found this information in the Help system. And, if you have the AutoList Members option turned on, you can often get some assistance while you enter your code (see Figure 6-2). In many cases, VBA lists all the constants that you can assign to a property.

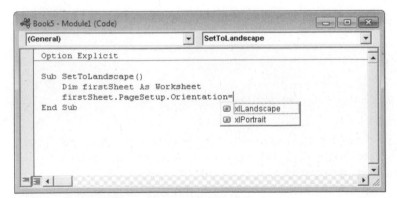

Figure 6-2: VBA displays a list of constants that you can assign to a property.

The actual value for xlLandscape is 2 (which you can discover by using the Immediate window). The other built-in constant for changing paper orientation is xlPortrait, which has a value of 1. Obviously, if you use the built-in constants, you don't really need to know their values.

Note

> Object Browser, which I discuss briefly in Chapter 5, can display a list of all Excel and VBA constants. In VBE, press F2 to bring up Object Browser.

Working with strings

Like Excel, VBA can manipulate both numbers and text (strings). There are two types of strings in VBA:

> ➤ *Fixed-length strings* are declared with a specified number of characters. The maximum length is 65,535 characters.

> ➤ *Variable-length strings* theoretically can hold up to 2 billion characters.

Each character in a string requires 1 byte of storage, plus a small amount of storage for the header of each string. When you declare a variable with a Dim statement as data type String, you can specify the length if you know it (that is, a fixed-length string), or you can let VBA handle it dynamically (a variable-length string).

In the following example, the MyString variable is declared to be a string with a maximum length of 50 characters. YourString is also declared as a string; but it's a variable-length string, so its length is not fixed.

```
Dim MyString As String * 50
Dim YourString As String
```

Working with dates

You can use a string variable to store a date, but if you do, it's not a real date (meaning you can't perform date calculations with it). Using the Date data type is a better way to work with dates.

A variable defined as a date uses 8 bytes of storage and can hold dates ranging from January 1, 0100, to December 31, 9999. That's a span of nearly 10,000 years — more than enough for even the most aggressive financial forecast! The Date data type is also useful for storing time-related data. In VBA, you specify dates and times by enclosing them between two hash marks (#).

About Excel's date bug

It is commonly known that Excel has a date bug: It incorrectly assumes that the year 1900 is a leap year. Even though there was no February 29, 1900, Excel accepts the following formula and displays the result as the 29th day of February, 1900:

```
=Date(1900,2,29)
```

VBA doesn't have this date bug. The VBA equivalent of Excel's DATE function is DateSerial. The following expression (correctly) returns March 1, 1900:

```
DateSerial(1900,2,29)
```

Therefore, Excel's date serial number system doesn't correspond exactly to the VBA date serial number system. These two systems return different values for dates between January 1, 1900, and February 28, 1900.

Note

The range of dates that VBA can handle is much larger than Excel's own date range, which begins with January 1, 1900, and extends through December 31, 9999. Therefore, be careful that you don't attempt to use a date in a worksheet that is outside Excel's acceptable date range.

Cross-Ref

In Chapter 8, I describe some relatively simple VBA functions that enable you to create formulas that work with pre-1900 dates in a worksheet.

Here are some examples of declaring variables and constants as Date data types:

```
Dim Today As Date
Dim StartTime As Date
Const FirstDay As Date = #1/1/2013#
Const Noon = #12:00:00#
```

Caution

Dates are always defined using month/day/year format, even if your system is set to display dates in a different format (for example, day/month/year).

If you use a message box to display a date, it's displayed according to your system's short date format. Similarly, a time is displayed according to your system's time format (either 12- or 24-hour). You can modify these system settings by using the Regional Settings option in the Windows Control Panel.

Assignment Statements

An *assignment statement* is a VBA instruction that evaluates an expression and assigns the result to a variable or an object. Excel's Help system defines *expression* as "a combination of keywords, operators, variables, and constants that yields a string, number, or object. An expression can perform a calculation, manipulate characters, or test data."

I couldn't have said it better myself. Much of the work done in VBA involves developing (and debugging) expressions. If you know how to create formulas in Excel, you'll have no trouble creating expressions in VBA. With a worksheet formula, Excel displays the result in a cell. The result of a VBA expression, on the other hand, can be assigned to a variable or used as a property value.

VBA uses the equal sign (=) as its assignment operator. The following are examples of assignment statements (the expressions are to the right of the equal sign):

```
x = 1
x = x + 1
x = (y * 2) / (z  * 2)
FileOpen = True
FileOpen = Not FileOpen
Range("TheYear").Value = 2010
```

Tip

Expressions can be complex. You may want to use the line continuation sequence (space followed by an underscore) to make lengthy expressions easier to read.

Often, expressions use functions. These functions can be built-in VBA functions, Excel's worksheet functions, or custom functions that you develop in VBA. I discuss built-in VBA functions later in this chapter (see the upcoming section "Built-in Functions").

Operators play a major role in VBA. Familiar operators describe mathematical operations, including addition (+), multiplication (*), division (/), subtraction (–), exponentiation (^), and string concatenation (&). Less familiar operators are the backslash (\) operator (used in integer division) and the Mod operator (used in modulo arithmetic). The Mod operator returns the remainder of one number divided by another. For example, the following expression returns 2:

```
17 Mod 3
```

VBA also supports the same comparison operators used in Excel formulas: equal to (=), greater than (>), less than (<), greater than or equal to (>=), less than or equal to (<=), and not equal to (<>).

With one exception, the order of precedence for operators in VBA is exactly the same as in Excel (see Table 6-3). And, of course, you can use parentheses to change the natural order of precedence.

Caution

The negation operator (a minus sign) is handled differently in VBA. In Excel, the following formula returns 25:

```
=-5^2
```

In VBA, x equals –25 after this statement is executed:

```
x = -5 ^ 2
```

VBA performs the exponentiation operation first and then applies the negation operator. The following statement returns 25:

```
x = (-5) ^ 2
```

Table 6-3: Operator Precedence

Operator	Operation	Order of Precedence
^	Exponentiation	1
* and /	Multiplication and division	2
+ and -	Addition and subtraction	3
&	Concatenation	4
=, <, >, <=, >=, <>	Comparison	5

In the statement that follows, x is assigned the value 10 because the multiplication operator has a higher precedence than the addition operator:

```
x = 4 + 3 * 2
```

To avoid ambiguity, you may prefer to write the statement as follows:

```
x = 4 + (3 * 2)
```

In addition, VBA provides a full set of logical operators, shown in Table 6-4. For complete details on these operators (including examples), use the VBA Help system.

Table 6-4: VBA Logical Operators

Operator	What It Does
Not	Performs a logical negation on an expression
And	Performs a logical conjunction on two expressions
Or	Performs a logical disjunction on two expressions
Xor	Performs a logical exclusion on two expressions
Eqv	Performs a logical equivalence on two expressions
Imp	Performs a logical implication on two expressions

The following instruction uses the Not operator to toggle the gridline display in the active window. The DisplayGridlines property takes a value of either True or False. Therefore, using the Not operator changes False to True and True to False.

```
ActiveWindow.DisplayGridlines = Not ActiveWindow.DisplayGridlines
```

The following expression performs a logical And operation. The MsgBox statement displays True only when Sheet1 is the active sheet *and* the active cell is in Row 1. If either or both of these conditions aren't true, the MsgBox statement displays False.

```
MsgBox ActiveSheet.Name = "Sheet1" And ActiveCell.Row = 1
```

The following expression performs a logical Or operation. The MsgBox statement displays True when either Sheet1 *or* Sheet2 is the active sheet.

```
MsgBox ActiveSheet.Name = "Sheet1" Or ActiveSheet.Name = "Sheet2"
```

Arrays

An *array* is a group of elements of the same type that have a common name. You refer to a specific element in the array by using the array name and an index number. For example, you can define an array of 12 string variables so that each variable corresponds to the name of a month. If you name the array MonthNames, you can refer to the first element of the array as MonthNames(0), the second element as MonthNames(1), and so on, up to MonthNames(11).

Declaring arrays

You declare an array with a Dim or Public statement, just as you declare a regular variable. You can also specify the number of elements in the array. You do so by specifying the first index number, the keyword To, and the last index number — all inside parentheses. For example, here's how to declare an array comprising exactly 100 integers:

```
Dim MyArray(1 To 100) As Integer
```

Tip

When you declare an array, you need to specify only the upper index, in which case VBA assumes that 0 is the lower index. Therefore, the two statements that follow have the same effect:

```
Dim MyArray(0 to 100) As Integer
Dim MyArray(100) As Integer
```

In both cases, the array consists of 101 elements.

By default, VBA assumes zero-based arrays. If you would like VBA to assume that 1 is the lower index for all arrays that declare only the upper index, include the following statement before any procedures in your module:

```
Option Base 1
```

Declaring multidimensional arrays

The array examples in the preceding section are one-dimensional arrays. VBA arrays can have up to 60 dimensions, although you'll rarely need more than three dimensions (a 3-D array). The following statement declares a 100-integer array with two dimensions (2-D):

```
Dim MyArray(1 To 10, 1 To 10) As Integer
```

You can think of the preceding array as occupying a 10-x-10 matrix. To refer to a specific element in a 2-D array, you need to specify two index numbers. For example, here's how you can assign a value to an element in the preceding array:

```
MyArray(3, 4) = 125
```

Following is a declaration for a 3-D array that contains 1,000 elements (visualize this array as a cube):

```
Dim MyArray(1 To 10, 1 To 10, 1 To 10) As Integer
```

Reference an item in the array by supplying three index numbers:

```
MyArray(4, 8, 2) = 0
```

Declaring dynamic arrays

A *dynamic array* doesn't have a preset number of elements. You declare a dynamic array with a blank set of parentheses:

```
Dim MyArray() As Integer
```

Before you can use a dynamic array in your code, however, you must use the ReDim statement to tell VBA how many elements are in the array. You can use a variable to assign the number of elements in an array. Often the value of the variable isn't known until the procedure is executing. For example, if the variable x contains a number, you can define the array's size by using this statement:

```
ReDim MyArray (1 To x)
```

You can use the ReDim statement any number of times, changing the array's size as often as you need to. When you change an array's dimensions the existing values are destroyed. If you want to preserve the existing values, use ReDim Preserve. For example:

```
ReDim Preserve MyArray (1 To y)
```

Arrays crop up later in this chapter when I discuss looping (the section "Looping blocks of instructions").

Object Variables

An *object variable* is a variable that represents an entire object, such as a range or a worksheet. Object variables are important for two reasons:

➤ They can simplify your code significantly.

➤ They can make your code execute more quickly.

Object variables, like normal variables, are declared with the Dim or Public statement. For example, the following statement declares InputArea as a Range object variable:

```
Dim InputArea As Range
```

Use the Set keyword to assign an object to the variable. For example:

```
Set InputArea = Range("C16:E16")
```

To see how object variables simplify your code, examine the following procedure, which doesn't use an object variable:

```
Sub NoObjVar()
    Worksheets("Sheet1").Range("A1").Value = 124
    Worksheets("Sheet1").Range("A1").Font.Bold = True
    Worksheets("Sheet1").Range("A1").Font.Italic = True
    Worksheets("Sheet1").Range("A1").Font.Size = 14
    Worksheets("Sheet1").Range("A1").Font.Name = "Cambria"
End Sub
```

This routine enters a value into cell A1 of Sheet1 on the active workbook, applies some formatting, and changes the fonts and size. That's a lot of typing. To reduce wear and tear on your fingers (and make your code more efficient), you can condense the routine with an object variable:

```
Sub ObjVar()
    Dim MyCell As Range
    Set MyCell = Worksheets("Sheet1").Range("A1")
    MyCell.Value = 124
    MyCell.Font.Bold = True
    MyCell.Font.Italic = True
    MyCell.Font.Size = 14
    MyCell.Font.Name = "Cambria"
End Sub
```

After the variable MyCell is declared as a Range object, the Set statement assigns an object to it. Subsequent statements can then use the simpler MyCell reference in place of the lengthy Worksheets("Sheet1").Range("A1") reference.

Tip

After an object is assigned to a variable, VBA can access it more quickly than it can a normal, lengthy reference that has to be resolved. So when speed is critical, use object variables. One way to think about code efficiency is in terms of dot processing. Every time VBA encounters a dot, as in Sheets(1).Range("A1"), it takes time to resolve the reference. Using an object variable reduces the number of dots to be processed. The fewer the dots, the faster the processing time. Another way to improve the speed of your code is by using the With-End With construct, which also reduces the number of dots to be processed. I discuss this construct later in this chapter.

The true value of object variables becomes apparent when I discuss looping later in this chapter.

User-Defined Data Types

VBA lets you create custom, or *user-defined,* data types. A user-defined data type can ease your work with some types of data. For example, if your application deals with customer information, you may want to create a user-defined data type named CustomerInfo:

```
Type CustomerInfo
    Company As String
    Contact As String
    RegionCode As Long
    Sales As Double
End Type
```

Note

You define custom data types at the top of your module, before any procedures.

After you create a user-defined data type, you use a Dim statement to declare a variable as that type. Usually, you define an array. For example:

```
Dim Customers(1 To 100) As CustomerInfo
```

Each of the 100 elements in this array consists of four components (as specified by the user-defined data type, CustomerInfo). You can refer to a particular component of the record as follows:

```
Customers(1).Company = "Acme Tools"
Customers(1).Contact = "Tim Robertson"
Customers(1).RegionCode = 3
Customers(1).Sales = 150674.98
```

You can also work with an element in the array as a whole. For example, to copy the information from Customers(1) to Customers(2), use this instruction:

```
Customers(2) = Customers(1)
```

The preceding example is equivalent to the following instruction block:

```
Customers(2).Company = Customers(1).Company
Customers(2).Contact = Customers(1).Contact
Customers(2).RegionCode = Customers(1).RegionCode
Customers(2).Sales = Customers(1).Sales
```

Built-in Functions

Like most programming languages, VBA has a variety of built-in functions that simplify calculations and operations. Many VBA functions are similar (or identical) to Excel worksheet functions. For example, the VBA function UCase, which converts a string argument to uppercase, is equivalent to the Excel worksheet function UPPER.

Cross-Ref

Appendix A contains a complete list of VBA functions, with a brief description of each. All are thoroughly described in the VBA Help system.

Tip

To get a list of VBA functions while you're writing your code, type VBA followed by a period (.).VBE displays a list of all its members, including functions (see Figure 6-3). The functions are preceded by a green icon. If this technique doesn't work for you, make sure that the Auto List Members option is selected. Choose Tools➜Options and then click the Editor tab.

You use functions in VBA expressions in much the same way that you use functions in worksheet formulas. Here's a simple procedure that calculates the square root of a variable (using the VBA Sqr function), stores the result in another variable, and then displays the result:

```
Sub ShowRoot()
    Dim MyValue As Double
    Dim SquareRoot As Double
    MyValue = 25
    SquareRoot = Sqr(MyValue)
    MsgBox SquareRoot
End Sub
```

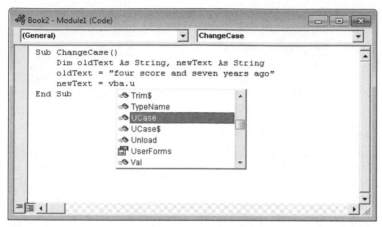

Figure 6-3: Displaying a list of VBA functions in VBE.

The VBA Sqr function is equivalent to the Excel SQRT worksheet function.

You can use many (but not all) of Excel's worksheet functions in your VBA code. The WorksheetFunction object, which is contained in the Application object, holds all the worksheet functions that you can call from your VBA procedures.

To use a worksheet function in a VBA statement, just precede the function name with

```
Application.WorksheetFunction
```

The following example demonstrates how to use an Excel worksheet function in a VBA procedure. Excel's infrequently used ROMAN function converts a decimal number into a roman numeral.

```
Sub ShowRoman()
    Dim DecValue As Long
    Dim RomanValue As String
    DecValue = 1939
    RomanValue = Application.WorksheetFunction.Roman(DecValue)
    MsgBox RomanValue
End Sub
```

When you execute this procedure, the MsgBox function displays the string MCMXXXIX.

By the way, fans of old movies will be pleased to learn that Excel 2013 includes a new function to convert a Roman numeral to its decimal equivalent. The following formula returns 1939:

```
=ARABIC("MCMXXXIX")
```

Keep in mind that you can't use worksheet functions that have an equivalent VBA function. For example, VBA can't access the Excel SQRT worksheet function because VBA has its own version of that function: Sqr. Therefore, the following statement generates an error:

```
MsgBox Application.WorksheetFunction.Sqrt(123)    'error
```

Cross-Ref

As I describe in Chapter 8, you can use VBA to create custom worksheet functions that work just like Excel's built-in worksheet functions.

The MsgBox function

The MsgBox function is one of the most useful VBA functions. Many of the examples in this chapter use this function to display the value of a variable.

This function often is a good substitute for a simple custom dialog box. It's also a useful debugging tool because you can insert MsgBox functions at any time to pause your code and display the result of a calculation or an assignment.

Most functions return a single value, which you assign to a variable. The MsgBox function not only returns a value but also displays a dialog box to which the user can respond. The value returned by the MsgBox function represents the user's response to the dialog box. You can use the MsgBox function even when you have no interest in the user's response but want to take advantage of the message display.

The official syntax of the MsgBox function has five arguments (those in square brackets are optional):

```
MsgBox(prompt[, buttons][, title][, helpfile, context])
```

- prompt: Required. The message displayed in the pop-up display.
- buttons: Optional. A value that specifies which buttons and which icons, if any, appear in the message box. Use built-in constants — for example, vbYesNo.
- title: Optional. The text that appears in the message box's title bar. The default is Microsoft Excel.
- helpfile: Optional. The name of the Help file associated with the message box.
- context: Optional. The context ID of the Help topic, which represents a specific Help topic to display. If you use the context argument, you must also use the helpfile argument.

You can assign the value returned to a variable, or you can use the function by itself without an assignment statement. This example assigns the result to the variable Ans:

```
Dim Ans As Long
Ans = MsgBox("Continue?", vbYesNo + vbQuestion, "Tell me")
If Ans = vbNo Then Exit Sub
```

Note that I used the sum of two built-in constants (vbYesNo + vbQuestion) for the buttons argument. Using vbYesNo displays two buttons in the message box: one labeled Yes and one labeled No. Adding vbQuestion to the argument also displays a question mark icon. When the first statement is executed, Ans contains one of two values, represented by the constant vbYes or vbNo. In this example, if the user clicks the No button, the procedure ends.

See Chapter 10 for more information about the MsgBox function.

Manipulating Objects and Collections

As an Excel programmer, you'll spend a lot of time working with objects and collections. Therefore, you want to know the most efficient ways to write your code to manipulate these objects and collections. VBA offers two important constructs that can simplify working with objects and collections:

➤ With-End With constructs

➤ For Each-Next constructs

With-End With constructs

The With-End With construct enables you to perform multiple operations on a single object. To start understanding how the With-End With construct works, examine the following procedure, which modifies six properties of a selection's formatting (the selection is assumed to be a Range object):

```
Sub ChangeFont1()
    Selection.Font.Name = "Cambria"
    Selection.Font.Bold = True
    Selection.Font.Italic = True
    Selection.Font.Size = 12
    Selection.Font.Underline = xlUnderlineStyleSingle
    Selection.Font.ThemeColor = xlThemeColorAccent1
End Sub
```

You can rewrite this procedure using the With-End With construct. The following procedure performs exactly like the preceding one:

```
Sub ChangeFont2()
    With Selection.Font
        .Name = "Cambria"
        .Bold = True
        .Italic = True
        .Size = 12
        .Underline = xlUnderlineStyleSingle
        .ThemeColor = xlThemeColorAccent1
    End With
End Sub
```

Some people think that the second incarnation of the procedure is more difficult to read. Remember, though, that the objective is increased speed. Although the first version may be more straightforward and easier to understand, a procedure that uses the With-End With construct to change several properties of an object can be faster than the equivalent procedure that explicitly references the object in each statement.

Note

> When you record a VBA macro, Excel uses the With-End With construct every chance it gets. To see a good example of this construct, try recording your actions while you change the page orientation using the Page Layout➜Page Setup➜Orientation command.

For Each-Next constructs

Recall from the preceding chapter that a *collection* is a group of related objects. For example, the Workbooks collection is a collection of all open Workbook objects. You can also work with many other collections.

Suppose that you want to perform some action on all objects in a collection. Or suppose that you want to evaluate all objects in a collection and take action under certain conditions. These occasions are perfect for the For Each-Next construct because you don't have to know how many elements are in a collection to use the For Each-Next construct.

The syntax of the For Each-Next construct is

```
For Each element In collection
    [instructions]
    [Exit For]
    [instructions]
Next [element]
```

The following procedure uses the For Each-Next construct with the Worksheets collection in the active workbook. When you execute the procedure, the MsgBox function displays each worksheet's Name property. (If five worksheets are in the active workbook, the MsgBox function is called five times.)

```
Sub CountSheets()
    Dim Item as Worksheet
    For Each Item In ActiveWorkbook.Worksheets
        MsgBox Item.Name
    Next Item
End Sub
```

Note

In the preceding example, Item is an object variable (more specifically, a Worksheet object). There's nothing special about the name Item; you can use any valid variable name in its place.

The next example uses For Each-Next to cycle through all objects in the Windows collection and count the number of windows that are hidden:

```
Sub HiddenWindows()
    Dim Cnt As Integer
    Dim Win As Window
    Cnt = 0
    For Each Win In Windows
        If Not Win.Visible Then Cnt = Cnt + 1
    Next Win
    MsgBox Cnt & " hidden windows."
End Sub
```

For each window, if the window is hidden, the Cnt variable is incremented. When the loop ends, the message box displays the value of Cnt.

Here's an example that closes all workbooks except the active workbook. This procedure uses the If-Then construct to evaluate each workbook in the Workbooks collection:

```
Sub CloseInactive()
    Dim Book as Workbook
    For Each Book In Workbooks
        If Book.Name <> ActiveWorkbook.Name Then Book.Close
    Next Book
End Sub
```

A common use for the For Each-Next construct is to loop through all cells in a range. The next example of For Each-Next is designed to be executed after the user selects a range of cells. Here, the Selection object acts as a collection that consists of Range objects because each cell in the selection is a Range object. The procedure evaluates each cell and uses the VBA UCase function to convert its contents to uppercase. (Numeric cells are not affected.)

```
Sub MakeUpperCase()
    Dim Cell as Range
    For Each Cell In Selection
        Cell.Value = UCase(Cell.Value)
    Next Cell
End Sub
```

VBA provides a way to exit a For-Next loop before all the elements in the collection are evaluated. Do this with an Exit For statement. The example that follows selects the first negative value in Row 1 of the active sheet:

```
Sub SelectNegative()
    Dim Cell As Range
    For Each Cell In Range("1:1")
        If Cell.Value < 0 Then
            Cell.Select
            Exit For
        End If
    Next Cell
End Sub
```

This example uses an If-Then construct to check the value of each cell. If a cell is negative, it's selected, and then the loop ends when the Exit For statement is executed.

Controlling Code Execution

Some VBA procedures start at the top and progress line by line to the bottom. Macros that you record, for example, always work in this fashion. Often, however, you need to control the flow of your routines by skipping over some statements, executing some statements multiple times, and testing conditions to determine what the routine does next.

The preceding section describes the For Each-Next construct, which is a type of loop. This section discusses the additional ways of controlling the execution of your VBA procedures:

> ➤ GoTo statements

> ➤ If-Then constructs

> ➤ Select Case constructs

➤ For-Next loops

➤ Do While loops

➤ Do Until loops

GoTo statements

The most straightforward way to change the flow of a program is to use a GoTo statement. This statement simply transfers program execution to a new instruction, which must be preceded by a label (a text string followed by a colon, or a number with no colon). VBA procedures can contain any number of labels, but a GoTo statement can't branch outside a procedure.

The following procedure uses the VBA InputBox function to get the user's name. If the name is not *Howard,* the procedure branches to the WrongName label and ends. Otherwise, the procedure executes some additional code. The Exit Sub statement causes the procedure to end.

```
Sub GoToDemo()
    UserName = InputBox("Enter Your Name:")
    If UserName <> "Howard" Then GoTo WrongName
    MsgBox ("Welcome Howard...")
'   -[More code here] -
    Exit Sub
WrongName:
    MsgBox "Sorry. Only Howard can run this macro."
End Sub
```

This simple procedure works, but it's not an example of good programming. In general, you should use the GoTo statement only when you have no other way to perform an action. In fact, the only time you *really* need to use a GoTo statement in VBA is for error handling (refer to Chapter 7).

Finally, it goes without saying that the preceding example is *not* intended to demonstrate an effective security technique!

If-Then constructs

Perhaps the most commonly used instruction grouping in VBA is the If-Then construct. This common instruction is one way to endow your applications with decision-making capability. Good decision-making is the key to writing successful programs.

The basic syntax of the If-Then construct is

```
If condition Then true_instructions [Else false_instructions]
```

The If-Then construct is used to execute one or more statements conditionally. The Else clause is optional. If included, the Else clause lets you execute one or more instructions when the condition that you're testing isn't True.

The following procedure demonstrates an If-Then structure without an Else clause. The example deals with time, and VBA uses a date-and-time serial number system similar to Excel's. The time of day is expressed as a fractional value — for example, noon is represented as .5. The VBA Time function returns a value that represents the time of day, as reported by the system clock. In the following example, a message is displayed if the time is before noon. If the current system time is greater than or equal to .5, the procedure ends, and nothing happens.

```
Sub GreetMe1()
    If Time < 0.5 Then MsgBox "Good Morning"
End Sub
```

Another way to code this routine is to use multiple statements, as follows:

```
Sub GreetMe1a()
    If Time < 0.5 Then
        MsgBox "Good Morning"
    End If
End Sub
```

Note that the If statement has a corresponding End If statement. In this example, only one statement is executed if the condition is True. You can, however, place any number of statements between the If and End If statements.

If you want to display a different greeting when the time of day is after noon, add another If-Then statement, like so:

```
Sub GreetMe2()
    If Time < 0.5 Then MsgBox "Good Morning"
    If Time >= 0.5 Then MsgBox "Good Afternoon"
End Sub
```

Notice that I used >= (greater than or equal to) for the second If-Then statement. This covers the remote chance that the time is precisely 12:00 noon.

Another approach is to use the Else clause of the If-Then construct. For example,

```
Sub GreetMe3()
    If Time < 0.5 Then MsgBox "Good Morning" Else _
      MsgBox "Good Afternoon"
End Sub
```

Notice that I used the line continuation sequence; If-Then-Else is actually a single statement.

If you need to execute multiple statements based on the condition, use this form:

```
Sub GreetMe3a()
    If Time < 0.5 Then
        MsgBox "Good Morning"
        ' Other statements go here
    Else
        MsgBox "Good Afternoon"
        ' Other statements go here
    End If
End Sub
```

If you need to expand a routine to handle three conditions (for example, morning, afternoon, and evening), you can use either three If-Then statements or a form that uses ElseIf. The first approach is simpler:

```
Sub GreetMe4()
    If Time < 0.5 Then MsgBox "Good Morning"
    If Time >= 0.5 And Time < 0.75 Then MsgBox "Good Afternoon"
    If Time >= 0.75 Then MsgBox "Good Evening"
End Sub
```

The value 0.75 represents 6:00 p.m. — three-quarters of the way through the day and a good point at which to call it an evening.

In the preceding examples, every instruction in the procedure gets executed, even if the first condition is satisfied (that is, it's morning). A more efficient procedure would include a structure that ends the routine when a condition is found to be True. For example, it might display the Good Morning message in the morning and then exit without evaluating the other, superfluous conditions. True, the difference in speed is inconsequential when you design a procedure as small as this routine. But for more complex applications, you need another syntax:

```
If condition Then
    [true_instructions]
[ElseIf condition-n Then
    [alternate_instructions]]
[Else
    [default_instructions]]
End If
```

Here's how you can use this syntax to rewrite the GreetMe procedure:

```
Sub GreetMe5()
    If Time < 0.5 Then
        MsgBox "Good Morning"
    ElseIf Time >= 0.5 And Time < 0.75 Then
        MsgBox "Good Afternoon"
    Else
        MsgBox "Good Evening"
    End If
End Sub
```

With this syntax, when a condition is True, the conditional statements are executed, and the If-Then construct ends. In other words, the extraneous conditions aren't evaluated. Although this syntax makes for greater efficiency, some find the code to be more difficult to understand.

The following procedure demonstrates yet another way to code this example. It uses nested If-Then-Else constructs (without using ElseIf). This procedure is efficient and also easy to understand. Note that each If statement has a corresponding End If statement.

```
Sub GreetMe6()
    If Time < 0.5 Then
        MsgBox "Good Morning"
    Else
        If Time >= 0.5 And Time < 0.75 Then
            MsgBox "Good Afternoon"
        Else
            If Time >= 0.75 Then
                MsgBox "Good Evening"
            End If
        End If
    End If
End Sub
```

The following is another example that uses the simple form of the If-Then construct. This procedure prompts the user for a value for Quantity and then displays the appropriate discount based on that value. Note that Quantity is declared as a Variant data type. This is because Quantity contains an empty string (not a numeric value) if InputBox is cancelled. To keep the procedure simple, it doesn't perform any other error checking. For example, it doesn't ensure that the quantity entered is a non-negative numeric value.

```
Sub Discount1()
    Dim Quantity As Variant
    Dim Discount As Double
    Quantity = InputBox("Enter Quantity: ")
    If Quantity = "" Then Exit Sub
    If Quantity >= 0 Then Discount = 0.1
    If Quantity >= 25 Then Discount = 0.15
    If Quantity >= 50 Then Discount = 0.2
    If Quantity >= 75 Then Discount = 0.25
    MsgBox "Discount: " & Discount
End Sub
```

Notice that each If-Then statement in this procedure is always executed, and the value for Discount can change. The final value, however, is the desired value.

The following procedure is the previous one rewritten to use the alternate syntax. In this case, the procedure ends after executing the True instruction block.

```
Sub Discount2()
    Dim Quantity As Variant
    Dim Discount As Double
    Quantity = InputBox("Enter Quantity: ")
    If Quantity = "" Then Exit Sub
    If Quantity >= 0 And Quantity < 25 Then
        Discount = 0.1
    ElseIf Quantity < 50 Then
        Discount = 0.15
    ElseIf Quantity < 75 Then
        Discount = 0.2
    Else
        Discount = 0.25
    End If
    MsgBox "Discount: " & Discount
End Sub
```

I find nested If-Then structures cumbersome. As a result, I usually use the If-Then structure only for simple binary decisions. When you need to choose among three or more alternatives, the Select Case structure (discussed next) is often a better construct to use.

VBA's IIf function

VBA offers an alternative to the If-Then construct: the IIf function. This function takes three arguments and works much like Excel's IF worksheet function. The syntax is

```
IIf(expr, truepart, falsepart)
```

- expr: (Required) Expression you want to evaluate.
- truepart: (Required) Value or expression returned if expr is True.
- falsepart: (Required) Value or expression returned if expr is False.

The following instruction demonstrates the use of the IIf function. The message box displays Zero if cell A1 contains a 0 or is empty and displays Nonzero if cell A1 contains anything else.

```
MsgBox IIf(Range("A1") = 0, "Zero", "Nonzero")
```

It's important to understand that the third argument (falsepart) is always evaluated, even if the first argument (expr) is True. Therefore, the following statement generates a Division By Zero error if the value of n is 0 (zero):

```
MsgBox IIf(n = 0, 0, 1 / n)
```

Select Case constructs

The Select Case construct is useful for choosing among three or more options. this construct also works with two options and is a good alternative to If-Then-Else. The syntax for Select Case is as follows:

```
Select Case testexpression
    [Case expressionlist-n
        [instructions-n]]
    [Case Else
        [default_instructions]]
End Select
```

The following example of a Select Case construct shows another way to code the GreetMe examples that I presented in the preceding section:

```
Sub GreetMe()
    Dim Msg As String
    Select Case Time
        Case Is < 0.5
            Msg = "Good Morning"
```

```
            Case 0.5 To 0.75
                Msg = "Good Afternoon"
            Case Else
                Msg = "Good Evening"
        End Select
        MsgBox Msg
    End Sub
```

And here's a rewritten version of the Discount example using a Select Case construct. This procedure assumes that Quantity is always an integer value. For simplicity, the procedure performs no error checking.

```
Sub Discount3()
    Dim Quantity As Variant
    Dim Discount As Double
    Quantity = InputBox("Enter Quantity: ")
    Select Case Quantity
        Case ""
            Exit Sub
        Case 0 To 24
            Discount = 0.1
        Case 25 To 49
            Discount = 0.15
        Case 50 To 74
            Discount = 0.2
        Case Is >= 75
            Discount = 0.25
    End Select
    MsgBox "Discount: " & Discount
End Sub
```

The Case statement also can use a comma to separate multiple values for a single case. The following procedure uses the VBA WeekDay function to determine whether the current day is a weekend (that is, the Weekday function returns 1 or 7). The procedure then displays an appropriate message.

```
Sub GreetUser1()
    Select Case Weekday(Now)
        Case 1, 7
            MsgBox "This is the weekend"
        Case Else
            MsgBox "This is not the weekend"
    End Select
End Sub
```

The following example shows another way to code the previous procedure:

```
Sub GreetUser2()
    Select Case Weekday(Now)
        Case 2, 3, 4, 5, 6
            MsgBox "This is not the weekend"
        Case Else
            MsgBox "This is the weekend"
    End Select
End Sub
```

Here's another way to code the procedure, using the To keyword to specify a range of values.

```
Sub GreetUser3()
    Select Case Weekday(Now)
        Case 2 To 6
            MsgBox "This is not the weekend"
        Case Else
            MsgBox "This is the weekend"
    End Select
End Sub
```

And to demonstrate the flexibility of VBA, a final example in which each case is evaluated until one of the expressions evaluates to True:

```
Sub GreetUser4()
    Select Case True
        Case Weekday(Now) = 1
            MsgBox "This is the weekend"
        Case Weekday(Now) = 7
            MsgBox "This is the weekend"
        Case Else
            MsgBox "This is not the weekend"
    End Select
End Sub
```

Any number of instructions can be written below each Case statement, and they're all executed if that case evaluates to True. If you use only one instruction per case, as in the preceding example, you might want to put the instruction on the same line as the Case keyword (but don't forget the VBA statement-separator character, the colon). This technique makes the code more compact. For example:

```
Sub Discount3()
    Dim Quantity As Variant
    Dim Discount As Double
    Quantity = InputBox("Enter Quantity: ")
    Select Case Quantity
        Case "": Exit Sub
        Case  0 To 24: Discount = 0.1
        Case 25 To 49: Discount = 0.15
        Case 50 To 74: Discount = 0.2
        Case Is >= 75: Discount = 0.25
    End Select
    MsgBox "Discount: " & Discount
End Sub
```

Tip

VBA exits a Select Case construct as soon as a True case is found. Therefore, for maximum efficiency, you should check the most likely case first.

Select Case structures can also be nested. The following procedure, for example, uses the VBA TypeName function to determine what is selected (a range, nothing, or anything else). If a range is selected, the procedure executes a nested Select Case and tests for the number of cells in the range. If one cell is selected, it displays One cell is selected. Otherwise, it displays a message with the number of selected rows.

```
Sub SelectionType()
    Select Case TypeName(Selection)
        Case "Range"
            Select Case Selection.Count
                Case 1
                    MsgBox "One cell is selected"
                Case Else
                    MsgBox Selection.Rows.Count & " rows"
            End Select
        Case "Nothing"
            MsgBox "Nothing is selected"
        Case Else
            MsgBox "Something other than a range"
    End Select
End Sub
```

This procedure also demonstrates the use of Case Else, a catch-all case. You can nest Select Case constructs as deeply as you need, but make sure that each Select Case statement has a corresponding End Select statement.

This procedure demonstrates the value of using indentation in your code to clarify the structure. For example, take a look at the same procedure without the indentations:

```
Sub SelectionType()
Select Case TypeName(Selection)
Case "Range"
Select Case Selection.Count
Case 1
MsgBox "One cell is selected"
Case Else
MsgBox Selection.Rows.Count & " rows"
End Select
Case "Nothing"
MsgBox "Nothing is selected"
Case Else
MsgBox "Something other than a range"
End Select
End Sub
```

Fairly incomprehensible, eh?

Looping blocks of instructions

Looping is the process of repeating a block of instructions. You might know the number of times to loop, or the number may be determined by the values of variables in your program.

The following code, which enters consecutive numbers into a range, demonstrates what I call a *bad loop*. The procedure uses two variables to store a starting value (StartVal) and the total number of cells to fill (NumToFill). This loop uses the GoTo statement to control the flow. If the Cnt variable, which keeps track of how many cells are filled, is less than the value of NumToFill, the program control loops back to DoAnother.

```
Sub BadLoop()
    Dim StartVal As Integer
    Dim NumToFill As Integer
    Dim Cnt As Integer
    StartVal = 1
    NumToFill = 100
    ActiveCell.Value = StartVal
    Cnt = 1
DoAnother:
    ActiveCell.Offset(Cnt, 0).Value = StartVal + Cnt
    Cnt = Cnt + 1
    If Cnt < NumToFill Then GoTo DoAnother Else Exit Sub
End Sub
```

This procedure works as intended, so why is it an example of bad looping? Programmers generally frown on using a GoTo statement when not absolutely necessary. Using GoTo statements to loop is contrary to the concept of structured coding. (See the "What is structured programming?" sidebar.) A GoTo statement makes the code much more difficult to read because representing a loop using line indentations is almost impossible. In addition, this type of unstructured loop makes the procedure more susceptible to error. Furthermore, using lots of labels results in *spaghetti code* — code that appears to have little or no structure and has a tangled flow.

Because VBA has several structured looping commands, you almost never have to rely on GoTo statements for your decision-making.

For-Next loops

The simplest type of a good loop is a For-Next loop. Its syntax is

```
For counter = start To end [Step stepval]
    [instructions]
    [Exit For]
    [instructions]
Next [counter]
```

What is structured programming?

Hang around with programmers, and sooner or later you'll hear the term *structured programming*. You'll also discover that structured programs are considered superior to unstructured programs.

So what is structured programming? And can you do it with VBA?

The basic premise of structured programming is that a routine or code segment should have only one entry point and one exit point. In other words, a body of code should be a stand-alone unit, and program control should not jump into or exit from the middle of this unit. As a result, structured programming rules out the GoTo statement. When you write structured code, your program progresses in an orderly manner and is easy to follow — as opposed to spaghetti code, in which a program jumps around.

A structured program is easier to read and understand than an unstructured one. More important, it's also easier to modify.

VBA is a structured language. It offers standard structured constructs, such as If-Then-Else and Select Case and the For-Next, Do Until, and Do While loops. Furthermore, VBA fully supports modular code construction.

If you're new to programming, form good structured programming habits early.

Following is an example of a For-Next loop that doesn't use the optional Step value or the optional Exit For statement. This routine executes the Sum = Sum + Sqr(Count) statement 100 times and displays the result — that is, the sum of the square roots of the first 100 integers.

```
Sub SumSquareRoots()
    Dim Sum As Double
    Dim Count As Integer
    Sum = 0
    For Count = 1 To 100
        Sum = Sum + Sqr(Count)
    Next Count
    MsgBox Sum
End Sub
```

In this example, Count (the loop counter variable) starts out as 1 and increases by 1 each time the loop repeats. The Sum variable simply accumulates the square roots of each value of Count.

Caution

When you use For-Next loops, it's important to understand that the loop counter is a normal variable — nothing special. As a result, it's possible to change the value of the loop counter in the block of code executed between the For and Next statements. Changing the loop counter inside a loop, however, is a bad practice and can cause unpredictable results. You should take precautions to ensure that your code doesn't change the loop counter.

You can also use a Step value to skip some values in the loop. Here's the same procedure rewritten to sum the square roots of the odd numbers between 1 and 100:

```
Sub SumOddSquareRoots()
    Dim Sum As Double
    Dim Count As Integer
    Sum = 0
    For Count = 1 To 100 Step 2
        Sum = Sum + Sqr(Count)
    Next Count
    MsgBox Sum
End Sub
```

In this procedure, Count starts out as 1 and then takes on values of 3, 5, 7, and so on. The final value of Count used in the loop is 99. When the loop ends, the value of Count is 101.

A Step value in a For-Next loop can also be negative. The procedure that follows deletes Rows 2, 4, 6, 8, and 10 of the active worksheet:

```
Sub DeleteRows()
    Dim RowNum As Long
    For RowNum = 10 To 2 Step -2
        Rows(RowNum).Delete
    Next RowNum
End Sub
```

You may wonder why I used a negative Step value in the DeleteRows procedure. If you use a positive Step value, as shown in the following procedure, incorrect rows are deleted. That's because the rows below a deleted row get a new row number. For example, when Row 2 is deleted, Row 3 becomes the new Row 2. Using a negative Step value ensures that the correct rows are deleted.

```
Sub DeleteRows2()
    Dim RowNum As Long
    For RowNum = 2 To 10 Step 2
        Rows(RowNum).Delete
    Next RowNum
End Sub
```

The following procedure performs the same task as the BadLoop example at the beginning of the "Looping blocks of instructions" section. I eliminate the GoTo statement, however, converting a bad loop into a good loop that uses the For-Next structure.

```
Sub GoodLoop()
    Dim StartVal As Integer
    Dim NumToFill As Integer
    Dim Cnt As Integer
    StartVal = 1
    NumToFill = 100
    For Cnt = 0 To NumToFill - 1
        ActiveCell.Offset(Cnt, 0).Value = StartVal + Cnt
    Next Cnt
End Sub
```

For-Next loops can also include one or more Exit For statements in the loop. When this statement is encountered, the loop terminates immediately and control passes to the statement following the Next statement of the current For-Next loop. The following example demonstrates the use of the Exit For statement. This procedure determines which cell has the largest value in Column A of the active worksheet:

```
Sub ExitForDemo()
    Dim MaxVal As Double
    Dim Row As Long
    MaxVal = Application.WorksheetFunction.Max(Range("A:A"))
    For Row = 1 To 1048576
        If Cells(Row, 1).Value = MaxVal Then
            Exit For
        End If
    Next Row
    MsgBox "Max value is in Row " & Row
    Cells(Row, 1).Activate
End Sub
```

The maximum value in the column is calculated by using the Excel MAX function, and the value is assigned to the MaxVal variable. The For-Next loop checks each cell in the column. If the cell being checked is equal to MaxVal, the Exit For statement terminates the loop and the statements following the Next statement are executed. These statements display the row of the maximum value and activate the cell.

Note

The ExitForDemo procedure is presented to demonstrate how to exit from a For-Next loop. However, it's not the most efficient way to activate the largest value in a range. In fact, a single statement does the job:

```
Range("A:A").Find(Application.WorksheetFunction.Max _
    (Range("A:A"))).Activate
```

The previous examples use relatively simple loops. But you can have any number of statements in the loop, and you can even nest For-Next loops inside other For-Next loops. Here's an example that uses nested For-Next loops to initialize a 10 x 10 x 10 array with the value –1. When the procedure is finished, each of the 1,000 elements in MyArray contains –1.

```
Sub NestedLoops()
    Dim MyArray(1 to 10, 1 to 10, 1 to 10)
    Dim i As Integer, j As Integer, k As Integer
    For i = 1 To 10
        For j = 1 To 10
            For k = 1 To 10
                MyArray(i, j, k) = -1
            Next k
        Next j
    Next i
'   [More code goes here]
End Sub
```

Do While loops

This section describes another type of looping structure available in VBA. Unlike a For-Next loop, a Do While loop executes as long as a specified condition is met.

A Do While loop can have either of two syntaxes:

```
Do [While condition]
    [instructions]
    [Exit Do]
    [instructions]
Loop
```

or

```
Do
    [instructions]
    [Exit Do]
    [instructions]
Loop [While condition]
```

As you can see, VBA lets you put the While condition at the beginning or the end of the loop. The difference between these two syntaxes involves the point at which the condition is evaluated. In the first syntax, the contents of the loop may never be executed. In the second syntax, the statements inside the loop are always executed at least one time.

The following examples insert a series of dates into the active worksheet. The dates correspond to the days in the current month, and the dates are entered in a column beginning at the active cell.

Note

These examples use some VBA date-related functions:

- **Date returns the current date.**
- **Month returns the month number for a date supplied as its argument.**
- **DateSerial returns a date for the year, month, and day supplied as arguments.**

The first example demonstrates a Do While loop that tests the condition at the beginning of the loop: The EnterDates1 procedure writes the dates of the current month to a worksheet column, beginning with the active cell.

```
Sub EnterDates1()
'   Do While, with test at the beginning
    Dim TheDate As Date
    TheDate = DateSerial(Year(Date), Month(Date), 1)
    Do While Month(TheDate) = Month(Date)
        ActiveCell = TheDate
        TheDate = TheDate + 1
        ActiveCell.Offset(1, 0).Activate
    Loop
End Sub
```

This procedure uses a variable, TheDate, which contains the dates that are written to the worksheet. This variable is initialized with the first day of the current month. Inside the loop, the value of TheDate is entered into the active cell, TheDate is incremented, and the next cell is activated. The loop continues while the month of TheDate is the same as the month of the current date.

The following procedure has the same result as the EnterDates1 procedure, but it uses the second Do While loop syntax, which checks the condition at the end of the loop.

```
Sub EnterDates2()
'   Do While, with test at the end
    Dim TheDate As Date
    TheDate = DateSerial(Year(Date), Month(Date), 1)
    Do
        ActiveCell = TheDate
        TheDate = TheDate + 1
        ActiveCell.Offset(1, 0).Activate
    Loop While Month(TheDate) = Month(Date)
End Sub
```

The following is another Do While loop example. This procedure opens a text file, reads each line, converts the text to uppercase, and then stores it in the active sheet, beginning with cell A1 and continuing down the column. The procedure uses the VBA EOF function, which returns True when the end of the file has been reached. The final statement closes the text file.

```
Sub DoWhileDemo1()
    Dim LineCt As Long
    Dim LineOfText As String
    Open "c:\data\textfile.txt" For Input As #1
    LineCt = 0
    Do While Not EOF(1)
      Line Input #1, LineOfText
      Range("A1").Offset(LineCt, 0) = UCase(LineOfText)
      LineCt = LineCt + 1
    Loop
    Close #1
End Sub
```

Cross-Ref For additional information about reading and writing text files using VBA, see Chapter 25.

Do While loops can also contain one or more Exit Do statements. When an Exit Do statement is encountered, the loop ends immediately and control passes to the statement following the Loop statement.

Do Until loops

The Do Until loop structure is similar to the Do While structure. The difference is evident only when the condition is tested. In a Do While loop, the loop executes *while* the condition is True; in a Do Until loop, the loop executes *until* the condition is True.

Do Until also has two syntaxes:

```
Do [Until condition]
    [instructions]
    [Exit Do]
    [instructions]
Loop
```

or

```
Do
    [instructions]
    [Exit Do]
    [instructions]
Loop [Until condition]
```

The two examples that follow perform the same action as the Do While date entry examples in the previous section. The difference in these two procedures is where the condition is evaluated (at the beginning or the end of the loop).

```
Sub EnterDates3()
'   Do Until, with test at beginning
    Dim TheDate As Date
    TheDate = DateSerial(Year(Date), Month(Date), 1)
    Do Until Month(TheDate) <> Month(Date)
        ActiveCell = TheDate
        TheDate = TheDate + 1
        ActiveCell.Offset(1, 0).Activate
    Loop
End Sub
```

```
Sub EnterDates4()
'    Do Until, with test at end
    Dim TheDate As Date
    TheDate = DateSerial(Year(Date), Month(Date), 1)
    Do
        ActiveCell = TheDate
        TheDate = TheDate + 1
        ActiveCell.Offset(1, 0).Activate
    Loop Until Month(TheDate) <> Month(Date)
End Sub
```

The following example was originally presented for the Do While loop but has been rewritten to use a Do Until loop. The only difference is the line with the Do statement. This example makes the code a bit clearer because it avoids the negative required in the Do While example.

```
Sub DoUntilDemo1()
    Dim LineCt As Long
    Dim LineOfText As String
    Open "c:\data\textfile.txt" For Input As #1
    LineCt = 0
    Do Until EOF(1)
        Line Input #1, LineOfText
        Range("A1").Offset(LineCt, 0) = UCase(LineOfText)
        LineCt = LineCt + 1
    Loop
    Close #1
End Sub
```

Note

VBA supports yet another type of loop, While Wend. This looping structure is included primarily for compatibility purposes. I mention it here in case you ever encounter such a loop. Here's how the date entry procedure looks when it's coded to use a While Wend loop:

```
Sub EnterDates5()
    Dim TheDate As Date
    TheDate = DateSerial(Year(Date), Month(Date), 1)
    While Month(TheDate) = Month(Date)
        ActiveCell = TheDate
        TheDate = TheDate + 1
        ActiveCell.Offset(1, 0).Activate
    Wend
End Sub
```

Working with VBA Sub Procedures

In This Chapter

- Declaring and creating VBA Sub procedures
- Executing procedures
- Passing arguments to a procedure
- Using error-handling techniques
- An example of developing a useful procedure

About Procedures

A *procedure* is a series of VBA statements that resides in a VBA module, which you access in Visual Basic Editor (VBE). A module can hold any number of procedures. A procedure holds a group of VBA statements that accomplishes a desired task. Most VBA code is contained in procedures.

You have a number of ways to *call,* or execute, procedures. A procedure is executed from beginning to end, but it can also be ended prematurely.

Tip

A procedure can be any length, but many people prefer to avoid creating extremely long procedures that perform many different operations. You may find it easier to write several smaller procedures, each with a single purpose. Then, design a main procedure that calls those other procedures. This approach can make your code easier to maintain.

Some procedures are written to receive arguments. An *argument* is information that is used by the procedure and that is passed to the procedure when it is executed. Procedure arguments work much like the arguments that you use in Excel worksheet functions. Instructions within the procedure perform operations using these arguments, and the results of the procedure are usually based on those arguments.

Cross-Ref

Although this chapter focuses on Sub procedures, VBA also supports Function procedures, which I discuss in Chapter 8. Chapter 9 has many additional examples of procedures, both Sub and Function, that you can incorporate into your work.

Declaring a Sub procedure

A procedure declared with the Sub keyword must adhere to the following syntax:

```
[Private | Public][Static] Sub name ([arglist])
    [instructions]
    [Exit Sub]
    [instructions]
End Sub
```

Here's a description of the elements that make up a Sub procedure:

➤ Private: Optional. Indicates that the procedure is accessible only to other procedures in the same module.

➤ Public: Optional. Indicates that the procedure is accessible to all other procedures in all other modules in the workbook. If used in a module that contains an Option Private Module statement, the procedure is not available outside the project.

➤ Static: Optional. Indicates that the procedure's variables are preserved when the procedure ends.

➤ Sub: Required. The keyword that indicates the beginning of a procedure.

➤ *name*: Required. Any valid procedure name.

➤ *arglist*: Optional. Represents a list of variables, enclosed in parentheses, that receive arguments passed to the procedure. Use a comma to separate arguments. If the procedure uses no arguments, a set of empty parentheses is required.

➤ *instructions:* Optional. Represents valid VBA instructions.

➤ Exit Sub: Optional. Forces an immediate exit from the procedure prior to its formal completion.

➤ End Sub: Required. Indicates the end of the procedure.

Note

With a few exceptions, all VBA instructions in a module must be contained in procedures. Exceptions include module-level variable declarations, user-defined data type definitions, and a few other instructions that specify module-level options (for example, Option Explicit).

Naming procedures

Every procedure must have a name. The rules governing procedure names are generally the same as those for variable names. Ideally, a procedure's name should describe what its contained processes do. A good rule is to use a name that includes a verb and a noun (for example, ProcessDate, PrintReport, Sort_Array, or CheckFilename). Unless you're writing a quick and dirty procedure that you'll use once and delete, avoid meaningless names such as DoIt, Update, and Fix.

Some programmers use sentence-like names that describe the procedure (for example, WriteReportToTextFile and Get_Print_Options_ and_Print_Report).

Scoping a procedure

In the preceding chapter, I note that a variable's *scope* determines the modules and procedures in which you can use the variable. Similarly, a procedure's scope determines which other procedures can call it.

Public procedures

By default, procedures are *public* — that is, they can be called by other procedures in any module in the workbook. It's not necessary to use the Public keyword, but programmers often include it for clarity. The following two procedures are both public:

```
Sub First()
'    ... [code goes here] ...
End Sub

Public Sub Second()
'    ... [code goes here] ...
End Sub
```

Private procedures

Private procedures can be called by other procedures in the same module but not by procedures in other modules.

Note

When a user displays the Macro dialog box (by pressing Alt+F8), Excel shows only public procedures. Therefore, if you have procedures that are designed to be called only by other procedures in the same module, you should make sure that those procedures are declared as Private. Doing so prevents the user from running these procedures from the Macro dialog box.

The following example declares a private procedure named MySub:

```
Private Sub MySub()
'    ... [code goes here] ...
End Sub
```

Tip

You can force all procedures in a module to be private — even those declared with the Public keyword — by including the following statement before your first Sub statement:

```
Option Private Module
```

If you write this statement in a module, you can omit the Private keyword from your Sub declarations.

Excel's macro recorder creates new Sub procedures called Macro1, Macro2, and so on. Unless you modify the recorded code, these procedures are all public procedures, and they will never use any arguments.

Executing Sub Procedures

In this section, I describe the various ways to *execute,* or call, a VBA Sub procedure:

➤ With the Run➜Run Sub/UserForm command (in the VBE menu). Or you can press the F5 shortcut key, or click the Run Sub/UserForm button on the Standard toolbar. These methods all assume that the cursor is within a procedure.

➤ From Excel's Macro dialog box.

➤ By using the Ctrl key shortcut assigned to the procedure (assuming that you assigned one).

➤ By clicking, on a worksheet, a button or shape assigned to the procedure.

➤ From another procedure that you write. Sub and Function procedures can execute other procedures.

➤ From an icon added to the Quick Access toolbar.

➤ From a button added to the Ribbon.

➤ From a customized shortcut menu.

➤ When an event occurs, such as opening the workbook, saving the workbook, closing the workbook, changing a cell's value, or activating a sheet.

➤ From the Immediate window in VBE. Just type the name of the procedure, including any arguments that may apply, and press Enter.

I discuss these methods of executing procedures in the following sections.

Note

In many cases, a procedure won't work properly unless it's executed in the appropriate context. For example, if a procedure is designed to work with the active worksheet, it will fail if a chart sheet is active. A good procedure incorporates code that checks for the appropriate context and exits gracefully if it can't proceed.

Executing a procedure with the Run Sub/UserForm command

The VBE Run➔Run Sub/UserForm menu command is used primarily to test a procedure while you're developing it. You would never require a user to activate VBE to execute a procedure. Choose Run➔Run Sub/UserForm in VBE to execute the current procedure (in other words, the procedure that contains the cursor). Or press F5, or use the Run Sub/UserForm button on the Standard toolbar.

If the cursor isn't located within a procedure, VBE displays its Macro dialog box so that you can select a procedure to execute.

Executing a procedure from the Macro dialog box

Choose Excel's View➔Macros➔Macros command to display the Macro dialog box, as shown in Figure 7-1. You can also press Alt+F8, or choose Developer➔Code➔Macros to access this dialog box. Use the Macros In drop-down box to limit the scope of the macros displayed (for example, show only the macros in the active workbook).

Figure 7-1: The Macro dialog box.

The Macro dialog box does *not* display

➤ Function procedures

➤ Sub procedures declared with the Private keyword

➤ Sub procedures that require one or more arguments

➤ Sub procedures contained in add-ins

➤ Event procedures stored in code modules for objects such as ThisWorkbook, Sheet1, or UserForm1

Tip

Even though procedures stored in an add-in are not listed in the Macro dialog box, you still can execute such a procedure if you know the name. Simply type the procedure name in the Macro Name field in the Macro dialog box and then click Run.

Executing a procedure with a Ctrl+shortcut key combination

You can assign a Ctrl+shortcut key combination to any Sub procedure that doesn't use any arguments. If you assign the Ctrl+U key combo to a procedure named UpdateCustomerList, for example, pressing Ctrl+U executes that procedure.

When you begin recording a macro, the Record Macro dialog box gives you the opportunity to assign a shortcut key. However, you can assign a shortcut key at any time. To assign a Ctrl shortcut key to a procedure (or to change a procedure's shortcut key), follow these steps:

1. Activate Excel and display the Macro dialog box (Alt+F8 is one way to do that).

2. Select the appropriate procedure from the list box in the Macro dialog box.

3. Click the Options button to display the Macro Options dialog box (see Figure 7-2).

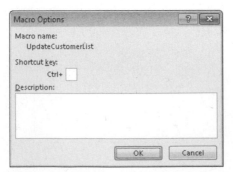

Figure 7-2: The Macro Options dialog box lets you assign a Ctrl key shortcut and an optional description to a procedure.

4. Enter a character into the Ctrl+ text box.

   Note: The character that you enter into the Ctrl+ text box is case-sensitive. If you enter a lowercase *s,* the shortcut key combo is Ctrl+S. If you enter an uppercase *S,* the shortcut key combo is Ctrl+Shift+S.

5. Enter a description (optional). If you enter a description for a macro, it's displayed at the bottom of the Macro dialog box when the procedure is selected in the list box.

6. Click OK to close the Macro Options dialog box and then click Cancel to close the Macro dialog box.

Caution

If you assign one of Excel's predefined shortcut key combinations to a procedure, your key assignment takes precedence over the predefined key assignment. For example, Ctrl+S is the Excel predefined shortcut key for saving the active workbook. But if you assign Ctrl+S to a procedure, pressing Ctrl+S no longer saves the active workbook when that macro is available.

Tip

The following keyboard keys are not used by Excel 2013 for Ctrl+key combinations: J, M, and Q. Excel doesn't use too many Ctrl+Shift+key combinations, and they are used for obscure commands.

Executing a procedure from the Ribbon

Excel's Ribbon user interface was introduced in Excel 2007. In that version, customizing the Ribbon required writing XML code to add a new button (or other control) to the Ribbon. Note that you modify the Ribbon in this way outside of Excel, and you can't do it using VBA.

Beginning with Excel 2010, users can modify the Ribbon directly from Excel. Just right-click any part of the Ribbon and choose Customize the Ribbon from the shortcut menu. It's a simple matter to add a new control to the Ribbon and assign a VBA macro to the control. However, this must be done manually. In other words, it's not possible to use VBA to add a control to the Ribbon.

Cross-Ref

Refer to Chapter 20 for more information about customizing the Ribbon.

Executing a procedure from a customized shortcut menu

You can also execute a macro by clicking a menu item in a customized shortcut menu. A shortcut menu appears when you right-click an object or range in Excel. It's fairly easy to write VBA code that adds a new item to any of Excel's shortcut menus.

Refer to Chapter 21 for more information about customizing shortcut menus.

Cross-Ref

Executing a procedure from another procedure

One of the most common ways to execute a procedure is to call it from another VBA procedure. You have three ways to do this:

> ➤ Enter the procedure's name, followed by its arguments (if any) separated by commas. Do not enclose the argument list in parentheses.

> ➤ Use the Call keyword followed by the procedure's name and then its arguments (if any) enclosed in parentheses and separated by commas.

> ➤ Use the Run method of the Application object. The Run method is useful when you need to run a procedure whose name is assigned to a variable. You can then pass the variable as an argument to the Run method.

Here's a simple Sub procedure that takes two arguments. The procedure displays the product of the two arguments.

```
Sub AddTwo (arg1, arg2)
    MsgBox arg1 * arg2
End Sub
```

The following three statements demonstrate three different ways to execute the AddTwo procedure and pass two arguments. All three have the same result.

```
AddTwo 12, 6
Call AddTwo (12, 6)
Run "AddTwo", 12, 6
```

Even though it's optional, some programmers always use the Call keyword just to make it perfectly clear that another procedure is being called.

Perhaps the best reason to use the Run method is when the procedure name is assigned to a variable. In fact, it's the only way to execute a procedure in such a way. The following oversimplified example demonstrates this. The Main procedure uses the VBA WeekDay function to determine the day of the week (an integer between 1 and 7, beginning with Sunday). The SubToCall variable is assigned a string that represents a procedure name. The Run method then calls the appropriate procedure (either WeekEnd or Daily).

```
Sub Main()
    Dim SubToCall As String
    Select Case WeekDay(Now)
        Case 1, 7: SubToCall = "WeekEnd"
        Case Else: SubToCall = "Daily"
    End Select
    Application.Run SubToCall
End Sub

Sub WeekEnd()
    MsgBox "Today is a weekend"
'   Code to execute on the weekend
'   goes here
End Sub

Sub Daily()
    MsgBox "Today is not a weekend"
'   Code to execute on the weekdays
'   goes here
End Sub
```

Calling a procedure in a different module

If VBA can't locate a called procedure in the current module, it looks for public procedures in other modules in the same workbook.

If you need to call a private procedure from another procedure, both procedures must reside in the same module.

You can't have two procedures with the same name in the same module, but you can have identically named procedures in different modules within the project. You can force VBA to execute an *ambiguously named* procedure — that is, another procedure in a different module that has the same name. To do so, precede the procedure name with the module name and a dot.

For example, assume that you define procedures named MySub in Module1 and Module2. If you want a procedure in Module2 to call the MySub in Module1, you can use either of the following statements:

```
Module1.MySub
Call Module1.MySub
```

If you do not differentiate between procedures that have the same name, you get the aptly named Ambiguous name detected error message.

Calling a procedure in a different workbook

In some cases, you may need your procedure to execute another procedure defined in a different workbook. To do so, you have two options: Either establish a reference to the other workbook or use the Run method and specify the workbook name explicitly.

To add a reference to another workbook, choose VBE's Tools➔References command. Excel displays the References dialog box (see Figure 7-3), which lists all available references, including all open workbooks. Select the box that corresponds to the workbook that you want to add as a reference and then click OK. After you establish a reference, you can call procedures in the workbook as if they were in the same workbook as the calling procedure.

A referenced workbook doesn't have to be open when you create the reference; the referenced workbook is treated like a separate object library. Use the Browse button in the References dialog box to establish a reference to a workbook that isn't open.

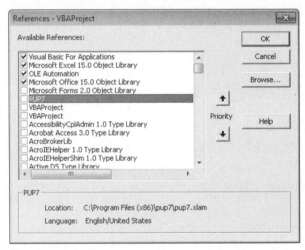

Figure 7-3: The References dialog box lets you establish a reference to another workbook.

When you open a workbook that contains a reference to another workbook, the referenced workbook is opened automatically.

Note

the workbook names that appear in the list of references are listed by their VBE project names. By default, every project is initially named VBAProject. Therefore, the list may contain several identically named items (but the full path of the selected item appears at the bottom of the dialog box). To distinguish a project, change its name in the Project Properties dialog box. Click the project name in the Project window and then choose Tools➔xxxx Properties (where xxxx is the current project name). In the Project Properties dialog box, click the General tab and change the name displayed in the Project Name field.

The list of references displayed in the References dialog box also includes object libraries and ActiveX controls that are registered on your system. Your Excel workbooks always include references to the following object libraries:

➤ Visual Basic for Applications

➤ Microsoft Excel 15.0 Object Library

➤ OLE Automation

➤ Microsoft Office 15.0 Object Library

➤ Microsoft Forms 2.0 Object Library (this reference is included only if your project includes a UserForm)

Note   **Any additional references to other workbooks that you add are also listed in your project outline in the Project Explorer window in VBE. These references are listed under a node called References.**

If you've established a reference to a workbook that contains the YourSub procedure, for example, you can use either of the following statements to call YourSub:

```
YourSub
Call YourSub
```

To precisely identify a procedure in a different workbook, specify the project name, module name, and procedure name by using the following syntax:

```
YourProject.YourModule.YourSub
```

Alternatively, you can use the Call keyword:

```
Call YourProject.YourModule.YourSub
```

Another way to call a procedure in a different workbook is to use the Run method of the Application object. This technique doesn't require that you establish a reference, but the workbook that contains the procedure must be open. The following statement executes the Consolidate procedure located in a workbook named budget macros.xlsm:

```
Application.Run "'budget macros.xlsm'!Consolidate"
```

Note that the workbook name is enclosed in single quotes. That syntax is necessary only if the file-name includes one or more space characters. Here's an example of calling a procedure in a workbook that doesn't have any spaces:

```
Application.Run "budgetmacros.xlsm!Consolidate"
```

Executing a procedure by clicking an object

Excel provides a variety of objects that you can place on a worksheet or chart sheet; you can attach a macro to any of these objects. These objects fall into several classes:

➤ ActiveX controls

➤ Forms controls

➤ Inserted objects (Shapes, SmartArt, WordArt, charts, and pictures)

 Why call other procedures?

If you're new to programming, you may wonder why anyone would ever want to call a procedure from another procedure. You may ask, "Why not just put the code from the called procedure into the calling procedure and keep things simple?"

One reason is to clarify your code. The simpler your code, the easier it is to maintain and modify. Smaller routines are easier to decipher and then debug. Examine the accompanying procedure, which does nothing but call other procedures. This procedure is easy to follow.

```
Sub Main()
    Call GetUserOptions
    Call ProcessData
    Call CleanUp
    Call CloseAllFiles
End Sub
```

Calling other procedures also eliminates redundancy. Suppose that you need to perform an operation at ten different places in your routine. Rather than enter the code ten times, you can write a procedure to perform the operation and then simply call the procedure ten times. Also, if you need to make a change, you make it only one time rather that ten times.

Also, you may have a series of general-purpose procedures that you use frequently. If you store these in a separate module, you can import the module to your current project and then call these procedures as needed — which is much easier than copying and pasting the code into your new procedures.

Creating several small procedures rather than a single large one is often considered good programming practice. A modular approach not only makes your job easier but also makes life easier for the people who wind up working with your code.

Note

The Developer➔Controls➔Insert drop-down list contains two types of controls that you can insert on a worksheet: Form controls and ActiveX controls. The ActiveX controls are similar to the controls that you use in a UserForm. The Forms controls were designed for Excel 5 and Excel 95, but you can still use them in later versions (and they may be preferable in some cases).

Unlike the Form controls, you can't use the ActiveX controls to execute an arbitrary macro. An ActiveX control executes a specially named macro. For example, if you insert an ActiveX button control named CommandButton1, clicking the button executes a macro named CommandButton1_Click, which must be located in the code module for the sheet on which the control was inserted.

Refer to Chapter 11 for information about using controls on worksheets.

To assign a procedure to a Button object from the Form controls, follow these steps:

1. Choose Developer➔Controls➔Insert and click the button icon in the Form Controls group.

2. Click the worksheet to create the button.

   Or you can drag your mouse on the worksheet to change the default size of the button.

   Excel jumps right in and displays the Assign Macro dialog box (see Figure 7-4). It proposes a macro based on the button's name (for example, Button1_Click).

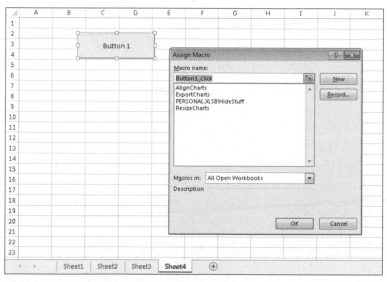

Figure 7-4: Assigning a macro to a button.

3. Select the macro that you want to assign to the button and then click OK.

You can always change the macro assignment by right-clicking the button and choosing Assign Macro.

To assign a macro to a Shape, SmartArt, WordArt, or picture, right-click the object and choose Assign Macro from the shortcut menu.

To assign a macro to an embedded chart, press Ctrl and click the chart (to select the chart as an object). Then right-click and choose Assign Macro from the shortcut menu.

Executing a procedure when an event occurs

You might want a procedure to execute when a particular event occurs, such as opening a workbook, entering data into a worksheet, saving a workbook, or clicking a CommandButton ActiveX control. A procedure that is executed when an event occurs is an *event-handler* procedure. Event-handler procedures are characterized by the following:

➤ They have special names that are made up of an object, an underscore, and the event name. For example, the procedure that is executed when a workbook is opened is Workbook_Open.

➤ They're stored in the Code module for the particular object (for example, ThisWorkbook or Sheet1).

Cross-Ref

Chapter 17 is devoted to event-handler procedures.

Executing a procedure from the Immediate window

You also can execute a procedure by entering its name in the Immediate window of VBE. (If the Immediate window isn't visible, press Ctrl+G.) The Immediate window executes VBA statements while you enter them. To execute a procedure, simply enter the name of the procedure in the Immediate window and press Enter.

This method can be useful when you're developing a procedure because you can insert commands to display results in the Immediate window. The following procedure demonstrates this technique:

```
Sub ChangeCase()
    Dim MyString As String
    MyString = "This is a test"
    MyString = UCase(MyString)
    Debug.Print MyString
End Sub
```

Figure 7-5 shows what happens when you enter **ChangeCase** in the Immediate window: The Debug.Print statement displays the result immediately.

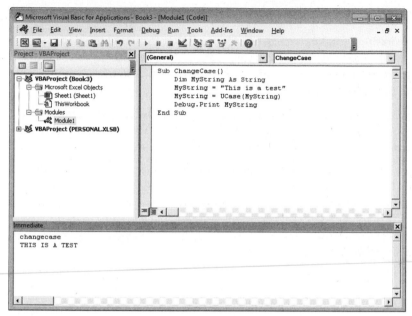

Figure 7-5: Executing a procedure by entering its name in the Immediate window.

Passing Arguments to Procedures

A procedure's *arguments* provide it with data that it uses in its instructions. The data that's passed by an argument can be any of the following:

➤ A variable

➤ A constant

➤ An expression

➤ An array

➤ An object

You are probably familiar with many of Excel's worksheet functions. Arguments for procedures are similar:

➤ A procedure may not require any arguments.

➤ A procedure may require a fixed number of arguments.

➤ A procedure may accept an indefinite number of arguments.

➤ A procedure may require some arguments, leaving others optional.

➤ A procedure may have all optional arguments.

For example, a few of Excel's worksheet functions, such as RAND and NOW, use no arguments. Others, such as COUNTIF, require two arguments. Others still, such as SUM, can use up to 255 arguments. Still other worksheet functions have optional arguments. The PMT function, for example, can have five arguments (three are required; two are optional).

Most of the procedures that you've seen so far in this book have been declared without arguments. They were declared with just the Sub keyword, the procedure's name, and a set of empty parentheses. Empty parentheses indicate that the procedure does not accept arguments.

The following example shows two procedures. The Main procedure calls the ProcessFile procedure three times (the Call statement is in a For-Next loop). Before calling ProcessFile, however, a three-element array is created. Inside the loop, each element of the array becomes the argument for the procedure call. The ProcessFile procedure takes one argument (named TheFile). Note that the argument goes inside parentheses in the Sub statement. When ProcessFile finishes, program control continues with the statement after the Call statement.

```vba
Sub Main()
    Dim File(1 To 3) As String
    Dim i as Integer
    File(1) = "dept1.xlsx"
    File(2) = "dept2.xlsx"
    File(3) = "dept3.xlsx"
    For i = 1 To 3
        Call ProcessFile(File(i))
    Next i
End Sub

Sub ProcessFile(TheFile)
    Workbooks.Open FileName:=TheFile
'   ...[more code here]...
End Sub
```

You can also pass *literals* (that is, not variables) to a procedure. For example:

```vba
Sub Main()
    Call ProcessFile("budget.xlsx")
End Sub
```

You can pass an argument to a procedure in two ways:

➤ **By reference:** Passing an argument by reference passes the memory address of the variable. Changes to the argument within the procedure are made to the original variable. This is the default method of passing an argument.

➤ **By value:** Passing an argument by value passes a *copy* of the original variable. Consequently, changes to the argument within the procedure are not reflected in the original variable.

The following example demonstrates this concept. The argument for the Process procedure is passed by reference (the default method). After the Main procedure assigns a value of 12 to MyValue, it calls the Process procedure and passes MyValue as the argument. The Process procedure multiplies the value of its argument (named YourValue) by 10. When Process ends and program control passes back to Main, the MsgBox function displays 120.

```
Sub Main()
    Dim MyValue As Integer
    MyValue = 12
    Call Process(MyValue)
    MsgBox MyValue
End Sub

Sub Process(YourValue)
    YourValue = YourValue * 10
End Sub
```

If you don't want the called procedure to modify any variables passed as arguments, you can modify the called procedure's argument list so that arguments are passed to it by *value* rather than by *reference*. To do so, precede the argument with the ByVal keyword. This technique causes the called routine to work with a copy of the passed variable's data — not the data itself. In the following procedure, for example, the changes made to YourValue in the Process procedure do not affect the MyValue variable in Main. As a result, the MsgBox function displays12 and not 120.

```
Sub Process(ByVal YourValue)
    YourValue = YourValue * 10
End Sub
```

In most cases, you'll be content to use the default reference method of passing arguments. However, if your procedure needs to use data passed to it in an argument — and you must keep the original data intact — you'll want to pass the data by value.

Using public variables versus passing arguments to a procedure

In Chapter 6, I point out how a variable declared as Public (at the top of the module) is available to all procedures in the module. In some cases, you may want to access a Public variable rather than pass the variable as an argument when calling another procedure.

For example, the procedure that follows passes the value of MonthVal to the ProcessMonth procedure:

```
Sub MySub()
    Dim MonthVal as Integer
'    ... [code goes here]
    MonthVal = 4
    Call ProcessMonth(MonthVal)
'    ... [code goes here]
End Sub
```

An alternative approach, which doesn't use an argument, is

```
Public MonthVal as Integer

Sub MySub()
'    ... [code goes here]
    MonthVal = 4
    Call ProcessMonth2
'    ... [code goes here]
End Sub
```

In the revised code, because MonthVal is a public variable, the ProcessMonth2 procedure can access it, thus eliminating the need for an argument for the ProcessMonth2 procedure.

A procedure's arguments can mix and match by value and by reference. Arguments preceded with ByVal are passed by value; all others are passed by reference.

 Note If you pass a variable defined as a user-defined data type to a procedure, it must be passed by reference. Attempting to pass it by value generates an error.

Because I didn't declare a data type for any of the arguments in the preceding examples, all the arguments have been of the Variant data type. But a procedure that uses arguments can define the data types directly in the argument list. The following is a Sub statement for a procedure with two arguments of different data types. The first is declared as an integer, and the second is declared as a string.

```
Sub Process(Iterations As Integer, TheFile As String)
```

When you pass arguments to a procedure, the data that is passed as the argument must match the argument's data type. For example, if you call Process in the preceding example and pass a string variable for the first argument, you get an error: ByRef argument type mismatch.

Note

Arguments are relevant to both Sub procedures and Function procedures. In fact, arguments are more often used in Function procedures. In Chapter 8, where I focus on Function procedures, I provide additional examples of using arguments with your routines, including how to handle optional arguments.

Error-Handling Techniques

When a VBA procedure is running, errors can (and probably will) occur. These include either *syntax errors* (which you must correct before you can execute a procedure) or *runtime errors* (which occur while the procedure is running). This section deals with runtime errors.

Caution

for error-handling procedures to work, the Break on All Errors setting must be turned off. In VBE, choose Tools→Options and click the General tab in the Options dialog box. If Break on All Errors is selected, VBA ignores your error-handling code. You'll usually want to use the Break on Unhandled Errors option.

Normally, a runtime error causes VBA to stop, and the user sees a dialog box that displays the error number and a description of the error. A good application doesn't make the user deal with these messages. Rather, it incorporates error-handling code to trap errors and take appropriate actions. At the very least, your error-handling code can display a more meaningful error message than the one VBA pops up.

Cross-Ref

Appendix B lists all the VBA error codes and descriptions.

Trapping errors

You can use the On Error statement to specify what happens when an error occurs. Basically, you have two choices:

➤ **Ignore the error and let VBA continue.** Your code can later examine the Err object to determine what the error was and then take action, if necessary.

➤ **Jump to a special error-handling section of your code to take action.** This section is placed at the end of the procedure and is also marked by a label.

To cause your VBA code to continue when an error occurs, insert the following statement in your code:

```
On Error Resume Next
```

Some errors are inconsequential, and you can ignore them without causing a problem. But you might want to determine what the error was. When an error occurs, you can use the Err object to determine the error number. You can use the VBA Error function to display the text that corresponds to the Err.Number value. For example, the following statement displays the same information as the normal Visual Basic error dialog box (the error number and the error description):

```
MsgBox "Error " & Err & ": " & Error(Err.Number)
```

Figure 7-6 shows a VBA error message, and Figure 7-7 shows the same error displayed in a message box. You can, of course, make the error message a bit more meaningful to your end users by using more descriptive text.

Figure 7-6: VBA error messages aren't always user friendly.

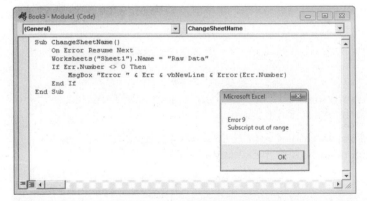

Figure 7-7: You can create a message box to display the error code and description.

Note

Referencing Err is equivalent to accessing the Number property of the Err object. Therefore, the following two statements have the same effect:

```
MsgBox Err
MsgBox Err.Number
```

You also use the On Error statement to specify a location in your procedure to jump to when an error occurs. You use a label to mark the location. For example:

```
On Error GoTo ErrorHandler
```

Error-handling examples

The first example demonstrates an error that you can safely ignore. The SpecialCells method selects cells that meet a certain criterion.

Note

The SpecialCells method is equivalent to choosing the Home➜Editing➜Find & Select➜ Go To Special command. The Go To Special dialog box provides you with a number of choices. For example, you can select cells that contain a numeric constant (nonformula).

In the example that follows, which doesn't use any error handling, the SpecialCells method selects all the cells in the current range selection that contain a formula. If no cells in the selection qualify, VBA displays the error message shown in Figure 7-8.

```
Sub SelectFormulas()
    Selection.SpecialCells(xlFormulas).Select
'    ...[more code goes here]
End Sub
```

Microsoft Visual Basic

Run-time error '1004':

No cells were found.

| Continue | End | Debug | Help |

Figure 7-8: The SpecialCells method generates this error if no cells are found.

Following is a variation that uses the On Error Resume Next statement to prevent the error message from appearing:

```
Sub SelectFormulas2()
    On Error Resume Next
    Selection.SpecialCells(xlFormulas).Select
    On Error GoTo 0
'    ...[more code goes here]
End Sub
```

The On Error GoTo 0 statement restores normal error handling for the remaining statements in the procedure.

The following procedure uses an additional statement to determine whether an error did occur. If so, the user is informed by a message.

```
Sub SelectFormulas3()
    On Error Resume Next
    Selection.SpecialCells(xlFormulas).Select
    If Err.Number = 1004 Then MsgBox "No formula cells were found."
    On Error GoTo 0
'    ...[more code goes here]
End Sub
```

If the Number property of Err is equal to anything other than 0, an error occurred. The If statement checks to see if Err.Number is equal to 1004 and displays a message box if it is. In this example, the code is checking for a specific error number. To check for any error, use a statement like this:

```
If Err.Number <> 0 Then MsgBox "An error occurred."
```

The next example demonstrates error handling by jumping to a label:

```
Sub ErrorDemo()
    On Error GoTo Handler
    Selection.Value = 123
    Exit Sub
Handler:
    MsgBox "Cannot assign a value to the selection."
End Sub
```

The procedure attempts to assign a value to the current selection. If an error occurs (for example, a range isn't selected or the sheet is protected), the assignment statement results in an error. The On Error statement specifies a jump to the Handler label if an error occurs. Note the use of the Exit Sub statement before the label. This statement prevents the error-handling code from being executed if no error occurs. If this statement is omitted, the error message is displayed even if an error does not occur.

Sometimes, you can take advantage of an error to get information. The example that follows simply checks whether a particular workbook is open. It doesn't use any error handling.

```vba
Sub CheckForFile1()
    Dim FileName As String
    Dim FileExists As Boolean
    Dim book As Workbook
    FileName = "BUDGET.XLSX"
    FileExists = False

'    Cycle through all open workbooks
    For Each book In Workbooks
        If UCase(book.Name) = FileName Then FileExists = True
    Next book

'    Display appropriate message
    If FileExists Then
        MsgBox FileName & " is open."
    Else
        MsgBox FileName & " is not open."
    End If
End Sub
```

Here, a For Each-Next loop cycles through all objects in the Workbooks collection. If the workbook is open, the FileExists variable is set to True. Finally, a message is displayed that tells the user whether the workbook is open.

You can rewrite the preceding routine to use error handling to determine whether the file is open. In the example that follows, the On Error Resume Next statement causes VBA to ignore any errors. The next instruction attempts to reference the workbook by assigning the workbook to an object variable (by using the Set keyword). If the workbook isn't open, an error occurs. The If-Then-Else structure checks the value property of Err and displays the appropriate message. This procedure uses no looping, so it's slightly more efficient.

```
Sub CheckForFile()
    Dim FileName As String
    Dim x As Workbook
    FileName = "BUDGET.XLSX"
    On Error Resume Next
    Set x = Workbooks(FileName)
    If Err = 0 Then
        MsgBox FileName & " is open."
    Else
        MsgBox FileName & " is not open."
    End If
    On Error GoTo 0
End Sub
```

Cross-Ref

Chapter 9 includes several additional examples that use error handling.

A Realistic Example That Uses Sub Procedures

In this chapter, I describe the basics of creating Sub procedures. Most of the previous examples, I will admit, have been wimpy. The remainder of this chapter is a real-life exercise that demonstrates many of the concepts covered in this and the preceding two chapters.

This section describes the development of a useful utility. More important, I demonstrate the *process* of analyzing a problem and then solving it with VBA. I wrote this section with VBA newcomers in mind. In addition to presenting the code, I show how to find what you need to know to develop the code.

On the Web

You can find the completed application, named sheet sorter.xlsm, on this book's website.

The goal

The goal of this exercise is to develop a utility that rearranges a workbook by alphabetizing its sheets (something that Excel can't do on its own). If you tend to create workbooks that consist of many sheets, you know that locating a particular sheet can be difficult. If the sheets are ordered alphabetically, however, it's easier to find a desired sheet.

Project requirements

Where to begin? One way to get started is to list the requirements for your application. When you develop your application, you can check your list to ensure that you're covering all the bases.

Here's the list of requirements that I compiled for this example application:

➤ It should sort the sheets (that is, worksheets and chart sheets) in the active workbook in ascending order of their names.

➤ It should be easy to execute.

➤ It should always be available. In other words, the user shouldn't have to open a workbook to use this utility.

➤ It should work properly for any workbook that's open.

➤ It should trap errors gracefully, and not display any cryptic VBA error messages.

What you know

Often, the most difficult part of a project is figuring out where to start. In this case, I started by listing things that I know about Excel that may be relevant to the project requirements:

➤ Excel doesn't have a command that sorts sheets, so I'm not reinventing the wheel.

➤ I can't create this type of macro by recording my actions. However, a recorded macro might provide some key information.

➤ Sorting the sheets will require moving some or all of them. I can move a sheet easily by dragging its sheet tab.

Mental note: Turn on the macro recorder and drag a sheet to a new location to find out what kind of code this action generates.

➤ Excel also has a Move or Copy dialog box, which is displayed when I right-click a sheet tab and choose Move or Copy. Would recording a macro of this command generate different code than moving a sheet manually?

➤ I'll need to know how many sheets are in the active workbook. I can get this information with VBA.

➤ I'll need to know the names of all the sheets. Again, I can get this information with VBA.

➤ Excel has a command that sorts data in worksheet cells.

Mental note: Maybe I can transfer the sheet names to a range and use this feature. Or maybe VBA has a sorting method that I can take advantage of.

➤ Thanks to the Macro Options dialog box, it's easy to assign a shortcut key to a macro.

➤ If a macro is stored in the Personal Macro Workbook, it will always be available.

➤ I need a way to test the application while I develop it. I don't want to be testing it using the same workbook in which I'm developing the code.

Mental note: Create a dummy workbook for testing.

➤ If I develop the code properly, VBA won't display any errors.

Mental note: Wishful thinking.

The approach

Although I still didn't know exactly how to proceed, I could devise a preliminary, skeleton plan that describes the general tasks required:

1. Identify the active workbook.

2. Get a list of all the sheet names in the workbook.

3. Count the sheets.

4. Sort the sheet names (somehow).

5. Rearrange the sheets so they correspond to the sorted sheet names.

What you need to know

I saw a few holes in the plan. I knew that I had to determine how to

➤ Identify the active workbook

➤ Count the sheets in the active workbook

➤ Get a list of the sheet names

➤ Sort the list

➤ Rearrange the sheets according to the sorted list

Tip

When you lack critical information about specific methods or properties, you can consult this book or the VBA Help system. You may eventually discover what you need to know. Your best bet, however, is to turn on the macro recorder and examine the code that it generates when you perform some relevant actions. You'll almost always get some clues as to how to proceed.

Some preliminary recording

Here's an example of using the macro recorder to learn about VBA. I started with a workbook that contained three worksheets. Then I turned on the macro recorder and specified my Personal Macro Workbook as the destination for the macro. With the macro recorder running, I dragged the third worksheet to the first sheet position. Here's the code that was generated by the macro recorder:

```
Sub Macro1()
    Sheets("Sheet3").Select
    Sheets("Sheet3").Move Before:=Sheets(1)
End Sub
```

I searched the VBA Help system for *Move* and discovered that it's a method that moves a sheet to a new location in the workbook. It also takes an argument that specifies the location for the sheet. This information is relevant to the task at hand. Curious, I then turned on the macro recorder to see whether using the Move or Copy dialog box would generate different code. It didn't.

Next, I needed to find out how many sheets were in the active workbook. I searched Help for the word *Count* and found out that it's a property of a collection. I activated the Immediate window in VBE and typed the following statement:

```
? ActiveWorkbook.Count
```

Error! After a little more thought, I realized that I needed to get a count of the sheets within a workbook. So I tried this:

```
? ActiveWorkbook.Sheets.Count
```

Success. Figure 7-9 shows the result. More useful information.

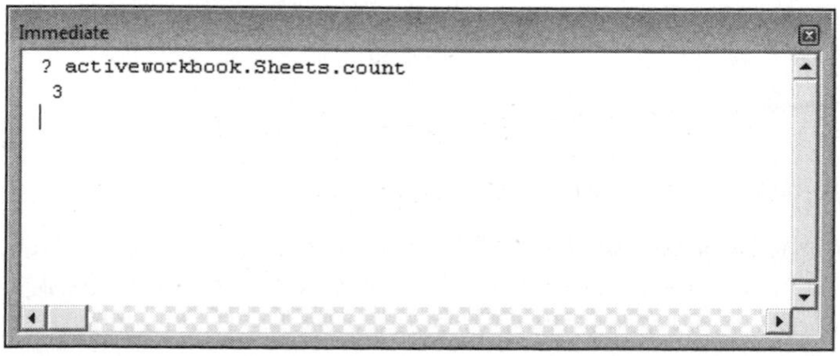

Figure 7-9: Using the VBE Immediate window to test a statement.

What about the sheet names? Time for another test. I entered the following statement in the Immediate window:

```
? ActiveWorkbook.Sheets(1).Name
```

This told me that the name of the first sheet is Sheet3, which is correct (because I'd moved it). More good information to keep in mind.

Then I remembered something about the For Each-Next construct: It's useful for cycling through each member of a collection. After consulting the Help system, I created a short procedure to test it:

```
Sub Test()
    For Each Sht In ActiveWorkbook.Sheets
        MsgBox Sht.Name
    Next Sht
End Sub
```

Another success. This macro displayed three message boxes, each showing a different sheet name.

Finally, it was time to think about sorting options. From the Help system, I learned that the Sort method applies to a Range object. So one option was to transfer the sheet names to a range and then sort the range, but that seemed like overkill for this application. I thought that a better option was to dump the sheet names into an array of strings and then sort the array by using VBA code.

Initial setup

Now I knew enough to get started writing some serious code. Before doing so, however, I needed to do some initial setup work. To recreate my steps, follow these instructions:

1. Create an empty workbook with five worksheets, named Sheet1, Sheet2, Sheet3, Sheet4, and Sheet5.

2. Move the sheets around randomly so that they aren't in any particular order. Just click and drag the sheet tabs.

3. Save the workbook as Test.xlsx.

4. Activate VBE and select the Personal.xlsb project in the Project window.

   If Personal.xlsb doesn't appear in the Project window in VBE, it means that you've never used the Personal Macro Workbook. To have Excel create this workbook for you, simply record a macro (any macro) and specify the Personal Macro Workbook as the destination for the macro.

5. Insert a new VBA module in Personal.xlsb (choose Insert➜Module).

6. Create an empty Sub procedure called SortSheets (see Figure 7-10).

   You can store this macro in any module in the Personal Macro Workbook. However, keeping each group of related macros in a separate module is a good idea. That way, you can easily export the module and import it into a different project later on.

7. Activate Excel and choose Developer➜Code➜Macros to display the Macro dialog box.

8. In the Macro dialog box, select the SortSheets procedure and click the Options button to assign a shortcut key to this macro.

   The Ctrl+Shift+S key combination is a good choice.

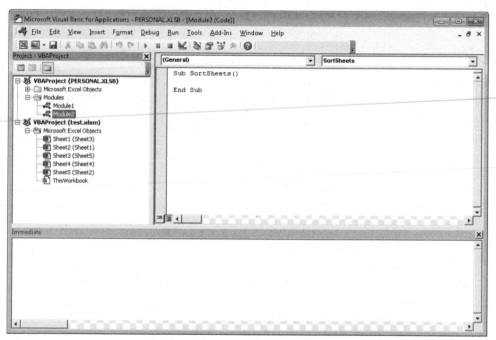

Figure 7-10: An empty procedure in a module located in the Personal Macro Workbook.

Code writing

Now it's time to write some code. I knew that I needed to put the sheet names into an array of strings. Because I didn't know yet how many sheets were in the active workbook, I used a Dim statement with empty parentheses to declare the array. I knew that I could use ReDim afterward to redimension the array for the actual number of elements.

I entered the following code, which inserted the sheet names into the SheetNames array. I also added a MsgBox function within the loop just to assure me that the sheets' names were indeed being entered into the array.

```
Sub SortSheets()
'    Sorts the sheets of the active workbook
    Dim SheetNames() as String
    Dim i as Long
    Dim SheetCount as Long
    SheetCount = ActiveWorkbook.Sheets.Count
    ReDim SheetNames(1 To SheetCount)
    For i = 1 To SheetCount
        SheetNames(i) = ActiveWorkbook.Sheets(i).Name
        MsgBox SheetNames(i)
    Next i
End Sub
```

To test the preceding code, I activated the Test.xlsx workbook and pressed Ctrl+Shift+S. Five message boxes appeared, each displaying the name of a sheet in the active workbook. So far, so good.

By the way, I'm a major proponent of testing your work as you go. I tend to work in small steps and set things up so that I'm convinced that each small step is working properly before I continue. When you're convinced that your code is working correctly, remove the MsgBox statement. (These message boxes become annoying after a while.)

Tip

Rather than use the MsgBox function to test your work, you can use the Print method of the Debug object to display information in the Immediate window. For this example, use the following statement in place of the MsgBox statement:

```
Debug.Print SheetNames(i)
```

This technique is much less intrusive than using MsgBox statements. Just make sure that you remember to remove the statement when you're finished.

At this point, the SortSheets procedure simply creates an array of sheet names corresponding to the sheets in the active workbook. Two steps remain: Sort the elements in the SheetNames array and then rearrange the sheets to correspond to the sorted array.

Writing the Sort procedure

It was time to sort the SheetNames array. One option was to insert the sorting code in the SortSheets procedure, but I thought a better approach was to write a general-purpose sorting procedure that I could reuse with other projects. (Sorting arrays is a common operation.)

You might be daunted by the thought of writing a sorting procedure. The good news is that the Internet makes it easy to find commonly used routines that you can use or adapt.

You can sort an array in many ways. I chose the *bubble sort* method; although it's not a fast technique, it's easy to code. Blazing speed isn't a requirement in this application.

The bubble sort method uses a nested For-Next loop to evaluate each array element. If the array element is greater than the next element, the two elements swap positions. The code includes a nested loop, so this evaluation is repeated for every pair of items (that is, $n-1$ times).

Cross-Ref

In Chapter 9, I present some other sorting routines and compare them in terms of speed.

Here's the sorting procedure I developed (after consulting a few programming websites to get some ideas):

```
Sub BubbleSort(List() As String)
'    Sorts the List array in ascending order
    Dim First As Long, Last As Long
    Dim i As Long, j As Long
    Dim Temp As String
    First = LBound(List)
    Last = UBound(List)
    For i = First To Last - 1
        For j = i + 1 To Last
            If List(i) > List(j) Then
                Temp = List(j)
                List(j) = List(i)
                List(i) = Temp
            End If
        Next j
    Next i
End Sub
```

This procedure accepts one argument: a one-dimensional array named List. An array passed to a procedure can be of any length. I used the LBound function to assign the lower bound of the array and the UBound function to assign the upper bound of the array to the variables First and Last, respectively.

Here's a little temporary procedure that I used to test the BubbleSort procedure:

```
Sub SortTester()
    Dim x(1 To 5) As String
    Dim i As Long
    x(1) = "dog"
    x(2) = "cat"
    x(3) = "elephant"
    x(4) = "aardvark"
    x(5) = "bird"
    Call BubbleSort(x)
    For i = 1 To 5
        Debug.Print i, x(i)
    Next i
End Sub
```

The SortTester routine creates an array of five strings, passes the array to BubbleSort, and then displays the sorted array in the Immediate window (see Figure 7-11). I eventually deleted this code because it served its purpose.

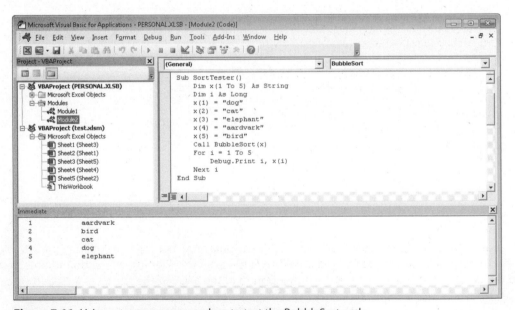

Figure 7-11: Using a temporary procedure to test the BubbleSort code.

When I was satisfied that this procedure worked reliably, I modified SortSheets by adding a call to the BubbleSort procedure, passing the SheetNames array as an argument. At this point, my module looked like this:

```
Sub SortSheets()
    Dim SheetNames() As String
    Dim SheetCount as Long
    Dim i as Long
    SheetCount = ActiveWorkbook.Sheets.Count
    ReDim SheetNames(1 To SheetCount)
    For i = 1 To SheetCount
        SheetNames(i) = ActiveWorkbook.Sheets(i).Name
    Next i
    Call BubbleSort(SheetNames)
End Sub

Sub BubbleSort(List() As String)
'    Sorts the List array in ascending order
    Dim First As Long, Last As Long
    Dim i As Long, j As Long
    Dim Temp As String
    First = LBound(List)
    Last = UBound(List)
    For i = First To Last - 1
        For j = i + 1 To Last
            If List(i) > List(j) Then
                Temp = List(j)
                List(j) = List(i)
                List(i) = Temp
            End If
        Next j
    Next i
End Sub
```

When the SheetSort procedure ends, it contains an array that consists of the sorted sheet names in the active workbook. To verify this, you can display the array contents in the VBE Immediate window by adding the following code at the end of the SortSheets procedure (if the Immediate window is not visible, press Ctrl+G):

```
For i = 1 To SheetCount
    Debug.Print SheetNames(i)
Next i
```

So far, so good. Next step: Write some code to rearrange the sheets to correspond to the sorted items in the SheetNames array.

The code that I recorded earlier proved useful. Remember the instruction that was recorded when I moved a sheet to the first position in the workbook?

```
Sheets("Sheet3").Move Before:=Sheets(1)
```

After a little thought, I was able to write a For-Next loop that would go through each sheet and move it to its corresponding sheet location, specified in the SheetNames array:

```
For i = 1 To SheetCount
    Sheets(SheetNames(i)).Move Before:=Sheets(i)
Next i
```

For example, the first time through the loop, the loop counter i is 1. The first element in the sorted SheetNames array is (in this example) Sheet1. Therefore, the expression for the Move method in the loop evaluates to

```
Sheets("Sheet1").Move Before:= Sheets(1)
```

The second time through the loop, the expression evaluates to

```
Sheets("Sheet2").Move Before:= Sheets(2)
```

I then added the new code to the SortSheets procedure:

```
Sub SortSheets()
    Dim SheetNames() As String
    Dim SheetCount as Long
    Dim i as Long
    SheetCount = ActiveWorkbook.Sheets.Count
    ReDim SheetNames(1 To SheetCount)
    For i = 1 To SheetCount
        SheetNames(i) = ActiveWorkbook.Sheets(i).Name
    Next i
    Call BubbleSort(SheetNames)
    For i = 1 To SheetCount
        ActiveWorkbook.Sheets(SheetNames(i)).Move _
            Before:=ActiveWorkbook.Sheets(i)
    Next i
End Sub
```

I did some testing, and the procedure seemed to work just fine for the Test.xlsx workbook.

Time to clean things up. I made sure that all the variables used in the procedures were declared, and then I added a few comments and blank lines to make the code easier to read. The SortSheets procedure looked like the following:

```
Sub SortSheets()
'   This routine sorts the sheets of the
'   active workbook in ascending order.
'   Use Ctrl+Shift+S to execute

    Dim SheetNames() As String
    Dim SheetCount As Long
    Dim i As Long

'   Determine the number of sheets & ReDim array
    SheetCount = ActiveWorkbook.Sheets.Count
    ReDim SheetNames(1 To SheetCount)

'   Fill array with sheet names
    For i = 1 To SheetCount
        SheetNames(i) = ActiveWorkbook.Sheets(i).Name
    Next i

'   Sort the array in ascending order
    Call BubbleSort(SheetNames)

'   Move the sheets
    For i = 1 To SheetCount
        ActiveWorkbook.Sheets(SheetNames(i)).Move _
            Before:= ActiveWorkbook.Sheets(i)
    Next i
End Sub
```

Everything seemed to be working. To test the code further, I added a few more sheets to Test.xlsx and changed some of the sheet names. It worked like a charm.

More testing

I was tempted to call it a day. However, just because the procedure worked with the Test.xlsx workbook didn't mean that it would work with all workbooks. To test it further, I loaded a few other workbooks and retried the routine. I soon discovered that the application wasn't perfect. In fact, it was far from perfect. I compiled a list of problems:

➤ Workbooks with many sheets took a long time to sort because the screen was continually updated during the move operations.

➤ The sorting didn't always work. For example, in one of my tests, a sheet named SUMMARY (all uppercase) appeared before a sheet named Sheet1. This problem was caused by the BubbleSort procedure — an uppercase *U* is "greater than" a lowercase *h*.

➤ If Excel had no visible workbook windows, pressing the Ctrl+Shift+S shortcut key combo caused the macro to fail.

➤ If the workbook's structure was protected, the Move method failed.

➤ After sorting, the last sheet in the workbook became the active sheet. Changing the user's active sheet isn't a good practice; it's better to keep the user's original sheet active.

➤ If I interrupted the macro by pressing Ctrl+Break, VBA displayed an error message.

➤ The macro can't be reversed (that is, the Undo command is disabled when a macro is executed). If the user accidentally presses Ctrl+Shift+S, the workbook sheets are sorted, and the only way to get them back to their original order is by doing it manually.

Fixing the problems

Fixing the screen-updating problem was a breeze. I inserted the following instruction to turn off screen updating while the sheets were being moved:

```
Application.ScreenUpdating = False
```

This statement causes Excel's windows to freeze while the macro is running. A beneficial side effect is that it also speeds up the macro considerably. After the macro completes it operation, screen updating is turned back on automatically.

It was also easy to fix the problem with the BubbleSort procedure: I used VBA's UCase function to convert the sheet names to uppercase for the comparison. This caused all the comparisons to be made by using uppercase versions of the sheet names. The corrected line read as follows:

```
If UCase(List(i)) > UCase(List(j)) Then
```

Tip

Another way to solve the "case" problem is to add the following statement to the top of your module:

```
Option Compare Text
```

This statement causes VBA to perform string comparisons based on a case-insensitive text sort order. In other words, A is considered the same as a.

To prevent the error message that appears when no workbooks are visible, I added some error checking. I used On Error Resume Next to ignore the error and then checked the value of Err. If Err is not equal to 0, an error occurred. Therefore, the procedure ends. The error-checking code is

```
On Error Resume Next
SheetCount = ActiveWorkbook.Sheets.Count
If Err <> 0 Then Exit Sub ' No active workbook
```

It occurred to me that I could avoid using On Error Resume Next. The following statement is a more direct approach to determining whether a workbook isn't visible and doesn't require any error handling. This statement can go at the top of the SortSheets procedure:

```
If ActiveWorkbook Is Nothing Then Exit Sub
```

There's usually a good reason that a workbook's structure is protected. I decided that the best approach was to not attempt to unprotect the workbook. Rather, the code should display a message box warning and let the user unprotect the workbook and re-execute the macro. Testing for a protected workbook structure was easy — the ProtectStructure property of a Workbook object returns True if a workbook is protected. I added the following block of code:

```
'   Check for protected workbook structure
    If ActiveWorkbook.ProtectStructure Then
        MsgBox ActiveWorkbook.Name & " is protected.", _
            vbCritical, "Cannot Sort Sheets."
        Exit Sub
    End If
```

If the workbook's structure is protected, the user sees a message box like the one shown in Figure 7-12.

Figure 7-12: This message box tells the user that the sheets cannot be sorted.

To reactivate the original active sheet after the sorting was performed, I wrote code that assigned the original sheet to an object variable (OldActiveSheet) and then activated that sheet when the routine was finished. Here's the statement that assigns the variable:

```
Set OldActive = ActiveSheet
```

This statement activates the original active worksheet:

```
OldActive.Activate
```

Pressing Ctrl+Break normally halts a macro, and VBA usually displays an error message. But because one of my goals was to avoid VBA error messages, I inserted a command to prevent this situation. From the VBA Help system, I discovered that the Application object has an EnableCancelKey property that can disable Ctrl+Break. So I added the following statement at the top of the routine:

```
Application.EnableCancelKey = xlDisabled
```

 Caution **Be careful when you disable the Cancel key. If your code gets caught in an infinite loop, you can't break out of it. For best results, insert this statement only after you're sure that everything is working properly.**

To prevent the problem of accidentally sorting the sheets, I added the following statement to the procedure, before the Ctrl+Break key is disabled:

```
If MsgBox("Sort the sheets in the active workbook?", _
    vbQuestion + vbYesNo) <> vbYes Then Exit Sub
```

When users execute the SortSheets procedure, they see the message box in Figure 7-13.

Figure 7-13: This message box appears before the sheets are sorted.

After I made all these corrections, the SortSheets procedure looked like this:

```
Option Explicit
Sub SortSheets()
'   This routine sorts the sheets of the
'   active workbook in ascending order.
'   Use Ctrl+Shift+S to execute

    Dim SheetNames() As String
    Dim i As Long
```

```
    Dim SheetCount As Long
    Dim OldActiveSheet As Object

    If ActiveWorkbook Is Nothing Then Exit Sub ' No active workbook
    SheetCount = ActiveWorkbook.Sheets.Count

'   Check for protected workbook structure
    If ActiveWorkbook.ProtectStructure Then
        MsgBox ActiveWorkbook.Name & " is protected.", _
            vbCritical, "Cannot Sort Sheets."
        Exit Sub
    End If

'   Make user verify
    If MsgBox("Sort the sheets in the active workbook?", _
      vbQuestion + vbYesNo) <> vbYes Then Exit Sub

'   Disable Ctrl+Break
    Application.EnableCancelKey = xlDisabled

'   Get the number of sheets
    SheetCount = ActiveWorkbook.Sheets.Count

'   Redimension the array
    ReDim SheetNames(1 To SheetCount)

'   Store a reference to the active sheet
    Set OldActiveSheet = ActiveSheet

'   Fill array with sheet names
    For i = 1 To SheetCount
        SheetNames(i) = ActiveWorkbook.Sheets(i).Name
    Next i

'   Sort the array in ascending order
    Call BubbleSort(SheetNames)

'   Turn off screen updating
    Application.ScreenUpdating = False

'   Move the sheets
    For i = 1 To SheetCount
        ActiveWorkbook.Sheets(SheetNames(i)).Move _
            Before:=ActiveWorkbook.Sheets(i)
    Next i

'   Reactivate the original active sheet
    OldActiveSheet.Activate
End Sub
```

Utility availability

Because the SortSheets macro is stored in the Personal Macro Workbook, it's available whenever Excel is running. At this point, you can execute the macro by selecting the macro's name from the Macro dialog box (Alt+F8 displays this dialog box) or by pressing Ctrl+Shift+S. Another option is to add a command to the Ribbon.

To add a command, follow these steps:

1. Right-click any area of the Ribbon and choose Customize the Ribbon.

2. In the Customize Ribbon tab of the Excel Options dialog box, choose Macros from the Choose Commands From drop-down list.

3. Click the item labeled PERSONAL.XLSB!SortSheets.

4. Use the controls in the box on the right to specify the Ribbon tab and create a new group.

   (You can't add a command to an existing group.)

I created a group named Sheets in the View tab, and renamed the new item to Short Sheets (see Figure 7-14).

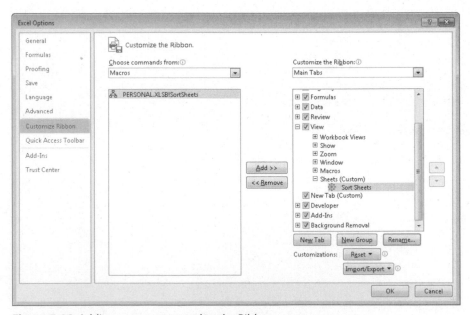

Figure 7-14: Adding a new command to the Ribbon.

Evaluating the project

So there you have it. The utility meets all the original project requirements: It sorts all sheets in the active workbook, it can be executed easily, it's always available, it seems to work for any workbook, and I have yet to see it display a VBA error message.

Note

The procedure still has one slight problem: The sorting is strict and may not always be "logical." For example, after sorting, Sheet10 is placed before Sheet2. Most would want Sheet2 to be listed before Sheet10. Solving that problem is possible but beyond the scope of this introductory exercise

Creating Function Procedures

In This Chapter

- Understanding the difference between Sub procedures and Function procedures

- Creating custom functions

- Looking at Function procedures and function arguments

- Creating a function that emulates Excel's SUM function

- Using functions that enable you to work with pre-1900 dates in your worksheets

- Debugging functions, dealing with the Insert Function dialog box, and using add-ins to store custom functions

- Calling the Windows Application Programming Interface (API) to perform otherwise impossible feats

Sub Procedures versus Function Procedures

A VBA Function is a procedure that performs calculations and returns a value. You can use these functions in your Visual Basic for Applications (VBA) code or in worksheet formulas.

VBA enables you to create Sub procedures and Function procedures. You can think of a Sub procedure as a command that either the user or another procedure can execute. Function procedures, on the other hand, usually return a single value (or an array), just like Excel worksheet functions and VBA built-in functions. As with built-in functions, your Function procedures can use arguments.

Function procedures are versatile, and you can use them in two situations:

➤ As part of an expression in a VBA procedure

➤ In formulas that you create in a worksheet

In fact, you can use a Function procedure anywhere that you can use an Excel worksheet function or a VBA built-in function. As far as I know, the only exception is that you can't use a VBA function in a data validation formula. You can, however, use a custom VBA function in a conditional formatting formula.

I cover Sub procedures in the preceding chapter and Function procedures in this chapter.

Cross-Ref

Chapter 9 has many useful and practical examples of Function procedures. You can incorporate many of these techniques into your work.

Why Create Custom Functions?

You're undoubtedly familiar with Excel worksheet functions; even novices know how to use the most common worksheet functions, such as SUM, AVERAGE, and IF. Excel 2013 includes more than 450 predefined worksheet functions that you can use in formulas. In addition, you can create custom functions by using VBA.

With all the functions available in Excel and VBA, you might wonder why you'd ever need to create new functions. The answer: to simplify your work. With a bit of planning, custom functions are useful in worksheet formulas and VBA procedures.

Often, for example, you can create a custom function that can significantly shorten your formulas. And shorter formulas are more readable and easier to work with. The trade-off, however, is that custom functions are usually much slower than built-in functions. And, of course, the user must enable macros to use these functions.

When you create applications, you may notice that some procedures repeat certain calculations. In such cases, consider creating a custom function that performs the calculation. Then you can call the function from your procedure. A custom function can eliminate the need for duplicated code, thus reducing errors.

Although many cringe at the thought of creating custom worksheet functions, the process isn't difficult. In fact, I *enjoy* creating custom functions. I especially like how my custom functions appear in the Insert Function dialog box along with Excel built-in functions, as if I'm re-engineering the software in some way.

In this chapter, I tell you what you need to know to start creating custom functions, and I provide lots of examples.

An Introductory Function Example

Without further ado, this section presents an example of a VBA Function procedure.

The following is a custom function defined in a VBA module. This function, named REMOVEVOWELS, uses a single argument. The function returns the argument, but with all the vowels removed.

```
Function REMOVEVOWELS(Txt) As String
' Removes all vowels from the Txt argument
    Dim i As Long
    RemoveVowels = ""
    For i = 1 To Len(Txt)
        If Not UCase(Mid(Txt, i, 1)) Like "[AEIOU]" Then
            REMOVEVOWELS = REMOVEVOWELS & Mid(Txt, i, 1)
        End If
    Next i
End Function
```

This function certainly isn't the most useful one I've written, but it demonstrates some key concepts related to functions. I explain how this function works later, in the "Analyzing the custom function" section.

Caution   When you create custom functions that will be used in a worksheet formula, make sure that the code resides in a normal VBA module (use Insert➜Module to create a normal VBA module). If you place your custom functions in a code module for a UserForm, a Sheet, or ThisWorkbook, they won't work in your formulas. Your formulas will return a #NAME? error.

Using the function in a worksheet

When you enter a formula that uses the REMOVEVOWELS function, Excel executes the code to get the result that's returned by the function. Here's an example of how you'd use the function in a formula:

```
=REMOVEVOWELS(A1)
```

See Figure 8-1 for examples of this function in action. The formulas are in column B, and they use the text in column A as their arguments. As you can see, the function returns the single argument, but with the vowels removed.

◢	A	B	C
1	Every good boy does fine.	vry gd by ds fn.	
2	antidisestablishmentarianism	ntdsstblshmntrnsm	
3	Microsoft Excel	Mcrsft xcl	
4	abcdefghijklmnopqrstuvwxyz	bcdfghjklmnpqrstvwxyz	
5	A failure to communicate.	flr t cmmnct.	
6	This sentence has no vowels.	Ths sntnc hs n vwls.	
7	Vowels: AEIOU	Vwls:	
8	Humuhumunukunukuapua'a is a fish	Hmhmnknkp's fsh	
9	Honorificabilitudinitatibus	Hnrfcbltdnttbs	
10	Do you like custom worksheet functions?	D y lk cstm wrksht fnctns?	
11			
12			
13			

Sheet1   ⊕

Figure 8-1: Using a custom function in a worksheet formula.

Actually, the function works like any built-in worksheet function. You can insert it in a formula by choosing Formulas➔Function Library➔Insert Function or by clicking the Insert Function Wizard icon to the left of the formula bar. Either of these actions displays the Insert Function dialog box. In the Insert Function dialog box, your custom functions are located, by default, in the User Defined category.

You can also nest custom functions and combine them with other elements in your formulas. For example, the following formula nests the REMOVEVOWELS function inside Excel's UPPER function. The result is the original string (sans vowels), converted to uppercase.

```
=UPPER(REMOVEVOWELS(A1))
```

Using the function in a VBA procedure

In addition to using custom functions in worksheet formulas, you can use them in other VBA procedures. The following VBA procedure, which is defined in the same module as the custom REMOVEVOWELS function, first displays an input box to solicit text from the user. Then the procedure uses the VBA built-in MsgBox function to display the user input after the REMOVEVOWELS function processes it (see Figure 8-2). The original input appears as the caption in the message box.

```
Sub ZapTheVowels()
    Dim UserInput as String
    UserInput = InputBox("Enter some text:")
    MsgBox REMOVEVOWELS(UserInput), vbInformation, UserInput
End Sub
```

Figure 8-2 shows text entered into an input box, and the result displayed in a message box .

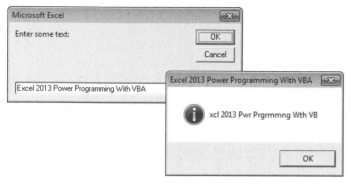

Figure 8-2: Using a custom function in a VBA procedure.

Analyzing the custom function

Function procedures can be as complex as you need them to be. Most of the time, they're more complex and much more useful than this sample procedure. Nonetheless, an analysis of this example may help you understand what is happening.

Here's the code, again:

```
Function REMOVEVOWELS(Txt) As String
' Removes all vowels from the Txt argument
    Dim i As Long
    REMOVEVOWELS = ""
    For i = 1 To Len(Txt)
        If Not UCase(Mid(Txt, i, 1)) Like "[AEIOU]" Then
            REMOVEVOWELS = REMOVEVOWELS & Mid(Txt, i, 1)
        End If
    Next i
End Function
```

Note that the procedure starts with the keyword Function, rather than Sub, followed by the name of the function (REMOVEVOWELS). This custom function uses only one argument (Txt), enclosed in parentheses. As String defines the data type of the function's return value. Excel uses the Variant data type if no data type is specified.

The second line is an optional comment that describes what the function does. This line is followed by a Dim statement, which declares the variable (i) used in the procedure as type Long.

Note

I use the function name as a variable and initialize it to an empty string. When a function ends, it always returns the current value of the variable that corresponds to the function's name.

The next five instructions make up a For-Next loop. The procedure loops through each character in the input and builds the string. The first instruction in the loop uses VBA's Mid function to return a single character from the input string and converts this character to uppercase. That character is then compared to a list of characters by using Excel's Like operator. In other words, the If clause is true if the character isn't A, E, I, O, or U. In such a case, the character is appended to the REMOVEVOWELS variable.

When the loop is finished, REMOVEVOWELS consists of the input string with all vowels removed. This string is the value that the function returns.

The procedure ends with an End Function statement.

Keep in mind that you can do the coding for this function in a number of different ways. Here's a function that accomplishes the same result but is coded differently:

```
Function REMOVEVOWELS(txt) As String
' Removes all vowels from the Txt argument
    Dim i As Long
    Dim TempString As String
    TempString = ""
    For i = 1 To Len(txt)
        Select Case ucase(Mid(txt, i, 1))
            Case "A", "E", "I", "O", "U"
                'Do nothing
            Case Else
                TempString = TempString & Mid(txt, i, 1)
        End Select
    Next i
    REMOVEVOWELS = TempString
End Function
```

In this version, I used a string variable (TempString) to store the vowel-less string as it's being constructed. Then, before the procedure ends, I assigned the contents of TempString to the function's name. This version also uses a Select Case construct rather than an If-Then construct.

On the Web

Both versions of this function are available at this book's website. The file is named **remove vowels.xlsm.**

What custom worksheet functions can't do

When you develop custom functions, it's important to understand a key distinction between functions that you call from other VBA procedures and functions that you use in worksheet formulas. Function procedures used in worksheet formulas must be passive. For example, code in a Function procedure can't manipulate ranges or change things on the worksheet. An example can help make this limitation clear.

You may be tempted to write a custom worksheet function that changes a cell's formatting. For example, it may be useful to have a formula that uses a custom function to change the color of text in a cell based on the cell's value. Try as you might, however, such a function is impossible to write. No matter what you do, the function won't change the worksheet. Remember, a function simply returns a value. It can't perform actions with objects.

That said, I should point out one notable exception. You can change the text in a cell *comment* by using a custom VBA function. I'm not sure if this behavior is intentional or if it's a bug in Excel. In any case, modifying a comment via a function seems to work reliably. Here's the function:

```
Function MODIFYCOMMENT(Cell As Range, Cmt As String)
    Cell.Comment.Text Cmt
End Function
```

Here's an example of using this function in a formula. The formula replaces the comment in cell A1 with new text. The function won't work if cell A1 doesn't have a comment.

```
=MODIFYCOMMENT(A1,"Hey, I changed your comment")
```

Function Procedures

A Function procedure has much in common with a Sub procedure. (For more information on Sub procedures, see Chapter 7.)

The syntax for declaring a function is as follows:

```
[Public | Private][Static] Function name ([arglist])[As type]
    [instructions]
    [name = expression]
    [Exit Function]
    [instructions]
    [name = expression]
End Function
```

The Function procedure contains the following elements:

➤ Public: Optional. Indicates that the Function procedure is accessible to all other procedures in all other modules in all active Excel VBA projects.

➤ Private: Optional. Indicates that the Function procedure is accessible only to other procedures in the same module.

➤ Static: Optional. Indicates that the values of variables declared in the Function procedure are preserved between calls.

➤ Function: Required. Indicates the beginning of a procedure that returns a value or other data.

➤ *name*: Required. Any valid Function procedure name, which must follow the same rules as a variable name.

➤ *arglist*: Optional. A list of one or more variables that represent arguments passed to the Function procedure. The arguments are enclosed in parentheses. Use a comma to separate pairs of arguments.

➤ *type*: Optional. The data type returned by the Function procedure.

➤ *instructions*: Optional. Any number of valid VBA instructions.

➤ Exit Function: Optional. A statement that forces an immediate exit from the Function procedure before its completion.

➤ End Function: Required. A keyword that indicates the end of the Function procedure.

A key point to remember about a custom function written in VBA is that a value is always assigned to the function's name a minimum of one time, generally when it has completed execution.

To create a custom function, start by inserting a VBA module. You can use an existing module, as long as it's a normal VBA module. Enter the keyword Function, followed by the function name and a list of its arguments (if any) in parentheses. You can also declare the data type of the return value by using the As keyword (this step is optional but recommended). Insert the VBA code that performs the work, making sure that the appropriate value is assigned to the term corresponding to the function name at least once in the body of the Function procedure. End the function with an End Function statement.

Function names must adhere to the same rules as variable names. If you plan to use your custom function in a worksheet formula, be careful if the function name is also a cell address. For example, if you use something such as ABC123 as a function name, you can't use the function in a worksheet formula because ABC123 is a cell address. If you do so, Excel displays a #REF! error.

The best advice is to avoid using function names that are also cell references, including named ranges. And avoid using function names that correspond to Excel's built-in function names. In the case of a function name conflict, Excel always uses its built-in function.

A function's scope

In Chapter 7, I discuss the concept of a procedure's scope (public or private). The same discussion applies to functions: A function's scope determines whether it can be called by procedures in other modules or in worksheets.

Here are a few things to keep in mind about a function's scope:

➤ If you don't declare a function's scope, its default scope is Public.

➤ Functions declared As Private don't appear in Excel's Insert Function dialog box. Therefore, when you create a function that should be used only in a VBA procedure, you should declare it Private so that users don't try to use it in a formula.

➤ If your VBA code needs to call a function that's defined in another workbook, set up a reference to the other workbook by choosing the Visual Basic Editor (VBE) Tools➔References command.

➤ You do not have to establish a reference if the function is defined in an add-in. Such a function is available for use in all workbooks.

Executing function procedures

Although you can execute a Sub procedure in many ways, you can execute a Function procedure in only four ways:

➤ Call it from another procedure

➤ Use it in a worksheet formula

➤ Use it in a formula that's used to specify conditional formatting

➤ Call it from the VBE Immediate window

From a procedure

You can call custom functions from a VBA procedure the same way that you call built-in functions. For example, after you define a function called SUMARRAY, you can enter a statement like the following:

```
Total = SUMARRAY(MyArray)
```

This statement executes the SUMARRAY function with MyArray as its argument, returns the function's result, and assigns it to the Total variable.

You also can use the Run method of the Application object. Here's an example:

```
Total = Application.Run ("SUMARRAY", "MyArray")
```

The first argument for the Run method is the function name. Subsequent arguments represent the arguments for the function. The arguments for the Run method can be literal strings (as shown in the preceding), numbers, expressions, or variables.

In a worksheet formula

Using custom functions in a worksheet formula is like using built-in functions except that you must ensure that Excel can locate the Function procedure. If the Function procedure is in the same workbook, you don't have to do anything special. If it's in a different workbook, you may have to tell Excel where to find it.

You can do so in three ways:

> **Precede the function name with a file reference.** For example, if you want to use a function called COUNTNAMES that's defined in an open workbook named Myfuncs.xlsm, you can use the following reference:

```
=Myfuncs.xlsm!COUNTNAMES(A1:A1000)
```

If you insert the function with the Insert Function dialog box, the workbook reference is inserted automatically.

> **Set up a reference to the workbook.** You do so by choosing the VBE Tools➜References command. If the function is defined in a referenced workbook, you don't need to use the worksheet name. Even when the dependent workbook is assigned as a reference, the Paste Function dialog box continues to insert the workbook reference (although it's not necessary).

> **Create an add-in.** When you create an add-in from a workbook that has Function procedures, you don't need to use the file reference when you use one of the functions in a formula. The add-in must be installed, however. I discuss add-ins in Chapter 19.

You'll notice that unlike Sub procedures, your Function procedures don't appear in the Macro dialog box when you issue the Developer➜Code➜Macros command. In addition, you can't choose a function when you issue the VBE Run➜Sub/UserForm command (or press F5) if the cursor is located in a Function procedure. (You get the Macro dialog box that lets you choose a macro to run.) Therefore, you need to do a bit of extra up-front work to test your functions while you're developing them. One approach is to set up a simple procedure that calls the function. If the function is designed to be used in worksheet formulas, you'll want to enter a simple formula to test it.

In a conditional formatting formula

When you specify conditional formatting, one of the options is to create a formula. The formula must be a logical formula (that is, it must return either TRUE or FALSE). If the formula returns TRUE, the condition is met and formatting is applied to the cell.

You can use custom VBA functions in your conditional formatting formulas. For example, here's a simple VBA function that returns TRUE if its argument is a cell that contains a formula:

```
Function CELLHASFORMULA(cell) As Boolean
    CELLHASFORMULA = cell.HasFormula
End Function
```

After defining this function in a VBA module, you can set up a conditional formatting rule so that cells that contain a formula contain different formatting:

1. Select the range that will contain the conditional formatting.

    For example, select A1:G20.

2. Choose Home➜Styles➜Conditional Formatting➜New Rule.

3. In the New Formatting Rule dialog box, select the option labeled Use a Formula to Determine Which Cells to Format.

4. Enter this formula in the formula box — but make sure that the cell reference argument corresponds to the upper-left cell in the range that you selected in Step 1:

    ```
    =CELLHASFORMULA(A1)
    ```

5. Click the Format button to specify the formatting for cells that meet this condition.

6. Click OK to apply the conditional formatting rule to the selected range.

Cells in the range that contain a formula will display the formatting you specified. In the New Formatting Rule dialog box shown in Figure 8-3, I am specifying a custom function in a formula.

Note   ISFORMULA, one of the new worksheet functions introduced in Excel 2013, works exactly like the custom CELLHASFORMULA function. But the CELLHASFORMULA function is still useful if you plan to share your workbook with others who haven't upgraded to Excel 2013.

Figure 8-3: Using a custom VBA function for conditional formatting.

From the VBE Immediate Window

The final way to call a Function procedure is from the VBE Immediate window. This method is generally used only for testing. Figure 8-4 shows an example. The ? character is a shortcut for print.

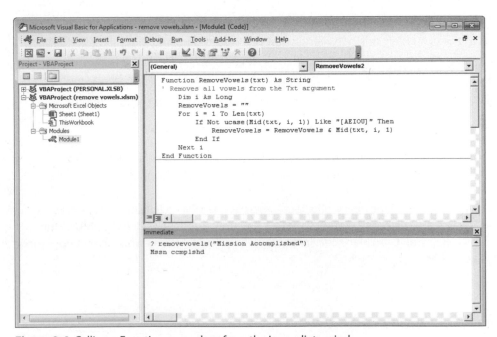

Figure 8-4: Calling a Function procedure from the Immediate window.

Reinventing the wheel

Just for fun, I wrote my own version of Excel's UPPER function (which converts a string to all upper-case) and named it UpCase:

```
Function UPCASE(InString As String) As String
'    Converts its argument to all uppercase.
    Dim StringLength As Long
    Dim i As Long
    Dim ASCIIVal As Long
    Dim CharVal As Long

    StringLength = Len(InString)
    UPCASE = InString
    For i = 1 To StringLength
        ASCIIVal = Asc(Mid(InString, i, 1))
        CharVal = 0
        If ASCIIVal >= 97 And ASCIIVal <= 122 Then
            CharVal = -32
            Mid(UPCASE, i, 1) = Chr(ASCIIVal + CharVal)
        End If
    Next i
End Function
```

Note: A workbook that contains this function is on this book's website, in a file named upper case.xlsm.

Note that I resisted the urge to take the easy route — using the VBA UCase function.

I was curious to see how the custom function differed from the built-in function, so I created a worksheet that called the function 20,000 times, using random names. The worksheet took about 20 seconds to calculate. I then substituted Excel's UPPER function and ran the test again. The recalculation time was virtually instantaneous. I don't claim that my UpCase function is the optimal algorithm for this task, but it's safe to say that a custom function will never match the speed of Excel's built-in functions.

For another example of reinventing the wheel, see the section "Emulating Excel's SUM Function," later in this chapter.

Function Arguments

Keep in mind the following points about Function procedure arguments:

➤ Arguments can be variables (including arrays), constants, literals, or expressions.

➤ Some functions don't have arguments.

➤ Some functions have a fixed number of required arguments (from 1 to 60).

➤ Some functions have a combination of required and optional arguments.

Note

If your formula uses a custom worksheet function and it returns #VALUE!, your function has an error. The error may be caused by logical errors in your code or by passing incorrect arguments to the function. See the section "Debugging Functions," later in this chapter.

Function Examples

In this section, I present a series of examples that demonstrate how to use arguments effectively with functions. By the way, this discussion applies also to Sub procedures.

Functions with no argument

Like Sub procedures, Function procedures need not have arguments. Excel, for example, has a few built-in functions that don't use arguments, including RAND, TODAY, and NOW. You can create similar functions.

This section contains examples of functions that don't use an argument.

On the Web

A workbook that contains these functions is available on this book's website. The file is named no argument.xlsm.

Here's a simple example of a function that doesn't use an argument. The following function returns the UserName property of the Application object. This is the name that appears in the Excel Options dialog box (General tab) and is stored in the Windows Registry.

```
Function USER()
'   Returns the name of the current user
    USER = Application.UserName
End Function
```

When you enter the following formula, the cell returns the name of the current user:

```
=USER()
```

When you use a function with no arguments in a worksheet formula, you must include a set of empty parentheses. This requirement isn't necessary if you call the function in a VBA procedure, although including the empty parentheses does make it clear that you're calling a function.

There is no need to use this function in another procedure because you can simply access the UserName property directly in your code.

The USER function demonstrates how you can create a *wrapper* function that returns a property or the result of a VBA function. Following are three additional wrapper functions that take no argument:

```
Function EXCELDIR() As String
'    Returns the directory in which Excel is installed
     EXCELDIR = Application.Path
End Function

Function SHEETCOUNT()
'    Returns the number of sheets in the workbook
     SHEETCOUNT = Application.Caller.Parent.Parent.Sheets.Count
End Function

Function SHEETNAME()
'    Returns the name of the worksheet
     SHEETNAME = Application.Caller.Parent.Name
End Function
```

You can probably think of other potentially useful wrapper functions. For example, you can write a function to display the template's location (Application.TemplatesPath), the default file location (Application.DefaultFilePath), and the version of Excel (Application.Version). Also, note that Excel 2013 introduced a new worksheet function, SHEETS, that makes the SHEETCOUNT function obsolete.

Here's another example of a function that doesn't take an argument. I used to use Excel's RAND function to quickly fill a range of cells with values. But I didn't like the fact that the random numbers changed whenever the worksheet was recalculated, so I converted the formulas to values.

Then I realized that I could create a custom function that returned random numbers that didn't change. I used the VBA built-in Rnd function, which returns a random number between 0 and 1. The custom function follows:

```
Function STATICRAND()
'    Returns a random number that doesn't
'    change when recalculated
     STATICRAND = Rnd()
End Function
```

If you want to generate a series of random integers between 0 and 1,000, you can use a formula such as this:

```
=INT(STATICRAND()*1000)
```

The values produced by this formula never change when the worksheet is calculated normally. However, you can force the formula to recalculate by pressing Ctrl+Alt+F9.

 # Controlling function recalculation

When you use a custom function in a worksheet formula, when is it recalculated?

Custom functions behave like Excel's built-in worksheet functions. Normally, a custom function is recalculated only when it needs to be — which is only when any of the function's arguments are modified. You can, however, force functions to recalculate more frequently. Adding the following statement to a Function procedure makes the function recalculate whenever the sheet is recalculated. If you're using automatic calculation mode, a calculation occurs whenever any cell is changed.

```
Application.Volatile True
```

The Volatile method of the Application object has one argument (either True or False). Marking a Function procedure as volatile forces the function to be calculated whenever recalculation occurs for any cell in the worksheet.

For example, the custom STATICRAND function can be changed to emulate Excel's RAND function using the Volatile method:

```
Function NONSTATICRAND()
'    Returns a random number that changes with each calculation
    Application.Volatile True
    NONSTATICRAND = Rnd()
End Function
```

Using the False argument of the Volatile method causes the function to be recalculated only when one or more of its arguments change as a result of a recalculation. (If a function has no arguments, this method has no effect.)

To force an entire recalculation, including nonvolatile custom functions, press Ctrl+Alt+F9. This key combination will, for example, generate new random numbers for the STATICRAND function presented in this chapter.

A function with one argument

This section describes a function for sales managers who need to calculate the commissions earned by their sales forces. The calculations in this example are based on the following table:

Monthly Sales	Commission Rate
0–$9,999	8.0%
$10,000–$19,999	10.5%
$20,000–$39,999	12.0%
$40,000+	14.0%

Note that the commission rate is nonlinear and also depends on the month's total sales. Employees who sell more earn a higher commission rate.

You can calculate commissions for various sales amounts entered in a worksheet in several ways. If you're not thinking too clearly, you can waste lots of time and come up with a lengthy formula such as this one:

```
=IF(AND(A1>=0,A1<=9999.99),A1*0.08,
  IF(AND(A1>=10000,A1<=19999.99),A1*0.105,
  IF(AND(A1>=20000,A1<=39999.99),A1*0.12,
  IF(A1>=40000,A1*0.14,0))))
```

This approach is bad for a couple of reasons. First, the formula is overly complex, making it difficult to understand. Second, the values are hard-coded into the formula, making the formula difficult to modify.

A better (non-VBA) approach is to use a lookup table function to compute the commissions. For example, the following formula uses VLOOKUP to retrieve the commission value from a range named Table and multiplies that value by the value in cell A1:

```
=VLOOKUP(A1,Table,2)*A1
```

Yet another approach (which eliminates the need to use a lookup table) is to create a custom function such as the following:

```
Function COMMISSION(Sales)
    Const Tier1 = 0.08
    Const Tier2 = 0.105
    Const Tier3 = 0.12
    Const Tier4 = 0.14
'    Calculates sales commissions
```

continued

```
    Select Case Sales
        Case 0 To 9999.99: COMMISSION = Sales * Tier1
        Case 10000 To 19999.99: COMMISSION = Sales * Tier2
        Case 20000 To 39999.99: COMMISSION = Sales * Tier3
        Case Is >= 40000: COMMISSION = Sales * Tier4
    End Select
End Function
```

After you enter this function in a VBA module, you can use it in a worksheet formula or call the function from other VBA procedures.

Entering the following formula into a cell produces a result of 3,000; the amount (25,000) qualifies for a commission rate of 12 percent:

```
=COMMISSION(25000)
```

Even if you don't need custom functions in a worksheet, creating Function procedures can make your VBA coding much simpler. For example, if your VBA procedure calculates sales commissions, you can use the same function and call it from a VBA procedure. Here's a tiny procedure that asks the user for a sales amount and then uses the COMMISSION function to calculate the commission due:

```
Sub CalcComm()
    Dim Sales as Long
    Sales = InputBox("Enter Sales:")
    MsgBox "The commission is " & COMMISSION(Sales)
End Sub
```

The CalcComm procedure starts by displaying an input box that asks for the sales amount. Then it displays a message box with the calculated sales commission for that amount.

This Sub procedure works, but it's crude. Following is an enhanced version with a bit of error handling. It also displays formatted values and keeps looping until the user clicks No (see Figure 8-5).

```
Sub CalcComm()
    Dim Sales As Long
    Dim Msg As String, Ans As String

'   Prompt for sales amount
    Sales = Val(InputBox("Enter Sales:", _
     "Sales Commission Calculator"))

'   Exit if canceled
    If Sales = 0 Then Exit Sub
```

```
'    Build the Message
    Msg = "Sales Amount:" & vbTab & Format(Sales, "$#,##0.00")
    Msg = Msg & vbCrLf & "Commission:" & vbTab
    Msg = Msg & Format(COMMISSION(Sales), "$#,##0.00")
    Msg = Msg & vbCrLf & vbCrLf & "Another?"

'    Display the result and prompt for another
    Ans = MsgBox(Msg, vbYesNo, "Sales Commission Calculator")
    If Ans = vbYes Then CalcComm
End Sub
```

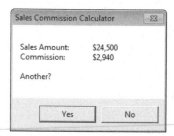

Figure 8-5: Using a function to display the result of a calculation.

This function uses two VBA built-in constants: vbTab represents a tab (to space the output), and vbCrLf specifies a carriage return and line feed (to skip to the next line). VBA's Format function displays a value in a specified format (in this case, with a dollar sign, a comma, and two decimal places).

In both examples, the Commission function must be available in the active workbook; otherwise, Excel displays an error message saying that the function isn't defined.

 ## Use arguments, not cell references

All ranges that are used in a custom function should be passed as arguments. Consider the following function, which returns the value in A1, multiplied by 2:

```
Function DOUBLECELL()
    DOUBLECELL = Range("A1") * 2
End Function
```

Although this function works, at times it may return an incorrect result. Excel's calculation engine can't account for ranges in your code that aren't passed as arguments. Therefore, in some cases, all precedents may not be calculated before the function's value is returned. The DOUBLECELL function should be written as follows, with A1 passed as the argument:

```
Function DOUBLECELL(cell)
    DOUBLECELL = cell * 2
End Function
```

A function with two arguments

Imagine that the aforementioned hypothetical sales managers implement a new policy to help reduce turnover: The total commission paid is increased by 1 percent for every year that the salesperson has been with the company.

I modified the custom COMMISSION function (defined in the preceding section) so that it takes two arguments. The new argument represents the number of years. Call this new function COMMISSION2:

```
Function COMMISSION2(Sales, Years)
'    Calculates sales commissions based on
'    years in service
     Const Tier1 = 0.08
     Const Tier2 = 0.105
     Const Tier3 = 0.12
     Const Tier4 = 0.14
     Select Case Sales
         Case 0 To 9999.99: COMMISSION2 = Sales * Tier1
         Case 10000 To 19999.99: COMMISSION2 = Sales * Tier2
         Case 20000 To 39999.99: COMMISSION2 = Sales * Tier3
         Case Is >= 40000: COMMISSION2 = Sales * Tier4
     End Select
     COMMISSION2 = COMMISSION2 + (COMMISSION2 * Years / 100)
End Function
```

Pretty simple, eh? I just added the second argument (Years) to the Function statement and included an additional computation that adjusts the commission.

Here's an example of how you can write a formula using this function (it assumes that the sales amount is in cell A1 and the number of years the salesperson has worked is in cell B1):

```
=COMMISSION2(A1,B1)
```

On the Web

All commission-related examples are available on this book's website, in a file named **commission functions.xlsm.**

A function with an array argument

A Function procedure also can accept one or more arrays as arguments, process the array(s), and return a single value. The array can also consist of a range of cells.

The following function accepts an array as its argument and returns the sum of its elements:

```
Function SUMARRAY(List) As Double
    Dim Item As Variant
    SumArray = 0
    For Each Item In List
        If WorksheetFunction.IsNumber(Item) Then _
            SUMARRAY = SUMARRAY + Item
    Next Item
End Function
```

Excel's ISNUMBER function checks to see whether each element is a number before adding it to the total. Adding this simple error-checking statement eliminates the type-mismatch error that occurs when you try to perform arithmetic with something other than a number.

The following procedure demonstrates how to call this function from a Sub procedure. The MakeList procedure creates a 100-element array and assigns a random number to each element. Then the MsgBox function displays the sum of the values in the array by calling the SUMARRAY function.

```
Sub MakeList()
    Dim Nums(1 To 100) As Double
    Dim i As Integer
    For i = 1 To 100
        Nums(i) = Rnd * 1000
    Next i
    MsgBox SUMARRAY(Nums)
End Sub
```

Note that the SUMARRAY function doesn't declare the data type of its argument (it's a variant). Because it's not declared as a specific numeric type, the function also works in your worksheet formulas in which the argument is a Range object. For example, the following formula returns the sum of the values in A1:C10:

```
=SUMARRAY(A1:C10)
```

You might notice that, when used in a worksheet formula, the SUMARRAY function works very much like Excel's SUM function. One difference, however, is that SUMARRAY doesn't accept multiple arguments. Understand that this example is for educational purposes only. Using the SUMARRAY function in a formula offers no advantages over the Excel SUM function.

On the Web

This example, named array argument.xlsm, is available on this book's website.

UPPERCASE functions?

You've probably noticed that Excel's built-in worksheet functions always use uppercase. Even if you enter a function naming using lowercase characters, Excel converts it to uppercase.

When you create custom worksheet formulas, you can use uppercase, lowercase, or mixed case. When I create functions that are intended to be used in worksheet formulas, I like to make them uppercase so that they match Excel's style.

Sometimes, however, when I enter a formula that uses a custom function, Excel will not match the case that I used in the VBA code. This behavior was a mystery, but I figured out a workaround. Assume you have a function named MYFUNC, and its function declaration uses uppercase for the name. But when you type the function in a formula, Excel does *not* display it in uppercase. Here's how to fix it.

In Excel, choose Formulas➜Defined Names➜Define Name, and then create a name called MYFUNC (in uppercase letters). What the name refers to doesn't matter. Now, all formulas that use the MYFUNC function will display an error (as expected). But note that the formula now displays MYFUNC in uppercase characters.

The final step is to choose Formulas➜Defined Names➜Name Manager, and then *delete* the MYFUNC name. The formulas will no longer display an error — and they will retain uppercase letters for the function name.

I can't tell you *why* this trick works, but it does seem to work every time.

A function with optional arguments

Many of Excel's built-in worksheet functions use optional arguments. An example is the LEFT function, which returns characters from the left side of a string. Its syntax is

```
LEFT(text,num_chars)
```

The first argument is required, but the second is optional. If the optional argument is omitted for the LEFT function, Excel assumes a value of 1. Therefore, the following two formulas return the same result:

```
=LEFT(A1,1)
=LEFT(A1)
```

The custom functions that you develop in VBA also can have optional arguments. You specify an optional argument by preceding the argument's name with the keyword Optional. In the argument list, optional arguments must appear after any required arguments.

Following is a simple function example that returns the user's name. The function's argument is optional.

```
Function USER(Optional UpperCase As Variant)
    If IsMissing(UpperCase) Then UpperCase = False
    USER = Application.UserName
    If UpperCase Then USER = UCase(USER)
End Function
```

If the argument is False or omitted, the user's name is returned without any changes. If the argument is True, the user's name is converted to uppercase (using the VBA UCase function) before it's returned. Note that the first statement in the procedure uses the VBA IsMissing function to determine whether the argument was supplied. If the argument is missing, the statement sets the UpperCase variable to False (the default value).

All the following formulas are valid, and the first two produce the same result:

```
=USER()
=USER(False)
=USER(True)
```

Note

If you need to determine whether an optional argument was passed to a function, you must declare the optional argument as a Variant data type. Then you can use the IsMissing function in the procedure, as demonstrated in this example. In other words, the argument for the IsMissing function must always be a Variant data type.

The following is another example of a custom function that uses an optional argument. This function randomly chooses one cell from an input range and returns that cell's contents. If the second argument is True, the selected value changes whenever the worksheet is recalculated (that is, the function is made volatile). If the second argument is False (or omitted), the function isn't recalculated unless one of the cells in the input range is modified.

```
Function DRAWONE(Rng As Variant, Optional Recalc As Variant = False)
'    Chooses one cell at random from a range

'    Make function volatile if Recalc is True
    Application.Volatile Recalc

'    Determine a random cell
    DRAWONE = Rng(Int((Rng.Count) * Rnd + 1))
End Function
```

Note that the second argument for DRAWONE includes the Optional keyword, along with a default value.

All the following formulas are valid, and the first two have the same effect:

```
=DRAWONE(A1:A100)
=DRAWONE(A1:A100,False)
=DRAWONE(A1:A100,True)
```

This function might be useful for choosing lottery numbers, picking a winner from a list of names, and so on.

On the Web

This function is available on this book's website. The filename is draw.xlsm.

A function that returns a VBA array

VBA includes a useful function called Array. The Array function returns a variant that contains an array (that is, multiple values). If you're familiar with array formulas in Excel, you have a head start on understanding VBA's Array function. You enter an array formula into a cell by pressing Ctrl+Shift+Enter. Excel inserts curly braces around the formula to indicate that it's an array formula.

Cross-Ref

See Chapter 2 for more details on array formulas.

Note

It's important to understand that the array returned by the Array function isn't the same as a normal array made up of elements of the Variant data type. In other words, a variant array isn't the same as an array of variants.

The MONTHNAMES function, which follows, is a simple example that uses VBA's Array function in a custom function:

```
Function MONTHNAMES ()
    MONTHNAMES = Array("Jan", "Feb", "Mar", "Apr","May", "Jun", _
        "Jul", "Aug", "Sep", "Oct", "Nov", "Dec")
End Function
```

The MONTHNAMES function returns a horizontal array of month names. You can create a multicell array formula that uses the MONTHNAMES function. Here's how to use it: Make sure that the function code is present in a VBA module. Next, in a worksheet, select multiple cells in a row (start by selecting 12 cells). Then enter the formula that follows (without the braces) and press Ctrl+Shift+Enter:

```
{=MONTHNAMES()}
```

What if you'd like to generate a vertical list of month names? No problem; just select a vertical range, enter the following formula (without the braces), and then press Ctrl+Shift+Enter:

```
{=TRANSPOSE(MONTHNAMES())}
```

This formula uses the Excel TRANSPOSE function to convert the horizontal array to a vertical array.

The following example is a variation on the MONTHNAMES function:

```
Function MonthNames(Optional MIndex)
    Dim AllNames As Variant
    Dim MonthVal As Long
    AllNames = Array("Jan", "Feb", "Mar", "Apr", "May", "Jun", _
        "Jul", "Aug", "Sep", "Oct", "Nov", "Dec")
    If IsMissing(MIndex) Then
        MONTHNAMES = AllNames
    Else
        Select Case MIndex
            Case Is >= 1
                Determine month value (for example, 13=1)
                MonthVal = ((MIndex - 1) Mod 12)
                MONTHNAMES = AllNames(MonthVal)
            Case Is <= 0 ' Vertical array
                MONTHNAMES = Application.Transpose(AllNames)
        End Select
    End If
End Function
```

Note that I use the VBA IsMissing function to test for a missing argument. In this situation, it isn't possible to specify the default value for the missing argument in the argument list of the function because the default value is defined in the function. You can use the IsMissing function only if the optional argument is a variant.

This enhanced function uses an optional argument that works as follows:

> ➤ **If the argument is missing,** the function returns a horizontal array of month names.

> ➤ **If the argument is less than or equal to 0,** the function returns a vertical array of month names. It uses Excel's TRANSPOSE function to convert the array.

> ➤ **If the argument is greater than or equal to 1,** the function returns the month name that corresponds to the argument value.

Note

This procedure uses the Mod operator to determine the month value. The Mod operator returns the remainder after dividing the first operand by the second. Keep in mind that the AllNames array is zero-based and that indices range from 0 to 11. In the statement that uses the Mod operator, 1 is subtracted from the function's argument. Therefore, an argument of 13 returns 0 (corresponding to Jan), and an argument of 24 returns 11 (corresponding to Dec).

You can use this function in a number of ways, as illustrated in Figure 8-6.

A1			✕ ✓ *fx*	{=MONTHNAMES()}									
	A	B	C	D	E	F	G	H	I	J	K	L	M
1	Jan	Feb	Mar	Apr	May	Jun	Jul	Aug	Sep	Oct	Nov	Dec	
2													
3	1	Jan		Jan		Mar							
4	2	Feb		Feb									
5	3	Mar		Mar									
6	4	Apr		Apr									
7	5	May		May									
8	6	Jun		Jun									
9	7	Jul		Jul									
10	8	Aug		Aug									
11	9	Sep		Sep									
12	10	Oct		Oct									
13	11	Nov		Nov									
14	12	Dec		Dec									
15													
16													

Sheet1   ⊕

Figure 8-6: Different ways of passing an array or a single value to a worksheet.

Range A1:L1 contains the following formula entered as an array. Start by selecting A1:L1, enter the formula (without the braces), and then press Ctrl+Shift+Enter.

```
{=MONTHNAMES()}
```

Range A3:A14 contains integers from 1 to 12. Cell B3 contains the following (nonarray) formula, which was copied to the 11 cells below it:

```
=MONTHNAMES(A3)
```

Range D3:D14 contains the following formula entered as an array:

```
{=MONTHNAMES(-1)}
```

Cell F3 contains this (nonarray) formula:

```
=MONTHNAMES(3)
```

Note

To enter an array formula, you must press Ctrl+Shift+Enter (and don't enter the curly braces).

Note

The lower bound of an array, created using the Array function, is determined by the lower bound specified with the Option Base statement at the top of the module. If there is no Option Base statement, the default lower bound is 0.

On the Web

A workbook that demonstrates the MONTHNAMES function is available on this book's website. The file is named month names.xslm.

A function that returns an error value

In some cases, you might want your custom function to return a particular error value. Consider the REMOVEVOWELS function, which I presented earlier in this chapter:

```
Function REMOVEVOWELS(Txt) As String
' Removes all vowels from the Txt argument
    Dim i As Long
    RemoveVowels = ""
    For i = 1 To Len(Txt)
        If Not UCase(Mid(Txt, i, 1)) Like "[AEIOU]" Then
            REMOVEVOWELS = REMOVEVOWELS & Mid(Txt, i, 1)
        End If
    Next i
End Function
```

When used in a worksheet formula, this function removes the vowels from its single-cell argument. If the argument is a numeric value, this function returns the value as a string. You may prefer that the function returns an error value (#N/A), rather than the numeric value converted to a string.

You may be tempted simply to assign a string that looks like an Excel formula error value. For example:

```
REMOVEVOWELS = "#N/A"
```

Although the string *looks* like an error value, other formulas that may reference it don't treat it as such. To return a *real* error value from a function, use the VBA CVErr function, which converts an error number to a real error.

Fortunately, VBA has built-in constants for the errors that you want to return from a custom function. These errors are Excel formula error values and not VBA runtime error values. These constants are as follows:

- ➤ xlErrDiv0 (for #DIV/0!)
- ➤ xlErrNA (for #N/A)
- ➤ xlErrName (for #NAME?)
- ➤ xlErrNull (for #NULL!)
- ➤ xlErrNum (for #NUM!)
- ➤ xlErrRef (for #REF!)
- ➤ xlErrValue (for #VALUE!)

To return a #N/A error from a custom function, you can use a statement like this:

```
REMOVEVOWELS = CVErr(xlErrNA)
```

The revised REMOVEVOWELS function follows. This function uses an If-Then construct to take a different action if the argument isn't text. It uses Excel's ISTEXT function to determine whether the argument is text. If the argument is text, the function proceeds normally. If the cell doesn't contain text (or is empty), the function returns the #N/A error.

```
Function REMOVEVOWELS (Txt) As Variant
' Removes all vowels from the Txt argument
' Returns #VALUE if Txt is not a string
    Dim i As Long
    RemoveVowels = ""
    If Application.WorksheetFunction.IsText(Txt) Then
        For i = 1 To Len(Txt)
            If Not UCase(Mid(Txt, i, 1)) Like "[AEIOU]" Then
                REMOVEVOWELS = REMOVEVOWELS & Mid(Txt, i, 1)
            End If
        Next i
    Else
        REMOVEVOWELS = CVErr(xlErrNA)
    End If
End Function
```

Note

Note that I also changed the data type for the function's return value. Because the function can now return something other than a string, I changed the data type to Variant.

A function with an indefinite number of arguments

Some Excel worksheet functions take an indefinite number of arguments. A familiar example is the SUM function, which has the following syntax:

```
SUM(number1,number2,...)
```

The first argument is required, but you can specify as many as 254 additional arguments. Here's an example of a SUM function with four range arguments:

```
=SUM(A1:A5,C1:C5,E1:E5,G1:G5)
```

You can even mix and match the argument types. For example, the following example uses three arguments: the first is a range, the second is a value, and the third is an expression.

```
=SUM(A1:A5,12,24*3)
```

You can create Function procedures that have an indefinite number of arguments. The trick is to use an array as the last (or only) argument, preceded by the keyword ParamArray.

Note

ParamArray can apply only to the last argument in the procedure's argument list. It's always a Variant data type and always an optional argument (although you don't use the Optional keyword).

Following is a function that can have any number of single-value arguments. (It doesn't work with multicell range arguments.) It simply returns the sum of the arguments.

```
Function SIMPLESUM(ParamArray arglist() As Variant) As Double
    For Each arg In arglist
        SIMPLESUM = SIMPLESUM + arg
    Next arg
End Function
```

To modify this function so that it works with multicell range arguments, you need to add another loop, which processes each cell in each of the arguments:

```
Function SIMPLESUM (ParamArray arglist() As Variant) As Double
    Dim cell As Range
    For Each arg In arglist
        For Each cell In arg
            SIMPLESUM = SIMPLESUM + cell
        Next cell
    Next arg
End Function
```

The SIMPLESUM function is similar to Excel's SUM function, but it's not nearly as flexible. Try it by using various types of arguments, and you'll see that it fails if any of the cells contain a nonvalue, or even if you use a literal value for an argument.

Emulating Excel's SUM function

In this section, I present a custom function called MYSUM. Unlike the SIMPLESUM function listed in the preceding section, the MYSUM function emulates Excel's SUM function (almost) perfectly.

Before you look at the code for MYSUM, take a minute to think about the Excel SUM function. It is versatile: It can have as many as 255 arguments (even "missing" arguments), and the arguments can be numerical values, cells, ranges, text representations of numbers, logical values, and even embedded functions. For example, consider the following formula:

```
=SUM(B1,5,"6",,TRUE,SQRT(4),A1:A5,D:D,C2*C3)
```

This perfectly valid formula contains all the following types of arguments, listed here in the order of their presentation:

- ➤ A single-cell reference
- ➤ A literal value
- ➤ A string that looks like a value
- ➤ A missing argument
- ➤ A logical TRUE value
- ➤ An expression that uses another function
- ➤ A simple range reference

➤ A range reference that includes an entire column

➤ An expression that calculates the product of two cells

The MYSUM function (see Listing 8-1) handles all these argument types.

On the Web

A workbook containing the MYSUM function is available on this book's website. The file is named mysum function.xlsm.

Listing 8-1: MYSUM Function

```
Function MYSUM(ParamArray args() As Variant) As Variant
' Emulates Excel's SUM function

' Variable declarations
  Dim i As Variant
  Dim TempRange As Range, cell As Range
  Dim ECode As String
  Dim m, n
  MYSUM = 0

' Process each argument
  For i = 0 To UBound(args)
'   Skip missing arguments
    If Not IsMissing(args(i)) Then
'     What type of argument is it?
      Select Case TypeName(args(i))
        Case "Range"
'         Create temp range to handle full row or column ranges
          Set TempRange = Intersect(args(i).Parent.UsedRange, args(i))
          For Each cell In TempRange
            If IsError(cell) Then
              MYSUM = cell ' return the error
              Exit Function
            End If
            If cell = True Or cell = False Then
              MYSUM = MYSUM + 0
            Else
              If IsNumeric(cell) Or IsDate(cell) Then _
                MYSUM = MYSUM + cell
              End If
            End If
          Next cell
        Case "Variant()"
          n = args(i)
          For m = LBound(n) To UBound(n)
            MYSUM = MYSUM(MYSUM, n(m)) 'recursive call
          Next m
```

continued

Listing 8-1: MYSUM Function *(continued)*

```
        Case "Null"  'ignore it
        Case "Error" 'return the error
          MYSUM = args(i)
          Exit Function
        Case "Boolean"
          Check for literal TRUE and compensate
          If args(i) = "True" Then MYSUM = MYSUM + 1
        Case "Date"
          MYSUM = MYSUM + args(i)
        Case Else
          MYSUM = MYSUM + args(i)
      End Select
    End If
  Next i
End Function
```

Figure 8-7 shows a workbook with various formulas that use SUM (column E) and MYSUM (column G). As you can see, the functions return identical results.

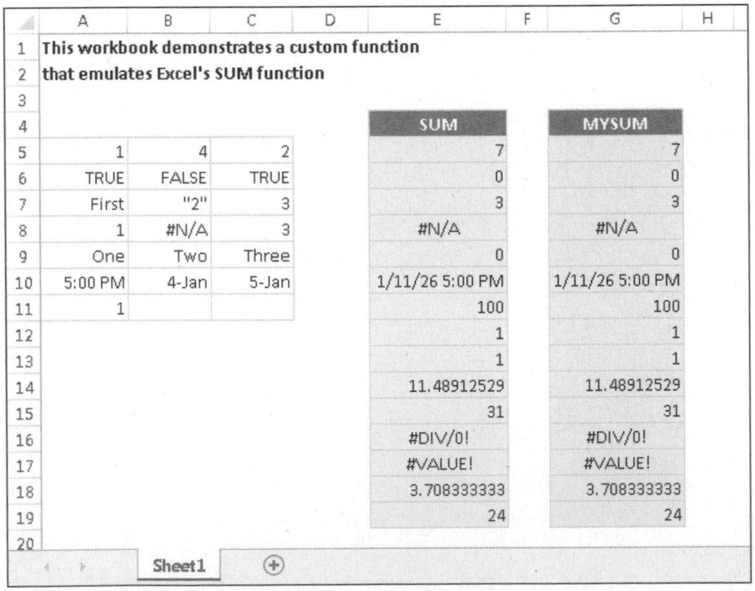

	A	B	C	D	E	F	G	H
1	This workbook demonstrates a custom function							
2	that emulates Excel's SUM function							
3								
4					SUM		MYSUM	
5	1	4	2		7		7	
6	TRUE	FALSE	TRUE		0		0	
7	First	"2"	3		3		3	
8	1	#N/A	3		#N/A		#N/A	
9	One	Two	Three		0		0	
10	5:00 PM	4-Jan	5-Jan		1/11/26 5:00 PM		1/11/26 5:00 PM	
11	1				100		100	
12					1		1	
13					1		1	
14					11.48912529		11.48912529	
15					31		31	
16					#DIV/0!		#DIV/0!	
17					#VALUE!		#VALUE!	
18					3.708333333		3.708333333	
19					24		24	
20								

Sheet1 ⊕

Figure 8-7: Comparing SUM with MYSUM.

MYSUM is a close emulation of the SUM function, but it's not perfect. It cannot handle operations on arrays. For example, this array formula returns the sum of the squared values in range A1:A4:

```
{=SUM(A:A4^2)}
```

This formula returns a #VALUE! error:

```
{=MYSUM(A1:A4^2)}
```

If you're interested in learning how the MYSUM function works, create a formula that uses the function. Then set a breakpoint in the code and step through the statements line by line. (See the section "Debugging Functions," later in this chapter.) Try this for several different argument types, and you'll soon have a good feel for how the MYSUM function works.

As you study the code for MYSUM, keep the following points in mind:

➤ Missing arguments (determined by the IsMissing function) are simply ignored.

➤ The procedure uses the VBA TypeName function to determine the type of argument (Range, Error, and so on). Each argument type is handled differently.

➤ For a range argument, the function loops through each cell in the range, determines the type of data in the cell, and (if appropriate) adds its value to a running total.

➤ The data type for the function is Variant because the function needs to return an error if any of its arguments are an error value.

➤ If an argument contains an error (for example, #DIV/0!), the MYSUM function simply returns the error — just as Excel's SUM function does.

➤ Excel's SUM function considers a text string to have a value of 0 unless it appears as a literal argument (that is, as an actual value, not a variable). Therefore, MYSUM adds the cell's value only if it can be evaluated as a number. (The VBA IsNumeric function is used to determine whether a string can be evaluated as a number.)

➤ For range arguments, the function uses the Intersect method to create a temporary range that consists of the intersection of the range and the sheet's used range. This technique handles cases in which a range argument consists of a complete row or column, which would take forever to evaluate.

You may be curious about the relative speeds of SUM and MYSUM. The MYSUM function, of course, is much slower, but just how much slower depends on the speed of your system and the formulas themselves. On my system, a worksheet with 5,000 SUM formulas recalculates instantly. After I replace the SUM functions with MySum functions, the recalculation takes about eight seconds. MYSUM may be improved a bit, but it can never come close to SUM's speed.

By the way, I hope you understand that the point of this example is *not* to create a new SUM function. Rather, it demonstrates how to create custom worksheet functions that look and work like those built into Excel.

Extended Date Functions

A common complaint among Excel users is the inability to work with dates prior to 1900. For example, genealogists often use Excel to keep track of birth and death dates. If either of those dates occurs in a year prior to 1900, calculating the number of years the person lived isn't possible.

I created a series of functions that take advantage of the fact that VBA can work with a much larger range of dates. The earliest date recognized by VBA is January 1, 0100.

Caution

Beware of calendar changes if you use dates prior to 1752. Differences between the historical American, British, Gregorian, and Julian calendars can result in inaccurate computations.

The functions are

> ➤ **XDATE(y,m,d,fmt):** Returns a date for a given year, month, and day. As an option, you can provide a date-formatting string.

> ➤ **XDATEADD(xdate1,days,fmt):** Adds a specified number of days to a date. As an option, you can provide a date-formatting string.

> ➤ **XDATEDIF(xdate1,xdate2):** Returns the number of days between two dates.

> ➤ **XDATEYEARDIF(xdate1,xdate2):** Returns the number of full years between two dates (useful for calculating ages).

> ➤ **XDATEYEAR(xdate1):** Returns the year of a date.

> ➤ **XDATEMONTH(xdate1):** Returns the month of a date.

> ➤ **XDATEDAY(xdate1):** Returns the day of a date.

> ➤ **XDATEDOW(xdate1):** Returns the day of the week of a date (as an integer between 1 and 7).

Figure 8-8 shows a workbook that uses some of these functions.

Keep in mind that the date returned by these functions is a *string*, not a real date. Therefore, you can't perform mathematical operations on the returned value using Excel's standard operators. You can, however, use the return value as an argument for other Extended Date functions.

The functions are surprisingly simple. For example, here's the listing for the XDATE function:

```
Function XDATE(y, m, d, Optional fmt As String) As String
    If IsMissing(fmt) Then fmt = "Short Date"
    XDATE = Format(DateSerial(y, m, d), fmt)
End Function
```

E11	▼	:	×	✓	*fx*	=XDATE(B11,C11,D11,"mmmm d, yyyy")		

▲	A	B	C	D	E	F	G	H
5								
6	President	Year	Month	Day	XDATE	XDATEDIF	XDATEYEARDIF	XDATEDOW
7	George Washington	1732	2	22	February 22, 1732	102,475	280	Friday
8	John Adams	1735	10	30	October 30, 1735	101,129	276	Sunday
9	Thomas Jefferson	1743	4	13	April 13, 1743	98,407	269	Saturday
10	James Madison	1751	3	16	March 16, 1751	95,513	261	Tuesday
11	James Monroe	1758	4	28	April 28, 1758	92,913	254	Friday
12	John Quincy Adams	1767	7	11	July 11, 1767	89,552	245	Saturday
13	Andrew Jackson	1767	3	15	March 15, 1767	89,670	245	Sunday
14	Martin Van Buren	1782	12	5	December 5, 1782	83,926	229	Thursday
15	William Henry Harrison	1773	2	9	February 9, 1773	87,512	239	Tuesday
16	John Tyler	1790	3	29	March 29, 1790	81,255	222	Monday
17	James K. Polk	1795	11	2	November 2, 1795	79,211	216	Monday
18	Zachary Taylor	1784	11	24	November 24, 1784	83,206	227	Wednesday
19	Millard Fillmore	1800	1	7	January 7, 1800	77,684	212	Tuesday
20	Franklin Pierce	1804	11	23	November 23, 1804	75,903	207	Friday
21	James Buchanan	1791	4	23	April 23, 1791	80,865	221	Saturday
22	Abraham Lincoln	1809	2	12	February 12, 1809	74,361	203	Sunday
23	Andrew Johnson	1808	12	29	December 29, 1808	74,406	203	Thursday
24	Ulysses S. Grant	1822	4	27	April 27, 1822	69,539	190	Saturday
25	Rutherford B. Hayes	1822	10	4	October 4, 1822	69,379	189	Friday
26	James A. Garfield	1831	11	19	November 19, 1831	66,046	180	Saturday

Sheet1   Sheet2   ⊕

Figure 8-8: The Extended Date functions used in formulas.

The arguments for XDATE are

➤ y: Required. A four-digit year (0100–9999).

➤ m: Required. A month number (1–12).

➤ d: Required. A day number (1–31).

➤ fmt: Optional. A date format string.

If the fmt argument is omitted, the date is displayed using the system's *short date* setting (as specified in the Windows Control Panel).

If the m or d argument exceeds a valid number, date rolls over into the next year or month. For example, a month of 13 is interpreted as January of the next year.

On the Web

The VBA code for the Extended Data functions is available on this book's website. The filename is extended date function.xlsm. You can also download documentation for these functions in the extended date functions help.pdf document.

Debugging Functions

When you're using a formula in a worksheet to test a Function procedure, VBA runtime errors don't appear in the all-too-familiar, pop-up error box. If an error occurs, the formula simply returns an error value (#VALUE!). The lack of a pop-up error message doesn't present a problem for debugging functions because you have several possible workarounds:

➤ **Place MsgBox functions at strategic locations to monitor the value of specific variables.** Message boxes in Function procedures *do* pop up when the procedure is executed. But make sure that you have only one formula in the worksheet that uses your function; otherwise, message boxes will appear for each formula that is evaluated, which will quickly become annoying.

➤ **Test the procedure by calling it from a Sub procedure, not from a worksheet formula.** Runtime errors are displayed in the usual manner, and you can either fix the problem (if you know it) or jump right into using Debugger.

➤ **Set a breakpoint in the function, and then step through the function.** You then can access all standard VBA debugging tools. To set a breakpoint, move the cursor to the statement at which you want to pause execution and then choose Debug➜Toggle Breakpoint (or press F9). When the function is executing, press F8 to step through the procedure line-by-line.

➤ **Use one or more temporary Debug.Print statements in your code to write values to the VBE Immediate window.** For example, if you want to monitor a value inside a loop, use something like the following routine:

```
Function VOWELCOUNT(r) As Long
    Dim Count As Long
    Dim i As Long
    Dim Ch As String * 1
    Count = 0
    For i = 1 To Len(r)
        Ch = UCase(Mid(r, i, 1))
        If Ch Like "[AEIOU]" Then
            Count = Count + 1
            Debug.Print Ch, i
        End If
    Next i
    VOWELCOUNT = Count
End Function
```

In this case, the values of two variables, Ch and i, are printed to the Immediate window whenever the Debug.Print statement is encountered. Figure 8-9 shows the result when the function has an argument of Tucson, Arizona.

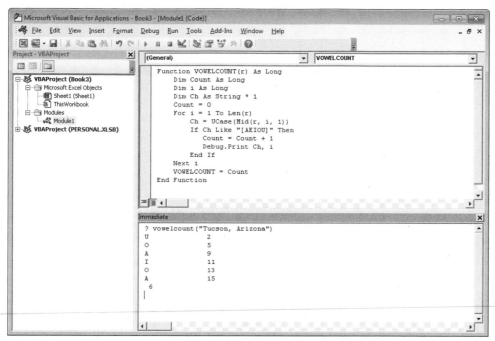

Figure 8-9: Use the Immediate window to display results while a function is running.

Dealing with the Insert Function Dialog Box

Excel's Insert Function dialog box is a handy tool. When you're creating a worksheet formula, this tool lets you select a particular worksheet function from a list of functions. These functions are grouped into various categories to make locating a particular function easier. When you select a function and click OK, the Function Arguments dialog box appears to help insert the function's arguments. Figure 8-10 shows both dialog boxes.

The Insert Function dialog box also displays your custom worksheet functions. By default, custom functions are listed under the User Defined category. The Function Arguments dialog box prompts you for a custom function's arguments.

The Insert Function dialog box enables you to search for a function by keyword. Unfortunately, you can't use this search feature to locate custom functions created in VBA.

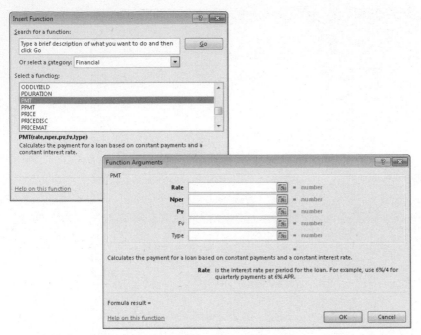

Figure 8-10: The Insert Function dialog box makes it easy to enter a function into a formula, and the Function Arguments dialog box prompts for the arguments.

Note
Custom Function procedures defined with the Private keyword don't appear in the Insert Function dialog box. If you develop a function that's intended to be used only in your other VBA procedures, you should declare it by using the Private keyword. However, declaring the function as Private doesn't prevent it from being used in a worksheet formula. It just prevents the display of the function in the Insert Function dialog box.

Using the MacroOptions method

You can use the MacroOptions method of the Application object to make your functions appear just like built-in functions. Specifically, this method enables you to

> ➤ Provide a description of the function

> ➤ Specify a function category

> ➤ Provide descriptions for the function arguments

Following is an example of a procedure that uses the MacroOptions method to provide information about a function:

```
Sub DescribeFunction()
    Dim FuncName As String
    Dim FuncDesc As String
    Dim FuncCat As Long
    Dim Arg1Desc As String, Arg2Desc As String

    FuncName = "DRAWONE"
    FuncDesc = "Displays the contents of a random cell from a range"
    FuncCat = 5
    Arg1Desc = "The range that contains the values"
    Arg2Desc = "(Optional) If False or missing, a new cell is selected when
  "
    Arg2Desc = Arg2Desc & "recalculated. If True, a new cell is selected "
    Arg2Desc = Arg2Desc & "when recalculated."

    Application.MacroOptions _
        Macro:=FuncName, _
        Description:=FuncDesc, _
        Category:=FuncCat, _
        ArgumentDescriptions:=Array(Arg1Desc, Arg2Desc)
End Sub
```

This procedure uses variables to store the information, and the variables are used as arguments for the MacroOptions method. The function is assigned to function category 5 (Lookup & Reference). Note that descriptions for the two arguments are indicated by using an array as the last argument for the MacroOptions method.

Note

The capability to provide argument descriptions was introduced in Excel 2010. If the workbook that contains the function is opened in a version prior to Excel 2010, the arguments won't display the descriptions.

Figure 8-11 shows the Insert Function and Function Arguments dialog boxes after executing this procedure.

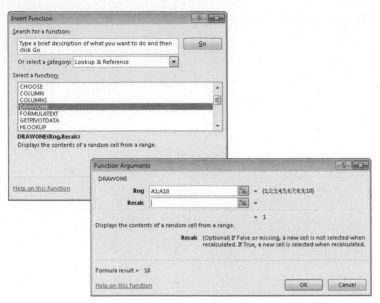

Figure 8-11: The Insert Function and Function Arguments dialog boxes for a custom function.

You need to execute the DescribeFunction procedure only one time. After doing so, the information assigned to the function is stored in the workbook. You can also omit arguments for the MacroOptions method. For example, if you don't need the arguments to have descriptions, just omit the ArgumentDescriptions argument in the code.

Cross-Ref

For information on creating a custom help topic accessible from the Insert Function dialog box, refer to Chapter 22.

Specifying a function category

If you don't use the MacroOptions method to specify a different category, your custom worksheet functions appear in the User Defined category in the Insert Function dialog box. You may prefer to assign your function to a different category. Assigning a function to a category also causes it to appear in the drop-down controls in the Formulas➜Function Library group on the Ribbon.

Table 8-1 lists the category numbers that you can use for the Category argument for the MacroOptions method. A few of these categories (10 through 13) aren't normally displayed in the Insert Function dialog box. If you assign your function to one of these categories, the category will appear in the dialog box.

Table 8-1: Function Categories

Category Number	Category Name
0	All (no specific category)
1	Financial
2	Date & Time
3	Math & Trig
4	Statistical
5	Lookup & Reference
6	Database
7	Text
8	Logical
9	Information
10	Commands
11	Customizing
12	Macro Control
13	DDE/External
14	User Defined
15	Engineering
16	Cube
17	Compatibility*
18	Web**

*The Compatibility category was introduced in Excel 2010.
** The Web category was introduced in Excel 2013.

Tip

You can also create custom function categories. Instead of using a number for the Category argument for MacroOptions, use a text string. The statement that follows creates a new function category named VBA Functions and assigns the COMMISSION function to this category:

```
Application.MacroOptions Macro:="COMMISSION",_
    Category:="VBA Functions"
```

Adding a function description manually

As an alternative to using the MacroOptions method to provide a function description, you can use the Macro dialog box.

Note

If you don't provide a description for your custom function, the Insert Function dialog box displays No help available.

Follow these steps to provide a description for a custom function:

1. Create your function in VBE.

2. Activate Excel, making sure that the workbook that contains the function is the active workbook.

3. Choose Developer→Code→Macros (or press Alt+F8).

   The Macro dialog box lists available procedures, but your function won't be in the list.

4. In the Macro Name box, type the name of your function.

5. Click the Options button to display the Macro Options dialog box.

6. In the Description box, enter the function description (see Figure 8-12).

   The Shortcut Key field is irrelevant for functions.

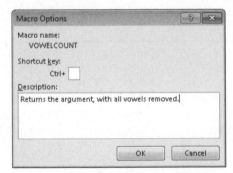

Figure 8-12: Provide a function description in the Macro Options dialog box.

7. Click OK and then click Cancel.

After you perform the preceding steps, the Insert Function dialog box displays the description that you entered in Step 6 when the function is selected.

Using Add-ins to Store Custom Functions

You may prefer to store frequently used custom functions in an add-in file. A primary advantage is that you can use those functions in any workbook when the add-in is installed.

In addition, you can use the functions in formulas without a filename qualifier. Assume that you have a custom function named ZAPSPACES that is stored in Myfuncs.xlsm. To use this function in a formula in a workbook other than Myfuncs.xlsm, you need to enter the following formula:

```
=Myfuncs.xlsm!ZAPSPACES(A1)
```

If you create an add-in from Myfuncs.xlsm and the add-in is loaded, you can omit the file reference and enter a formula such as the following:

```
=ZAPSPACES(A1)
```

Cross-Ref

I discuss add-ins in Chapter 19.

Caution

A potential problem with using add-ins to store custom functions is that your workbook is dependent on the add-in file. If you need to share your workbook with a colleague, you also need to share a copy of the add-in that contains the functions.

Using the Windows API

VBA can borrow methods from other files that have nothing to do with Excel or VBA — for example, the Dynamic Link Library (DLL) files that Windows and other software use. As a result, you can do things with VBA that would otherwise be outside the language's scope.

The Windows *Application Programming Interface* (API) is a set of functions available to Windows programmers. When you call a Windows function from VBA, you're accessing the Windows API. Many of the Windows resources used by Windows programmers are available in DLLs, which store programs and functions and are linked at runtime rather than at compile time.

64-bit Excel and API functions

Beginning with Excel 2010, using Windows API functions in your code became a bit more challenging because Excel 2010 and Excel 2013 are available also in 64-bit versions. If you want your code to be compatible with the 32-bit and the 64-bit versions of Excel, you need to declare your API functions twice, using compiler directives to ensure that the correct declaration is used.

For example, the following declaration works with 32-bit Excel versions but causes a compile error with 64-bit Excel 2010 or 64-bit Excel 2013:

```
Declare Function GetWindowsDirectoryA Lib "kernel32" _
  (ByVal lpBuffer As String, ByVal nSize As Long) As Long
```

In many cases, making the declaration compatible with 64-bit Excel is as simple as adding PtrSafe after the Declare keyword. The following declaration is compatible with both the 32-bit and 64-bit versions of Excel 2010 and Excel 2013:

```
 Declare PtrSafe Function GetWindowsDirectoryA Lib "kernel32" _
   (ByVal lpBuffer As String, ByVal nSize As Long) As Long
```

However, the code will fail in Excel 2007 (and earlier versions) because the PtrSafe keyword is not recognized by those versions.

In Chapter 24, I describe how to make API function declarations compatible with all versions of 32-bit Excel as well as 64-bit Excel 2010 and Excel 2013.

Windows API examples

Before you can use a Windows API function, you must declare the function at the top of your code module. If the code module is for UserForm, Sheet, or ThisWorkbook, you must declare the API function as Private.

An API function must be declared precisely. The declaration statement tells VBA

> ➤ Which API function you're using
> ➤ In which library the API function is located
> ➤ The API function's arguments

After you declare an API function, you can use it in your VBA code.

Determining the Windows directory

This section contains an example of an API function that displays the name of the Windows directory — something that's not possible using standard VBA statements. This code works with Excel 2010 and later.

Here's the API function declaration:

```
Declare PtrSafe Function GetWindowsDirectoryA Lib "kernel32" _
  (ByVal lpBuffer As String, ByVal nSize As Long) As Long
```

This function, which has two arguments, returns the name of the directory in which Windows is installed. After calling the function, the Windows directory is contained in lpBuffer, and the length of the directory string is contained in nSize.

After inserting the Declare statement at the top of your module, you can access the function by calling the GetWindowsDirectoryA function. The following is an example of calling the function and displaying the result in a message box:

```
Sub ShowWindowsDir()
    Dim WinPath As String * 255
    Dim WinDir As String
    WinPath = Space(255)
    WinDir = Left(WinPath, GetWindowsDirectoryA (WinPath, Len(WinPath)))
    MsgBox WinDir, vbInformation, "Windows Directory"
End Sub
```

Executing the ShowWindowsDir procedure displays a message box with the Windows directory.

Often, you'll want to create a *wrapper* for API functions. In other words, you create your own function that uses the API function. This greatly simplifies using the API function. Here's an example of a wrapper VBA function:

```
Function WINDOWSDIR() As String
'   Returns the Windows directory
    Dim WinPath As String * 255
    WinPath = Space(255)
    WINDOWSDIR=Left(WinPath, GetWindowsDirectoryA (WinPath, Len(WinPath)))
End Function
```

After declaring this function, you can call it from another procedure:

```
MsgBox WINDOWSDIR()
```

You can even use the function in a worksheet formula:

```
=WINDOWSDIR()
```

On the Web

This example is available on this book's website. The filename is windows directory. xlsm, and the API function declaration is compatible with Excel 2007 and later.

The reason for using API calls is to perform actions that would otherwise be impossible (or at least very difficult). If your application needs to find the path of the Windows directory, you could search all day and not find a function in Excel or VBA to do the trick. But knowing how to access the Windows API may solve your problem.

Caution

When you work with API calls, system crashes during testing aren't uncommon, so save your work often.

Detecting the Shift key

Here's another example of using an API function. Suppose that you've written a VBA macro that will be executed by clicking a button on a worksheet. Furthermore, suppose that you want the macro to perform differently if the user presses the Shift key when the button is clicked. VBA doesn't provide a way to detect whether the Shift key is pressed. But you can use the GetKeyState API function to find out. The GetKeyState function tells you whether a particular key is pressed. It takes a single argument, nVirtKey, which represents the code for the key in which you're interested.

The following code demonstrates how to detect whether the Shift key is pressed when the Button_Click event-handler procedure is executed. Note that I define a constant for the Shift key (using a hexadecimal value) and then use this constant as the argument for GetKeyState. If GetKeyState returns a value less than zero, it means that the Shift key was pressed; otherwise, the Shift key wasn't pressed. This code isn't compatible with Excel 2007.

```
Declare PtrSafe Function GetKeyState Lib "user32" _
   (ByVal nVirtKey As Long) As Integer

Sub Button_Click()
    Const VK_SHIFT As Integer = &H10
    If GetKeyState(VK_SHIFT) < 0 Then
        MsgBox "Shift is pressed"
    Else
        MsgBox "Shift is not pressed"
    End If
End Sub
```

On the Web

A workbook named key press.xlsm, available on this book's website, demonstrates how to detect the Ctrl, Shift, and Alt keys (as well as any combinations). The API function declaration in this workbook is compatible with Excel 2007 and later. Figure 8-13 shows the message from this procedure.

Figure 8-13: Using Windows API functions to determine which keys were pressed.

Learning more about API functions

Working with the Windows API functions can be tricky. Many programming reference books list the declarations for common API calls and often provide examples. Usually, you can simply copy the declarations and use the functions without understanding the details. Many Excel programmers take a cookbook approach to API functions. The Internet has dozens of reliable examples that you can copy and paste. Or search the web for a file named Win32API_PtrSafe.txt. This file, from Microsoft, contains many examples of declaration statements.

Cross-Ref

Chapter 9 has several additional examples of using Windows API functions.

VBA Programming Examples and Techniques

In This Chapter

- Using VBA to work with ranges

- Using VBA to work with workbooks and sheets

- Creating custom functions for use in your VBA procedures and in worksheet formulas

- Trying miscellaneous VBA tricks and techniques

- Using Windows Application Programming Interface (API) functions

Learning by Example

I believe that learning programming concepts is accelerated by a heavy emphasis on examples. And based on the feedback that I've received from readers of previous editions of this book, I have plenty of company. VBA programmers especially benefit from a hands-on approach. A well-thought-out example usually communicates a concept much better than a description of the underlying theory. I decided, therefore, not to write a reference book that painstakingly describes every nuance of VBA. Rather, I prepared numerous examples to demonstrate useful Excel programming techniques.

The previous chapters in this part provide enough information to get you started. The Help system provides all the details that I left out. In this chapter, I pick up the pace and present examples that solve practical problems while furthering your knowledge of VBA.

Using the examples in this chapter

Not all the examples in this chapter are intended to be stand-alone programs. They are, however, set up as usable procedures that you can adapt for your own applications.

I urge you to follow along on your computer as you read this chapter. Better yet, modify the examples and see what happens. I guarantee that this hands-on experience will help you more than reading a reference book.

I've grouped this chapter's examples into six categories:

➤ Working with ranges

➤ Working with workbooks and sheets

➤ VBA techniques

➤ Functions that are useful in your VBA procedures

➤ Functions that you can use in worksheet formulas

➤ Windows API calls

Cross-Ref   Subsequent chapters in this book present additional feature-specific examples: charts, pivot tables, events, UserForms, and so on.

Working with Ranges

The examples in this section demonstrate how to manipulate worksheet ranges with VBA.

Specifically, I provide examples of copying a range, moving a range, selecting a range, identifying types of information in a range, prompting for a cell value, determining the first empty cell in a column, pausing a macro to allow the user to select a range, counting cells in a range, looping through the cells in a range, and several other commonly used range-related operations.

Copying a range

Excel's macro recorder is useful not so much for generating usable code but for discovering the names of relevant objects, methods, and properties. The code that's generated by the macro recorder isn't always the most efficient, but it can usually provide you with several clues.

For example, recording a simple copy-and-paste operation generates five lines of VBA code:

```
Sub Macro1()
    Range("A1").Select
    Selection.Copy
    Range("B1").Select
    ActiveSheet.Paste
    Application.CutCopyMode = False
End Sub
```

Note that the generated code selects cell A1, copies it, and then selects cell B1 and performs the paste operation. But in VBA, you don't need to select an object to work with it. You would never learn this important point by mimicking the preceding recorded macro code, where two statements incorporate the Select method. You can replace this procedure with the following much simpler routine, which doesn't select any cells. It also takes advantage of the fact that the Copy method can use an argument that represents the destination for the copied range.

```
Sub CopyRange()
    Range("A1").Copy Range("B1")
End Sub
```

Both macros assume that a worksheet is active and that the operation takes place on the active worksheet. To copy a range to a different worksheet or workbook, simply qualify the range reference for the destination. The following example copies a range from Sheet1 in File1.xlsx to Sheet2 in File2.xlsx. Because the references are fully qualified, this example works regardless of which workbook is active.

```
Sub CopyRange2()
    Workbooks("File1.xlsx").Sheets("Sheet1").Range("A1").Copy _
        Workbooks("File2.xlsx").Sheets("Sheet2").Range("A1")
End Sub
```

Another way to approach this task is to use object variables to represent the ranges, as shown in the code that follows. Using object variables is especially useful when your code will use the ranges at some other point.

```
Sub CopyRange3()
    Dim Rng1 As Range, Rng2 As Range
    Set Rng1 = Workbooks("File1.xlsx").Sheets("Sheet1").Range("A1")
    Set Rng2 = Workbooks("File2.xlsx").Sheets("Sheet2").Range("A1")
    Rng1.Copy Rng2
End Sub
```

As you might expect, copying isn't limited to one single cell at a time. The following procedure, for example, copies a large range. Note that the destination consists of only a single cell (which represents the upper-left cell for the destination). Using a single cell for the destination works just like it does when you copy and paste a range manually in Excel.

```
Sub CopyRange4()
    Range("A1:C800").Copy Range("D1")
End Sub
```

Moving a range

The VBA instructions for moving a range are similar to those for copying a range, as the following example demonstrates. The difference is that you use the Cut method instead of the Copy method. Note that you need to specify only the upper-left cell for the destination range.

The following example moves 18 cells (in A1:C6) to a new location, beginning at cell H1:

```
Sub MoveRange1()
    Range("A1:C6").Cut Range("H1")
End Sub
```

Copying a variably sized range

In many cases, you need to copy a range of cells, but you don't know the exact row and column dimensions of the range. For example, you might have a workbook that tracks weekly sales, and the number of rows changes weekly when you add new data.

Figure 9-1 shows a common type of worksheet. This range consists of several rows, and the number of rows changes each week. Because you don't know the exact range address at any given time, writing a macro to copy the range requires additional coding.

	A	B	C	D
1	Week	Total Sales	New Customers	
2	1	21,094	45	
3	2	20,309	64	
4	3	19,374	80	
5	4	21,050	72	
6	5	22,227	92	
7	6	24,970	99	
8	7	27,259	111	
9				
10				
11				

Sheet1 | Sheet2

Figure 9-1: The number of rows in the data range changes every week.

The following macro demonstrates how to copy this range from Sheet1 to Sheet2 (beginning at cell A1). It uses the CurrentRegion property, which returns a Range object that corresponds to the block of cells around a particular cell (in this case, A1).

```
Sub CopyCurrentRegion2()
    Range("A1").CurrentRegion.Copy Sheets("Sheet2").Range("A1")
End Sub
```

Note

Using the CurrentRegion property is equivalent to choosing the Home→Editing→Find & Select→Go To Special command and selecting the Current Region option (or by using the Ctrl+Shift+* shortcut to select the current region). To see how the CurrentRegion selection works, record your actions while you issue that command. Generally, the CurrentRegion property setting consists of a rectangular block of cells surrounded by one or more blank rows or columns.

▶ Tips for working with ranges

When you work with ranges, keep the following points in mind:

- Your code doesn't need to select a range to work with it.

- You can't select a range that's not on the active worksheet. So if your code *does* select a range, its worksheet must be active. You can use the Activate method of the Worksheets collection to activate a particular sheet.

- Remember that the macro recorder doesn't always generate the most efficient code. Often, you can create your macro by using the recorder and then edit the code to make it more efficient.

- Using named ranges in your VBA code is a good idea. For example, refer to Range("Total") rather than Range("D45"). In the latter case, if you add a row above row 45, the cell address will change. You would then need to modify the macro so that it uses the correct range address (D46).

- If you rely on the macro recorder when selecting ranges, make sure that you record the macro using relative references. Choose Developer→Code→Use Relative References to toggle this setting.

- When running a macro that works on each cell in the current range selection, the user might select entire columns or rows. In most cases, you don't want to loop through every cell in the selection. Your macro should create a subset of the selection consisting of only the nonblank cells. See the section "Looping through a selected range efficiently," later in this chapter.

- Excel allows multiple selections. For example, you can select a range, press Ctrl, and select another range. You can test for multiple selections in your macro and take appropriate action. See the section "Determining the type of selected range," later in this chapter.

If the range to be copied is a table (specified by choosing Insert➜Tables➜Table), you can use code like this (assuming the table is named Table1):

```
Sub CopyTable()
    Range("Table1[#All]").Copy Sheets("Sheet2").Range("A1")
End Sub
```

Selecting or otherwise identifying various types of ranges

Much of the work that you'll do in VBA will involve working with ranges — either selecting a range or identifying a range so that you can do something with the cells.

In addition to the CurrentRegion property (which I discussed earlier), you should also be aware of the End method of the Range object. The End method takes one argument, which determines the direction in which the selection is extended. The following statement selects a range from the active cell to the last nonempty cell in that column:

```
Range(ActiveCell, ActiveCell.End(xlDown)).Select
```

Here's a similar example that uses a specific cell as the starting point:

```
Range(Range("A2"), Range("A2").End(xlDown)).Select
```

As you might expect, three other constants simulate key combinations in the other directions: xlUp, xlToLeft, and xlToRight.

Caution

Be careful when using the End method with the ActiveCell property. If the active cell is at the perimeter of a range or if the range contains one or more empty cells, the End method may not produce the desired results.

On the Web

This book's website includes a workbook that demonstrates several common types of range selections. When you open this workbook, named range selections.xlsm, the code adds a new menu item to the shortcut menu that appears when you right-click a cell: Selection Demo. This menu contains commands that enable the user to make various types of selections, as shown in Figure 9-2.

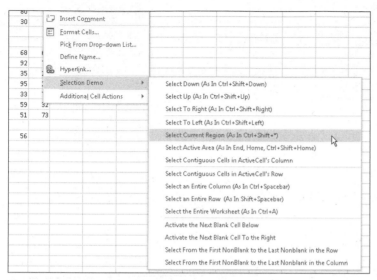

Figure 9-2: This workbook uses a custom shortcut menu to demonstrate how to select variably sized ranges by using VBA.

The following macro is in the example workbook. The SelectCurrentRegion macro simulates pressing Ctrl+Shift+*.

```
Sub SelectCurrentRegion()
    ActiveCell.CurrentRegion.Select
End Sub
```

Often, you won't want to select the cells. Rather, you'll want to work with them in some way (for example, format them). You can easily adapt the cell-selecting procedures. The following procedure was adapted from SelectCurrentRegion. This procedure doesn't select cells; it applies formatting to the range defined as the current region around the active cell. You can adapt the other procedures in the example workbook in this manner.

```
Sub FormatCurrentRegion()
    ActiveCell.CurrentRegion.Font.Bold = True
End Sub
```

Another way to refer to a range

If you look at VBA code written by others, you may notice a different way to reference a range. For example, the following statement selects a range:

```
[C2:D8].Select
```

The range address is surrounded by square brackets, and the range address is not enclosed in quote marks. The preceding statement is equivalent to

```
Range("C2:D8").Select
```

Using square brackets is a shortcut for the Evaluate method of the Application object. In this example, it's a shortcut for

```
Application.Evaluate("C2:D8").Select
```

I've never used this type of "square bracket" range referencing because I think it can be confusing. The sole purpose seems to be to save a few keystrokes when entering the code. However, using square brackets is also about 70 percent slower than the normal type of referencing (according to tests I performed) because it takes time to evaluate a text string and determine that it's a range reference.

Resizing a range

The Resize property of a Range object makes it easy to change the size of a range. The Resize property takes two arguments that represent the total number of rows and the total number of columns in the resized range.

For example, after executing the following statement, the MyRange object variable is 20 rows by 5 columns (range A1:E20):

```
Set MyRange = Range("A1")
Set MyRange = MyRange.Resize(20, 5)
```

After the following statement is executed, the size of MyRange is increased by one row. Note that the second argument is omitted, so the number of columns does not change.

```
Set MyRange = MyRange.Resize(MyRange.Rows.Count + 1)
```

A more practical example involves changing the definition of a range name. Assume a workbook has a range named Data. Your code needs to extend the named range by adding an additional row. This code snippet will do the job:

```
With Range("Data")
   .Resize(.Rows.Count + 1).Name = "Data"
End With
```

Prompting for a cell value

The following procedure demonstrates how to ask the user for a value and then insert it into cell A1 of the active worksheet:

```
Sub GetValue1()
    Range("A1").Value = InputBox("Enter the value")
End Sub
```

Figure 9-3 shows how the input box looks.

Figure 9-3: The InputBox function gets a value from the user to be inserted into a cell.

This procedure has a problem, however. If the user clicks the Cancel button in the input box, the procedure deletes any data already in the cell. The following modification takes no action if the Cancel button is clicked (which results in an empty string for the UserEntry variable):

```
Sub GetValue2()
    Dim UserEntry As Variant
    UserEntry = InputBox("Enter the value")
    If UserEntry <> "" Then Range("A1").Value = UserEntry
End Sub
```

In many cases, you'll need to validate the user's entry in the input box. For example, you may require a number between 1 and 12. The following example demonstrates one way to validate the user's entry. In this example, an invalid entry is ignored, and the input box is displayed again. This cycle keeps repeating until the user enters a valid number or clicks Cancel.

```
Sub GetValue3()
    Dim UserEntry As Variant
    Dim Msg As String
    Const MinVal As Integer = 1
    Const MaxVal As Integer = 12
    Msg = "Enter a value between " & MinVal & " and " & MaxVal
    Do
        UserEntry = InputBox(Msg)
        If UserEntry = "" Then Exit Sub
```

continued

```
        If IsNumeric(UserEntry) Then
            If UserEntry >= MinVal And UserEntry <= MaxVal Then Exit Do
        End If
        Msg = "Your previous entry was INVALID."
        Msg = Msg & vbNewLine
        Msg = Msg & "Enter a value between " & MinVal & " and " & MaxVal
    Loop
    ActiveSheet.Range("A1").Value = UserEntry
End Sub
```

As you can see in Figure 9-4, the code also changes the message displayed if the user makes an invalid entry.

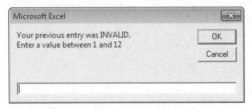

Figure 9-4: Validate a user's entry with the VBA InputBox function.

On the Web

The three **GetValue** procedures are available on this book's website in the **inputbox demo.xlsm** file.

Entering a value in the next empty cell

A common requirement is to enter a value into the next empty cell in a column or row. The following example prompts the user for a name and a value and then enters the data into the next empty row (see Figure 9-5).

```
Sub GetData()
    Dim NextRow As Long
    Dim Entry1 As String, Entry2 As String
  Do
    'Determine next empty row
    NextRow = Cells(Rows.Count, 1).End(xlUp).Row + 1

'   Prompt for the data
    Entry1 = InputBox("Enter the name")
    If Entry1 = "" Then Exit Sub
    Entry2 = InputBox("Enter the amount")
```

```
        If Entry2 = "" Then Exit Sub

'       Write the data
        Cells(NextRow, 1) = Entry1
        Cells(NextRow, 2) = Entry2
    Loop
End Sub
```

	A	B	C	D	E	F	G	H	I	J
1	Name	Amount								
2	Allen	983								
3	Bill	409								
4	Clara	773								
5	Dave	0								
6	Elisa	412								
7	Frank	551								
8	George	895								
9	Jim	545								
10	Keith	988								
11	Pat	545								
12	Paul	344								
13										
14										
15										

Microsoft Excel — Enter the name — OK — Cancel

Figure 9-5: A macro for inserting data into the next empty row in a worksheet.

To keep things simple, this procedure doesn't perform any validation. The loop continues indefinitely. I use Exit Sub statements to get out of the loop when the user clicks Cancel in the input box.

On the Web

The GetData procedure is available on the book's website in the next empty cell.xlsm file.

Note the statement that determines the value of the NextRow variable. If you don't understand how this statement works, try the manual equivalent: Activate the last cell in column A (cell A1048576), press End, and then press the up-arrow key. At this point, the last nonblank cell in column A will be selected. The Row property returns this row number, which is incremented by 1 to get the row of the cell below it (the next empty row). Rather than hard-code the last cell in column A, I used Rows.Count so that this procedure will work with previous versions of Excel (which have fewer rows).

This technique of selecting the next empty cell has a slight glitch. If the column is empty, it will calculate row 2 as the next empty row. Writing additional code to account for this possibility would be fairly easy.

Pausing a macro to get a user-selected range

In some situations, you may need an interactive macro. For example, you can create a macro that pauses while the user specifies a range of cells. The procedure in this section describes how to do this with Excel's InputBox method.

Note

Don't confuse Excel's InputBox method with VBA's InputBox function. Although these two items have the same name, they're not the same.

The Sub procedure that follows demonstrates how to pause a macro and let the user select a range. The code then inserts a formula in each cell of the specified range.

```vba
Sub GetUserRange()
    Dim UserRange As Range

    Prompt = "Select a range for the random numbers."
    Title = "Select a range"

'   Display the Input Box
    On Error Resume Next
    Set UserRange = Application.InputBox( _
        Prompt:=Prompt, _
        Title:=Title, _
        Default:=ActiveCell.Address, _
        Type:=8) 'Range selection
    On Error GoTo 0

'   Was the Input Box canceled?
    If UserRange Is Nothing Then
        MsgBox "Canceled."
    Else
        UserRange.Formula = "=RAND()"
    End If
End Sub
```

The input box is shown in Figure 9-6.

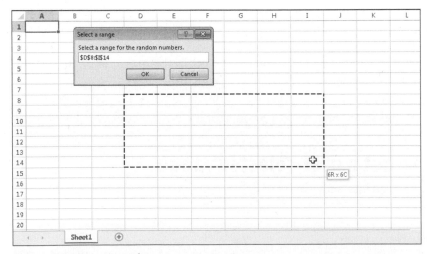

Figure 9-6: Use an input box to pause a macro.

This example, named **prompt for a range.xlsm, is available on this book's website.**

Specifying a Type argument of 8 for the InputBox method is the key to this procedure. Also note the use of On Error Resume Next. This statement ignores the error that occurs if the user clicks the Cancel button. If the user clicks Cancel, the UserRange object variable isn't defined. This example displays a message box with the text Canceled. If the user clicks OK, the macro continues. Using On Error GoTo 0 resumes normal error handling.

By the way, you don't need to check for a valid range selection. Excel takes care of this task for you. If the user types an invalid range address, Excel displays a message box with instructions on how to select a range.

Caution

Make sure that screen updating isn't turned off when you use the InputBox method to select a range. Otherwise, every movement of the input box leaves an ugly trail, as shown in Figure 9-7. Use the ScreenUpdating property of the Application object to control screen updating while a macro is running.

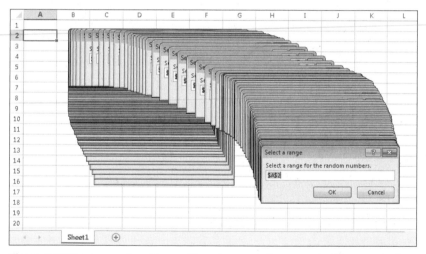

Figure 9-7: Moving an input box with screen updating turned off leaves a trail.

Counting selected cells

You can create a macro that works with the range of cells selected by the user. Use the Count property of the Range object to determine how many cells are contained in a range selection (or any range, for that matter). For example, the following statement displays a message box that contains the number of cells in the current selection:

```
MsgBox Selection.Count
```

Caution

With the larger worksheet size introduced in Excel 2007, the Count property can generate an error. The Count property uses the Long data type, so the largest value that it can store is 2,147,483,647. For example, if the user selects 2,048 complete columns (2,147,483,648 cells), the Count property generates an error. Fortunately, Microsoft added a new property beginning with Excel 2007: CountLarge. CountLarge uses the Double data type, which can handle values up to 1.79+E^308.

Bottom line? In the vast majority of situations, the Count property will work fine. If there's a chance that you may need to count more cells (such as all cells in a worksheet), use CountLarge instead of Count.

If the active sheet contains a range named Data, the following statement assigns the number of cells in the Data range to a variable named CellCount:

```
CellCount = Range("Data").Count
```

You can also determine how many rows or columns are contained in a range. The following expression calculates the number of columns in the currently selected range:

```
Selection.Columns.Count
```

And, of course, you can use the Rows property to determine the number of rows in a range. The following statement counts the number of rows in a range named Data and assigns the number to a variable named RowCount:

```
RowCount = Range("Data").Rows.Count
```

Determining the type of selected range

Excel supports several types of range selections:

- ➤ A single cell
- ➤ A contiguous range of cells
- ➤ One or more entire columns
- ➤ One or more entire rows
- ➤ The entire worksheet
- ➤ Any combination of the preceding (that is, a multiple selection)

As a result, when your VBA procedure processes a user-selected range, you can't make any presumptions about what that range might be. For example, the range selection might consist of two areas, say A1:A10 and C1:C10. (To make a multiple selection, press Ctrl while you select the ranges with your mouse.)

In the case of a multiple range selection, the Range object comprises separate areas. To determine whether a selection is a multiple selection, use the Areas method, which returns an Areas collection. This collection represents all the ranges in a multiple range selection.

You can use an expression such as the following to determine whether a selected range has multiple areas:

```
NumAreas = Selection.Areas.Count
```

If the NumAreas variable contains a value greater than 1, the selection is a multiple selection.

Following is a function named AreaType, which returns a text string that describes the type of range selection:

```
Function AreaType(RangeArea As Range) As String
'    Returns the type of a range in an area
     Select Case True
         Case RangeArea.Cells.CountLarge = 1
             AreaType = "Cell"
         Case RangeArea.CountLarge = Cells.CountLarge
             AreaType = "Worksheet"
         Case RangeArea.Rows.Count = Cells.Rows.Count
             AreaType = "Column"
         Case RangeArea.Columns.Count = Cells.Columns.Count
             AreaType = "Row"
         Case Else
             AreaType = "Block"
     End Select
End Function
```

This function accepts a Range object as its argument and returns one of five strings that describe the area: Cell, Worksheet, Column, Row, or Block. The function uses a Select Case construct to determine which of five comparison expressions is True. For example, if the range consists of a single cell, the function returns Cell. If the number of cells in the range is equal to the number of cells in the worksheet, it returns Worksheet. If the number of rows in the range equals the number of rows in the worksheet, it returns Column. If the number of columns in the range equals the number of columns in the worksheet, the function returns Row. If none of the Case expressions is True, the function returns Block.

Note that I used the CountLarge property when counting cells. As I noted previously in this chapter, the number of selected cells could potentially exceed the limit of the Count property.

On the Web

This example is available on this book's website in a file named about range selection. xlsm. The workbook contains a procedure (named RangeDescription) that uses the AreaType function to display a message box that describes the current range selection. Figure 9-8 shows an example. Understanding how this routine works will give you a good foundation for working with Range objects.

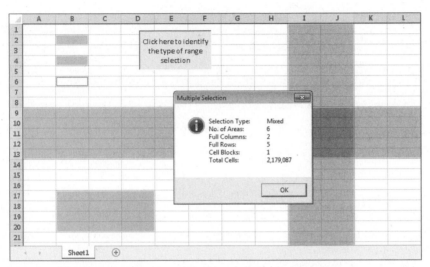

Figure 9-8: A VBA procedure analyzes the currently selected range.

Note

You might be surprised to discover that Excel allows multiple selections to be identical. For example, if you hold down Ctrl and click five times in cell A1, the selection will have five identical areas. The RangeDescription procedure takes this possibility into account and doesn't count the same cell multiple times. Also note that a new feature causes Excel 2013 to display progressively darker shading for overlapping range selections.

Looping through a selected range efficiently

A common task is to create a macro that evaluates each cell in a range and performs an operation if the cell meets a certain criterion. The procedure that follows is an example of such a macro. The ColorNegative procedure sets the cell's background color to red for cells that contain a negative value. For non-negative value cells, it sets the background color to none.

Note

This example is for educational purposes only. Using Excel's conditional formatting feature is a much better approach.

```
Sub ColorNegative()
'    Makes negative cells red
    Dim cell As Range
    If TypeName(Selection) <> "Range" Then Exit Sub
    Application.ScreenUpdating = False
    For Each cell In Selection
        If cell.Value < 0 Then
            cell.Interior.Color = RGB(255, 0, 0)
        Else
            cell.Interior.Color = xlNone
        End If
    Next cell
End Sub
```

The ColorNegative procedure certainly works, but it has a serious flaw. For example, what if the used area on the worksheet were small, but the user selects an entire column? Or ten columns? Or the entire worksheet? You don't need to process all those empty cells, and the user would probably give up long before your code churns through all those cells.

A better solution (ColorNegative2) follows. In this revised procedure, I create a Range object variable, WorkRange, which consists of the intersection of the user's selected range and the worksheet's used range.

```
Sub ColorNegative2()
'    Makes negative cells red
    Dim WorkRange As Range
    Dim cell As Range
    If TypeName(Selection) <> "Range" Then Exit Sub
    Application.ScreenUpdating = False
    Set WorkRange = Application.Intersect(Selection, ActiveSheet.UsedRange)
    For Each cell In WorkRange
        If cell.Value < 0 Then
            cell.Interior.Color = RGB(255, 0, 0)
        Else
            cell.Interior.Color = xlNone
        End If
    Next cell
End Sub
```

Figure 9-9 shows an example; the entire column D is selected (1,048,576 cells). The range used by the worksheet, however, is B2:I16. Therefore, the intersection of these ranges is D2:D16, which is a much smaller range than the original selection. Needless to say, the time difference between processing 15 cells versus processing 1,048,576 cells is significant.

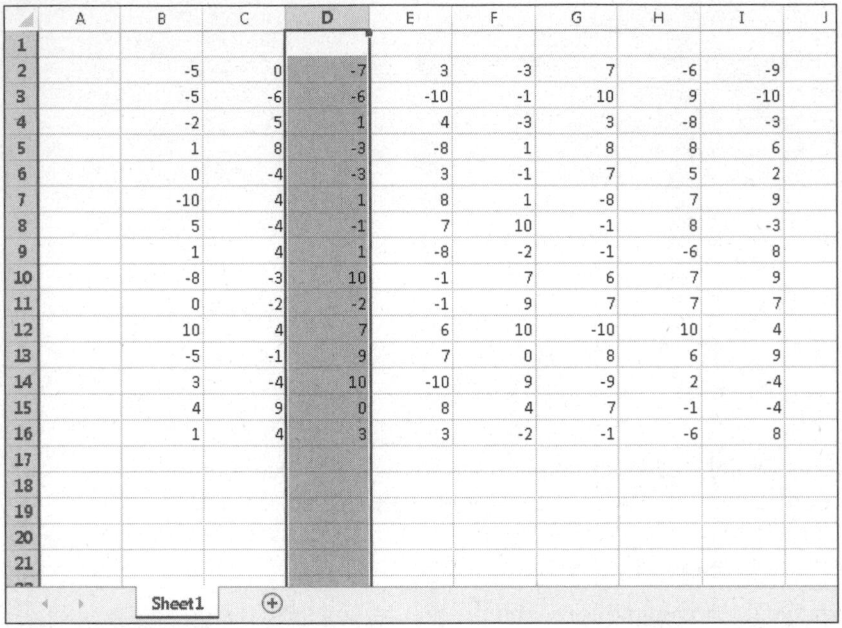

	A	B	C	D	E	F	G	H	I	J
1										
2		-5	0	-7	3	-3	7	-6	-9	
3		-5	-6	-6	-10	-1	10	9	-10	
4		-2	5	1	4	-3	3	-8	-3	
5		1	8	-3	-8	1	8	8	6	
6		0	-4	-3	3	-1	7	5	2	
7		-10	4	1	8	1	-8	7	9	
8		5	-4	-1	7	10	-1	8	-3	
9		1	4	1	-8	-2	-1	-6	8	
10		-8	-3	10	-1	7	6	7	9	
11		0	-2	-2	-1	9	7	7	7	
12		10	4	7	6	10	-10	10	4	
13		-5	-1	9	7	0	8	6	9	
14		3	-4	10	-10	9	-9	2	-4	
15		4	9	0	8	4	7	-1	-4	
16		1	4	3	3	-2	-1	-6	8	
17										
18										
19										
20										
21										

Sheet1 ⊕

Figure 9-9: Using the intersection of the used range and the selected ranged results in fewer cells to process.

The ColorNegative2 procedure is an improvement, but it's still not as efficient as it could be because it processes empty cells. A third revision, ColorNegative3, is quite a bit longer but much more efficient. I use the SpecialCells method to generate two subsets of the selection: One subset (ConstantCells) includes only the cells with numeric constants; the other subset (FormulaCells) includes only the cells with numeric formulas. The code processes the cells in these subsets by using two For Each-Next constructs. The net effect: Only nonblank, nontext cells are evaluated, thus speeding up the macro considerably.

```
Sub ColorNegative3()
'   Makes negative cells red
    Dim FormulaCells As Range, ConstantCells As Range
    Dim cell As Range
    If TypeName(Selection) <> "Range" Then Exit Sub
    Application.ScreenUpdating = False

'   Create subsets of original selection
    On Error Resume Next
    Set FormulaCells = Selection.SpecialCells(xlFormulas, xlNumbers)
    Set ConstantCells = Selection.SpecialCells(xlConstants, xlNumbers)
    On Error GoTo 0

'   Process the formula cells
    If Not FormulaCells Is Nothing Then
        For Each cell In FormulaCells
            If cell.Value < 0 Then
                cell.Interior.Color = RGB(255, 0, 0)
```

```
            Else
                cell.Interior.Color = xlNone
            End If
            Next cell
    End If

'   Process the constant cells
    If Not ConstantCells Is Nothing Then
        For Each cell In ConstantCells
            If cell.Value < 0 Then
                cell.Interior.Color = RGB(255, 0, 0)
            Else
                cell.Interior.Color = xlNone
            End If
        Next cell
    End If
End Sub
```

Note

The On Error statement is necessary because the SpecialCells method generates an error if no cells qualify.

On the Web

A workbook that contains the three ColorNegative procedures is available on this book's website in the efficient looping.xlsm file.

Deleting all empty rows

The following procedure deletes all empty rows in the active worksheet. This routine is fast and efficient because it doesn't check all rows. It checks only the rows in the used range, which is determined by using the UsedRange property of the Worksheet object.

```
Sub DeleteEmptyRows()
    Dim LastRow As Long
    Dim r As Long
    Dim Counter As Long
    Application.ScreenUpdating = False
    LastRow = ActiveSheet.UsedRange.Rows.Count+ActiveSheet.UsedRange.Rows(1).Row - 1
    For r = LastRow To 1 Step -1
        If Application.WorksheetFunction.CountA(Rows(r)) = 0 Then
            Rows(r).Delete
            Counter = Counter + 1
        End If
    Next r
    Application.ScreenUpdating = True
    MsgBox Counter & " empty rows were deleted."
End Sub
```

The first step is to determine the last used row and then assign this row number to the LastRow variable. This calculation isn't as simple as you might think because the used range may or may not begin in row 1. Therefore, LastRow is calculated by determining the number of rows in the used range, adding the first row number in the used range, and subtracting 1.

The procedure uses Excel's COUNTA worksheet function to determine whether a row is empty. If this function returns 0 for a particular row, the row is empty. Note that the procedure works on the rows from bottom to top and also uses a negative step value in the For-Next loop. This negative step value is necessary because deleting rows causes all subsequent rows to move up in the worksheet. If the looping occurred from top to bottom, the counter in the loop wouldn't be accurate after a row is deleted.

The macro uses another variable, Counter, to keep track of how many rows were deleted. This number is displayed in a message box when the procedure ends.

On the Web A workbook that contains this example is available on this book's website in a file named **delete empty rows.xlsm.**

Duplicating rows a variable number of times

The example in this section demonstrates how to use VBA to create duplicates of a row. Figure 9-10 shows a worksheet for an office raffle. Column A contains the name, and column B contains the number of tickets purchased by each person. Column C contains a random number (generated by the RAND function). The winner will be determined by sorting the data based on column C (the highest random number wins).

	A	B	C	D
1	Name	No. Tickets	Random	
2	Alan	1	0.54149729	
3	Barbara	2	0.8477736	
4	Charlie	1	0.20355509	
5	Dave	5	0.21869392	
6	Frank	3	0.53989374	
7	Gilda	1	0.86832302	
8	Hubert	1	0.90946248	
9	Inez	2	0.42000917	
10	Mark	1	0.77526214	
11	Norah	10	0.43757829	
12	Penelope	2	0.64897258	
13	Rance	1	0.29826416	
14	Wendy	2	0.88803093	
15				
16				

Sheet1 ⊕

Figure 9-10: The goal is to duplicate rows based on the value in column B.

The macro duplicates the rows so that each person will have a row for each ticket purchased. For example, Barbara purchased two tickets, so she should have two rows (and two chances to win).

The procedure to insert the new rows is shown here:

```
Sub DupeRows()
  Dim cell As Range
' First cell with number of tickets
  Set cell = Range("B2")
  Do While Not IsEmpty(cell)
    If cell > 1 Then
        Range(cell.Offset(1, 0), cell.Offset(cell.Value - 1, _
          0)).EntireRow.Insert
        Range(cell, cell.Offset(cell.Value - 1, 1)).EntireRow.FillDown
    End If
    Set cell = cell.Offset(cell.Value, 0)
    Loop
  End Sub
```

The cell object variable is initialized to cell B2, the first cell that has a number. The loop inserts new rows and then copies the row using the FillDown method. The cell variable is incremented to the next person, and the loop continues until an empty cell is encountered. Figure 9-11 shows a portion of the worksheet after running this procedure.

	A	B	C	D
1	Name	No. Tickets	Random	
2	Alan	1	0.35393487	
3	Barbara	2	0.49222915	
4	Barbara	2	0.44158491	
5	Charlie	1	0.13574781	
6	Dave	5	0.99112971	
7	Dave	5	0.81786031	
8	Dave	5	0.08615939	
9	Dave	5	0.55590457	
10	Dave	5	0.56925493	
11	Frank	3	0.71547138	
12	Frank	3	0.80488384	
13	Frank	3	0.12447761	
14	Gilda	1	0.23517351	
15	Hubert	1	0.0140915	
16	Inez	2	0.37960838	
17	Inez	2	0.80498449	
18	Mark	1	0.45096235	
19	Norah	10	0.53623758	
20	Norah	10	0.52188045	
21	Norah	10	0.97845782	
22	Norah	10	0.59028777	
23	Norah	10	0.21613136	
24	Norah	10	0.7526961	

Figure 9-11: New rows were added, according to the value in column B.

On the Web A workbook that contains this example is available on this book's website in the dupli-cate rows.xlsm file.

Determining whether a range is contained in another range

The following InRange function accepts two arguments, both Range objects. The function returns True if the first range is contained in the second range. This function can be used in a worksheet for-mula, but it's more useful when called by another procedure.

```
Function InRange(rng1, rng2) As Boolean
'    Returns True if rng1 is a subset of rng2
    On Error GoTo ErrHandler
    If Union(rng1, rng2).Address = rng2.Address Then
        InRange = True
        Exit Function
    End If
ErrHandler:
    InRange = False
End Function
```

The Union method of the Application object returns a Range object that represents the union of two Range objects. The union consists of all the cells from both ranges. If the address of the union of the two ranges is the same as the address of the second range, the first range is contained in the second range.

If the two ranges are in different worksheets, the Union method generates an error. The On Error statement handles this situation.

On the Web A workbook that contains this function is available on this book's website in the inrange function.xlsm file.

Determining a cell's data type

Excel provides a number of built-in functions that can help determine the type of data contained in a cell. Examples of these functions are ISTEXT, ISLOGICAL, and ISERROR. In addition, VBA includes func-tions such as IsEmpty, IsDate, and IsNumeric.

The following function, named CellType, accepts a range argument and returns a string (Blank, Text, Logical, Error, Date, Time, or Number) that describes the data type of the upper-left cell in the range.

```
Function CellType(Rng) As String
'    Returns the cell type of the upper left cell in a range
    Dim TheCell As Range
    Set TheCell = Rng.Range("A1")
    Select Case True
        Case IsEmpty(TheCell)
            CELLTYPE = "Blank"
        Case TheCell.NumberFormat = "@"
            CELLTYPE = "Text"
        Case Application.IsText(TheCell)
            CELLTYPE = "Text"
        Case Application.IsLogical(TheCell)
            CELLTYPE = "Logical"
        Case Application.IsErr(TheCell)
            CELLTYPE = "Error"
        Case IsDate(TheCell)
            CELLTYPE = "Date"
        Case InStr(1, TheCell.Text, ":") <> 0
            CELLTYPE = "Time"
        Case IsNumeric(TheCell)
            CELLTYPE = "Number"
    End Select
End Function
```

You can use this function in a worksheet formula or from another VBA procedure. In Figure 9-12, the function is used in formulas in column B. These formulas use data in column A as the argument. Column C is just a description of the data.

	A	B	C	D
1	145.4	Number	A simple value	
2	8.6	Number	Formula that returns a value	
3	Budget Sheet	Text	Simple text	
4	FALSE	Logical	Logical formula	
5	TRUE	Logical	Logical value	
6	#DIV/0!	Error	Formula error	
7	9/17/2012	Date	Formula that returns a date	
8	4:00 PM	Time	A time	
9	1/13/10 5:25 AM	Date	A date and a time	
10	143	Text	Value preceded by apostrophe	
11	434	Text	Cell formatted as Text	
12	A1:C4	Text	Text with a colon	
13		Blank	Empty cell	
14		Text	Cell with a single space	
15		Text	Cell with an empty string (single apostrophe)	
16				

| ◂ ▸ | Sheet1 | ⊕ |

Figure 9-12: Using a function to determine the type of data in a cell.

Note the use of the Set TheCell statement. The CellType function accepts a range argument of any size, but this statement causes it to operate on only the upper-left cell in the range (which is represented by the TheCell variable).

On the Web

A workbook that contains this function is available on this book's website in the celltype function.xlsm file.

Reading and writing ranges

Many VBA tasks involve transferring values either from an array to a range or from a range to an array. Excel reads from ranges much faster than it writes to ranges because (presumably) the latter operation involves the calculation engine. The WriteReadRange procedure that follows demonstrates the relative speeds of writing and reading a range.

This procedure creates an array and then uses For-Next loops to write the array to a range and then read the range back into the array. It calculates the time required for each operation by using the VBA Timer function.

```
Sub WriteReadRange()
    Dim MyArray()
    Dim Time1 As Double
    Dim NumElements As Long, i As Long
    Dim WriteTime As String, ReadTime As String
    Dim Msg As String

    NumElements = 250000
    ReDim MyArray(1 To NumElements)

'   Fill the array
    For i = 1 To NumElements
        MyArray(i) = i
    Next i

'   Write the array to a range
    Time1 = Timer
    For i = 1 To NumElements
        Cells(i, 1) = MyArray(i)
    Next i
    WriteTime = Format(Timer - Time1, "00:00")

'   Read the range into the array
    Time1 = Timer
    For i = 1 To NumElements
        MyArray(i) = Cells(i, 1)
    Next i
```

```
    ReadTime = Format(Timer - Time1, "00:00")

'   Show results
    Msg = "Write: " & WriteTime
    Msg = Msg & vbCrLf
    Msg = Msg & "Read: " & ReadTime
    MsgBox Msg, vbOKOnly, NumElements & " Elements"
End Sub
```

The results are shown in Figure 9-13. On my system, it took 14 seconds to write a 250,000-element array to a range but less than 1 second to read the range into an array.

Figure 9-13: Displaying the time to write to a range and read from a range, using a loop.

A better way to write to a range

The example in the preceding section uses a For-Next loop to transfer the contents of an array to a worksheet range. In this section, I demonstrate a more efficient way to accomplish this task.

Start with the example that follows, which illustrates the most obvious (but not the most efficient) way to fill a range. This example uses a For-Next loop to insert its values in a range.

```
Sub LoopFillRange()
'   Fill a range by looping through cells

    Dim CellsDown As Long, CellsAcross As Integer
    Dim CurrRow As Long, CurrCol As Integer
    Dim StartTime As Double
    Dim CurrVal As Long

'   Get the dimensions
    CellsDown = InputBox("How many cells down?")
    If CellsDown = 0 Then Exit Sub
    CellsAcross = InputBox("How many cells across?")
    If CellsAcross = 0 Then Exit Sub

'   Record starting time
    StartTime = Timer
```

continued

```
'    Loop through cells and insert values
     CurrVal = 1
     Application.ScreenUpdating = False
     For CurrRow = 1 To CellsDown
         For CurrCol = 1 To CellsAcross
             ActiveCell.Offset(CurrRow - 1, _
             CurrCol - 1).Value = CurrVal
             CurrVal = CurrVal + 1
         Next CurrCol
     Next CurrRow

'    Display elapsed time
     Application.ScreenUpdating = True
     MsgBox Format(Timer - StartTime, "00.00") & " seconds"
End Sub
```

The example that follows demonstrates a much faster way to produce the same result. This code inserts the values into an array and then uses a single statement to transfer the contents of an array to the range.

```
Sub ArrayFillRange()
'    Fill a range by transferring an array

     Dim CellsDown As Long, CellsAcross As Integer
     Dim i As Long, j As Integer
     Dim StartTime As Double
     Dim TempArray() As Long
     Dim TheRange As Range
     Dim CurrVal As Long

'    Get the dimensions
     CellsDown = InputBox("How many cells down?")
     If CellsDown = 0 Then Exit Sub
     CellsAcross = InputBox("How many cells across?")
     If CellsAcross = 0 Then Exit Sub

'    Record starting time
     StartTime = Timer

'    Redimension temporary array
     ReDim TempArray(1 To CellsDown, 1 To CellsAcross)

'    Set worksheet range
     Set TheRange = ActiveCell.Range(Cells(1, 1), _
         Cells(CellsDown, CellsAcross))

'    Fill the temporary array
     CurrVal = 0
```

```
    Application.ScreenUpdating = False
    For i = 1 To CellsDown
        For j = 1 To CellsAcross
            TempArray(i, j) = CurrVal + 1
            CurrVal = CurrVal + 1
        Next j
    Next i

'   Transfer temporary array to worksheet
    TheRange.Value = TempArray

'   Display elapsed time
    Application.ScreenUpdating = True
    MsgBox Format(Timer - StartTime, "00.00") & " seconds"
End Sub
```

On my system, using the loop method to fill a 1000 x 250–cell range (250,000 cells) took 15.80 seconds. The array transfer method took only 0.15 seconds to generate the same results — more than 100 times faster! The moral of this story? If you need to transfer large amounts of data to a worksheet, avoid looping whenever possible.

Note

The timing results are highly dependent on the presence of formulas. Generally, you'll get faster transfer times if no workbooks are open that contain formulas or if you set the calculation mode to Manual.

On the Web

A workbook that contains the WriteReadRange, LoopFillRange, and ArrayFillRange procedures is available on this book's website. The file is named loop vs array fill range. xlsm.

Transferring one-dimensional arrays

The example in the preceding section involves a two-dimensional array, which works out nicely for row-and-column-based worksheets.

When transferring a one-dimensional array to a range, the range must be horizontal — that is, one row with multiple *columns*. If you need the data in a vertical range instead, you must first transpose the array to make it vertical. You can use Excel's TRANSPOSE function to do this. The following example transfers a 100-element array to a vertical worksheet range (A1:A100):

```
Range("A1:A100").Value = Application.WorksheetFunction.Transpose(MyArray)
```

Transferring a range to a variant array

This section discusses yet another way to work with worksheet data in VBA. The following example transfers a range of cells to a two-dimensional variant array. Then message boxes display the upper bounds for each dimension of the variant array.

```
Sub RangeToVariant()
    Dim x As Variant
    x = Range("A1:L600").Value
    MsgBox UBound(x, 1)
    MsgBox UBound(x, 2)
End Sub
```

In this example, the first message box displays 600 (the number of rows in the original range), and the second message box displays 12 (the number of columns). You'll find that transferring the range data to a variant array is virtually instantaneous.

The following example reads a range (named data) into a variant array, performs a simple multiplication operation on each element in the array, and then transfers the variant array back to the range:

```
Sub RangeToVariant2()
    Dim x As Variant
    Dim r As Long, c As Integer

'   Read the data into the variant
    x = Range("data").Value

'   Loop through the variant array
    For r = 1 To UBound(x, 1)
        For c = 1 To UBound(x, 2)
'           Multiply by 2
            x(r, c) = x(r, c) * 2
        Next c
    Next r

'   Transfer the variant back to the sheet
    Range("data") = x
End Sub
```

You'll find that this procedure runs amazingly fast. Working with 30,000 cells took less than 1 second.

On the Web

A workbook that contains this example is available on this book's website in the variant transfer.xlsm file.

Selecting cells by value

The example in this section demonstrates how to select cells based on their value. Oddly, Excel doesn't provide a direct way to perform this operation. My SelectByValue procedure follows. In this example, the code selects cells that contain a negative value, but you can easily change the code to select cells based on other criteria.

```vba
Sub SelectByValue()
    Dim Cell As Object
    Dim FoundCells As Range
    Dim WorkRange As Range

    If TypeName(Selection) <> "Range" Then Exit Sub

'   Check all or selection?
    If Selection.CountLarge = 1 Then
        Set WorkRange = ActiveSheet.UsedRange
    Else
        Set WorkRange = Application.Intersect(Selection, ActiveSheet.UsedRange)
    End If

'   Reduce the search to numeric cells only
    On Error Resume Next
    Set WorkRange = WorkRange.SpecialCells(xlConstants, xlNumbers)
    If WorkRange Is Nothing Then Exit Sub
    On Error GoTo 0

'   Loop through each cell, add to the FoundCells range if it qualifies
    For Each Cell In WorkRange
        If Cell.Value < 0 Then
            If FoundCells Is Nothing Then
                Set FoundCells = Cell
            Else
                Set FoundCells = Union(FoundCells, Cell)
            End If
        End If
    Next Cell

'   Show message, or select the cells
    If FoundCells Is Nothing Then
        MsgBox "No cells qualify."
    Else
        FoundCells.Select
        MsgBox "Selected " & FoundCells.Count & " cells."
    End If
End Sub
```

The procedure starts by checking the selection. If it's a single cell, the entire worksheet is searched. If the selection is at least two cells, only the selected range is searched. The range to be searched is further refined by using the SpecialCells method to create a Range object that consists only of the numeric constants.

The code in the For-Next loop examines the cell's value. If it meets the criterion (less than 0), the cell is added to the FoundCells Range object by using the Union method. Note that you can't use the Union method for the first cell. If the FoundCells range contains no cells, attempting to use the Union method will generate an error. Therefore, the code checks whether FoundCells is Nothing.

When the loop ends, the FoundCells object will consist of the cells that meet the criterion (or will be Nothing if no cells were found). If no cells are found, a message box appears. Otherwise, the cells are selected.

On the Web

This example is available on this book's website in the select by value.xlsm file.

Copying a noncontiguous range

If you've ever attempted to copy a noncontiguous range selection, you discovered that Excel doesn't support such an operation. Attempting to do so displays the following error message: *That command cannot be used on multiple selections.*

An exception is when you attempt to copy a multiple selection that consists of entire rows or columns, or when the multiple selections are in the same row(s) or same column(s). Excel *does* allow those operations. But when you paste the copied cells, all blanks are removed.

When you encounter a limitation in Excel, you can often circumvent it by creating a macro. The example in this section is a VBA procedure that allows you to copy a multiple selection to another location.

```
Sub CopyMultipleSelection()
    Dim SelAreas() As Range
    Dim PasteRange As Range
    Dim UpperLeft As Range
    Dim NumAreas As Long, i As Long
    Dim TopRow As Long, LeftCol As Long
    Dim RowOffset As Long, ColOffset As Long

    If TypeName(Selection) <> "Range" Then Exit Sub

'   Store the areas as separate Range objects
    NumAreas = Selection.Areas.Count
    ReDim SelAreas(1 To NumAreas)
    For i = 1 To NumAreas
        Set SelAreas(i) = Selection.Areas(i)
    Next

'   Determine the upper-left cell in the multiple selection
```

```
    TopRow = ActiveSheet.Rows.Count
    LeftCol = ActiveSheet.Columns.Count
    For i = 1 To NumAreas
        If SelAreas(i).Row < TopRow Then TopRow = SelAreas(i).Row
        If SelAreas(i).Column < LeftCol Then LeftCol = SelAreas(i).Column
    Next
    Set UpperLeft = Cells(TopRow, LeftCol)

'   Get the paste address
    On Error Resume Next
    Set PasteRange = Application.InputBox _
      (Prompt:="Specify the upper-left cell for the paste range:", _
      Title:="Copy Multiple Selection", _
      Type:=8)
    On Error GoTo 0
'   Exit if canceled
    If TypeName(PasteRange) <> "Range" Then Exit Sub

'   Make sure only the upper-left cell is used
    Set PasteRange = PasteRange.Range("A1")

'   Copy and paste each area
    For i = 1 To NumAreas
        RowOffset = SelAreas(i).Row - TopRow
        ColOffset = SelAreas(i).Column - LeftCol
        SelAreas(i).Copy PasteRange.Offset(RowOffset, ColOffset)
    Next i
End Sub
```

Figure 9-14 shows the prompt to select the destination location.

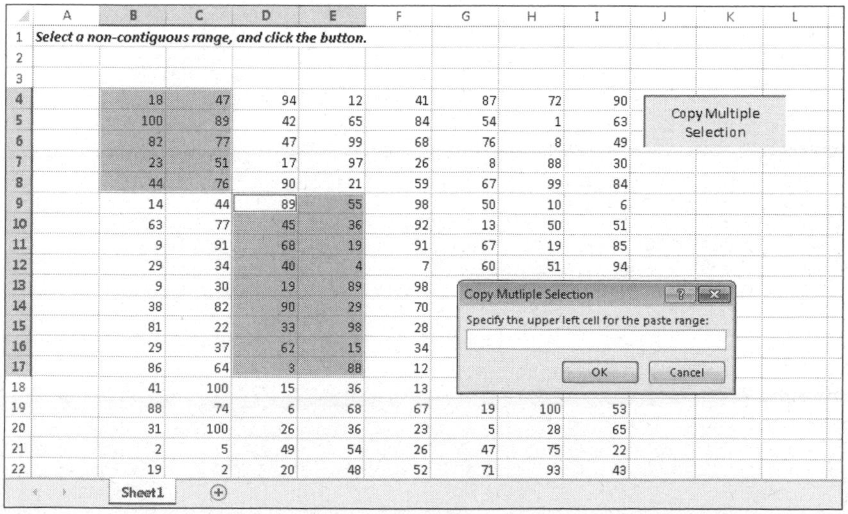

Figure 9-14: Using Excel's InputBox method to prompt for a cell location.

On the Web This book's website contains a workbook with this example, plus another version that warns the user if data will be overwritten. The file is named copy multiple selection.xlsm.

Working with Workbooks and Sheets

The examples in this section demonstrate various ways to use VBA to work with workbooks and worksheets.

Saving all workbooks

The following procedure loops through all workbooks in the Workbooks collection and saves each file that has been saved previously:

```
Public Sub SaveAllWorkbooks()
    Dim Book As Workbook
    For Each Book In Workbooks
        If Book.Path <> "" Then Book.Save
    Next Book
End Sub
```

Note the use of the Path property. If a workbook's Path property is empty, the file has never been saved (it's a newly created workbook). This procedure ignores such workbooks and saves only the workbooks that have a nonempty Path property.

A more efficient approach also checks the Saved property. This property is True if the workbook has not been changed since it was last saved. The SaveAllWorkbooks2 procedure doesn't save files that don't need to be saved.

```
Public Sub SaveAllWorkbooks2()
    Dim Book As Workbook
    For Each Book In Workbooks
        If Book.Path <> "" Then
            If Book.Saved <> True Then
                Book.Save
            End If
        End If
    Next Book
End Sub
```

Saving and closing all workbooks

The following procedure loops through the Workbooks collection. The code saves and closes all workbooks.

```
Sub CloseAllWorkbooks()
    Dim Book As Workbook
    For Each Book In Workbooks
        If Book.Name <> ThisWorkbook.Name Then
            Book.Close savechanges:=True
        End If
    Next Book
    ThisWorkbook.Close savechanges:=True
End Sub
```

The procedure uses an If statement in the For-Next loop to determine whether the workbook is the workbook that contains the code. This statement is necessary because closing the workbook that contains the procedure would end the code, and subsequent workbooks wouldn't be affected. After all the other workbooks are closed, the workbook that contains the code closes itself.

Hiding all but the selection

The example in this section hides all rows and columns in a worksheet except those in the current range selection:

```
Sub HideRowsAndColumns()
    Dim row1 As Long, row2 As Long
    Dim col1 As Long, col2 As Long

    If TypeName(Selection) <> "Range" Then Exit Sub

'   If last row or last column is hidden, unhide all and quit
    If Rows(Rows.Count).EntireRow.Hidden Or _
      Columns(Columns.Count).EntireColumn.Hidden Then
        Cells.EntireColumn.Hidden = False
        Cells.EntireRow.Hidden = False
        Exit Sub
    End If

    row1 = Selection.Rows(1).Row
    row2 = row1 + Selection.Rows.Count - 1
```

continued

```
    col1 = Selection.Columns(1).Column
    col2 = col1 + Selection.Columns.Count - 1

    Application.ScreenUpdating = False
    On Error Resume Next
'   Hide rows
    Range(Cells(1, 1), Cells(row1 - 1, 1)).EntireRow.Hidden = True
    Range(Cells(row2 + 1, 1), Cells(Rows.Count, 1)).EntireRow.Hidden = True
'   Hide columns
    Range(Cells(1, 1), Cells(1, col1 - 1)).EntireColumn.Hidden = True
    Range(Cells(1, col2 + 1), Cells(1, Columns.Count)).EntireColumn.Hidden = True
End Sub
```

Figure 9-15 shows an example. If the range selection consists of a noncontiguous range, the first area is used as the basis for hiding rows and columns. Note that it's a toggle. Executing the procedures when the last row or last column is hidden unhides all rows and columns.

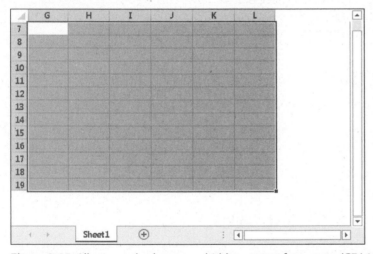

Figure 9-15: All rows and columns are hidden, except for a range (G7:L19).

On the Web

A workbook with this example is available on this book's website in the hide rows and columns.xlsm file.

Creating a hyperlink table of contents

The CreateTOC procedure inserts a new worksheet at the beginning of the active workbook. It then creates a table of contents, in the form of a list of hyperlinks to each worksheet.

```
Sub CreateTOC()
    Dim i As Integer
    Sheets.Add Before:=Sheets(1)
    For i = 2 To Worksheets.Count
      ActiveSheet.Hyperlinks.Add _
        Anchor:=Cells(i, 1), _
        Address:="", _
        SubAddress:="'" & Worksheets(i).Name & "'!A1", _
        TextToDisplay:=Worksheets(i).Name
    Next i
End Sub
```

It's not possible to create a hyperlink to a chart sheet, so the code uses the Worksheet collection rather than the Sheets collection.

Figure 9-16 shows an example of a hyperlink table of contents that contains worksheets comprised of month names.

◢	A	B	C	D	E	F	G	H	I
1									
2	January								
3	February								
4	March								
5	April								
6	May								
7	June								
8	July								
9	August								
10	September								
11	October								
12	November								
13	December								
14									

Sheet1 | January | February | March | April | May | June | Jul ⋯ ⊕

Figure 9-16: Hyperlinks to each worksheet, created by a macro.

On the Web

A workbook with this example is available on this book's website in the create hyperlinks.xlsm file.

Synchronizing worksheets

If you use multisheet workbooks, you probably know that Excel can't synchronize the sheets in a workbook. In other words, there is no automatic way to force all sheets to have the same selected range and upper-left cell. The VBA macro that follows uses the active worksheet as a base and then performs the following on all other worksheets in the workbook:

➤ Selects the same range as the active sheet

➤ Makes the upper-left cell the same as the active sheet

Following is the listing for the procedure:

```vba
Sub SynchSheets()
'    Duplicates the active sheet's active cell and upper left cell
'    Across all worksheets
    If TypeName(ActiveSheet) <> "Worksheet" Then Exit Sub
    Dim UserSheet As Worksheet, sht As Worksheet
    Dim TopRow As Long, LeftCol As Integer
    Dim UserSel As String

    Application.ScreenUpdating = False

'    Remember the current sheet
    Set UserSheet = ActiveSheet

'    Store info from the active sheet
    TopRow = ActiveWindow.ScrollRow
    LeftCol = ActiveWindow.ScrollColumn
    UserSel = ActiveWindow.RangeSelection.Address

'    Loop through the worksheets
    For Each sht In ActiveWorkbook.Worksheets
        If sht.Visible Then 'skip hidden sheets
            sht.Activate
            Range(UserSel).Select
            ActiveWindow.ScrollRow = TopRow
            ActiveWindow.ScrollColumn = LeftCol
        End If
    Next sht

'    Restore the original position
    UserSheet.Activate
    Application.ScreenUpdating = True
End Sub
```

On the Web

A workbook with this example is available on this book's website in the synchronize sheets.xlsm file.

VBA Techniques

The examples in this section illustrate common VBA techniques that you might be able to adapt to your own projects.

Toggling a Boolean property

A *Boolean property* is one that is either True or False. The easiest way to toggle a Boolean property is to use the Not operator, as shown in the following example, which toggles the WrapText property of a selection:

```
Sub ToggleWrapText()
'    Toggles text wrap alignment for selected cells
    If TypeName(Selection) = "Range" Then
       Selection.WrapText = Not ActiveCell.WrapText
    End If
End Sub
```

You can modify this procedure to toggle other Boolean properties.

Note that the active cell is used as the basis for toggling. When a range is selected and the property values in the cells are inconsistent (for example, some cells are bold and others are not), Excel uses the active cell to determine how to toggle. If the active cell is bold, for example, all cells in the selection are made not bold when you click the Bold button. this simple procedure mimics the way Excel works, which is usually the best practice.

Note also that this procedure uses the TypeName function to check whether the selection is a range. If the selection isn't a range, nothing happens.

You can use the Not operator to toggle many other properties. For example, to toggle the display of row and column borders in a worksheet, use the following code:

```
ActiveWindow.DisplayHeadings = Not ActiveWindow.DisplayHeadings
```

To toggle the display of gridlines in the active worksheet, use the following code:

```
ActiveWindow.DisplayGridlines = Not ActiveWindow.DisplayGridlines
```

Displaying the date and time

If you understand the serial number system that Excel uses to store dates and times, you won't have any problems using dates and times in your VBA procedures.

The DateAndTime procedure displays a message box with the current date and time, as depicted in Figure 9-17. This example also displays a personalized message in the message box's title bar.

Figure 9-17: A message box displaying the date and time.

The procedure uses the Date function as an argument for the Format function. The result is a string with a nicely formatted date. I used the same technique to get a nicely formatted time.

```vba
Sub DateAndTime()
    Dim TheDate As String, TheTime As String
    Dim Greeting As String
    Dim FullName As String, FirstName As String
    Dim SpaceInName As Long

    TheDate = Format(Date, "Long Date")
    TheTime = Format(Time, "Medium Time")

'   Determine greeting based on time
    Select Case Time
        Case Is < TimeValue("12:00"): Greeting = "Good Morning, "
        Case Is >= TimeValue("17:00"): Greeting = "Good Evening, "
        Case Else: Greeting = "Good Afternoon, "
    End Select

'   Append user's first name to greeting
    FullName = Application.UserName
    SpaceInName = InStr(1, FullName, " ", 1)

'   Handle situation when name has no space
    If SpaceInName = 0 Then SpaceInName = Len(FullName)
    FirstName = Left(FullName, SpaceInName)
    Greeting = Greeting & FirstName

'   Show the message
    MsgBox TheDate & vbCrLf & vbCrLf & "It's " & TheTime, vbOKOnly, Greeting
End Sub
```

In the preceding example, I used named formats (Long Date and Medium Time) to ensure that the macro will work properly regardless of the user's international settings. You can, however, use other formats. For example, to display the date in mm/dd/yy format, you can use a statement like the following:

```
TheDate = Format(Date, "mm/dd/yy")
```

I used a Select Case construct to base the greeting displayed in the message box's title bar on the time of day. VBA time values work just as they do in Excel. If the time is less than .5 (noon), it's morning. If it's greater than .7083 (5 p.m.), it's evening. Otherwise, it's afternoon. I took the easy way out and used VBA's TimeValue function, which returns a time value from a string.

The next series of statements determines the user's first name, as recorded in the General tab in Excel's Options dialog box. I used the VBA InStr function to locate the first space in the user's name. When I first wrote this procedure, I didn't consider a username that has no space. So when I ran this procedure on a machine with a username of *Nobody,* the code failed — which goes to show you that I can't think of everything, and even the simplest procedures can run aground. (By the way, if the user's name is left blank, Excel always substitutes the name *User.*) The solution to this problem was to use the length of the full name for the SpaceInName variable so that the Left function extracts the full name.

The MsgBox function concatenates the date and time but uses the built-in vbCrLf constant to insert a line break between them. vbOKOnly is a predefined constant that returns 0, causing the message box to appear with only an OK button. The final argument is the Greeting, constructed earlier in the procedure.

On the Web   The DateAndTime procedure is available on this book's website, in a file named date and time.xlsm.

Displaying friendly time

If you're not a stickler for 100 percent accuracy, you might like the FT function, listed here. FT, which stands for *friendly time,* displays a time difference in words.

```
Function FT(t1, t2)
    Dim SDif As Double, DDif As Double

    If Not (IsDate(t1) And IsDate(t2)) Then
        FT = CVErr(xlErrValue)
        Exit Function
    End If
```

continued

```
    DDif = Abs(t2 - t1)
    SDif = DDif * 24 * 60 * 60

    If DDif < 1 Then
        If SDif < 10 Then FT = "Just now": Exit Function
        If SDif < 60 Then FT = SDif & " seconds ago": Exit Function
        If SDif < 120 Then FT = "a minute ago": Exit Function
        If SDif < 3600 Then FT = Round(SDif / 60, 0) & "minutes ago": Exit
Function
        If SDif < 7200 Then FT = "An hour ago": Exit Function
        If SDif < 86400 Then FT = Round(SDif / 3600, 0) & " hours ago": Exit
Function
    End If
    If DDif = 1 Then FT = "Yesterday": Exit Function
    If DDif < 7 Then FT = Round(DDif, 0) & " days ago": Exit Function
    If DDif < 31 Then FT = Round(DDif / 7, 0) & " weeks ago": Exit Function
    If DDif < 365 Then FT = Round(DDif / 30, 0) & " months ago": Exit
Function
    FT = Round(DDif / 365, 0) & " years ago"
End Function
```

Figure 9-18 shows examples of this function used in formulas. If you actually have a need for such a way to display time differences, this procedure leaves lots of room for improvement. For example, you can write code to prevent displays such as *1 months ago* and *1 years ago*.

	A	B	C
1	**Time1**	**Time 2**	**Time Difference**
2	3/30/2013 8:45 AM	3/30/2013 8:46 AM	a minute ago
3	3/30/2013 8:45 AM	4/1/2013 1:33 AM	2 days ago
4	3/30/2013 8:45 AM	4/13/2013 1:47 AM	2 weeks ago
5	3/30/2013 8:45 AM	5/1/2013 2:20 PM	1 months ago
6	3/30/2013 8:45 AM	6/28/2013 2:04 PM	3 months ago
7	3/30/2013 8:45 AM	1/24/2014 11:37 AM	10 months ago
8	3/30/2013 8:45 AM	4/21/2014 11:09 PM	1 years ago
9	3/30/2013 8:45 AM	6/16/2021 4:25 PM	8 years ago
10			

Sheet1 ⊕

Figure 9-18: Using a function to display time differences in a friendly manner.

On the Web

This example is available on this book's website. The file is named **friendly time.xlsm**.

Getting a list of fonts

If you need to get a list of all installed fonts, you'll find that Excel doesn't provide a direct way to retrieve that information. The technique described here takes advantage of the fact that Excel 2013 still supports the old CommandBar properties and methods for compatibility with pre–Excel 2007 versions. These properties and methods were used to work with toolbars and menus.

The ShowInstalledFonts macro displays a list of the installed fonts in column A of the active worksheet. It creates a temporary toolbar (a CommandBar object), adds the Font control, and reads the font names from that control. The temporary toolbar is then deleted.

```
Sub ShowInstalledFonts()
    Dim FontList As CommandBarControl
    Dim TempBar As CommandBar
    Dim i As Long

'   Create temporary CommandBar
    Set TempBar = Application.CommandBars.Add
    Set FontList = TempBar.Controls.Add(ID:=1728)

'   Put the fonts into column A
    Range("A:A").ClearContents
    For i = 0 To FontList.ListCount - 1
        Cells(i + 1, 1) = FontList.List(i + 1)
    Next i

'   Delete temporary CommandBar
    TempBar.Delete
End Sub
```

Tip

As an option, you can display each font name in the actual font (as shown in Figure 9-19). To do so, add this statement inside the For-Next loop:

```
Cells(i+1,1).Font.Name = FontList.List(i+1)
```

Be aware, however, that using many fonts in a workbook can eat up lots of system resources and could even crash your system.

On the Web

This procedure is available on the book's website in the list fonts.xlsm file.

Figure 9-19: Listing font names in the actual fonts.

Sorting an array

Although Excel has a built-in command to sort worksheet ranges, VBA doesn't offer a method to sort arrays. One viable (but cumbersome) workaround is to transfer your array to a worksheet range, sort it by using Excel's commands, and then return the result to your array. This method is surprisingly fast, but if you need something faster, use a sorting routine written in VBA.

In this section, I cover four different sorting techniques:

➤ *Worksheet sort* transfers an array to a worksheet range, sorts it, and transfers it back to the array. This procedure accepts an array as its only argument.

➤ *Bubble sort* is a simple sorting technique (also used in the Chapter 7 sheet-sorting example). Although easy to program, the bubble-sorting algorithm tends to be slow, especially with many elements.

➤ *Quick sort* is a much faster sorting routine than bubble sort, but it is also more difficult to understand. This technique works only with Integer and Long data types.

➤ *Counting sort* is lightning fast but difficult to understand. Like the quick sort, this technique works only with Integer and Long data types.

On the Web

The book's website includes a workbook application that demonstrates these sorting methods. This workbook, named sorting demo.xlsm, is useful for comparing these techniques with arrays of varying sizes. However, you can also copy the procedures and use them in your code.

Figure 9-20 shows the dialog box for this project. I tested the sorting procedures with seven array sizes, ranging from 500 to 100,000 elements. The arrays contained random numbers (of type Long).

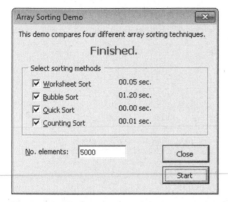

Figure 9-20: Comparing the time required to perform sorts of various array sizes.

Table 9-1 shows the results of my tests. A 0.00 entry means that the sort was virtually instantaneous (less than .01 second).

Table 9-1: Sorting Times (in Seconds) for Four Sort Algorithms Using Randomly Filled Arrays

Array Elements	Excel Worksheet Sort	VBA Bubble Sort	VBA Quick Sort	VBA Counting Sort
500	0.01	0.01	0.00	0.00
1,000	0.02	0.05	0.00	0.01
5,000	0.05	1.20	0.00	0.01
10,000	0.07	4.82	0.01	0.01
25,000	0.16	29.19	0.04	0.01
50,000	0.31	112.05	0.07	0.02
100,000	0.63	418.38	0.17	0.04

The worksheet sort algorithm is amazingly fast, especially when you consider that the array is transferred to the sheet, sorted, and then transferred back to the array.

The bubble sort algorithm is the simplest and is reasonably fast with small arrays, but for larger arrays (more than 10,000 elements), forget it. The quick sort and counting sort algorithms are blazingly fast, but they're limited to Integer and Long data types.

Processing a series of files

One common use for macros is to perform repetitive tasks. The example in this section demonstrates how to execute a macro that operates on several different files stored on disk. This example — which may help you set up your own routine for this type of task — prompts the user for a file specification and then processes all matching files. In this case, processing consists of importing the file and entering a series of summary formulas that describe the data in the file.

```vba
Sub BatchProcess()
    Dim FileSpec As String
    Dim i As Integer
    Dim FileName As String
    Dim FileList() As String
    Dim FoundFiles As Integer

'   Specify path and file spec
    FileSpec = ThisWorkbook.Path & "\" & "text??.txt"
    FileName = Dir(FileSpec)

'   Was a file found?
    If FileName <> "" Then
        FoundFiles = 1
        ReDim Preserve FileList(1 To FoundFiles)
        FileList(FoundFiles) = FileName
    Else
        MsgBox "No files were found that match " & FileSpec
        Exit Sub
    End If

'   Get other filenames
    Do
        FileName = Dir
        If FileName = "" Then Exit Do
        FoundFiles = FoundFiles + 1
        ReDim Preserve FileList(1 To FoundFiles)
        FileList(FoundFiles) = FileName & "*"
    Loop

'   Loop through the files and process them
    For i = 1 To FoundFiles
        Call ProcessFiles(FileList(i))
    Next i
End Sub
```

This example, named batch processing.xlsm, is available on the book's website. It uses three additional files (also available for download): text01.txt, text02.txt, and text03.txt. You'll need to modify the routine to import other text files.

The matching filenames are stored in an array named FoundFiles, and the procedure uses a For-Next loop to process the files. Within the loop, the processing is done by calling the ProcessFiles procedure, which follows. This simple procedure uses the OpenText method to import the file and then inserts five formulas. You may, of course, substitute your own routine in place of this one:

```vba
Sub ProcessFiles(FileName As String)
'    Import the file
    Workbooks.OpenText FileName:=FileName, _
        Origin:=xlWindows, _
        StartRow:=1, _
        DataType:=xlFixedWidth, _
        FieldInfo:= _
        Array(Array(0, 1), Array(3, 1), Array(12, 1))
'    Enter summary formulas
    Range("D1").Value = "A"
    Range("D2").Value = "B"
    Range("D3").Value = "C"
    Range("E1:E3").Formula = "=COUNTIF(B:B,D1)"
    Range("F1:F3").Formula = "=SUMIF(B:B,D1,C:C)"
End Sub
```

Cross-Ref

For more information about working with files using VBA, refer to Chapter 25.

Some Useful Functions for Use in Your Code

In this section, I present some custom utility functions that you may find useful in your own applications and that may provide inspiration for creating similar functions. These functions are most useful when called from another VBA procedure. Therefore, they're declared by using the Private keyword so that they won't appear in Excel's Insert Function dialog box.

The examples in this section are available on the book's website in the VBA utility functions.xlsm file.

The FileExists function

The FileExists function takes one argument (a path with a filename) and returns True if the file exists:

```
Private Function FileExists(fname) As Boolean
'    Returns TRUE if the file exists
    FileExists = (Dir(fname) <> "")
End Function
```

The FileNameOnly function

The FileNameOnly function accepts one argument (a path with a filename) and returns only the filename. In other words, it strips out the path.

```
Private Function FileNameOnly(pname) As String
'    Returns the filename from a path/filename string
    Dim temp As Variant
    length = Len(pname)
    temp = Split(pname, Application.PathSeparator)
    FileNameOnly = temp(UBound(temp))
End Function
```

The function uses the VBA Split function, which accepts a string (that includes delimiter characters), and returns a variant array that contains the elements between the delimiter characters. In this case the temp variable contains an array that consists of each text string between the Application.PathSeparator (usually a backslash character). For another example of the Split function, see the section "Extracting the nth element from a string," later in this chapter.

If the argument is c:\excel files\2013\backup\budget.xlsx, the function returns the string budget.xlsx.

The FileNameOnly function works with any path and filename (even if the file *does not* exist). If the file exists, the following function is a simpler way to strip the path and return only the filename:

```
Private Function FileNameOnly2(pname) As String
    FileNameOnly2 = Dir(pname)
End Function
```

The PathExists function

The PathExists function accepts one argument (a path) and returns True if the path exists:

```
Private Function PathExists(pname) As Boolean
' Returns TRUE if the path exists
  If Dir(pname, vbDirectory) = "" Then
    PathExists = False
  Else
    PathExists = (GetAttr(pname) And vbDirectory) = vbDirectory
  End If
End Function
```

The RangeNameExists function

The RangeNameExists function accepts a single argument (a range name) and returns True if the range name exists in the active workbook:

```
Private Function RangeNameExists(nname) As Boolean
'    Returns TRUE if the range name exists
    Dim n As Name
    RangeNameExists = False
    For Each n In ActiveWorkbook.Names
        If UCase(n.Name) = UCase(nname) Then
            RangeNameExists = True
            Exit Function
        End If
    Next n
End Function
```

Another way to write this function follows. This version attempts to create an object variable using the name. If doing so generates an error, the name doesn't exist.

```
Private Function RangeNameExists2(nname) As Boolean
'    Returns TRUE if the range name exists
    Dim n As Range
    On Error Resume Next
    Set n = Range(nname)
    If Err.Number = 0 Then RangeNameExists2 = True _
        Else RangeNameExists2 = False
End Function
```

The SheetExists function

The SheetExists function accepts one argument (a worksheet name) and returns True if the worksheet exists in the active workbook:

```
Private Function SheetExists(sname) As Boolean
'   Returns TRUE if sheet exists in the active workbook
    Dim x As Object
    On Error Resume Next
    Set x = ActiveWorkbook.Sheets(sname)
    If Err.Number = 0 Then SheetExists = True Else SheetExists = False
End Function
```

 ## Testing for membership in a collection

The following function procedure is a generic function that you can use to determine whether an object is a member of a collection:

```
Private Function IsInCollection _
   (Coln As Object, Item As String) As Boolean
    Dim Obj As Object
    On Error Resume Next
    Set Obj = Coln(Item)
    IsInCollection = Not Obj Is Nothing
End Function
```

This function accepts two arguments: the collection (an object) and the item (a string) that might or might not be a member of the collection. The function attempts to create an object variable that represents the item in the collection. If the attempt is successful, the function returns True; otherwise, it returns False.

You can use the IsInCollection function in place of three other functions listed in this chapter: RangeNameExists, SheetExists, and WorkbookIsOpen. To determine whether a range named Data exists in the active workbook, call the IsInCollection function with this statement:

```
MsgBox IsInCollection(ActiveWorkbook.Names, "Data")
```

To determine whether a workbook named Budget is open, use this statement:

```
MsgBox IsInCollection(Workbooks, "budget.xlsx")
```

To determine whether the active workbook contains a sheet named Sheet1, use this statement:

```
MsgBox IsInCollection(ActiveWorkbook.Worksheets, "Sheet1")
```

The WorkbookIsOpen function

The WorkbookIsOpen function accepts one argument (a workbook name) and returns True if the workbook is open:

```
Private Function WorkbookIsOpen(wbname) As Boolean
'    Returns TRUE if the workbook is open
     Dim x As Workbook
     On Error Resume Next
     Set x = Workbooks(wbname)
     If Err.Number = 0 Then WorkbookIsOpen = True _
         Else WorkbookIsOpen = False
End Function
```

Retrieving a value from a closed workbook

VBA doesn't include a method to retrieve a value from a closed workbook file. You can, however, take advantage of Excel's capability to work with linked files. This section contains a custom VBA function (GetValue, which follows) that retrieves a value from a closed workbook. It does so by calling an *XLM macro,* which is an old-style macro used in versions before Excel 5. Fortunately, Excel still supports this old macro system.

```
Private Function GetValue(path, file, sheet, ref)
'    Retrieves a value from a closed workbook
     Dim arg As String

'    Make sure the file exists
     If Right(path, 1) <> "\" Then path = path & "\"
     If Dir(path & file) = "" Then
         GetValue = "File Not Found"
         Exit Function
     End If

'    Create the argument
     arg = "'" & path & "[" & file & "]" & sheet & "'!" & _
       Range(ref).Range("A1").Address(, , xlR1C1)

'    Execute an XLM macro
     GetValue = ExecuteExcel4Macro(arg)
End Function
```

The GetValue function takes four arguments:

➤ path: The drive and path to the closed file (for example, "d:\files")

➤ file: The workbook name (for example, "budget.xlsx")

➤ sheet: The worksheet name (for example, "Sheet1")

➤ ref: The cell reference (for example, "C4")

The following Sub procedure demonstrates how to use the GetValue function. It displays the value in cell A1 in Sheet1 of a file named 2013budget.xlsx, located in the XLFiles\Budget directory on drive C.

```
Sub TestGetValue()
    Dim p As String, f As String
    Dim s As String, a As String

    p = "c:\XLFiles\Budget"
    f = "2013budget.xlsx"
    s = "Sheet1"
    a = "A1"
    MsgBox GetValue(p, f, s, a)
End Sub
```

Another example follows. This procedure reads 1,200 values (100 rows and 12 columns) from a closed file and then places the values into the active worksheet.

```
Sub TestGetValue2()
    Dim p As String, f As String
    Dim s As String, a As String
    Dim r As Long, c As Long

    p = "c:\XLFiles\Budget"
    f = "2013Budget.xlsx"
    s = "Sheet1"
    Application.ScreenUpdating = False
    For r = 1 To 100
        For c = 1 To 12
            a = Cells(r, c).Address
            Cells(r, c) = GetValue(p, f, s, a)
        Next c
    Next r
End Sub
```

An alternative is to write code that turns off screen updating, opens the file, gets the value, and then closes the file. Unless the file is very large, the user won't even notice that a file is being opened.

Note

The GetValue function doesn't work in a worksheet formula. However, there is no need to use this function in a formula. You can simply create a link formula to retrieve a value from a closed file.

On the Web

This example is available on this book's website in the value from a closed workbook. xlsm file. The example uses a file named myworkbook.xlsx for the closed file.

Some Useful Worksheet Functions

The examples in this section are custom functions that you can use in worksheet formulas. Remember, you must define these Function procedures in a VBA module (not a code module associated with ThisWorkbook, a Sheet, or a UserForm).

On the Web

The examples in this section are available on the book's website in the worksheet functions.xlsm file.

Returning cell formatting information

This section contains a number of custom functions that return information about a cell's formatting. These functions are useful if you need to sort data based on formatting (for example, sort in such a way that all bold cells are together).

Caution

You'll find that these functions aren't always updated automatically because changing formatting doesn't trigger Excel's recalculation engine. To force a global recalculation (and update all custom functions), press Ctrl+Alt+F9.

Alternatively, you can add the following statement to your function:

```
Application.Volatile
```

When this statement is present, pressing F9 will recalculate the function.

The following function returns TRUE if its single-cell argument has bold formatting. If a range is passed as the argument, the function uses the upper-left cell of the range.

```
Function ISBOLD(cell) As Boolean
'   Returns TRUE if cell is bold
    ISBOLD = cell.Range("A1").Font.Bold
End Function
```

Note that this function works only with explicitly applied formatting. It doesn't work for formatting applied using conditional formatting. Excel 2010 introduced DisplayFormat, a new object that takes conditional formatting into account. Here's the ISBOLD function rewritten so that it works also with bold formatting applied as a result of conditional formatting:

```
Function ISBOLD (cell) As Boolean
'   Returns TRUE if cell is bold, even if from conditional formatting
    ISBOLD = cell.Range("A1").DisplayFormat.Font.Bold
End Function
```

The following function returns TRUE if its single-cell argument has italic formatting:

```
Function ISITALIC(cell) As Boolean
'   Returns TRUE if cell is italic
    ISITALIC = cell.Range("A1").Font.Italic
End Function
```

Both functions will return an error if the cell has mixed formatting — for example, if only *some* characters are bold. The following function returns TRUE only if all characters in the cell are bold:

```
Function ALLBOLD(cell) As Boolean
'   Returns TRUE if all characters in cell are bold
    If IsNull(cell.Font.Bold) Then
        ALLBOLD = False
    Else
        ALLBOLD = cell.Font.Bold
    End If
End Function
```

You can simplify the ALLBOLD function as follows:

```
Function ALLBOLD (cell) As Boolean
'   Returns TRUE if all characters in cell are bold
    ALLBOLD = Not IsNull(cell.Font.Bold)
End Function
```

The FILLCOLOR function returns an integer that corresponds to the color index of the cell's interior. The actual color depends on the applied workbook theme. If the cell's interior isn't filled, the function returns −4142. This function doesn't work with fill colors applied in tables (created with Insert➜Tables➜Table) or pivot tables. You need to use the DisplayFormat object to detect that type of fill color, as I described previously.

```
Function FILLCOLOR(cell) As Integer
'   Returns an integer corresponding to
'   cell's interior color
    FILLCOLOR = cell.Range("A1").Interior.ColorIndex
End Function
```

A talking worksheet

The SAYIT function uses Excel's text-to-speech generator to "speak" its argument (which can be literal text or a cell reference):

```
Function SAYIT(txt)
    Application.Speech.Speak (txt)
    SAYIT = txt
End Function
```

This function has some amusing possibilities, but it can also be useful. For example, use the function in a formula like this:

```
=IF(SUM(A:A)>25000,SAYIT("Goal Reached"))
```

If the sum of the values in column A exceeds 25,000, you'll hear the synthesized voice tell you that the goal has been reached. You can use the Speak method also at the end of a lengthy procedure. That way, you can do something else and get an audible notice when the procedure ends.

Displaying the date when a file was saved or printed

An Excel workbook contains several built-in document properties, accessible from the BuiltinDocumentProperties property of the Workbook object. The following function returns the date and time that the workbook was last saved:

```
Function LASTSAVED()
    Application.Volatile
    LASTSAVED = ThisWorkbook. _
      BuiltinDocumentProperties("Last Save Time")
End Function
```

The date and time returned by this function are the same date and time that appear in the Related Dates section of Backstage view when you choose File➜Info. Note that the AutoSave feature also affects this value. In other words, "Last Save Time" is not necessarily the last time the file was saved by the *user*.

The following function is similar to LASTSAVED, but it returns the date and time when the workbook was last printed or previewed. If the workbook has never been printed or previewed, the function returns a #VALUE error.

```
Function LASTPRINTED()
    Application.Volatile
    LASTPRINTED = ThisWorkbook. _
      BuiltinDocumentProperties("Last Print Date")
End Function
```

If you use these functions in a formula, you might need to force a recalculation (by pressing F9) to get the current values of these properties.

Note

Quite a few additional built-in properties are available, but Excel doesn't use all of them. For example, attempting to access the Number of Bytes property will generate an error. For a list of all built-in properties, consult the Help system.

The preceding LASTSAVED and LASTPRINTED functions are designed to be stored in the workbook in which they're used. In some cases, you may want to store the function in a different workbook (for example, personal.xlsb) or in an add-in. Because these functions reference ThisWorkbook, they won't work correctly. Following are more general-purpose versions of these functions. These functions use Application.Caller, which returns a Range object that represents the cell that calls the function. The use of Parent.Parent returns the workbook (that is, the parent of the parent of the Range object — a Workbook object). This topic is explained further in the next section.

```
Function LASTSAVED2()
    Application.Volatile
    LASTSAVED2 = Application.Caller.Parent.Parent. _
      BuiltinDocumentProperties("Last Save Time")
End Function
```

Understanding object parents

As you know, Excel's object model is a hierarchy: Objects are contained in other objects. At the top of the hierarchy is the Application object. Excel contains other objects, and these objects contain other objects, and so on. The following hierarchy depicts how a Range object fits into this scheme:

> Application object
>> Workbook object
>>> Worksheet object
>>>> Range object

In the lingo of object-oriented programming, a Range object's parent is the Worksheet object that contains it. A Worksheet object's parent is the Workbook object that contains the worksheet, and a Workbook object's parent is the Application object.

How can you put this information to use? Examine the SheetName VBA function that follows. This function accepts a single argument (a range) and returns the name of the worksheet that contains the range. It uses the Parent property of the Range object. The Parent property returns an object: the object that contains the Range object.

```
Function SHEETNAME(ref) As String
    SHEETNAME = ref.Parent.Name
End Function
```

The next function, WORKBOOKNAME, returns the name of the workbook for a particular cell. Note that it uses the Parent property twice. the first Parent property returns a Worksheet object, and the second Parent property returns a Workbook object.

```
Function WORKBOOKNAME(ref) As String
    WORKBOOKNAME = ref.Parent.Parent.Name
End Function
```

The APPNAME function that follows carries this exercise to the next logical level, accessing the Parent property three times (the parent of the parent of the parent). This function returns the name of the Application object for a particular cell. It will, of course, always return Microsoft Excel.

```
Function APPNAME(ref) As String
    APPNAME = ref.Parent.Parent.Parent.Name
End Function
```

Counting cells between two values

The following function, named COUNTBETWEEN, returns the number of values in a range (first argument) that fall between values represented by the second and third arguments:

```
Function COUNTBETWEEN(InRange, num1, num2) As Long
'    Counts number of values between num1 and num2
    With Application.WorksheetFunction
        If num1 <= num2 Then
            COUNTBETWEEN = .CountIfs(InRange, ">=" & num1, _
                InRange, "<=" & num2)
        Else
            COUNTBETWEEN = .CountIfs(InRange, ">=" & num2, _
                InRange, "<=" & num1)
        End If
    End With
End Function
```

Note that this function uses Excel's COUNTIFS function. The CountBetween function is essentially a wrapper that can simplify your formulas.

Note

COUNTIFS was introduced in Excel 2007, so this function won't work with previous versions of Excel.

Following is an example formula that uses the COUNTBETWEEN function. The formula returns the number of cells in A1:A100 that are greater than or equal to 10 and less than or equal to 20.

```
=COUNTBETWEEN(A1:A100,10,20)
```

The function accepts the two numeric argument in either order. The following formula is equivalent to the preceding one:

```
=COUNTBETWEEN(A1:A100,20,10)
```

Using this VBA function is simpler than entering the following (somewhat confusing) formula:

```
=COUNTIFS(A1:A100,">=10",A1:A100,"<=20")
```

The formula approach is faster, however.

Determining the last nonempty cell in a column or row

In this section, I present two useful functions: LASTINCOLUMN returns the contents of the last non-empty cell in a column, and LASTINROW returns the contents of the last nonempty cell in a row. Each function accepts a range as its single argument. The range argument can be a complete column (for LASTINCOLUMN) or a complete row (for LASTINROW). If the supplied argument isn't a complete column or row, the function uses the column or row of the upper-left cell in the range. For example, the following formula returns the last value in column B:

```
=LASTINCOLUMN(B5)
```

The following formula returns the last value in row 7:

```
=LASTINROW(C7:D9)
```

The LASTINCOLUMN function follows:

```
Function LASTINCOLUMN(rng As Range)
'    Returns the contents of the last non-empty cell in a column
    Dim LastCell As Range
    Application.Volatile
    With rng.Parent
        With .Cells(.Rows.Count, rng.Column)
            If Not IsEmpty(.Value) Then
                LASTINCOLUMN = .Value
            ElseIf IsEmpty(.End(xlUp)) Then
                LASTINCOLUMN = ""
            Else
                LASTINCOLUMN = .End(xlUp).Value
            End If
        End With
    End With
End Function
```

This function is complicated, so here are a few points that may help you understand it:

➤ Application.Volatile causes the function to be executed whenever the sheet is calculated.

➤ Rows.Count returns the number of rows in the worksheet. I used the Count property rather than hard-coding the value because not all worksheets have the same number of rows.

➤ rng.Column returns the column number of the upper-left cell in the rng argument.

➤ Using rng.Parent causes the function to work properly even if the rng argument refers to a different sheet or workbook.

➤ The End method (with the xlUp argument) is equivalent to activating the last cell in a column, pressing End, and then pressing the up-arrow key.

➤ The IsEmpty function checks whether the cell is empty. If so, it returns an empty string. Without this statement, an empty cell would be returned as 0.

The LASTINROW function follows. This function is similar to the LASTINCOLUMN function.

```
Function LASTINROW(rng As Range)
'    Returns the contents of the last non-empty cell in a row
    Application.Volatile
    With rng.Parent
        With .Cells(rng.Row, .Columns.Count)
            If Not IsEmpty(.Value) Then
                LASTINROW = .Value
            ElseIf IsEmpty(.End(xlToLeft)) Then
                LASTINROW = ""
            Else
                LASTINROW = .End(xlToLeft).Value
            End If
        End With
    End With
End Function
```

Does a string match a pattern?

The ISLIKE function is simple but also useful. This function returns TRUE if a text string matches a specified pattern.

```
Function ISLIKE(text As String, pattern As String) As Boolean
'    Returns true if the first argument is like the second
    ISLIKE = text Like pattern
End Function
```

The function is remarkably simple. It is essentially a wrapper that lets you take advantage of VBA's powerful Like operator in your formulas.

This ISLIKE function takes two arguments:

➤ text: A text string or a reference to a cell that contains a text string

➤ pattern: A string that contains wildcard characters according to the following list:

Character(s) in Pattern	Matches in Text
?	Any single character
*	Zero or more characters
#	Any single digit (0–9)
[charlist]	Any single character in charlist
[!charlist]	Any single character not in charlist

The following formula returns TRUE because * matches any number of characters. The formula returns TRUE if the first argument is any text that begins with g.

```
=ISLIKE("guitar","g*")
```

The following formula returns TRUE because ? matches any single character. If the first argument were "Unit12", the function would return FALSE.

```
=ISLIKE("Unit1","Unit?")
```

The next formula returns TRUE because the first argument is a single character in the second argument:

```
=ISLIKE("a","[aeiou]")
```

The following formula returns TRUE if cell A1 contains *a, e, i, o, u, A, E, I, O,* or *U*. Using the UPPER function for the arguments makes the formula not case-sensitive.

```
=ISLIKE(UPPER(A1), UPPER("[aeiou]"))
```

The following formula returns TRUE if cell A1 contains a value that begins with 1 and has exactly three digits (that is, any integer between 100 and 199):

```
=ISLIKE(A1,"1##")
```

Extracting the nth element from a string

EXTRACTELEMENT is a custom worksheet function (which you can also call from a VBA procedure) that extracts an element from a text string. For example, if a cell contains the following text, you can use the EXTRACTELEMENT function to extract any of the substrings between the hyphens.

```
123-456-789-0133-8844
```

The following formula, for example, returns 0133, which is the fourth element in the string. The string uses a hyphen (-) as the separator.

```
=EXTRACTELEMENT("123-456-789-0133-8844",4,"-")
```

The EXTRACTELEMENT function uses three arguments:

> ➤ Txt: The text string from which you're extracting. It can be a literal string or a cell reference.

> ➤ n: An integer that represents the element to extract.

> ➤ Separator: A single character used as the separator.

Note

If you specify a space as the Separator argument, multiple spaces are treated as a single space, which is almost always what you want. If n exceeds the number of elements in the string, the function returns an empty string.

The VBA code for the EXTRACTELEMENT function follows:

```
Function EXTRACTELEMENT(Txt, n, Separator) As String
'    Returns the nth element of a text string, where the
'    elements are separated by a specified separator character
    Dim AllElements As Variant
    AllElements = Split(Txt, Separator)
    EXTRACTELEMENT = AllElements(n - 1)
End Function
```

This function uses the VBA Split function, which returns a variant array that contains each element of the text string. This array begins with 0 (not 1), so using n - 1 references the desired element.

Spelling out a number

The SPELLDOLLARS function returns a number spelled out in text — as on a check. For example, the following formula returns the string *One hundred twenty-three and 45/100 dollars:*

```
=SPELLDOLLARS(123.45)
```

Figure 9-21 shows some additional examples of the SPELLDOLLARS function. Column C contains formulas that use the function. For example, the formula in C1 is

```
=SPELLDOLLARS(A1)
```

Note that negative numbers are spelled out and enclosed in parentheses.

	A	B	C	D	E	F	G	H	I	J
1	32		Thirty-Two and 00/100 Dollars							
2	37.56		Thirty-Seven and 56/100 Dollars							
3	-32		(Thirty-Two and 00/100 Dollars)							
4	-26.44		(Twenty-Six and 44/100 Dollars)							
5	-4		(Four and 00/100 Dollars)							
6	1.87341		One and 87/100 Dollars							
7	1.56		One and 56/100 Dollars							
8	1		One and 00/100 Dollars							
9	6.56		Six and 56/100 Dollars							
10	12.12		Twelve and 12/100 Dollars							
11	1000000		One Million and 00/100 Dollars							
12	10000000000		Ten Billion and 00/100 Dollars							
13	1111111111		One Billion One Hundred Eleven Million One Hundred Eleven Thousand One Hundred Eleven and 00/100 Dollars							
14										
15										

Sheet1

Figure 9-21: Examples of the SPELLDOLLARS function.

The SPELLDOLLARS function is too lengthy to list here, but you can view the complete listing in spelldollars function.xlsm on the book's website.

A multifunctional function

The next example describes a technique that may be helpful in some situations: making a single worksheet function act like multiple functions. The following VBA listing is for a custom function called STATFUNCTION, which takes two arguments: the range (rng) and the operation (op). Depending on the value of op, the function returns a value computed using any of the following worksheet functions: AVERAGE, COUNT, MAX, MEDIAN, MIN, MODE, STDEV, SUM, or VAR.

For example, you can use this function in your worksheet as follows:

```
=STATFUNCTION(B1:B24,A24)
```

The result of the formula depends on the contents of cell A24, which should be a string such as Average, Count, or Max. You can adapt this technique for other types of functions.

```
Function STATFUNCTION (rng, op)
    Select Case UCase(op)
        Case "SUM"
            STATFUNCTION = WorksheetFunction.Sum(rng)
        Case "AVERAGE"
            STATFUNCTION = WorksheetFunction.Average(rng)
        Case "MEDIAN"
            STATFUNCTION = WorksheetFunction.Median(rng)
        Case "MODE"
            STATFUNCTION = WorksheetFunction.Mode(rng)
        Case "COUNT"
            STATFUNCTION = WorksheetFunction.Count(rng)
        Case "MAX"
            STATFUNCTION = WorksheetFunction.Max(rng)
        Case "MIN"
            STATFUNCTION = WorksheetFunction.Min(rng)
        Case "VAR"
            STATFUNCTION = WorksheetFunction.Var(rng)
        Case "STDEV"
            STATFUNCTION = WorksheetFunction.StDev(rng)
        Case Else
            STATFUNCTION = CVErr(xlErrNA)
    End Select
End Function
```

The SHEETOFFSET function

You probably know that Excel's support for 3-D workbooks is limited. For example, if you need to refer to a different worksheet in a workbook, you must include the worksheet's name in your formula. Adding the worksheet name isn't a big problem . . . until you attempt to copy the formula across other worksheets. The copied formulas continue to refer to the original worksheet name, and the sheet references aren't adjusted as they would be in a true 3-D workbook.

The example discussed in this section is the VBA SHEETOFFSET function, which enables you to address worksheets in a relative manner. For example, you can refer to cell A1 on the previous worksheet by using this formula:

```
=SHEETOFFSET(-1,A1)
```

The first argument represents the relative sheet, and it can be positive, negative, or zero. The second argument must be a reference to a single cell. You can copy this formula to other sheets, and the relative referencing will be in effect in all the copied formulas.

The VBA code for the SHEETOFFSET function follows:

```
Function SHEETOFFSET (Offset As Long, Optional Cell As Variant)
'    Returns cell contents at Ref, in sheet offset
    Dim WksIndex As Long, WksNum As Long
    Dim wks As Worksheet
    Application.Volatile
    If IsMissing(Cell) Then Set Cell = Application.Caller
    WksNum = 1
    For Each wks In Application.Caller.Parent.Parent.Worksheets
        If Application.Caller.Parent.Name = wks.Name Then
            SHEETOFFSET = Worksheets(WksNum + Offset).Range(Cell(1).Address)
            Exit Function
        Else
            WksNum = WksNum + 1
        End If
    Next wks
End Function
```

Returning the maximum value across all worksheets

If you need to determine the maximum value in cell B1 across a number of worksheets, you would use a formula such as this:

```
=MAX(Sheet1:Sheet4!B1)
```

This formula returns the maximum value in cell B1 for Sheet1, Sheet4, and all the sheets in between.

But what if you add a new sheet (Sheet5) after Sheet4? Your formula won't adjust automatically, so you need to edit the formula to include the new sheet reference:

```
=MAX(Sheet1:Sheet5!B1)
```

The MaxAllSheets function accepts a single-cell argument and returns the maximum value in that cell across all worksheets in the workbook. The formula that follows, for example, returns the maximum value in cell B1 for all sheets in the workbook:

```
=MAXALLSHEETS(B1)
```

If you add a new sheet, you don't need to edit the formula:

```
Function MAXALLSHEETS (cell)
    Dim MaxVal As Double
    Dim Addr As String
    Dim Wksht As Object
    Application.Volatile
    Addr = cell.Range("A1").Address
    MaxVal = -9.9E+307
    For Each Wksht In cell.Parent.Parent.Worksheets
        If Wksht.Name = cell.Parent.Name And _
          Addr = Application.Caller.Address Then
        ' avoid circular reference
        Else
            If IsNumeric(Wksht.Range(Addr)) Then
                If Wksht.Range(Addr) > MaxVal Then _
                    MaxVal = Wksht.Range(Addr).Value
            End If
        End If
    Next Wksht
    If MaxVal = -9.9E+307 Then MaxVal = 0
    MAXALLSHEETS = MaxVal
End Function
```

The For Each statement uses the following expression to access the workbook:

```
cell.Parent.Parent.Worksheets
```

The parent of the cell is a worksheet, and the parent of the worksheet is the workbook. Therefore, the For Each-Next loop cycles among all worksheets in the workbook. The first If statement inside the loop performs a check to see whether the cell being checked is the cell that contains the function. If so, that cell is ignored to avoid a circular reference error.

Note   You can easily modify this function to perform other cross-worksheet calculations, such as minimum, average, and sum.

Returning an array of nonduplicated random integers

The function in this section, RANDOMINTEGERS, returns an array of nonduplicated integers. The function is intended to be used in a multicell array formula.

```
{=RANDOMINTEGERS()}
```

Select a range and then enter the formula by pressing Ctrl+Shift+Enter. The formula returns an array of nonduplicated integers, arranged randomly. For example, if you enter the formula into a 50-cell range, the formulas will return nonduplicated integers from 1 to 50.

The code for RANDOMINTEGERS follows:

```
Function RANDOMINTEGERS()
    Dim FuncRange As Range
    Dim V() As Variant, ValArray() As Variant
    Dim CellCount As Double
    Dim i As Integer, j As Integer
    Dim r As Integer, c As Integer
    Dim Temp1 As Variant, Temp2 As Variant
    Dim RCount As Integer, CCount As Integer

'   Create Range object
    Set FuncRange = Application.Caller

'   Return an error if FuncRange is too large
    CellCount = FuncRange.Count
    If CellCount > 1000 Then
        RANDOMINTEGERS = CVErr(xlErrNA)
        Exit Function
    End If

'   Assign variables
    RCount = FuncRange.Rows.Count
    CCount = FuncRange.Columns.Count
    ReDim V(1 To RCount, 1 To CCount)
    ReDim ValArray(1 To 2, 1 To CellCount)

'   Fill array with random numbers
'   and consecutive integers
    For i = 1 To CellCount
        ValArray(1, i) = Rnd
        ValArray(2, i) = i
    Next i

'   Sort ValArray by the random number dimension
    For i = 1 To CellCount
        For j = i + 1 To CellCount
            If ValArray(1, i) > ValArray(1, j) Then
                Temp1 = ValArray(1, j)
                Temp2 = ValArray(2, j)
                ValArray(1, j) = ValArray(1, i)
                ValArray(2, j) = ValArray(2, i)
                ValArray(1, i) = Temp1
                ValArray(2, i) = Temp2
            End If
```

continued

```
        Next j
    Next i

'   Put the randomized values into the V array
    i = 0
    For r = 1 To RCount
        For c = 1 To CCount
            i = i + 1
            V(r, c) = ValArray(2, i)
        Next c
    Next r
    RANDOMINTEGERS = V
End Function
```

Randomizing a range

The RANGERANDOMIZE function, which follows, accepts a range argument and returns an array that consists of the input range — in random order:

```
Function RANGERANDOMIZE(rng)
    Dim V() As Variant, ValArray() As Variant
    Dim CellCount As Double
    Dim i As Integer, j As Integer
    Dim r As Integer, c As Integer
    Dim Temp1 As Variant, Temp2 As Variant
    Dim RCount As Integer, CCount As Integer

'   Return an error if rng is too large
    CellCount = rng.Count
    If CellCount > 1000 Then
        RANGERANDOMIZE = CVErr(xlErrNA)
        Exit Function
    End If

'   Assign variables
    RCount = rng.Rows.Count
    CCount = rng.Columns.Count
    ReDim V(1 To RCount, 1 To CCount)
    ReDim ValArray(1 To 2, 1 To CellCount)

'   Fill ValArray with random numbers
'   and values from rng
    For i = 1 To CellCount
        ValArray(1, i) = Rnd
        ValArray(2, i) = rng(i)
    Next i

'   Sort ValArray by the random number dimension
    For i = 1 To CellCount
```

```
            For j = i + 1 To CellCount
                If ValArray(1, i) > ValArray(1, j) Then
                    Temp1 = ValArray(1, j)
                    Temp2 = ValArray(2, j)
                    ValArray(1, j) = ValArray(1, i)
                    ValArray(2, j) = ValArray(2, i)
                    ValArray(1, i) = Temp1
                    ValArray(2, i) = Temp2
                End If
            Next j
        Next i

'       Put the randomized values into the V array
        i = 0
        For r = 1 To RCount
            For c = 1 To CCount
                i = i + 1
                V(r, c) = ValArray(2, i)
            Next c
        Next r
        RANGERANDOMIZE = V
End Function
```

The code is similar to that for the RANDOMINTEGERS function.

Figure 9-22 shows the function in use. The array formula in B2:B11 is

```
{=RANGERANDOMIZE(A2:A11)}
```

This formula returns the contents of A2:A11, but in random order.

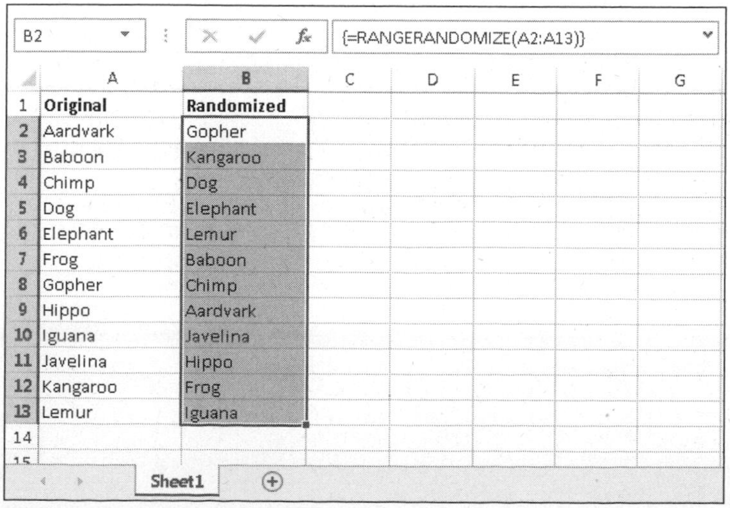

Figure 9-22: The RANGERANDOMIZE function returns the contents of a range, in random order.

Sorting a range

The SORTED function accepts a single-column range argument and returns the range, sorted:

```
Function SORTED(Rng)
    Dim SortedData() As Variant
    Dim Cell As Range
    Dim Temp As Variant, i As Long, j As Long
    Dim NonEmpty As Long

'   Transfer data to SortedData
    For Each Cell In Rng
        If Not IsEmpty(Cell) Then
            NonEmpty = NonEmpty + 1
            ReDim Preserve SortedData(1 To NonEmpty)
            SortedData(NonEmpty) = Cell.Value
        End If
    Next Cell

'   Sort the array
    For i = 1 To NonEmpty
        For j = i + 1 To NonEmpty
            If SortedData(i) > SortedData(j) Then
                Temp = SortedData(j)
                SortedData(j) = SortedData(i)
                SortedData(i) = Temp
            End If
        Next j
    Next i

'   Transpose the array and return it
    SORTED = Application.Transpose(SortedData)
End Function
```

Figure 9-23 shows the SORTED function in use. It's entered as a multicell array formula.

The SORTED function starts by creating an array named SortedData. This array contains all nonblank values in the argument range. Next, the array is sorted, using a bubble sort algorithm. Because the array is a horizontal array, it must be transposed before it is returned by the function.

The SORTED function works with a range of any size, as long as it's in a single column or row. If the unsorted data is in a row, your formula needs to use Excel's TRANSPOSE function to display the sorted data horizontally. For example:

```
=TRANSPOSE(SORTED(A16:L16))
```

Figure 9-23: The SORTED function returns the contents of a range, sorted.

Windows API Calls

VBA has the capability to use functions that are stored in Dynamic Link Libraries (DLLs). The examples in this section use common Windows API calls to DLLs.

Note

For simplicity, the API function declarations presented in this section work only with Excel 2010 and Excel 2013 (both the 32-bit and 64-bit versions). However, the example files on the book's website use compiler directives so they will work with previous versions of Excel.

Determining file associations

In Windows, many file types are associated with a particular application. This association makes it possible to double-click the file to load it into its associated application.

The following function, named GetExecutable, uses a Windows API call to get the full path to the application associated with a particular file. For example, your system has many files with a .txt extension — one named Readme.txt is probably in your Windows directory right now. You can use the GetExecutable function to determine the full path of the application that opens when the file is double-clicked.

Note   **Windows API declarations must appear at the top of your VBA module.**

```
Private Declare PtrSafe Function FindExecutableA Lib "shell32.dll" _
    (ByVal lpFile As String, ByVal lpDirectory As String, _
    ByVal lpResult As String) As Long
```

```
Function GetExecutable(strFile As String) As String
    Dim strPath As String
    Dim intLen As Integer
    strPath = Space(255)
    intLen = FindExecutableA(strFile, "\", strPath)
    GetExecutable = Trim(strPath)
End Function
```

Figure 9-24 shows the result of calling the GetExecutable function, with an argument of the filename for an MP3 audio file. The function returns the full path of the application associated with the file.

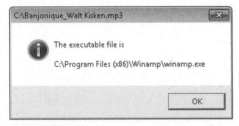

Figure 9-24: Determining the path and name of the application associated with a particular file.

On the Web

This example is available on this book's website in the file association.xlsm file.

Determining disk drive information

VBA doesn't have a way to directly get information about disk drives. But with the assistance of three API functions, you can get all the information you need.

Figure 9-25 shows the output from a VBA procedure that identifies all connected drives, determines the drive type, and calculates total space, used space, and free space.

On the Web

The code is lengthy, so I don't list it here, but the interested reader should be able to figure it out by examining the code in the example file, drive information.xlsm, on the book's website.

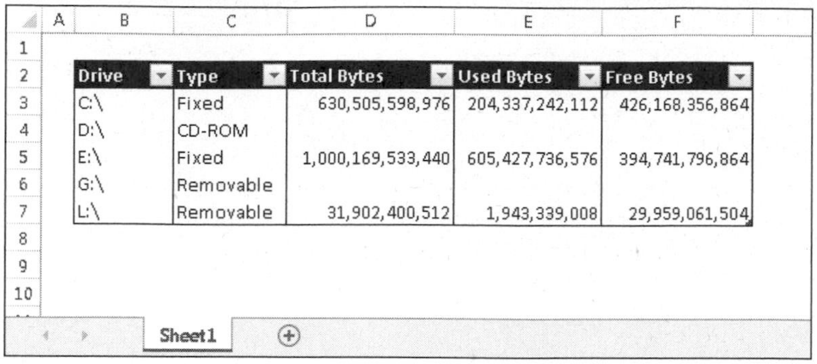

Drive	Type	Total Bytes	Used Bytes	Free Bytes
C:\	Fixed	630,505,598,976	204,337,242,112	426,168,356,864
D:\	CD-ROM			
E:\	Fixed	1,000,169,533,440	605,427,736,576	394,741,796,864
G:\	Removable			
L:\	Removable	31,902,400,512	1,943,339,008	29,959,061,504

Figure 9-25: Using Windows API functions to get disk drive information.

Determining default printer information

The example in this section uses a Windows API function to return information about the active printer. The information is contained in a single text string. The example parses the string and displays the information in a more readable format.

```
Private Declare PtrSafe Function GetProfileStringA Lib "kernel32" _
   (ByVal lpAppName As String, ByVal lpKeyName As String, _
    ByVal lpDefault As String, ByVal lpReturnedString As _
    String, ByVal nSize As Long) As Long

Sub DefaultPrinterInfo()
    Dim strLPT As String * 255
    Dim Result As String
    Call GetProfileStringA _
      ("Windows", "Device", "", strLPT, 254)

    Result = Application.Trim(strLPT)
    ResultLength = Len(Result)

    Comma1 = InStr(1, Result, ",", 1)
    Comma2 = InStr(Comma1 + 1, Result, ",", 1)

'   Gets printer's name
    Printer = Left(Result, Comma1 - 1)

'   Gets driver
    Driver = Mid(Result, Comma1 + 1, Comma2 - Comma1 - 1)

'   Gets last part of device line
    Port = Right(Result, ResultLength - Comma2)
```

continued

```
'    Build message
     Msg = "Printer:" & Chr(9) & Printer & Chr(13)
     Msg = Msg & "Driver:" & Chr(9) & Driver & Chr(13)
     Msg = Msg & "Port:" & Chr(9) & Port

'    Display message
     MsgBox Msg, vbInformation, "Default Printer Information"
End Sub
```

Note The ActivePrinter property of the Application object returns the name of the active printer (and lets you change it), but there's no direct way to determine what printer driver or port is being used. That's why this function may be useful.

Figure 9-26 shows a sample message box returned by this procedure.

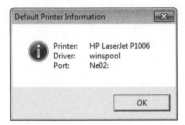

Figure 9-26: Getting information about the active printer by using a Windows API call.

On the Web This example is available on this book's website in the printer info.xlsm file.

Determining video display information

The example in this section uses Windows API calls to determine a system's current video mode for the primary display monitor. If your application needs to display a certain amount of information on one screen, knowing the display size helps you scale the text accordingly. In addition, the code determines the number of monitors. If more than one monitor is installed, the procedure reports the virtual screen size.

```
Declare PtrSafe Function GetSystemMetrics Lib "user32" _
  (ByVal nIndex As Long) As Long

Public Const SM_CMONITORS = 80
Public Const SM_CXSCREEN = 0
Public Const SM_CYSCREEN = 1
```

```vba
Public Const SM_CXVIRTUALSCREEN = 78
Public Const SM_CYVIRTUALSCREEN = 79

Sub DisplayVideoInfo()
    Dim numMonitors As Long
    Dim vidWidth As Long, vidHeight As Long
    Dim virtWidth As Long, virtHeight As Long
    Dim Msg As String

    numMonitors = GetSystemMetrics(SM_CMONITORS)
    vidWidth = GetSystemMetrics(SM_CXSCREEN)
    vidHeight = GetSystemMetrics(SM_CYSCREEN)
    virtWidth = GetSystemMetrics(SM_CXVIRTUALSCREEN)
    virtHeight = GetSystemMetrics(SM_CYVIRTUALSCREEN)

    If numMonitors > 1 Then
        Msg = numMonitors & " display monitors" & vbCrLf
        Msg = Msg & "Virtual screen: " & virtWidth & " X "
        Msg = Msg & virtHeight & vbCrLf & vbCrLf
        Msg = Msg & "The video mode on the primary display is: "
        Msg = Msg & vidWidth & " X " & vidHeight
    Else
        Msg = Msg & "The video display mode: "
        Msg = Msg & vidWidth & " X " & vidHeight
    End If
    MsgBox Msg
End Sub
```

Figure 9-27 shows the message box returned by this procedure when running on a dual-monitor system.

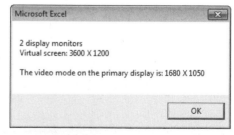

Figure 9-27: Using a Windows API call to determine the video display mode.

On the Web This example is available on the book's website in the video mode.xlsm file.

Reading from and writing to the Registry

Most Windows applications use the Windows Registry database to store settings. Your VBA procedures can read values from the Registry and write new values to the Registry. Doing so requires the following Windows API declarations:

```
Private Declare PtrSafe Function RegOpenKeyA Lib "ADVAPI32.DLL" _
    (ByVal hKey As Long, ByVal sSubKey As String, _
    ByRef hkeyResult As Long) As Long

Private Declare PtrSafe Function RegCloseKey Lib "ADVAPI32.DLL" _
    (ByVal hKey As Long) As Long

Private Declare PtrSafe Function RegSetValueExA Lib "ADVAPI32.DLL" _
    (ByVal hKey As Long, ByVal sValueName As String, _
    ByVal dwReserved As Long, ByVal dwType As Long, _
    ByVal sValue As String, ByVal dwSize As Long) As Long

Private Declare PtrSafe Function RegCreateKeyA Lib "ADVAPI32.DLL" _
    (ByVal hKey As Long, ByVal sSubKey As String, _
    ByRef hkeyResult As Long) As Long

Private Declare PtrSafe Function RegQueryValueExA Lib "ADVAPI32.DLL" _
    (ByVal hKey As Long, ByVal sValueName As String, _
    ByVal dwReserved As Long, ByRef lValueType As Long, _
    ByVal sValue As String, ByRef lResultLen As Long) As Long
```

On the Web

I developed two wrapper functions that simplify the task of working with the Registry: GetRegistry and WriteRegistry. These functions are available on this book's website in a file named windows registry.xlsm. This workbook includes a procedure that demonstrates reading from the Registry and writing to the Registry.

Reading from the Registry

The GetRegistry function returns a setting from the specified location in the Registry. It takes three arguments:

➤ RootKey: A string that represents the branch of the Registry to address. This string can be one of the following:

- HKEY_CLASSES_ROOT
- HKEY_CURRENT_USER

- HKEY_LOCAL_MACHINE
- HKEY_USERS
- HKEY_CURRENT_CONFIG

➤ Path: The full path of the Registry category being addressed.

➤ RegEntry: The name of the setting to retrieve.

Here's an example. If you'd like to find which graphic file, if any, is being used for the desktop wallpaper, you can call GetRegistry as follows. (Note that the arguments aren't case-sensitive.)

```
RootKey = "hkey_current_user"
Path = "Control Panel\Desktop"
RegEntry = "Wallpaper"
MsgBox GetRegistry(RootKey, Path, RegEntry), _
    vbInformation, Path & "\RegEntry"
```

The message box will display the path and filename of the graphic file (or an empty string if wallpaper isn't used).

Writing to the Registry

The WriteRegistry function writes a value to the Registry at a specified location. If the operation is successful, the function returns True; otherwise, it returns False. WriteRegistry takes the following arguments (all of which are strings):

➤ RootKey: A string that represents the branch of the Registry to address. This string may be one of the following:

- HKEY_CLASSES_ROOT
- HKEY_CURRENT_USER
- HKEY_LOCAL_MACHINE
- HKEY_USERS
- HKEY_CURRENT_CONFIG

➤ Path: The full path in the Registry. If the path doesn't exist, it is created.

➤ RegEntry: The name of the Registry category to which the value will be written. If it doesn't exist, it is added.

➤ RegVal: The value that you're writing.

An easier way to access the Registry

If you want to use the Windows Registry to store and retrieve settings for your Excel applications, you don't have to bother with the Windows API calls. Rather, you can use the VBA GetSetting and SaveSetting functions. Using these functions is *much* easier than using the API calls.

These two functions are described in the Help system, so I won't cover the details here. However, it's important to understand that these functions work only with the following key name:

HKEY_CURRENT_USER\Software\VB and VBA Program Settings

In other words, you can't use these functions to access any key in the registry. Rather, these functions are most useful for storing information about your Excel application that you need to maintain between sessions.

Here's an example that writes to the Registry a value representing the time and date Excel was started. The information is written in the area that stores Excel's settings.

```
Sub Workbook_Open()
    RootKey = "hkey_current_user"
    Path = "software\microsoft\office\15.0\excel\LastStarted"
    RegEntry = "DateTime"
    RegVal = Now()
    If WriteRegistry(RootKey, Path, RegEntry, RegVal) Then
        msg = RegVal & " has been stored in the registry."
    Else
        msg = "An error occurred"
    End If
    MsgBox msg
End Sub
```

If you store this routine in the ThisWorkbook module in your Personal Macro Workbook, the setting is automatically updated whenever you start Excel.

Working with UserForms

Custom Dialog Box Alternatives

In This Chapter

- Using an input box to get user input
- Using a message box to display messages or get a simple response
- Selecting a file from a dialog box
- Selecting a directory
- Displaying Excel's built-in dialog boxes

Before You Create That UserForm . . .

Dialog boxes are a key user interface element in many Windows programs. Virtually every Windows program uses them, and most users have a good understanding of how they work. Excel developers implement custom dialog boxes by creating UserForms. However, VBA provides the means to display some built-in dialog boxes, with minimal programming required.

Before I get into the nitty-gritty of creating UserForms (beginning with Chapter 11), you might find it helpful to understand some of Excel's built-in tools that display dialog boxes. The sections that follow describe various dialog boxes that you can display using VBA, and without creating a UserForm.

Using an Input Box

An *input box* is a simple dialog box that allows the user to make a single entry. For example, you can use an input box to let the user enter text or a number or even select a range. You can generate an InputBox in two ways: by using a VBA function and by using a method of the Application object. These are two different objects, and I explain each in the sections that follow.

The VBA InputBox function

The syntax for VBA's InputBox function is

```
InputBox(prompt[,title][,default][,xpos][,ypos][,helpfile, context])
```

➤ prompt: Required. The text displayed in the input box.

➤ title: Optional. The caption displayed in the title bar of the input box.

➤ default: Optional. The default value to be displayed in the input box.

➤ xpos, ypos: Optional. The screen coordinates of the upper-left corner of the input box.

➤ helpfile, context: Optional. The help file and help topic.

The InputBox function prompts the user for a single piece of information. The function always returns a string, so your code may need to convert the results to a value.

The prompt can consist of up to 1,024 characters. In addition, you can provide a title for the dialog box, provide a default value, and even specify the dialog box's display position on the screen. You can also specify a custom Help topic; if you do, the input box includes a Help button.

The following example, which generates the dialog box shown in Figure 10-1, uses the VBA InputBox function to ask the user for his or her full name. The code then extracts the first name and displays a greeting in a message box.

Figure 10-1: The VBA InputBox function at work.

```
Sub GetName()
    Dim UserName As String
    Dim FirstSpace As Integer
    Do Until UserName <> ""
        UserName = InputBox("Enter your full name: ", "Identify Yourself")
    Loop
    FirstSpace = InStr(UserName, " ")
    If FirstSpace <> 0 Then
        UserName = Left(UserName, FirstSpace - 1)
    End If
    MsgBox "Hello " & UserName
End Sub
```

Note that this InputBox function is written in a Do Until loop to ensure that something is entered when the input box appears. If the user clicks Cancel or doesn't enter any text, UserName contains an empty string, and the input box reappears. The procedure then attempts to extract the first name by searching for the first space character (by using the InStr function) and then using the Left function to extract all characters before the first space. If a space character isn't found, the entire name is used as entered.

Figure 10-2 shows another example of the VBA InputBox function. The user is asked to fill in the missing word. This example also illustrates the use of named arguments. The prompt text is retrieved from a worksheet cell and is assigned to a variable (p).

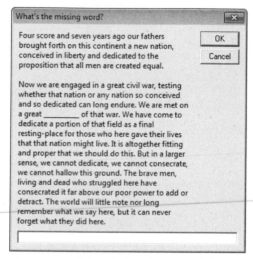

Figure 10-2: Using the VBA InputBox function with a long prompt.

```
Sub GetWord()
    Dim TheWord As String
    Dim p As String
    Dim t As String
    p = Range("A1")
    t = "What's the missing word?"
    TheWord = InputBox(prompt:=p, Title:=t)
    If UCase(TheWord) = "BATTLEFIELD" Then
        MsgBox "Correct."
    Else
        MsgBox "That is incorrect."
    End If
End Sub
```

As I mentioned, the InputBox function always returns a string. If the string returned by the InputBox function looks like a number, you can convert it to a value by using the VBA Val function or just perform a mathematical operation on the string.

The following code uses the InputBox function to prompt for a numeric value. It uses the IsNumeric function to determine if the string can be interpreted as a number. If so, it displays the user's input multiplied by 12.

```
Sub GetValue()
    Dim Monthly As String
    Dim Annual As Double
    Monthly = InputBox("Enter your monthly salary:")
    If Monthly = "" Then Exit Sub
    On Error Resume Next
    If IsNumeric(Monthly) Then
        MsgBox "Annualized: " & Monthly * 12
    Else
        MsgBox "Invalid input"
    End If
End Sub
```

On the Web

The three examples in this section are available on the book's website in the VBA inputbox.xlsm file.

The Excel InputBox method

Using Excel's InputBox method rather than the VBA InputBox function offers three advantages:

> ➤ You can specify the data type returned (it doesn't have to be a String).

> ➤ The user can specify a worksheet range by dragging in the worksheet.

> ➤ Input validation is performed automatically.

The syntax for the Excel InputBox method is

```
InputBox(Prompt [,Title][,Default][,Left][,Top][,HelpFile, HelpContextID]
    [,Type])
```

> ➤ Prompt: Required. The text displayed in the input box.

> ➤ Title: Optional. The caption in the title bar of the input box.

> ➤ Default: Optional. The default value to be returned by the function if the user enters nothing.

> ➤ Left, Top: Optional. The screen coordinates of the upper-left corner of the window.

> ➤ HelpFile, HelpContextID: Optional. The Help file and Help topic.

> ➤ Type: Optional. A code for the data type returned, as listed in Table 10-1.

Note

Apparently, the Left, Top, HelpFile, and HelpContextID arguments are no longer supported. You can specify these arguments, but they have no effect.

Table 10-1: Codes to Determine the Data Type Returned by Excel's Inputbox Method

Code	Meaning
0	A formula
1	A number
2	A string (text)
4	A logical value (True or False)
8	A cell reference, as a range object
16	An error value, such as #N/A
64	An array of values

Excel's InputBox method is versatile. To allow more than one data type to be returned, use the sum of the pertinent codes. For example, to display an input box that can accept text or numbers, set type equal to 3 (that is, 1 + 2, or number plus text). If you use 8 for the type argument, the user can enter a cell or range address (or a named cell or range) manually or point to a range in the worksheet.

The EraseRange procedure, which follows, uses the InputBox method to allow the user to select a range to erase (see Figure 10-3). The user can either type the range address manually or use the mouse to select the range in the sheet.

Figure 10-3: Using the InputBox method to specify a range.

The InputBox method with a type argument of 8 returns a Range object (note the Set keyword). This range is then erased (by using the Clear method). The default value displayed in the input box is the current selection's address. The On Error statement ends the procedure if the input box is canceled.

```
Sub EraseRange()
    Dim UserRange As Range
    On Error GoTo Canceled
    Set UserRange = Application.InputBox _
        (Prompt:="Range to erase:", _
        Title:="Range Erase", _
        Default:=Selection.Address, _
        Type:=8)
    UserRange.Clear
    UserRange.Select
Canceled:
End Sub
```

Yet another advantage of using Excel's InputBox method is that Excel performs input validation automatically. If you enter something other than a range address in the GetRange example, Excel displays a message and lets the user try again (see Figure 10-4).

Figure 10-4: Excel's InputBox method performs validation automatically.

The following code is similar to the GetValue procedure in the preceding section, but this procedure uses the Excel Inputbox method. Although I specified the type argument to be 1 (a numeric value), I declare the Monthly variable to be a variant. That's because clicking the Cancel button returns False. If the user makes a non-numeric entry, Excel displays a message and lets the user try again (see Figure 10-5).

```
Sub GetValue2()
    Dim Monthly As Variant
    Monthly = Application.InputBox _
        (Prompt:="Enter your monthly salary:", _
        Type:=1)
    If Monthly = False Then Exit Sub
    MsgBox "Annualized: " & Monthly * 12
End Sub
```

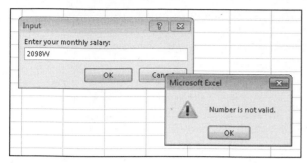

Figure 10-5: Another example of validating an entry in Excel's InputBox.

On the Web

The two examples in this section are available on the book's website in a file named inputbox method.xlsm.

The VBA MsgBox Function

VBA's MsgBox function is an easy way to display a message to the user or to get a simple response (such as OK or Cancel). I use the MsgBox function in many of the examples in this book as a way to display a variable's value.

Keep in mind that MsgBox is a function, and your code is halted until the message box is dismissed by the user.

Tip

When a message box is displayed, you can press Ctrl+C to copy the contents of the message box to the Windows clipboard.

The official syntax for MsgBox is as follows:

```
MsgBox(prompt[,buttons][,title][,helpfile, context])
```

> prompt: Required. The text displayed in the message box.

> buttons: Optional. A numeric expression that determines which buttons and icon are displayed in the message box. See Table 10-2.

> title: Optional. The caption in the message box window.

> helpfile, context: Optional. The helpfile and Help topic.

You can easily customize your message boxes because of the flexibility of the buttons argument. (Table 10-2 lists the many constants that you can use for this argument.) You can specify which buttons to display, whether an icon appears, and which button is the default.

Table 10-2: Constants Used for Buttons in the MsgBox Function

Constant	Value	Description
vbOKOnly	0	Display OK button only.
vbOKCancel	1	Display OK and Cancel buttons.
vbAbortRetryIgnore	2	Display Abort, Retry, and Ignore buttons.
vbYesNoCancel	3	Display Yes, No, and Cancel buttons.
vbYesNo	4	Display Yes and No buttons.
vbRetryCancel	5	Display Retry and Cancel buttons.
vbCritical	16	Display Critical Message icon.
vbQuestion	32	Display Warning Query icon.
vbExclamation	48	Display Warning Message icon.
vbInformation	64	Display Information Message icon.
vbDefaultButton1	0	First button is default.
vbDefaultButton2	256	Second button is default.
vbDefaultButton3	512	Third button is default.
vbDefaultButton4	768	Fourth button is default.
vbSystemModal	4096	All applications are suspended until the user responds to the message box (might not work under all conditions).
vbMsgBoxHelpButton	16384	Display a Help button. To display help when this button is clicked, use the helpfile and context arguments.

You can use the MsgBox function by itself (to simply display a message) or assign its result to a variable. When you use the MsgBox function to return a result, the value represents the button clicked by the user. The following example displays a message and an OK button but doesn't return a result:

```
Sub MsgBoxDemo()
    MsgBox "Macro finished with no errors."
End Sub
```

Note that the single argument is not enclosed in parentheses because the MsgBox result is not assigned to a variable.

To get a response from a message box, you can assign the results of the MsgBox function to a variable. In this situation, the arguments must be in parentheses. In the following code, I use some built-in constants (described in Table 10-3) to make it easier to work with the values returned by MsgBox:

```
Sub GetAnswer()
    Dim Ans As Integer
    Ans = MsgBox("Continue?", vbYesNo)
    Select Case Ans
        Case vbYes
'           ...[code if Ans is Yes]...
        Case vbNo
'           ...[code if Ans is No]...
    End Select
End Sub
```

Table 10-3: Constants Used for MsgBox Return Value

Constant	Value	Button Clicked
vbOK	1	OK
vbCancel	2	Cancel
vbAbort	3	Abort
vbRetry	4	Retry
vbIgnore	5	Ignore
vbYes	6	Yes
vbNo	7	No

The variable returned by the MsgBox function is an Integer data type. Actually, you don't even need to use a variable to utilize the result of a message box. The following procedure is another way of coding the GetAnswer procedure:

```
Sub GetAnswer2()
    If MsgBox("Continue?", vbYesNo) = vbYes Then
'           ...[code if Ans is Yes]...
    Else
'           ...[code if Ans is No]...
    End If
End Sub
```

The following function example uses a combination of constants to display a message box with a Yes button, a No button, and a question mark icon; the second button is designated as the default button (see Figure 10-6). For simplicity, I assigned these constants to the Config variable.

```
Private Function ContinueProcedure() As Boolean
    Dim Config As Integer
    Dim Ans As Integer
    Config = vbYesNo + vbQuestion + vbDefaultButton2
    Ans = MsgBox("An error occurred. Continue?", Config)
    If Ans = vbYes Then ContinueProcedure = True _
        Else ContinueProcedure = False
End Function
```

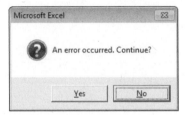

Figure 10-6: The buttons argument of the MsgBox function determines which buttons appear.

You can call the ContinueProcedure function from another procedure. For example, the following statement calls the ContinueProcedure function (which displays the message box). If the function returns False (that is, the user selects No), the procedure ends. Otherwise, the next statement is executed.

```
If Not ContinueProcedure() Then Exit Sub
```

The width of the message box depends on your video resolution. Figure 10-7 shows a message box displaying lengthy text with no forced line breaks.

If you'd like to force a line break in the message, use the vbCrLf (or vbNewLine) constant in the text. The following example displays the message in three lines:

```
Sub MultiLine()
    Dim Msg As String
    Msg = "This is the first line of text." & vbCrLf & vbCrLf
    Msg = Msg & "This is the second line." & vbCrLf
    Msg = Msg & "And this is the last line."
    MsgBox Msg
End Sub
```

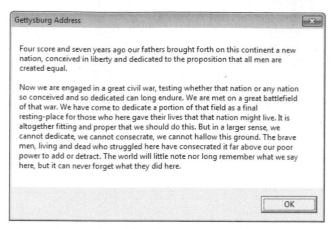

Figure 10-7: Displaying lengthy text in a message box.

You can also insert a tab character by using the vbTab constant. The following procedure uses a message box to display the values in a 13 x 3 range of cells in A1:C13 (see Figure 10-8). It separates the columns by using a vbTab constant and inserts a new line by using the vbCrLf constant. The MsgBox function accepts a maximum string length of 1,023 characters, which will limit the number of cells that you can display. Also, note that the tab stops are fixed, so if a cell contains more than 11 characters, the columns won't be aligned.

```
Sub ShowRange()
    Dim Msg As String
    Dim r As Integer, c As Integer
    Msg = ""
    For r = 1 To 12
        For c = 1 To 3
            Msg = Msg & Cells(r, c).Text
            If c <> 3 Then Msg = Msg & vbTab
        Next c
        Msg = Msg & vbCrLf
    Next r
    MsgBox Msg
End Sub
```

On the Web

Examples from this section are available on the book's website, in a file named message box examples.xlsm.

Cross-Ref

Chapter 13 includes a UserForm example that emulates the MsgBox function.

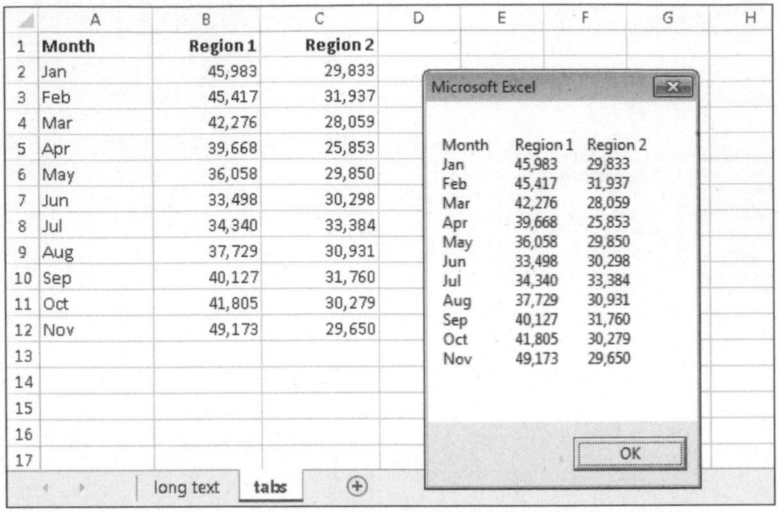

Figure 10-8: This message box displays text with tabs and line breaks.

The Excel GetOpenFilename Method

If your application needs to ask the user for a filename, you can use the InputBox function. But this approach is tedious and error-prone because the user must type the filename (with no browsing capability). A better approach is to use the GetOpenFilename method of the Application object, which ensures that your application gets a valid filename (as well as its complete path).

This method displays the normal Open dialog box, but it does *not* actually open the file specified. Rather, the method returns a string that contains the path and filename selected by the user. Then you can write code to do whatever you want with the filename.

The syntax for the GetOpenFilename method is as follows:

```
Application.GetOpenFilename(FileFilter, FilterIndex, Title, ButtonText,
    MultiSelect)
```

➤ FileFilter: Optional. A string specifying file-filtering criteria.

➤ FilterIndex: Optional. The index number of the default file-filtering criteria.

➤ Title: Optional. The title of the dialog box. If omitted, the title is Open.

➤ ButtonText: For Macintosh only.

➤ MultiSelect: Optional. If True, you can select multiple filenames. The default value is False.

The FileFilter argument determines what file types appear in the dialog box's Files of Type drop-down list. The argument consists of pairs of file filter strings followed by the wildcard file filter specification, with each part and each pair separated by commas. If omitted, this argument defaults to the following:

```
"All Files (*.*),*.*"
```

Note that the first part of this string (All Files (*.*)) is the text displayed in the Files of Type drop-down list. The second part (*.*) determines which files are displayed.

The following instruction assigns a string to a variable named Filt. You can then use this string as a FileFilter argument for the GetOpenFilename method. In this case, the dialog box will allow the user to select from four file types (plus an All Files option). Note that I used the VBA line continuation sequence to set up the Filt variable; doing so makes it much easier to work with this rather complicated argument.

```
Filt = "Text Files (*.txt),*.txt," & _
       "Lotus Files (*.prn),*.prn," & _
       "Comma Separated Files (*.csv),*.csv," & _
       "ASCII Files (*.asc),*.asc," & _
       "All Files (*.*),*.*"
```

The FilterIndex argument specifies which FileFilter is the default, and the Title argument is text that is displayed in the title bar. If the MultiSelect argument is True, the user can select multiple files, all of which are returned in an array.

The following example prompts the user for a filename. It defines five file filters.

```
Sub GetImportFileName()
    Dim Filt As String
    Dim FilterIndex As Integer
    Dim Title As String
    Dim FileName As Variant

'   Set up list of file filters
    Filt = "Text Files (*.txt),*.txt," & _
           "Lotus Files (*.prn),*.prn," & _
           "Comma Separated Files (*.csv),*.csv," & _
           "ASCII Files (*.asc),*.asc," & _
           "All Files (*.*),*.*"

'   Display *.* by default
    FilterIndex = 5

'   Set the dialog box caption
    Title = "Select a File to Import"
```

continued

```
'    Get the file name
    FileName = Application.GetOpenFilename _
        (FileFilter:=Filt, _
        FilterIndex:=FilterIndex, _
        Title:=Title)

'    Exit if dialog box canceled
    If FileName = False Then
        MsgBox "No file was selected."
        Exit Sub
    End If

'    Display full path and name of the file
    MsgBox "You selected " & FileName
End Sub
```

Figure 10-9 shows the dialog box that appears when this procedure is executed and the user selects the Text Files filter.

Figure 10-9: The GetOpenFilename method displays a dialog box used to specify a file.

The following example is similar to the preceding one. The difference is that the user can press Ctrl or Shift and select multiple files when the dialog box is displayed. I check for the Cancel button click by determining whether FileName is an array. If the user doesn't click Cancel, the result is an array that consists of at least one element. In this example, a list of the selected files is displayed in a message box.

```
Sub GetImportFileName2()
    Dim Filt As String
    Dim FilterIndex As Integer
    Dim FileName As Variant
    Dim Title As String
    Dim i As Integer
    Dim Msg As String
'   Set up list of file filters
    Filt = "Text Files (*.txt),*.txt," & _
           "Lotus Files (*.prn),*.prn," & _
           "Comma Separated Files (*.csv),*.csv," & _
           "ASCII Files (*.asc),*.asc," & _
           "All Files (*.*),*.*"
'   Display *.* by default
    FilterIndex = 5

'   Set the dialog box caption
    Title = "Select a File to Import"

'   Get the file name
    FileName = Application.GetOpenFilename _
        (FileFilter:=Filt, _
         FilterIndex:=FilterIndex, _
         Title:=Title, _
         MultiSelect:=True)

'   Exit if dialog box canceled
    If Not IsArray(FileName) Then
        MsgBox "No file was selected."
        Exit Sub
    End If

'   Display full path and name of the files
    For i = LBound(FileName) To UBound(FileName)
        Msg = Msg & FileName(i) & vbCrLf
    Next i
    MsgBox "You selected:" & vbCrLf & Msg
End Sub
```

The FileName variable is defined as a Variant data type (not a String, as in the previous examples). I use Variant because FileName can potentially hold an array rather than a single filename.

On the Web

The two examples in this section are available on the book's website in the prompt for file.xlsm file.

The Excel GetSaveAsFilename Method

The GetSaveAsFilename method, which is similar to the GetOpenFilename method, displays a Save As dialog box and lets the user select (or specify) a file. The GetSaveAsFilename method returns a filename and path but doesn't take any action.

The syntax for this method is

```
Application.GetSaveAsFilename(InitialFilename, FileFilter, FilterIndex,
    Title, ButtonText)
```

The arguments are

- ➤ InitialFilename: Optional. Specifies the suggested filename.
- ➤ FileFilter: Optional. A string specifying file-filtering criteria.
- ➤ FilterIndex: Optional. The index number of the default file-filtering criteria.
- ➤ Title: Optional. The title of the dialog box.
- ➤ ButtonText: For Macintosh only.

Prompting for a Directory

If you need to get a filename, the simplest solution is to use the GetOpenFileName method, as I describe earlier. But if you need to get a directory name only (no file), you can use Excel's FileDialog object.

The following procedure displays a dialog box that allows the user to select a directory. The selected directory name (or Canceled) is then displayed by using the MsgBox function.

```
Sub GetAFolder ()
    With Application.FileDialog(msoFileDialogFolderPicker)
        .InitialFileName = Application.DefaultFilePath & "\"
        .Title = "Select a location for the backup"
        .Show
        If .SelectedItems.Count = 0 Then
            MsgBox "Canceled"
        Else
            MsgBox .SelectedItems(1)
        End If
    End With
End Sub
```

The FileDialog object lets you specify the starting directory by providing a value for the InitialFileName property. In this example, the code uses Excel's default file path as the starting directory.

Displaying Excel's Built-In Dialog Boxes

Code that you write in VBA can execute many Excel Ribbon commands. And, if the command normally leads to a dialog box, your code can "make choices" in the dialog box (although the dialog box itself isn't displayed). For example, the following VBA statement is equivalent to choosing the Home➜Editing➜Find & Select➜Go To command, specifying the range A1:C3, and clicking OK:

```
Application.Goto Reference:=Range("A1:C3")
```

But when you execute this statement, the Go To dialog box never appears (which is almost always what you want).

In some cases, however, you may want to display one of Excel's built-in dialog boxes so that the user can make the choices. You can do so by writing code that executes a Ribbon command.

Note

Using the Dialogs collection of the Application object is another way to display an Excel dialog box. However, Microsoft has not kept this feature up-to-date, so I don't even discuss it. The method I describe in this section is a much better solution.

In previous versions of Excel, programmers created custom menus and toolbars by using the CommandBar object. In Excel 2007 and later versions, the CommandBar object is still available, but it doesn't work like it has in the past.

Cross-Ref

Refer to Chapters 20 and 21 for more information about the CommandBar object.

The CommandBar object has also been enhanced, beginning with Excel 2007. You can use the CommandBar object to execute Ribbon commands using VBA. Many of the Ribbon commands display a dialog box. For example, the following statement displays the Unhide dialog box (see Figure 10-10):

```
Application.CommandBars.ExecuteMso("SheetUnhide")
```

Figure 10-10: This dialog box was displayed with a VBA statement.

Keep in mind that your code cannot get any information about the user's action. For example, when this statement is executed, there is no way to know which sheet was selected or whether the user clicked the Cancel button. And, of course, code that executes a Ribbon command is not compatible with versions prior to Excel 2007.

The ExecuteMso method accepts one argument: an idMso parameter, which represents a Ribbon control. Unfortunately, these parameters aren't listed in the Help system.

If you try to display a built-in dialog box in an incorrect context, Excel displays an error message. For example, here's a statement that displays the Format Number dialog box:

```
Application.CommandBars.ExecuteMso ("NumberFormatsDialog")
```

 ## Executing an old menu item directly

You can display a built-in dialog box by using the ExecuteMso method. Another way to display a built-in dialog box requires knowledge of the pre-Excel 2007 toolbars, which are officially known as CommandBar objects. Although Excel no longer uses CommandBar objects, they're still supported for compatibility.

The following statement, for example, is equivalent to selecting the Format➜Sheet➜Unhide command in the Excel 2003 menu:

```
Application.CommandBars("Worksheet Menu Bar"). _
  Controls("Format").Controls("Sheet"). _
  Controls("Unhide...").Execute
```

This statement, when executed, displays the Unhide dialog box. Note that the menu item captions must match exactly (including the three dots following Unhide).

Here's another example. This statement displays the Format Cells dialog box:

```
Application.CommandBars("Worksheet Menu Bar"). _
    Controls("Format").Controls("Cells...").Execute
```

It's probably not a good idea to rely on CommandBar objects because they may be removed from a future version of Excel.

If you execute this statement when it's not appropriate (for example, when a shape is selected), Excel displays an error message because that dialog box is appropriate only for worksheet cells.

Excel has thousands of commands. How can you find the name of the one you need? One way is to use the Customize Ribbon tab of the Excel Options dialog box (right-click any Ribbon control and choose Customize the Ribbon from the shortcut menu). Virtually every command available in Excel is listed in the left panel. Find the command you need, hover your mouse cursor over it, and you'll see its command name in parentheses in the tooltip. Figure 10-11 shows an example. In this case, I learned how to display the Define Name dialog box:

```
Application.CommandBars.ExecuteMso ("NameDefine")
```

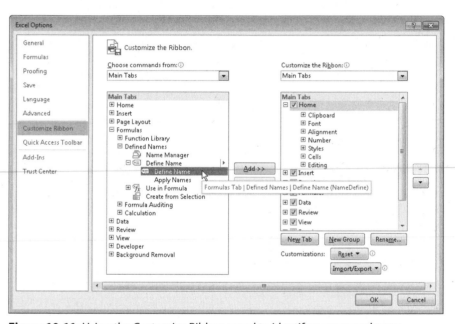

Figure 10-11: Using the Customize Ribbon panel to identify a command name.

Displaying a Data Form

Many people use Excel to manage lists in which the information is arranged in tabular form. Excel offers a simple way to work with this type of data through the use of a built-in data entry form that Excel can create automatically. This data form works with either a normal range of data or a range that has been designated as a table (by choosing the Insert→Tables→Table command). Figure 10-12 shows an example of a data form in use.

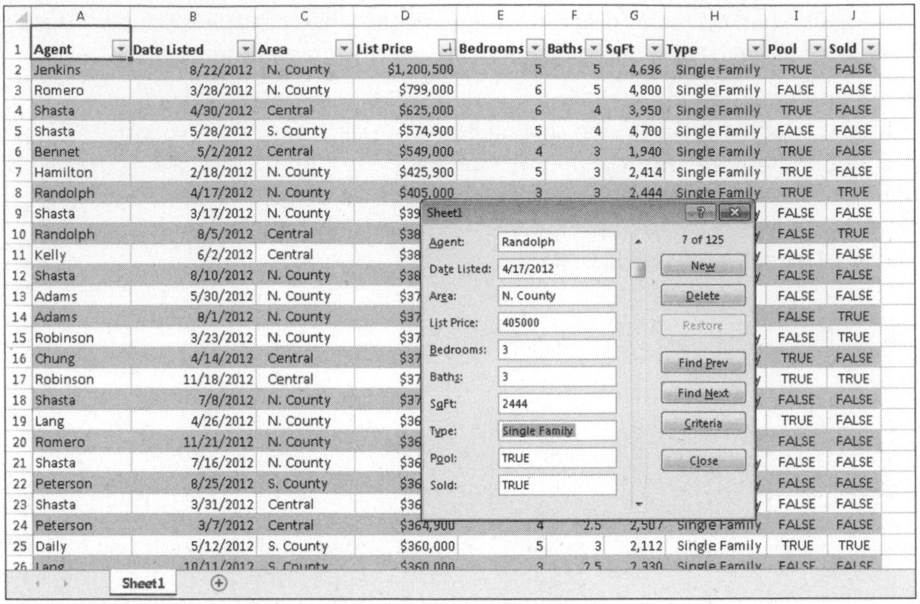

Figure 10-12: Some users prefer to use Excel's built-in data form for data-entry tasks.

Making the data form accessible

For some reason, the command to access the data form isn't on the Excel Ribbon. To access the data form from Excel's user interface, you must add it to your Quick Access toolbar or to the Ribbon. Following are instructions to add this command to the Quick Access toolbar:

1. Right-click the Quick Access toolbar and choose Customize Quick Access Toolbar.

   The Quick Access Toolbar panel of the Excel Options dialog box appears.

2. In the Choose Commands From drop-down list, select Commands Not in the Ribbon.

3. In the list box on the left, select Form.

4. Click the Add button to add the selected command to your Quick Access toolbar.

5. Click OK to close the Excel Options dialog box.

   After performing these steps, a new icon will appear on your Quick Access toolbar.

To use a data entry form, you must arrange your data so that Excel can recognize it as a table. Start by entering headings for the columns in the first row of your data entry range. Select any cell in the table and click the Form button on your Quick Access toolbar. Excel then displays a dialog box customized to your data. You can use the Tab key to move between text boxes and supply information. If a cell contains a formula, the formula result appears as text (not as an edit box). In other words, you can't modify formulas from the data entry form.

When you complete the data form, click the New button. Excel enters the data into a row in the worksheet and clears the dialog box for the next row of data.

Displaying a data form by using VBA

Use the ShowDataForm method to display Excel's data form. The only requirement is that the data table must begin in cell A1. Alternatively, the data range can have a range name of Database.

The following code displays the data form:

```
Sub DisplayDataForm()
    ActiveSheet.ShowDataForm
End Sub
```

This macro will work even if the Form command has not been added to the Ribbon or the Quick Access toolbar.

On the Web

A workbook with this example is available on the book's website in the data form example.xlsm file. If you like the idea of a general-purpose data entry form, check out my Enhanced Data Form add-in, which I created using VBA. You can download it from my website: `http://spreadsheetpage.com/index.php/dataform/`.

Introducing UserForms

11

In This Chapter

- Creating, showing, and unloading UserForms
- Exploring the UserForm controls available to you
- Setting the properties of UserForm controls
- Controlling UserForms with VBA procedures
- Creating a UserForm
- Introducing the types of events relevant to UserForms and controls
- Customizing your control Toolbox
- Going over a handy checklist for creating UserForms

How Excel Handles Custom Dialog Boxes

Excel makes creating custom dialog boxes for your applications relatively easy. In fact, you can duplicate the look and feel of many of Excel's dialog boxes. A custom dialog box is created on a UserForm, and you access UserForms in Visual Basic Editor (VBE).

Following is the typical sequence that you'll follow when you create a UserForm:

1. Insert a new UserForm into your workbook's VB Project.

2. Add controls to the UserForm.

3. Adjust some of the properties of the controls that you added.

4. Write event-handler procedures for the controls.

   These procedures, which are located in the code window for the UserForm, are executed when various events (such as a button click) occur.

5. Write a procedure that will display the UserForm.

    This procedure will be located in a VBA module (not in the code module for the UserForm).

6. Add a way to make it easy for the user to execute the procedure you created in Step 5.

    You can add a button to a worksheet, create a shortcut menu command, and so on.

Inserting a New UserForm

To insert a new UserForm, activate VBE (press Alt+F11), select your workbook's project from the Project window, and then choose Insert➔UserForm. UserForms have default names: UserForm1, UserForm2, and so on.

Tip

You can change the name of a UserForm to make it easier to identify and more descriptive. Select the form and use the Properties window to change the Name property. (Press F4 if the Properties window isn't displayed.) Figure 11-1 shows the Properties window when an empty UserForm is selected.

A workbook can have any number of UserForms, and each UserForm holds a single custom dialog box.

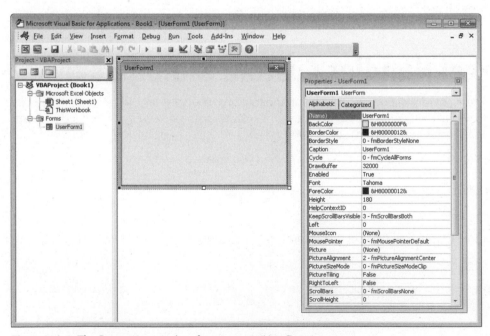

Figure 11-1: The Properties window for an empty UserForm.

Adding Controls to a UserForm

To add controls to a UserForm, use the Toolbox, as shown in Figure 11-2. (VBE doesn't have menu commands that add controls.) If the Toolbox isn't displayed, choose View➜Toolbox. The Toolbox is a floating window, so you can move it to a convenient location.

Figure 11-2: Use the Toolbox to add controls to a UserForm.

Click the Toolbox button that corresponds to the control that you want to add and then click inside the dialog box to create the control (using its default size). Or you can click the control and then drag in the dialog box to specify the dimensions for the control.

When you add a new control, it's assigned a name that combines the control type with the numeric sequence for that type of control. For example, if you add a CommandButton control to an empty UserForm, it's named CommandButton1. If you then add a second CommandButton control, it's named CommandButton2.

Tip

Renaming all the controls that you'll be manipulating with your VBA code is a good idea. Doing so lets you refer to meaningful names (such as ProductListBox) rather than generic names (such as ListBox1). To change the name of a control, use the Properties window in VBE. Just select the object and change the Name property.

Toolbox Controls

In the sections that follow, I briefly describe the controls available to you in the Toolbox.

On the Web

Figure 11-3 shows a UserForm that contains one of each control. This workbook, named all userform controls.xlsm, is available on the book's website.

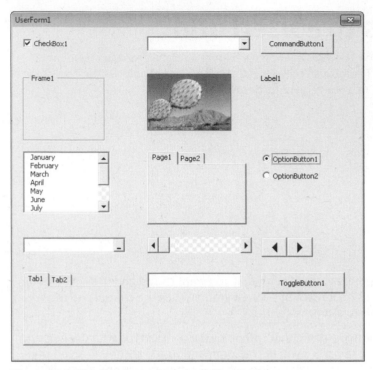

Figure 11-3: This UserForm displays all 15 controls.

Tip

Your UserForms can also use other ActiveX controls that aren't included with Excel. See "Customizing the Toolbox," later in this chapter.

CheckBox

A CheckBox control is useful for getting a binary choice: yes or no, true or false, on or off, and so on. When a CheckBox is checked, it has a value of True; when it's not checked, the CheckBox value is False.

ComboBox

A ComboBox control presents a list of items in a drop-down box and displays only one item at a time. Unlike a ListBox control, you can set up a ComboBox to allow the user to enter a value that doesn't appear in the list of items.

CommandButton

Every dialog box that you create will probably have at least one CommandButton control. Usually, your UserForms will have one CommandButton labeled OK and another labeled Cancel.

Frame

A Frame control is used to enclose other controls. You enclose controls either for aesthetic purposes or to logically group a set of controls. A Frame is particularly useful when the dialog box contains more than one set of OptionButton controls.

Image

You can use an Image control to display a graphic image, which can come from a file or can be pasted from the Clipboard. You may want to use an Image control to display your company's logo in a dialog box. The graphics image is stored in the workbook. That way, if you distribute your workbook to someone else, you don't have to include a copy of the graphics file.

Caution

Some graphics files are very large, and using such images can make your workbook increase dramatically in size. For best results, use graphics sparingly or use small graphics files.

Label

A Label control simply displays text in your dialog box.

ListBox

The ListBox control presents a list of items, and the user can select an item (or multiple items). ListBox controls are very flexible. For example, you can specify a worksheet range that holds the ListBox items, and this range can consist of multiple columns. Or you can fill the ListBox with items by using VBA.

MultiPage

A MultiPage control lets you create tabbed dialog boxes, such as the Format Cells dialog box. By default, a MultiPage control has two pages, but you can add any number of additional pages.

OptionButton

OptionButton controls are useful when the user needs to select one item from a small number of choices. OptionButtons are always used in groups of at least two. When one OptionButton is selected, the other OptionButtons in its group are deselected.

If your UserForm contains more than one set of OptionButtons, the OptionButtons in each set must share a unique GroupName property value. Otherwise, all OptionButtons become part of the same set. Alternatively, you can enclose the OptionButtons in a Frame control, which automatically groups the OptionButtons contained in the frame.

RefEdit

The RefEdit control is used when you need to let the user select a range in a worksheet. This control accepts a typed range address or a range address generated by pointing to the range in a worksheet.

ScrollBar

The ScrollBar control is similar to a SpinButton control. The difference is that the user can drag the ScrollBar button to change the control's value in larger increments. The ScrollBar control is most useful for selecting a value that extends across a wide range of possible values.

SpinButton

The SpinButton control lets the user select a value by clicking either of two arrows: one to increase the value and the other to decrease the value. A SpinButton is often used with a TextBox control or Label control, which displays the current value of the SpinButton. A SpinButton can be oriented horizontally or vertically.

TabStrip

A TabStrip control is similar to a MultiPage control, but it's not as easy to use. A TabStrip control, unlike a MultiPage control, doesn't serve as a container for other objects. Generally, you'll find that the MultiPage control is much more versatile.

TextBox

A TextBox control lets the user type text or a value.

ToggleButton

A ToggleButton control has two states: on and off. Clicking the button toggles between these two states, and the button changes its appearance. Its value is either True (pressed) or False (not pressed). I never use this control because I think a CheckBox is much clearer.

Using controls on a worksheet

You can embed many of the UserForm controls directly into a worksheet. You can access these controls by using Excel's Developer➜Controls➜Insert command. Adding such controls to a worksheet requires much less effort than creating a UserForm. In addition, you may not have to create any macros because you can link a control to a worksheet cell. For example, if you insert a CheckBox control on a worksheet, you can link it to a particular cell by setting its LinkedCell property. When the CheckBox is checked, the linked cell displays TRUE. When the CheckBox is unchecked, the linked cell displays FALSE.

The accompanying figure shows a worksheet that contains some ActiveX controls. This workbook, named activex worksheet controls.xlsx, is available on this book's website. The workbook uses linked cells and contains no macros.

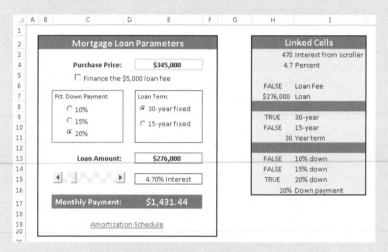

Adding controls to a worksheet can be a bit confusing because controls can come from two sources:

- **Form controls:** These controls are insertable objects.
- **ActiveX controls:** These controls are a subset of those that are available for use on UserForms.

You can use the controls from either of these sources, but it's important that you understand the distinctions between them. The Form controls work much differently than the ActiveX controls.

When you add an ActiveX control to a worksheet, Excel goes into *design mode*. In this mode, you can adjust the properties of any controls on your worksheet, add or edit event-handler procedures for the control, or change its size or position. To display the Properties window for an ActiveX control, use the Developer➜Controls➜Properties command.

For simple buttons, I often use the Button control from the Form controls because I can attach any macro to it. If I use a CommandButton control from the ActiveX controls, clicking it will execute its event-handler procedure (for example, CommandButton1_Click) in the code module for the Sheet object — you can't attach just any macro to it.

When Excel is in design mode, you can't try out the controls. To test the controls, you must exit design mode by clicking the Developer➜Controls➜Design mode button (which is a toggle).

Adjusting UserForm Controls

After you place a control in a UserForm, you can move and resize the control by using standard mouse techniques.

Tip **You can select multiple controls by Shift-clicking or by clicking and dragging to lasso a group of controls.**

A UserForm can contain vertical and horizontal gridlines (displayed as dots) that help you align the controls that you add. When you add or move a control, it *snaps* to the grid to help you line up the controls. If you don't like to see these gridlines, you can turn them off by choosing Tools➜Options in VBE. In the Options dialog box, select the General tab and set your desired options in the Form Grid Settings section. These gridlines are for design only and do not appear when the dialog box is displayed to the user.

The Format menu in the VBE window provides several commands to help you precisely align and space the controls in a dialog box. Before you use these commands, select the controls with which you want to work. These commands work just as you'd expect, so I don't explain them here. Figure 11-4 shows a dialog box with several OptionButton controls about to be aligned. Figure 11-5 shows the controls after they are aligned and assigned equal vertical spacing.

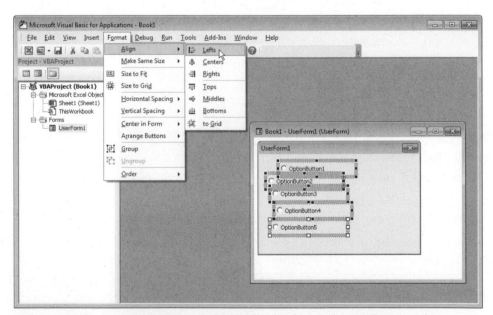

Figure 11-4: Use the Format➜Align command to change the alignment of controls.

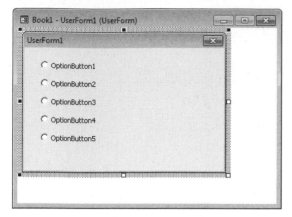

Figure 11-5: The OptionButton controls, aligned and evenly spaced.

Tip

When you select multiple controls, the last control that you select appears with white handles rather than the normal black handles. The control with the white handles is used as the basis for sizing or positioning.

Adjusting a Control's Properties

Every control has a number of properties that determine how the control looks and behaves. You can change a control's properties, as follows:

➤ **At design time** when you're developing the UserForm. You use the Properties window to make design time changes.

➤ **During runtime** when the UserForm is being displayed for the user. You use VBA instructions to change a control's properties at runtime.

Using the Properties window

In VBE, the Properties window adjusts to display the properties of the selected item (which can be a control or the UserForm itself). In addition, you can select a control from the drop-down list at the top of the Properties window. Figure 11-6 shows the Properties window for an OptionButton control.

Figure 11-6: The Properties window for an OptionButton control.

Note The Properties window has two tabs. The Alphabetic tab displays the properties for the selected object in alphabetical order, and the Categorized tab displays the properties grouped into logical categories. Both tabs contain the same properties but in a different order.

To change a property, just click it and specify the new property. Some properties can take on a finite number of values, selectable from a list. If so, the Properties window will display a button with a downward-pointing arrow when that property is selected. Click the button, and you'll be able to select the property's value from the list. For example, the TextAlign property can have any of the following values: 1 - fmTextAlignLeft, 2 - fmTextAlignCenter, or 3 - fmTextAlignRight.

A few properties (for example, Font and Picture) display a small button with an ellipsis when selected. Click the button to display a dialog box associated with the property.

The Image control Picture property is worth mentioning because you can either select a graphic file that contains the image or paste an image from the Clipboard. When pasting an image, first copy it to the Clipboard, and then select the Picture property for the Image control and press Ctrl+V to paste the Clipboard contents.

Note

If you select two or more controls at once, the Properties window displays only the properties that are common to the selected controls.

Tip

The UserForm itself has many properties that you can adjust. Some of these properties are then used as defaults for controls that you add to the UserForm. For example, if you change the UserForm Font property, all controls added to the UserForm will use that font. Note, however, that controls already on the UserForm aren't affected.

Common properties

Although each control has its own unique set of properties, many controls have some common properties. For example, every control has a Name property and properties that determine its size and position (Height, Width, Left, and Right).

If you're going to manipulate a control by using VBA, you'll probably want to provide a meaningful name for the control. For example, the first OptionButton that you add to a UserForm has a default name of OptionButton1. You refer to this object in your code with a statement such as the following:

```
OptionButton1.Value = True
```

But if you give the OptionButton a more meaningful name (such as obLandscape), you can use a statement such as this one:

```
obLandscape.Value = True
```

Tip

Many people find it helpful to use a name that also identifies the type of object. In the preceding example, I use ob as the prefix to identify the control as an OptionButton. I'm not aware of any standard prefixes, so feel free to invent your own.

You can adjust the properties of several controls at once. For example, you might have several OptionButtons that you want left-aligned. You can simply select all the OptionButtons and then change the Left property in the Properties box. All the selected controls will then take on that new Left property value.

The best way to learn about the various properties for a control is to use the Help system. Simply click a property in the Property window and press F1.

Accommodating keyboard users

Many users prefer to navigate through a dialog box by using the keyboard: The Tab and Shift+Tab keystrokes cycle through the controls, and pressing a *hot key* (an underlined letter) operates the control. To make sure that your dialog box works properly for keyboard users, you must be mindful of two issues: tab order and accelerator keys.

Changing the tab order of controls

The *tab order* determines the sequence in which the controls are activated when the user presses Tab or Shift+Tab. It also determines which control has the initial *focus*. If a user is entering text in a TextBox control, for example, the TextBox has the focus. If the user clicks an OptionButton, the OptionButton has the focus. The control that's first in the tab order has the focus when a dialog box is first displayed.

To set the tab order of your controls, choose View➜Tab Order or right-click the UserForm and choose Tab Order from the shortcut menu. In either case, Excel displays the Tab Order dialog box, which lists all the controls, the sequence of which corresponds to the order in which controls pass the focus between each other in the UserForm. To move a control, select it and click the arrow keys up or down. You can choose more than one control (by Shift- or Ctrl-clicking) and move them all at once.

Alternatively, you can set an individual control's position in the tab order by using the Properties window. The first control in the tab order has a TabIndex property of 0. Changing the TabIndex property for a control may also affect the TabIndex property of other controls. These adjustments are made automatically to ensure that no control has a TabIndex greater than the number of controls. If you want to remove a control from the tab order, set its TabStop property to False.

Note

Some controls, such as Frame and MultiPage, act as containers for other controls. The controls inside a container have their own tab order. To set the tab order for a group of OptionButtons inside a Frame control, select the Frame control before you choose the View➜Tab Order command. Figure 11-7 shows the Tab Order dialog box when a Frame is selected.

Testing a UserForm

You'll usually want to test your UserForm while you're developing it. You can test a UserForm in three ways without actually calling it from a VBA procedure:

* Choose the Run➜Run Sub/UserForm command.
* Press F5.
* Click the Run Sub/UserForm button on the Standard toolbar.

These three techniques all trigger the UserForm's Initialize event. When a dialog box is displayed in this test mode, you can try out the tab order and the accelerator keys.

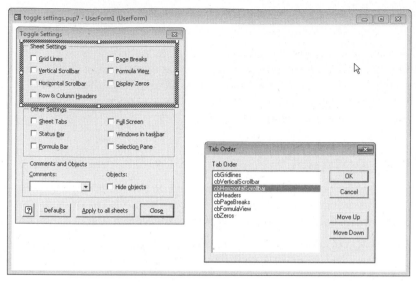

Figure 11-7: Use the Tab Order dialog box to specify the tab order of the controls in a Frame control.

Setting hot keys

You can assign an accelerator key, or hot key, to most dialog box controls. An accelerator key allows the user to access the control by pressing Alt and the hot key. Use the Accelerator property in the Properties window for this purpose.

Tip

Some controls, such as a TextBox, don't have an Accelerator property because they don't display a caption. You still can allow direct keyboard access to these controls by using a Label control. Assign an accelerator key to the Label and put it before the TextBox in the tab order.

Displaying a UserForm

To display a UserForm from VBA, you create a procedure that uses the Show method of the UserForm object. If your UserForm is named UserForm1, the following procedure displays the dialog box on that form:

```
Sub ShowForm()
    UserForm1.Show
End Sub
```

This procedure must be located in a standard VBA module and not in the code module for the UserForm.

When the UserForm is displayed, it remains visible on-screen until it's dismissed. Usually, you'll add a CommandButton control to the UserForm that executes a procedure that dismisses the UserForm. The procedure can either unload the UserForm (with the Unload command) or hide the UserForm (with the Hide method of the UserForm object). This concept will become clearer as you work through various examples in this and subsequent chapters.

Adjusting the display position

The StartUpPosition property of the UserForm object determines where on the screen the dialog box will be displayed. You can specify this property in the Properties box or at runtime. The default value is 1 – CenterOwner, which displays the dialog box in the center of the Excel window.

If you use a dual-monitor system, however, you'll find that sometimes the StartUpPosition property seems to be ignored. Specifically, if the Excel window is on the secondary monitor, the UserForm may appear on the left edge of the primary window.

The following code ensures that the UserForm is always displayed in the center of the Excel window:

```
With UserForm1
  .StartUpPosition = 0
  .Left = Application.Left + (0.5 * Application.Width) - (0.5 * .Width)
  .Top = Application.Top + (0.5 * Application.Height) - (0.5 * .Height)
  .Show
End With
```

Displaying a modeless UserForm

By default, UserForms are displayed modally. This means that the UserForm must be dismissed before the user can do anything in the worksheet. You can also display a modeless UserForm. When a modeless UserForm is displayed, the user can continue working in Excel, and the UserForm remains visible. To display a modeless UserForm, use the following syntax:

```
UserForm1.Show vbModeless
```

New Feature

The single-document interface introduced in Excel 2013 affects modeless UserForms. In previous Excel versions, a modeless UserForm is visible regardless of which workbook window is active. In Excel 2013, a modeless UserForm is associated with the workbook window that's active when the UserForm appears. If you switch to a different workbook window, the UserForm may not be visible. Chapter 13 has an example that demonstrates how to make a modeless UserForm visible in all workbook windows.

Displaying a UserForm based on a variable

In some cases, you may have several UserForms, and your code makes a decision regarding which of them to display. If the name of the UserForm is stored as a string variable, you can use the Add method to add the UserForm to the UserForms collection and then use the Show method of the UserForms collection. Here's an example that assigns the name of a UserForm to the MyForm variable and then displays the UserForm:

```
MyForm = "UserForm1"
UserForms.Add(MyForm).Show
```

Loading a UserForm

VBA also has a Load statement. Loading a UserForm loads it into memory and triggers the UserForm's Initialize event. But the dialog box is not visible until you use the Show method. To load a UserForm, use a statement like this:

```
Load UserForm1
```

If you have a complex UserForm that takes a bit of time to initialize, you might want to load it into memory before it's needed so that it will appear more quickly when you use the Show method. In the majority of situations, however, you don't need to use the Load statement.

About event-handler procedures

After the UserForm is displayed, the user interacts with it — selecting an item from a ListBox, clicking a CommandButton, and so on. In official terminology, the user causes an *event* to occur. For example, clicking a CommandButton causes the Click event for the CommandButton control. You need to write procedures that execute when these events occur. These procedures are sometimes known as *event-handler* procedures.

Note

Event-handler procedures must be located in the code window for the UserForm. However, your event-handler procedure can call another procedure that's located in a standard VBA module.

Your VBA code can change the properties of the controls while the UserForm is displayed (that is, at runtime). For example, you could assign to a ListBox control a procedure that changes the text in a Label when an item is selected. This type of manipulation is the key to making dialog boxes interactive, and will become clearer later in this chapter.

Closing a UserForm

To close a UserForm, use the Unload command, as shown in this example:

```
Unload UserForm1
```

Or, if the code is located in the code module for the UserForm, you can use the following:

```
Unload Me
```

In this case, the keyword Me refers to the UserForm. Using Me rather than the UserForm's name eliminates the need to modify your code if you change the name of the UserForm.

Normally, your VBA code should include the Unload command after the UserForm has performed its actions. For example, your UserForm may have a CommandButton control that functions as an OK button. Clicking this button executes a macro, and one of the statements in the macro will unload the UserForm. The UserForm remains visible on the screen until the macro that contains the Unload statement finishes.

When a UserForm is unloaded, its controls are reset to their original values. In other words, your code won't be able to access the user's choices after the UserForm is unloaded. If the user's choice must be used later on (after the UserForm is unloaded), you need to store the value in a Public variable, declared in a standard VBA module. Or you could store the value in a worksheet cell or even in the Windows registry.

Note

> A UserForm is automatically unloaded when the user clicks the Close button (the X in the UserForm title bar). This action also triggers a UserForm QueryClose event, followed by a UserForm Terminate event.

UserForms also have a Hide method. When you invoke this method, the UserForm disappears, but it remains loaded in memory, so your code can still access the various properties of the controls. Here's an example of a statement that hides a UserForm:

```
UserForm1.Hide
```

Or, if the code is in the code module for the UserForm, you can use the following:

```
Me.Hide
```

If for some reason you'd like your UserForm to disappear immediately while its macro is executing, use the Hide method at the top of the procedure. For example, in the following procedure, the UserForm disappears immediately when CommandButton1 is clicked. The last statement in the procedure unloads the UserForm.

```
Private Sub CommandButton1_Click()
    Me.Hide
    Application.ScreenUpdating = True
    For r = 1 To 10000
        Cells(r, 1) = r
    Next r
    Unload Me
End Sub
```

In this example, I set ScreenUpdating to True to force Excel to hide the UserForm completely. Without that statement, the UserForm may actually remain visible.

Cross-Ref

In Chapter 13, I describe how to display a progress indicator, which takes advantage of the fact that a UserForm remains visible while the macro executes.

Creating a UserForm: An Example

If you've never created a UserForm, you might want to walk through the example in this section. The example includes step-by-step instructions for creating a simple dialog box and developing a VBA procedure to support the dialog box.

This example uses a UserForm to obtain two pieces of information: a person's name and sex. The dialog box uses a TextBox control to get the name and three OptionButtons to get the sex (Male, Female, or Unknown). The information collected in the dialog box is then sent to the next blank row in a worksheet.

Creating the UserForm

Figure 11-8 shows the completed UserForm for this example.

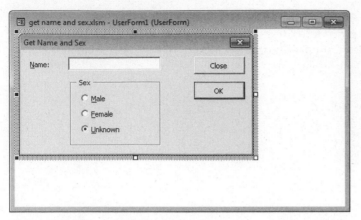

Figure 11-8: This dialog box asks the user to enter a name and a sex.

For best results, start with a new workbook with only one worksheet in it. Then follow these steps:

1. Press Alt+F11 to activate VBE.

2. In the Project window, select the workbook's project and choose Insert➔UserForm to add an empty UserForm.

   The UserForm's Caption property will have its default value: UserForm1.

3. Use the Properties window to change the UserForm's Caption property to Get Name and Sex.

   (If the Properties window isn't visible, press F4.)

4. Add a Label control and adjust the properties as follows:

Property	Value
Accelerator	N
Caption	Name:
TabIndex	0

5. Add a TextBox control and adjust the properties as follows:

Property	Value
Name	TextName
TabIndex	1

6. Add a Frame control and adjust the properties as follows:

Property	Value
Caption	Sex
TabIndex	2

7. Add an OptionButton control inside the frame and adjust the properties as follows:

Property	Value
Accelerator	M
Caption	Male
Name	OptionMale
TabIndex	0

8. Add another OptionButton control inside the frame and adjust the properties as follows:

Property	Value
Accelerator	F
Caption	Female
Name	OptionFemale
TabIndex	1

9. Add yet another OptionButton control inside the Frame and adjust the properties as follows:

Property	Value
Accelerator	U
Caption	Unknown
Name	OptionUnknown
TabIndex	2
Value	True

10. Add a CommandButton control *outside* the Frame and adjust the properties as follows:

Property	Value
Caption	OK
Default	True
Name	OKButton
TabIndex	3

11. Add another CommandButton control and adjust the properties as follows:

Property	Value
Caption	Close
Cancel	True
Name	CloseButton
TabIndex	4

Tip

When you're creating several controls that are similar, you may find it easier to copy an existing control rather than create a new one. To copy a control, press Ctrl while you drag the control to make a new copy of it. Then adjust the properties for the copied control.

Writing code to display the dialog box

Next, you add an ActiveX CommandButton to the worksheet. This button will execute a procedure that displays the UserForm. Here's how:

1. Activate Excel.

   (Alt+F11 is the shortcut key combination.)

2. Choose Developer➜Controls➜Insert and click CommandButton from the ActiveX Controls section (the bottom group of controls).

3. Drag in the worksheet to create the button.

   If you like, you can change the caption for the worksheet CommandButton. To do so, right-click the button and choose CommandButton Object➜Edit from the shortcut menu. You can then edit the text that appears on the CommandButton. To change other properties of the object, right-click and choose Properties. Then make the changes in the Properties box.

4. Double-click the CommandButton.

   This step activates VBE. More specifically, the code module for the worksheet will be displayed, with an empty event-handler procedure for the worksheet's CommandButton control.

5. Enter a single statement in the CommandButton1_Click procedure (see Figure 11-9).

   This short procedure uses the Show method of an object (UserForm1) to display the UserForm.

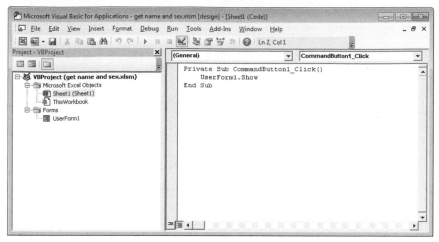

Figure 11-9: The CommandButton1_Click procedure is executed when the button on the worksheet is clicked.

Testing the dialog box

The next step is to reactivate Excel and try out the procedure that displays the dialog box.

Note When you click the CommandButton on the worksheet, you'll find that nothing happens. Instead, the button is selected. That's because Excel is still in design mode — which happens automatically when you insert an ActiveX control. To exit design mode, click the Design Mode button in the Developer➜Controls group. To make any changes to your CommandButton, you'll need to put Excel back into design mode.

When you exit design mode, clicking the button will display the UserForm (see Figure 11-10).

When the dialog box is displayed, enter some text in the text box and click OK. Nothing happens — which is understandable because you haven't yet created an event-handler procedure for the OK button.

Note Click the X (Close) button in the UserForm title bar to dismiss the dialog box.

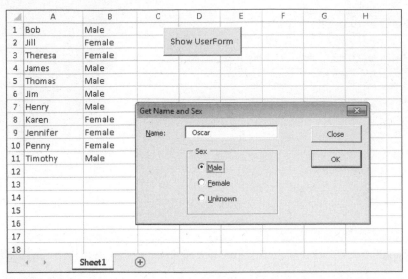

Figure 11-10: The CommandButton's Click event procedure displays the UserForm.

Adding event-handler procedures

In this section, I explain how to write the procedures that will handle the events that occur while the UserForm is displayed. To continue the example, do the following:

1. Press Alt+F11 to activate VBE.

2. Make sure the UserForm is displayed and double-click the CommandButton captioned Close.

   This step activates the code window for the UserForm and inserts an empty procedure named CloseButton_Click. Note that this procedure consists of the object's name, an underscore character, and the event that it handles.

3. Modify the procedure as follows. (This is the event handler for the CloseButton's Click event.)

```
Private Sub CloseButton_Click()
    Unload UserForm1
End Sub
```

   This procedure, which is executed when the user clicks the Close button, simply unloads the UserForm.

4. Press Shift+F7 to redisplay UserForm1 (or click the View Object icon at the top of the Project Explorer window).

5. Double-click the OK button and enter the following procedure. (This is the event handler for the OKButton's Click event.)

```
Private Sub OKButton_Click()
    Dim NextRow As Long
'   Make sure Sheet1 is active
    Sheets("Sheet1").Activate

'   Determine the next empty row
    NextRow = _
        Application.WorksheetFunction.CountA(Range("A:A")) + 1
'   Transfer the name
    Cells(NextRow, 1) = TextName.Text

'   Transfer the sex
    If OptionMale Then Cells(NextRow, 2) = "Male"
    If OptionFemale Then Cells(NextRow, 2) = "Female"
    If OptionUnknown Then Cells(NextRow, 2) = "Unknown"

'   Clear the controls for the next entry
    TextName.Text = ""
    OptionUnknown = True
    TextName.SetFocus
End Sub
```

6. Activate Excel and click the CommandButton again to display the UserForm and then run the procedure again.

You'll find that the UserForm controls now function correctly. You can use them to add new names to the two-column list in the worksheet.

Here's how the OKButton_Click procedure works: First, the procedure makes sure that the proper worksheet (Sheet1) is active. It then uses the Excel COUNTA function to determine the next blank cell in column A. Next, it transfers the text from the TextBox control to column A. It then uses a series of If statements to determine which OptionButton was selected and writes the appropriate text (Male, Female, or Unknown) to column B. Finally, the dialog box is reset to make it ready for the next entry. Note that clicking OK doesn't close the dialog box. To end data entry (and unload the UserForm), click the Close button.

Validating the data

Play around with this example some more, and you'll find that it has a small problem: It doesn't ensure that the user enters a name in the text box. To make sure that the user enters a name (well, at least some text) in the TextBox, insert the following code in the OKButton_Click procedure, before the text is transferred to the worksheet. If the TextBox is empty, a message appears, and the focus is set to the TextBox so that the user can try again. The Exit Sub statement ends the procedure with no further action.

```
'   Make sure a name is entered
    If TextName.Text = "" Then
        MsgBox "You must enter a name."
        TextName.SetFocus
        Exit Sub
    End If
```

The finished dialog box

After making all these modifications, you'll find that the dialog box works flawlessly. (Don't forget to test the hot keys.) In real life, you'd probably need to collect more information than just the name and sex. The same basic principles apply; you would just need to deal with more UserForm controls.

On the Web

A workbook with this example is available on this book's website in the get name and sex.xlsm file.

Understanding UserForm Events

Each UserForm control (as well as the UserForm itself) is designed to respond to certain types of events, and a user or Excel can trigger these events. For example, clicking a CommandButton generates a Click event for the CommandButton. You can write code that is executed when a particular event occurs.

Some actions generate multiple events. For example, clicking the up arrow of a SpinButton control generates a SpinUp event and also a Change event. When a UserForm is displayed by using the Show method, Excel generates an Initialize event and an Activate event for the UserForm. (Actually, the Initialize event occurs when the UserForm is loaded into memory and before it's actually displayed.)

Cross-Ref

Excel also supports events associated with a Sheet object, Chart objects, and the ThisWorkbook object. I discuss these types of events in Chapter 17.

Learning about events

To find out which events are supported by a particular control, do the following:

1. Add a control to a UserForm.

2. Double-click the control to activate the code module for the UserForm.

   VBE inserts an empty event-handler procedure for the default event for the control.

3. Click the drop-down list in the upper-right corner of the module window.

   You see a complete list of events for the control. Figure 11-11 shows the list of events for a CheckBox control.

4. Select an event from the list.

   VBE creates an empty event-handler procedure for you.

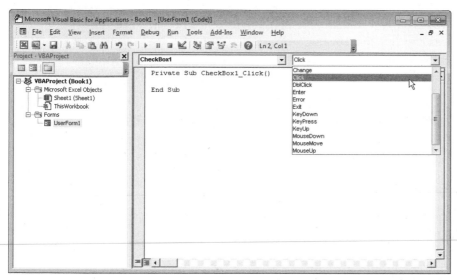

Figure 11-11: The event list for a CheckBox control.

To find out specific details about an event, consult the Help system. The Help system also lists the events available for each control.

Caution

Event-handler procedures incorporate the name of the object in the procedure's name. If you change the name of a control, you'll also need to make the appropriate changes to the control's event-handler procedure(s) because the name changes aren't performed automatically. To make things easy on yourself, it's a good idea to provide names for your controls before you begin creating event-handler procedures.

UserForm events

A UserForm has quite a few events. Here are the events associated with showing and unloading a UserForm:

➤ Initialize: Occurs before a UserForm is loaded or shown but doesn't occur if the UserForm was previously hidden

➤ Activate: Occurs when a UserForm is shown

➤ Deactivate: Occurs when a UserForm is deactivated but doesn't occur if the form is hidden

➤ QueryClose: Occurs before a UserForm is unloaded

➤ Terminate: Occurs after the UserForm is unloaded

Note

Often, it's critical that you choose the appropriate event for your event-handler procedure and that you understand the order in which the events occur. Using the Show method invokes the Initialize and Activate events (in that order). Using the Load command invokes only the Initialize event. Using the Unload command triggers the QueryClose and Terminate events (in that order), but using the Hide method doesn't trigger either event.

On the Web

The book's website contains the userform events.xlsm workbook, which monitors all these events and displays a message box when an event occurs. If you're confused about UserForm events, studying the code in this workbook should clear things up.

SpinButton events

To help clarify the concept of events, this section takes a close look at the events associated with a SpinButton control. Some of these events are associated with other controls, and some are unique to the SpinButton control.

On the Web

The book's website contains a workbook that demonstrates the sequence of events that occur for a SpinButton and the UserForm that contains it. The workbook, named spinbutton events.xlsm, contains a series of event-handler routines — one for each SpinButton and UserForm event. Each routine simply displays a message box that tells you which event just fired.

Table 11-1 lists all the events for the SpinButton control.

Table 11-1: SpinButton Events

Event	Description
AfterUpdate	Occurs after the control is changed through the user interface
BeforeDragOver	Occurs when a drag-and-drop operation is in progress
BeforeDropOrPaste	Occurs when the user is about to drop or paste data onto the control
BeforeUpdate	Occurs before the control is changed
Change	Occurs when the Value property changes
Enter	Occurs before the control receives the focus from a control on the same UserForm
Error	Occurs when the control detects an error and can't return the error information to a calling program

Event	Description
Exit	Occurs immediately before a control loses the focus to another control on the same form
KeyDown	Occurs when the user presses a key and the object has the focus
KeyPress	Occurs when the user presses any key that produces a typeable character
KeyUp	Occurs when the user releases a key and the object has the focus
SpinDown	Occurs when the user clicks the lower (or left) SpinButton arrow
SpinUp	Occurs when the user clicks the upper (or right) SpinButton arrow

A user can operate a SpinButton control by clicking it with the mouse or (if the control has the focus) by using the arrow keys.

Mouse-initiated events

When the user clicks the upper SpinButton arrow, the following events occur in this order:

1. Enter (triggered only if the SpinButton did not already have the focus)
2. Change
3. SpinUp

Keyboard-initiated events

The user can also press Tab to set the focus to the SpinButton and then use the arrow keys to increment or decrement the control. If so, the following events occur (in this order):

1. Enter (occurs when the SpinButton gets the focus)
2. KeyDown
3. Change
4. SpinUp (or SpinDown)
5. KeyUp

What about code-initiated events?

The SpinButton control can also be changed by VBA code — which also triggers the appropriate event(s). For example, the following statement sets the SpinButton1 Value property to 0 and also triggers the Change event for the SpinButton control — but only if the SpinButton value was not already 0:

```
SpinButton1.Value = 0
```

You might think that you could disable events by setting the EnableEvents property of the Application object to False. Unfortunately, this property applies only to events that involve true Excel objects: Workbooks, Worksheets, and Charts.

Pairing a SpinButton with a TextBox

A SpinButton has a Value property, but this control doesn't have a caption in which to display its value. In many cases, however, you'll want the user to see the SpinButton value. And sometimes you'll want the user to be able to change the SpinButton value directly instead of clicking the SpinButton repeatedly.

The solution is to pair a SpinButton with a TextBox, which enables the user to specify a value either by typing it in the TextBox directly or by clicking the SpinButton to increment or decrement the value in the TextBox.

Figure 11-12 shows a simple example. The SpinButton's Min property is -10, and its Max property is 10. Therefore, clicking the SpinButton's arrows will change its value to an integer between -10 and 10.

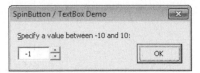

Figure 11-12: This SpinButton is paired with a TextBox.

 The example is available on the book's website in the spinbutton and textbox.xlsm file.

The code required to link a SpinButton with a TextBox is relatively simple. It's basically a matter of writing event-handler procedures to ensure that the SpinButton's Value property is always in sync with the TextBox's Text property. In the following code, the controls have their default names (SpinButton1 and TextBox1).

The following procedure is executed whenever the SpinButton's Change event is triggered. That is, the procedure is executed when the user clicks the SpinButton or changes its value by pressing an arrow key.

```
Private Sub SpinButton1_Change()
    TextBox1.Text = SpinButton1.Value
End Sub
```

The procedure assigns the SpinButton's Value to the Text property of the TextBox control. If the user enters a value directly in the TextBox, its Change event is triggered, and the following procedure is executed:

```
Private Sub TextBox1_Change()
    Dim NewVal As Integer
    If IsNumeric(TextBox1.Text) Then
        NewVal = Val(TextBox1.Text)
        If NewVal >= SpinButton1.Min And _
            NewVal <= SpinButton1.Max Then _
            SpinButton1.Value = NewVal
    End If
End Sub
```

This procedure starts by determining whether the entry in the TextBox is a number. If so, the procedure continues and the text is assigned to the NewVal variable. The next statement determines whether the value is within the proper range for the SpinButton. If so, the SpinButton's Value property is set to the value entered in the TextBox. If the entry is not numeric or is out of range, nothing happens.

The example is set up so that clicking the OK button (which is named OKButton) transfers the SpinButton's value to the active cell. The event handler for this CommandButton's Click event is as follows:

```
Private Sub OKButton_Click()
'    Enter the value into the active cell
    If CStr(SpinButton1.Value) = TextBox1.Text Then
        ActiveCell = SpinButton1.Value
        Unload Me
    Else
        MsgBox "Invalid entry.", vbCritical
        TextBox1.SetFocus
        TextBox1.SelStart = 0
        TextBox1.SelLength = Len(TextBox1.Text)
    End If
End Sub
```

This procedure does one final check: It makes sure that the text entered in the TextBox matches the SpinButton's value. This check is necessary in the case of an invalid entry. For example, if the user enters 3r in the TextBox, the SpinButton's value would not be changed, and the result placed in the active cell would not be what the user intended. Note that the SpinButton's Value property is converted to a string by using the CStr function. This conversion ensures that the comparison won't generate an error if a value is compared with text. If the SpinButton's value doesn't match the TextBox's contents, a message box is displayed. Notice that the focus is set to the TextBox object, and the contents are selected (by using the SelStart and SelLength properties). This setup makes it easy for the user to correct the entry.

About the Tag property

Every UserForm and control has a Tag property. This property doesn't represent anything specific, and, by default, is empty. You can use the Tag property to store information for your own use.

For example, you may have a series of TextBox controls in a UserForm. The user may be required to enter text in some but not all of them. You can use the Tag property to identify (for your own use) which fields are required. In this case, you can set the Tag property to a string such as Required. Then when you write code to validate the user's entries, you can refer to the Tag property.

The following example is a function that examines all TextBox controls on UserForm1 and returns the number of required TextBox controls that are empty: If the function returns a number greater than 0, it means that all required fields were not completed.

```
Function EmptyCount()
  Dim ctl As Control
  EmptyCount= 0
  For Each ctl In UserForm1.Controls
    If TypeName(ctl) = "TextBox" Then
      If ctl.Tag = "Required" Then
        If ctl.Text = "" Then
          EmptyCount = EmptyCount + 1
        End If
      End If
    End If
 Next ctl
End Function
```

As you work with UserForms, you'll probably think of other uses for the Tag property.

Referencing UserForm Controls

When working with controls on a UserForm, the event-handler VBA code is usually contained in the code window for the UserForm. In such a case, you do not need to qualify references to the controls because the controls are assumed to belong to the UserForm.

You can also refer to UserForm controls from a general VBA module. To do so, you need to qualify the reference to the control by specifying the UserForm name. For example, consider the following procedure, which is located in a VBA module. It simply displays the UserForm named UserForm1.

```
Sub GetData()
    UserForm1.Show
End Sub
```

Assume that UserForm1 contains a text box (named TextBox1), and you want to provide a default value for the text box. You could modify the procedure as follows:

```
Sub GetData()
    UserForm1.TextBox1.Value = "John Doe"
    UserForm1.Show
End Sub
```

Another way to set the default value is to take advantage of the UserForm's Initialize event. You can write code in the UserForm_Initialize procedure, which is located in the code module for the UserForm. Here's an example:

```
Private Sub UserForm_Initialize()
    TextBox1.Value = "John Doe"
End Sub
```

Note that when the control is referenced in the code module for the UserForm, you don't need to qualify the references with the UserForm name. However, qualifying references to controls does have an advantage: You'll then be able to take advantage of the Auto List Members feature, which lets you choose the control names from a drop-down list.

 ## Understanding the controls collection

The controls on a UserForm make up a collection. For example, the following statement displays the number of controls on UserForm1:

```
MsgBox UserForm1.Controls.Count
```

VBA does *not* maintain a collection of each control type. For example, there is no collection of CommandButton controls. However, you can determine the type of control by using the TypeName function. The following procedure uses a For Each structure to loop through the Controls collection and then displays the number of CommandButton controls on UserForm1:

```
Sub CountButtons()
    Dim cbCount As Integer
    Dim ctl as Control
    cbCount = 0
    For Each ctl In UserForm1.Controls
        If TypeName(ctl) = "CommandButton" Then cbCount = cbCount + 1
    Next ctl
    MsgBox cbCount
End Sub
```

Tip

> Rather than use the actual name of the UserForm, it's preferable to use Me. Then, if you change the name of the UserForm, you won't need to replace the references in your code.

Customizing the Toolbox

When a UserForm is active in VBE, the Toolbox displays the controls that you can add to the UserForm. If the Toolbox isn't visible, choose View→Toolbox to display it. This section describes ways to customize the Toolbox.

Adding new pages to the Toolbox

The Toolbox initially contains a single tab. Right-click this tab and choose New Page to add a new tab to the Toolbox. You can also change the text displayed on the tab by choosing Rename from the shortcut menu.

Customizing or combining controls

A handy feature lets you customize a control and then save it for future use. You can, for example, create a CommandButton control that's set up to serve as an OK button. Set the following properties to customize the CommandButton: Width, Height, Caption, Default, and Name. Then drag the customized CommandButton to the Toolbox to create a new control. Right-click the new control to rename it or change its icon.

You can also create a new Toolbox entry that consists of multiple controls. For example, you can create two CommandButtons that represent a UserForm's OK and Cancel buttons. Customize them as you like and then select them both and drag them to the Toolbox. Then, you can use this new Toolbox control to add two customized buttons in one fell swoop.

This type of customization also works with controls that act as containers. For example, create a Frame control and add four customized OptionButtons, neatly spaced and aligned. Then drag the Frame to the Toolbox to create a customized Frame control.

To help identify customized controls, right-click the control and choose Customize *xxx* from the shortcut menu (where *xxx* is the control's name). You see a new dialog box that lets you change the ToolTip text, edit the icon, or load a new icon image from a file.

Tip

> You may want to place your customized controls on a separate page in the Toolbox. Then you can export the entire page so that you can share it with other Excel users. To export a Toolbox page, right-click the tab and choose Export Page.

Figure 11-13 shows a new page with eight customized controls:

> ➤ A Frame with four OptionButtons
> ➤ A TextBox and Spinner
> ➤ Six Checkboxes
> ➤ A "critical" red X icon
> ➤ An exclamation point icon
> ➤ A question mark icon
> ➤ An Information icon

The four icons are the same images displayed by the MsgBox function.

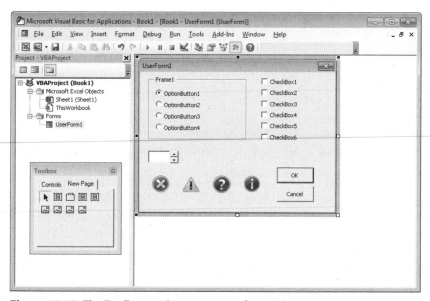

Figure 11-13: The Toolbox, with a new page of controls.

On the Web You can find these customized controls on the book's website in the newcontrols.pag file. To import the PAG file as a new page in your Toolbox, right-click a tab, choose Import Page, and then locate and choose the file.

Adding new ActiveX controls

UserForms can use other ActiveX controls developed by Microsoft or other vendors. To add an additional ActiveX control to the Toolbox, right-click the Toolbox and choose Additional Controls. You see the dialog box shown in Figure 11-14.

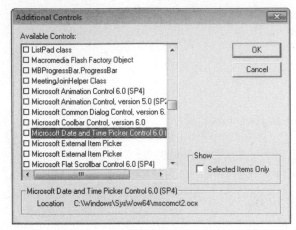

Figure 11-14: The Additional Controls dialog box lets you add other ActiveX controls.

The Additional Controls dialog box lists all ActiveX controls installed on your system. Select the control(s) that you want to add and then click OK to add an icon for each selected control.

Caution

Most ActiveX controls installed on your system will probably not work in Excel UserForms. Also, some controls require a license to use them in an application. If you (or the users of your application) aren't licensed to use a particular control, an error will occur.

Creating UserForm Templates

You may find that when you design a new UserForm, you tend to add the same controls each time. For example, every UserForm might have two CommandButtons that serve as OK and Cancel buttons. In the preceding section, I describe how to create a new control that combines these two (customized) buttons into a single control. Another option is to create your UserForm template and then export it so that you can import it into other projects. An advantage is that the event-handler code for the controls is stored with the template.

Start by creating a UserForm that contains all the controls and customizations that you'd need to reuse in other projects. Then make sure that the UserForm is selected and choose File➜Export File (or press Ctrl+E). You'll be prompted for a filename.

Then, when you start your next project, choose File➜Import File to load the saved UserForm.

Emulating Excel's dialog boxes

The look and feel of Windows dialog boxes differs from program to program. When developing applications for Excel, it's best to try to mimic Excel's dialog box style whenever possible.

A good way to learn how to create effective dialog boxes is to try to copy one of Excel's dialog boxes down to the smallest detail. For example, make sure that you get all the hot keys defined and be sure that the tab order is the same. To recreate one of Excel's dialog boxes, you need to test it under various circumstances and see how it behaves. I guarantee that your analysis of Excel's dialog boxes will improve your own dialog boxes.

On the other hand, you'll find that it's impossible to duplicate some of Excel's dialog boxes. For example, it's not possible to duplicate the Convert Text to Columns Wizard dialog box, which is displayed when you choose Data➜Data Tools➜Text to Columns. This dialog box uses controls that are not available to VBA users.

A UserForm Checklist

Before you unleash a UserForm on end users, be sure that everything is working correctly. The following checklist should help you identify potential problems:

> ➤ Are similar controls the same size?

> ➤ Are the controls evenly spaced?

> ➤ Is the dialog box overwhelming? If so, you may want to group the controls by using a MultiPage control.

> ➤ Can every control be accessed with a hot key?

> ➤ Are any hot keys duplicated?

> ➤ Is the tab order set correctly?

> ➤ Will your VBA code take appropriate action if the user presses Esc or clicks the Close button on the UserForm?

> ➤ Is any text misspelled?

> ➤ Does the dialog box have an appropriate caption?

> ➤ Will the dialog box display properly at all video resolutions?

> ➤ Are the controls grouped logically (by function)?

> ➤ Do ScrollBar and SpinButton controls allow only valid values?

> ➤ Does the UserForm use any controls that might not be installed on every system?

> ➤ Are ListBoxes set properly (Single, Multi, or Extended)? See Chapter 12 for details on ListBox controls.

UserForm Examples

In This Chapter

- Using a UserForm for a simple menu
- Selecting ranges from a UserForm
- Using a UserForm as a splash screen
- Changing the size of a UserForm while it's displayed
- Zooming and scrolling a sheet from a UserForm
- Understanding various techniques that involve a ListBox control
- Using an external control
- Using the MultiPage control
- Animating a Label control

Creating a UserForm "Menu"

Sometimes, you might want to use a UserForm as a type of menu. In other words, the UserForm presents some options, and the user makes a choice. This section presents two ways to do this: using CommandButtons or using a ListBox.

Cross-Ref

Chapter 13 contains additional examples of more advanced UserForm techniques.

Using CommandButtons in a UserForm

Figure 12-1 shows an example of a UserForm that uses CommandButton control as a simple menu.

Figure 12-1: This dialog box uses CommandButtons as a menu.

Setting up this sort of UserForm is easy, and the code behind the UserForm is straightforward. Each CommandButton has its own event-handler procedure. For example, the following procedure is executed when CommandButton1 is clicked:

```
Private Sub CommandButton1_Click()
    Me.Hide
    Call Macro1
    Unload Me
End Sub
```

This procedure hides the UserForm, calls Macro1, and then closes the UserForm. The other buttons have similar event-handler procedures.

Using a ListBox in a UserForm

Figure 12-2 shows another example that uses a ListBox as a menu.

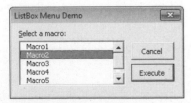

Figure 12-2: This dialog box uses a ListBox as a menu.

This style is easier to maintain because you can easily add new menu items without adjusting the size of the UserForm. Before the UserForm is displayed, its Initialize event-handler procedure is called. This procedure, which follows, uses the AddItem method to add six items to the ListBox:

```
Private Sub UserForm_Initialize()
    With ListBox1
        .AddItem "Macro1"
        .AddItem "Macro2"
        .AddItem "Macro3"
        .AddItem "Macro4"
        .AddItem "Macro5"
        .AddItem "Macro6"
    End With
End Sub
```

The Execute button also has a procedure to handle its Click event:

```
Private Sub ExecuteButton_Click()
    Select Case ListBox1.ListIndex
        Case -1
            MsgBox "Select a macro from the list."
            Exit Sub
        Case 0: Call Macro1
        Case 1: Call Macro2
        Case 2: Call Macro3
        Case 3: Call Macro4
        Case 4: Call Macro5
        Case 5: Call Macro6
    End Select
    Unload Me
End Sub
```

This procedure accesses the ListIndex property of the ListBox to determine which item is selected. The procedure uses a Select Case structure to execute the appropriate macro. If the ListIndex is –1, nothing is selected in the ListBox, and the user sees a message.

In addition, this UserForm has a procedure to handle the double-click event for the ListBox. Double-clicking an item in the ListBox executes the corresponding macro.

On the Web

The two examples in this section are available on the book's website in the userform menus.xlsm file.

Cross-Ref

Chapter 13 shows a similar example in which you can use a UserForm to simulate a toolbar.

Selecting Ranges from a UserForm

Many of Excel's built-in dialog boxes allow the user to specify a range. For example, the Goal Seek dialog box (displayed by choosing Data➜Data Tools➜What-If Analysis➜Goal Seek) asks the user to select two single-cell ranges. The user can either type the range addresses (or names) directly or use the mouse to point and click in a sheet to make a range selection.

Your UserForms can also provide this type of functionality, thanks to the RefEdit control. The RefEdit control doesn't look exactly like the range selection control used in Excel's built-in dialog boxes, but it works in a similar manner. If the user clicks the small button on the right side of the control, the dialog box disappears temporarily, and a small range selector is displayed — which is exactly what happens with Excel's built-in dialog boxes.

Note

Unfortunately, the RefEdit control has a few quirks that still haven't been fixed. You'll find that this control doesn't allow the user to use shortcut range-selection keys (for example, pressing End, followed by Shift+↓ will not select cells to the end of the column). In addition, the control is mouse-centric. After clicking the small button on the right side of the control (to temporarily hide the dialog box), you're limited to mouse selections only. You can't use the keyboard to make a selection.

Figure 12-3 shows a UserForm that contains a RefEdit control. This dialog box enables the user to perform a simple mathematical operation on all nonformula (and nonempty) cells in the selected range. The operation that's performed corresponds to the selected OptionButton.

⊿	A	B	C	D	E	F	G	H	I	J
1	-91	-43	92	-60	-73					
2	-26	49	53	29	-9					
3	38	11	58	10	3					
4	45	12	-23	-14	-41					
5	-85	-51	-94	-76	93					
6	72	93	55	-90	63					
7	81	23	-76	-89	-97					
8	47	63	-74	42	87					
9	46	83	-17	77	69					
10	-84	-62	-10	55	-79					
11	16	15	-81	58	-6	-51	77			
12	-42	36	29	30	-55	-24	-21			
13	69	-54	89	-40	29	-77	-96			
14	-71	93	-12	-10	-75	-37	32			
15	18	-24	26	-34	52	-97	19			
16	-4	89	-94	-57	41	-64	66			
17										
18										

Range Selection Demo

Select the range to modify:

Sheet1!$B$3:$D$8

Cancel

OK

Operation

⊙ Add   ○ Multiply

○ Subtract   ○ Divide

Operand:

6R x 3C

Sheet1   Sheet2   ⊕

Figure 12-3: The RefEdit control shown here allows the user to select a range.

On the Web

This example is available on the book's website in a file named range selection demo.xlsm.

Following are a few things to keep in mind when using a RefEdit control:

➤ The RefEdit control returns a text string that represents a range address. You can convert this string to a Range object by using a statement such as

```
Set UserRange = Range(RefEdit1.Text)
```

➤ Initializing the RefEdit control to display the current range selection is good practice. You can do so in the UserForm_Initialize procedure by using a statement such as

```
RefEdit1.Text = ActiveWindow.RangeSelection.Address
```

➤ For best results, avoid using a RefEdit control inside a Frame or a MultiPage control. Doing so may cause Excel to crash.

➤ Don't assume that RefEdit will always return a valid range address. Pointing to a range isn't the only way to get text into this control. The user can type any text and can also edit or delete the displayed text. Therefore, you need to make sure that the range is valid. The following code is an example of a way to check for a valid range. If an invalid range is detected, the user is given a message, and focus is set to the RefEdit control so that the user can try again.

```
On Error Resume Next
Set UserRange = Range(RefEdit1.Text)
If Err.Number <> 0 Then
    MsgBox "Invalid range selected"
    RefEdit1.SetFocus
    Exit Sub
End If
On Error GoTo 0
```

➤ The user can also click the worksheet tabs while selecting a range with the RefEdit control. Therefore, you can't assume that the selection is on the active sheet. However, if a different sheet is selected, the range address is preceded by a sheet name. For example:

```
Sheet2!$A$1:$C$4
```

➤ If you need to get a single cell selection from the user, you can isolate the upper-left cell of a selected range by using a statement such as

```
Set OneCell = Range(RefEdit1.Text).Range("A1")
```

Cross-Ref

As I discuss in Chapter 10, you can also use Excel's InputBox method to allow the user to select a range.

Creating a Splash Screen

Some developers like to display introductory information when the application is opened. This display is commonly known as a *splash screen*.

You can create a splash screen for your Excel application with a UserForm. This example is essentially a UserForm that is displayed automatically when the workbook is opened, and then dismisses itself after five seconds.

On the Web

This book's website contains a workbook that demonstrates this procedure in a file named splash screen.xlsm.

Follow these instructions to create a splash screen for your project:

1. Create your workbook.

2. Activate Visual Basic Editor (VBE) and insert a new UserForm into the project.

    The code in this example assumes that this form is named UserForm1.

3. Place any controls that you like on UserForm1.

    For example, you may want to insert an Image control that has your company's logo. Figure 12-4 shows an example.

XYZ Pet Supply

Customer
Tracking
System

Copyright 2013. Company Confidential

Figure 12-4: This splash screen is displayed briefly when the workbook is opened.

4. Insert the following procedure into the code module for the ThisWorkbook object:

```
Private Sub Workbook_Open()
    UserForm1.Show
End Sub
```

5. Insert the following procedure into the code module for UserForm1.

   For a delay other than five seconds, change the argument for the TimeValue function.

```
Private Sub UserForm_Activate()
    Application.OnTime Now + _
      TimeValue("00:00:05"), "KillTheForm"
End Sub
```

6. Insert the following procedure into a general VBA module:

```
Private Sub KillTheForm()
    Unload UserForm1
End Sub
```

When the workbook is opened, the Workbook_Open procedure is executed. The procedure in Step 4 displays the UserForm. At that time, the UserForm's Activate event occurs, which triggers the UserForm_Activate procedure (see Step 5). This procedure uses the OnTime method of the Application object to execute a procedure named KillTheForm at a particular time. In this case, the time is five seconds after the activation event. The KillTheForm procedure simply unloads the UserForm.

7. As an option, you can add a small CommandButton named CancelButton, set its Cancel property to True, and insert the following event-handler procedure in the UserForm's code module:

```
Private Sub CancelButton_Click()
    Unload Me
End Sub
```

Doing so lets the user cancel the splash screen before the time has expired by pressing Esc. In the example, I placed this small button behind another object so that it's not visible.

 Caution

Keep in mind that the splash screen isn't displayed until the workbook is entirely loaded. In other words, if you'd like to display the splash screen to give the user something to look at while a large workbook is loading, this technique won't fill the bill.

 Tip

If your application needs to run some VBA procedures at start-up, you can display the UserForm modeless so that the code will continue running while the UserForm is displayed. To do so, change the Workbook_Open procedure as follows:

```
Private Sub Workbook_Open()
    UserForm1.Show vbModeless
    ' other code goes here
End Sub
```

Disabling a UserForm's Close Button

When a UserForm is displayed, clicking the Close button (the X in the upper-right corner) will unload the form. You might have a situation in which you don't want the Close button to unload the form. For example, you might require that the UserForm be closed only by clicking a particular CommandButton.

Although you can't actually disable the Close button, you can prevent the user from closing a UserForm by clicking it. You can do so by monitoring the UserForm's QueryClose event.

The following procedure, which is located in the code module for the UserForm, is executed before the form is closed (that is, when the QueryClose event occurs):

```
Private Sub UserForm_QueryClose _
    (Cancel As Integer, CloseMode As Integer)
    If CloseMode = vbFormControlMenu Then
        MsgBox "Click the OK button to close the form."
        Cancel = True
    End If
End Sub
```

The UserForm_QueryClose procedure uses two arguments. The CloseMode argument contains a value that indicates the cause of the QueryClose event. If CloseMode is equal to vbFormControlMenu (a built-in constant), the user clicked the Close button. If a message is displayed, the Cancel argument is set to True, and the form isn't actually closed.

On the Web

The example in this section is available on the books website in a file named queryclose demo.xlsm.

Note

Keep in mind that a user can press Ctrl+Break to break out of the macro. In this example, pressing Ctrl+Break while the UserForm is displayed dismisses the UserForm. To prevent this occurrence, execute the following statement prior to displaying the UserForm:

```
Application.EnableCancelKey = xlDisabled
```

Make sure that your application is debugged before you add this statement. Otherwise, you'll find that it's impossible to break out of an accidental endless loop.

Changing a UserForm's Size

Many applications use dialog boxes that change their own size. For example, Excel's Find and Replace dialog box (displayed when you choose Home→Editing→Find & Select→Replace) increases its height when the user clicks the Options button.

The example in this section demonstrates how to get a UserForm to change its size dynamically. Changing a dialog box's size is done by altering the Width or Height property of the UserForm object. This example displays a list of worksheets in the active workbook and lets the user select which sheets to print.

Cross-Ref

Refer to Chapter 13 for an example that allows the user to change the UserForm's size by dragging the lower-right corner.

Figure 12-5 shows the two states of the dialog box: as it is first displayed and after the user clicks the Options button. Note that the button's caption changes, depending on the size of the UserForm.

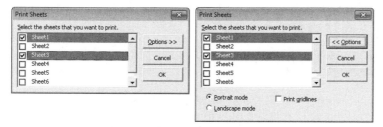

Figure 12-5: A dialog box before and after displaying options.

While you're creating the UserForm, set it to its largest size to enable you to work with the controls. Then use the UserForm_Initialize procedure to set the UserForm to its default (smaller) size.

The code uses two constants, defined at the top of the module:

```
Const SmallSize As Integer = 124
Const LargeSize As Integer = 164
```

Following is the event handler that's executed when the CommandButton named OptionsButton is clicked:

```
Private Sub OptionsButton_Click()
    If OptionsButton.Caption = "Options >>" Then
        Me.Height = LargeSize
        OptionsButton.Caption = "<< Options"
    Else
        Me.Height = SmallSize
        OptionsButton.Caption = "Options >>"
    End If
End Sub
```

This procedure examines the Caption of the CommandButton and sets the UserForm's Height property accordingly.

Note

When controls aren't displayed because they're outside the visible portion of the UserForm, the accelerator keys for such controls continue to function. In this example, the user can press the Alt+L hot key (to select landscape mode) even if that option isn't visible. To block access to nondisplayed controls, you can write code to disable the controls when they aren't displayed.

On the Web

The example in this section is available on the book's website in the file named change userform size.xlsm.

Zooming and Scrolling a Sheet from a UserForm

The example in this section demonstrates how to use ScrollBar controls to allow sheet scrolling and zooming while a dialog box is displayed. Figure 12-6 shows how the example dialog box is set up. When the UserForm is displayed, the user can adjust the worksheet's zoom factor (from 10% to 400%) by using the ScrollBar at the top. The two ScrollBars in the bottom section of the dialog box allow the user to scroll the worksheet horizontally and vertically.

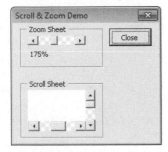

Figure 12-6: Here, ScrollBar controls allow zooming and scrolling of the worksheet.

On the Web

This example, named zoom and scroll sheet.xlsm, is available on the book's website.

The code for this example is remarkably simple. The controls are initialized in the UserForm_Initialize procedure, which follows:

```
Private Sub UserForm_Initialize()
    LabelZoom.Caption = ActiveWindow.Zoom & "%"
'   Zoom
    With ScrollBarZoom
        .Min = 10
        .Max = 400
        .SmallChange = 1
        .LargeChange = 10
        .Value = ActiveWindow.Zoom
    End With

'   Horizontally scrolling
    With ScrollBarColumns
        .Min = 1
        .Max = ActiveSheet.UsedRange.Columns.Count
        .Value = ActiveWindow.ScrollColumn
        .LargeChange = 25
        .SmallChange = 1
    End With

'   Vertically scrolling
    With ScrollBarRows
        .Min = 1
        .Max = ActiveSheet.UsedRange.Rows.Count
        .Value = ActiveWindow.ScrollRow
        .LargeChange = 25
        .SmallChange = 1
    End With
End Sub
```

This procedure sets various properties of the ScrollBar controls by using values based on the active window.

When the ScrollBarZoom control is used, the ScrollBarZoom_Change procedure (which follows) is executed. This procedure sets the ScrollBar control's Value to the ActiveWindow's Zoom property value. It also changes a label to display the current zoom factor.

```
Private Sub ScrollBarZoom_Change()
    With ActiveWindow
        .Zoom = ScrollBarZoom.Value
        LabelZoom = .Zoom & "%"
    End With
End Sub
```

Worksheet scrolling is accomplished by the two procedures that follow. These procedures set the ScrollRow or ScrollColumns property of the ActiveWindow object equal to the appropriate ScrollBar control value.

```
Private Sub ScrollBarColumns_Change()
    ActiveWindow.ScrollColumn = ScrollBarColumns.Value
End Sub

Private Sub ScrollBarRows_Change()
    ActiveWindow.ScrollRow = ScrollBarRows.Value
End Sub
```

Tip

If you use the Scroll event rather than use the Change event in the preceding procedures, the event will be triggered when the ScrollBars are dragged — resulting in smooth zooming and scrolling. To use the Scroll event, just make the Change part of the procedure name Scroll.

ListBox Techniques

The ListBox control is versatile, but it can be tricky to work with. This section contains of a number of examples that demonstrate common techniques that involve the ListBox control.

Note

In most cases, the techniques described in this section work also with a ComboBox control.

Following are a few points to keep in mind when working with ListBox controls. Examples in the sections that follow demonstrate many of these points:

➤ You can retrieve the items in a ListBox from a range of cells (specified by the RowSource property), or you can add them by using VBA code (using the AddItem method).

➤ You can set up a ListBox to allow a single selection or a multiple selection. You use the MultiSelect property to specify the type of selection allowed.

➤ If a ListBox isn't set up for a multiple selection, you can link the value of the ListBox to a worksheet cell by using the ControlSource property.

➤ You can display a ListBox with no items selected (the ListIndex property will be −1). However, after an item is selected, the user can't deselect all items. The exception is if the MultiSelect property is True.

➤ A ListBox can contain multiple columns (controlled by the ColumnCount property) and even a descriptive header (controlled by the ColumnHeads property).

➤ The vertical height of a ListBox displayed in a UserForm window at design time isn't always the same as the vertical height when the UserForm is displayed.

➤ You can display the items in a ListBox either as check boxes (if multiple selections are allowed) or as option buttons (if a single selection is allowed). The display type is controlled by the ListStyle property.

For complete details on the properties and methods for a ListBox control, consult the Help system.

Adding items to a ListBox control

Before displaying a UserForm that uses a ListBox control, you need to fill the ListBox with items. You can fill a ListBox at design time using items stored in a worksheet range or at runtime using VBA.

The two examples in this section presume that

➤ You have a UserForm named UserForm1.

➤ This UserForm contains a ListBox control named ListBox1.

➤ The workbook contains a sheet named Sheet1, and range A1:A12 contains the items to be displayed in the ListBox.

Adding items to a ListBox at design time

To add items to a ListBox at design time, the ListBox items must be stored in a worksheet range. Use the RowSource property to specify the range that contains the ListBox items. Figure 12-7 shows the Properties window for a ListBox control. The RowSource property is set to Sheet1!A1:A12. When the UserForm is displayed, the ListBox will contain the 12 items in this range. The items appear in the ListBox at design time as soon as you specify the range for the RowSource property.

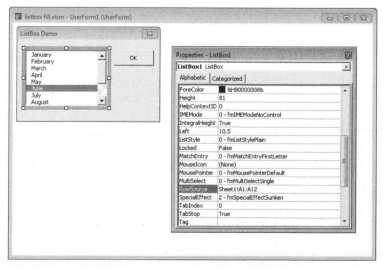

Figure 12-7: Setting the RowSource property at design time.

Caution

In most cases, you'll want to include the worksheet name when you specify the RowSource property; otherwise, the ListBox will use the specified range on the active worksheet. In some cases, you may need to fully qualify the range by including the workbook name. For example:

```
[budget.xlsx]Sheet1!A1:A12
```

A better practice is to define a workbook-level name for the range and use that name in your code. This habit will ensure that the proper range is used even if rows above the range are added or deleted.

Adding items to a ListBox at runtime

To add ListBox items at runtime, you have two choices:

➤ Set the RowSource property to a range address by using code.

➤ Write code that uses the AddItem method to add the ListBox items.

As you might expect, you can set the RowSource property through code rather than with the Properties window. For example, the following procedure sets the RowSource property for a ListBox before displaying the UserForm. In this case, the items consist of the cell entries in a range named Categories in the Budget worksheet.

```
UserForm1.ListBox1.RowSource = "Budget!Categories"
UserForm1.Show
```

If the ListBox items aren't contained in a worksheet range, you can write VBA code to fill the ListBox before the dialog box appears. The following procedure fills the ListBox with the names of the months by using the AddItem method:

```
Sub ShowUserForm2()
'   Fill the list box
    With UserForm1.ListBox1
        .RowSource=""
        .AddItem "January"
        .AddItem "February"
        .AddItem "March"
        .AddItem "April"
        .AddItem "May"
        .AddItem "June"
        .AddItem "July"
        .AddItem "August"
```

```
        .AddItem "September"
        .AddItem "October"
        .AddItem "November"
        .AddItem "December"
    End With
    UserForm1.Show
End Sub
```

Caution

In the preceding code, note that I set the RowSource property to an empty string. This setting avoids a potential error that occurs if the Properties window has a nonempty RowSource setting. If you try to add items to a ListBox that has a non-null RowSource setting, you'll get a Permission denied error.

You can also retrieve items from a range, and use the AddItem method to add them to the ListBox. Here's an example that fills a ListBox with the contents of A1:A12 on Sheet1:

```
For Row = 1 To 12
  UserForm1.ListBox1.AddItem Sheets("Sheet1").Cells(Row, 1)
Next Row
```

Using the List property is even simpler. The statement that follows has the same effect as the preceding For Next loop:

```
UserForm1.ListBox1.List = _
    Application.Transpose(Sheets("Sheet1").Range("A1:A12"))
```

Note that I used the Transpose function because the List property expects a horizontal array and the range is in a column rather than a row.

You can use the List property also if your data is stored in a one-dimensional array. For example, assume that you have an array named MyList that contains 50 elements. The following statement will create a 50-item list in ListBox1:

```
UserForm1.ListBox1.List = MyList
```

On the Web

The examples in this section are available on the book's website in the file named listbox fill.xlsm.

Adding only unique items to a ListBox

In some cases, you may need to fill a ListBox with *unique* (nonduplicated) items from a list. For example, assume that you have a worksheet that contains customer data. One of the columns might contain the state (see Figure 12-8). You'd like to fill a ListBox with the state names of your customers, but you don't want to include duplicate state names.

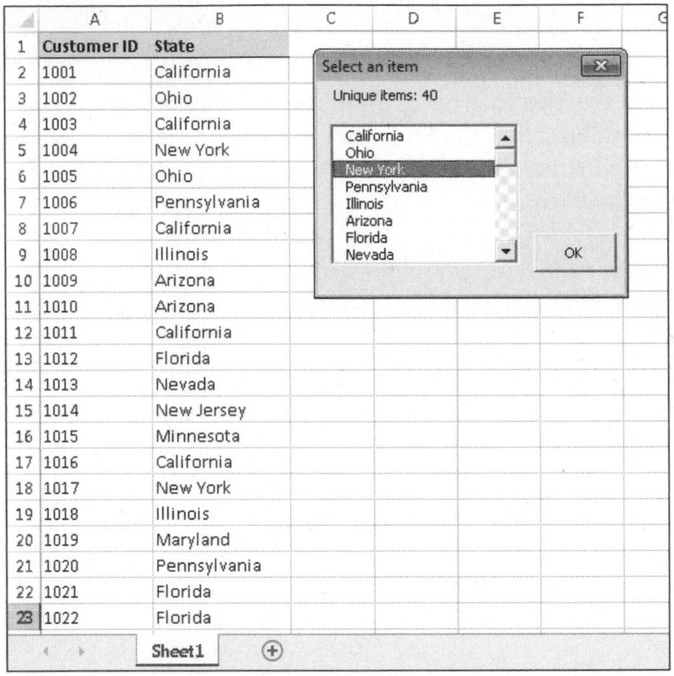

Figure 12-8: A Collection object is used to fill a ListBox with the unique items from column B.

One fast and efficient technique involves using a Collection object. After creating a new Collection object, you can add items to the object with the following syntax:

```
object.Add item, key, before, after
```

The key argument, if used, must be a unique text string that specifies a separate key that you can use to access a member of the collection. The important word here is *unique*. If you attempt to add a nonunique key to a collection, an error occurs and the item isn't added. You can take advantage of this situation and use it to create a collection that consists only of unique items.

The following procedure starts by declaring a new Collection object named NoDupes. It assumes that a range named Data contains a list of items, some of which may be duplicated.

The code loops through the cells in the range and attempts to add the cell's value to the NoDupes collection. It also uses the cell's value (converted to a string) for the key argument. Using the On Error Resume Next statement causes VBA to ignore the error that occurs if the key isn't unique. When an error occurs, the item isn't added to the collection — which is just what you want. The procedure then transfers the items in the NoDupes collection to the ListBox. The UserForm also contains a label that displays the number of unique items.

```
Sub RemoveDuplicates1()
    Dim AllCells As Range, Cell As Range
    Dim NoDupes As New Collection

    On Error Resume Next
    For Each Cell In Range("State")
        NoDupes.Add Cell.Value, CStr(Cell.Value)
    Next Cell
    On Error GoTo 0

'   Add the non-duplicated items to a ListBox
    For Each Item In NoDupes
        UserForm1.ListBox1.AddItem Item
    Next Item

'   Display the count
    UserForm1.Label1.Caption = "Unique items: " & NoDupes.Count

'   Show the UserForm
    UserForm1.Show
End Sub
```

On the Web

This example, named listbox unique items1.xlsm, is available on the book's website. A workbook named listbox unique items2.xlsm has a slightly more sophisticated version of this technique and displays the items sorted.

Determining the selected item in a ListBox

The examples in the preceding sections merely display a UserForm with a ListBox filled with various items. These procedures omit a key point: how to determine which item or items were selected by the user.

Note

This discussion assumes a single-selection ListBox object — one whose MultiSelect property is set to 0.

To determine which item was selected, access the ListBox's Value property. The statement that follows, for example, displays the text of the selected item in ListBox1.

```
MsgBox ListBox1.Value
```

If no item is selected, this statement will generate an error.

If you need to know the position of the selected item in the list (rather than the content of that item), you can access the ListBox's ListIndex property. The following example uses a message box to display the item number of the selected ListBox item:

```
MsgBox "You selected item #" & ListBox1.ListIndex
```

If no item is selected, the ListIndex property will return –1.

Note The numbering of items in a ListBox begins with 0, not 1. Therefore, the ListIndex of the first item is 0, and the ListIndex of the last item is equivalent to the value of the ListCount property minus 1.

Determining multiple selections in a ListBox

A ListBox's MultiSelect property can be any of three values:

➤ 0 (fmMultiSelectSingle): Only one item can be selected. This setting is the default.

➤ 1 (fmMultiSelectMulti): Pressing the spacebar or clicking selects or deselects an item in the list.

➤ 2 (fmMultiSelectExtended): Press Ctrl and click to select multiple items. Shift-clicking extends the selection from the previously selected item to the current item. You can also use Shift and one of the arrow keys to extend the selected items.

If the ListBox allows multiple selections (that is, if its MultiSelect property is either 1 or 2), trying to access the ListIndex or Value property will result in an error. Instead, you need to use the Selected property, which returns an array whose first item has an index of 0. For example, the following statement displays True if the first item in the ListBox list is selected:

```
MsgBox ListBox1.Selected(0)
```

This book's website contains a workbook that demonstrates how to identify the selected item(s) in a ListBox. It works for single-selection and multiple-selection ListBoxes. The file is named **listbox selected items.xlsm.**

The following code, from the example workbook on the website, loops through each item in the ListBox. If the item was selected, the item's text is appended to a variable called Msg. Finally, the names of all selected items are displayed in a message box.

```
Private Sub OKButton_Click()
    Msg = ""
    For i = 0 To ListBox1.ListCount - 1
        If ListBox1.Selected(i) Then _
            Msg = Msg & ListBox1.List(i) & vbCrLf
    Next i
    MsgBox "You selected: " & vbCrLf & Msg
    Unload Me
End Sub
```

Figure 12-9 shows the result when multiple ListBox items are selected.

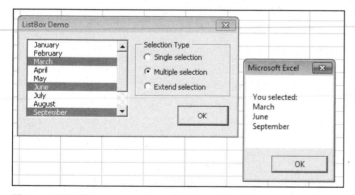

Figure 12-9: This message box displays a list of items selected in a ListBox.

Multiple lists in a single ListBox

This example demonstrates how to create a ListBox in which the contents change depending on the user's selection from a group of OptionButtons.

The ListBox gets its items from a worksheet range. The procedures that handle the Click event for the OptionButton controls simply set the ListBox's RowSource property to a different range. One of these procedures follows:

```
Private Sub obMonths_Click()
    ListBox1.RowSource = "Sheet1!Months"
End Sub
```

Figure 12-10 shows the UserForm.

▲	A	B	C	D	E	F	G	H	I
1	January	Jeep	Red						
2	February	Ford	Orange						
3	March	Chevrolet	Yellow						
4	April	Toyota	Green						
5	May	Nissan	Blue						
6	June	Volkswagen	Indigo						
7	July		Violet						
8	August								
9	September								
10	October								
11	November								
12	December								
13									
14									
15									

ListBox Demo

Show
○ Months
○ Cars
● Colors

Red
Orange
Yellow
Green
Blue

OK

Sheet1   ⊕

Figure 12-10: The contents of this ListBox depend on the OptionButton selected.

Clicking the OptionButton named obMonths changes the RowSource property of the ListBox to use a range named Months on Sheet1.

On the Web   **This example, named listbox multiple lists.xlsm, is available on the book's website.**

ListBox item transfer

Some applications require a user to select several items from a list. It's often useful to create a new list of the selected items and display the new list in another ListBox. For an example of this situation, check out the Quick Access Toolbar tab of the Excel Options dialog box.

Figure 12-11 shows a dialog box with two ListBoxes. The Add button adds the item selected in the left ListBox to the right ListBox. The Remove button removes the selected item from the list on the right. A check box determines the behavior when a duplicate item is added to the list: Namely, if the Allow Duplicates check box isn't marked, nothing happens if the user attempts to add an item that's already on the list.

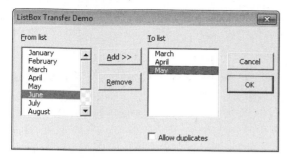

Figure 12-11: Building a list from another list.

The code for this example is simple. Here's the procedure that is executed when the user clicks the Add button:

```
Private Sub AddButton_Click()
    If ListBox1.ListIndex = -1 Then Exit Sub
    If Not cbDuplicates Then
'        See if item already exists
        For i = 0 To ListBox2.ListCount - 1
            If ListBox1.Value = ListBox2.List(i) Then Exit Sub
        Next i
    End If
    ListBox2.AddItem ListBox1.Value
End Sub
```

The code for the Remove button is even simpler:

```
Private Sub RemoveButton_Click()
    If ListBox2.ListIndex <> -1 Then
        ListBox2.RemoveItem ListBox2.ListIndex
    End If
    If ListBox2.ListIndex = -1 Then RemoveButton.Enabled = False
End Sub
```

Note that both routines check to make sure that an item is actually selected. If the ListBox's ListIndex property is –1, no items are selected, and the procedure ends. When the Remove button is clicked, the code checks to see whether any items remain. If there are no items, the Remove button is disabled.

This example has two additional procedures that control whether the Remove button is enabled or disabled. These events are triggered when the ListBox is entered (by a keystroke or a mouse click). The net effect is that the Remove button is enabled only when the user is working in ListBox2.

```
Private Sub ListBox1_Enter()
    RemoveButton.Enabled = False
End Sub

Private Sub ListBox2_Enter()
    RemoveButton.Enabled = True
End Sub
```

This example, named listbox item transfer.xlsm, is available on the book's website.

On the Web

Moving items in a ListBox

Often, the order of items in a list is important. The example in this section demonstrates how to allow the user to move items up or down in a ListBox. VBE uses this type of technique to let you control the tab order of the items in a UserForm. (Right-click a UserForm and choose Tab Order from the shortcut menu.)

Figure 12-12 shows a dialog box that contains a ListBox and two CommandButtons. Clicking the Move Up button moves the selected item up in the ListBox; clicking the Move Down button moves the selected item down.

Figure 12-12: The buttons allow the user to move items up or down in the ListBox.

This example, named listbox move items.xlsm, is available on the book's website.

On the Web

The event-handler procedures for the two CommandButtons follow:

```
Private Sub MoveUpButton_Click()
    Dim NumItems As Integer, i As Integer, ItemNum As Integer
    Dim TempItem As String, TempList()
    If ListBox1.ListIndex <= 0 Then Exit Sub
```

```
        NumItems = ListBox1.ListCount
    Dim TempList()
    ReDim TempList(0 To NumItems - 1)
'     Fill array with list box items
    For i = 0 To NumItems - 1
        TempList(i) = ListBox1.List(i)
    Next i
'     Selected item
    ItemNum = ListBox1.ListIndex
'     Exchange items
    TempItem = TempList(ItemNum)
    TempList(ItemNum) = TempList(ItemNum - 1)
    TempList(ItemNum - 1) = TempItem
    ListBox1.List = TempList
'     Change the list index
    ListBox1.ListIndex = ItemNum - 1
End Sub

Private Sub MoveDownButton_Click()
    Dim NumItems As Integer, i As Integer, ItemNum As Integer
    Dim TempItem As String, TempList()
    If ListBox1.ListIndex = ListBox1.ListCount - 1 Then Exit Sub
    NumItems = ListBox1.ListCount
    Dim TempList()
    ReDim TempList(0 To NumItems - 1)
'     Fill array with list box items
    For i = 0 To NumItems - 1
        TempList(i) = ListBox1.List(i)
    Next i
'     Selected item
    ItemNum = ListBox1.ListIndex
'     Exchange items
    TempItem = TempList(ItemNum)
    TempList(ItemNum) = TempList(ItemNum + 1)
    TempList(ItemNum + 1) = TempItem
    ListBox1.List = TempList
'     Change the list index
    ListBox1.ListIndex = ItemNum + 1
End Sub
```

I noticed that, for some reason, rapid clicking of the Move Up or the Move Down button didn't register as multiple clicks. To fix this problem, I added two more procedures that respond to the Double Click event for each button. These procedures simply call the appropriate Click event procedure listed previously.

Working with multicolumn ListBox controls

A normal ListBox has a single column for its items. You can, however, create a ListBox that displays multiple columns and (optionally) column headers. Figure 12-13 shows an example of a multicolumn ListBox that gets its data from a worksheet range.

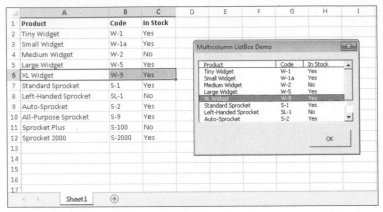

Figure 12-13: This ListBox displays a three-column list with column headers.

On the Web **This example, named listbox multicolumn1.xlsm, is available on the book's website.**

To set up a multicolumn ListBox that uses data stored in a worksheet range, follow these steps:

1. Make sure that the ListBox's ColumnCount property is set to the correct number of columns.

2. Specify the correct multicolumn range in the Excel worksheet as the ListBox's RowSource property.

3. If you want to display column headers, set the ColumnHeads property to True.

   Do not include the column headings on the worksheet in the range setting for the RowSource property. VBA will instead automatically use the row directly above the first row of the RowSource range.

4. Adjust the column widths by assigning a series of values, specified in *points* (½ of 1 inch) and separated by semicolons, to the ColumnWidths property. This will almost always require some trial and error.

   For example, for a three-column list box, the ColumnWidths property might be set to the following text string:

```
110 pt;40 pt;30 pt
```

5. Specify the appropriate column as the BoundColumn property.

The bound column specifies which column is referenced when an instruction polls the ListBox's Value property.

To fill a ListBox with multicolumn data without using a range, you first create a two-dimensional array and then assign the array to the ListBox's List property. The following statements demonstrate this using a 12-row-by-2-column array named Data. The two-column ListBox shows the month names in column 1 and the number of the days in the month in column 2 (see Figure 12-14). Note that the procedure sets the ColumnCount property to 2.

```vba
Private Sub UserForm_Initialize()
'    Fill the list box
    Dim Data(1 To 12, 1 To 2)
    For i = 1 To 12
        Data(i, 1) = Format(DateSerial(2012, i, 1), "mmmm")
    Next i
    For i = 1 To 12
        Data(i, 2) = Day(DateSerial(2012, i + 1, 1) - 1)
    Next i
    ListBox1.ColumnCount = 2
    ListBox1.List = Data
End Sub
```

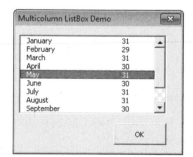

Figure 12-14: A two-column ListBox filled with data stored in an array.

On the Web

This example is available on the book's website in the file named listbox multicolumn2. xlsm.

Note

There appears to be no way to specify column headers for the ColumnHeads property when the list source is a VBA array.

Using a ListBox to select worksheet rows

The example in this section displays a ListBox that consists of the entire used range of the active worksheet (see Figure 12-15). The user can select multiple items in the ListBox. Clicking the All button selects all items, and clicking the None button deselects all items. Clicking OK selects those corresponding rows in the worksheet. You might find that selecting multiple noncontiguous rows is easier when using this method rather than by pressing Ctrl while you click the row borders..

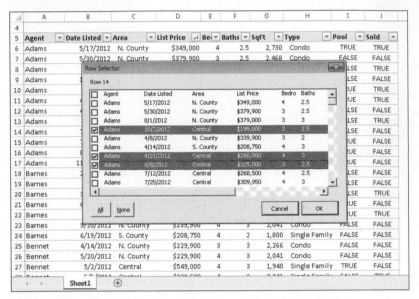

Figure 12-15: This ListBox makes selecting rows in a worksheet easy.

On the Web

This example, named listbox select rows.xlsm, is available on the book's website.

Selecting multiple items is possible because the ListBox's MultiSelect property is set to 1 - fmMultiSelectMulti. The check boxes on each item are displayed because the ListBox's ListStyle property is set to 1 - fmListStyleOption.

The UserForm's Initialize procedure follows. This procedure creates a Range object named rng that consists of the active sheet's used range. Additional code sets the ListBox's ColumnCount and RowSource properties and adjusts the ColumnWidths property so that the ListBox columns are proportional to the column widths in the worksheet.

```
Private Sub UserForm_Initialize()
    Dim ColCnt As Integer
    Dim rng As Range
    Dim cw As String
    Dim c As Integer
```

```
    ColCnt = ActiveSheet.UsedRange.Columns.Count
    Set rng = ActiveSheet.UsedRange
    With ListBox1
        .ColumnCount = ColCnt
        .RowSource = rng.Address
        cw = ""
        For c = 1 To .ColumnCount
            cw = cw & rng.Columns(c).Width & ";"
        Next c
        .ColumnWidths = cw
        .ListIndex = 0
    End With
End Sub
```

The All and None buttons (named SelectAllButton and SelectNoneButton, respectively) have simple event-handler procedures:

```
Private Sub SelectAllButton_Click()
    Dim r As Integer
    For r = 0 To ListBox1.ListCount - 1
        ListBox1.Selected(r) = True
    Next r
End Sub

Private Sub SelectNoneButton_Click()
    Dim r As Integer
    For r = 0 To ListBox1.ListCount - 1
        ListBox1.Selected(r) = False
    Next r
End Sub
```

The OKButton_Click procedure follows. This procedure creates a Range object named RowRange that consists of the rows that correspond to the selected items in the ListBox. To determine whether a row was selected, the code examines the Selected property of the ListBox control. Note that it uses the Union function to add ranges to the RowRange object.

```
Private Sub OKButton_Click()
    Dim RowRange As Range
    Dim RowCnt As Integer, r As Integer
    RowCnt = 0
    For r = 0 To ListBox1.ListCount - 1
        If ListBox1.Selected(r) Then
            RowCnt = RowCnt + 1
            If RowCnt = 1 Then
                Set RowRange = ActiveSheet.UsedRange.Rows(r + 1)
```

continued

```
            Else
                Set RowRange = _
                    Union(RowRange, ActiveSheet.UsedRange.Rows(r + 1))
            End If
        End If
    Next r
    If Not RowRange Is Nothing Then RowRange.Select
    Unload Me
End Sub
```

On the Web

This example is available on the book's website in the file named listbox select rows. xlsm.

Using a ListBox to activate a sheet

The example in this section is just as useful as it is instructive. This example uses a multicolumn ListBox to display a list of sheets in the active workbook. The columns represent

➤ The sheet's name

➤ The type of sheet (worksheet, chart sheet, or Excel 5/95 dialog sheet)

➤ The number of nonempty cells in the sheet

➤ Whether the sheet is visible

Figure 12-16 shows an example of the dialog box.

Figure 12-16: This dialog box lets the user activate a sheet.

The code in the UserForm_Initialize procedure (which follows) creates a two-dimensional array and collects the information by looping through the sheets in the active workbook. It then transfers this array to the ListBox.

```vba
Public OriginalSheet As Object

Private Sub UserForm_Initialize()
    Dim SheetData() As String, Sht As Object
    Dim ShtCnt As Integer, ShtNum As Integer, ListPos As Integer

    Set OriginalSheet = ActiveSheet
    ShtCnt = ActiveWorkbook.Sheets.Count
    ReDim SheetData(1 To ShtCnt, 1 To 4)
    ShtNum = 1
    For Each Sht In ActiveWorkbook.Sheets
        If Sht.Name = ActiveSheet.Name Then _
          ListPos = ShtNum - 1
        SheetData(ShtNum, 1) = Sht.Name
        Select Case TypeName(Sht)
            Case "Worksheet"
                SheetData(ShtNum, 2) = "Sheet"
                SheetData(ShtNum, 3) = _
                  Application.CountA(Sht.Cells)
            Case "Chart"
                SheetData(ShtNum, 2) = "Chart"
                SheetData(ShtNum, 3) = "N/A"
            Case "DialogSheet"
                SheetData(ShtNum, 2) = "Dialog"
                SheetData(ShtNum, 3) = "N/A"
        End Select
        If Sht.Visible Then
            SheetData(ShtNum, 4) = "True"
        Else
            SheetData(ShtNum, 4) = "False"
        End If
        ShtNum = ShtNum + 1
    Next Sht
    With ListBox1
        .ColumnWidths = "100 pt;30 pt;40 pt;50 pt"
        .List = SheetData
        .ListIndex = ListPos
    End With
End Sub
```

The ListBox1_Click procedure follows:

```
Private Sub ListBox1_Click()
    If cbPreview Then Sheets(ListBox1.Value).Activate
End Sub
```

The value of the CheckBox control (named cbPreview) determines whether the selected sheet is previewed when the user clicks an item in the ListBox.

Clicking the OK button (named OKButton) executes the OKButton_Click procedure, which follows:

```
Private Sub OKButton_Click()
    Dim UserSheet As Object
    Set UserSheet = Sheets(ListBox1.Value)
    If UserSheet.Visible Then
        UserSheet.Activate
    Else
        If MsgBox("Unhide sheet?", _
          vbQuestion + vbYesNoCancel) = vbYes Then
            UserSheet.Visible = True
            UserSheet.Activate
        Else
            OriginalSheet.Activate
        End If
    End If
    Unload Me
End Sub
```

The OKButton_Click procedure creates an object variable that represents the selected sheet. If the sheet is visible, it's activated. If it's not visible, the user is presented with a message box asking whether it should be unhidden. If the user responds in the affirmative, the sheet is unhidden and activated. Otherwise, the original sheet (stored in a public object variable named OriginalSheet) is activated.

Double-clicking an item in the ListBox has the same result as clicking the OK button. The ListBox1_DblClick procedure, which follows, simply calls the OKButton_Click procedure.

```
Private Sub ListBox1_DblClick(ByVal Cancel As MSForms.ReturnBoolean)
    Call OKButton_Click
End Sub
```

Using the MultiPage Control in a UserForm

The MultiPage control is useful for UserForms that must display many controls because it enables you to group choices and place each group on a separate tab.

Figure 12-17 shows an example of a UserForm that contains a MultiPage control. In this case, the control has three pages, each with its own tab.

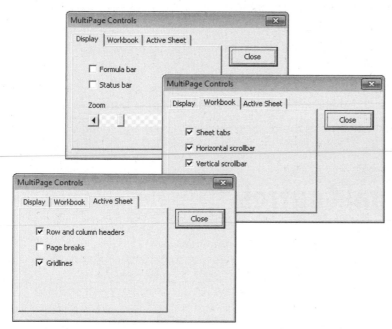

Figure 12-17: MultiPage groups your controls on pages, making them accessible from a tab.

Note

The Toolbox also contains a control named TabStrip, which resembles a MultiPage control. However, unlike the MultiPage control, the TabStrip control isn't a container for other objects. The MultiPage control is more versatile, and I've never had a need to use the TabStrip control.

Using a MultiPage control can be tricky. The following are some things to keep in mind when using this control:

➤ The tab (or page) that's displayed up front is determined by the control's Value property. A value of 0 displays the first tab, a value of 1 displays the second tab, and so on.

➤ By default, a MultiPage control has two pages. To add a new page in VBE, right-click a tab and choose New Page from the shortcut menu.

➤ When you're working with a MultiPage control, just click a tab to set the properties for that particular page. The Properties window will display the properties that you can adjust.

➤ You may find it difficult to select the actual MultiPage control because clicking the control selects a page within the control. To select the control itself, click its border. Or you can use the Tab key to cycle among all the controls. Yet another option is to choose the MultiPage control from the drop-down list in the Properties window.

➤ If your MultiPage control has lots of tabs, you can set its MultiRow property to True to display the tabs in more than one row.

➤ If you prefer, you can display buttons instead of tabs. Just change the Style property to 1. If the Style property value is 2, the MultiPage control won't display tabs or buttons.

➤ The TabOrientation property determines the location of the tabs on the MultiPage control.

Using an External Control

The example in this section uses the Windows Media Player ActiveX control. Although this control isn't an Excel control (it's installed with Windows), it works fine in a UserForm.

To make this control available, add a UserForm to a workbook and follow these steps:

1. Activate VBE.

2. Right-click the Toolbox and choose Additional Controls.

   Choose View➜Toolbox if the Toolbox isn't visible.

3. In the Additional Controls dialog box, scroll down and place a check mark next to Windows Media Player.

4. Click OK.

   Your Toolbox will display a new control.

Figure 12-18 shows the Windows Media Player control in a UserForm, along with the Property window. The URL property represents the media item being played (music or video). If the item is on your hard drive, the URL property will contain the full path along with the filename.

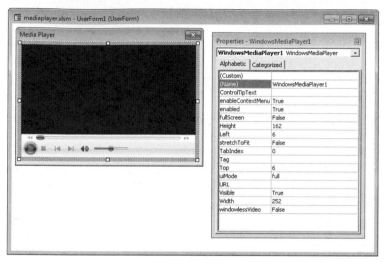

Figure 12-18: The Windows Media Player control in a UserForm.

Figure 12-19 shows this control being used. The video is showing a visualization that changes in time to the audio. I added a ListBox, which is filled with MP3 audio filenames. Clicking the Play button plays the selected file. Clicking the Close button stops the sound and closes the UserForm. This UserForm is displayed modeless, so the user can continue working when the dialog box is displayed.

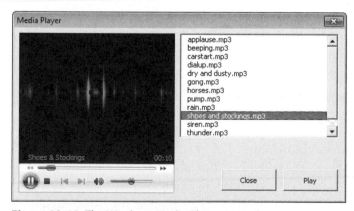

Figure 12-19: The Windows Media Player control.

On the Web   This example is available on the book's website in the mediaplayer.xlsm file, which is in a separate directory that includes public domain MP3 sound files.

This example was easy to create. The UserForm_Initialize procedure adds the MP3 filenames to the ListBox. To keep things simple, it reads the files that are in the same directory as the workbook. A more versatile approach is to let the user select a directory.

```
Private Sub UserForm_Initialize()
    Dim FileName As String
'   Fill listbox with MP3 files
    FileName = Dir(ThisWorkbook.Path & "\*.mp3", vbNormal)
    Do While Len(FileName) > 0
        ListBox1.AddItem FileName
        FileName = Dir()
    Loop
    ListBox1.ListIndex = 0
End Sub
```

Cross-Ref   See Chapter 25 for more information about using the Dir command.

The PlayButton_Click event-handler code consists of a single statement, which assigns the selected filename to the URL property of the WindowsMediaPlayer1 object:

```
Private Sub PlayButton_Click()
'   URL property loads track, and starts player
    WindowsMediaPlayer1.URL = _
        ThisWorkbook.Path & "\" & ListBox1.List(ListBox1.ListIndex)
End Sub
```

You can probably think of lots of enhancements for this simple application. Also note that this control responds to many events.

Animating a Label

The final example in this chapter demonstrates how to animate a Label control. The UserForm shown in Figure 12-20 is an interactive random number generator.

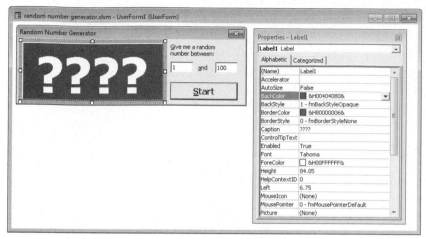

Figure 12-20: Generating a random number.

Two TextBox controls hold the lower and upper values for the random number. A Label control initially displays four question marks, but the text is animated to show random numbers when the user clicks the Start button. The Start button changes to a Stop button, and clicking it again stops the animation and displays the random number. Figure 12-21 shows the dialog box displaying a random number between -1,000 and 1000.

Figure 12-21: A random number has been chosen.

The code that's attached to the button is as follows:

```
Dim Stopped As Boolean

Private Sub StartStopButton_Click()
    Dim Low As Double, Hi As Double

    If StartStopButton.Caption = "Start" Then
'       validate low and hi values
        If Not IsNumeric(TextBox1.Text) Then
            MsgBox "Non-numeric starting value.", vbInformation
            With TextBox1
                .SelStart = 0
                .SelLength = Len(.Text)
                .SetFocus
```

continued

```
            End With
            Exit Sub
        End If

        If Not IsNumeric(TextBox2.Text) Then
            MsgBox "Non-numeric ending value.", vbInformation
            With TextBox2
                .SelStart = 0
                .SelLength = Len(.Text)
                .SetFocus
            End With
            Exit Sub
        End If

'       Make sure they aren't in the wrong order
        Low = Application.Min(Val(TextBox1.Text), Val(TextBox2.Text))
        Hi = Application.Max(Val(TextBox1.Text), Val(TextBox2.Text))

'       Adjust font size, if necessary
        Select Case Application.Max(Len(TextBox1.Text), Len(TextBox2.Text))
            Case Is < 5: Label1.Font.Size = 72
            Case 5: Label1.Font.Size = 60
            Case 6: Label1.Font.Size = 48
            Case Else: Label1.Font.Size = 36
        End Select

        StartStopButton.Caption = "Stop"
        Stopped = False
        Randomize
        Do Until Stopped
            Label1.Caption = Int((Hi - Low + 1) * Rnd + Low)
            DoEvents ' Causes the animation
        Loop
    Else
        Stopped = True
        StartStopButton.Caption = "Start"
    End If
End Sub
```

Because the button serves two purposes (starting and stopping), the procedure uses a public variable, Stopped, to keep track of the state. The first part of the procedure consists of two If-Then structures to validate the contents of the TextBox controls. Two more statements ensure that the low value is in fact less than the high value. The next section adjusts the Label control's font size, based on the maximum value. The Do Until loop is responsible for generating and displaying the random numbers.

Note the DoEvents statement. This statement causes Excel to "yield" to the operating system. Without the statement, the Label control wouldn't display each random number as it's generated. In other words, the DoEvents statement makes the animation possible.

The UserForm also contains a CommandButton that serves as a Cancel button. This control is positioned off the UserForm so that it's not visible. This CommandButton has its Cancel property set to True, so pressing Esc is equivalent to clicking the button. Its click event-handler procedure simply sets the Stopped variable to True and unloads the UserForm:

```
Private Sub CancelButton_Click()
    Stopped = True
    Unload Me
End Sub
```

This example, named random number generator.xlsm, is available on the book's website.

On the Web

Advanced UserForm Techniques

In This Chapter

- Using modeless UserForms
- Displaying a progress indicator
- Creating a *wizard* — an interactive series of dialog boxes
- Creating a function that emulates VBA's MsgBox function
- Allowing users to move UserForm controls
- Displaying a UserForm with no title bar
- Simulating a toolbar with a Userform
- Emulating a task pane with a Userform
- Allowing users to resize a UserForm
- Handling multiple controls with a single event handler
- Using a dialog box to select a color
- Displaying a chart in a UserForm
- Using an Enhanced Data Form
- Creating a moving tile puzzle

A Modeless Dialog Box

Most dialog boxes that you encounter are *modal* dialog boxes, which you must dismiss from the screen before the user can do anything with the underlying application. Some dialog boxes, however, are *modeless,* which means the user can continue to work in the application while the dialog box is displayed.

To display a modeless UserForm, use a statement such as

```
UserForm1.Show vbModeless
```

The word vbModeless is a built-in constant that has a value of 0. Therefore, the following statement works identically:

```
UserForm1.Show 0
```

Figure 13-1 shows a modeless dialog box that displays information about the active cell. When the dialog box is displayed, the user is free to move the cell cursor, activate other sheets, and perform other Excel actions. The information displayed in the dialog box changes when the active cell changes.

	A	B	C	D	E	F	G	H	I	J
1	9/23/2012									
2										
3	**Product**	**Sales**	**Units**	**Per Unit**	**Pct of Total**					
4	Widgets	$1,322.50	20	$66.13	89.7%					
5	Shapholytes	$902.44	6	$150.41	204.1%					
6	Hinkers	$322.40	8	$40.30	54.7%					
7	Ralimongers	$32.00	1	$32.00	43.4%					
8	Total:	$2,579.34	35	$73.70						
9										
10										
11										

Cell: D5

Formula:	=B5/C5
Number Format:	$#,##0.00_);($#,##0.00)
Locked:	True

Close

Sheet1 Sheet2 Chart1 +

Figure 13-1: This modeless dialog box remains visible while the user continues working.

On the Web

This example, named **modeless userform1.xlsm, is available on the book's website.**

The key to making this UserForm work is determining when to update the information in the dialog box. To do so, the code in the example monitors two workbook events: SheetSelectionChange and SheetActivate. These event-handler procedures are located in the code module for the ThisWorkbook object.

Cross-Ref   Refer to Chapter 17 for additional information about events.

The event-handler procedures are simple:

```
Private Sub Workbook_SheetSelectionChange _
  (ByVal Sh As Object, ByVal Target As Range)
    Call UpdateBox
End Sub

Private Sub Workbook_SheetActivate(ByVal Sh As Object)
    Call UpdateBox
End Sub
```

The two previous procedures call the UpdateBox procedure, which follows:

```
Sub UpdateBox()
    With UserForm1
'       Make sure a worksheet is active
        If TypeName(ActiveSheet) <> "Worksheet" Then
            .lblFormula.Caption = "N/A"
            .lblNumFormat.Caption = "N/A"
            .lblLocked.Caption = "N/A"
            Exit Sub
        End If
        .Caption = "Cell: " & ActiveCell.Address(False, False)
'       Formula
        If ActiveCell.HasFormula Then
            .lblFormula.Caption = ActiveCell.Formula
        Else
            .lblFormula.Caption = "(none)"
        End If
'       Number format
        .lblNumFormat.Caption = ActiveCell.NumberFormat
'       Locked
        .lblLocked.Caption = ActiveCell.Locked
    End With
End Sub
```

The UpdateBox procedure changes the UserForm's caption to show the active cell's address; then it updates the three Label controls (lblFormula, lblNumFormat, and lblLocked).

Following are a few points to help you understand how this example works:

➤ The UserForm is displayed modeless so that you can still access the worksheet while it's displayed.

➤ Code at the top of the procedure checks to make sure that the active sheet is a worksheet. If the sheet isn't a worksheet, the Label controls are assigned the text N/A.

➤ The workbook monitors the active cell by using a Selection_Change event (which is located in the ThisWorkbook code module).

➤ The information is displayed in Label controls on the UserForm.

Figure 13-2 shows a more sophisticated version of this example. This version displays quite a bit of additional information about the selected cell. The code is too lengthy to display here, but you can view the well-commented code in the example workbook.

	A	B	C	D	E	F	G	H	I	J
1										
2										
3										
4		Product-A	Product-B	Product-C	Total	Pct Change				
5	January	3,331	2,122	2,791	8,244	#N/A				
6	February	2,909	1,892	3,111	7,912	-4.0%				
7	March	2,579	2,321	3,856	8,756	10.7%				
8	Quarter Total	$ 8,819	$ 6,335	$ 9,758	$ 24,912					
9										
10										
11										
12	19									
13										
14	This workbook c <-- Lengthy text									
15										
16										
17	#DIV/0!									
18	#REF!									
19										
20										
21										
22										
23										
24										
25										
26										

InfoBox for cell: B8 (R8C2)

Options
☑ Auto update
☐ Show formulas in R1C1 notation

Close
Update

Value: 8819
Displayed As: $ 8,819
Cell Type: Currency
Number Format: _($* #,##0_);_($* (#,##0);_($* "-"??_);_(@_)
Formula: =SUM(B5:B7)
Name: (none)
Protection: Locked
Cell Comment: (none)
Dependent Cells: 1
Dir Dependents: 1
Precedent Cells: 3
Dir Precedents: 3

Sheet1 | Sheet2 | Chart1 | ⊕

Figure 13-2: This modeless UserForm displays various information about the active cell.

Modeless UserForms in Excel 2013

The single-document interface introduced in Excel 2013 adds a new wrinkle to modeless UserForms. When a modeless UserForm is displayed, it's associated with the active workbook window. So if you switch to a different workbook window, the modeless dialog box may not be visible. Even if it *is* visible, it will not work as you intended if a different workbook is active.

If you would like a modeless UserForm to be available in all workbook windows, you need to do some extra work. A workbook (modeless SDI.xlsm) one the book's website demonstrates the technique.

The example uses a Windows API function to get the Windows handle of the modeless UserForm. The workbook uses a class module to monitor all Window Activate events. When a window is activated, another Windows API function sets the UserForm's parent to the new workbook window. As a result, the UserForm always appears on top of the active window.

Following are some key points about this more sophisticated version:

➤ The UserForm has a check box (Auto Update). When this check box is selected, the UserForm is updated automatically. When Auto Update isn't turned on, the user can use the Update button to refresh the information.

➤ The workbook uses a class module to monitor two events for all open workbooks: the SheetSelectionChange event and the SheetActivate event. As a result, the code to display the information about the current cell is executed automatically whenever these events occur in any workbook (assuming that the Auto Update option is in effect). Some actions (such as changing a cell's number format) do not trigger either of these events. Therefore, the UserForm also contains an Update button.

Cross-Ref   **Refer to Chapter 27 for more information about class modules.**

➤ The counts displayed for the cell precedents and dependents fields include cells in the active sheet only, due to a limitation of the Precedents and Dependents properties.

➤ Because the length of the information will vary, VBA code is used to size and vertically space the labels — and also change the height of the UserForm if necessary.

Displaying a Progress Indicator

One of the most common requests among Excel developers involves progress indicators. A *progress indicator* is a graphical thermometer-type display that shows the progress of a task, such as a lengthy macro.

In this section, I describe how to create three types of progress indicators for

> ➤ A macro that's not initiated by a UserForm (a stand-alone progress indicator).

> ➤ A macro that is initiated by a UserForm. In this case, the UserForm uses a MultiPage control that displays the progress indicator while the macro is running.

> ➤ A macro that is initiated by a UserForm. In this case, the UserForm increases in height while the macro is running, and the progress indicator appears at the bottom of the dialog box.

Using a progress indicator requires that your code gauge how far along your macro is in completing its given task. How you do this will vary, depending on the macro. For example, if your macro writes data to cells and you know the number of cells that will be written to, it's a simple matter to write code that calculates the percent completed. Even if you can't accurately gauge the progress of a macro, it's a good idea to give the user some indication that the macro is still running and Excel hasn't crashed.

Caution

A progress indicator will slow down your macro a bit because of the extra overhead of having to update it. If speed is absolutely critical, you might prefer to forgo using a progress indicator.

 ## Displaying progress in the status bar

A simple way to display the progress of a macro is to use Excel's status bar. The advantage is that a status bar is easy to program. However, the disadvantage is that most users aren't accustomed to watching the status bar and prefer a more visual display.

To write text to the status bar, use a statement such as

```
Application.StatusBar = "Please wait..."
```

You can, of course, update the status bar while your macro progresses. For example, if you have a variable named Pct that represents the percent completed, you can write code that periodically executes a statement such as this:

```
Application.StatusBar = "Processing… " & Pct & "% Completed"
```

When your macro finishes, you must reset the status bar to its normal state with the following statement:

```
Application.StatusBar = False
```

If you don't reset the status bar, the final message will continue to be displayed.

Creating a stand-alone progress indicator

This section describes how to set up a stand-alone progress indicator — that is, one that isn't initiated by displaying a UserForm — to display the progress of a macro. The macro in this example clears the worksheet and writes 20,000 random numbers to a range of cells:

```
Sub GenerateRandomNumbers()
'   Inserts random numbers on the active worksheet
    Const RowMax As Long = 500
    Const ColMax As Long = 40
    Dim r As Long, c As Long
    If TypeName(ActiveSheet) <> "Worksheet" Then Exit Sub
    Cells.Clear
    For r = 1 To RowMax
        For c = 1 To ColMax
            Cells(r, c) = Int(Rnd * 1000)
        Next c
    Next r
End Sub
```

After you make a few modifications to this macro (described in the next section), the UserForm, shown in Figure 13-3, displays the progress.

	A	B	C	D	E	F	G	H	I	J	K	L
1	89	670	300	727	183	545	459	149	468	286	694	3
2	604	43	927	112	730	296	520	521	185	131	670	3
3	338	152	172	160	742	298	907	682	240	854	341	3
4	543	735	324	502	822	233	73	771	715	707	448	5
5	616	107	937	974	968	612	987	380	333	21	500	8
6	592	660	334	112	67	272	635	54	958	705	271	5
7	647	367	10	Progress				791	94	745	301	5
8	598	275	58	Entering random numbers...				545	387	707	395	8
9	403	13	41	66%				719	122	233	123	2
10	660	287	96					671	725	545	322	7
11	107	379	88					212	264	943	594	
12	124	653	591	642	579	437	46	107	945	302	806	
13	231	46	763	562	3	105	716	573	617	580	593	2
14	589	579	848	763	541	574	561	780	268	309	853	6
15	499	846	555	609	595	135	207	351	529	102	250	6
16	902	523	363	170	458	409	294	864	168	149	715	9
17	882	862	15	717	815	843	979	348	598	717	943	9
18	161	192	17	226	240	213	435	786	368	652	896	3
19	604	424	145	874	699	122	349	614	671	880	301	3
20	714	544	937	544	47	504	425	222	840	902	150	5
21	136	116	200	320	531	118	883	450	847	300	203	1
22	157	784	503	989	289	52	957	96	806	231	482	5
23	203	769	683	542	848	224	398	408	472	933	778	9
24	340	370	343	672	626	877	971	586	740	220	145	7

Sheet1

Figure 13-3: A UserForm displays the progress of a macro.

On the Web

This example, named **progress indicator1.xlsm**, is available on the book's website.

Building the stand-alone progress indicator UserForm

Follow these steps to create the UserForm that will be used to display the progress of your task:

1. Insert a new UserForm and change its Caption property setting to Progress.

2. Add a Frame control and name it FrameProgress.

3. Add a Label control inside the Frame, name it LabelProgress, remove the label's caption, and make its background color (BackColor property) something that will stand out.

   The label's size and placement don't matter for now.

4. Optional. Add another label above the frame to describe what's going on.

   In this example, the label reads, *Entering random numbers....*

5. Adjust the UserForm and controls so that they look something like Figure 13-4.

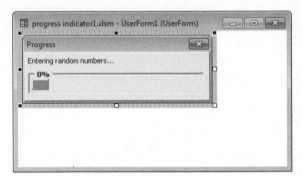

Figure 13-4: This UserForm will serve as a progress indicator.

You can, of course, apply any other type of formatting to the controls. For example, I changed the SpecialEffect property for the Frame control to make it appear sunken.

Creating the event-handler procedures for the stand-alone progress indicator

The trick in creating the stand-alone progress indicator 's event handlers involves running a procedure automatically when the UserForm is displayed. One option is to use the Initialize event. However, this event occurs *before* the UserForm is displayed, so it's not appropriate. The Activate event, on the other hand, is triggered when the UserForm is displayed, so it's perfect for this application.

Insert the following procedure in the code window for the UserForm. This procedure simply calls a procedure named GenerateRandomNumbers when the UserForm is displayed. This procedure, which is stored in a VBA module, is the macro that runs while the progress indicator is displayed.

```
Private Sub UserForm_Activate()
    Call GenerateRandomNumbers
End Sub
```

The modified version of the GenerateRandomNumber procedure (which was presented earlier) follows. Note that additional code keeps track of the progress and stores it in a variable named PctDone.

```
Sub GenerateRandomNumbers()
'    Inserts random numbers on the active worksheet
    Dim Counter As Long
    Const RowMax As Long = 500
    Const ColMax As Long = 40
    Dim r As Integer, c As Long
    Dim PctDone As Double

    If TypeName(ActiveSheet) <> "Worksheet" Then Exit Sub
    Cells.Clear
    Counter = 1    For r = 1 To RowMax
        For c = 1 To ColMax
            Cells(r, c) = Int(Rnd * 1000)
            Counter = Counter + 1
        Next c
        PctDone = Counter / (RowMax * ColMax)
        Call UpdateProgress(PctDone)
    Next r
    Unload UserForm1
End Sub
```

The GenerateRandomNumbers procedure contains two loops. In the inner loop is a call to the UpdateProgress procedure, which takes one argument (the PctDone variable, which represents the progress of the macro). PctDone will contain a value between 0 and 100.

```
Sub UpdateProgress(Pct)
    With UserForm1
      .FrameProgress.Caption = Format(Pct, "0%")
      .LabelProgress.Width = Pct * (.FrameProgress.Width - 10)
      .Repaint
    End With
End Sub
```

Creating the start-up procedure for a stand-alone progress indicator

All that's missing is a procedure to display the UserForm. Enter the following procedure in a VBA module:

```
Sub ShowUserForm()
    With UserForm1
        .LabelProgress.Width = 0
        .Show
    End With
End Sub
```

Tip

An additional accoutrement is to make the progress bar color match the workbook's current theme. To do so, just add this statement to the ShowUserForm procedure:

```
.LabelProgress.BackColor = ActiveWorkbook.Theme. _
    ThemeColorScheme.Colors(msoThemeAccent1)
```

How the stand-alone progress indicator works

When you execute the ShowUserForm procedure, the Label object's width is set to 0. Then the Show method of the UserForm1 object displays the UserForm (which is the progress indicator). When the UserForm is displayed, its Activate event is triggered, which executes the GenerateRandomNumbers procedure. The GenerateRandomNumbers procedure contains code that calls the UpdateProgress procedure every time the r loop counter variable changes. Note that the UpdateProgress procedure uses the Repaint method of the UserForm object. Without this statement, the changes to the label would not be updated. Before the GenerateRandomNumbers procedure ends, the last statement unloads the UserForm.

To customize this technique, you need to figure out how to determine the percentage completed and assign it to the PctDone variable. This calculation will vary, depending on your application. If your code runs in a loop (as in this example), determining the percentage completed is easy. If your code is not in a loop, you might need to estimate the progress completed at various points in your code.

Showing a progress indicator by using a MultiPage control

In the preceding example, a UserForm didn't initiate the macro. In many cases, your lengthy macro is kicked off when the user clicks the OK button on a UserForm. The technique that I describe in this section is a better solution and assumes the following:

➤ Your project is completed and debugged.

➤ Your project uses a UserForm (without a MultiPage control) to initiate a lengthy macro.

➤ You have a way to gauge the progress of your macro.

This book's website demonstrates this technique in the progress indicator2.xlsm file.

Like the previous example, this one enters random numbers into a worksheet. The difference here is that the application contains a UserForm that allows the user to specify the number of rows and columns for the random numbers (see Figure 13-5).

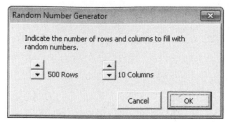

Figure 13-5: The user specifies the number of rows and columns for the random numbers.

Modifying your UserForm for a progress indicator with a MultiPage control

This step assumes that you have a UserForm all set up. You'll add a MultiPage control. The first page of the MultiPage control will contain all your original UserForm controls. The second page will contain the controls that display the progress indicator. When the macro begins executing, VBA code will change the Value property of the MultiPage control to effectively hide the original controls and display the progress indicator.

The first step is to add a MultiPage control to your UserForm. Then move all the existing controls on the UserForm to Page1 of the MultiPage control.

Next, activate Page2 of the MultiPage control and set it up as shown in Figure 13-6. This is essentially the same combination of controls used in the example in the previous section.

Follow these steps to set up the MultiPage control:

1. Add a Frame control and name it FrameProgress.

2. Add a Label control inside the Frame, name it LabelProgress, remove the label's caption, and make its background color red.

3. Optional. Add another label to describe what's going on.

4. Next, activate the MultiPage control itself (not a page on the control) and set its Style property to 2 – fmTabStyleNone.

   (This will hide the tabs.) You'll probably need to adjust the size of the MultiPage control to account for the fact that the tabs aren't displayed.

The easiest way to select the MultiPage control when the tabs are hidden is to use the drop-down list in the Properties window. To select a particular page, specify a Value for the MultiPage control: 0 for Page1, 1 for Page2, and so on.

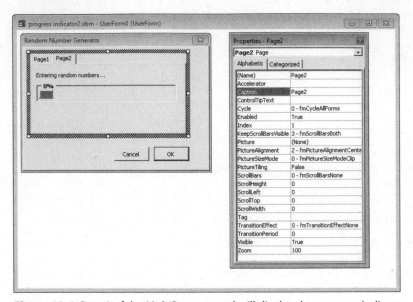

Figure 13-6: Page2 of the MultiPage control will display the progress indicator.

Inserting the UpdateProgress procedure for a progress indicator with a MultiPage control

Insert the following procedure in the code module for the UserForm:

```
Sub UpdateProgress(Pct)
    With UserForm1
        .FrameProgress.Caption = Format(Pct, "0%")
        .LabelProgress.Width = Pct * (.FrameProgress.Width - 10)
        .Repaint
    End With
End Sub
```

The UpdateProgress procedure is called from the macro that's executed when the user clicks the OK button and performs the updating of the progress indicator.

Modifying your procedure for a progress indicator with a MultiPage control

You need to modify the procedure that is executed when the user clicks the OK button — the Click event-handler procedure for the button named OKButton_Click. First, insert the following statement at the top of your procedure:

```
MultiPage1.Value = 1
```

This statement activates Page2 of the MultiPage control (the page that displays the progress indicator).

In the next step, you're pretty much on your own. You need to write code to calculate the percent completed and assign this value to a variable named PctDone. Most likely, this calculation will be performed inside a loop. Then insert the following statement, which will update the progress indicator:

```
Call UpdateProgress(PctDone)
```

How a progress indicator with a MultiPage control works

Using a MultiPage control as a progress indicator is straightforward and, as you've seen, it involves only one UserForm. The code switches pages of the MultiPage control and converts your normal dialog box into a progress indicator. Because the MultiPage tabs are hidden, it doesn't even resemble a MultiPage control.

Showing a progress indicator without using a MultiPage control

The example in this section is similar to the example in the preceding section. However, this technique is simpler because it doesn't use a MultiPage control. Rather, the progress indicator is stored at the bottom of the UserForm — but the UserForm's height is reduced so that the progress indicator controls aren't visible. When it's time to display the progress indicator, the UserForm's height is increased, which makes the progress indicator visible.

On the Web

This book's website demonstrates this technique in the progress indicator3.xlsm file.

Figure 13-7 shows the UserForm in VBE.

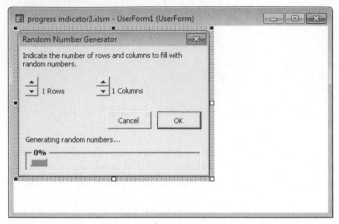

Figure 13-7: The progress indicator will be hidden by reducing the height of the UserForm.

The Height property of the UserForm is 172. However, before the UserForm is displayed, the VBA code changes the Height to 124 (which means the progress indicator controls aren't visible to the user). When the user clicks OK, the VBA code changes the Height property to 172 with the following statement:

```
Me.Height = 172
```

Figure 13-8 shows the UserForm with the progress indicator section unhidden.

Figure 13-8: The progress indicator in action.

Creating Wizards

Many applications incorporate wizards to guide users through an operation. Excel's Text Import Wizard is a good example. A *wizard* is essentially a series of dialog boxes that solicit information from the user. Usually, the user's choices in earlier dialog boxes influence the contents of later dialog boxes. In most wizards, the user is free to go forward or backward through the dialog box sequence or to click the Finish button to accept all defaults.

You can create wizards by using VBA and a series of UserForms. However, I've found that the most efficient way to create a wizard is to use a single UserForm and a MultiPage control with the tabs hidden.

Figure 13-9 shows an example of a simple four-step wizard, which consists of a single UserForm that contains a MultiPage control. Each step of the wizard displays a different page in the MultiPage control.

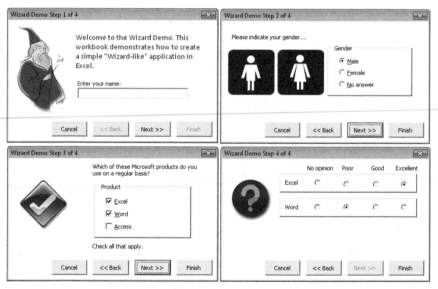

Figure 13-9: This four-step wizard uses a MultiPage control.

On the Web

The wizard example in this section is available on the book's website. in a file named wizard demo.xlsm.

The sections that follow describe how I created the sample wizard.

Setting up the MultiPage control for the wizard

Start with a new UserForm and add a MultiPage control. By default, this control contains two pages. Right-click the MultiPage tab and insert enough new pages to handle your wizard (one page for each wizard step). The example is a four-step wizard, so the MultiPage control has four pages. The captions of the MultiPage tabs are irrelevant because they won't be seen. The MultiPage control's Style property will eventually be set to 2 - fmTabStyleNone.

Tip

While working on the UserForm, you'll want to keep the MultiPage tabs visible to make it easier to access various pages.

Next, add the desired controls to each page of the MultiPage control. These controls will, of course, vary depending on your application. You may need to resize the MultiPage control while you work to have room for the controls.

Adding the buttons to the wizard's UserForm

Now add the buttons that control the progress of the wizard. These buttons are placed outside the MultiPage control because they're used while any of the pages are displayed. Most wizards have four buttons:

- ➤ **Cancel:** Cancels the wizard and performs no action.
- ➤ **Back:** Returns to the previous step. During Step 1 of the wizard, this button should be disabled.
- ➤ **Next:** Advances to the next step. During the last wizard step, this button should be disabled.
- ➤ **Finish:** Finishes the wizard.

In the example, these CommandButtons are named CancelButton, BackButton, NextButton, and FinishButton.

Note

In some cases, the user is allowed to click the Finish button at any time and accept the defaults for items that were skipped. In other cases, the wizard requires a user response for some items, so the Finish button is disabled until all required input is made. The example requires an entry in the TextBox in Step 1.

Programming the wizard's buttons

Each of the four wizard buttons requires a procedure to handle its Click event. The event handler for the CancelButton control follows.

```
Private Sub CancelButton_Click()
    Dim Msg As String
    Dim Ans As Integer
    Msg = "Cancel the wizard?"
    Ans = MsgBox(Msg, vbQuestion + vbYesNo, APPNAME)
    If Ans = vbYes Then Unload Me
End Sub
```

This procedure uses a MsgBox function (see Figure 13-10) to verify that the user really wants to exit. If the user clicks the Yes button, the UserForm is unloaded with no action taken. This type of verification, of course, is optional.

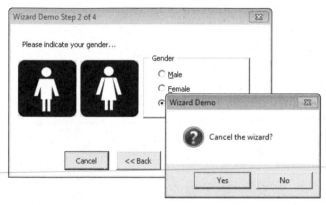

Figure 13-10: Clicking the Cancel button displays a confirmation message box.

The event-handler procedures for the Back and Next buttons follow:

```
Private Sub BackButton_Click()
    MultiPage1.Value = MultiPage1.Value - 1
    UpdateControls
End Sub

Private Sub NextButton_Click()
    MultiPage1.Value = MultiPage1.Value + 1
    UpdateControls
End Sub
```

These two procedures are simple. They change the Value property of the MultiPage control and then call another procedure named UpdateControls (which follows).

The UpdateControls procedure is responsible for enabling and disabling the BackButton and NextButton controls.

```
Sub UpdateControls()
    Select Case MultiPage1.Value
        Case 0
            BackButton.Enabled = False
            NextButton.Enabled = True
        Case MultiPage1.Pages.Count - 1
            BackButton.Enabled = True
            NextButton.Enabled = False
        Case Else
            BackButton.Enabled = True
            NextButton.Enabled = True
    End Select

'    Update the caption
    Me.Caption = APPNAME & " Step " _
      & MultiPage1.Value + 1 & " of " _
      & MultiPage1.Pages.Count

'    The Name field is required
    If tbName.Text = "" Then
        FinishButton.Enabled = False
    Else
        FinishButton.Enabled = True
    End If
End Sub
```

The procedure changes the UserForm's caption to display the current step and the total number of steps. APPNAME is a public constant, defined in Module1. The procedure then examines the name field on the first page (a TextBox named tbName). This field is required, so if it's empty the user can't click the Finish button. If the TextBox is empty, the FinishButton is disabled; otherwise, it's enabled.

Programming dependencies in a wizard

In most wizards, a user's response on a particular step can affect what's displayed in a subsequent step. In this example, the users indicate which products they use in Step 3 and then rate those products in Step 4. The OptionButtons for a product's rating are visible only if the users have indicated a particular product.

Programmatically, you accomplish this task by monitoring the MultiPage's Change event. Whenever the value of the MultiPage is changed (by clicking the Back or Next button), the MultiPage1_Change procedure is executed. If the MultiPage control is on the last tab (Step 4), the procedure examines the values of the CheckBox controls in Step 3 and makes the appropriate adjustments in Step 4.

In this example, the code uses two arrays of controls — one for the product CheckBox controls (Step 3) and one for the Frame controls (Step 4). The code uses a For-Next loop to hide the Frames for the products that aren't used and then adjusts their vertical positioning. If none of the check boxes in Step 3 are checked, everything in Step 4 is hidden except a TextBox that displays Click Finish to exit (if a name is entered in Step 1) or A name is required in Step 1 (if a name isn't entered in Step 1). The MultiPage1_Change procedure follows:

```vba
Private Sub MultiPage1_Change()
    Dim TopPos As Long
    Dim FSpace As Long
    Dim AtLeastOne As Boolean
    Dim i As Long

'   Set up the Ratings page?
    If MultiPage1.Value = 3 Then
'       Create an array of CheckBox controls
        Dim ProdCB(1 To 3) As MSForms.CheckBox
        Set ProdCB(1) = cbExcel
        Set ProdCB(2) = cbWord
        Set ProdCB(3) = cbAccess

'       Create an array of Frame controls
        Dim ProdFrame(1 To 3) As MSForms.Frame
        Set ProdFrame(1) = FrameExcel
        Set ProdFrame(2) = FrameWord
        Set ProdFrame(3) = FrameAccess

        TopPos = 22
        FSpace = 8
        AtLeastOne = False

'       Loop through all products
        For i = 1 To 3
            If ProdCB(i) Then
                ProdFrame(i).Visible = True
                ProdFrame(i).Top = TopPos
                TopPos = TopPos + ProdFrame(i).Height + FSpace
                AtLeastOne = True
            Else
                ProdFrame(i).Visible = False
            End If
```

continued

```
        Next i

'       Uses no products?
        If AtLeastOne Then
            lblHeadings.Visible = True
            Image4.Visible = True
            lblFinishMsg.Visible = False
        Else
            lblHeadings.Visible = False
            Image4.Visible = False
            lblFinishMsg.Visible = True
            If tbName = "" Then
                lblFinishMsg.Caption = _
                    "A name is required in Step 1."
            Else
                lblFinishMsg.Caption = _
                    "Click Finish to exit."
            End If
        End If
    End If
End Sub
```

Performing the task with the wizard

When the user clicks the Finish button, the wizard performs its task: transferring the information from the UserForm to the next empty row in the worksheet. This procedure, named FinishButton_Click, is straightforward. It starts by determining the next empty worksheet row and assigns this value to a variable (r). The remainder of the procedure simply translates the values of the controls and enters data into the worksheet.

```
Private Sub FinishButton_Click()
    Dim r As Long
    r = Application.WorksheetFunction. _
      CountA(Range("A:A")) + 1

'   Insert the name
    Cells(r, 1) = tbName.Text

'   Insert the gender
    Select Case True
        Case obMale: Cells(r, 2) = "Male"
        Case obFemale: Cells(r, 2) = "Female"
        Case obNoAnswer: Cells(r, 2) = "Unknown"
```

```
      End Select

'     Insert usage
      Cells(r, 3) = cbExcel
      Cells(r, 4) = cbWord
      Cells(r, 5) = cbAccess

'     Insert ratings
      If obExcel1 Then Cells(r, 6) = ""
      If obExcel2 Then Cells(r, 6) = 0
      If obExcel3 Then Cells(r, 6) = 1
      If obExcel4 Then Cells(r, 6) = 2
      If obWord1 Then Cells(r, 7) = ""
      If obWord2 Then Cells(r, 7) = 0
      If obWord3 Then Cells(r, 7) = 1
      If obWord4 Then Cells(r, 7) = 2
      If obAccess1 Then Cells(r, 8) = ""
      If obAccess2 Then Cells(r, 8) = 0
      If obAccess3 Then Cells(r, 8) = 1
      If obAccess4 Then Cells(r, 8) = 2

'     Unload the form
      Unload Me
End Sub
```

After you test your wizard, and everything is working properly, you can set the MultiPage control's Style property to 2 - fmTabStyleNone to hide the tabs.

Emulating the MsgBox Function

The VBA MsgBox function (discussed in Chapter 10) is a bit unusual because, unlike most functions, it displays a dialog box. But, similar to other functions, it also returns a value: an integer that represents which button the user clicked.

This section describes a custom function that I created that emulates the VBA MsgBox function. On first thought, creating such a function might seem easy. Think again! The MsgBox function is extraordinarily versatile because of the arguments that it accepts. Consequently, creating a function to emulate MsgBox is no small feat.

Note

The point of this exercise is not to create an alternative messaging function. Rather, it's to demonstrate how to develop a complex function that also incorporates a UserForm. However, some people might like the idea of being able to customize their messages. If so, you'll find that this function is easy to customize. For example, you can change the font, colors, button text, and so on.

I named my pseudo-MsgBox function MyMsgBox. The emulation is close but not perfect. The MyMsgBox function has the following limitations:

➤ It does not support the Helpfile argument (which adds a Help button that, when clicked, opens a Help file).

➤ It does not support the Context argument (which specifies the context ID for the Help file).

➤ It does not support the *system modal* option, which puts everything in Windows on hold until you respond to the dialog box.

➤ It does not play a sound when it is called.

The syntax for MyMsgBox is

```
MyMsgBox(prompt[, buttons] [, title])
```

This syntax is the same as the MsgBox syntax except it doesn't use the last two optional arguments (Helpfile and Context). MyMsgBox also uses the same predefined constants as MsgBox: vbOKOnly, vbQuestion, vbDefaultButton1, and so on.

Note   If you're not familiar with the VBA MsgBox function, consult the Help system to become acquainted with its arguments.

MsgBox emulation: MyMsgBox code

The MyMsgBox function uses a UserForm named MyMsgBoxForm. The function itself, which follows, is short. The bulk of the work is done in the UserForm_Initialize procedure.

```
Public Prompt1 As String
Public Buttons1 As Integer
Public Title1 As String
Public UserClick As Integer

Function MyMsgBox(ByVal Prompt As String, _
  Optional ByVal Buttons As Integer, _
  Optional ByVal Title As String) As Integer
    Prompt1 = Prompt
    Buttons1 = Buttons
    Title1 = Title
    MyMsgBoxForm.Show
    MyMsgBox = UserClick
End Function
```

On the Web

The complete code for the MyMsgBox function is too lengthy to list here, but it's available in a workbook named msgbox emulation.xlsm, available on the book's website. The workbook is set up so that you can easily try various options.

Figure 13-11 shows MyMsgBox in use. It looks similar to the VBA message box, but I used a different font for the message text and also used some different icons.

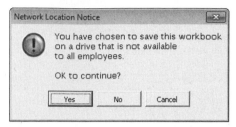

Figure 13-11: The result of the MsgBox emulation function.

If you use a multiple monitor system, the position of the displayed UserForm may not be centered in Excel's window. To solve that problem, use the following code to display MyMsgBoxForm:

```
With MyMsgBoxForm
    .StartUpPosition = 0
    .Left = Application.Left + (0.5 * Application.Width) - (0.5 * .Width)
    .Top = Application.Top + (0.5 * Application.Height) - (0.5 * .Height)
    .Show
End With
```

Here's the code that I used to execute the function:

```
Prompt = "You have chosen to save this workbook" & vbCrLf
Prompt = Prompt & "on a drive that is not available to"  & vbCrLf
Prompt = Prompt & "all employees." & vbCrLf & vbCrLf
Prompt = Prompt & "OK to continue?"
Buttons = vbQuestion + vbYesNo
Title = "Network Location Notice"
Ans = MyMsgBox(Prompt, Buttons, Title)
```

How the MyMsgBox function works

In The MyMsgBox function, note the use of four Public variables. The first three (Prompt1, Buttons1, and Title1) represent the arguments that are passed to the function. The other variable (UserClick) represents the values returned by the function. The UserForm_Initialize procedure needs a way to get this information and send it back to the function, and using Public variables is the only way to accomplish that.

The UserForm (shown in Figure 13-12) contains four Label controls. Each of these Label controls has an image, which I pasted into the Picture property. The UserForm also has three CommandButton controls and a TextBox control.

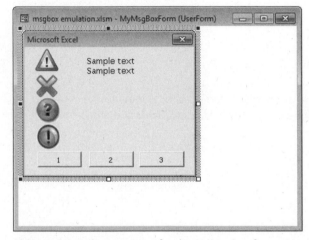

Figure 13-12: The UserForm for the MyMsgBox function.

Note

I originally used Image controls to hold the four icons, but the images displayed with a faint outline. I switched to Label controls because the image is not displayed with an outline.

The code in the UserForm_Initialize procedure examines the arguments and does the following:

➤ Determines which, if any, image to display (and hides the others)

➤ Determines which button(s) to display (and hides the others)

➤ Determines which button is the default button

➤ Centers the buttons in the dialog box

➤ Determines the captions for the CommandButtons

➤ Determines the position of the text within the dialog box

➤ Determines the width and height of the dialog box (by using an API function call to get the video resolution)

➤ Displays the UserForm

Three additional event-handler procedures are included (one for each CommandButton). These routines determine which button was clicked and return a value for the function by setting a value for the UserClick variable.

Interpreting the second argument (buttons) is challenging. This argument can consist of a number of constants added together. For example, the second argument can be something like this:

```
VbYesNoCancel + VbQuestion + VbDefaultButton3
```

This argument creates a three-button MsgBox (with Yes, No, and Cancel buttons), displays the question mark icon, and makes the third button the default button. The actual argument is 547 (3 + 32 + 512).

The challenge was pulling three pieces of information from a single number. The solution involves converting the argument to a binary number and then examining specific bits. For example, 547 in binary is 1000100011. Binary digits 4 through 6 determine the image displayed; digits 8 through 10 determine which buttons to display; and digits 1 and 2 determine which button is the default button.

Using the MyMsgBox function

To use this function in your own project, export the MyMsgBoxMod module and the MyMsgBoxForm UserForm. Then import these two files into your project. You can then use the MyMsgBox function in your code just as you'd use the MsgBox function.

A UserForm with Movable Controls

The UserForm shown in Figure 13-13 contains three Image controls. The user can use the mouse to drag these images around in the dialog box. I'm not sure of the practical significance of this technique, but the example in this section will help you understand mouse-related events.

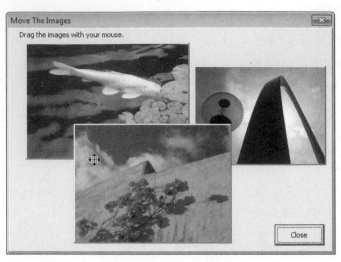

Figure 13-13: You can drag and rearrange the three Image controls by using the mouse.

On the Web   **This example is available on the book's website in a file named move controls.xlsm.**

Each Image control has two associated event procedures: MouseDown and MouseMove. The event procedures for the Image1 control are shown here. (The others are identical except for the control names.)

```
Private Sub Image1_MouseDown(ByVal Button As Integer, _
    ByVal Shift As Integer, ByVal X As Single, ByVal Y As Single)
'   Starting position when button is pressed
    OldX = X
    OldY = Y
    Image1.ZOrder 0
End Sub

Private Sub Image1_MouseMove(ByVal Button As Integer, _
    ByVal Shift As Integer, ByVal X As Single, ByVal Y As Single)
'   Move the image
    If Button = 1 Then
        Image1.Left = Image1.Left + (X - OldX)
        Image1.Top = Image1.Top + (Y - OldY)
    End If
End Sub
```

When the mouse button is pressed, the MouseDown event occurs, and the X and Y positions of the mouse pointer are stored. Two public variables are used to keep track of the original position of the controls: OldX and OldY. This procedure also changes the ZOrder property, which puts the image on top of the others.

When the mouse is being moved, the MouseMove event occurs repeatedly. The event procedure checks the mouse button. If the Button argument is 1, it means that the left mouse button is depressed. If so, then the Image control is shifted relative to its old position.

Also note that the mouse pointer changes when it's over an image. That's because the MousePointer property is set to 15 - fmMousePointerSizeAll, a mouse pointer style that's commonly used to indicate that an item can be dragged.

A UserForm with No Title Bar

Excel provides no direct way to display a UserForm without its title bar. But this feat is possible with the help of a few API functions. Figure 13-14 shows a UserForm with no title bar.

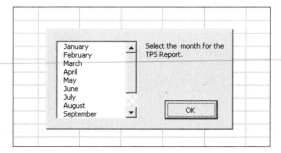

Figure 13-14: This UserForm lacks a title bar.

Another example of a UserForm without a title bar is in Figure 13-15. This dialog box contains an Image control and a CommandButton control.

On the Web

Both examples are in a workbook named no title bar.xlsm, which is available on the book's website. Also available is another version of the splash screen example presented in Chapter 12. This version, named splash screen2.xlsm, displays the UserForm without a title bar.

Figure 13-15: Another UserForm without a title bar.

Displaying a UserForm without a title bar requires four windows API functions: GetWindowLong, SetWindowLong, DrawMenuBar, and FindWindowA (see the example file for the function declarations). The UserForm_Initialize procedure calls these functions:

```
Private Sub UserForm_Initialize()
    Dim lngWindow As Long, lFrmHdl As Long
    lFrmHdl = FindWindowA(vbNullString, Me.Caption)
    lngWindow = GetWindowLong(lFrmHdl, GWL_STYLE)
    lngWindow = lngWindow And (Not WS_CAPTION)
    Call SetWindowLong(lFrmHdl, GWL_STYLE, lngWindow)
    Call DrawMenuBar(lFrmHdl)
End Sub
```

One problem is that the user has no way to reposition a dialog box without a title bar. The solution is to use the MouseDown and MouseMove events, as described in the preceding section.

Note

Because the FindWindowA function uses the UserForm's caption, this technique won't work if the Caption property is set to an empty string.

Simulating a Toolbar with a UserForm

Creating a custom toolbar in versions prior to Excel 2007 was relatively easy. Beginning with Excel 2007, you can no longer create custom toolbars. More accurately, you can still create custom toolbars with VBA, but Excel ignores many of your VBA instructions. Beginning with Excel 2007, all custom toolbars are displayed in the Add-Ins➜Custom Toolbars Ribbon group. You can't move, float, resize, or dock these toolbars.

This section describes how to create a toolbar alternative: a modeless UserForm that simulates a floating toolbar. Figure 13-16 shows a UserForm that may substitute for a toolbar. It uses Windows API calls to make the title bar a bit shorter than normal, and also displays the UserForm with square (rather than rounded) corners. The Close button is also smaller.

⊿	E	F	G	H	I	J	K	L	M
1	134	346	257	194	248	320	274	72	
2	143						160	183	
3	247						304	248	
4	260						205	343	
5	251						305	263	
6	144	154	245	316			28	227	
7	184	97	61	191				319	
8	317	291	194	19	221	219	126	69	
9	247	198	269	89	340	88	23	207	
10	321	343	122	311	211	94	255	187	
11	152	190	130	248	27	204	286	224	

UserForm Posing As A Toolbar — Click here to exceute Macro 6

Figure 13-16: A UserForm set up to function as a toolbar.

On the Web   **This example, named simulated toolbar.xlm, is available on the book's website.**

The UserForm contains eight Image controls, and each executes a macro. Figure 13-17 shows the UserForm in VBE. Note that

➤ The controls aren't aligned.

➤ The images displayed are not the final images

➤ The UserForm isn't the final size.

➤ The title bar is the standard size.

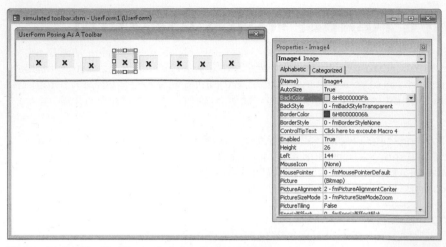

Figure 13-17: The UserForm that simulates a toolbar.

The VBA code takes care of the cosmetic details, including borrowing images from Excel's Ribbon. For example, this statement assign an image to the Image1 control:

```
Image1.Picture = Application.CommandBars. _
   GetImageMso("ReviewAcceptChange", 32, 32)
```

See Chapter 20 for more information about accessing images from the Ribbon.

The code also aligns the controls and adjusts the size of the UserForm to eliminate wasted space. In addition, the code uses Windows API functions to make the UserForm's title bar smaller — just like a real toolbar. To make the UserForm look even more like a toolbar, I also set the ControlTipText property of each Image control — which displays a toolbar-like tooltip when the mouse cursor is hovered over the control.

If you open the example file, you'll also notice that the images increase in size slightly when the mouse cursor is hovered over them. That's because each Image control has an associated MouseMove event handler that changes the size. Here's the MouseMove event handler procedure for Image1 (the others are identical):

```
Private Sub Image1_MouseMove(ByVal Button As Integer, _
   ByVal Shift As Integer, ByVal X As Single, ByVal Y As Single)
   Call NormalSize
   Image1.Width = 26
   Image1.Height = 26
End Sub
```

This procedure calls the NormalSize procedure, which returns each image to its normal size:

```
Private Sub NormalSize()
'   Make all controls normal size
    Dim ctl As Control
    For Each ctl In Controls
        ctl.Width = 24
        ctl.Height = 24
    Next ctl
End Sub
```

The net effect is that the user gets some visual feedback when the mouse cursor moves over a control — just like a real toolbar. The toolbar simulation only goes so far, however. You can't resize the UserForm (for example, make the images display vertically rather than horizontally). And, of course, you can't dock the pseudotoolbar to one of the Excel window borders.

Emulating a Task Pane with a UserForm

In Office 2013, task panes take on an expanded role and are used for adjusting formatting for many objects, including charts and images. The task panes also have a new look.

I spent some time to try to emulate the look of a task pane in a UserForm. The result is shown in Figure 13-18. The example is the same as the modeless UserForm example at the beginning of the chapter (refer to Figure 13-2). You can move the UserForm by dragging its title (the same way your move a task pane). The UserForm also has an X (Close) button in the upper-right corner. And, like a task pane, it displays a vertical scrollbar only when needed.

```
Me.BackColor = RGB(255, 255, 255)
Frame1.BackColor = RGB(255, 255, 255)
Frame2.BackColor = RGB(255, 255, 255)
```

Frame controls cannot have a transparent background, so I had to set the background color of the two Frame controls separately.

To create a UserForm that has a background color that matches the Light Gray theme, use this expression:

```
RGB(240, 240, 240)
```

To emulate the Dark Gray theme, use this expression:

```
RGB(222, 222, 222)
```

⁄	A	B	C	D	E	F	G	H	I
16	8	$573.34	$4,586.75	$91.89	$815.13	$481.45	$3,771.61	14,728.39	
17	9	$573.34	$5,160.09	$88.98	$904.12	$484.36	$4,255.97	14,244.03	
18	10	$573.34	$5,733.43	$86.06					
19	11	$573.34	$6,306.78	$83.11	$1,				
20	12	$573.34	$6,880.12	$80.15	$1,				
21	13	$573.34	$7,453.46	$77.17	$1,				
22	14	$573.34	$8,026.81	$74.17	$1,				
23	15	$573.34	$8,600.15	$71.16	$1,				
24	16	$573.34	$9,173.49	$68.12	$1,				
25	17	$573.34	$9,746.84	$65.07	$1,				
26	18	$573.34	$10,320.18	$62.00	$1,				
27	19	$573.34	$10,893.52	$58.91	$1,				
28	20	$573.34	$11,466.87	$55.80	$1,				
29	21	$573.34	$12,040.21	$52.68	$1,				
30	22	$573.34	$12,613.55	$49.53	$1,				
31	23	$573.34	$13,186.90	$46.37	$1,				
32	24	$573.34	$13,760.24	$43.18	$1,				
33	25	$573.34	$14,333.58	$39.98	$1,				
34	26	$573.34	$14,906.93	$36.76	$1,				
35	27	$573.34	$15,480.27	$33.52	$1,				
36	28	$573.34	$16,053.61	$30.25	$2,				
37	29	$573.34	$16,626.96	$26.97	$2,043.10	$546.37	$14,581.66	3,918.14	
38	30	$573.34	$17,200.30	$23.67	$2,068.77	$549.67	$15,131.53	3,368.47	
39	31	$573.34	$17,773.64	$20.35	$2,089.12	$552.99	$15,684.52	2,815.48	
40	32	$573.34	$18,346.99	$17.01	$2,106.13	$556.33	$16,240.85	2,259.15	
41	33	$573.34	$18,920.33	$13.65	$2,119.70	$559.69	$16,800.55	1,699.45	

InfoBox for cell D29 (R29C4)   ✕

▸ OPTIONS

☐ Formulas in R1C1 notation   ☑ Auto update

▸ CELL INFORMATION

Value:	52.6773
Displayed As:	$52.68
Cell Type:	Currency
Number Format:	$#,##0.00_);[Red]($#,##0.00)
Formula:	=IPMT($C$2*($C$3/12),A29,$C$4,-$C$1)
Name:	(none)
Protection:	Locked
Cell Comment:	(none)
Dependent Cells:	460
Dir Dependents:	1
Precedent Cells:	26
Dir Precedents:	5

◂ ▸   **Sheet1**   Sheet2   ⊕

Figure 13-18: A UserForm designed to look like a task pane.

I think I managed to capture the basic look of a task pane, but it falls short in terms of behavior. For example, the sections cannot be collapsed and it's not possible to dock the UserForm to the side of the screen. Also, it's not resizable by the user — but it could be (see the next section).

On the Web

This example, named **emulate task pane.xlm, is available on the book's website.**

A Resizable UserForm

Excel uses several resizable dialog boxes. For example, you can resize the Name Manager dialog box by clicking and dragging the bottom-right corner.

If you'd like to create a resizable UserForm, you'll eventually discover that there's no direct way to do it. One solution is to resort to Windows API calls. That method works, but it's complicated to set up and doesn't generate any events, so your code can't respond when the UserForm is resized. In this section, I present a much simpler technique for creating a user-resizable UserForm.

Note **Credit for this technique goes to Andy Pope, an Excel expert and Microsoft MVP who lives in the UK. Andy is one of the most creative Excel developers I've ever met. For a real treat (and lots of interesting downloads), visit his website at** `http://andypope.info.`

Figure 13-19 shows the UserForm that's described in this section. It contains a ListBox control that displays data from a worksheet. The scrollbars on the ListBox indicate that the ListBox contains information that doesn't fit. In addition, a (perhaps) familiar sizing control appears in the bottom-right corner of the dialog box.

Resizable UserForm

Resize the UserForm by dragging the bottom right corner.

Product	Jan	Feb
Artichoke	6,507	8,218
Asparagus	8,995	6,216
Aubergene	7,708	5,542
Beans	7,628	5,744
Beets	5,295	6,084
Broccoli	5,254	7,271

Close

Figure 13-19: This UserForm is resizable.

Figure 13-20 shows the same UserForm after the user resized it. The size of the ListBox is also increased, and the Close button remains in the same relative position. You can stretch this UserForm to the limits of your monitor.

Resizable UserForm

Resize the UserForm by dragging the bottom right corner.

Product	Jan	Feb	Mar	Apr	May	Jun
Artichoke	6,507	8,218	6,584	5,942	8,763	7,085
Asparagus	8,995	6,216	5,829	6,268	7,422	5,830
Aubergene	7,708	5,542	9,407	5,369	9,578	8,903
Beans	7,628	5,744	7,261	8,673	7,294	9,585
Beets	5,295	6,084	5,817	8,853	5,735	6,060
Broccoli	5,254	7,271	5,852	6,469	6,721	9,120
Brussel sprouts	8,634	9,301	8,106	5,105	7,357	9,452
Cabbage	5,483	8,870	9,898	5,373	7,133	9,407
Carrot	5,773	7,729	8,764	7,720	5,461	6,608
Cauliflower	9,989	5,609	8,701	9,338	7,390	7,323
Celeriac	5,022	5,086	5,586	8,434	8,657	7,892
Celery	6,775	9,352	9,243	6,467	7,143	5,487
Chard	9,642	9,654	5,530	8,669	7,849	8,981
Chicory	7,818	6,437	6,372	9,133	8,779	5,092
Collards	7,325	6,469	9,372	9,757	9,300	5,584
Corn	6,180	6,494	9,307	6,365	5,354	6,070
Cress	9,902	8,386	8,034	6,426	8,643	6,244

Close

Figure 13-20: The UserForm after it was increased.

This example is available on the book's website in the resizable userform.xlsm file.

The sizing control at the bottom-right corner is actually a Label control that displays a single character: The letter *o* (character 111) from the Marlett font, character set 2. This control (named objResizer) is added to the UserForm in the UserForm_Initialize procedure at runtime:

```
Private Sub UserForm_Initialize()
'    Add a resizing control to bottom right corner of UserForm
    Set objResizer = Me.Controls.Add("Forms.label.1", MResizer, True)
    With objResizer
        .Caption = Chr(111)
        .Font.Name = "Marlett"
        .Font.Charset = 2
        .Font.Size = 14
        .BackStyle = fmBackStyleTransparent
        .AutoSize = True
        .ForeColor = RGB(100, 100, 100)
        .MousePointer = fmMousePointerSizeNWSE
        .ZOrder
        .Top = Me.InsideHeight - .Height
        .Left = Me.InsideWidth - .Width
    End With
End Sub
```

Note

Although the Label control is added at runtime, the event-handler code for the object is contained in the module. Including code for an object that doesn't exist does not present a problem.

This technique relies on these facts:

➤ The user can move a control on a UserForm (see "A UserForm with Movable Controls," earlier in this chapter).

➤ Events exist that can identify mouse movements and pointer coordinates. Specifically, these events are MouseDown and MouseMove.

➤ VBA code can change the size of a UserForm at runtime, but a user cannot.

Do a bit of creative thinking about these facts, and you see that it's possible to translate the user's movement of a Label control into information that you can use to resize a UserForm.

When the user clicks the objResizer Label object, the objResizer_MouseDown event-handler procedure is executed:

```
Private Sub objResizer_MouseDown(ByVal Button As Integer, _
    ByVal Shift As Integer, ByVal X As Single, ByVal Y As Single)
    If Button = 1 Then
        LeftResizePos = X
        TopResizePos = Y
    End If
End Sub
```

This procedure executes only if the left mouse button is pressed (that is, the Button argument is 1) and the cursor is on the objResizer label. The X and Y mouse coordinates at the time of the button click are stored in module-level variables: LeftResizePos and TopResizePos.

Subsequent mouse movements fire the MouseMove event, and the objResizer_MouseMove event handler kicks into action. Here's an initial take on this procedure:

```
Private Sub objResizer_MouseMove(ByVal Button As Integer, _
    ByVal Shift As Integer, ByVal X As Single, ByVal Y As Single)
    If Button = 1 Then
        With objResizer
            .Move .Left + X - LeftResizePos, .Top + Y - TopResizePos
            Me.Width = Me.Width + X - LeftResizePos
            Me.Height = Me.Height + Y - TopResizePos
            .Left = Me.InsideWidth - .Width
            .Top = Me.InsideHeight - .Height
        End With
    End If
End Sub
```

If you study the code, you'll see that the UserForm's Width and Height properties are adjusted based on the movement of the objResizer Label control. Figure 13-21 shows how the UserForm looks after the user moves the Label control down and to the right.

The problem, of course, is that the other controls in the UserForm don't respond to the UserForm's new size. The ListBox should be expanded, and the CommandButton should be relocated so that it remains in the lower-left corner.

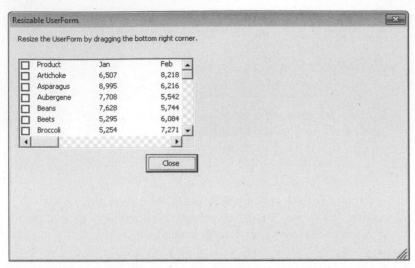

Figure 13-21: VBA code converts Label control movements into new Width and Height properties for the UserForm.

More VBA code is needed to adjust the controls in the UserForm when the UserForm size is changed. The location for this new code is in the objResizer_MouseMove event-handler procedure. The statements that follow do the job:

```
'    Adjust the ListBox
     On Error Resume Next
     With ListBox1
         .Width = Me.Width - 22
         .Height = Me.Height - 100
     End With
     On Error GoTo 0

'    Adjust the Close Button
     With CloseButton
         .Left = Me.Width - 70
         .Top = Me.Height - 54
     End With
```

These two controls are adjusted relative to the UserForm's size (that is, Me). After adding this new code, the dialog box works like a charm. The user can make the dialog box as large as needed, and the controls adjust.

It should be clear that the most challenging part of creating a resizable dialog box is figuring out how to adjust the controls. When you have more than two or three controls, coding can get complicated.

Handling Multiple UserForm Controls with One Event Handler

Every CommandButton on a UserForm must have its own procedure to handle its events. For example, if you have two CommandButtons, you'll need two event-handler procedures for the controls' click events:

```
Private Sub CommandButton1_Click()
' Code goes here
End Sub

Private Sub CommandButton2_Click()
' Code goes here
End Sub
```

In other words, you can't assign a macro to execute when *any* CommandButton is clicked. Each Click event handler is hard-wired to its CommandButton. You can, however, have each event handler call another all-inclusive macro in the event-handler procedures, but you'll need to pass an argument to indicate which button was clicked. In the following examples, clicking either CommandButton1 or CommandButton2 executes the ButtonClick procedure, and the single argument tells the ButtonClick procedure which button was clicked:

```
Private Sub CommandButton1_Click()
    Call ButtonClick(1)
End Sub

Private Sub CommandButton2_Click()
    Call ButtonClick(2)
End Sub
```

If your UserForm has many CommandButtons, setting up all these event handlers can get tedious. You might prefer to have a single procedure that can determine which button was clicked and take the appropriate action.

This section describes a way around this limitation by using a class module to define a new class.

On the Web   **This example, named multiple buttons.xlsm, is available on the book's website.**

The following steps describe how to re-create the example UserForm shown in Figure 13-22:

1. Create your UserForm as usual and add several CommandButtons.

   (The example contains 16 CommandButton controls.) This example assumes that the form is named UserForm1.

Figure 13-22: Multiple CommandButtons with a single event-handler procedure.

2. Insert a class module into your project (choose Insert→Class Module), give it the name BtnClass, and enter the following code.

```
Public WithEvents ButtonGroup As MsForms.CommandButton

Private Sub ButtonGroup_Click()
    Dim Msg As String
    Msg = "You clicked " & ButtonGroup.Name & vbCrLf & vbCrLf
    Msg = Msg & "Caption: " & ButtonGroup.Caption & vbCrLf
    Msg = Msg & "Left Position: " & ButtonGroup.Left & vbCrLf
    Msg = Msg & "Top Position: " & ButtonGroup.Top
    MsgBox Msg, vbInformation, ButtonGroup.Name
End Sub
```

You will need to customize the ButtonGroup_Click procedure.

Tip You can adapt this technique to work with other types of controls. You need to change the type name in the Public WithEvents declaration. For example, if you have OptionButtons instead of CommandButtons, use a declaration statement like this:

```
Public WithEvents ButtonGroup As MsForms.OptionButton
```

3. Insert a normal VBA module and enter the following code:

```
Sub ShowDialog()
    UserForm1.Show
End Sub
```

This routine simply displays the UserForm.

4. In the code module for the UserForm, enter the UserForm_Initialize code that follows.

```
Dim Buttons() As New BtnClass

Private Sub UserForm_Initialize()
    Dim ButtonCount As Integer
    Dim ctl As Control

'    Create the Button objects
    ButtonCount = 0
    For Each ctl In UserForm1.Controls
        If TypeName(ctl) = "CommandButton" Then
            'Skip the OKButton
            If ctl.Name <> "OKButton" Then
                ButtonCount = ButtonCount + 1
                ReDim Preserve Buttons(1 To ButtonCount)
                Set Buttons(ButtonCount).ButtonGroup = ctl
            End If
        End If
    Next ctl
End Sub
```

This procedure is triggered by the UserForm's Initialize event. Note that the code excludes a button named OKButton from the button group. Therefore, clicking the OK button doesn't execute the ButtonGroup_Click procedure.

After performing these steps, you can execute the ShowDialog procedure to display the UserForm. Clicking any CommandButton (except the OK button) executes the ButtonGroup_Click procedure. Figure 13-23 shows an example of the message displayed when a button is clicked.

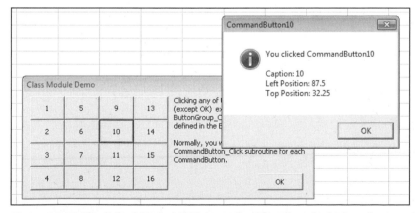

Figure 13-23: The ButtonGroup_Click procedure describes the button that was clicked.

Selecting a Color in a UserForm

The example in this section is a function that displays a dialog box (similar in concept to the MyMsgBox function, presented earlier). The function, named GetAColor, returns a color value:

```
Public ColorValue As Variant

Function GetAColor() As Variant
    UserForm1.Show
    GetAColor = ColorValue
End Function
```

You can use the GetAColor function with a statement like the following:

```
UserColor = GetAColor()
```

Executing this statement displays the UserForm. The user selects a color and clicks OK. The function then assigns the user's selected color value to the UserColor variable.

The UserForm, shown in Figure 13-24, contains three ScrollBar controls — one for each of the color components (red, green, and blue). The value range for each ScrollBar is from 0 to 255. The module contains procedures for the ScrollBar Change events. For example, here's the procedure that's executed when the first ScrollBar is changed:

```
Private Sub ScrollBarRed_Change()
    LabelRed.BackColor = RGB(ScrollBarRed.Value, 0, 0)
    Call UpdateColor
End Sub
```

The UpdateColor procedure adjusts the color sample displayed, and also updates the RGB values.

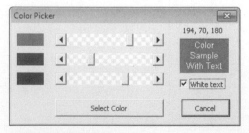

Figure 13-24: This dialog box lets the user select a color by specifying the red, green, and blue components.

On the Web

This example, named getacolor function.xlsm, is available on the book's website.

The GetAColor UserForm has another twist: It remembers the last color that was selected. When the function ends, the three ScrollBar values are stored in the Windows Registry, using this code (APPNAME is a string defined in Module1):

```
SaveSetting APPNAME, "Colors", "RedValue", ScrollBarRed.Value
SaveSetting APPNAME, "Colors", "BlueValue", ScrollBarBlue.Value
SaveSetting APPNAME, "Colors", "GreenValue", ScrollBarGreen.Value
```

The UserForm_Initialize procedure retrieves these values and assigns them to the scrollbars:

```
ScrollBarRed.Value = GetSetting(APPNAME, "Colors", "RedValue", 128)
ScrollBarGreen.Value = GetSetting(APPNAME, "Colors", "GreenValue", 128)
ScrollBarBlue.Value = GetSetting(APPNAME, "Colors", "BlueValue", 128)
```

The last argument for the GetSetting function is the default value, which is used if the Registry key is not found. In this case, each color defaults to 128, which produces middle gray.

The SaveSetting and GetSetting functions always use this Registry key:

```
HKEY_CURRENT_USER\Software\VB and VBA Program Settings\
```

Figure 13-25 shows the Registry data, displayed with the Windows Regedit.exe program.

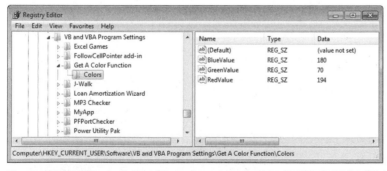

Figure 13-25: The user's ScrollBar values are stored in the Windows Registry and retrieved the next time the GetAColor function is used.

Cross-Ref

To learn more about how Excel uses colors, refer to Chapter 28.

Displaying a Chart in a UserForm

Excel provides no direct way to display a chart in a UserForm. You can, of course, copy the chart and paste it to the Picture property of an Image control, but this creates a static image of the chart, so it won't display any changes that are made to the chart.

This section describes a technique to display a chart in a UserForm. Figure 13-26 shows a UserForm with a chart displayed in an Image object. The chart resides on a worksheet, and the UserForm always displays the current chart. This technique works by copying the chart to a temporary graphics file and then using the LoadPicture function to specify that file for the Image control's Picture property.

On the Web

This workbook is available on the book's website in the chart in userform.xlsm file.

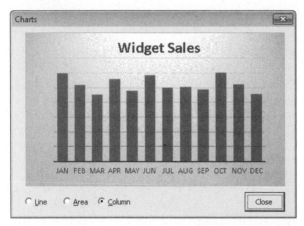

Figure 13-26: With a bit of trickery, a UserForm can display "live" charts.

To display a chart in a UserForm, follow these general steps:

1. Create your chart or charts as usual.

2. Insert a UserForm and then add an Image control.

3. Write VBA code to save the chart as a GIF file and then set the Image control's Picture property to the GIF file.

   You need to use VBA's LoadPicture function to do this task.

4. Add other bells and whistles as desired.

   For example, the UserForm in the demo file contains controls that let you change the chart type. Alternatively, you could write code to display multiple charts.

Saving a chart as a GIF file

The following code demonstrates how to create a GIF file (named temp.gif) from a chart (in this case, the first chart object on the sheet named Data):

```
Set CurrentChart = Sheets("Data").ChartObjects(1).Chart
Fname = ThisWorkbook.Path & "\temp.gif"
CurrentChart.Export FileName:=Fname, FilterName:="GIF"
```

Changing the Image control's Picture property

If the Image control on the UserForm is named Image1, the following statement loads the image (represented by the Fname variable) into the Image control:

```
Image1.Picture = LoadPicture(Fname)
```

Note

This technique works fine, but you may notice a slight delay when the chart is saved and then retrieved. On a fast system, however, this delay is hardly noticeable.

Making a UserForm Semitransparent

Normally, a UserForm is opaque — it completely hides whatever is underneath it. However, you can make a UserForm semitransparent, such that the user can see the worksheet under the UserForm.

Creating a semitransparent UserForm requires a number of Windows API functions. You can set the transparency level using values that range from 0 (UserForm is invisible) to 255 (UserForm is completely opaque, as usual). Values in between 0 and 255 specify a level of semitransparency.

Figure 13-27 shows an example of a UserForm with a transparency level of about 128.

On the Web

This workbook is available on the book's website. The filename is semi-transparent userform.xlsm.

⁄	A	B	C	D	E	F	G	H	I	J	K	L
4												
5	80	39	68	20	63	80	100	20				
6	61	13	76	84	88	57	66	10				
7	98	89	74	5	30	37	32	46				
8	60	58	95	83	47	18						
9	15	70	31	79	44	20	80	64				
10	9	42	59	23	18	2						
11	21	90	22	85	3	42						
12	90	11	42	86	97	80	32	19				
13	2	98	28	83	9	64	7	87				
14	80	43	91	36	24	29	55	46				
15	59	71	52	73	82	25	67	71				
16	91	65	60	54	15	93	46	93				
17	70	27	39	23	18	19	71					
18	20	48	1	7	7	16	19	38				
19	28	77	25	84	61	37	69	2				
20	69	94	90	71	28	60	72	11				
21	94	81	58	57	37	89	76					
22	40	66	32	29	6	77	30	89				
23	71	68	44	98	66	10	24	90				

Use the scroll bar to specify the level of transparency.

0   255

(If the UserForm disappears, press Esc to close it)

Close

Sheet1

Figure 13-27: A semitransparent UserForm.

What good is a semitransparent UserForm? After giving this question some thought, I came up with a potential use for this technique: creating a *light-box effect*. You've probably seen websites that use the light-box effect. The web page is dimmed (as if the lights are lowered), and an image or a pop-up is displayed. This effect serves to focus the user's attention to a specific item on the screen.

Figure 13-28 shows an Excel workbook that uses the light-box effect. Excel's window is dimmed, but the message box is displayed normally. How does it work? I created a UserForm with a black background. Then I wrote code to resize and position the UserForm so that it covers Excel's window. Here's the code to accomplish the cover-up:

```
With Me
  .Height = Application.Height
  .Width = Application.Width
  .Left = Application.Left
  .Top = Application.Top
End With
```

Then, I made the UserForm semitransparent, which gives Excel's window a dimmed appearance. The message box (or another UserForm) is displayed on top of the semitransparent UserForm.

On the Web

This workbook is available on the book's website in the excel light-box.xlsm file.

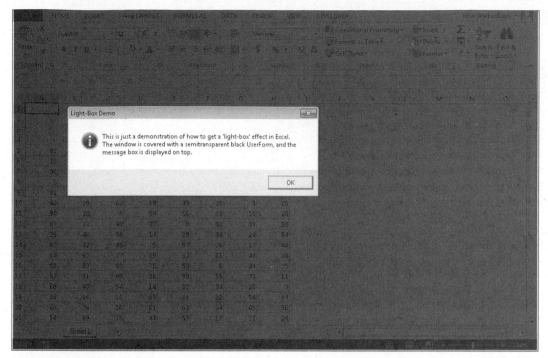

Figure 13-28: Creating a light-box effect in Excel.

An Enhanced Data Form

The example in this section is probably one of the more complex UserForms that you'll encounter. I designed it as a replacement for Excel's built-in Data Form, which is shown in Figure 13-29.

Note

Displaying Excel's Data Form is not easy in recent versions of Excel. This command isn't part of Excel's user interface, so you need to add the command to the Ribbon or to the Quick Access toolbar. To add it to the Quick Access toolbar, right-click the Quick Access toolbar and choose Customize Quick Access Toolbar. Then, in the Excel Options dialog box, add the Form command from the Commands Not in the Ribbon group.

Like Excel's Data Form, my Enhanced Data Form works with a list in a worksheet. But as you can see in Figure 13-30, it has a dramatically different appearance and offers several advantages.

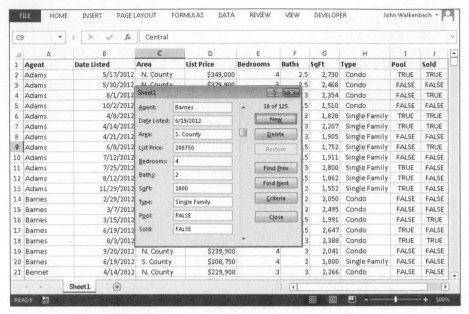

Figure 13-29: Excel's Data Form.

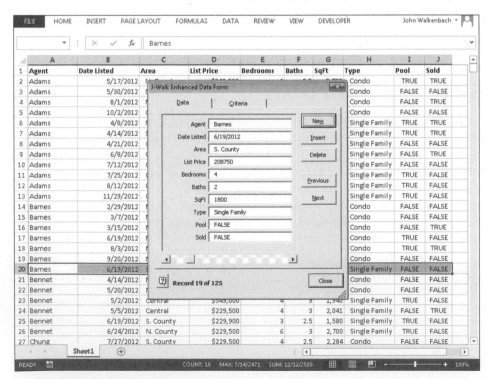

Figure 13-30: My Enhanced Data Form.

About the Enhanced Data Form

The Enhanced Data Form features the enhancements listed in Table 13-1.

Table 13-1: Comparing the Enhanced Data Form with the Excel Data Form

Enhanced Data Form	Excel Data Form
Handles any number of records and fields.	Limited to 32 fields.
Dialog box can be displayed in any size that you like and can be resized by the user.	Dialog box adjusts its size based on the number of fields. In fact, it can take up the entire screen!
Fields can consist of either InputBox or ComboBox controls.	Uses only InputBox controls.
Can modify the width of the descriptive column headers.	Can't change column header fields.
Can easily change the language used in the dialog box (VBA password required).	Can't change language.
Record displayed in the dialog box is always visible on-screen and is highlighted so that you know exactly where you are.	Doesn't scroll the screen for you and doesn't high-light the current record.
At start-up, the dialog box always displays the record at the active cell.	Always starts with the first record in the database.
When you close the dialog box, the current record is selected for you.	Doesn't change your selection when you exit.
Lets you insert a new record at any position in the database.	Adds new records only at the end of the database.
Includes an Undo button for Data Entry, Insert Record, Delete Record, and New Record.	Includes only a Restore button.
Search criteria are stored in a separate panel, so you always know exactly what you're searching for.	The search criteria aren't always apparent.
Supports approximate matches while searching (*, ?, and #).	Doesn't support wildcard characters.
The complete VBA source code is available, so you can customize it to your needs.	Isn't written in VBA and can't be customized.

On the Web

The Enhanced Data Form is a commercial product (sort of). Versions for Excel 97 and later are available on the book's website. These files may be distributed freely.

If you'd like to customize the code or UserForm, access to the complete VBA source is available for a modest fee. You can find out the details at http://spreadsheetpage.com.

Installing the Enhanced Data Form add-in

To try out the Enhanced Data Form, install the add-in:

1. Download the dataform3.xlam file to your hard drive.

2. In Excel, press Alt+TI to display the Add-Ins dialog box.

3. In the Add-Ins dialog box, click Browse and locate the dataform3.xlam file in the directory from Step 1.

After performing these steps, you can access the Enhanced Data Form by choosing Data➜ DataForm➜J-Walk Enhanced DataForm. You can use the Enhanced Data Form to work with any worksheet list or table.

A Puzzle on a UserForm

The example in this section is a familiar sliding puzzle, displayed on a UserForm (see Figure 13-31). This puzzle was invented by Noyes Chapman in the late 1800s. In addition to providing a few minutes of amusement, you may find the coding instructive.

Figure 13-31: A sliding tile puzzle in a UserForm.

The goal is to arrange the shuffled tiles (CommandButton controls) in numerical order. Click a button next to the empty space, and the button moves to the empty space. The ComboBox control lets the user choose from three configurations: 3 x 3, 4 x 4, and 5 x 5. The New button shuffles the tiles, and a Label control keeps track of the number of moves.

This application uses a class module to handle all button events (see "Handling Multiple UserForm Controls with One Event Handler," earlier in this chapter).

The VBA code is lengthy, so it's not listed here. Here are a few points to keep in mind when examining the code:

➤ The CommandButton controls are added to the UserForm via code. The number and size of the buttons are determined by the ComboBox value.

➤ The tiles are shuffled by simulating a few thousand random clicks on the buttons. Another option is to simply assign random numbers, but that could result in some unsolvable games.

➤ The blank space in the tile grid is actually a CommandButton with its Visible property set to False.

➤ The class module contains one event procedure (MouseUp), which is executed whenever the user clicks a tile.

➤ When the user clicks a CommandButton tile, its Caption is swapped with the hidden button. The code doesn't actually move any buttons.

On the Web   **This workbook, named sliding tile puzzle.xlsm, is available on the book's website.**

Video Poker on a UserForm

And finally, proof that Excel doesn't have to be boring. Figure 13-32 shows a UserForm set up as a casino-style video poker game.

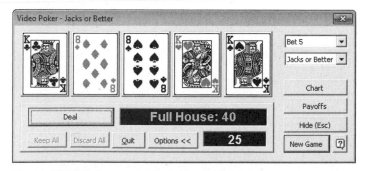

Figure 13-32: A feature-packed video poker game.

The game features

> ➤ A choice between two games: Joker's Wild and Jacks or Better

> ➤ A chart that shows your winning (or losing) history

> ➤ The capability to change the payoffs

> ➤ Help (displayed on a worksheet)

> ➤ An emergency button that quickly hides the UserForm

All that's missing is the casino noise.

On the Web   **This workbook, named video poker.xlsm, is available on the book's website.**

As you might expect, the code is much too lengthy to list here, but if you examine the workbook, you'll find lots of useful UserForm tips — including a class module example.

PART IV

Advanced Programming Techniques

Developing Excel Utilities with VBA

In This Chapter

- Exploring Excel utilities and utilities in general

- Developing utilities with VBA

- Creating good utilities

- Manipulating text in cells

- Finding additional Excel utilities

About Excel Utilities

A *utility,* in general, is something that enhances software, adding useful features or making existing features more accessible. A utility isn't an end product, such as a quarterly report. Rather, it's a tool that helps you produce an end product. An Excel utility is (almost always) an add-in that enhances Excel with new features or capabilities.

Excel is a great product, but many users soon develop a wish list of features that they'd like to see added to the software. For example, users who work with dates may want a pop-up calendar feature to facilitate entering dates into cells. And some users desire an easier way to export a range of data to a separate file or to save a chart as a graphics file. These are all examples of features that aren't currently available in Excel. You can, however, add these features by creating a utility.

Utilities don't need to be complicated. Some of the most useful ones are very simple. For example, have you noticed that Excel 2013 doesn't have a Ribbon command to toggle the page break display in a worksheet? If you don't like to see those dotted lines in your worksheet, a trip to the Excel Options dialog box to turn them off is required. Even worse, you can't add that command to the Ribbon or Quick Access toolbar.

Here's a simple VBA macro that toggles the page break display:

```
Sub TogglePageBreaks()
  With ActiveSheet
    .DisplayPageBreaks = Not .DisplayPageBreaks
  End With
End Sub
```

You can store this macro in your Personal Macro Workbook so that it's always available. Or you may prefer to package your favorite utilities in an add-in. For quicker access, you can assign your utility macros to a shortcut key or a right-click shortcut menu or modify your Quick Access toolbar or the Ribbon.

As you'll see, creating utilities for Excel is an excellent way to make a great product even better.

Using VBA to Develop Utilities

Excel 5, released in 1992, was the first version of Excel to include VBA. When I received the beta version of Excel 5, I was impressed by VBA's potential. VBA was light-years ahead of Excel's powerful (but cryptic) XLM macro language, and I decided that I wanted to explore this new language and see its capabilities.

In an effort to learn VBA, I wrote a collection of Excel utilities by using only VBA. I figured that I would learn the language more quickly if I gave myself a tangible goal. The result was a product that I call the *Power Utility Pak for Excel,* which is available to you at a discounted price as a benefit of buying this book. (Use the coupon in the back of the book to order your copy.)

I learned several things from my initial efforts on this project:

➤ VBA can be difficult to grasp at first, but it becomes much easier with practice.

➤ Experimentation is the key to mastering VBA. Every project that I undertake usually involves dozens of small coding experiments that eventually lead to a finished product.

➤ VBA enables you to extend Excel in a way that is consistent with Excel's look and feel, including custom worksheet functions and dialog boxes. And, if you're willing to step outside VBA, you can write XML code to customize the Ribbon automatically when your application is opened.

➤ Excel can do almost anything. When you reach a dead end, chances are that another path leads to a solution, especially if you're creative and know where to look for help.

Few other software packages include such an extensive set of tools that enable the end user to extend the software.

What Makes a Good Utility?

An Excel utility, of course, should ultimately make your job easier or more efficient. But if you're developing utilities for other users, what makes an Excel utility valuable? I've put together a list of elements that are common to good utilities:

➤ **It adds something to Excel.** This addition could be a new feature, a way to combine existing features, or just a way to make an existing feature easier to use.

➤ **It's general in nature.** Ideally, a utility should be useful under a wide variety of conditions. Of course, writing a general-purpose utility is more difficult than it is to write one that works in a highly defined environment.

➤ **It's flexible.** The best utilities provide many options to handle various situations.

➤ **It looks, works, and feels like an Excel command.** Although adding your own special touch to utilities is tempting, other users will find them easier to use if they look and act like familiar Excel commands and dialog boxes.

➤ **It provides help for the user when needed.** In other words, the utility should have documentation that's thorough and accessible.

➤ **It traps errors.** An end user should never see a VBA error message. Any error messages that appear should be ones that you write.

➤ **Users can undo its effects.** Users who don't like the result caused by your utility should be able to reverse their path.

Text Tools: The Anatomy of a Utility

In this section, I describe an Excel utility that I developed and use frequently. It's also part of my Power Utility Pak add-in. The Text Tools utility enables the user to manipulate text in a selected range of cells. Specifically, this utility enables the user to do the following:

➤ Change the case of the text (uppercase, lowercase, proper case, sentence case, or toggle case).

➤ Add characters to the text (at the beginning, at the end, or at a specific character position).

➤ Remove characters from the text (from the beginning, from the end, or from a specific position within the string).

➤ Remove spaces from the text (either all spaces or excess spaces).

➤ Delete characters from the text (nonprinting characters, alphabetic characters, non-numeric characters, nonalphabetic characters, or numeric characters).

Figure 14-1 shows the Text Tools Utility dialog box.

Figure 14-1: Use the Text Tools utility to change the case of selected text.

On the Web

The Text Tools utility is available on the book's website. It's a stand-alone version of the tool included with the Power Utility Pak. The file, named text tools.xlam, is a standard Excel add-in. When installed, it adds a new command to the Ribbon: Home➔Utilities➔ Text Tools. The VBA project isn't protected with a password, so you can examine the code to see how it works or make changes to better suit your needs.

Background for Text Tools

Excel has many worksheet functions that can manipulate text strings in useful ways. For example, you can make the text in a cell uppercase (UPPER), add characters to text (CONCATENATE), and remove spaces (TRIM). But to perform any of these operations, you need to write formulas, copy them, convert the formulas to values, and then paste the values over the original text. In other words, Excel doesn't make modifying text particularly easy. Wouldn't it be nice if Excel had some text manipulation tools that didn't require formulas?

By the way, many good utility ideas come from statements that begin, "Wouldn't it be nice if . . .?"

Project goals for Text Tools

The first step in designing a utility is to envision exactly how you want the utility to work. Here's my original plan, stated in the form of a dozen goals:

> ➤ Its main features will be those listed at the beginning of this section.

> ➤ It will enable the user to specify that the preceding types of changes work with nontext cells as well as with text cells.

➤ It will have the same look and feel of other Excel commands. In other words, it will have a dialog box that looks like Excel's dialog boxes.

➤ It will be in the form of an add-in and will also be accessible from the Ribbon.

➤ It will operate with the current selection of cells (including multiple selections) and will enable the user to modify the range selection while the dialog box is displayed.

➤ It will remember the last operation used and display those settings the next time the dialog box is invoked.

➤ It will have no effect on cells that contain formulas.

➤ It will be fast and efficient. For example, if the user selects an entire column, the utility will ignore the empty cells in the column.

➤ It will use a modeless dialog box so that the user can keep the dialog box on-screen and ready to use.

➤ It will be compact in size so that it doesn't hide too much of the worksheet.

➤ It will enable the user to undo changes.

➤ Comprehensive help will be available.

The Text Tools workbook

The Text Tools utility is an XLAM add-in file. During development, I worked with the file as a macro-enabled XLSM workbook. When I was satisfied that all was working properly, I saved the workbook as an add-in.

The Text Tools workbook consists of the following components:

➤ **One worksheet:** Every workbook (including add-ins) must have at least one worksheet. I take advantage of this fact and use this worksheet to store information used in the Undo procedure (see "Implementing Undo," later in this chapter).

➤ **One VBA module:** This module contains public variable and constant declarations, the code to display the UserForm, and the code to handle the undo procedure.

➤ **One UserForm:** This component contains the dialog box. The code that does the text manipulation is stored in the code module for the UserForm.

Note

The file also contains some manual modifications that I made to display the command on the Ribbon. See "Adding the RibbonX code," later in this chapter. Unfortunately, you can't modify Excel's Ribbon using only VBA.

Installing an add-in

To install an add-in, including the text tools.xlam add-in, follow these steps:

1. Choose File➜ Options.

2. In the Excel Options dialog box, click the Add-Ins tab.

3. In the drop-down list labeled Manage, choose Excel Add-Ins and then click Go to display the Add-Ins dialog box.

4. If the add-in that you want to install is listed in the Add-Ins Available list, place a check mark next to the item.

   If the add-in isn't listed, click Browse to locate the XLAM or XLA add-in file.

5. Click OK.

   The add-in will be installed and will remain installed until you deselect it from the list.

In the preceding instructions, you can skip Steps 1 through 3 and press Alt+TI, which is the pre-Excel 2007 keyboard sequence to display the Add-Ins dialog box. Or if the Developer tab is displayed on the Ribbon, choose Developer➜Add-Ins➜Addins.

How the Text Tools utility works

The Text Tools add-in contains some RibbonX code that creates a new item in the Ribbon: Home➜Utilities➜Text Tools. Choosing this command sequence executes the StartTextTools procedure, which calls the ShowTextToolsDialog procedure.

Cross-Ref

To find out why this utility requests both the StartTextTools procedure and the ShowTextToolsDialog procedure, see "Adding the RibbonX code," later in this chapter.

The user can specify various text modifications and click the Apply button to perform them. The changes are visible in the worksheet, and the dialog box remains displayed. Each operation can be undone, or the user can perform additional text modifications. Clicking the Help button displays a Help window, and clicking the Close button dismisses the dialog box. Note that this is a *modeless* dialog box. In other words, you can keep working in Excel while the dialog box is displayed. In that sense, a modeless dialog box is similar to a toolbar.

Note

If you use this utility in Excel 2013, the Text Tools dialog box will not be available if you switch to a different workbook window. To use the utility in a different workbook, you must close the Text Tools dialog box, activate the other window, and then issue the command to display the dialog box again.

The UserForm for the Text Tools utility

When I create a utility, I usually begin by designing the user interface. In this example, the user interface is the dialog box that's displayed to the user. Creating the dialog box forces me to think through the project one more time.

Figure 14-2 shows the UserForm for the Text Tools utility.

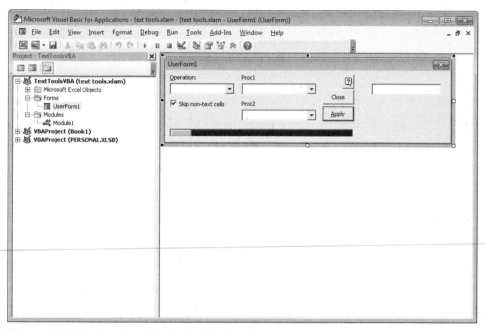

Figure 14-2: The UserForm for the Text Tools utility.

Note that the controls on this UserForm are laid out differently from how they appear to the user. That's because some options use different controls, and the positioning of the controls is handled dynamically in the code. The controls are listed and described next:

> ➤ **The Operation ComboBox:** This control always appears on the left, and you use it to select the operation to be performed.

> ➤ **Proc1 ComboBox:** Most of the text manipulation options use this ComboBox to further specify the operation.

> ➤ **Proc2 ComboBox:** Two of the text manipulation options use this ComboBox to specify the operation even further. Specifically, this additional ComboBox is used by Add Text and Remove by Position.

> ➤ **Check box:** The Skip Non-Text Cells check box is an option relevant to some of the operations.

➤ **Help button:** Clicking this CommandButton displays help.

➤ **Close button:** Clicking this CommandButton unloads the UserForm.

➤ **Apply button:** Clicking this CommandButton applies the selected text manipulation option.

➤ **Progress bar:** This control consists of a Label control inside a Frame control.

➤ **Text box:** This text box is used for the Add Text option.

Figure 14-3 shows how the UserForm looks for each of the five operations. Note that the configuration of the controls varies, depending on which option is selected.

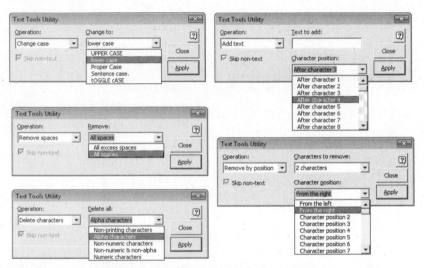

Figure 14-3: The UserForm layout changes for each operation.

The Module1 VBA module

The Module1 VBA module contains the declarations, a simple procedure that starts the utility, and a procedure that handles the undo operation.

Declarations in the Module1 VBA module

Following are the declarations at the top of the Module1 module:

```
Public Const APPNAME As String = "Text Tools Utility"
Public Const PROGRESSTHRESHOLD = 2000
Public UserChoices(1 To 8) As Variant 'stores user's last choices
Public UndoRange As Range ' For undoing
Public UserSelection As Range 'For undoing
```

I declare a Public constant containing a string that stores the name of the application. This string is used in the UserForm caption and in various message boxes.

The PROGRESSTHRESHOLD constant specifies the number of cells that will display the progress indicator. When this constant is 2,000, the progress indicator will be shown only if the utility is working on 2,000 or more cells.

The UserChoices array holds the value of each control. This information is stored in the Windows Registry when the user closes the dialog box and is retrieved when the utility is executed again. I added this convenience feature because I found that many users tend to perform the same operation every time they use the utility.

Two other Range object variables are used to store information used for undoing.

The ShowTextToolsDialog procedure in the Module1 VBA module

The ShowTextToolsDialog procedure follows:

```
Sub ShowTextToolsDialog()
    Dim InvalidContext As Boolean
    If Val(Application.Version) < 12 Then
        MsgBox "This utility requires Excel 2007 or later.", vbCritical
        Exit Sub
    End If
    If ActiveSheet Is Nothing Then InvalidContext = True
    If TypeName(ActiveSheet) <> "Worksheet" Then InvalidContext = True
    If InvalidContext Then
        MsgBox "Select some cells in a range.", vbCritical, APPNAME
    Else
        UserForm1.Show vbModeless
    End If
End Sub
```

The procedure starts by checking the version of Excel. If the version is prior to Excel 2007, the user is informed that the utility requires Excel 2007 or later.

Note

For simplicity, I made this utility an application for Excel 2007 or later. However, you can design this utility so that it also works with previous versions of Excel.

If the user is running the appropriate version of Excel, the ShowTextToolsDialog procedure checks to make sure that a sheet is active, and then it makes sure that the sheet is a worksheet. If either one isn't true, the InvalidContext variable is set to True. The If-Then-Else construct checks this variable and displays either a message (see Figure 14-4) or the UserForm. The Show method uses the vbModeless argument, which makes it a *modeless* UserForm (that is, the user can keep working in Excel while it's displayed).

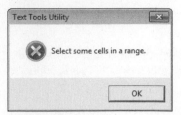

Figure 14-4: This message is displayed if no workbook is active or if the active sheet isn't a worksheet.

Note that the code doesn't ensure that a range is selected. This additional error handling is included in the code that's executed when the Apply button is clicked.

Tip

While I was developing this utility, I assigned a keyboard shortcut (Ctrl+Shift+T) to the ShowTextToolsDialog procedure because I saved the Ribbon modification task for last and I needed a way to test the utility. After I added the Ribbon button, I removed the keyboard shortcut.

To assign a keyboard shortcut to a macro, press Alt+F8 to display the Macro dialog box. Type ShowTextToolsDialog in the Macro Name box and then click Options. Use the Macro Options dialog box to assign (or unassign) the shortcut key combination.

The UndoTextTools procedure in the Module1 VBA module

The UndoTextTools procedure is executed when the user clicks the Undo button (or presses Ctrl+Z). This technique is explained later in this chapter (see "Implementing Undo").

The UserForm1 code module

All the real work is done by VBA code in the code module for UserForm1. Here, I briefly describe each procedure in this module. The code is too lengthy to list here, but you can view it by opening the text tools.xlam file available on the book's website.

The UserForm_Initialize procedure in the UserForm1 code module

The UserForm_Initialize procedure is executed before the UserForm is displayed. It sizes the UserForm and retrieves (from the Windows Registry) the previously selected values for the controls. It also adds the list items to the ComboBox (named ComboBoxOperation) that determines which operation will be performed. These items are

- ➤ Change case
- ➤ Add text
- ➤ Remove by position
- ➤ Remove spaces
- ➤ Delete characters

The ComboBoxOperation_Change procedure in the UserForm1 code module

The ComboBoxOperation_Change procedure is executed whenever the user selects an item in the ComboBoxOperation. It does the work of displaying or hiding the other controls. For example, if the user selects the Change Case option, the code unhides the second ComboBox control (named ComboProc1) and fills it with the following choices:

> ➤ UPPER CASE

> ➤ lower case

> ➤ Proper Case

> ➤ Sentence case

> ➤ tOGGLE cASE

The ApplyButton_Click procedure in the UserForm1 code module

The ApplyButton_Click procedure is executed when the Apply button is clicked. It does some error checking to ensure that a range is selected and then calls the CreateWorkRange function to make sure that empty cells aren't included in the cells to be processed. See the upcoming section, "Making the Text Tools utility efficient."

The ApplyButton_Click procedure also calls the SaveForUndo procedure, which saves the current data in case the user needs to undo the operation. See "Implementing Undo," later in this chapter.

The procedure then uses a Select Case construct to call the appropriate procedure to perform the operation. It calls one of the following Sub procedures:

> ➤ ChangeCase

> ➤ AddText

> ➤ RemoveText

> ➤ RemoveSpaces

> ➤ RemoveCharacters

Some of these procedures make calls to function procedures. For example, the ChangeCase procedure might call the ToggleCase or SentenceCase procedure.

The CloseButton_Click procedure in the UserForm1 code module

The CloseButton_Click procedure is executed when the Close button is clicked. The procedure saves the current control settings to the Windows Registry and then unloads the UserForm.

The HelpButton_Click procedure in the UserForm1 code module

The HelpButton_Click procedure is executed when the Help button is clicked. This procedure simply displays the Help file (which is a standard compiled HTML help file).

Making the Text Tools utility efficient

The procedures in the Text Tools utility work by looping through a range of cells. It makes no sense to loop through cells that will not be changed — for example, empty cells and cells that contain a formula. Therefore, I added code to improve the efficiency of the cell processing.

The ApplyButton_Click procedure calls a Function procedure named CreateWorkRange. This function creates and returns a Range object that consists of all nonempty and nonformula cells in the user's selected range. For example, assume that column A contains text in the range A1:A12. If the user selects the entire column, the CreateWorkRange function would convert that complete column range into a subset that consists of only the nonempty cells (that is, the range A:A would be converted to A1:A12). This conversion makes the code much more efficient because empty cells and formulas need not be included in the loop.

The CreateWorkRange function accepts two arguments:

➤ Rng: A Range object that represents the range selected by the user.

➤ TextOnly: A Boolean value. If True, the function returns only text cells. Otherwise, it returns all nonempty cells.

```
Private Function CreateWorkRange(Rng, TextOnly)
'    Creates and returns a Range object
    Set CreateWorkRange = Nothing
'    Single cell, has a formula
    If Rng.Count = 1 And Rng.HasFormula Then
        Set CreateWorkRange = Nothing
        Exit Function
    End If
'    Single cell, or single merged cell
    If Rng.Count = 1 Or Rng.MergeCells = True Then
        If TextOnly Then
            If Not IsNumeric(Rng(1).Value) Then
                Set CreateWorkRange = Rng
                Exit Function
            Else
                Set CreateWorkRange = Nothing
                Exit Function
            End If
        Else
            If Not IsEmpty(Rng(1)) Then
                Set CreateWorkRange = Rng
                Exit Function
             End If
```

```
        End If
    End If
    On Error Resume Next
    Set Rng = Intersect(Rng, Rng.Parent.UsedRange)
    If TextOnly = True Then
        Set CreateWorkRange = Rng.SpecialCells(xlConstants, xlTextValues)
        If Err <> 0 Then
            Set CreateWorkRange = Nothing
            On Error GoTo 0
            Exit Function
        End If
    Else
        Set CreateWorkRange = Rng.SpecialCells _
          (xlConstants, xlTextValues + xlNumbers)
        If Err <> 0 Then
            Set CreateWorkRange = Nothing
            On Error GoTo 0
            Exit Function
        End If
    End If
End Function
```

Note

The CreateWorkRange function makes heavy use of the SpecialCells property. To learn more about the SpecialCells property, try recording a macro while making various selections in Excel's Go To Special dialog box. You can display this dialog box by pressing F5 and then clicking the Special button in the Go To dialog box.

It's important to understand how the Go To Special dialog box works. Normally, it operates on the current range selection. For example, if an entire column is selected, the result is a subset of that column. But if a single cell is selected, it operates on the entire worksheet. Because of this, the CreateWorkRange function checks the number of cells in the range passed to it.

Saving the Text Tools utility settings

The Text Tools utility has a useful feature: It remembers the last settings that you used. This feature is handy because many people tend to use the same option each time they invoke it.

The most recently used settings are stored in the Windows Registry. When the user clicks the Close button, the code uses VBA's SaveSetting function to save the value of each control. When the Text Tools utility is started, it uses the GetSetting function to retrieve those values and set the controls accordingly.

In the Windows Registry, the settings are stored at the following location:

```
HKEY_CURRENT_USER\Software\VB and VBA Program Settings\
Text Tools Utility\Settings
```

Figure 14-5 shows these settings in the Windows Registry Editor program (regedit.exe).

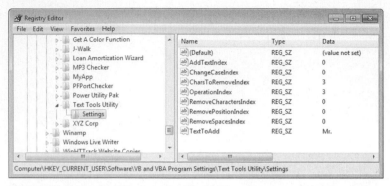

Figure 14-5: Use the Windows Registry Editor program to view the settings stored in the Registry.

If you examine the code for the Text Tools utility, you'll find that I used an eight-element array (named UserChoices) to store the settings. I could have used separate variables for each setting, but using an array made the coding a bit easier.

The following VBA code reads the settings from the Registry and stores them in the UserChoices array:

```
'    Get previous settings
    UserChoices(1) = GetSetting(APPNAME, "Settings", "OperationIndex", 0)
    UserChoices(2) = GetSetting(APPNAME, "Settings", "ChangeCaseIndex", 0)
    UserChoices(3) = GetSetting(APPNAME, "Settings", "TextToAdd", "")
    UserChoices(4) = GetSetting(APPNAME, "Settings", "AddTextIndex", 0)
    UserChoices(5) = GetSetting(APPNAME, "Settings", "CharsToRemoveIndex", 0)
    UserChoices(6) = GetSetting(APPNAME, "Settings", "RemovePositionIndex", 0)
    UserChoices(7) = GetSetting(APPNAME, "Settings", "RemoveSpacesIndex", 0)
    UserChoices(8) = GetSetting(APPNAME, "Settings", "RemoveCharactersIndex", 0)
    cbSkipNonText.Value = GetSetting(APPNAME, "cbSkipNonText", 0)
```

The code that follows is executed when the dialog box is closed. These statements retrieve the values from the UserChoices array and write them to the Registry.

```
'    Store settings
    SaveSetting APPNAME, "Settings", "OperationIndex", UserChoices(1)
    SaveSetting APPNAME, "Settings", "ChangeCaseIndex", UserChoices(2)
    SaveSetting APPNAME, "Settings", "TextToAdd", UserChoices(3)
    SaveSetting APPNAME, "Settings", "AddTextIndex", UserChoices(4)
    SaveSetting APPNAME, "Settings", "CharsToRemoveIndex", UserChoices(5)
    SaveSetting APPNAME, "Settings", "RemovePositionIndex", UserChoices(6)
    SaveSetting APPNAME, "Settings", "RemoveSpacesIndex", UserChoices(7)
    SaveSetting APPNAME, "Settings", "RemoveCharactersIndex", UserChoices(8)
    SaveSetting APPNAME, "Settings", "cbSkipNonText", cbSkipNonText.Value * -1
```

Implementing Undo

Unfortunately, Excel doesn't provide a direct way to undo an operation performed using VBA. Undoing a VBA macro is often possible, but it usually takes quite a bit of work. And, unlike Excel's Undo feature, the undo technique used in the Text Tools utility is a single level. In other words, the user can undo only the most recent operation. Refer to the sidebar, "Undoing a VBA procedure," for additional information about using Undo with your applications.

The Text Tools utility implements Undo by saving the original data in a worksheet. If the user undoes the operation, that data is then copied back to the user's workbook.

In the Text Tools utility, recall that the Module1 VBA module declared two public variables for handling undo:

```
Public UndoRange As Range
Public UserSelection As Range
```

Before modifying any data, the ApplyButton_Click procedure calls the SaveForUndo procedure. The procedure starts with three statements:

```
Set UserSelection = Selection
Set UndoRange = WorkRange
ThisWorkbook.Sheets(1).UsedRange.Clear
```

The UserSelection object variable saves the user's current selection so that you can reselect it after the undo operation. WorkRange is a Range object that's returned by the CreateWorkRange function. The range consists of the nonempty and nonformula cells in the user's selection. The preceding third statement erases any existing saved data from the worksheet.

Next, the following loop is executed:

```
For Each RngArea In WorkRange.Areas
    ThisWorkbook.Sheets(1).Range(RngArea.Address).Formula = RngArea.Formula
Next RngArea
```

This code loops through each area of WorkRange and stores the data in the worksheet. (If WorkRange consists of a contiguous range of cells, it will contain only one area.)

After the specified operation is performed, the code then uses the OnUndo method to specify the procedure to execute if the user chooses Undo. For example, after performing a case change operation, this statement is executed:

```
Application.OnUndo "Undo Change Case", "UndoTextTools"
```

Excel's Undo drop-down list will then contain a menu item: Undo Change Case (see Figure 14-6). If the user selects the command, the UndoTextTools procedure, shown next, will be executed.

```
Private Sub UndoTextTools()
'   Undoes the last operation
    Dim a As Range
    On Error GoTo ErrHandler
    Application.ScreenUpdating = False
    With UserSelection
        .Parent.Parent.Activate
        .Parent.Activate
        .Select
    End With
    For Each a In UndoRange.Areas
        a.Formula = ThisWorkbook.Sheets(1).Range(a.Address).Formula
    Next a
    Application.ScreenUpdating = True
    On Error GoTo 0
    Exit Sub
ErrHandler:
    Application.ScreenUpdating = True
    MsgBox "Can't undo", vbInformation, APPNAME
    On Error GoTo 0
End Sub
```

Figure 14-6: The Text Tools utility includes a single level of undo.

The UndoTextTools procedure first ensures that the correct workbook and worksheet are activated and then selects the original range selected by the user. Then it loops through each area of the stored data (which is available because of the UndoRange public variable) and puts the data back to its original location (overwriting the changes, of course).

On the Web   **The book's website contains a simpler example that demonstrates how to enable the Undo command after a VBA procedure is executed. This example, named simple undo demo.xlsm, stores the data in an array rather than a worksheet. The array is made up of a custom data type that includes the value and address of each cell.**

Undoing a VBA procedure

Computer users have become accustomed to being able to undo an operation. You can undo almost every operation that you perform in Excel. Even better, beginning with Excel 2007, Microsoft increased the number of undo levels from 16 to 100.

If you program in VBA, you may have wondered whether you can undo the effects of a procedure. Although the answer is *yes,* the qualified answer is *it's not always easy.*

Making the effects of your VBA procedures undoable isn't automatic. Your procedure needs to store the previous state so that it can be restored if the user chooses the Undo command (which is located in the Quick Access toolbar). How you store the previous state can vary depending on what the procedure does. You can save the old information in a worksheet or in an array. In extreme cases, you may need to save an entire worksheet. If your procedure modifies a range, for example, you need to save only the contents of that range.

Also, keep in mind that executing a VBA Sub procedure that changes a workbook wipes out Excel's undo stack. In other words, after you run such a macro, it's impossible to undo any previous operations.

The Application object contains an OnUndo method, which lets the programmer specify text to appear on the Undo drop-down list and a procedure to execute if the user chooses the Undo command. For example, the following statement causes the Undo drop-down list to display Undo my cool macro. If the user chooses Undo→Undo My Cool Macro, the UndoMyMacro procedure is executed:

```
Application.OnUndo "Undo my cool macro", "UndoMyMacro"
```

Displaying the Help file

I created a simple compiled HTML Help file named texttools.chm for this utility. Clicking the HelpButton on the UserForm executes this procedure:

```
Private Sub HelpButton_Click()
    Application.Help (ThisWorkbook.Path & "\" & "texttools.chm", 0)
End Sub
```

Figure 14-7 shows one of the Help screens.

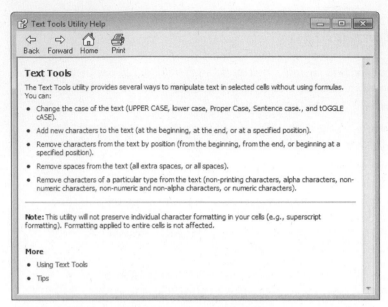

Figure 14-7: A Help screen for the Text Tools utility.

The book's website includes all the source files that were used to create the Help file. These files are in a directory named \helpsource. If you're not familiar with HTML Help files, refer to Chapter 22 for additional information.

On the Web

Adding the RibbonX code

The final task in creating this utility is to provide a way to execute it. Before Excel 2007, inserting a new menu command or toolbar button was relatively easy. But, with the new Ribbon user interface, this once-simple job is significantly more challenging.

I used the Custom UI Editor for Microsoft Office to add the RibbonX code that generates a new Ribbon group and command. The Custom UI Editor isn't included with Microsoft Office, but you can locate and download the program on the Internet.

Chapter 20 contains additional information about working with the Ribbon and the Custom UI Editor.

Cross-Ref

Figure 14-8 shows a portion of the Ribbon with a new group (called Utilities) added to the end of the Home tab. This group contains a single control that, when clicked, executes this procedure:

```
Sub StartTextTools(control As IRibbonControl)
    Call ShowTextToolsDialog
End Sub
```

Figure 14-8: The Ribbon contains a new group in the Home tab.

Figure 14-9 shows the RibbonX code in the Custom UI Editor.

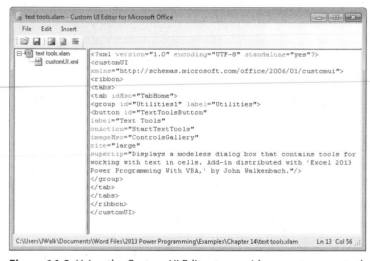

Figure 14-9: Using the Custom UI Editor to provide a way to execute the utility from the Ribbon.

Note

When a workbook has a customized Ribbon, the Ribbon customizations appear only when that workbook is active. But, fortunately, this rule has an exception. When the Ribbon customization is contained in an XLAM add-in file (as in this example), the Ribbon modifications appear as long as the add-in file is opened, regardless of which workbook is active.

Post-mortem of the project

The previous sections describe each component of the Text Tools utility. At this point, it's useful to revisit the original project goals to see whether they were met. The original goals, along with my comments, are as follows:

> ➤ **Its main features will be those listed at the beginning of this section.** Accomplished.

> ➤ **It will enable the user to specify that the preceding types of changes work with nontext cells as well as with text cells.** Accomplished.

> ➤ **It will have the same look and feel of other Excel commands. In other words, it will have a dialog box that looks like Excel's dialog boxes.** The Text Tools utility deviates from Excel's normal look and feel by using an Apply button rather than an OK button. And, unlike most of Excel's dialog boxes, Text Tools uses a modeless, stay-on-top dialog box. In light of the enhanced usability, I think these deviations are quite reasonable.

> ➤ **It will be in the form of an add-in and will also be accessible from the Ribbon.** Accomplished.

> ➤ **It will operate with the current selection of cells (including multiple selections) and will enable the user to modify the range selection while the dialog box is displayed.** Accomplished. And because the dialog box need not be dismissed, it didn't require the use of a RefEdit control.

> ➤ **It will remember the last operation used and display those settings the next time the dialog box is invoked.** Accomplished (thanks to the Windows Registry).

> ➤ **It will have no effect on cells that contain formulas.** Accomplished.

> ➤ **It will be fast and efficient. For example, if the user selects an entire column, the utility will ignore empty cells in the column.** Accomplished.

> ➤ **It will use a modeless dialog box so that the user can keep the dialog box on-screen and ready to use.** Accomplished.

> ➤ **It will be compact in size so that it doesn't hide too much of the worksheet.** Accomplished.

> ➤ **It will enable the user to undo changes.** Accomplished.

> ➤ **Comprehensive help will be available.** Accomplished.

Understand the Text Tools utility

If you don't fully understand how the Text Tools utility works, I urge you to load the add-in and use the Debugger to step through the code. Try out the utility with different types of selections, including an entire worksheet. You'll see that regardless of the size of the original selection, only the appropriate cells are processed and empty cells are ignored. If a worksheet has only one cell with text in it, the utility operates just as quickly whether you select that cell or the entire worksheet.

If you convert the add-in to a standard workbook, you'll be able to see how the original data is stored in the worksheet for undo. To convert the add-in to a workbook, double-click the ThisWorkbook code module in the Properties window. Press F4 to display the Properties box and then change the IsAddin property to False.

More about Excel Utilities

If you are interested in creating Excel utilities, I urge you to download a trial copy of Power Utility Pak. This product includes about 60 useful utilities (plus many custom worksheet functions). If you find it helpful, you can use the coupon in the back of this book to order a copy at a discounted price. The complete VBA source code also is available for a small fee.

In addition to the Power Utility Pak, many other utilities are available, and you can download most of them from the Internet.

Working with Pivot Tables

In This Chapter

- Creating pivot tables with VBA

- Looking at examples of VBA procedures that create pivot tables

- Using VBA to create a worksheet table from a summary table

An Introductory Pivot Table Example

Excel's pivot table feature is, arguably, the most innovative and powerful feature in Excel. Pivot tables first appeared in Excel 5, and the feature has been improved in every subsequent version. This chapter is not an introduction to pivot tables. I assume that you're familiar with this feature and its terminology and that you know how to create and modify pivot tables manually.

As you probably know, creating a pivot table from a database or list enables you to summarize data in ways that otherwise would not be possible — and is amazingly fast and requires no formulas. You also can write VBA code to generate and modify pivot tables.

This section gets the ball rolling with a simple example of using VBA to create a pivot table.

Figure 15-1 shows a simple worksheet range that contains four fields: SalesRep, Region, Month, and Sales. Each record describes the sales for a particular sales representative in a particular month.

On the Web

This workbook, named simple pivot table.xlsm, is available on the book's website.

	A	B	C	D	E
1	**SalesRep**	**Region**	**Month**	**Sales**	
2	Amy	North	Jan	33,488	
3	Amy	North	Feb	47,008	
4	Amy	North	Mar	32,128	
5	Bob	North	Jan	34,736	
6	Bob	North	Feb	92,872	
7	Bob	North	Mar	76,128	
8	Chuck	South	Jan	41,536	
9	Chuck	South	Feb	23,192	
10	Chuck	South	Mar	21,736	
11	Doug	South	Jan	44,834	
12	Doug	South	Feb	32,002	
13	Doug	South	Mar	23,932	
14					
15					

Sheet1 ⊕

Figure 15-1: This table is a good candidate for a pivot table.

Creating a pivot table

Figure 15-2 shows a pivot table created from the data, along with the PivotTable Field List task pane. This pivot table summarizes the sales performance by sales representative and month. This pivot table is set up with the following fields:

➤ **Region:** A report filter field in the pivot table

➤ **SalesRep:** A row field in the pivot table

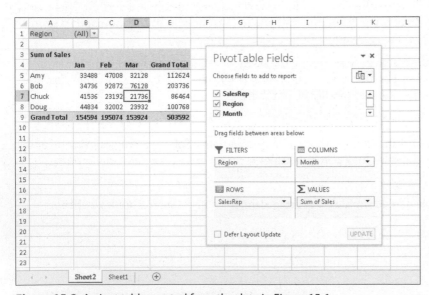

Figure 15-2: A pivot table created from the data in Figure 15-1.

➤ **Month:** A column field in the pivot table

➤ **Sales:** A values field in the pivot table that uses the Sum function

I turned on the macro recorder before I created this pivot table and specified a new worksheet for the pivot table location. The code that was generated follows:

```
Sub CreatePivotTable()
    Sheets.Add
    ActiveWorkbook.PivotCaches.Create _
        (SourceType:=xlDatabase, _
        SourceData:="Sheet1!R1C1:R13C4", _
        Version:=xlPivotTableVersion15).CreatePivotTable _
        TableDestination:="Sheet2!R3C1", _
        TableName:="PivotTable1", _
        DefaultVersion:=xlPivotTableVersion15
    Sheets("Sheet2").Select
    Cells(3, 1).Select
    With ActiveSheet.PivotTables("PivotTable1").PivotFields("Region")
        .Orientation = xlPageField
        .Position = 1
    End With
    With ActiveSheet.PivotTables("PivotTable1").PivotFields("SalesRep")
        .Orientation = xlRowField
        .Position = 1
    End With
    With ActiveSheet.PivotTables("PivotTable1").PivotFields("Month")
        .Orientation = xlColumnField
        .Position = 1
    End With
    ActiveSheet.PivotTables("PivotTable1").AddDataField _
        ActiveSheet.PivotTables("PivotTable1").PivotFields("Sales"), _
        "Sum of Sales", xlSum
End Sub
```

If you execute this macro, it will almost certainly end with an error. Examine the code, and you'll see that the macro recorder hard-coded the worksheet name (Sheet2) for the pivot table. If that sheet already exists (or if the new sheet that's added has a different name), the macro ends with an error. But a more serious problem is that the macro recorder also hard-coded the pivot table name. The new pivot table's name won't be PivotTable1 if the workbook has other pivot tables.

But even though the recorded macro doesn't work, it's not completely useless. The code provides lots of insight for writing code to generate pivot tables.

Data appropriate for a pivot table

A pivot table requires that your data be in the form of a rectangular database. You can store the database in either a worksheet range (which can be a table or just a normal range) or an external database file. Although Excel can generate a pivot table from any database, not all databases benefit from this treatment.

In general, fields in a database table consist of two types:

- **Data:** Contains a value or data to be summarized. For the sales example, the Sales field is a data field.
- **Category:** Describes the data. For the sales data, the SalesRep, Region, and Month fields are category fields because they describe the data in the Sales field.

A database table that's appropriate for a pivot table is said to be *normalized*. In other words, each record (or row) contains information that describes the data.

A single database table can have any number of data fields and category fields. When you create a pivot table, you usually want to summarize one or more of the data fields. Conversely, the values in the category fields appear in the pivot table as rows, columns, or filters.

If you're not clear on the concept, check out the normalized data.xlsx workbook on the book's website. This workbook contains an example of a range of data before and after being normalized to make it suitable for a pivot table.

Examining the recorded code for the pivot table

VBA code that works with pivot tables can be confusing. to make any sense of the recorded macro, you need to know about a few relevant objects, all of which are explained in the Help system.

➤ PivotCaches: A collection of PivotCache objects in a Workbook object (the data used by a pivot table is stored in a pivot cache).

➤ PivotTables: A collection of PivotTable objects in a Worksheet object.

➤ PivotFields: A collection of fields in a PivotTable object.

➤ PivotItems: A collection of individual data items within a field category.

➤ CreatePivotTable: A method that creates a pivot table by using the data in a pivot cache.

Cleaning up the recorded pivot table code

As with most recorded macros, the preceding example isn't as efficient as it could be. And, as I noted, it's likely to generate an error. You can simplify the code to make it more understandable and also to prevent the error. The hand-crafted code that follows generates the same pivot table as the procedure previously listed:

```
Sub CreatePivotTable()
    Dim PTCache As PivotCache
    Dim PT As PivotTable

'   Create the cache
    Set PTCache = ActiveWorkbook.PivotCaches.Create( _
        SourceType:=xlDatabase, _
        SourceData:=Range("A1").CurrentRegion)

'   Add a new sheet for the pivot table
    Worksheets.Add

'   Create the pivot table
    Set PT = ActiveSheet.PivotTables.Add( _
        PivotCache:=PTCache, _
        TableDestination:=Range("A3"))

'   Specify the fields
    With PT
        .PivotFields("Region").Orientation = xlPageField
        .PivotFields("Month").Orientation = xlColumnField
        .PivotFields("SalesRep").Orientation = xlRowField
        .PivotFields("Sales").Orientation = xlDataField

        'no field captions
        .DisplayFieldCaptions = False
    End With
End Sub
```

The CreatePivotTable procedure is simplified (and might be easier to understand) because it declares two object variables: PTCache and PT. A new PivotCache object is created by using the Create method. A worksheet is added, and it becomes the active sheet (the destination for the pivot table). Then a new PivotTable object is created by using the Add method of the PivotTables collection. The last section of the code adds the four fields to the pivot table and specifies their location within it by assigning a value to the Orientation property.

Pivot table compatibility

If you plan to share a workbook that contains a pivot table with users of previous versions of Excel, you need to pay careful attention to compatibility. If you look at the recorded macro in the "Creating a pivot table" section, you see the following statement:

```
DefaultVersion:=xlPivotTableVersion15
```

If your workbook is in compatibility mode, the recorded statement is

```
DefaultVersion:=xlPivotTableVersion10
```

You'll also find that the recorded code is completely different because Microsoft has made significant changes in pivot tables beginning with Excel 2007.

Assume that you create a pivot table in Excel 2013 and give the workbook to a coworker who has Excel 2003. The coworker will see the pivot table, but it will not be refreshable. In other words, it's just a dead table of numbers.

To create a backward-compatible pivot table in Excel 2013, you must save your file in XLS format and then reopen it. After doing so, pivot tables that you create will work with versions prior to Excel 2007. But, of course, you won't be able to take advantage of all the new pivot table features introduced in later versions of Excel.

Fortunately, Excel's Compatibility Checker will alert you regarding this type of compatibility issue (see the accompanying figure). However, it won't check your pivot table–related macros for compatibility. The macros in this chapter do *not* generate backward-compatible pivot tables.

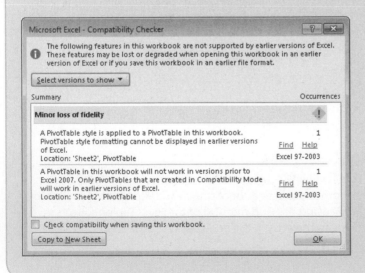

The original macro hard-coded both the data range used to create the PivotCache object ('Sheet1!R1C1:R13C4') and the pivot table location (Sheet2). In the CreatePivotTable procedure, the pivot table is based on the current region surrounding cell A1. This ensures that the macro will continue to work properly if more data is added.

Adding the worksheet before the pivot table is created eliminates the need to hard-code the sheet reference. Yet another difference is that the hand-written macro doesn't specify a pivot table name. Because the PT object variable is created, your code doesn't ever have to refer to the pivot table by name.

Note

The code could be more general through the use of indices rather than literal strings for the PivotFields collections. This way, if the user changes the column headings, the code will still work. For example, more general code would use PivotFields(1) rather than PivotFields('Region').

As always, the best way to master this topic is to record your actions in a macro to find out its relevant objects, methods, and properties. Then study the Help topics to understand how everything fits together. In almost every case, you'll need to modify the recorded macros. Or, after you understand how to work with pivot tables, you can write code from scratch and avoid the macro recorder.

Creating a More Complex Pivot Table

In this section, I present VBA code to create a relatively complex pivot table.

Figure 15-3 shows part of a large worksheet table. This table has 15,840 rows and consists of hierarchical budget data for a corporation. The corporation has 5 divisions, and each division contains 11 departments. Each department has 4 budget categories, and each budget category contains several budget items. Budgeted and actual amounts are included for each of the 12 months. The goal is to summarize this information with a pivot table.

On the Web

This workbook is available on the book's website in a file named budget pivot table. xlsm.

Figure 15-4 shows a pivot table created from the data. Note that the pivot table contains a calculated field named Variance. This field is the difference between the Budget amount and the Actual amount.

	A	B	C	D	E	F	G
1	Division	Department	Category	Item	Month	Budget	Actual
2	N. America	Data Processing	Compensation	Salaries	Jan	2583	3165
3	N. America	Data Processing	Compensation	Benefits	Jan	4496	2980
4	N. America	Data Processing	Compensation	Bonuses	Jan	3768	3029
5	N. America	Data Processing	Compensation	Commissions	Jan	3133	2815
6	N. America	Data Processing	Compensation	Payroll Taxes	Jan	3559	3770
7	N. America	Data Processing	Compensation	Training	Jan	3099	3559
8	N. America	Data Processing	Compensation	Conferences	Jan	2931	3199
9	N. America	Data Processing	Compensation	Entertainment	Jan	2632	2633
10	N. America	Data Processing	Facility	Rent	Jan	2833	2508
11	N. America	Data Processing	Facility	Lease	Jan	3450	2631
12	N. America	Data Processing	Facility	Utilities	Jan	4111	3098
13	N. America	Data Processing	Facility	Maintenance	Jan	3070	2870
14	N. America	Data Processing	Facility	Telephone	Jan	3827	4329
15	N. America	Data Processing	Facility	Other	Jan	3843	3322
16	N. America	Data Processing	Supplies & Services	General Office	Jan	2642	3218
17	N. America	Data Processing	Supplies & Services	Computer Supplies	Jan	3052	4098
18	N. America	Data Processing	Supplies & Services	Books & Subs	Jan	4346	3361
19	N. America	Data Processing	Supplies & Services	Outside Services	Jan	2869	3717
20	N. America	Data Processing	Supplies & Services	Other	Jan	3328	3116
21	N. America	Data Processing	Equipment	Computer Hardware	Jan	3088	2728
22	N. America	Data Processing	Equipment	Software	Jan	4226	2675
23	N. America	Data Processing	Equipment	Photocopiers	Jan	3780	3514
24	N. America	Data Processing	Equipment	Telecommunication	Jan	3893	3664
25	N. America	Data Processing	Equipment	Other	Jan	2851	4380
26	N. America	Human Resources	Compensation	Salaries	Jan	3604	3501
27	N. America	Human Resources	Compensation	Benefits	Jan	2859	4493
28	N. America	Human Resources	Compensation	Bonuses	Jan	3020	2676

Sheet1

Figure 15-3: The data in this workbook will be summarized in a pivot table.

	A	B	C	D	E	F	G	H	I	J	K	L	M	N
1	Division	(All)												
2	Category	(All)												
3														
4		Jan	Feb	Mar	Apr	May	Jun	Jul	Aug	Sep	Oct	Nov	Dec	Grand Total
5	Accounting													
6	Budget	422,455	433,317	420,522	417,964	411,820	414,012	427,431	418,530	412,134	421,678	426,602	418,445	5,044,910
7	Actual	422,662	413,163	416,522	420,672	431,303	429,993	425,879	415,253	417,401	417,806	425,271	420,026	5,055,951
8	Variance	-0,207	20,154	4,000	-2,708	-19,483	-15,981	1,552	3,277	-5,267	3,872	1,331	-1,581	-11,041
9	Advertising													
10	Budget	424,590	419,331	417,949	420,324	427,150	424,169	421,183	420,245	429,454	412,078	411,896	423,101	5,051,470
11	Actual	416,008	420,828	425,437	417,310	419,996	428,330	428,958	420,856	416,067	419,232	411,739	424,492	5,049,253
12	Variance	8,582	-1,497	-7,488	3,014	7,154	-4,161	-7,775	-0,611	13,387	-7,154	0,157	-1,391	2,217
13	Data Processing													
14	Budget	422,197	422,057	419,659	417,260	422,848	421,038	421,676	418,093	419,999	418,752	421,106	428,679	5,053,364
15	Actual	414,743	438,990	430,545	424,214	411,775	421,909	420,210	414,966	419,913	430,262	417,478	408,644	5,053,649
16	Variance	7,454	-16,933	-10,886	-6,954	11,073	-0,871	1,466	3,127	0,086	-11,510	3,628	20,035	-0,285
17	Human Resources													
18	Budget	422,053	425,313	418,634	423,038	423,514	419,602	415,197	419,701	422,762	413,741	410,972	422,746	5,037,273
19	Actual	424,934	429,275	407,053	429,187	410,258	421,870	428,551	422,469	422,252	421,838	415,125	417,222	5,050,034
20	Variance	-2,881	-3,962	11,581	-6,149	13,256	-2,268	-13,354	-2,768	0,510	-8,097	-4,153	5,524	-12,761
21	Operations													
22	Budget	413,530	427,975	419,527	422,299	415,298	414,805	413,149	425,287	412,284	414,242	427,521	420,190	5,026,107
23	Actual	415,819	406,592	426,827	418,223	431,307	413,201	416,350	411,339	422,584	416,132	424,041	426,461	5,028,876
24	Variance	-2,289	21,383	-7,300	4,076	-16,009	1,604	-3,201	13,948	-10,300	-1,890	3,480	-6,271	-2,769
25	Public Relations													
26	Budget	424,896	414,507	415,179	417,100	426,223	408,425	422,138	416,146	429,216	410,282	414,608	421,044	5,019,764
27	Actual	413,526	414,084	415,476	414,040	396,652	416,201	423,826	427,949	423,197	408,537	425,103	412,853	4,991,444
28	Variance	11,370	0,423	-0,297	3,060	29,571	-7,776	-1,688	-11,803	6,019	1,745	-10,495	8,191	28,320
29	R&D													
30	Budget	417,771	429,880	424,066	421,539	417,440	421,174	417,151	413,086	417,919	417,782	419,949	419,881	5,037,638
31	Actual	432,019	426,644	419,595	427,567	412,038	425,932	426,686	424,366	411,557	421,449	423,256	428,113	5,079,222
32	Variance	-14,248	3,236	4,471	-6,028	5,402	-4,758	-9,535	-11,280	6,362	-3,667	-3,307	-8,232	-41,584
33	Sales													
34	Budget	420,659	421,962	417,814	420,302	422,409	426,802	428,460	420,879	422,334	426,271	408,725	411,322	5,047,939
35	Actual	431,565	421,251	408,661	408,912	425,620	428,596	424,737	416,638	408,030	417,463	415,480	413,360	5,020,313

PivotSheet | Sheet1

Figure 15-4: A pivot table created from the budget data.

Note

Another option is to insert a new column in the table and create a formula to calculate the difference between the budget and actual amounts. If the data is from an external source (rather than in a worksheet), that option may not be possible.

The code that created the pivot table

Here's the VBA code that created the pivot table:

```
Sub CreatePivotTable()
    Dim PTcache As PivotCache
    Dim PT As PivotTable

    Application.ScreenUpdating = False
'   Delete PivotSheet if it exists
    On Error Resume Next
    Application.DisplayAlerts = False
    Sheets("PivotSheet").Delete
    On Error GoTo 0

'   Create a Pivot Cache
    Set PTcache = ActiveWorkbook.PivotCaches.Create( _
        SourceType:=xlDatabase, _
        SourceData:=Range("A1").CurrentRegion.Address)

'   Add new worksheet
    Worksheets.Add
    ActiveSheet.Name = "PivotSheet"
    ActiveWindow.DisplayGridlines = False

'   Create the Pivot Table from the Cache
    Set PT = ActiveSheet.PivotTables.Add( _
        PivotCache:=PTcache, _
        TableDestination:=Range("A1"), _
        TableName:="BudgetPivot")

    With PT
'       Add fields
        .PivotFields("Category").Orientation = xlPageField
        .PivotFields("Division").Orientation = xlPageField
        .PivotFields("Department").Orientation = xlRowField
        .PivotFields("Month").Orientation = xlColumnField
        .PivotFields("Budget").Orientation = xlDataField
        .PivotFields("Actual").Orientation = xlDataField
        .DataPivotField.Orientation = xlRowField

'       Add a calculated field to compute variance
        .CalculatedFields.Add "Variance", "=Budget-Actual"
        .PivotFields("Variance").Orientation = xlDataField
```

continued

```
'       Specify a number format
        .DataBodyRange.NumberFormat = "0,000"

'       Apply a style
        .TableStyle2 = "PivotStyleMedium2"

'       Hide Field Headers
        .DisplayFieldCaptions = False

'       Change the captions
        .PivotFields("Sum of Budget").Caption = " Budget"
        .PivotFields("Sum of Actual").Caption = " Actual"
        .PivotFields("Sum of Variance").Caption = " Variance"
    End With
End Sub
```

How the more complex pivot table works

The CreatePivotTable procedure starts by deleting the PivotSheet worksheet if it already exists. It then creates a PivotCache object, inserts a new worksheet named PivotSheet, and creates the pivot table from the PivotCache. The code then adds the following fields to the pivot table:

➤ **Category:** A report filter (page) field

➤ **Division:** A report filter (page) field

➤ **Department:** A row field

➤ **Month:** A column field

➤ **Budget:** A data field

➤ **Actual:** A data field

Note that the Orientation property of the DataPivotField is set to xlRowField in the following statement:

```
.DataPivotField.Orientation = xlRowField
```

This statement determines the overall orientation of the pivot table, and it represents the Sum Values field in the Pivot Table Fields task pane (see Figure 15-5). Try moving that field to the Columns section to see how it affects the pivot table layout.

Figure 15-5: The Pivot Table Fields task pane.

Next, the procedure uses the Add method of the CalculatedFields collection to create the calculated field Variance, which subtracts the Actual amount from the Budget amount. This calculated field is assigned as a data field.

Note **To add a calculated field to a pivot table manually, use the PivotTable➡Options➡ Calculations➡Fields, Items, & Sets➡Calculated Field command, which displays the Insert Calculated Field dialog box.**

Finally, the code makes a few cosmetic adjustments:

➤ Applies a number format to the DataBodyRange (which represents the entire pivot table data).

➤ Applies a style.

➤ Hides the captions (equivalent to the PivotTable Tools➡Options➡Show ➡Field Headers command).

➤ Changes the captions displayed in the pivot table. For example, Sum of Budget is replaced by Budget. Note that the Budget string is preceded by a space. Excel doesn't allow you to change a caption that corresponds to a field name, so adding a space gets around this restriction.

Note

While creating this procedure, I used the macro recorder extensively to learn about the various properties. That technique, combined with the information in the Help system (and a fair amount of trial and error), provided all the information I needed.

Creating Multiple Pivot Tables

The final example creates a series of pivot tables that summarize data collected in a customer survey. That data is stored in a worksheet (see Figure 15-6) and consists of 150 rows. Each row contains the respondent's sex plus a numerical rating using a 1–5 scale for each of the 14 survey items.

	A	B	C	D	E	F	G	H	I	J	K	L	M	N	O	P
1	Name	Sex	Store locations are convenient	Store hours are convenient	Stores are well-maintained	You are easy to reach by phone	I like your web site	Employees are friendly	Employees are helpful	Employee are knowledge able	Pricing is competitive	You have a good selection of products	I like your TV ads	You sell quality products	Overall, I am satisfied	I would recommend your company
2	Subject1	Male	1	4	4	4	1	1	2	1	1	2	5	2	2	1
3	Subject2	Female	2	5	1	1	4	2	4	3	3	2	2	5	2	3
4	Subject3	Male	1	1	4	2	3	3	2	1	2	3	2	4	3	2
5	Subject4	Male	2	1	3	5	1	2	3	4	2	1	3	4	1	2
6	Subject5	Female	2	2	5	5	4	2	1	5	5	2	3	4	2	5
7	Subject6	Female	2	4	3	3	1	1	4	4	4	2	2	2	2	4
8	Subject7	Female	2	4	5	4	5	3	2	5	4	4	1	5	4	4
9	Subject8	Male	3	2	1	2	3	4	3	1	2	4	3	4	4	2
10	Subject9	Female	3	4	4	4	5	1	4	1	4	1	2	1	1	4
11	Subject10	Male	2	1	5	5	5	1	4	1	2	2	5	2	2	2
12	Subject11	Male	4	3	3	2	1	2	4	2	1	4	2	2	4	1
13	Subject12	Female	2	1	4	5	5	5	3	1	4	1	2	3	4	4
14	Subject13	Female	4	3	4	3	2	5	3	3	2	2	5	2	4	2
15	Subject14	Female	2	3	4	2	1	1	4	2	1	3	3	1	3	1
16	Subject15	Female	1	3	5	1	2	2	4	1	3	4	2	5	4	3
17	Subject16	Male	1	4	1	3	4	3	4	4	5	3	4	1	3	3
18	Subject17	Female	3	4	3	5	5	4	4	3	2	4	2	2	4	2
19	Subject18	Male	1	5	5	3	5	3	4	2	3	2	3	3	2	3
20	Subject19	Female	1	3	5	4	5	5	5	1	1	5	3	2	5	1
21	Subject20	Male	2	2	5	2	2	5	5	3	1	5	2	4	5	1
22	Subject21	Male	3	4	1	4	5	1	3	1	4	1	2	1	1	4
23	Subject22	Male	2	1	5	5	5	1	2	1	2	2	5	2	2	2
24	Subject23	Male	4	3	4	2	1	2	1	2	1	4	4	1	4	2
25	Subject24	Female	1	1	2	5	5	5	3	1	4	1	2	3	1	2
26	Subject25	Female	2	3	4	3	2	5	3	3	2	2	5	2	1	2
27	Subject26	Male	1	3	4	2	1	1	3	2	1	3	2	1	1	1

SurveyData

Figure 15-6: Creating a series of pivot tables will summarize this survey data.

On the Web

This workbook, named survey data pivot tables.xlsm, is available on the book's website.

Figure 15-7 shows a few of the 28 pivot tables produced by the macro. Each survey item is summarized in 2 pivot tables (one showing percentages, and one showing the actual frequencies).

Store locations are convenient

Count of Store locations are convenient	Female	Male	Grand Total
Strongly Disagree	28	40	68
Disagree	20	16	36
Undecided	15	9	24
Agree	6	14	20
Strongly Agree	2		2
Grand Total	**71**	**79**	**150**

Store locations are convenient

Count of Store locations are convenient	Female	Male	Grand Total
Strongly Disagree	39.4%	50.6%	45.3%
Disagree	28.2%	20.3%	24.0%
Undecided	21.1%	11.4%	16.0%
Agree	8.5%	17.7%	13.3%
Strongly Agree	2.8%	0.0%	1.3%

Store hours are convenient

Count of Store hours are convenient	Female	Male	Grand Total
Strongly Disagree	11	13	24
Disagree	7	11	18
Undecided	30	26	56
Agree	20	22	42
Strongly Agree	3	7	10
Grand Total	**71**	**79**	**150**

Store hours are convenient

Count of Store hours are convenient	Female	Male	Grand Total
Strongly Disagree	15.5%	16.5%	16.0%
Disagree	9.9%	13.9%	12.0%
Undecided	42.3%	32.9%	37.3%
Agree	28.2%	27.8%	28.0%
Strongly Agree	4.2%	8.9%	6.7%

Stores are well-maintained

Count of Stores are well-maintained	Female	Male	Grand Total
Strongly Disagree	7	14	21
Disagree	7	4	11
Undecided	16	14	30
Agree	29	29	58
Strongly Agree	12	18	30
Grand Total	**71**	**79**	**150**

Stores are well-maintained

Count of Stores are well-maintained	Female	Male	Grand Total
Strongly Disagree	9.9%	17.7%	14.0%
Disagree	9.9%	5.1%	7.3%
Undecided	22.5%	17.7%	20.0%
Agree	40.8%	36.7%	38.7%
Strongly Agree	16.9%	22.8%	20.0%

Summary   SurveyData

Figure 15-7: Several pivot tables created by a VBA procedure.

The VBA code that created the pivot tables follows:

```
Sub MakePivotTables()
'   This procedure creates 28 pivot tables
    Dim PTCache As PivotCache
    Dim PT As PivotTable
    Dim SummarySheet As Worksheet
    Dim ItemName As String
    Dim Row As Long, Col As Long, i As Long

    Application.ScreenUpdating = False

'   Delete Summary sheet if it exists
    On Error Resume Next
    Application.DisplayAlerts = False
    Sheets("Summary").Delete
    On Error GoTo 0

'   Add Summary sheet
    Set SummarySheet = Worksheets.Add
    ActiveSheet.Name = "Summary"

'   Create Pivot Cache
```

continued

```vba
Set PTCache = ActiveWorkbook.PivotCaches.Create( _
  SourceType:=xlDatabase, _
  SourceData:=Sheets("SurveyData").Range("A1"). _
  CurrentRegion)

Row = 1
For i = 1 To 14
  For Col = 1 To 6 Step 5 '2 columns
    ItemName = Sheets("SurveyData").Cells(1, i + 2)
    With Cells(Row, Col)
        .Value = ItemName
        .Font.Size = 16
    End With

'   Create pivot table
    Set PT = ActiveSheet.PivotTables.Add( _
      PivotCache:=PTCache, _
      TableDestination:=SummarySheet.Cells(Row + 1, Col))

'   Add the fields
    If Col = 1 Then 'Frequency tables
        With PT.PivotFields(ItemName)
          .Orientation = xlDataField
          .Name = "Frequency"
          .Function = xlCount
        End With
    Else ' Percent tables
    With PT.PivotFields(ItemName)
        .Orientation = xlDataField
        .Name = "Percent"
        .Function = xlCount
        .Calculation = xlPercentOfColumn
        .NumberFormat = "0.0%"
    End With
    End If

    PT.PivotFields(ItemName).Orientation = xlRowField
    PT.PivotFields("Sex").Orientation = xlColumnField
    PT.TableStyle2 = "PivotStyleMedium2"
    PT.DisplayFieldCaptions = False
    If Col = 6 Then
'       add data bars to the last column
        PT.ColumnGrand = False
        PT.DataBodyRange.Columns(3).FormatConditions. _
          AddDatabar
    With pt.DataBodyRange.Columns(3).FormatConditions(1)
      .BarFillType = xlDataBarFillSolid
      .MinPoint.Modify newtype:=xlConditionValueNumber, newvalue:=0
      .MaxPoint.Modify newtype:=xlConditionValueNumber, newvalue:=1
    End With
```

```
        End If
    Next Col
        Row = Row + 10
    Next i

'   Replace numbers with descriptive text
    With Range("A:A,F:F")
        .Replace "1", "Strongly Disagree"
        .Replace "2", "Disagree"
        .Replace "3", "Undecided"
        .Replace "4", "Agree"
        .Replace "5", "Strongly Agree"
    End With
End Sub
```

Note that all these pivot tables were created from a single PivotCache object.

The pivot tables are created in a nested loop. The Col loop counter goes from 1 to 6 by using the Step parameter. The instructions vary a bit for the second column of pivot tables. Specifically, the pivot tables in the second column do the following:

➤ Display the count as a percent of the column

➤ Do not show grand totals for the rows

➤ Are assigned a number format

➤ Display conditional formatting data bars

The Row variable keeps track of the starting row of each pivot table. The final step is to replace the numeric categories in columns A and F with text. For example, 1 is replaced with *Strongly Agree*.

Creating a Reverse Pivot Table

A pivot table is a summary of data in a table. But what if you have a summary table, and you'd like to create a normalized table from the summary? Figure 15-8 shows an example. Range B2:F14 contains a summary table — similar to a very simple pivot table. Columns I:K contain a 48-row table created from the summary table. In the table, each row contains one data point, and the first two columns describe that data point. In other words, the transformed data is normalized. (See the sidebar, "Data appropriate for a pivot table," earlier in this chapter.)

	A	B	C	D	E	F	G	H	I	J	K
1									Column1 ▼	Column2 ▼	Column3 ▼
2		Month	Amy	Bob	Chuck	Doug			Jan	Amy	47,955
3		Jan	47,955	34,240	55,560	56,380			Jan	Bob	34,240
4		Feb	44,715	35,435	61,810	63,325			Jan	Chuck	55,560
5		Mar	41,635	34,005	58,655	60,055			Jan	Doug	56,380
6		Apr	48,515	32,065	63,530	57,700			Feb	Amy	44,715
7		May	53,945	39,225	67,860	57,900			Feb	Bob	35,435
8		Jun	50,990	38,305	64,370	61,760			Feb	Chuck	61,810
9		Jul	49,235	38,675	66,020	65,220			Feb	Doug	63,325
10		Aug	55,725	34,300	70,160	63,140			Mar	Amy	41,635
11		Sep	57,710	26,615	68,985	65,740			Mar	Bob	34,005
12		Oct	54,020	24,220	70,035	63,300			Mar	Chuck	58,655
13		Nov	52,055	19,365	65,240	62,905			Mar	Doug	60,055
14		Dec	48,690	20,440	64,165	54,915			Apr	Amy	48,515
15									Apr	Bob	32,065
16									Apr	Chuck	63,530
17									Apr	Doug	57,700
18									May	Amy	53,945
19									May	Bob	39,225
20									May	Chuck	67,860
21									May	Doug	57,900

Data ⊕

Figure 15-8: The summary table on the left will be converted to the table on the right.

Excel doesn't provide a way to transform a summary table into a normalized table, so it's a good job for a VBA macro. After I created this macro, I spent a bit more time and added a UserForm, shown in Figure 15-9. The UserForm gets the input and output ranges and also has an option to convert the output range to a table.

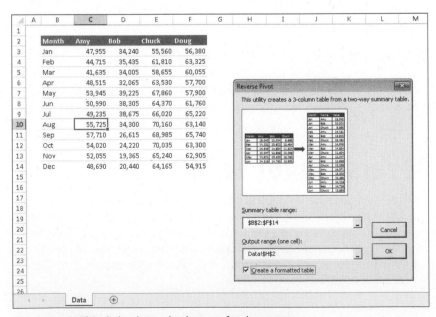

Figure 15-9: This dialog box asks the user for the ranges.

When the user clicks the OK button in the UserForm, VBA code validates the ranges and then calls the ReversePivot procedure with this statement:

```
Call ReversePivot(SummaryTable, OutputRange, cbCreateTable)
```

It passes three arguments:

➤ SummaryTable: A Range object that represents the summary table

➤ OutputRange: A Range object that represents the upper-left cell of the output range

➤ cbCreateTable: The Checkbox object on the UserForm

This procedure will work for any size summary table. The number of data rows in the output table will be equal to (r-1) * (c-1), where r and c represent the number of rows and columns in SummaryTable.

The code for the ReversePivot procedure follows:

```
Sub ReversePivot(SummaryTable As Range, _
  OutputRange As Range, CreateTable As Boolean)
    Dim r As Long, c As Long
    Dim OutRow As Long, OutCol As Long

'   Convert the range
    OutRow = 2
    Application.ScreenUpdating = False
    OutputRange.Range("A1:C3") = Array("Column1", "Column2", "Column3")
    For r = 2 To SummaryTable.Rows.Count
        For c = 2 To SummaryTable.Columns.Count
            OutputRange.Cells(OutRow, 1) = SummaryTable.Cells(r, 1)
            OutputRange.Cells(OutRow, 2) = SummaryTable.Cells(1, c)
            OutputRange.Cells(OutRow, 3) = SummaryTable.Cells(r, c)
            OutRow = OutRow + 1
        Next c
    Next r

'   Make it a table?
    If CreateTable Then _
      ActiveSheet.ListObjects.Add xlSrcRange, _
        OutputRange.CurrentRegion, , xlYes
End Sub
```

The procedure is fairly simple. The code loops through the rows and columns in the input range and then writes the data to the output range. The output range will always have three columns. The OutRow variable keeps track of the current row in the output range. Finally, if the user checked the check box, the output range is converted to a table by using the Add method of the ListObjects collection.

Working with Charts

In This Chapter

- Discovering essential background information on Excel charts
- Knowing the difference between embedded charts and chart sheets
- Understanding the Chart object model
- Using methods other than the macro recorder to help you learn about Chart objects
- Exploring examples of common charting tasks that use VBA
- Navigating more complex charting macros
- Finding out some interesting (and useful) chart-making tricks
- Working with Sparkline charts

Getting the Inside Scoop on Charts

Excel's charting feature lets you create a wide variety of charts using data that's stored in a worksheet. You have a great deal of control over nearly every aspect of each chart.

An Excel chart is simply packed with objects, each of which has its own properties and methods. Because of this, manipulating charts with Visual Basic for Applications (VBA) can be a bit of a challenge. In this chapter, I discuss the key concepts that you need to understand to write VBA code that generates or manipulates charts. The secret, as you'll see, is a good understanding of the object hierarchy for charts.

Chart locations

In Excel, a chart can be located in either of two places in a workbook:

> **As an embedded object on a worksheet:** A worksheet can contain any number of embedded charts.

> **In a separate chart sheet:** A chart sheet normally holds a single chart.

Compatibility note

The VBA code in this chapter uses the chart-related properties and methods that were introduced in Excel 2013. For example, Excel 2013 introduced the AddChart2 method. The AddChart method still works, but I focus on the most recent changes, which are often much easier to use. As a result, some of the code presented here won't work with versions prior to Excel 2013.

Most users create charts manually by using the commands in the Insert➜Charts group. But you can also create charts by using VBA. And, of course, you can use VBA to modify existing charts.

Tip

The fastest way to create a chart manually is to select your data and then press Alt+F1. Excel creates an embedded chart and uses the default chart type. To create a new default chart on a chart sheet, select the data and press F11.

A key concept when working with charts is the *active chart* — that is, the chart that's currently selected. When the user clicks an embedded chart or activates a chart sheet, a Chart object is activated. In VBA, the ActiveChart property returns the activated Chart object (if any). You can write code to work with this Chart object, much like you can write code to work with the Workbook object returned by the ActiveWorkbook property.

Here's an example: If a chart is activated, the following statement will display the Name property for the Chart object:

```
MsgBox ActiveChart.Name
```

If a chart isn't activated, the preceding statement generates an error.

Note

As you see later in this chapter, you don't need to activate a chart to manipulate it with VBA.

The macro recorder and charts

If you've read other chapters in the book, you know that I often recommend using the macro recorder to learn about objects, properties, and methods. As always, recorded macros are best viewed as a learning tool. The recorded code will almost always steer you to the relevant objects, properties, and methods.

The Chart object model

When you first start exploring the object model for a Chart object, you'll probably be confused — which isn't surprising because the object model *is* confusing. It's also deep.

For example, assume that you want to change the title displayed in an embedded chart. The top-level object, of course, is the Application object (Excel). The Application object contains a Workbook object, and the Workbook object contains a Worksheet object. The Worksheet object contains a ChartObject object, which contains a Chart object. The Chart object has a ChartTitle object, and the ChartTitle object has a Text property that stores the text displayed as the chart's title.

Here's another way to look at this hierarchy for an embedded chart:

```
Application
    Workbook
        Worksheet
            ChartObject
                Chart
                    ChartTitle
```

Your VBA code must, of course, follow this object model precisely. For example, to set a chart's title to YTD Sales, you can write a VBA instruction like this:

```
Worksheets(1).ChartObjects(1).Chart.ChartTitle.Text = "YTD Sales"
```

This statement assumes the active workbook is the Workbook object. The statement works with the first object in the ChartObjects collection on the first worksheet. The Chart property returns the actual Chart object, and the ChartTitle property returns the ChartTitle object. Finally, you get to the Text property.

Note that the preceding statement will fail if the chart doesn't have a title. To add a default title to the chart (which displays the text Chart Title), use this statement:

```
Worksheets("Sheet1").ChartObjects(1).Chart.HasTitle = True
```

For a chart sheet, the object hierarchy is a bit different because it doesn't involve the Worksheet object or the ChartObject object. For example, here's the hierarchy for the ChartTitle object for a chart in a chart sheet:

```
Application
    Workbook
        Chart
            ChartTitle
```

You can use this VBA statement to set the chart title in a chart sheet to YTD Sales:

```
Sheets("Chart1").ChartTitle.Text = "YTD Sales"
```

A chart sheet is essentially a Chart object, and it has no containing ChartObject object. Put another way, the parent object for an embedded chart is a ChartObject object, and the parent object for a chart on a separate chart sheet is a Workbook object.

Both of the following statements will display a message box that displays the word *Chart*:

```
MsgBox TypeName(Sheets("Sheet1").ChartObjects(1).Chart)
Msgbox TypeName(Sheets("Chart1"))
```

Note

When you create a new embedded chart, you're adding to the ChartObjects collection and the Shapes collection contained in a particular worksheet. (There is no Charts collection for a worksheet.) When you create a new chart sheet, you're adding to the Charts collection and the Sheets collection for a particular workbook.

Creating an Embedded Chart

A ChartObject is a special type of Shape object. Therefore, it's a member of the Shapes collection. To create a new chart, use the AddChart2 method of the Shapes collection. The following statement creates an empty embedded chart with all default settings:

```
ActiveSheet.Shapes.AddChart2
```

The AddChart2 method can use seven arguments (all are optional):

➤ **Style:** A numeric code that specifies the style (or overall look) of the chart.

➤ **xlChartType:** The type of chart. If omitted, the default chart type is used. Constants for all the chart types are provided (for example, xlArea and xlColumnClustered).

➤ **Left:** The left position of the chart, in points. If omitted, Excel centers the chart horizontally.

➤ **Top:** The top position of the chart, in points. If omitted, Excel centers the chart vertically.

➤ **Width:** The width of the chart, in points. If omitted, Excel uses 354.

➤ **Height:** The height of the chart, in points. If omitted, Excel uses 210.

➤ **NewLayout:** A numeric code that specifies the layout of the chart.

Here's a statement that creates a clustered column chart, using Style 2 and Layout 5, positioned 50 pixels from the left, 60 pixels from the top, 300 pixels wide, and 200 pixels high:

```
ActiveSheet.Shapes.AddChart2 201, xlColumnClustered, 50, 60, 300, 200, 5
```

In many cases, you may find it efficient to create an object variable when the chart is created. The following procedure creates a line chart that you can reference in code by using the MyChart object variable. Note that the AddChart2 method specifies only the first two arguments. The other five arguments use default values.

```
Sub CreateChart()
    Dim MyChart As Chart
    Set MyChart = ActiveSheet.Shapes.AddChart2(212,xlLineMarkers).Chart
End Sub
```

A chart without data isn't useful. You can specify data for a chart in two ways:

➤ Select cells before your code creates the chart
➤ Use the SetSourceData method of the Chart object after the chart is created

Here's a simple procedure that selects a range of data and then creates a chart:

```
Sub CreateChart2()
    Range("A1:B6").Select
    ActiveSheet.Shapes.AddChart2 201, xlColumnClustered
End Sub
```

The procedure that follows demonstrates the SetSourceData method. This procedure uses two object variables: DataRange (for the Range object that holds the data) and MyChart (for the Chart object). The MyChart object variable is created at the same time the chart is created.

```
Sub CreateChart3()
    Dim MyChart As Chart
    Dim DataRange As Range
    Set DataRange = ActiveSheet.Range("A1:B6")
    Set MyChart = ActiveSheet.Shapes.AddChart2.Chart
    MyChart.SetSourceData Source:=DataRange
End Sub
```

The code creates the chart shown in Figure 16-1. Note the AddChart2 method has no arguments, so a default chart is created.

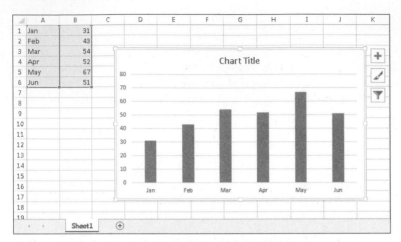

Figure 16-1: A few lines of VBA code created this chart.

Creating a Chart on a Chart Sheet

The preceding section describes the basic procedures for creating an embedded chart. To create a chart directly on a chart sheet, use the Add2 method of the Charts collection. The Add2 method of the Charts collection uses several optional arguments, but these arguments specify the position of the chart sheet — not chart-related information.

The example that follows creates a chart on a chart sheet and specifies the data range and chart type:

```
Sub CreateChartSheet()
    Dim MyChart As Chart
    Dim DataRange As Range
    Set DataRange = ActiveSheet.Range("A1:C7")
    Set MyChart = Charts.Add2
    MyChart.SetSourceData Source:=DataRange
    ActiveChart.ChartType = xlColumnClustered
End Sub
```

Figure 16-2 shows the result.

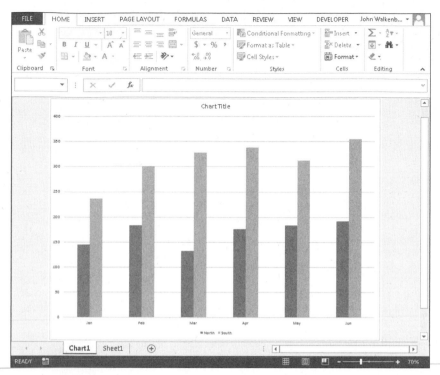

Figure 16-2: Creating a chart on a chart sheet.

Modifying Charts

Enhancements in Excel 2013 make it easier than ever for end users to create and modify charts. For example, when a chart is activated, Excel displays three icons on the right side of the chart: Chart Elements (used to add or remove elements from the chart), Style & Color (used to select a chart style or change the color palette), and Chart Filters (used to hide series or data points).

Your VBA code can perform all the actions available from the new chart controls. For example, if you turn on the macro recorder while you add or remove elements from a chart, you'll see that the relevant method is SetElement (a method of the Chart object). This method takes one argument, and predefined constants are available. For example, to add primary horizontal gridlines to the active chart, use this statement:

```
ActiveChart.SetElement msoElementPrimaryValueGridLinesMajor
```

To remove the primary horizontal gridlines, use this statement:

```
ActiveChart.SetElement msoElementPrimaryValueGridLinesNone
```

All the constants are listed in the Help system, or you can use the macro recorder to discover them.

Use the ChartStyle property to change the chart to a predefined style. The styles are numbers, and no descriptive constants are available. For example, this statement changes the style of the active chart to Style 215:

```
ActiveChart.ChartStyle = 215
```

Valid values for the ChartStyle property are 1–48 and 201–248. The latter group consists of new styles introduced in Excel 2013. Also, keep in mind that the actual appearance of the styles isn't consistent across Excel versions. For example, applying style 48 looks different in Excel 2010.

To change the color scheme used by a chart, set its ChartColor property to a value between 1 and 26. For example:

```
ActiveChart.ChartColor = 12
```

The ChartColor property is new to Excel 2013.

When you combine the 96 ChartStyle values with the 26 ChartColor options, you have 2,496 combinations — enough to satisfy just about anyone. And if those prebuilt choices aren't enough, you have control over every element in a chart. For example, the following code changes the fill color for one point in a chart series:

```
With ActiveChart.FullSeriesCollection(1).Points(2).Format.Fill
    .Visible = msoTrue
    .ForeColor.ObjectThemeColor = msoThemeColorAccent2
    .ForeColor.TintAndShade = 0.4
    .ForeColor.Brightness = -0.25
    .Solid
End With
```

Again, recording your actions while you make changes to a chart will give you the object model information you need to write your code.

Using VBA to Activate a Chart

When a user clicks any area of an embedded chart, the chart is activated. Your VBA code can activate an embedded chart with the Activate method. Here's a VBA statement that's the equivalent of licking an embedded chart to activate it:

```
ActiveSheet.ChartObjects("Chart 1").Activate
```

If the chart is on a chart sheet, use a statement like this:

```
Sheets("Chart1").Activate
```

Alternatively, you can activate a chart by selecting its containing Shape:

```
ActiveSheet.Shapes("Chart 1").Select
```

When a chart is activated, you can refer to it in your code by using the ActiveChart property (which returns a Chart object). For example, the following instruction displays the name of the active chart. If no active chart exists, the statement generates an error:

```
MsgBox ActiveChart.Name
```

To modify a chart with VBA, it's not necessary to activate it. The two procedures that follow have exactly the same effect. That is, they change the embedded chart named Chart 1 to an area chart. The first procedure activates the chart before performing the manipulations; the second one doesn't:

```
Sub ModifyChart1()
    ActiveSheet.ChartObjects("Chart 1").Activate
    ActiveChart.ChartType = xlArea
End Sub

Sub ModifyChart2()
    ActiveSheet.ChartObjects("Chart 1").Chart.ChartType = xlArea
End Sub
```

Moving a Chart

A chart embedded on a worksheet can be converted to a chart sheet. To do so manually, just activate the embedded chart and choose Chart Tools➜Design➜Location➜Move Chart. In the Move Chart dialog box, select the New Sheet option and specify a name.

You can also convert an embedded chart to a chart sheet by using VBA. Here's an example that converts the first ChartObject on a worksheet named Sheet1 to a chart sheet named MyChart:

```
Sub MoveChart1()
    Sheets("Sheet1").ChartObjects(1).Chart. _
      Location xlLocationAsNewSheet, "MyChart"
End Sub
```

The following example does just the opposite of the preceding procedure: It converts the chart on a chart sheet named MyChart to an embedded chart on the worksheet named Sheet1.

```
Sub MoveChart2()
    Charts("MyChart").Location xlLocationAsObject, "Sheet1"
End Sub
```

Note

Using the Location method also activates the relocated chart.

Using VBA to Deactivate a Chart

You can use the Activate method to activate a chart, but how do you deactivate (that is, deselect) a chart?

As far as I can tell, the only way to deactivate a chart by using VBA is to select something other than the chart. For an embedded chart, you can use the RangeSelection property of the ActiveWindow object to deactivate the chart and select the range that was selected before the chart was activated:

```
ActiveWindow.RangeSelection.Select
```

To deactivate a chart on a chart sheet, just write code that activates a different sheet.

What's your name?

Every ChartObject object has a name, and every Chart object contained in a ChartObject has a name. That statement seems straightforward, but chart names can be confusing. Create a new chart on Sheet1 and activate it. Then activate the VBA Immediate window and type a few commands:

```
? ActiveSheet.Shapes(1).Name
Chart 1
? ActiveSheet.ChartObjects(1).Name
Chart 1
? ActiveChart.Name
Sheet1 Chart 1
? Activesheet.ChartObjects(1).Chart.Name
Sheet1 Chart 1
```

If you change the name of the worksheet, the name of the chart also changes to include the new sheet name. You can also use the Name box (to the left of the Formula bar) to change a Chart object's name, and also change the name using VBA:

```
Activesheet.ChartObjects(1).Name = "New Name"
```

However, you can't change the name of a Chart object contained in a ChartObject. This statement generates an inexplicable "out of memory" error:

```
Activesheet.ChartObjects(1).Chart.Name = "New Name"
```

Oddly, Excel allows you to use the name of an existing ChartObject. In other words, you could have a dozen embedded charts on a worksheet, and every one of them can be named Chart 1. If you make a copy of an embedded chart, the new chart has the same name as the source chart.

Bottom line? Be aware of this quirk. If you find that your VBA charting macro isn't working, make sure that you don't have two identically named charts.

Determining Whether a Chart Is Activated

A common type of macro performs some manipulations on the active chart (the chart selected by a user). For example, a macro might change the chart's type, apply a style, add data labels, or export the chart to a graphics file.

The question is how can your VBA code determine whether the user has actually selected a chart? By selecting a chart, I mean either activating a chart sheet or activating an embedded chart by clicking it. Your first inclination might be to check the TypeName property of the Selection, as in this expression:

```
TypeName(Selection) = "Chart"
```

In fact, this expression never evaluates to True. When a chart is activated, the actual selection will be an object within the Chart object. For example, the selection might be a Series object, a ChartTitle object, a Legend object, or a PlotArea object.

The solution is to determine whether ActiveChart is Nothing. If so, a chart isn't active. The following code checks to ensure that a chart is active. If not, the user sees a message, and the procedure ends:

```
If ActiveChart Is Nothing Then
    MsgBox "Select a chart."
    Exit Sub
Else
    'other code goes here
End If
```

You may find it convenient to use a VBA function procedure to determine whether a chart is activated. The ChartIsSelected function, which follows, returns True if a chart sheet is active or if an embedded chart is activated, but returns False if a chart isn't activated:

```
Private Function ChartIsActivated() As Boolean
    ChartIsActivated = Not ActiveChart Is Nothing
End Function
```

Deleting from the ChartObjects or Charts Collection

To delete a chart on a worksheet, you must know the name or index of the ChartObject or the Shape object. This statement deletes the ChartObject named Chart 1 on the active worksheet:

```
ActiveSheet.ChartObjects("Chart 1").Delete
```

Keep in mind that multiple ChartObjects can have the same name. If that's the case, you can delete a chart by using its index number:

```
ActiveSheet.ChartObjects(1).Delete
```

To delete all ChartObject objects on a worksheet, use the Delete method of the ChartObjects collection:

```
ActiveSheet.ChartObjects.Delete
```

You can also delete embedded charts by accessing the Shapes collection. The following statement deletes the shape named Chart 1 on the active worksheet:

```
ActiveSheet.Shapes("Chart 1").Delete
```

This code deletes all embedded charts (and all other shapes) on the active sheet:

```
Dim shp as Shape
For Each shp In ActiveSheet.Shapes
    shp.Delete
Next shp
```

To delete a single chart sheet, you must know the chart sheet's name or index. The following statement deletes the chart sheet named Chart1:

```
Charts("Chart1").Delete
```

To delete all chart sheets in the active workbook, use the following statement:

```
ActiveWorkbook.Charts.Delete
```

Deleting sheets causes Excel to display a warning like the one shown in Figure 16-3. The user must reply to this prompt for the macro to continue.

Figure 16-3: Attempting to delete one or more chart sheets results in this message.

If you're deleting a sheet with a macro, you probably won't want this warning prompt to appear. To eliminate the prompt, use the following series of statements:

```
Application.DisplayAlerts = False
ActiveWorkbook.Charts.Delete
Application.DisplayAlerts = True
```

Looping through All Charts

In some cases, you may need to perform an operation on all charts. The following example applies changes to every embedded chart on the active worksheet. The procedure uses a loop to cycle through each object in the ChartObjects collection and then accesses the Chart object in each and changes several properties.

```
Sub FormatAllCharts()
    Dim ChtObj As ChartObject
    For Each ChtObj In ActiveSheet.ChartObjects
      With ChtObj.Chart
        .ChartType = xlLineMarkers
        .ApplyLayout 3
        .ChartStyle = 12
        .ClearToMatchStyle
        .SetElement msoElementChartTitleAboveChart
        .SetElement msoElementLegendNone
        .SetElement msoElementPrimaryValueAxisTitleNone
        .SetElement msoElementPrimaryCategoryAxisTitleNone
        .Axes(xlValue).MinimumScale = 0
        .Axes(xlValue).MaximumScale = 1000
        With .Axes(xlValue).MajorGridlines.Format.Line
            .ForeColor.ObjectThemeColor = msoThemeColorBackground1
            .ForeColor.TintAndShade = 0
            .ForeColor.Brightness = -0.25
            .DashStyle = msoLineSysDash
            .Transparency = 0
        End With
      End With
    Next ChtObj
End Sub
```

On the Web

This example is available on the book's website in the format all charts.xlsm file.

Figure 16-4 shows four charts that use a variety of different formatting; Figure 16-5 shows the same charts after running the FormatAllCharts macro.

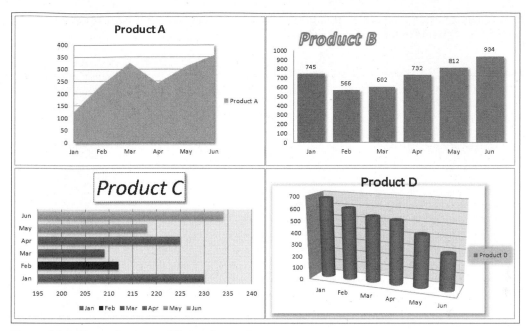

Figure 16-4: These charts use different formatting.

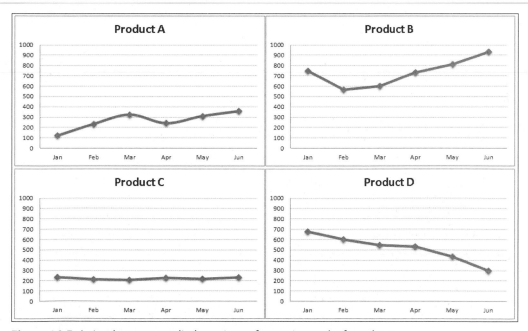

Figure 16-5: A simple macro applied consistent formatting to the four charts.

The following macro performs the same operation as the preceding FormatAllCharts procedure but works on all the chart sheets in the active workbook:

```
Sub FormatAllCharts2()
    Dim cht as Chart
    For Each cht In ActiveWorkbook.Charts
      With cht
        .ChartType = xlLineMarkers
        .ApplyLayout 3
        .ChartStyle = 12
        .ClearToMatchStyle
        .SetElement msoElementChartTitleAboveChart
        .SetElement msoElementLegendNone
        .SetElement msoElementPrimaryValueAxisTitleNone
        .SetElement msoElementPrimaryCategoryAxisTitleNone
        .Axes(xlValue).MinimumScale = 0
        .Axes(xlValue).MaximumScale = 1000
        With .Axes(xlValue).MajorGridlines.Format.Line
            .ForeColor.ObjectThemeColor = msoThemeColorBackground1
            .ForeColor.TintAndShade = 0
            .ForeColor.Brightness = -0.25
            .DashStyle = msoLineSysDash
            .Transparency = 0
        End With
      End With
    Next cht
End Sub
```

Sizing and Aligning ChartObjects

A ChartObject object has standard positional (Top and Left) and sizing (Width and Height) properties that you can access with your VBA code. The Excel Ribbon has controls (in the Chart Tools➜ Format➜Size group) to set the Height and Width, but not the Top and Left.

The following example resizes all ChartObject objects on a sheet so that they match the dimensions of the active chart. It also arranges the ChartObject objects into a user-specified number of columns.

```
Sub SizeAndAlignCharts()
    Dim W As Long, H As Long
    Dim TopPosition As Long, LeftPosition As Long
    Dim ChtObj As ChartObject
    Dim i As Long, NumCols As Long

    If ActiveChart Is Nothing Then
        MsgBox "Select a chart to be used as the base for the sizing"
        Exit Sub
    End If

    'Get columns
    On Error Resume Next
    NumCols = InputBox("How many columns of charts?")
    If Err.Number <> 0 Then Exit Sub
    If NumCols < 1 Then Exit Sub
    On Error GoTo 0

    'Get size of active chart
    W = ActiveChart.Parent.Width
    H = ActiveChart.Parent.Height

    'Change starting positions, if necessary
    TopPosition = 100
    LeftPosition = 20
    For i = 1 To ActiveSheet.ChartObjects.Count
        With ActiveSheet.ChartObjects(i)
            .Width = W
            .Height = H
            .Left = LeftPosition + ((i - 1) Mod NumCols) * W
            .Top = TopPosition + Int((i - 1) / NumCols) * H
        End With
    Next i
End Sub
```

If no chart is active, the user is prompted to activate a chart that will be used as the basis for sizing the other charts. I use an InputBox function to get the number of columns. The values for the Left and Top properties are calculated within the loop.

Figure 16-6 shows some charts, neatly sized and arranged.

On the Web   **This workbook, named size and align charts.xlsm, is available on the book's website.**

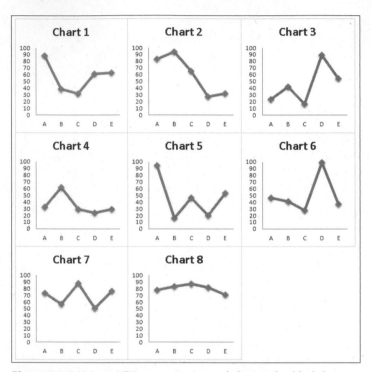

Figure 16-6: Using a VBA macro to size and align embedded charts.

Creating Lots of Charts

The example in this section demonstrates how to automate the task of creating multiple charts. Figure 16-7 shows part of the data to be charted. The worksheet contains data for 50 people, and the goal is to create 50 charts, consistently formatted and nicely aligned.

	A	B	C	D	E	F
1	**Name**	**Day 1**	**Day 2**	**Day 3**	**Day 4**	**Day 5**
2	Daisy Allen	37	56	70	72	88
3	Joe Perry	48	56	61	58	52
4	Joe Long	44	62	71	69	68
5	Stephen Mitchell	49	51	55	74	92
6	Thelma Carter	32	25	15	31	50
7	Susie Fitzgerald	47	67	85	92	99
8	Gerard Johnson	40	56	75	86	79
9	Mary Young	33	34	33	50	41
10	Robert Mcdonald	39	57	72	89	96
11	Robert Hall	39	54	49	45	41
12	Jennifer Head	58	50	43	45	56
13	Todd Fowler	32	42	40	42	55
14	Margaret Adams	56	71	75	72	71
15	William Smith	42	40	36	37	51
16	Douglas Taylor	45	46	46	56	67
17	Evelyn Reyes	39	36	41	34	49
18	Peter Gonzales	54	49	47	64	66
19	Victor Klein	36	42	33	50	43
20	Christopher Anderson	32	28	34	38	37
21	Raul Jones	31	25	30	22	33
22	Bernard Jones	45	48	52	66	67
23	Norma Young	53	67	57	50	64
24	Francis Valencia	49	68	65	68	64
25	Shannon Taylor	57	59	67	79	79

Sheet1   Sheet2   (+)

Figure 16-7: Each row of data will be used to create a chart.

I started out by creating the CreateChart procedure, which accepts the following arguments:

➤ **rng:** The range to be used for the chart

➤ **l:** The left position for the chart

➤ **t:** The top position for the chart

➤ **w:** The width of the chart

➤ **h:** The height of the chart

The CreateChart procedure uses these arguments to create a line chart with axis scale values ranging from 0 to 100.

```
Sub CreateChart(rng, l, t, w, h)
    With Worksheets("Sheet2").Shapes. _
      AddChart2(332, xlLineMarkers, l, t, w, h).Chart
        .SetSourceData Source:=rng
        .Axes(xlValue).MinimumScale = 0
        .Axes(xlValue).MaximumScale = 100
    End With
End Sub
```

When I was satisfied that this procedure worked, I wrote another procedure, Make50Charts, that uses a For-Next loop to call CreateChart 50 times. Note that the chart data consists of the first row (the headers), plus data in a row from 2 through 50. I used the Union method to join these two ranges into one Range object, which is passed to the CreateChart procedure. The other tricky part was writing code to determine the top and left position for each chart.

```
Sub Make50Charts()
    Dim ChartData As Range
    Dim i As Long
    Dim leftPos As Long, topPos As Long
'   Delete existing charts if they exist
    With Worksheets("Sheet2").ChartObjects
        If .Count > 0 Then .Delete
    End With

'   Initialize positions
    leftPos = 0
    topPos = 0

'   Loop through the data
    For i = 2 To 51
'       Determine the data range
        With Worksheets("Sheet1")
          Set ChartData = Union(.Range("A1:F1"), _
            .Range(.Cells(i, 1), .Cells(i, 6)))
        End With

'       Create a chart
        Call CreateChart(ChartData, leftPos, topPos, 180, 120)

'       Adjust positions
        If (i - 1) Mod 5 = 0 Then
            leftPos = 0
            topPos = topPos + 120
        Else
            leftPos = leftPos + 180
        End If
    Next i
End Sub
```

Figure 16-8 shows some of the 50 charts.

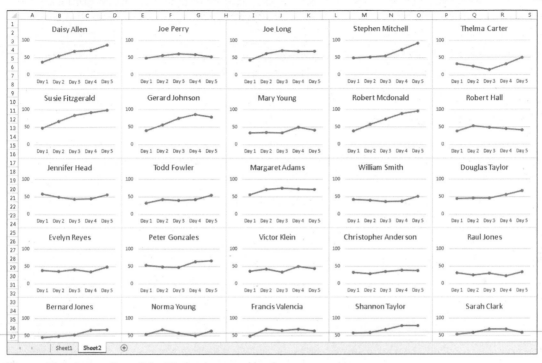

Figure 16-8: A sampling of the 50 charts created by the macro.

Exporting a Chart

In some cases, you may need an Excel chart in the form of a graphics file. For example, you may want to post the chart on a website. One option is to use a screen capture program and copy the pixels directly from the screen. Another choice is to write a simple VBA macro.

The procedure that follows uses the Export method of the Chart object to save the active chart as a GIF file:

```
Sub SaveChartAsGIF ()
  Dim Fname as String
  If ActiveChart Is Nothing Then Exit Sub
  Fname = ThisWorkbook.Path & "\" & ActiveChart.Name & ".gif"
  ActiveChart.Export FileName:=Fname, FilterName:="GIF"
End Sub
```

Other choices for the FilterName argument are "JPEG" and "PNG". Usually, GIF and PNG files look better. The Help system lists a third argument for the Export method: Interactive. If this argument is True, you're supposed to see a dialog box in which you can specify export options. However, this argument has no effect.

Keep in mind that the Export method will fail if the user doesn't have the specified graphics export filter installed. These filters are installed in the Office setup program.

Exporting all graphics

One way to export all graphic images from a workbook is to save the file in HTML format. Doing so creates a directory that contains GIF and PNG images of the charts, shapes, clipart, and even copied range images (created with Home➜Clipboard➜Paste➜Picture (U)).

Here's a VBA procedure that automates the process. It works with the active workbook:

```
Sub SaveAllGraphics()
    Dim FileName As String
    Dim TempName As String
    Dim DirName As String
    Dim gFile As String

    FileName = ActiveWorkbook.FullName
    TempName = ActiveWorkbook.Path & "\" & _
        ActiveWorkbook.Name & "graphics.htm"
    DirName = Left(TempName, Len(TempName) - 4) & "_files"

'   Save active workbookbook as HTML, then reopen original
    ActiveWorkbook.Save
    ActiveWorkbook.SaveAs FileName:=TempName, FileFormat:=xlHtml
    Application.DisplayAlerts = False
    ActiveWorkbook.Close
    Workbooks.Open FileName

'   Delete the HTML file
    Kill TempName

'   Delete all but *.PNG files in the HTML folder
    gFile = Dir(DirName & "\*.*")
    Do While gFile <> ""
        If Right(gFile, 3) <> "png" Then Kill DirName & "\" & gFile
        gFile = Dir
    Loop

'   Show the exported graphics
    Shell "explorer.exe " & DirName, vbNormalFocus
End Sub
```

The procedure starts by saving the active workbook. Then it saves the workbook as an HTML file, closes the file, and reopens the original workbook. Next, it deletes the HTML file because we're just interested in the folder that it creates (because that folder contains the images). The code then loops through the folder and deletes everything except the PNG files. Finally, it uses the Shell function to display the folder.

Cross-Ref

See Chapter 25 for more information about the file manipulation commands.

On the Web

This example is available on the book's website in the export all graphics.xlsm file.

Changing the Data Used in a Chart

The examples so far in this chapter have used the SourceData property to specify the complete data range for a chart. In many cases, you'll want to adjust the data used by a particular chart series. To do so, access the Values property of the Series object. The Series object also has an XValues property that stores the category axis values.

Note

The Values property corresponds to the third argument of the SERIES formula, and the XValues property corresponds to the second argument of the SERIES formula. See the sidebar, "Understanding a chart's SERIES formula."

Changing chart data based on the active cell

Figure 16-9 shows a chart that's based on the data in the row of the active cell. When the user moves the cell pointer, the chart is updated automatically.

This example uses an event handler for the Sheet1 object. The SelectionChange event occurs whenever the user changes the selection by moving the cell pointer. The event-handler procedure for this event (which is located in the code module for the Sheet1 object) is as follows:

```
Private Sub Worksheet_SelectionChange(ByVal Target As Excel.Range)
    If CheckBox1 Then Call UpdateChart
End Sub
```

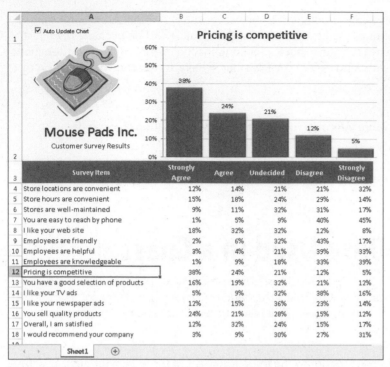

Figure 16-9: This chart always displays the data from the row of the active cell.

In other words, every time the user moves the cell cursor, the Worksheet_SelectionChange procedure is executed. If the Auto Update Chart check box (an ActiveX control on the sheet) is checked, this procedure calls the UpdateChart procedure, which follows:

```
Sub UpdateChart()
    Dim ChtObj As ChartObject
    Dim UserRow As Long
    Set ChtObj = ActiveSheet.ChartObjects(1)
    UserRow = ActiveCell.Row
    If UserRow < 4 Or IsEmpty(Cells(UserRow, 1)) Then
        ChtObj.Visible = False
    Else
        ChtObj.Chart.SeriesCollection(1).Values = _
            Range(Cells(UserRow, 2), Cells(UserRow, 6))
        ChtObj.Chart.ChartTitle.Text = Cells(UserRow, 1).Text
        ChtObj.Visible = True
    End If
End Sub
```

Understanding a chart's SERIES formula

The data used in each series in a chart is determined by its SERIES formula. When you select a data series in a chart, the SERIES formula appears in the formula bar. This is not a real formula: In other words, you can't use it in a cell, and you can't use worksheet functions within the SERIES formula. You can, however, edit the arguments in the SERIES formula.

A SERIES formula has the following syntax:

```
=SERIES(series_name, category_labels, values, order, sizes)
```

The arguments that you can use in the SERIES formula are

- series_name: Optional. A reference to the cell that contains the series name used in the legend. If the chart has only one series, the name argument is used as the title. This argument can also consist of text in quotation marks. If omitted, Excel creates a default series name (for example, Series 1).

- category_labels: Optional. A reference to the range that contains the labels for the category axis. If omitted, Excel uses consecutive integers beginning with 1. For XY charts, this argument specifies the X values. A noncontiguous range reference is also valid. The ranges' addresses are separated by a comma and enclosed in parentheses. The argument could also consist of an array of comma-separated values (or text in quotation marks) enclosed in curly brackets.

- values: Required. A reference to the range that contains the values for the series. For XY charts, this argument specifies the Y values. A noncontiguous range reference is also valid. The ranges' addresses are separated by a comma and enclosed in parentheses. The argument could also consist of an array of comma-separated values enclosed in curly brackets.

- order: Required. An integer that specifies the plotting order of the series. This argument is relevant only if the chart has more than one series. For example, in a stacked column chart, this parameter determines the stacking order. Using a reference to a cell is not allowed.

- sizes: Only for bubble charts. A reference to the range that contains the values for the size of the bubbles in a bubble chart. A noncontiguous range reference is also valid. The ranges' addresses are separated by a comma and enclosed in parentheses. The argument could also consist of an array of values enclosed in curly brackets.

Range references in a SERIES formula are always absolute, and they always include the sheet name. For example:

```
=SERIES(Sheet1!$B$1,,Sheet1!$B$2:$B$7,1)
```

A range reference can consist of a noncontiguous range. If so, each range is separated by a comma, and the argument is enclosed in parentheses. In the following SERIES formula, the values range consists of B2:B3 and B5:B7:

```
=SERIES(,,(Sheet1!$B$2:$B$3,Sheet1!$B$5:$B$7),1)
```

You can substitute range names for the range references. If you do so (and the name is a workbook-level name), Excel changes the reference in the SERIES formula to include the workbook. For example:

```
=SERIES(Sheet1!$B$1,,budget.xlsx!CurrentData,1)
```

The UserRow variable contains the row number of the active cell. The If statement checks that the active cell is in a row that contains data. (The data starts in row 4.) If the cell cursor is in a row that doesn't have data, the ChartObject object is hidden, and the underlying text is visible ("Cannot display chart"). Otherwise, the code sets the Values property for the Series object to the range in columns 2–6 of the active row. It also sets the ChartTitle object to correspond to the text in column A.

On the Web

This example, named chart active cell.xlsm, is available on the book's website.

Using VBA to determine the ranges used in a chart

The previous example demonstrated how to use the Values property of a Series object to specify the data used by a chart series. This section discusses using VBA macros to identify the ranges used by a series in a chart. For example, you might want to increase the size of each series by adding a new cell to the range.

Following is a description of three properties that are relevant to this task:

➤ Formula property: Returns or sets the SERIES formula for the Series. When you select a series in a chart, its SERIES formula is displayed in the formula bar. The Formula property returns this formula as a string.

➤ Values property: Returns or sets a collection of all the values in the series. This property can be specified as a range on a worksheet or as an array of constant values, but not a combination of both.

➤ XValues property: Returns or sets an array of X values for a chart series. The XValues property can be set to a range on a worksheet or to an array of values, but it can't be a combination of both. The XValues property can also be empty.

If you create a VBA macro that needs to determine the data range used by a particular chart series, you might think that the Values property of the Series object is just the ticket. Similarly, the XValues property seems to be the way to get the range that contains the X values (or category labels). In theory, that way of thinking certainly *seems* correct. But in practice, it doesn't work.

When you set the Values property for a Series object, you can specify a Range object or an array. But when you read this property, an array is always returned. Unfortunately, the object model provides no way to get a Range object used by a Series object.

One possible solution is to write code to parse the SERIES formula and extract the range addresses. This task sounds simple, but it's actually difficult because a SERIES formula can be complex. Following are a few examples of valid SERIES formulas:

```
=SERIES(Sheet1!$B$1,Sheet1!$A$2:$A$4,Sheet1!$B$2:$B$4,1)
=SERIES(,,Sheet1!$B$2:$B$4,1)
=SERIES(,Sheet1!$A$2:$A$4,Sheet1!$B$2:$B$4,1)
=SERIES("Sales Summary",,Sheet1!$B$2:$B$4,1)
=SERIES(,{"Jan","Feb","Mar"},Sheet1!$B$2:$B$4,1)
=SERIES(,(Sheet1!$A$2,Sheet1!$A$4),(Sheet1!$B$2,Sheet1!$B$4),1)
=SERIES(Sheet1!$B$1,Sheet1!$A$2:$A$4,Sheet1!$B$2:$B$4,1,Sheet1!$C$2:$C$4)
```

As you can see, a SERIES formula can have missing arguments, use arrays, and even use noncontiguous range addresses. And, to confuse the issue even more, a bubble chart has an additional argument (for example, the last SERIES formula in the preceding list). Attempting to parse the arguments is certainly not a trivial programming task.

I spent a lot of time working on this problem, and I eventually arrived at a solution that involves evaluating the SERIES formula by using a dummy function. This function accepts the same arguments as a SERIES formula and returns a 2 x 5 element array that contains all the information in the SERIES formula.

I simplified the solution by creating four custom VBA functions, each of which accepts one argument (a reference to a Series object) and returns a two-element array. These functions are the following:

> SERIESNAME_FROM_SERIES: The first array element contains a string that describes the data type of the first SERIES argument (Range, Empty, or String). The second array element contains a range address, an empty string, or a string.

> XVALUES_FROM_SERIES: The first array element contains a string that describes the data type of the second SERIES argument (Range, Array, Empty, or String). The second array element contains a range address, an array, an empty string, or a string.

> VALUES_FROM_SERIES: The first array element contains a string that describes the data type of the third SERIES argument (Range or Array). The second array element contains a range address or an array.

> BUBBLESIZE_FROM_SERIES: The first array element contains a string that describes the data type of the fifth SERIES argument (Range, Array, or Empty). The second array element contains a range address, an array, or an empty string. This function is relevant only for bubble charts.

Note that I did not create a function to get the fourth SERIES argument (plot order). You can obtain this argument directly by using the PlotOrder property of the Series object.

On the Web **The VBA code for these functions is too lengthy to be listed here, but the code is available on the book's website in a file named get series ranges.xlsm. These functions are documented in such a way that they can be easily adapted to other situations.**

The following example demonstrates the VALUES_FROM_SERIES function. It displays the address of the values range for the first series in the active chart.

```
Sub ShowValueRange()
    Dim Ser As Series
    Dim x As Variant
    Set Ser = ActiveChart.SeriesCollection(1)
    x = VALUES_FROM_SERIES(Ser)
    If x(1) = "Range" Then
        MsgBox Range(x(2)).Address
    End If
End Sub
```

The variable x is defined as a variant and will hold the two-element array that's returned by the VALUES_FROM_SERIES function. The first element of the x array contains a string that describes the data type. If the string is Range, the message box displays the address of the range contained in the second element of the x array.

Figure 16-10 shows another example. The chart has three data series. Buttons on the sheet execute macros that expand and contract each of the data ranges.

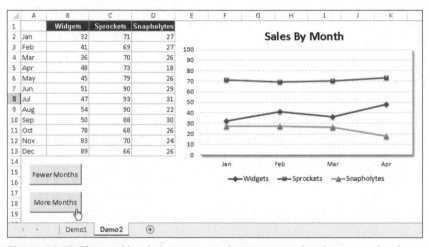

Figure 16-10: This workbook demonstrates how to expand and contract the chart series by using VBA macros.

The ContractAllSeries procedure follows. This procedure loops through the SeriesCollection collection and uses the XVALUE_FROM_SERIES and the VALUES_FROM_SERIES functions to retrieve the current ranges. It then uses the Resize method to decrease the size of the ranges.

```
Sub ContractAllSeries()
    Dim s As Series
    Dim Result As Variant
    Dim DRange As Range
```

```
    For Each s In ActiveSheet.ChartObjects(1).Chart.SeriesCollection
        Result = XVALUES_FROM_SERIES(s)
        If Result(1) = "Range" Then
            Set DRange = Range(Result(2))
            If DRange.Rows.Count > 1 Then
                Set DRange = DRange.Resize(DRange.Rows.Count - 1)
                s.XValues = DRange
            End If
        End If
        Result = VALUES_FROM_SERIES(s)
        If Result(1) = "Range" Then
            Set DRange = Range(Result(2))
            If DRange.Rows.Count > 1 Then
                Set DRange = DRange.Resize(DRange.Rows.Count - 1)
                s.Values = DRange
            End If
        End If
    Next s
End Sub
```

The ExpandAllSeries procedure is similar. When executed, it expands each range by one cell.

Using VBA to Display Arbitrary Data Labels on a Chart

Note

If you use Excel 2013 exclusively, I'm pleased to announce that this section is no longer relevant. Microsoft has finally responded to what must be thousands of requests for the capability to specify a range of data for chart data labels. That feature is now available in Excel 2013.

Here's how to specify a range of data labels for a chart series:

1. Create your chart and select the data series that will contain labels from a range.

2. Click the Chart Elements icon to the right of the chart and choose Data Labels.

3. Click the arrow to right of the Data Labels item and choose More Options.

   The Label Options section of the Format Data Labels task pane is displayed.

4. Select Value From Cells.

   Excel prompts you for the range that contains the labels.

Figure 16-11 shows an example. I specified range C2:C7 as the data labels for the series. In the past, specifying a range as data labels had to be done manually or with a VBA macro.

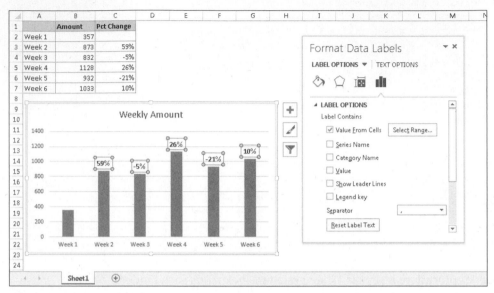

Figure 16-11: Data labels from an arbitrary range show the percent change for each week.

This feature is great but is not backward compatible. Figure 16-12 shows how the chart looks when I opened it in Excel 2010.

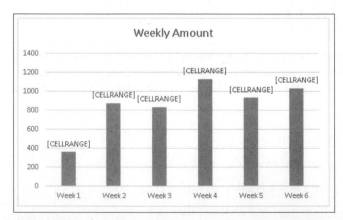

Figure 16-12: Data labels created from a range of data are not compatible with earlier versions of Excel.

The remainder of this section describes how to apply data labels from an arbitrary range using VBA. The data labels applied in this manner *are* compatible with previous versions of Excel.

Figure 16-13 shows an XY chart. It would be useful to display the associated name for each data point.

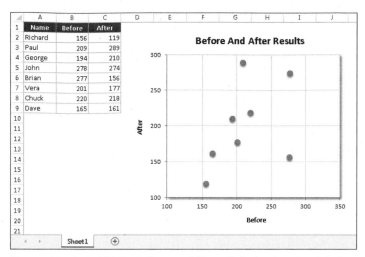

Figure 16-13: An XY chart that would benefit by having data labels.

The DataLabelsFromRange procedure works with the first chart on the active sheet. It prompts the user for a range and then loops through the Points collection and changes the Text property to the values found in the range.

```
Sub DataLabelsFromRange()
    Dim DLRange As Range
    Dim Cht As Chart
    Dim i As Integer, Pts As Integer

'    Specify chart
    Set Cht = ActiveSheet.ChartObjects(1).Chart

'    Prompt for a range
    On Error Resume Next
    Set DLRange = Application.InputBox _
      (prompt:="Range for data labels?", Type:=8)
    If DLRange Is Nothing Then Exit Sub
    On Error GoTo 0

'    Add data labels
    Cht.SeriesCollection(1).ApplyDataLabels _
      Type:=xlDataLabelsShowValue, _
      AutoText:=True, _
      LegendKey:=False

'    Loop through the Points, and set the data labels
    Pts = Cht.SeriesCollection(1).Points.Count
    For i = 1 To Pts
        Cht.SeriesCollection(1). _
          Points(i).DataLabel.Text = DLRange(i)
    Next i
End Sub
```

This example, named data labels.xlsm, is available on the book's website.

Figure 16-14 shows the chart after running the DataLabelsFromRange procedure and specifying A2:A9 as the data range.

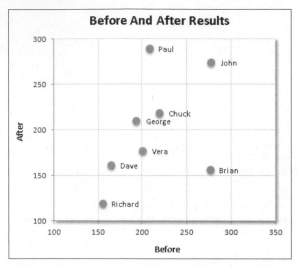

Figure 16-14: This XY chart has data labels, thanks to a VBA procedure.

A data label in a chart can also consist of a link to a cell. To modify the DataLabelsFromRange procedure so it creates cell links, just change the statement in the For-Next loop to

```
Cht.SeriesCollection(1).Points(i).DataLabel.Text = _
    "=" & "'" & DLRange.Parent.Name & "'!" & _
    DLRange(i).Address(ReferenceStyle:=xlR1C1)
```

The preceding procedure is crude and does little error checking. In addition, it works with only the first Series object. The book's website contains a stand-alone version of my Power Utility Pak utility, which is more sophisticated. Figure 16-15 shows the dialog box. The file-name is PUP chart data labeler.xlsm, and it could easily be converted to an add-in.

Figure 16-15: The dialog box for the PUP Chart Data Labeler utility.

Displaying a Chart in a UserForm

In Chapter 13, I describe a way to display a chart in a UserForm. The technique saves the chart as a GIF file and then loads the GIF file into an Image control on the UserForm.

The example in this section uses that same technique but adds a new twist: The chart is created on the fly and uses the data in the row of the active cell. Figure 16-16 shows an example.

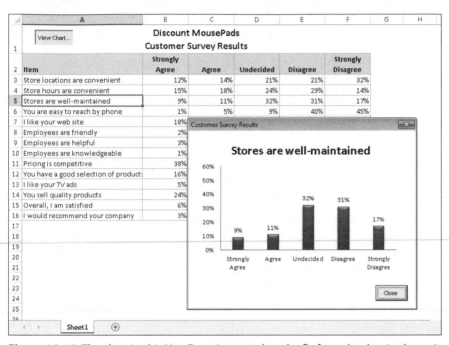

Figure 16-16: The chart in this UserForm is created on the fly from the data in the active row.

The UserForm for this example is simple. It contains an Image control and a CommandButton (Close). The worksheet that contains the data has a button that executes the following procedure:

```
Sub ShowChart()
    Dim UserRow As Long
    UserRow = ActiveCell.Row
    If UserRow < 2 Or IsEmpty(Cells(UserRow, 1)) Then
        MsgBox "Move the cell pointer to a row that contains data."
        Exit Sub
    End If
    CreateChart (UserRow)
    UserForm1.Show
End Sub
```

Because the chart is based on the data in the row of the active cell, the procedure warns the user if the cell pointer is in an invalid row. If the active cell is appropriate, ShowChart calls the CreateChart procedure to create the chart and then displays the UserForm.

The CreateChart procedure accepts one argument, which represents the row of the active cell. This procedure originated from a macro recording that I cleaned up to make more general.

```vba
Sub CreateChart(r)
    Dim TempChart As Chart
    Dim CatTitles As Range
    Dim SrcRange As Range, SourceData As Range
    Dim FName As String

    Set CatTitles = ActiveSheet.Range("A2:F2")
    Set SrcRange = ActiveSheet.Range(Cells(r, 1), Cells(r, 6))
    Set SourceData = Union(CatTitles, SrcRange)

'   Add a chart
    Application.ScreenUpdating = False
    Set TempChart = ActiveSheet.Shapes.AddChart2.Chart
        TempChart.SetSourceData Source:=SourceData

'   Fix it up
    With TempChart
        .ChartType = xlColumnClustered
        .SetSourceData Source:=SourceData, PlotBy:=xlRows
        .ChartStyle = 25
        .HasLegend = False
        .PlotArea.Interior.ColorIndex = xlNone
        .Axes(xlValue).MajorGridlines.Delete
        .ApplyDataLabels Type:=xlDataLabelsShowValue, LegendKey:=False
        .Axes(xlValue).MaximumScale = 0.6
        .ChartArea.Format.Line.Visible = False
    End With

'   Adjust the ChartObject's size
    With ActiveSheet.ChartObjects(1)
        .Width = 300
        .Height = 200
    End With

'   Save chart as GIF

    FName = Application.DefaultFilePath & Application.PathSeparator & "temp.gif"

    TempChart.Export Filename:=FName, filterName:="GIF"
    ActiveSheet.ChartObjects(1).Delete
    Application.ScreenUpdating = True
End Sub
```

When the CreateChart procedure ends, the worksheet contains a ChartObject with a chart of the data in the row of the active cell. However, the ChartObject isn't visible because ScreenUpdating is turned off. The chart is exported and deleted, and ScreenUpdating is turned back on.

The final instruction of the ShowChart procedure loads the UserForm. Following is the UserForm_Initialize procedure, which simply loads the GIF file into the Image control:

```
Private Sub UserForm_Initialize()
    Dim FName As String
    FName = Application.DefaultFilePath & _
        Application.PathSeparator & "temp.gif"
    UserForm1.Image1.Picture = LoadPicture(FName)
End Sub
```

On the Web

This workbook, named chart in userform.xlsm, is available on the book's website.

Understanding Chart Events

Excel supports several events associated with charts. For example, when a chart is activated, it generates an Activate event. The Calculate event occurs after the chart receives new or changed data. You can, of course, write VBA code that gets executed when a particular event occurs.

Cross-Ref

Refer to Chapter 17 for additional information about events.

Table 16-1 lists all the chart events.

Table 16-1: Events Recognized by the Chart Object

Event	Action That Triggers the Event
Activate	A chart sheet or embedded chart is activated.
BeforeDoubleClick	An embedded chart is double-clicked. This event occurs before the default double-click action.
BeforeRightClick	An embedded chart is right-clicked. The event occurs before the default right-click action.
Calculate	New or changed data is plotted on a chart.
Deactivate	A chart is deactivated.
MouseDown	A mouse button is pressed while the pointer is over a chart.

continued

Table 16-1: Events Recognized by the Chart Object *(continued)*

Event	Action That Triggers the Event
MouseMove	The position of the mouse pointer changes over a chart.
MouseUp	A mouse button is released while the pointer is over a chart.
Resize	A chart is resized.
Select	A chart element is selected.
SeriesChange	The value of a chart data point is changed.

An example of using Chart events

To program an event handler for an event taking place on a chart sheet, your VBA code must reside in the code module for the Chart object. To activate this code module, double-click the Chart item in the Project window. Then, in the code module, select Chart from the Object drop-down list on the left and select the event from the Procedure drop-down list on the right (see Figure 16-17).

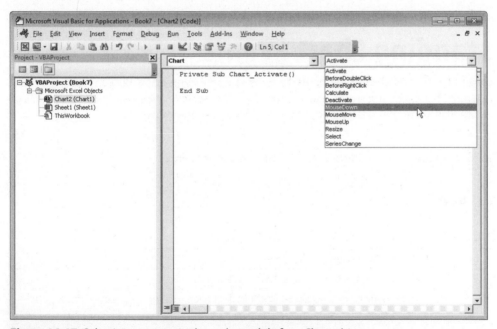

Figure 16-17: Selecting an event in the code module for a Chart object.

Note

Because an embedded chart doesn't have its own code module, the procedure that I describe in this section works only for chart sheets. You can also handle events for embedded charts, but you must do some initial setup work that involves creating a class module. This procedure is described later in "Enabling events for an embedded chart."

The example that follows simply displays a message when the user activates a chart sheet, deactivates a chart sheet, or selects any element on the chart. I created a workbook with a chart sheet; then I wrote three event-handler procedures named as follows:

➤ Chart_Activate: Executed when the chart sheet is activated

➤ Chart_Deactivate: Executed when the chart sheet is deactivated

➤ Chart_Select: Executed when an element on the chart sheet is selected

On the Web

This workbook, named events – chart sheet.xlsm, is available on the book's website.

The Chart_Activate procedure follows:

```
Private Sub Chart_Activate()
    Dim msg As String
    msg = "Hello " & Application.UserName & vbCrLf & vbCrLf
    msg = msg & "You are now viewing the six-month sales "
    msg = msg & "summary for Products 1-3." & vbCrLf & vbCrLf
    msg = msg & _
     "Click an item in the chart to find out what it is."
    MsgBox msg, vbInformation, ActiveWorkbook.Name
End Sub
```

This procedure displays a message whenever the chart is activated. See Figure 16-18.

The Chart_Deactivate procedure that follows also displays a message, but only when the chart sheet is deactivated:

```
Private Sub Chart_Deactivate()
    Dim msg As String
    msg = "Thanks for viewing the chart."
    MsgBox msg, , ActiveWorkbook.Name
End Sub
```

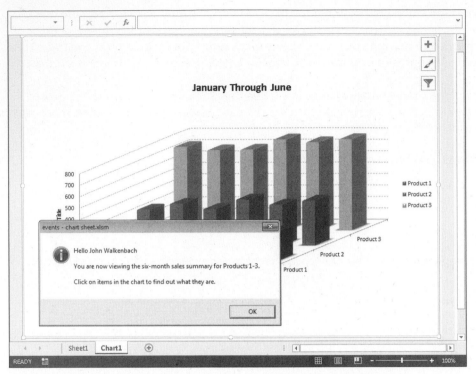

Figure 16-18: Activating the chart causes Chart_Activate to display this message.

The Chart_Select procedure that follows is executed whenever an item on the chart is selected:

```
Private Sub Chart_Select(ByVal ElementID As Long, _
  ByVal Arg1 As Long, ByVal Arg2 As Long)
    Dim Id As String
    Select Case ElementID
        Case xlAxis: Id = "Axis"
        Case xlAxisTitle: Id = "AxisTitle"
        Case xlChartArea: Id = "ChartArea"
        Case xlChartTitle: Id = "ChartTitle"
        Case xlCorners: Id = "Corners"
        Case xlDataLabel: Id = "DataLabel"
        Case xlDataTable: Id = "DataTable"
        Case xlDownBars: Id = "DownBars"
        Case xlDropLines: Id = "DropLines"
        Case xlErrorBars: Id = "ErrorBars"
        Case xlFloor: Id = "Floor"
        Case xlHiLoLines: Id = "HiLoLines"
        Case xlLegend: Id = "Legend"
        Case xlLegendEntry: Id = "LegendEntry"
```

```
            Case xlLegendKey: Id = "LegendKey"
            Case xlMajorGridlines: Id = "MajorGridlines"
            Case xlMinorGridlines: Id = "MinorGridlines"
            Case xlNothing: Id = "Nothing"
            Case xlPlotArea: Id = "PlotArea"
            Case xlRadarAxisLabels: Id = "RadarAxisLabels"
            Case xlSeries: Id = "Series"
            Case xlSeriesLines: Id = "SeriesLines"
            Case xlShape: Id = "Shape"
            Case xlTrendline: Id = "Trendline"
            Case xlUpBars: Id = "UpBars"
            Case xlWalls: Id = "Walls"
            Case xlXErrorBars: Id = "XErrorBars"
            Case xlYErrorBars: Id = "YErrorBars"
            Case Else:: Id = "Some unknown thing"
        End Select

        MsgBox "Selection type:" & Id & vbCrLf & Arg1 & vbCrLf & Arg2
    End Sub
```

This procedure displays a message box that contains a description of the selected item, plus the values for Arg1 and Arg2. When the Select event occurs, the ElementID argument contains an integer that corresponds to what was selected. The Arg1 and Arg2 arguments provide additional information about the selected item (see the Help system for details). The Select Case structure converts the built-in constants to descriptive strings.

Note

Because the code doesn't contain a comprehensive listing of all items that could appear in a Chart object, I included the Case Else statement.

Enabling events for an embedded chart

As I note in the preceding section, Chart events are automatically enabled for chart sheets but not for charts embedded in a worksheet. To use events with an embedded chart, you need to perform the following steps.

Create a class module

In the Visual Basic Editor (VBE) window, select your project in the Project window and choose Insert➔Class Module. This step adds a new (empty) class module to your project. Then use the Properties window to give the class module a more descriptive name (such as clsChart). Renaming the class module isn't necessary but is a good practice.

Declare a public Chart object

The next step is to declare a Public variable that will represent the chart. The variable should be of type Chart and must be declared in the class module by using the WithEvents keyword. If you omit the WithEvents keyword, the object will not respond to events. Following is an example of such a declaration:

```
Public WithEvents clsChart As Chart
```

Connect the declared object with your chart

Before your event-handler procedures will run, you must connect the declared object in the class module with your embedded chart. You do this by declaring an object of type clsChart (or whatever your class module is named). This should be a module-level object variable, declared in a regular VBA module (not in the class module). Here's an example:

```
Dim MyChart As New clsChart
```

Then you must write code to associate the clsChart object with a particular chart. The following statement accomplishes this task:

```
Set MyChart.clsChart = ActiveSheet.ChartObjects(1).Chart
```

After this statement is executed, the clsChart object in the class module points to the first embedded chart on the active sheet. Consequently, the event-handler procedures in the class module will execute when the events occur.

Write event-handler procedures for the chart class

In this section, I describe how to write event-handler procedures in the class module. Recall that the class module must contain a declaration such as the following:

```
Public WithEvents clsChart As Chart
```

After this new object has been declared with the WithEvents keyword, it appears in the Object drop-down list box in the class module. When you select the new object in the Object box, the valid events for that object are listed in the Procedure drop-down box on the right.

The following example is a simple event-handler procedure that is executed when the embedded chart is activated. This procedure simply pops up a message box that displays the name of the Chart object's parent (which is a ChartObject object).

```
Private Sub clsChart_Activate()
    MsgBox clsChart.Parent.Name & " was activated!"
End Sub
```

On the Web

The book's website contains a workbook that demonstrates the concepts that I describe in this section. The file is events – embedded chart.xlsm.

Example: Using Chart events with an embedded chart

The example in this section provides a practical demonstration of the information presented in the previous section. The example shown in Figure 16-19 consists of an embedded chart that functions as a clickable image map. When chart events are enabled, clicking one of the chart columns activates a worksheet that shows detailed data for the region.

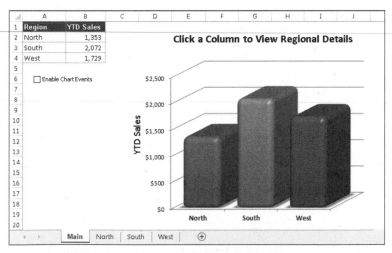

Figure 16-19: This chart serves as a clickable image map.

The workbook is set up with four worksheets. The sheet named Main contains the embedded chart. The other sheets are named North, South, and West. Formulas in B2:B4 sum the data in the respective sheets, and this summary data is plotted in the chart. Clicking a column in the chart triggers an event, and the event-handler procedure activates the appropriate sheet so that the user can view the details for the desired region.

The workbook contains both a class module named EmbChartClass and a normal VBA module named Module1. For demonstration purposes, the Main worksheet also contains a check box control (from the Forms group). Clicking the check box executes the CheckBox1_Click procedure, which turns event monitoring on and off:

In addition, each of the other worksheets contains a button that executes the ReturnToMain macro that reactivates the Main sheet.

The complete listing of Module1 follows:

```
Dim SummaryChart As New EmbChartClass

Sub CheckBox1_Click()
    If Worksheets("Main").CheckBoxes("Check Box 1") = xlOn Then
        'Enable chart events
        Range("A1").Select
        Set SummaryChart.myChartClass = _
          Worksheets(1).ChartObjects(1).Chart
    Else
        'Disable chart events
        Set SummaryChart.myChartClass = Nothing
        Range("A1").Select
    End If
End Sub

Sub ReturnToMain()
'   Called by worksheet button
    Sheets("Main").Activate
End Sub
```

The first instruction declares a new object variable SummaryChart to be of type EmbChartClass — which, as you recall, is the name of the class module. When the user clicks the Enable Chart Events button, the embedded chart is assigned to the SummaryChart object, which, in effect, enables the events for the chart. The contents of the class module for EmbChartClass follow:

```
Public WithEvents myChartClass As Chart

Private Sub myChartClass_MouseDown(ByVal Button As Long, _
  ByVal Shift As Long, ByVal X As Long, ByVal Y As Long)

    Dim IDnum As Long
    Dim a As Long, b As Long

'   The next statement returns values for
'   IDnum, a, and b
    myChartClass.GetChartElement X, Y, IDnum, a, b

'   Was a series clicked?
```

```
        If IDnum = xlSeries Then
            Select Case b
                Case 1
                    Sheets("North").Activate
                Case 2
                    Sheets("South").Activate
                Case 3
                    Sheets("West").Activate
            End Select
        End If
        Range("A1").Select
End Sub
```

Clicking the chart generates a MouseDown event, which executes the myChartClass_MouseDown procedure. This procedure uses the GetChartElement method to determine what element of the chart was clicked. The GetChartElement method returns information about the chart element at specified X and Y coordinates (information that is available through the arguments for the myChartClass_MouseDown procedure).

On the Web

This workbook, named chart image map.xlsm, is available on the book's website.

Discovering VBA Charting Tricks

This section contains a few charting tricks that I've discovered over the years. Some of these techniques might be useful in your applications, and others are simply for fun. At the very least, studying them could give you some new insights into the object model for charts.

Printing embedded charts on a full page

When an embedded chart is selected, you can print the chart by choosing File➡Print. The embedded chart will be printed on a full page by itself (just as if it were on a chart sheet), yet it will remain an embedded chart.

The following macro prints all embedded charts on the active sheet, and each chart is printed on a full page:

```
Sub PrintEmbeddedCharts()
    Dim ChtObj As ChartObject
    For Each ChtObj In ActiveSheet.ChartObjects
        ChtObj.Chart.PrintOut
    Next ChtObj
End Sub
```

Hiding series by hiding columns

By default, Excel charts don't display data contained in hidden rows or columns. The workbook shown in Figure 16-20 demonstrates an easy way to allow the user to hide and unhide particular chart series. The chart has seven data series, and it's a confusing mess.

Figure 16-20: Using CheckBox controls to specify which data series to display.

A few simple macros allow the user to use the ActiveX CheckBox to indicate which series they'd like to view. Figure 16-21 shows the chart with only three series displayed.

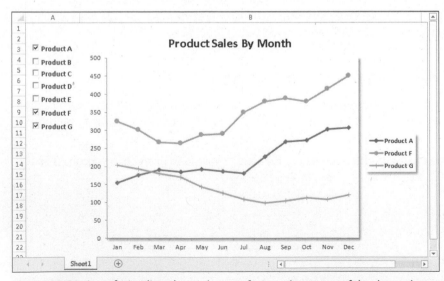

Figure 16-21: A confusing line chart is less confusing when some of the data columns are hidden.

Each series is in a named range: Product_A, Product_B, and so on. Each check box has its own Click event procedure. For example, the procedure that's executed when the user clicks the Product A check box is

```
Private Sub CheckBox1_Click()
    ActiveSheet.Range("Product_A").EntireColumn.Hidden = _
      Not ActiveSheet.OLEObjects(1).Object.Value
End Sub
```

Note

Excel 2013 includes a new feature that makes it easy to hide and unhide chart series. When a chart is selected, three icons appear to the right of the chart. The third icon, Chart Filters, contains a checkbox for each data series. Just deselect the series name to hide the series. You can also hide and unhide specific data points.

On the Web

This workbook, named hide and unhide series.xlsm, is available at this book's Web site.

Creating unlinked charts

Normally, an Excel chart uses data stored in a range. Change the data in the range, and the chart is updated automatically. In some cases, you might want to unlink the chart from its data ranges and produce a *dead chart* (a chart that never changes). For example, if you plot data generated by various what-if scenarios, you might want to save a chart that represents some baseline so that you can compare it with other scenarios.

The three ways to create such a chart are

> ➤ **Copy the chart as a picture.** Activate the chart and choose Home➜Clipboard➜Copy➜Copy As Picture. Accept the defaults in the Copy Picture dialog box. Then click a cell and choose Home➜Clipboard➜Paste. The result will be a picture of the copied chart.

> ➤ **Convert the range references to arrays.** Click a chart series and then click the formula bar. Press F9 to convert the ranges to an array, and press Enter. Repeat these steps for each series in the chart.

> ➤ **Use VBA to assign an array rather than a range to the XValues or Values properties of the Series object.** This technique is described next.

The following procedure creates a chart (see Figure 16-22) by using arrays. The data isn't stored in the worksheet. As you can see, the SERIES formula contains arrays and not range references.

```
Sub CreateUnlinkedChart()
    Dim MyChart As Chart
    Set MyChart = ActiveSheet.Shapes.AddChart2.Chart
    With MyChart
        .SeriesCollection.NewSeries
        .SeriesCollection(1).Name = "Sales"
        .SeriesCollection(1).XValues = Array("Jan", "Feb", "Mar")
        .SeriesCollection(1).Values = Array(125, 165, 189)
        .ChartType = xlColumnClustered
        .SetElement msoElementLegendNone
    End With
End Sub
```

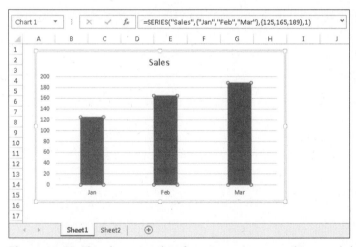

Figure 16-22: This chart uses data from arrays (not stored in a worksheet).

Because Excel imposes a limit to the length of a chart's SERIES formula, this technique works for only relatively small data sets.

The following procedure creates a picture of the active chart. (The original chart isn't deleted.) It works only with embedded charts.

```
Sub ConvertChartToPicture()
    Dim Cht As Chart
    If ActiveChart Is Nothing Then Exit Sub
    If TypeName(ActiveSheet) = "Chart" Then Exit Sub
    Set Cht = ActiveChart
```

```
    Cht.CopyPicture Appearance:=xlPrinter, _
        Size:=xlScreen, Format:=xlPicture
    ActiveWindow.RangeSelection.Select
    ActiveSheet.Paste
End Sub
```

When a chart is converted to a picture, you can create some interesting displays by choosing Picture Tools➜Format➜Picture Styles. See Figure 16-23 for an example.

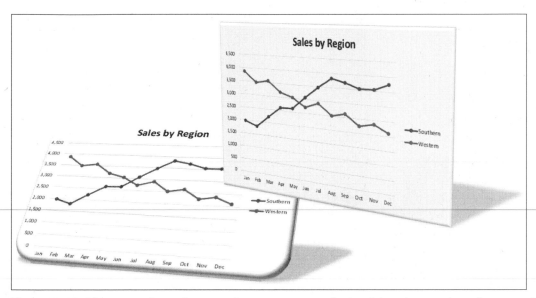

Figure 16-23: After converting a chart to a picture, you can manipulate it by using a variety of commands.

The two examples in this section are available on the book's website in the unlinked charts.xlsm file.

Displaying text with the MouseOver event

A common charting question deals with modifying chart tips. A *chart tip* is the small message that appears next to the mouse pointer when you move the mouse over an activated chart. The chart tip displays the chart element name and (for series) the value of the data point. The Chart object model does not expose these chart tips, so there is no way to modify them.

To turn chart tips on or off, choose File➜Options to display the Excel Options dialog box. Click the Advanced tab and locate the Chart section. The options are labeled Show Chart Element Names on Hover and Show Data Point Values on Hover.

This section describes an alternative to chart tips. Figure 16-24 shows a column chart that uses the MouseOver event. When the mouse pointer is positioned over a column, the text box (a Shape object) in the upper-left displays information about the data point. The information is stored in a range and can consist of anything you like.

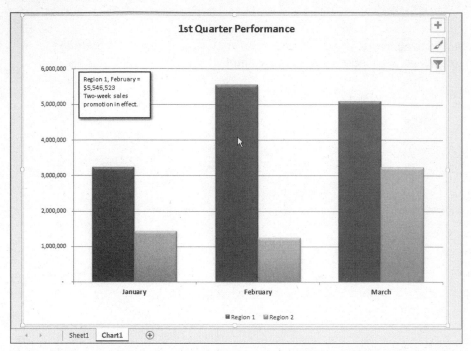

Figure 16-24: A text box displays information about the data point under the mouse pointer.

The event procedure that follows is located in the code module for the Chart sheet that contains the chart.

```
Private Sub Chart_MouseMove(ByVal Button As Long, ByVal Shift As Long, _
  ByVal X As Long, ByVal Y As Long)
    Dim ElementId As Long
    Dim arg1 As Long, arg2 As Long
    On Error Resume Next
    ActiveChart.GetChartElement X, Y, ElementId, arg1, arg2
    If ElementId = xlSeries Then
        ActiveChart.Shapes(1).Visible = msoCTrue
        ActiveChart.Shapes(1).TextFrame.Characters.Text = _
          Sheets("Sheet1").Range("Comments").Offset(arg2, arg1)
    Else
        ActiveChart.Shapes(1).Visible = msoFalse
    End If
End Sub
```

This procedure monitors all mouse movements on the Chart sheet. The mouse coordinates are contained in the X and Y variables, which are passed to the procedure. The Button and Shift arguments aren't used in this procedure.

As in the previous example, the key component in this procedure is the GetChartElement method. If ElementId is xlSeries, the mouse pointer is over a series. The TextBox is made visible and displays the text in a particular cell. This text contains descriptive information about the data point (see Figure 16-25). If the mouse pointer isn't over a series, the text box is hidden.

▲	A	B	C	D
1	**Month**	**Region 1**	**Region 2**	
2	January	3,245,151	1,434,343	
3	February	5,546,523	1,238,709	
4	March	5,083,204	3,224,855	
5				
6	**Comments**			
7		Region 1, January = $3,245,151	Region 2, January = $1,434,343	
8		Region 1, February = $5,546,523 Two-week sales promotion in effect.	Region 2, February = $1,238,709	
9		Region 1, March = $5,083,204	Region 2, March = $3,224,855 L.A. merger took place in week three.	
10				
11				

Sheet1 | Chart1 | ⊕

Figure 16-25: Range B7:C9 contains data point information that's displayed in the text box on the chart.

The example workbook also contains a Chart_Activate event procedure that turns off the normal ChartTip display, and a Chart_Deactivate procedure that turns the settings back on. The Chart_Activate procedure is

```
Private Sub Chart_Activate()
    Application.ShowChartTipNames = False
    Application.ShowChartTipValues = False
End Sub
```

On the Web

The book's website contains this example set up for an embedded chart (mouseover event - embedded.xlsm) and for a chart sheet (mouseover event - chart sheet.xlsm).

Animating Charts

Most people don't realize it, but Excel is capable of performing simple animations. For example, you can animate shapes and charts. Consider the XY chart shown in Figure 16-26.

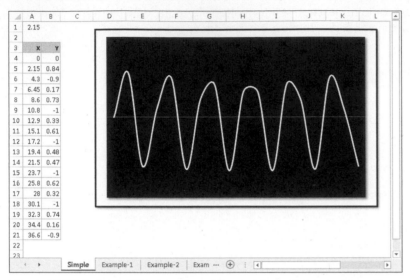

Figure 16-26: A simple VBA procedure will turn this graph into an interesting animation.

The X values (column A) depend on the value in cell A1. The value in each row is the previous row's value plus the value in A1. Column B contains formulas that calculate the SIN of the corresponding value in column A. The following simple procedure produces an interesting animation. It uses a loop to continually change the value in cell A1, which causes the values in the X and Y ranges to change. The effect is an animated chart.

```
Sub SimpleAnimation()
    Dim i As Long
    Range("A1") = 0
    For i = 1 To 150
        DoEvents
        Range("A1") = Range("A1") + 0.035
        DoEvents
    Next i
    Range("A1") = 0
End Sub
```

The key to chart animation is to use one or more DoEvents statements. This statement passes control to the operating system, which (apparently) causes the chart to be updated when control is passed back to Excel. Without the DoEvents statements, the chart's changes would not be displayed inside of the loop.

On the Web

The book's website contains a workbook that includes this animated chart, plus several other animation examples. The filename is animated charts.xlsm.

Scrolling a chart

Figure 16-27 shows a chart with 5,218 data points in each series. The chart shows only a portion of the data, but it can be scrolled to show additional values.

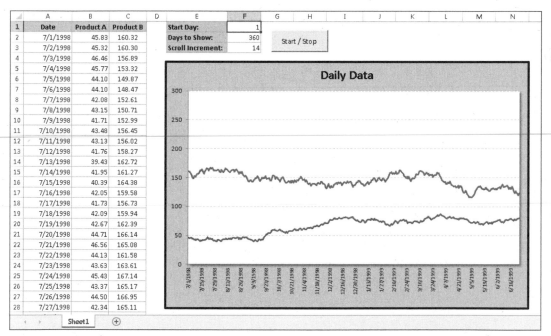

Figure 16-27: The values in column F determine which data to display in the chart.

The workbook contains six names:

> StartDay: A name for cell F1

> NumDays: A name for cell F2

> Increment: A name for cell F3 (used for automatic scrolling)

➤ Date: A named formula:

```
=OFFSET(Sheet1!$A$1,StartDay,0,NumDays,1)
```

➤ ProdA: A named formula:

```
=OFFSET(Sheet1!$B$1,StartDay,0,NumDays,1)
```

➤ ProdB: A named formula:

```
=OFFSET(Sheet1!$C$1,StartDay,0,NumDays,1)
```

Each SERIES formula in the chart uses names for the category values and the data. The SERIES formula for the Product A series is as follows (I deleted the sheet name and workbook name for clarity):

```
=SERIES($B$1,Date,ProdA,1)
```

The SERIES formula for the Product B series is

```
=SERIES($C$1,Date,ProdB,2)
```

Using these names enables the user to specify a value for StartDay and NumDays. The chart will display a subset of the data.

On the Web

The book's website contains a workbook that includes this animated chart. The filename is scrolling chart.xlsm.

A relatively simple macro makes the chart scroll. The button in the worksheet executes the following macro that scrolls (or stops scrolling) the chart:

```
Public AnimationInProgress As Boolean

Sub AnimateChart()
    Dim StartVal As Long, r As Long
    If AnimationInProgress Then
        AnimationInProgress = False
        End
    End If
    AnimationInProgress = True
    StartVal = Range("StartDay")
    For r = StartVal To 5219 - Range("NumDays")Step Range("Increment")
        Range("StartDay") = r
        DoEvents
    Next r
    AnimationInProgress = False
End Sub
```

The AnimateChart procedure uses a public variable (AnimationInProgress) to keep track of the animation status. The animation results from a loop that changes the value in the StartDay cell. Because the two chart series use this value, the chart is continually updated with a new starting value. The Scroll Increment setting determines how quickly the chart scrolls.

To stop the animation, I use an End statement rather than an Exit Sub statement. For some reason, Exit Sub doesn't work reliably and may even crash Excel.

Creating a hypocycloid chart

Even if you hated your high school trigonometry class, you'll probably like the example in this section, which relies heavily on trigonometric functions. The workbook shown in Figure 16-28 contains an XY chart that displays a nearly infinite number of dazzling hypocycloid curves. A *hypocycloid* curve is the path formed by a point on a circle that rolls inside of another circle. This, as you may recall from your childhood, is the same technique used in Hasbro's popular Spirograph toy.

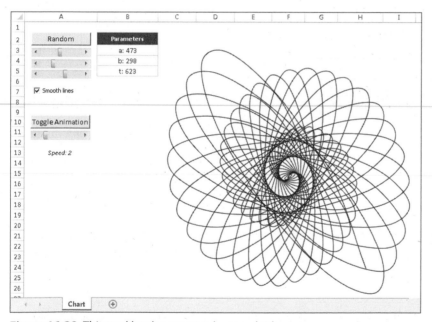

Figure 16-28: This workbook generates hypocycloid curves.

On the Web

This workbook is available on the book's website. The filename is hypocycloid - animate. xlsm.

The chart is an XY chart, and all chart elements are hidden except the data series. The X and Y data are generated by using formulas stored in cells to the right (not visible in the figure). The scroll bar controls at the top let you adjust the three parameters that drive the formulas and determine the look of the chart. In addition, clicking the Random button generates random values for the three parameters.

The chart itself is interesting enough, but it gets *really* interesting when it's animated. The animation occurs by changing the starting value for the series within a loop.

Creating a clock chart

Figure 16-29 shows an XY chart formatted to look like a clock. It not only looks like a clock but also functions as a clock. I can't think of a single reason why anyone would need to display a clock like this on a worksheet, but creating the workbook was challenging, and you might find it instructive.

Figure 16-29: This clock is fully functional and is actually an XY chart in disguise.

On the Web This workbook, named **vba clock chart.xlsm**, is available on the book's website.

Besides the clock chart, the workbook contains a text box that displays the time as a normal string, as shown in Figure 16-30. Normally the text box is hidden, but you can display it by deselecting the Analog Clock check box.

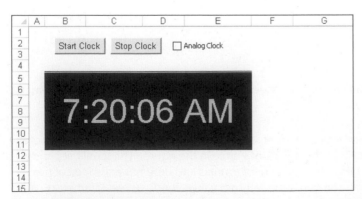

Figure 16-30: Displaying a digital clock in a worksheet is much easier but not as much fun to create.

As you explore this workbook, here are a few things to keep in mind:

➤ The ChartObject is named ClockChart, and it covers up a range named DigitalClock, which is used to display the time digitally.

➤ The two buttons on the worksheet are from the Forms toolbar, and each has a macro assigned (StartClock and StopClock).

➤ The CheckBox control (named cbClockType) on the worksheet is from the Forms toolbar — not from the Control Toolbox toolbar. Clicking the object executes a procedure named cbClockType_Click, which simply toggles the Visible property of ChartObject. When ChartObject is invisible, the digital clock is revealed.

➤ The chart is an XY chart with four Series objects. These series represent the hour hand, the minute hand, the second hand, and the 12 numbers. The numbers are data labels for the fourth series.

➤ The UpdateClock procedure is executed when the Start Clock button is clicked. The procedure also uses the OnTime method of the Application object to set up a new OnTime event that will occur in one second. In other words, the UpdateClock procedure is called every second.

➤ Unlike most charts, this one doesn't use any worksheet ranges for its data. Rather, the values are calculated in VBA and transferred directly to the Values and XValues properties of the chart's Series object.

Caution

Although this clock is an interesting demo, displaying a continually updating clock in a worksheet isn't feasible. The VBA macro must be running at all times in the background, which may interfere with other macros and reduce overall performance.

Creating an Interactive Chart without VBA

The example shown in Figure 16-31 is a useful application that allows the user to choose two U.S. cities (from a list of 284 cities) and view a chart that compares the cities by month in any of the following categories: average precipitation, average temperature, percent sunshine, and average wind speed.

The most interesting aspect of this application is that it uses no VBA macros. The interactivity is a result of using Excel's built-in features. The cities are chosen from a drop-down list, using Excel's Data Validation feature, and the data option is selected using four Option Button controls, which are linked to a cell. The pieces are all connected using a few formulas.

This example demonstrates that it is indeed possible to create a user-friendly, interactive application without the assistance of macros.

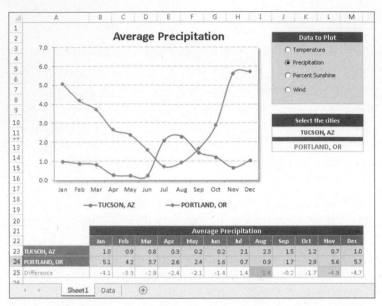

Figure 16-31: This application uses a variety of techniques (but no VBA code) to plot monthly climate data for two selected U.S. cities.

On the Web

This workbook, named climate data.xlsx, is available on the book's website.

The following sections describe the steps I took to set up this application.

Getting the data to create an interactive chart

I did a Web search and spent about five minutes locating the data I needed at the National Climatic Data Center. I copied the data from my browser window, pasted it in an Excel worksheet, and did a bit of clean-up work. The result was four 13-column tables of data, which I named PrecipitationData, TemperatureData, SunshineData, and WindData. To keep the interface as clean as possible, I put the data on a separate sheet (named Data).

Creating the Option Button controls for an interactive chart

I needed a way to allow the user to select the data to plot and decided to use OptionButton controls from the Forms group of controls. Because option buttons work as a group, the four OptionButton controls are all linked to the same cell: cell O3. Cell O3, therefore, contains a value from 1 to 4, depending on which option button is selected.

I needed a way to obtain the name of the data table based on the numeric value in cell O3. The solution was to write a formula (in cell O4) that uses Excel's CHOOSE function:

```
=CHOOSE(O3,"TemperatureData","PrecipitationData","SunshineData","WindData")
```

Therefore, cell O4 displays the name of one of the four named data tables. I then did some cell formatting behind the OptionButton controls to make them more visible.

Creating the city lists for the interactive chart

The next step is setting up the application: creating drop-down lists to enable the user to choose the cities to be compared in the chart. Excel's Data Validation feature makes creating a drop-down list in a cell easy. First, I did some cell merging to create a wider field. I merged cells J11:M11 for the first city list and gave them the name City1. I merged cells J13:M13 for the second city list and gave them the name City2.

To make working with the list of cities easier, I created a named range, CityList, which refers to the first column in the PrecipitationData table.

Following are the steps that I used to create the drop-down lists:

1. Select J11:M11.

   (Remember, these are merged cells.)

2. Choose Data➜Data Validation to display Excel's Data Validation dialog box.

3. Select the Settings tab in the Data Validation dialog box.

4. In the Allow field, choose List.

5. In the Source field, enter **=CityList**.

6. Click OK.

7. Copy J11:M11 to J13:M13.

   This duplicates the Data Validation settings for the second city.

Figure 16-32 shows the result.

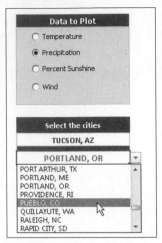

Figure 16-32: Use the Data Validation drop-down list to select a city.

Creating the interactive chart data range

The key to this application is that the chart uses data in a specific range. The data in this range is retrieved from the appropriate data table by using formulas that utilize the VLOOKUP function (see Figure 16-33).

	A	B	C	D	E	F	G	H	I	J	K	L	M
20													
21						Average Precipitation							
22		Jan	Feb	Mar	Apr	May	Jun	Jul	Aug	Sep	Oct	Nov	Dec
23	TUCSON, AZ	1.0	0.9	0.8	0.3	0.2	0.2	2.1	2.3	1.5	1.2	0.7	1.0
24	PORTLAND, OR	5.1	4.2	3.7	2.6	2.4	1.6	0.7	0.9	1.7	2.9	5.6	5.7
25	Difference	-4.1	-3.3	-2.9	-2.4	-2.1	-1.4	1.4	1.4	-0.2	-1.7	-4.9	-4.7
26													

Figure 16-33: The chart uses the data retrieved by formulas in A23:M24.

The formula in cell A23, which looks up data based on the contents of City1, is

```
=VLOOKUP(City1,INDIRECT(DataTable),COLUMN(),FALSE)
```

The formula in cell A24 is the same except that it looks up data based on the contents of City2:

```
=VLOOKUP(City2,INDIRECT(DataTable),COLUMN(),FALSE)
```

After entering these formulas, I simply copied them across to the next 12 columns.

Note

You may be wondering about the use of the COLUMN function for the third argument of the VLOOKUP function. This function returns the column number of the cell that contains the formula. This method avoids hard coding the column to be retrieved and allows the same formula to be used in each column.

Row 25 contains formulas that calculate the difference between the two cities for each month. I used conditional formatting to apply a different color background for the largest difference and the smallest difference.

The label above the month names is generated by a formula that refers to the DataTable cell and constructs a descriptive title: The formula is

```
="Average " & LEFT(DataTable,LEN(DataTable)-4)
```

Creating the interactive chart

After completing the previous tasks, the final step — creating the actual chart — is a breeze. The line chart has two data series and uses the data in A22:M24. The chart title is linked to cell B21. The data in A23:M24 changes, of course, whenever an OptionButton control is selected or a new city is selected from either Data Validation list.

Working with Sparkline Charts

I conclude this chapter with a brief discussion of Sparkline charts, a feature introduced in Excel 2010. A *Sparkline* is a small chart displayed in a cell. A Sparkline lets the viewer quickly spot time-based trends or variations in data. Because they're so compact, Sparklines are often used in a group.

Figure 16-34 shows examples of the three types of Sparklines supported by Excel.

Rather, you need to use the Cells property (which returns a range object):

```
MsgBox Cells.SparklineGroups.Count
```

The following example lists the address of each Sparkline group on the active worksheet:

```
Sub ListSparklineGroups()
    Dim sg As SparklineGroup
    Dim i As Long
    For i = 1 To Cells.SparklineGroups.Count
        Set sg = Cells.SparklineGroups(i)
        MsgBox sg.Location.Address
    Next i
End Sub
```

⧫	A	B	C	D	E	F	G	H
1	Line Sparklines							
2								
3	Fund Number	Jan	Feb	Mar	Apr	May	Jun	Sparklines
4	A-13	103.98	98.92	88.12	86.34	75.58	71.2	
5	C-09	212.74	218.7	202.18	198.56	190.12	181.74	
6	K-88	75.74	73.68	69.86	60.34	64.92	59.46	
7	W-91	91.78	95.44	98.1	99.46	98.68	105.86	
8	M-03	324.48	309.14	313.1	287.82	276.24	260.9	
9								
10	Column Sparklines							
11								
12	Fund Number	Jan	Feb	Mar	Apr	May	Jun	Sparklines
13	A-13	103.98	98.92	88.12	86.34	75.58	71.2	
14	C-09	212.74	218.7	202.18	198.56	190.12	181.74	
15	K-88	75.74	73.68	69.86	60.34	64.92	59.46	
16	W-91	91.78	95.44	98.1	99.46	98.68	105.86	
17	M-03	324.48	309.14	313.1	287.82	276.24	260.9	
18								
19	Win/Loss Sparklines							
20								
21	Fund Number	Jan	Feb	Mar	Apr	May	Jun	Sparklines
22	A-13	#N/A	-5.06	-10.8	-1.78	-10.76	-4.38	
23	C-09	#N/A	5.96	-16.52	-3.62	-8.44	-8.38	
24	K-88	#N/A	-2.06	-3.82	-9.52	4.58	-5.46	
25	W-91	#N/A	3.66	2.66	1.36	-0.78	7.18	
26	M-03	#N/A	-15.34	3.96	-25.28	-11.58	-15.34	
27								

Figure 16-34: Sparkline examples.

For some reason, you can't use the For Each construct to loop through the objects in the SparklineGroups collection. You need to refer to the objects by their index number.

Following is another example of working with Sparklines in VBA. The SparklineReport procedure lists information about each Sparkline on the active sheet.

```
Sub SparklineReport()
    Dim sg As SparklineGroup
    Dim sl As Sparkline
    Dim SGType As String
    Dim SLSheet As Worksheet
    Dim i As Long, j As Long, r As Long

    If Cells.SparklineGroups.Count = 0 Then
        MsgBox "No sparklines were found on the active sheet."
        Exit Sub
```

```
    End If

    Set SLSheet = ActiveSheet
'   Insert new worksheet for the report
    Worksheets.Add

'   Headings
    With Range("A1")
        .Value = "Sparkline Report: " & SLSheet.Name & " in " _
            & SLSheet.Parent.Name
        .Font.Bold = True
        .Font.Size = 16
    End With
    With Range("A3:F3")
        .Value = Array("Group #", "Sparkline Grp Range", _
            "# in Group", "Type", "Sparkline #", "Source Range")
        .Font.Bold = True
    End With
    r = 4

    'Loop through each sparkline group
    For i = 1 To SLSheet.Cells.SparklineGroups.Count
        Set sg = SLSheet.Cells.SparklineGroups(i)
        Select Case sg.Type
            Case 1: SGType = "Line"
            Case 2: SGType = "Column"
            Case 3: SGType = "Win/Loss"
        End Select
        ' Loop through each sparkline in the group
        For j = 1 To sg.Count
            Set sl = sg.Item(j)
            Cells(r, 1) = i 'Group #
            Cells(r, 2) = sg.Location.Address
            Cells(r, 3) = sg.Count
            Cells(r, 4) = SGType
            Cells(r, 5) = j 'Sparkline # within Group
            Cells(r, 6) = sl.SourceData
            r = r + 1
        Next j
        r = r + 1
    Next i
End Sub
```

Figure 16-35 shows the report generated for the worksheet in Figure 16-34.

	A	B	C	D	E	F
1	**Sparkline Report: Sheet1 in sparkline examples.xlsx**					
2						
3	**Group #**	**Sparkline Grp Range**	**# in Group**	**Type**	**Sparkline #**	**Source Range**
4	1	$H$22:$H$26	5	Win/Loss	1	B22:G22
5	1	$H$22:$H$26	5	Win/Loss	2	B23:G23
6	1	$H$22:$H$26	5	Win/Loss	3	B24:G24
7	1	$H$22:$H$26	5	Win/Loss	4	B25:G25
8	1	$H$22:$H$26	5	Win/Loss	5	B26:G26
9						
10	2	$H$13:$H$17	5	Column	1	B13:G13
11	2	$H$13:$H$17	5	Column	2	B14:G14
12	2	$H$13:$H$17	5	Column	3	B15:G15
13	2	$H$13:$H$17	5	Column	4	B16:G16
14	2	$H$13:$H$17	5	Column	5	B17:G17
15						
16	3	$H$4:$H$8	5	Line	1	B4:G4
17	3	$H$4:$H$8	5	Line	2	B5:G5
18	3	$H$4:$H$8	5	Line	3	B6:G6
19	3	$H$4:$H$8	5	Line	4	B7:G7
20	3	$H$4:$H$8	5	Line	5	B8:G8
21						
22						

Figure 16-35: The result of running the SparklineReport procedure.

On the Web

This workbook, named sparkline report.xlsm, is available on the book's website.

Understanding Excel's Events

In This Chapter

- Recognizing the types of events that Excel can monitor
- Figuring out what you need to know to work with events
- Exploring examples of Workbook events, Worksheet events, Chart events, and UserForm events
- Using Application events to monitor all open workbooks
- Seeing examples of processing time-based events and keystroke events

What You Should Know about Events

In several earlier chapters in this book, I present examples of VBA *event-handler procedures*, which are specially named procedures that are executed when a specific event occurs. An example is the CommandButton1_Click procedure, which is executed when the user clicks an object named CommandButton1 stored on a UserForm or on a worksheet. Clicking the button is an event that triggers the execution of the event-handler VBA code.

Excel is programmed to monitor many different events. These events can be classified as

➤ **Workbook events:** Events that occur for a particular workbook. Examples of such events include Open (the workbook is opened or created), BeforeSave (the workbook is about to be saved), and NewSheet (a new sheet is added).

➤ **Worksheet events:** Events that occur for a particular worksheet. Examples include Change (a cell on the sheet is changed), SelectionChange (the user moves the cell indicator), and Calculate (the worksheet is recalculated).

➤ **Chart events:** Events that occur for a particular chart. These events include Select (an object in the chart is selected) and SeriesChange (a value of a data point in a series is changed). To monitor events for an embedded chart, you use a class module, as I demonstrate in Chapter 16.

➤ **Application events:** Events that occur for the application (Excel). Examples include NewWorkbook (a new workbook is created), WorkbookBeforeClose (any workbook is about to be closed), and SheetChange (a cell in any open workbook is altered). To monitor Application-level events, you need to use a class module.

➤ **UserForm events:** Events that occur for a particular UserForm or an object contained on the UserForm. For example, a UserForm has an Initialize event (occurs before the UserForm is displayed), and a CommandButton on a UserForm has a Click event (occurs when the button is clicked).

➤ **Events not associated with objects:** The final category consists of two useful Application-level events that I call On events: OnTime and OnKey. These work in a different manner than other events.

This chapter is organized according to the preceding list. Within each section, I provide examples to demonstrate some of the events.

Understanding event sequences

Some actions trigger multiple events. For example, when you insert a new worksheet into a workbook, three Application-level events are triggered:

➤ WorkbookNewSheet: Occurs when a new worksheet is added

➤ SheetDeactivate: Occurs when the active worksheet is deactivated

➤ SheetActivate: Occurs when the newly added worksheet is activated

Note

Event sequencing is a bit more complicated than you might think. The preceding events are Application-level events. When adding a new worksheet, additional events occur at the Workbook level and at the Worksheet level.

At this point, just keep in mind that events fire in a particular sequence, and knowing that sequence may be critical when writing event-handler procedures. Later in this chapter, I describe how to determine the order of the events that occur for a particular action (see "Monitoring Application-level events").

Where to put event-handler procedures

VBA newcomers often wonder why their event-handler procedures aren't being executed when the corresponding event occurs. The answer is almost always because these procedures are located in the wrong place.

In the Visual Basic Editor (VBE) window, each project (one project per workbook) is listed in the Projects window. The project components are arranged in a collapsible list, as shown in Figure 17-1.

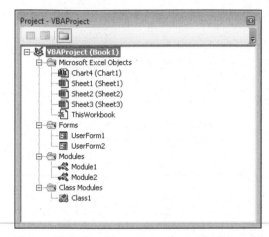

Figure 17-1: The components for each VBA project are listed in the Project window.

Each of the following components has its own code module:

> ➤ Sheet objects (for example, Sheet1, Sheet2, and so on): Use this module for event-handler code related to the particular worksheet.

> ➤ Chart objects (that is, chart sheets): Use this module for event-handler code related to the chart.

> ➤ ThisWorkbook object: Use this module for event-handler code related to the workbook.

> ➤ General VBA modules: You never put event-handler procedures in a general (that is, nonobject) module.

> ➤ UserForm objects: Use this module for event-handler code related to the UserForm or controls on the UserForm.

> ➤ Class modules: Use class modules for special-purpose event handlers, including application-level events and events for embedded charts.

Events in older versions of Excel

Versions of Excel prior to Office 97 also supported events, but the programming techniques required to take advantage of those were quite different from what I describe in this chapter.

For example, if you had a procedure named Auto_Open stored in a regular VBA module, this procedure would be executed when the workbook was opened. Beginning with Excel 97, the Auto_Open procedure was supplemented by the Workbook_Open event-handler procedure, which was stored in the code module for the ThisWorkbook object and was executed prior to Auto_Open.

Before Excel 97, you often needed to explicitly set up events. For example, if you needed to execute a procedure whenever data was entered in a cell, you would need to execute a statement such as the following:

```
Sheets("Sheet1").OnEntry = "ValidateEntry"
```

This statement instructs Excel to execute the procedure named ValidateEntry whenever data is entered in a cell. With Excel 97 and later, you simply create a procedure named Worksheet_Change and store it in the code module for the Sheet1 object.

For compatibility, Excel 97 and later versions still support the older event mechanism (although they are no longer documented in the Help system). I mention old events just in case you encounter a workbook that seems to have some odd statements.

Even though the event-handler procedure must be located in the correct module, the procedure can call other standard procedures stored in other modules. For example, the following event-handler procedure, located in the module for the ThisWorkbook object, calls a procedure named WorkbookSetup, which you can store in a regular VBA module:

```
Private Sub Workbook_Open()
    Call WorkbookSetup
End Sub
```

Disabling events

By default, all events are enabled. To disable all events, execute the following VBA instruction:

```
Application.EnableEvents = False
```

To enable events, use this one:

```
Application.EnableEvents = True
```

Note Disabling events does not apply to events triggered by UserForm controls — for example, the Click event generated by clicking a CommandButton control on a UserForm.

Why would you need to disable events? One common reason is to prevent an infinite loop of cascading events.

For example, suppose that cell A1 of your worksheet must always contain a value less than or equal to 12. You can write some code that is executed whenever data is entered in a cell to validate the cell's contents. In this case, you're monitoring the Change event for a Worksheet with a procedure named Worksheet_Change. Your procedure checks the user's entry, and, if the entry isn't less than or equal to 12, it displays a message and then clears that entry. The problem is that clearing the entry with your VBA code generates a new Change event, so your event-handler procedure is executed again. This is not what you want to happen, so you need to disable events before you clear the cell, and then enable events again so that you can monitor the user's next entry.

Another way to prevent an infinite loop of cascading events is to declare a Static Boolean variable at the beginning of your event-handler procedure, such as this:

```
Static AbortProc As Boolean
```

Whenever the procedure needs to make its own changes, set the AbortProc variable to True (otherwise, make sure that it's set to False). Insert the following code at the top of the procedure:

```
If AbortProc Then
    AbortProc = False
    Exit Sub
End if
```

The event procedure is reentered, but the True state of AbortProc causes the procedure to end. In addition, AbortProc is reset to False.

Cross-Ref For a practical example of validating data, see "Monitoring a range to validate data entry," later in this chapter.

Caution Disabling events in Excel applies to all workbooks. For example, if you disable events in your procedure and then open another workbook that has, say, a Workbook_Open procedure, that procedure will not execute.

Entering event-handler code

Every event-handler procedure has a predetermined name, and you can't change those names. Following are some examples of event-handler procedure names:

- ➤ Worksheet_SelectionChange
- ➤ Workbook_Open
- ➤ Chart_Activate
- ➤ Class_Initialize

You can declare the procedure by typing it manually, but a much better approach is to let VBE declare it for you.

Figure 17-2 shows the code module for the ThisWorkbook object. To insert a procedure declaration, select Workbook from the objects list on the left. Then select the event from the procedures list on the right. When you do so, you get a procedure shell that contains the procedure declaration line and an End Sub statement.

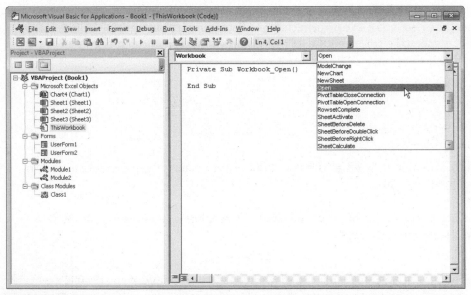

Figure 17-2: The best way to create an event procedure is to let VBE do it for you.

For example, if you select Workbook from the objects list and Open from the procedures list, VBE inserts the following (empty) procedure:

```
Private Sub Workbook_Open()

End Sub
```

Your VBA code, of course, goes between these two statements.

Note   Note that as soon as you select an item from the objects list (for example, Workbook or Worksheet), VBE inserts a procedure declaration automatically. Usually, the procedure definition is not the one you want. Simply choose the event you want from the procedures list on the right, and then delete the one that was generated automatically.

Event-handler procedures that use arguments

Some event-handler procedures use an argument list. For example, you may need to create an event-handler procedure to monitor the SheetActivate event for a workbook. If you use the technique described in the preceding section, VBE creates the following procedure in the code module for the ThisWorkbook object:

```
Private Sub Workbook_SheetActivate(ByVal Sh As Object)

End Sub
```

This procedure uses one argument (Sh), which represents the sheet that was activated. In this case, Sh is declared as an Object data type rather than a Worksheet data type because the activated sheet can also be a chart sheet.

Your code can use the data passed as an argument. The following procedure is executed whenever a sheet is activated. It displays the type and name of the activated sheet by using VBA's TypeName function and accessing the Name property of the object passed in the argument:

```
Private Sub Workbook_SheetActivate(ByVal Sh As Object)
    MsgBox TypeName(Sh) & vbCrLf & Sh.Name
End Sub
```

Figure 17-3 shows the message that appears when Sheet3 is activated.

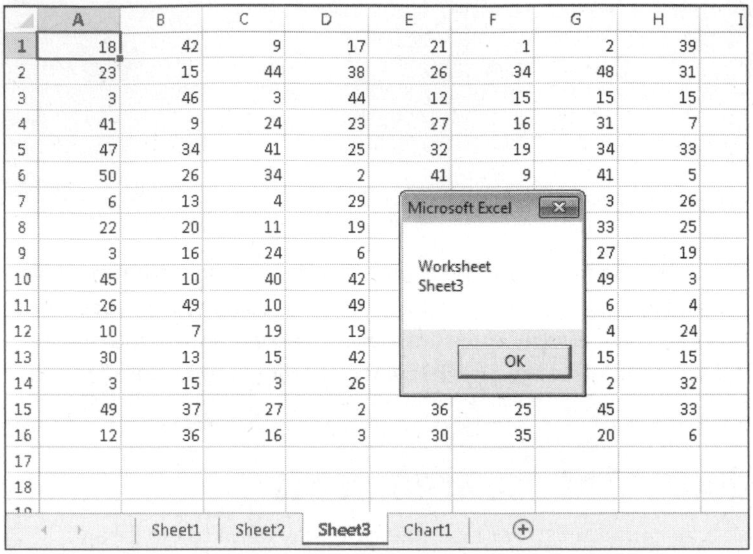

Figure 17-3: This message box was triggered by a SheetActivate event.

Several event-handler procedures use a Boolean argument named Cancel. For example, the declaration for a workbook's BeforePrint event is as follows:

```
Private Sub Workbook_BeforePrint(Cancel As Boolean)
```

The value of Cancel passed to the procedure is False. However, your code can set Cancel to True, which will cancel the printing. The following example demonstrates this:

```
Private Sub Workbook_BeforePrint(Cancel As Boolean)
    Dim Msg As String, Ans As Integer
    Msg = "Have you loaded the 5164 label stock?"
    Ans = MsgBox(Msg, vbYesNo, "About to print...")
    If Ans = vbNo Then Cancel = True
End Sub
```

The Workbook_BeforePrint procedure is executed before the workbook is printed. This routine displays the message box shown in Figure 17-4. If the user clicks the No button, Cancel is set to True, and nothing is printed.

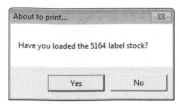

Figure 17-4: Clicking No cancels the print operation by changing the Cancel argument in the event-handler procedure.

Tip

The BeforePrint event also occurs when the user previews a worksheet.

Unfortunately, Excel doesn't provide a sheet-level BeforePrint event. Therefore, your code can't determine which sheet is about to be printed. Often, you can assume that the ActiveSheet is the sheet that will be printed. However, there is no way to detect if the user requests that the entire workbook be printed.

Getting Acquainted with Workbook-Level Events

Workbook-level events occur in a particular workbook. Table 17-1 lists the commonly used workbook events, along with a brief description of each. Consult the Help system for a complete list of Workbook-level events. Workbook event-handler procedures are stored in the code module for the ThisWorkbook object.

Table 17-1: Commonly Used Workbook Events

Event	Action That Triggers the Event
Activate	A workbook is activated.
AddinInstall	A workbook is installed as an add-in.
AddinUninstall	A workbook is uninstalled as an add-in.
AfterSave	A workbook has been saved.
BeforeClose	A workbook is about to be closed.
BeforePrint	A workbook (or anything in it) is about to be printed or previewed.
BeforeSave	A workbook is about to be saved.
Deactivate	A workbook is deactivated.
NewSheet	A new sheet is created in a workbook.

continued

Table 17-1: Commonly Used Workbook Events *(continued)*

Event	Action That Triggers the Event
Open	A workbook is opened.
SheetActivate	Any sheet is activated.
SheetBeforeDoubleClick	Any worksheet is double-clicked. This event occurs before the default double-click action.
SheetBeforeRightClick	Any worksheet is right-clicked. This event occurs before the default right-click action.
SheetCalculate	Any worksheet is calculated (or recalculated).
SheetChange	Any worksheet is changed by the user or by an external link.
SheetDeactivate	Any sheet is deactivated.
SheetFollowHyperlink	A hyperlink on a sheet is clicked.
SheetPivotTableUpdate	A pivot table is changed or refreshed.
SheetSelectionChange	The selection on any worksheet is changed.
WindowActivate	Any workbook window is activated.
WindowDeactivate	Any workbook window is deactivated.
WindowResize	Any workbook window is resized.

Cross-Ref

If you need to monitor events for any workbook, you need to work with Application-level events (see "Monitoring with Application Events," later in this chapter). The remainder of this section presents examples of using Workbook-level events. All the example procedures that follow must be located in the code module for the ThisWorkbook object. If you put them into any other type of code module, they won't work.

The Open event

One of the most common monitored events is the Open event for a workbook. This event is triggered when the workbook (or add-in) is opened and executes the procedure named Workbook_Open. A Workbook_Open procedure is often used for tasks such as these:

➤ Displaying welcome messages.

➤ Opening other workbooks.

➤ Setting up shortcut menus.

➤ Activating a particular sheet or cell.

➤ Ensuring that certain conditions are met. For example, a workbook may require that a particular add-in be installed.

➤ Setting up certain automatic features. For example, you can define key combinations (see "The OnKey event" section, later in this chapter).

➤ Setting a worksheet's ScrollArea property (which isn't stored with the workbook).

➤ Setting UserInterfaceOnly protection for worksheets so that your code can operate on protected sheets. This setting is an argument for the Protect method and isn't stored with the workbook.

Note

Creating event-handler procedures doesn't guarantee that they will be executed. If the user holds down the Shift key when opening a workbook, the workbook's Workbook_Open procedure won't execute. And, of course, the procedure won't execute if the workbook is opened with macros disabled.

Following is an example of a Workbook_Open procedure. It uses the VBA Weekday function to determine the day of the week. If it's Friday, a message box appears, reminding the user to submit a weekly report. If it's not Friday, nothing happens.

```
Private Sub Workbook_Open()
  If Weekday(Now) = vbFriday Then
      Msg = "Today is Friday. Make sure that you "
      Msg = Msg & "submit the TPS Report."
      MsgBox Msg, vbInformation
  End If
End Sub
```

The Activate event

The following procedure is executed whenever the workbook is activated. This procedure simply maximizes the active window. If the workbook window is already maximized, the procedure has no effect.

```
Private Sub Workbook_Activate()
    ActiveWindow.WindowState = xlMaximized
End Sub
```

The SheetActivate event

The following procedure is executed whenever the user activates any sheet in the workbook. If the sheet is a worksheet, the code selects cell A1. If the sheet isn't a worksheet, nothing happens. This procedure uses the VBA TypeName function to ensure that the activated sheet is a worksheet (as opposed to a chart sheet).

```
Private Sub Workbook_SheetActivate(ByVal Sh As Object)
    If TypeName(Sh) = "Worksheet" Then Range("A1").Select
End Sub
```

The following procedure demonstrates an alternative method that doesn't require checking the sheet type. In this procedure, the error is just ignored.

```
Private Sub Workbook_SheetActivate(ByVal Sh As Object)
    On Error Resume Next
    Range("A1").Select
End Sub
```

The NewSheet event

The following procedure is executed whenever a new sheet is added to the workbook. The sheet is passed to the procedure as an argument. Because a new sheet can be a worksheet or a chart sheet, this procedure determines the sheet type. If it's a worksheet, the code adjusts the width of all columns and inserts a date and time stamp in cell A1 on the new sheet.

```
Private Sub Workbook_NewSheet(ByVal Sh As Object)
    If TypeName(Sh) = "Worksheet" Then
        Sh.Cells.ColumnWidth = 35
        Sh.Range("A1") = "Sheet added " & Now()
    End If
End Sub
```

The BeforeSave event

The BeforeSave event occurs before the workbook is saved. As you know, choosing the File➜Save command sometimes brings up the Save As dialog box. This dialog box appears if the workbook has never been saved or if it was opened in read-only mode.

When the Workbook_BeforeSave procedure is executed, it receives an argument (SaveAsUI) that indicates whether the Save As dialog box will be displayed. The following example demonstrates how to use the SaveAsUI argument:

```
Private Sub Workbook_BeforeSave _
  (ByVal SaveAsUI As Boolean, Cancel As Boolean)
    If SaveAsUI Then
        MsgBox "Make sure you save this file on drive J."
    End If
End Sub
```

When the user attempts to save the workbook, the Workbook_BeforeSave procedure is executed. If the save operation will display Excel's Save As dialog box, the SaveAsUI variable is True. The Workbook_BeforeSave procedure checks this variable and displays a message only if the Save As dialog box will be displayed. If the procedure sets the Cancel argument to True, the file won't be saved (or the Save As dialog box won't be shown).

The Deactivate event

The following example demonstrates the Deactivate event. This procedure is executed whenever the workbook is deactivated and essentially never lets the user deactivate the workbook. One way to trigger the Deactivate event is to activate a different workbook window. When the Deactivate event occurs, the code reactivates the workbook and displays a message.

```
Private Sub Workbook_Deactivate()
    Me.Activate
    MsgBox "Sorry, you may not leave this workbook"
End Sub
```

Note

Procedures that attempt to "take over" Excel, such as this one, can be frustrating and confusing for the user, so I don't recommend using them. Instead, train the user in the correct use of your application.

This example also illustrates the importance of understanding event sequences. If you try out this procedure, you'll see that it works well if the user attempts to activate another workbook. However, it's important to understand that the workbook Deactivate event is also triggered by the following actions:

➤ Closing the workbook

➤ Opening a new workbook

➤ Minimizing the workbook

In other words, this procedure may not perform as it was originally intended. When programming event procedures, you need to make sure that you understand all the actions that can trigger the events.

The BeforePrint event

The BeforePrint event occurs when the user requests a print or a print preview but before the printing or previewing occurs. The event uses a Cancel argument, so your code can cancel the printing or previewing by setting the Cancel variable to True. Unfortunately, you can't determine whether the BeforePrint event was triggered by a print request or by a preview request.

Updating a header or footer

Excel's page header and footer options are flexible, but these options don't include a common request: the capability to print the contents of a specific cell in the header or footer. The Workbook_BeforePrint event provides a way to display the current contents of a cell in the header or footer when the workbook is printed. The following code updates each sheet's left footer whenever the workbook is printed or previewed. Specifically, it inserts the contents of cell A1 on Sheet1:

```
Private Sub Workbook_BeforePrint(Cancel As Boolean)
    Dim sht As Object
    For Each sht In ThisWorkbook.Sheets
        sht.PageSetup.LeftFooter = Worksheets("Sheet1").Range("A1")
    Next sht
End Sub
```

This procedure loops through each sheet in the workbook and sets the LeftFooter property of the PageSetup object to the value in cell A1 on Sheet1.

Hiding columns before printing

The example that follows uses a Workbook_BeforePrint procedure to hide columns B:D in Sheet1 before printing or previewing:

```
Private Sub Workbook_BeforePrint(Cancel As Boolean)
    'Hide columns B:D on Sheet1 before printing
    Worksheets("Sheet1").Range("B:D").EntireColumn.Hidden = True
  End Sub
```

Ideally, you would want to unhide the columns after printing has occurred. It would be nice if Excel provided an AfterPrint event, but that event doesn't exist. However, there is a way to unhide the columns automatically. The modified procedure that follows schedules an OnTime event, which calls a procedure named UnhideColumns five seconds after printing or previewing:

```
Private Sub Workbook_BeforePrint(Cancel As Boolean)
    'Hide columns B:D on Sheet1 before printing
    Worksheets("Sheet1").Range("B:D").EntireColumn.Hidden = True
    Application.OnTime Now()+ TimeValue("0:00:05"), "UnhideColumns"
End Sub
```

The UnhideColumns procedure goes in a standard VBA module:

```
Sub UnhideColumns()
    Worksheets("Sheet1").Range("B:D").EntireColumn.Hidden = False
End Sub
```

On the Web

This example, named hide columns before printing.xlsm, is available on the book's website.

Cross-Ref

For more information about OnTime events, see "The OnTime event," later in this chapter.

The BeforeClose event

The BeforeClose event occurs before a workbook is closed. This event is often used with a Workbook_Open event handler. For example, you might use the Workbook_Open procedure to add shortcut menu items for your workbook and then use the Workbook_BeforeClose procedure to delete the shortcut menu items when the workbook is closed. That way, the custom menu is available only when the workbook is open.

Unfortunately, the Workbook_BeforeClose event isn't implemented very well. For example, if you attempt to close a workbook that hasn't been saved, Excel displays a prompt asking whether you want to save the workbook before closing, as shown in Figure 17-5. The problem is that the Workbook_BeforeClose event has already occurred by the time the user sees this message. If the user cancels, your event-handler procedure has already executed.

Figure 17-5: When this message appears, Workbook_BeforeClose has already done its thing.

Consider this scenario: You need to display custom shortcut menus when a particular workbook is open. Therefore, your workbook uses a Workbook_Open procedure to create the menu items when the workbook is opened and a Workbook_BeforeClose procedure to remove the menu items when the workbook is closed. These two event-handler procedures follow. Both of these call other procedures, which aren't shown here.

```
Private Sub Workbook_Open()
    Call CreateShortcutMenuItems
End Sub

Private Sub Workbook_BeforeClose(Cancel As Boolean)
    Call DeleteShortcutMenuItems
End Sub
```

As I note earlier, the Excel save prompt is displayed *after* the Workbook_BeforeClose event handler runs. So, if the user clicks Cancel, the workbook remains open, but the custom menu items have already been deleted.

One solution to this problem is to bypass Excel's prompt and write your own code in the Workbook_BeforeClose procedure to ask the user to save the workbook. The following code demonstrates this solution:

```
Private Sub Workbook_BeforeClose(Cancel As Boolean)
    Dim Msg As String
    If Me.Saved = False Then
        Msg = "Do you want to save the changes you made to "
        Msg = Msg & Me.Name & "?"
        Ans = MsgBox(Msg, vbQuestion + vbYesNoCancel)
        Select Case Ans
            Case vbYes
                Me.Save
            Case vbCancel
                Cancel = True
                Exit Sub
        End Select
    End If
    Call DeleteShortcutMenuItems
    Me.Saved = True
End Sub
```

This procedure checks the Saved property of the Workbook object to determine whether the workbook has been saved. If so, no problem — the DeleteShortcutMenuItems procedure is executed, and the workbook is closed. But if the workbook hasn't been saved, the procedure displays a message box similar to the one that Excel would normally show (see Figure 17-6). The following lists details the effect of clicking each of the three buttons:

➤ **Yes:** The workbook is saved, the shortcut menu items are deleted, and the workbook is closed.

➤ **No:** The code sets the Saved property of the Workbook object to True (but doesn't actually save the file), deletes the menu items, and closes the file.

➤ **Cancel:** The BeforeClose event is canceled, and the procedure ends without deleting the shortcut menu items.

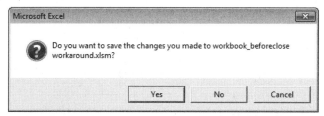

Figure 17-6: A message displayed by the Workbook_BeforeClose event procedure.

On the Web

A workbook with this example is available on the book's website in the workbook_ beforeclose workaround.xlsm file.

Examining Worksheet Events

The events for a Worksheet object are some of the most useful, because most of what happens in Excel occurs on a worksheet. Monitoring these events can make your applications perform feats that would otherwise be impossible.

Table 17-2 lists the most commonly used worksheet events, with a brief description of each.

Table 17-2: Commonly Used Worksheet Events

Event	Action That Triggers the Event
Activate	The worksheet is activated.
BeforeDelete	The worksheet is about to be deleted
BeforeDoubleClick	The worksheet is double-clicked.
BeforeRightClick	The worksheet is right-clicked.

continued

Table 17-2: Commonly Used Worksheet Events *(continued)*

Event	Action That Triggers the Event
Calculate	The worksheet is calculated (or recalculated).
Change	Cells on the worksheet are changed by the user or by an external link.
Deactivate	The worksheet is deactivated.
FollowHyperlink	A hyperlink on the sheet is clicked.
PivotTableUpdate	A pivot table on the sheet is updated.
SelectionChange	The selection on the worksheet is changed or refreshed.

Remember that the code for a worksheet event must be stored in the code module for the specific worksheet.

Tip

To quickly activate the code module for a worksheet, right-click the sheet tab and then choose View Code.

The Change event

The Change event occurs when any cell in a worksheet is changed by the user or by a VBA procedure. The Change event does not occur when a calculation generates a different value for a formula or when an object is added to the sheet.

When the Worksheet_Change procedure is executed, it receives a Range object as its Target argument. This Range object represents the changed cell or range that triggered the event. The following procedure is executed whenever the worksheet is changed. It displays a message box that shows the address of the Target range:

```
Private Sub Worksheet_Change(ByVal Target As Range)
    MsgBox "Range " & Target.Address & " was changed."
End Sub
```

To get a better feel for the types of actions that generate a Change event for a worksheet, enter the preceding procedure in the code module for a Worksheet object. After entering this procedure, activate Excel and make some changes to the worksheet by using various techniques. Every time the Change event occurs, you'll see a message box that displays the address of the range that was changed.

When I ran this procedure, I discovered some interesting quirks. Some actions that should trigger the event don't, and other actions that shouldn't trigger the event do!

➤ Changing the formatting of a cell doesn't trigger the Change event (as expected). But copying and pasting formatting *does* trigger the Change event. Choosing the Home➡Editing➡Clear➡Clear Formats command also triggers the event.

➤ Merging cells doesn't trigger the Change event, even if the contents of some of the merged cells are deleted in the process.

➤ Adding, editing, or deleting a cell comment doesn't trigger the Change event.

➤ Pressing Delete generates an event even if the cell is empty to start with.

➤ Cells that are changed by using Excel commands may or may not trigger the Change event. For example, sorting a range or using Goal Seeker to change a cell does not trigger the event. But using the spell checker does.

➤ If your VBA procedure changes the contents of a cell, it *does* trigger the Change event.

As you can see from the preceding list, it's not a good idea to rely on the Change event to detect cell changes for critical applications.

Monitoring a specific range for changes

The Change event occurs when any cell on the worksheet is changed. But, in most cases, all you care about are changes made to a specific cell or range. When the Worksheet_Change event handler procedure is called, it receives a Range object as its argument. This Range object represents the cell or cells that were changed.

Assume that your worksheet has a range named InputRange, and you'd like to monitor changes made only within this range. There is no Change event for a Range object, but you can perform a quick check in the Worksheet_Change procedure:

```
Private Sub Worksheet_Change(ByVal Target As Range)
    Dim MRange As Range
    Set MRange = Range("InputRange")
    If Not Intersect(Target, MRange) Is Nothing Then _
       MsgBox "A changed cell is in the input range."
End Sub
```

This example uses a Range object variable named MRange, which represents the worksheet range that you want to monitor for changes. The procedure uses the VBA Intersect function to determine whether the Target range (passed to the procedure in its argument) intersects with MRange. The Intersect function returns an object that consists of all cells contained in both of its arguments. If the Intersect function returns Nothing, the ranges have no cells in common. The Not operator is used so that the expression returns True if the ranges *do* have at least one cell in common. Therefore, if the changed range has any cells in common with the range named InputRange, a message box is displayed. Otherwise, the procedure ends, and nothing happens.

Monitoring a range to make formulas bold

The following example monitors a worksheet and also makes formula entries bold and nonformula entries not bold:

```
Private Sub Worksheet_Change(ByVal Target As Range)
    Dim cell As Range
    For Each cell In Target
        If cell.HasFormula Then cell.Font.Bold = True
    Next cell
End Sub
```

Because the object passed to the Worksheet_Change procedure can consist of a multicell range, the procedure loops through each cell in the Target range. If the cell has a formula, the cell is made bold. Otherwise, the Bold property is set to False.

The procedure works, but it has a problem. What if the user deletes a row or column? In such a case, the Target range consists of a huge number of cells. The For Each loop would take a long time to examine them all — and it wouldn't find any formulas.

The modified procedure listed next solves this problem by changing the Target range to the intersection of the Target range and the worksheet's used range. The check to ensure that Target is Not Nothing handles the case in which an empty row or column outside the used range is deleted.

```
Private Sub Worksheet_Change(ByVal Target As Range)
    Dim cell As Range
    Set Target = Intersect(Target, Target.Parent.UsedRange)
    If Not Target Is Nothing Then
        For Each cell In Target
            cell.Font.Bold = cell.HasFormula
        Next cell
    End If
End Sub
```

On the Web This example, named make formulas bold.xlsm, is available on the book's website.

Caution A Worksheet_Change procedure may affect Excel's Undo feature, a potentially serious side effect. Excel's Undo stack is destroyed whenever an event procedure makes a change to the worksheet. In the preceding example, making a cell entry triggers a formatting change — which destroys the Undo stack.

Monitoring a range to validate data entry

Excel's data validation feature is a useful tool, but it suffers from a potentially serious problem. When you paste data to a cell that uses data validation, the pasted value not only fails to get validated but also deletes the validation rules associated with the cell! This fact makes the data validation feature practically worthless for critical applications. In this section, I demonstrate how you can use the Change event for a worksheet to create your own data validation procedure.

On the Web

The book's website contains two versions of this example. One (named validate entry1. xlsm) uses the EnableEvents property to prevent cascading Change events; the other (named validate entry2.xlsm) uses a Static variable. See "Disabling events," earlier in this chapter.

The Worksheet_Change procedure that follows is executed when a user changes a cell. The validation is restricted to the range named InputRange. Values entered into this range must be integers between 1 and 12.

```
Private Sub Worksheet_Change(ByVal Target As Range)
    Dim VRange As Range, cell As Range
    Dim Msg As String
    Dim ValidateCode As Variant
    Set VRange = Range("InputRange")
    If Intersect(VRange, Target) Is Nothing Then Exit Sub
    For Each cell In Intersect(VRange, Target)
        ValidateCode = EntryIsValid(cell)
        If TypeName(ValidateCode) = "String" Then
            Msg = "Cell " & cell.Address(False, False) & ":"
            Msg = Msg & vbCrLf & vbCrLf & ValidateCode
            MsgBox Msg, vbCritical, "Invalid Entry"
            Application.EnableEvents = False
            cell.ClearContents
            cell.Activate
            Application.EnableEvents = True
        End If
    Next cell
End Sub
```

The Worksheet_Change procedure creates a Range object (named VRange) that represents the worksheet range that is validated. Then it loops through each cell in the Target argument, which represents the cell or cells that were changed. The code determines whether each cell is contained in the range to be validated. If so, it passes the cell as an argument to a custom function (EntryIsValid), which returns True if the cell is a valid entry.

If the entry isn't valid, the EntryIsValid function returns a string that describes the problem, and the user is informed by a message box (see Figure 17-7). When the message box is dismissed, the invalid entry is cleared from the cell and the cell is activated. Note that events are disabled before the cell is cleared. If events weren't disabled, clearing the cell would produce a Change event that causes an endless loop.

Also, note that entering an invalid value clears Excel's Undo stack.

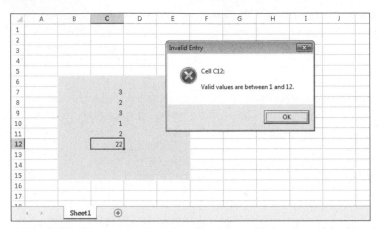

Figure 17-7: This message box describes the problem when the user makes an invalid entry.

The EntryIsValid function procedure is shown here:

```
Private Function EntryIsValid(cell) As Variant
'    Returns True if cell is an integer between 1 and 12
'    Otherwise it returns a string that describes the problem

'    Numeric?
    If Not WorksheetFunction.IsNumber (cell) Then
        EntryIsValid = "Non-numeric entry."
        Exit Function
    End If
'    Integer?
    If CInt(cell) <> cell Then
        EntryIsValid = "Integer required."
        Exit Function
    End If
'    Between 1 and 12?
    If cell < 1 Or cell > 12 Then
        EntryIsValid = "Valid values are between 1 and 12."
        Exit Function
    End If
'    It passed all the tests
    EntryIsValid = True
End Function
```

The preceding technique works, but setting it up is tedious. Wouldn't it be nice if you could take advantage of Excel's data validation feature, yet ensure that the data validation rules aren't deleted if the user pastes data into the validation range? The next example does the trick:

```
Private Sub Worksheet_Change(ByVal Target As Range)
    Dim VT As Long
    'Do all cells in the validation range
    'still have validation?
    On Error Resume Next
    VT = Range("InputRange").Validation.Type
    If Err.Number <> 0 Then
        Application.Undo
        MsgBox "Your last operation was canceled." & _
        "It would have deleted data validation rules.", vbCritical
    End If
End Sub
```

This event procedure checks the validation type of InputRange, the range that is *supposed* to contain the data validation rules. If the VT variable contains an error, one or more cells in the InputRange no longer contain data validation. In other words, the worksheet change probably resulted from data being copied into the range that contains data validation. If that's the case, the code executes the Undo method of the Application object and reverses the user's action. Then it displays the message box shown in Figure 17-8.

Note

This procedure works correctly only if all cells in the validation range contain the same type of data validation.

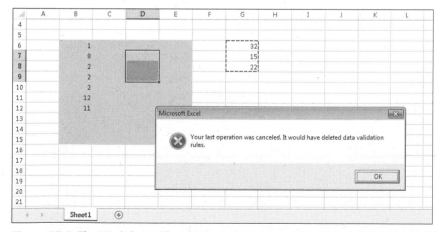

Figure 17-8: The Worksheet_Change procedure ensures that data validation isn't deleted.

Note A nice side-benefit to using this procedure is that the Undo stack isn't destroyed.

On the Web This example, named validate entry3.xlsm, is available on the book's website.

The SelectionChange event

The following procedure demonstrates the SelectionChange event. It's executed whenever the user makes a new selection in the worksheet.

```
Private Sub Worksheet_SelectionChange(ByVal Target As Range)
    Cells.Interior.ColorIndex = xlNone
    With ActiveCell
        .EntireRow.Interior.Color = RGB(219, 229, 241)
        .EntireColumn.Interior.Color = RGB(219, 229, 241)
    End With
End Sub
```

This procedure shades the row and column of the active cell, which makes identifying the active cell easy. The first statement removes the background color for all cells in the worksheet. Next, the entire row and column of the active cell is shaded light blue. Figure 17-9 shows the shading in effect.

	A	B	C	D	E	F	G	H	I	J	K	L
1		Project-1	Project-2	Project-3	Project-4	Project-5	Project-6	Project-7	Project-8	Project-9	Project-10	
2	Jan-2010	2158	1527	3870	4863	3927	3993	2175	2143	3965	2885	
3	Feb-2010	4254	28	4345	2108	412	2857	3098	87	2181	4461	
4	Mar-2010	3631	1240	4208	452	3443	2965	91	2935	170	3044	
5	Apr-2010	724	4939	1619	1721	3631	3487	3581	3082	3729	2335	
6	May-2010	3060	1034	1646	345	978	526	4422	1390	3566	3063	
7	Jun-2010	394	1241	2965	1411	3545	4499	2477	735	2533	4951	
8	Jul-2010	2080	3978	3304	1460	4533	3335	2675	1687	2475	3901	
9	Aug-2010	411	753	732	1207	1902	4009	1793	2262	916	2887	
10	Sep-2010	2711	95	2267	2634	1944	3920	2020	402	3183	3581	
11	Oct-2010	2996	4934	3932	2938	4730	1139	3776	3366	2239	1539	
12	Nov-2010	2837	1116	3879	1740	1466	3628	212	780	4518	4769	
13	Dec-2010	300	2917	321	1219	841	3554	1924	1786	3967	245	
14	Jan-2011	1604	768	2617	3414	4732	863	2993	4184	3432	1977	
15	Feb-2011	1662	1380	4590	531	4143	1758	2990	2938	4400	798	
16	Mar-2011	1001	3454	4611	4852	456	46	4475	1340	859	1334	
17	Apr-2011	4407	46	4185	4868	2313	2750	4948	4525	3896	473	
18	May-2011	3948	1292	1462	1977	2418	1816	4810	2803	4973	910	
19	Jun-2011	160	2908	3834	2396	4120	2231	3689	486	4751	3174	
20	Jul-2011	1131	118	3193	40	1965	424	4802	3379	3645	3293	
21	Aug-2011	2480	2564	373	3893	4932	4362	4472	3707	2411	3218	
22	Sep-2011	4949	2649	2335	9	2309	3454	657	3519	658	3619	
23	Oct-2011	3268	2652	2164	1898	1598	1237	1524	4752	1237	4708	
24	Nov-2011	794	4821	2885	102	2618	1086	3050	3121	2202	2375	
25	Dec-2011	2623	985	3737	666	3568	4685	4184	36	1830	4622	

Sheet1

Figure 17-9: Moving the cell cursor shades the active cell's row and column.

You won't want to use the procedure if your worksheet contains any background shading because the shading will be wiped out. The exceptions are tables with a style applied and background colors resulting from conditional formatting. In both these instances, the background color *is* maintained. Keep in mind, however, that executing the Worksheet_SelectionChange macro destroys the Undo stack, so using this technique essentially disables Excel's Undo feature.

On the Web

This example, named shade active row and column.xlsm, is available on the book's website.

The BeforeDoubleClick event

You can set up a VBA procedure to be executed when the user double-clicks a cell. In the following example (which is stored in the code window for a Sheet object), double-clicking a cell toggles the cell's style. If the cell style is "Normal", it applies the "Good" style. If the style is "Good", it applies the "Normal" style.

```
Private Sub Worksheet_BeforeDoubleClick _
    (ByVal Target As Range, Cancel As Boolean)
    If Target.Style = "Good" Then
        Target.Style = "Normal"
    Else
        Target.Style = "Good"
    End If
    Cancel = True
End Sub
```

If Cancel is set to True, the default double-click action doesn't occur. In other words, double-clicking the cell won't put Excel into cell edit mode. Keep in mind that every-double click also destroys the Undo stack.

The BeforeRightClick event

When the user right-clicks in a worksheet, Excel displays a shortcut menu. If, for some reason, you'd like to prevent the shortcut menu from appearing in a particular sheet, you can trap the RightClick event. The following procedure sets the Cancel argument to True, which cancels the RightClick event and thereby cancels the shortcut menu, and then displays a message box:

```
Private Sub Worksheet_BeforeRightClick _
    (ByVal Target As Range, Cancel As Boolean)
    Cancel = True
    MsgBox "The shortcut menu is not available."
End Sub
```

Keep in mind that the user can still access the shortcut menu by using Shift+F10. However, only a tiny percentage of Excel users are aware of that keystroke combination.

Cross-Ref

To find out how to intercept the Shift+F10 key combination, see "The OnKey event," later in this chapter. Chapter 21 describes other methods for disabling shortcut menus.

Following is another example that uses the BeforeRightClick event. This procedure checks to see whether the cell that was right-clicked contains a numeric value. If so, the code displays the Number tab of the Format Cells dialog box and sets the Cancel argument to True (avoiding the normal shortcut menu display). If the cell doesn't contain a numeric value, nothing special happens — the shortcut menu is displayed as usual.

```
Private Sub Worksheet_BeforeRightClick _
    (ByVal Target As Range, Cancel As Boolean)
    If IsNumeric(Target) And Not IsEmpty(Target) Then
        Application.CommandBars.ExecuteMso ("NumberFormatsDialog")
        Cancel = True
    End If
End Sub
```

Note that the code makes an additional check to determine if the cell is not empty. I added this check because VBA considers empty cells to be numeric.

Checking Out Chart Events

This section describes some of the events associated with charts. By default, events are enabled only for charts that reside on a chart sheet. To work with events for an embedded chart, you need to create a class module.

Cross-Ref

Refer to Chapter 16 for examples that deal with Chart events. Chapter 16 also describes how to create a class module to enable events for embedded charts.

Table 17-3 contains a list of the chart events as well as a brief description of each.

Table 17-3: Events Recognized by a Chart Sheet

Event	Action That Triggers the Event
Activate	The chart sheet or embedded chart is activated.
BeforeDoubleClick	The chart sheet or an embedded chart is double-clicked. This event occurs before the default double-click action.
BeforeRightClick	The chart sheet or an embedded chart is right-clicked. The event occurs before the default right-click action.
Calculate	New or changed data is plotted on a chart.

Event	Action That Triggers the Event
Deactivate	The chart is deactivated.
MouseDown	A mouse button is pressed while the pointer is over a chart.
MouseMove	The position of the mouse pointer changes over a chart.
MouseUp	A mouse button is released while the pointer is over a chart.
Resize	The chart is resized.
Select	A chart element is selected.
SeriesChange	The value of a chart data point is changed.

 Using Object Browser to locate events

Object Browser is a useful tool that can help you learn about objects and their properties and methods. It can also help you find out which objects support a particular event. For example, say you'd like to find out which objects support the MouseMove event. Activate VBE and press F2 to display the Object Browser window. Make sure that <All Libraries> is selected; then type **MouseMove** and click the binoculars icon (see the accompanying figure).

The Object Browser displays a list of matching items. Events are indicated with a small yellow lightning bolt. From this list, you can see which objects support the MouseMove event. Most of the located objects are controls in the MSForms library, which are UserForm controls. But you can also see that the Excel Chart object supports the MouseMove event.

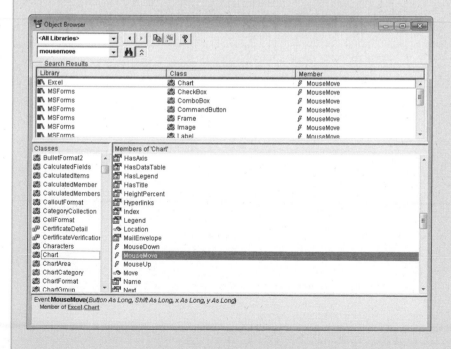

continued

continued

Note how the list is divided into three columns: Library, Class, and Member. The match for the item that you're searching for might appear in any of these columns. This fact brings up a crucial point: The name of an event or a term belonging to one library or class could be the same as an event or a term belonging to a different library or class — although they probably don't share the same functionality. So be sure to click each item in the Object Browser list and check the status bar at the bottom of the list for the syntax. You may find, for example, that one class or library treats an event differently.

Monitoring with Application Events

In earlier sections, I discuss Workbook events and Worksheet events. Those events are monitored for a particular workbook. If you want to monitor events for all open workbooks or all worksheets, you use Application-level events.

Note

Creating event-handler procedures to handle Application events always requires a class module and some setup work.

Table 17-4 lists commonly used Application events with a brief description of each. Consult the Help system for details.

Table 17-4: Commonly Used Events Recognized by the Application Object

Event	Action That Triggers the Event
AfterCalculate	A calculation has been completed and no outstanding queries exist.
NewWorkbook	A new workbook is created.
SheetActivate	Any sheet is activated.
SheetBeforeDoubleClick	Any worksheet is double-clicked. This event occurs before the default double-click action.
SheetBeforeRightClick	Any worksheet is right-clicked. This event occurs before the default right-click action.
SheetCalculate	Any worksheet is calculated (or recalculated).
SheetChange	Cells in any worksheet are changed by the user or by an external link.
SheetDeactivate	Any sheet is deactivated.
SheetFollowHyperlink	A hyperlink is clicked.
SheetPivotTableUpdate	Any pivot table is updated.
SheetSelectionChange	The selection changes on any worksheet except a chart sheet.
WindowActivate	Any workbook window is activated.

Event	Action That Triggers the Event
WindowDeactivate	Any workbook window is deactivated.
WindowResize	Any workbook window is resized.
WorkbookActivate	Any workbook is activated.
WorkbookAddinInstall	A workbook is installed as an add-in.
WorkbookAddinUninstall	Any add-in workbook is uninstalled.
WorkbookBeforeClose	Any open workbook is closed.
WorkbookBeforePrint	Any open workbook is printed.
WorkbookBeforeSave	Any open workbook is saved.
WorkbookDeactivate	Any open workbook is deactivated.
WorkbookNewSheet	A new sheet is created in any open workbook.
WorkbookOpen	A workbook is opened.

Enabling Application-level events

To use Application-level events, you need to do the following:

1. Insert a new class module.

2. Set a name for this class module in the Properties window under *Name*.

   By default, VBA gives each new class module a default name like Class1, Class2, and so on. You may want to give your class module a more meaningful name, such as clsApp.

3. In the class module, declare a public Application object by using the WithEvents keyword.

   For example:

```
Public WithEvents XL As Application
```

4. Create a variable that you'll use to refer to the declared Application object in the class module.

   It should be a module-level object variable declared in a regular VBA module (not in the class module). For example:

```
Dim X As New clsApp
```

5. Connect the declared object with the Application object.

   This step is often done in a Workbook_Open procedure. For example:

```
Set X.XL = Application
```

6. Write event-handler procedures for the XL object in the class module.

Cross-Ref

> This procedure is virtually identical to that required to use events with an embedded chart. See Chapter 16.

Determining when a workbook is opened

The example in this section keeps track of every workbook that is opened by storing information in a comma-separated variable (CSV) text file. You can import this file into Excel.

I start by inserting a new class module and naming it clsApp. The code in the class module is

```
Public WithEvents AppEvents As Application

Private Sub AppEvents_WorkbookOpen (ByVal Wb As Excel.Workbook)
    Call UpdateLogFile(Wb)
End Sub
```

This code declares AppEvents as an Application object with events. The AppEvents_WorkbookOpen procedure will be called whenever a workbook is opened. This event-handler procedure calls UpdateLogFile and passes the Wb variable, which represents the workbook that was opened. I then added a VBA module and inserted the following code:

```
Dim AppObject As New clsApp

Sub Init()
'   Called by Workbook_Open
    Set AppObject.AppEvents = Application
End Sub

Sub UpdateLogFile(Wb)
    Dim txt As String
    Dim Fname As String
    txt = Wb.FullName
    txt = txt & "," & Date & "," & Time
    txt = txt & "," & Application.UserName
    Fname = Application.DefaultFilePath & "\logfile.csv"
    Open Fname For Append As #1
    Print #1, txt
    Close #1
    MsgBox txt
End Sub
```

Note at the top that the AppObject variable is declared as type clsApp (the name of the class module). The call to Init is in the Workbook_Open procedure, which is in the code module for ThisWorkbook. This procedure is as follows:

```
Private Sub Workbook_Open()
    Call Init
End Sub
```

The UpdateLogFile procedure opens a text file — or creates the text file if it doesn't exist. The procedure then writes key information about the workbook that was opened: the filename and full path, the date, the time, and the username.

The Workbook_Open procedure calls the Init procedure. Therefore, when the workbook opens, the Init procedure creates the object variable. The final statement uses a message box to display the information that was written to the CSV file. You can delete this statement if you prefer not to see that message.

On the Web

This example, named log workbook open.xlsm, is available on the book's website.

Monitoring Application-level events

To get a feel for the event-generation process, you may find it helpful to see a list of events that get generated as you go about your work.

I created a workbook that displays (in a UserForm) a description of various Application-level events as they occur (see Figure 17-10). You might find this workbook helpful when learning about the types and sequence of events that occur.

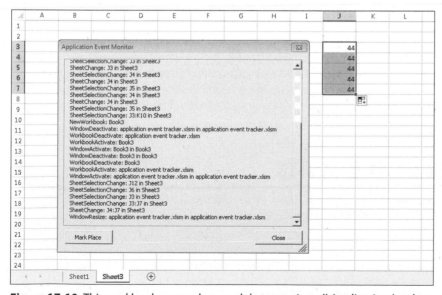

Figure 17-10: This workbook uses a class module to monitor all Application-level events.

This example is available on the book's website in the application event tracker .xlsm file.

The workbook contains a class module with 21 procedures defined, one for each of the commonly used Application-level events. Here's an example of one of them:

```
Private Sub XL_NewWorkbook(ByVal Wb As Excel.Workbook)
    LogEvent "NewWorkbook: " & Wb.Name
End Sub
```

Each of these procedures calls the LogEvent procedure and passes an argument that consists of the event name and the object. The LogEvent procedure follows:

```
Sub LogEvent(txt)
    EventNum = EventNum + 1
    With UserForm1
        With .lblEvents
            .AutoSize = False
            .Caption = .Caption & vbCrLf & txt
            .Width = UserForm1.FrameEvents.Width - 20
            .AutoSize = True
        End With
        .FrameEvents.ScrollHeight = .lblEvents.Height + 20
        .FrameEvents.ScrollTop = EventNum * 20
    End With
End Sub
```

The LogEvent procedure updates the UserForm by modifying the Caption property of the Label control named lblEvents. The procedure also adjusts the ScrollHeight and ScrollTop properties of the Frame named FrameEvents, which contains the Label. Adjusting these properties causes the most recently added text to be visible while older text scrolls out of view. You can also adjust the vertical size of this UserForm. The code uses the resizing technique described in Chapter 13.

Using UserForm Events

A UserForm supports quite a few events, and each control placed on a UserForm has its own set of events. Table 17-5 lists the UserForm events that you can use.

Table 17-5: Events Recognized by a UserForm

Event	Action That Triggers the Event
Activate	The UserForm is activated.
AddControl	A control is added at runtime.
BeforeDragOver	A drag-and-drop operation is in progress while the pointer is over the form.
BeforeDropOrPaste	The user is about to drop or paste data: that is, just before the user has released the mouse button.
Click	A mouse is clicked while the pointer is over the form.
DblClick	A mouse is double-clicked while the pointer is over the form.
Deactivate	The UserForm is deactivated.
Error	A control detects an error and can't return the error information to a calling program.
Initialize	The UserForm is about to be shown.
KeyDown	A key is pressed.
KeyPress	The user presses any ANSI key.
KeyUp	A key is released.
Layout	A UserForm changes size.
MouseDown	A mouse button is pressed.
MouseMove	The mouse is moved.
MouseUp	A mouse button is released.
QueryClose	Occurs before a UserForm closes.
RemoveControl	A control is removed from the UserForm at runtime.
Resize	The UserForm is resized.
Scroll	The UserForm is scrolled.
Terminate	The UserForm is terminated.
Zoom	The UserForm is zoomed.

Cross-Ref

Many of the examples in Chapters 11 through 13 demonstrate event handling for UserForms and UserForm controls.

Accessing Events Not Associated with an Object

The events that I discuss earlier in this chapter are all associated with an object (Application, Workbook, Sheet, and so on). In this section, I discuss two additional rogue events: OnTime and OnKey. Instead of being associated with an object, these events are accessed by using methods of the Application object.

Note

Unlike the other events discussed in this chapter, you program these On events in a general VBA module.

The OnTime event

The OnTime event occurs at a specified time of day. The following example demonstrates how to program Excel so that it beeps and displays a message at 3 p.m.:

```
Sub SetAlarm()
    Application.OnTime TimeValue("15:00:00"), "DisplayAlarm"
End Sub

Sub DisplayAlarm()
    Beep
    MsgBox "Wake up. It's time for your afternoon break!"
End Sub
```

In this example, the SetAlarm procedure uses the OnTime method of the Application object to set up the OnTime event. This method takes two arguments: the time (3 p.m., in the example) and the procedure to execute when the time occurs (DisplayAlarm in the example). After SetAlarm is executed, the DisplayAlarm procedure will be called at 3 p.m., displaying the message in Figure 17-11.

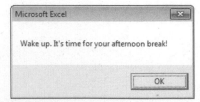

Figure 17-11: This message box was programmed to display at a particular time of day.

If you want to schedule an event relative to the current time — for example, 20 minutes from now — you can write an instruction like this:

```
Application.OnTime Now + TimeValue("00:20:00"), "DisplayAlarm"
```

You can also use the OnTime method to schedule a procedure on a particular day. The following statement runs the DisplayAlarm procedure at 12:01 a.m. on April 1, 2013:

```
Application.OnTime DateSerial(2013, 4, 1) + _
    TimeValue("00:00:01"), "DisplayAlarm"
```

Note

The OnTime method has two additional arguments. If you plan to use this method, you should refer to the online help for complete details.

The two procedures that follow demonstrate how to program a repeated event. In this case, cell A1 is updated with the current time every five seconds. Executing the UpdateClock procedure writes the time to cell A1 and also programs another event five seconds later. This event reruns the UpdateClock procedure. To stop the events, execute the StopClock procedure (which cancels the event). Note that NextTick is a module-level variable that stores the time for the next event.

On the Web

This example, named ontime event demo.xlsm, is available on the book's website.

```
Dim NextTick As Date

Sub UpdateClock()
'   Updates cell A1 with the current time
    ThisWorkbook.Sheets(1).Range("A1") = Time
'   Set up the next event five seconds from now
    NextTick = Now + TimeValue("00:00:05")
    Application.OnTime NextTick, "UpdateClock"
End Sub

Sub StopClock()
'   Cancels the OnTime event (stops the clock)
    On Error Resume Next
    Application.OnTime NextTick, "UpdateClock", , False
End Sub
```

Caution   The OnTime event persists even after the workbook is closed. In other words, if you close the workbook without running the StopClock procedure, the workbook will reopen itself in five seconds (assuming that Excel is still running). To prevent this, use a Workbook_BeforeClose event procedure that contains the following statement:

```
Call StopClock
```

Cross-Ref   To see an example of a repeating OnTime event, see the analog clock example in Chapter 16.

The OnKey event

While you're working, Excel constantly monitors what you type. Because of this monitoring, you can set up a keystroke or a key combination that, when pressed, executes a particular procedure. The only time these keystrokes won't be recognized is when you're entering a formula or working with a dialog box.

Caution   It's important to understand that creating a procedure to respond to an OnKey event isn't limited to a single workbook. The re-mapped keystroke is valid in all open workbooks, not just the one in which you created the event procedure.

Also, if you set up an OnKey event, make sure that you provide a way to cancel the event. A common way to do this is to use the Workbook_BeforeClose event procedure.

An OnKey event example

The following example uses the OnKey method to set up an OnKey event. This event reassigns the PgDn and PgUp keys. After the Setup_OnKey procedure is executed, pressing PgDn executes the PgDn_Sub procedure, and pressing PgUp executes the PgUp_Sub procedure. The net effect is that pressing PgDn moves the cursor down one row, and pressing PgUp moves the cursor up one row. Key combinations that use PgUp and PgDn aren't affected. So, for example, Ctrl+PgDn will continue to activate the next worksheet in a workbook.

```
Sub Setup_OnKey()
    Application.OnKey "{PgDn}", "PgDn_Sub"
    Application.OnKey "{PgUp}", "PgUp_Sub"
End Sub
```

```
Sub PgDn_Sub()
    On Error Resume Next
    ActiveCell.Offset(1, 0).Activate
End Sub

Sub PgUp_Sub()
    On Error Resume Next
    ActiveCell.Offset(-1, 0).Activate
End Sub
```

On the Web

This example, named onkey event demo.xlsm, is available on the book's website.

In the previous examples, I use On Error Resume Next to ignore any errors that are generated. For example, if the active cell is in the first row, trying to move up one row causes an error. Also, if the active sheet is a chart sheet, an error will occur because there is no such thing as an active cell in a chart sheet.

By executing the following procedure, you cancel the OnKey events and return these keys to their normal functionality:

```
Sub Cancel_OnKey()
    Application.OnKey "{PgDn}"
    Application.OnKey "{PgUp}"
End Sub
```

Contrary to what you might expect, using an empty string as the second argument for the OnKey method does *not* cancel the OnKey event. Rather, it causes Excel to simply ignore the keystroke and do nothing. For example, the following instruction tells Excel to ignore Alt+F4 (the percent sign represents the Alt key):

```
    Application.OnKey "%{F4}", ""
```

Cross-Ref

Although you can use the OnKey method to assign a shortcut key for executing a macro, it's better to use the Macro Options dialog box for this task. For more details, see Chapter 7.

Key Codes

In the previous section, note that the PgDn keystroke appears in braces. Table 17-6 shows the key codes that you can use in your OnKey procedures.

Table 17-6: Key Codes for the OnKey Event

Key	Code
Backspace	{BACKSPACE} or {BS}
Break	{BREAK}
Caps Lock	{CAPSLOCK}
Delete or Del	{DELETE} or {DEL}
Down Arrow	{DOWN}
End	{END}
Enter	~ (tilde)
Enter (on the numeric keypad)	{ENTER}
Escape	{ESCAPE} or {ESC}
Home	{HOME}
Ins	{INSERT}
Left Arrow	{LEFT}
NumLock	{NUMLOCK}
PgDn	{PGDN}
PgUp	{PGUP}
Right Arrow	{RIGHT}
Scroll Lock	{SCROLLLOCK}
Tab	{TAB}
Up Arrow	{UP}
F1 through F15	{F1} through {F15}

You can also specify keys combined with Shift, Ctrl, and Alt. To specify a key combined with another key or keys, use the following symbols:

➤ **Shift:** Plus sign (+)

➤ **Ctrl:** Caret (^)

➤ **Alt:** Percent sign (%)

For example, to assign a procedure to the Ctrl+Shift+A key, use this code:

```
Application.OnKey "^+A", "SubName"
```

To assign a procedure to Alt+F11 (which is normally used to switch to the VB Editor window), use this code:

```
Application.OnKey "%{F11}", "SubName"
```

Disabling shortcut menus

Earlier in this chapter, I discuss a Worksheet_BeforeRightClick procedure that disables the right-click shortcut menu. The following procedure is placed in the ThisWorkbook code module:

```
Private Sub Worksheet_BeforeRightClick _
   (ByVal Target As Range, Cancel As Boolean)Cancel = True
     MsgBox "The shortcut menu is not available."
End Sub
```

I also noted that the user could still display the shortcut menu by pressing Shift+F10. To intercept the Shift+F10 key combination, add these procedures to a standard VBA module:

```
Sub SetupNoShiftF10()
    Application.OnKey "+{F10}", "NoShiftF10"
End Sub

Sub TurnOffNoShiftF10()
    Application.OnKey "+{F10}"
End Sub

Sub NoShiftF10()
    MsgBox "Nice try, but that doesn't work either."
End Sub
```

After the SetupNoShiftF10 procedure is executed, pressing Shift+F10 displays the message box shown in Figure 17-12. Remember that the Worksheet_BeforeRightClick procedure is valid only in its own workbook. The Shift+F10 key event, on the other hand, applies to all open workbooks.

	A	B	C	D	E	F	G	H	I
22									
23		9	4	22	29	5	89	58	
24		76	10	93	35	20	21	91	
25		60	2	98	62	35	99	29	
26		13	58	93	34	10	51	59	
27		7	30	65					
28		60	74	64					
29		98	65	39					
30		93	71	41					
31		35	36	76					
32		78	15	66					
33		10	57	58					
34		68	68	2	42	56	35	4	
35		3	93	10	36	47	1	49	
36		11	48	86	99	90	84	62	
37		3	28	92	51	56	93	50	

Microsoft Excel

Nice try, but that doesn't work either.

OK

Sheet1

Figure 17-12: Pressing Shift+F10 displays this message.

Note

Some keyboards have a dedicated key that displays a shortcut menu. On my keyboard, that key is on the right side of the keyboard between the Windows key and the Ctrl key. I was surprised to discover that intercepting the Shit+F10 key combination also disables the dedicated shortcut menu key.

On the Web

The book's website contains a workbook that includes all the OnKey procedures. The file, named no shortcut menus.xlsm, includes workbook event-handler procedures: Workbook_Open executes the SetupNoShiftF10 procedure, and Workbook_BeforeClose calls the TurnOffNoShiftF10 procedure.

Interacting with Other Applications

In This Chapter

- Starting or activating another application from Excel
- Displaying Windows Control Panel dialog boxes
- Using Automation to control another application

Starting an Application from Excel

Launching another application from Excel is often useful. For example, you might want to execute another Microsoft Office application or even a DOS batch file from Excel. Or, as an application developer, you may want to make it easy for a user to access the Windows Control Panel to adjust system settings.

Using the VBA Shell function

The VBA Shell function makes launching other programs relatively easy. Following is an example of VBA code that launches the Windows Calculator application:

```
Sub StartCalc()
    Dim Program As String
    Dim TaskID As Double
    On Error Resume Next
    Program = "calc.exe"
    TaskID = Shell(Program, 1)
    If Err <> 0 Then
        MsgBox "Cannot start " & Program, vbCritical, "Error"
    End If
End Sub
```

You'll probably recognize the application that this procedure launches in Figure 18-1.

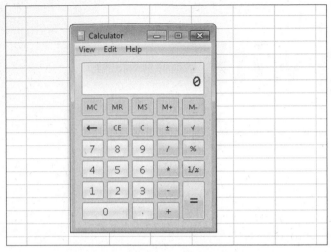

Figure 18-1: Running the Windows Calculator program from Excel.

The Shell function returns a task identification number for the application specified in the first argument. You can use this number later to activate the task. The second argument for the Shell function determines how the application is displayed. (1 is the code for a normal-size window that has the focus.) Refer to the Help system for other values for this argument.

If the Shell function isn't successful, it generates an error. Therefore, this procedure uses an On Error statement to display a message if the executable file can't be found or if some other error occurs.

It's important to understand that your VBA code doesn't pause while the application that was started with the Shell function is running. In other words, the Shell function runs the application *asynchronously*. If the procedure has more instructions after the Shell function is executed, these instructions are executed concurrently with the newly loaded program. If any instruction requires user intervention (for example, displaying a message box), Excel's title bar flashes while the other application is active.

In some cases, you may want to launch an application with the Shell function, but you need your VBA code to pause until the application is closed. For example, the launched application might generate a file that is used later in your code. Although you can't pause the execution of your code, you *can* create a loop that does nothing except monitor the application's status. The example that follows displays a message box when the application launched by the Shell function has ended:

```
Declare PtrSafe Function OpenProcess Lib "kernel32" _
    (ByVal dwDesiredAccess As Long, _
    ByVal bInheritHandle As Long, _
    ByVal dwProcessId As Long) As Long

Declare PtrSafe Function GetExitCodeProcess Lib "kernel32" _
    (ByVal hProcess As Long, _
```

```
        lpExitCode As Long) As Long

Sub StartCalc2()
    Dim TaskID As Long
    Dim hProc As Long
    Dim lExitCode As Long
    Dim ACCESS_TYPE As Integer, STILL_ACTIVE As Integer
    Dim Program As String

    ACCESS_TYPE = &H400
    STILL_ACTIVE = &H103

    Program = "Calc.exe"
    On Error Resume Next

'   Shell the task
    TaskID = Shell(Program, 1)

'   Get the process handle
    hProc = OpenProcess(ACCESS_TYPE, False, TaskID)

    If Err <> 0 Then
        MsgBox "Cannot start " & Program, vbCritical, "Error"
        Exit Sub
    End If

    Do  'Loop continuously
'       Check on the process
        GetExitCodeProcess hProc, lExitCode
'       Allow event processing
        DoEvents
    Loop While lExitCode = STILL_ACTIVE

'   Task is finished, so show message
    MsgBox Program & " was closed"
End Sub
```

While the launched program is running, this procedure continually calls the GetExitCodeProcess function from a Do-Loop structure, testing for its returned value (lExitCode). When the program is finished, lExitCode returns a different value, the loop ends, and the VBA code resumes executing.

On the Web

Both of the previous examples are available on the book's website. The filename is start calculator.xlsm.

Tip

Another way to launch an app is to create a hyperlink in a cell (VBA not required). For example, this formula creates a hyperlink in a cell that, when clicked, runs the Windows Calculator program:

```
=HYPERLINK("C:\Windows\System32\calc.exe","Windows Calculator")
```

You need to make sure that the link points to the correct location. And you'll probably get at least one security warning when you click the link. This technique works also for files, and loads the file into the default application for the file type. For example, clicking the hyperlink created by the following formula loads the file into the default app for text files:

```
=HYPERLINK("C:\files\data.txt","Open the data file")
```

Displaying a folder window

The Shell function is handy also if you need to display a particular directory using Windows Explorer. For example, the statement that follows displays the folder of the active workbook (but only if the workbook has been saved):

```
If ActiveWorkbook.Path <> "" Then _
  Shell "explorer.exe " & ActiveWorkbook.Path, vbNormalFocus
```

Using the Windows ShellExecute API function

ShellExecute is a Windows Application Programming Interface (API) function that is useful for starting other applications. Importantly, this function can start an application only if an associated file-name is known (assuming that the file type is registered with Windows). For example, you can use ShellExecute to display a web document by starting the default web browser. Or you can use an e-mail address to start the default e-mail client.

The API declaration follows (this code works only with Excel 2010 or later):

```
Private Declare PtrSafe Function ShellExecute Lib "shell32.dll" _
  Alias "ShellExecuteA" (ByVal hWnd As Long, _
  ByVal lpOperation As String, ByVal lpFile As String, _
  ByVal lpParameters As String, ByVal lpDirectory As String, _
  ByVal nShowCmd As Long) As Long
```

The following procedure demonstrates how to call the ShellExecute function. In this example, it opens a graphics file by using the graphics program that's set up to handle JPG files. If the result returned by the function is less than 32, an error occurred.

```
Sub ShowGraphic()
    Dim FileName As String
    Dim Result As Long
    FileName = ThisWorkbook.Path & "\flower.jpg"
```

```
    Result = ShellExecute(0&, vbNullString, FileName, _
        vbNullString, vbNullString, vbNormalFocus)
    If Result < 32 Then MsgBox "Error"
End Sub
```

The next procedure opens a text file, using the default text file program:

```
Sub OpenTextFile()
    Dim FileName As String
    Dim Result As Long
    FileName = ThisWorkbook.Path & "\textfile.txt"
    Result = ShellExecute(0&, vbNullString, FileName, _
        vbNullString, vbNullString, vbNormalFocus)
    If Result < 32 Then MsgBox "Error"
End Sub
```

The following example is similar, but it opens a web URL by using the default browser:

```
Sub OpenURL()
    Dim URL As String
    Dim Result As Long
    URL = "http://spreadsheetpage.com"
    Result = ShellExecute(0&, vbNullString, URL, _
        vbNullString, vbNullString, vbNormalFocus)
    If Result < 32 Then MsgBox "Error"
End Sub
```

You can use this technique also with an e-mail address. The following example opens the default e-mail client (if one exists) and then addresses an e-mail to the recipient:

```
Sub StartEmail()
    Dim Addr As String
    Dim Result As Long
    Addr = "mailto:nobody@example.com"
    Result = ShellExecute(0&, vbNullString, Addr, _
        vbNullString, vbNullString, vbNormalFocus)
    If Result < 32 Then MsgBox "Error"
End Sub
```

On the Web

These examples are available on the book's website in a file named shellexecute exam-ples.xlsm. This file uses API declarations that are compatible with all versions of Excel.

Activating an Application with Excel

In the preceding section, I discuss various ways to start an application. You may find that if an application is already running, using the Shell function may start another instance of it. In most cases, however, you want to *activate* the instance that's running — not start another instance of it.

Using AppActivate

The following StartCalculator procedure uses the AppActivate statement to activate an application (in this case, the Windows Calculator) if it's already running. The argument for AppActivate is the caption of the application's title bar. If the AppActivate statement generates an error, Calculator is not running and the routine starts the application.

```
Sub StartCalculator()
    Dim AppFile As String
    Dim CalcTaskID As Double

    AppFile = "Calc.exe"
    On Error Resume Next
    AppActivate "Calculator"
    If Err <> 0 Then
        Err = 0
        CalcTaskID = Shell(AppFile, 1)
        If Err <> 0 Then MsgBox "Can't start Calculator"
    End If
End Sub
```

On the Web

This example is available on the book's website. The filename is start calculator.xlsm.

Activating a Microsoft Office application

If the application that you want to start is one of several Microsoft applications, you can use the ActivateMicrosoftApp method of the Application object. For example, the following procedure starts Word:

```
Sub StartWord()
    Application.ActivateMicrosoftApp xlMicrosoftWord
End Sub
```

If Word is already running when the preceding procedure is executed, the application is activated. The other constants available for this method are

➤ xlMicrosoftPowerPoint

➤ xlMicrosoftMail (activates Outlook)

➤ xlMicrosoftAccess

➤ xlMicrosoftFoxPro

➤ xlMicrosoftProject

Running Control Panel Dialog Boxes

Windows provides quite a few system dialog boxes and wizards, most of which are accessible from the Windows Control Panel. You might need to display one or more of these from your Excel application. For example, you might want to display the Windows Date and Time dialog box, shown in Figure 18-2.

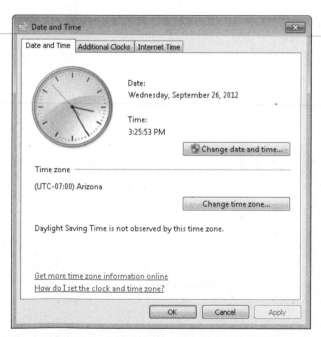

Figure 18-2: Use VBA to display a Control Panel dialog box.

The key to running other system dialog boxes is to execute the rundll32.exe application by using the VBA Shell function.

The following procedure displays the Date and Time dialog box:

```
Sub ShowDateTimeDlg()
  Dim Arg As String
  Dim TaskID As Double
  Arg = "rundll32.exe shell32.dll,Control_RunDLL timedate.cpl"
  On Error Resume Next
  TaskID = Shell(Arg)
  If Err <> 0 Then
      MsgBox ("Cannot start the application.")
  End If
End Sub
```

Following is the general format for the rundll32.exe application:

```
rundll32.exe shell32.dll,Control_RunDLL filename.cpl, n,t
```

where:

> filename.cpl: The name of one of the Control Panel *.CPL files

> n: The zero-based number of the applet in the *.CPL file

> t: The number of the tab (for multitabbed applets)

On the Web

A workbook that displays 12 additional Control Panel applets, depicted in Figure 18-3, is available on the book's website. The filename is control panel dialogs.xlsm.

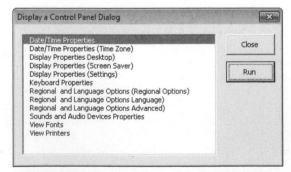

Figure 18-3: The workbook that displays this dialog box demonstrates how to run system dialog boxes from Excel.

Using Automation in Excel

You can write an Excel macro to control other applications, such as Microsoft Word. More accurately, the Excel macro will control Word's automation server. In such circumstances, Excel is the *client application* and Word is the *server application.* Or you can write a VBA application in Word to control Excel. The process of one application's controlling another is sometimes known as *Object Linking and Embedding (OLE),* or simply *automation.*

The concept behind automation is quite appealing. A developer who needs to generate a chart, for example, can just reach into another application's grab bag of objects, fetch a Chart object, and then manipulate its properties and use its methods. Automation, in a sense, blurs the boundaries between applications. An end user may be working with an Access object and not even realize it.

Note

Some applications, such as Excel, can function as either a client application or a server application. Other applications can function only as client applications or only as server applications.

In this section, I demonstrate how to use VBA to access and manipulate the objects exposed by other applications. The examples use Microsoft Word, but the concepts apply to any application that exposes its objects for automation — which accounts for an increasing number of applications.

Working with foreign objects using automation

As you may know, you can use Excel's Insert➜Text➜Object command to embed an object, such as a Word document, in a worksheet. In addition, you can create an object and manipulate it with VBA. (This action is the heart of automation.) When you do so, you usually have full access to the object. For developers, this technique is generally more beneficial than embedding the object in a worksheet. When an object is embedded, the user must know how to use the automation object's application. But when you use VBA to work with the object, you can program the object so that the user can manipulate it by an action as simple as a button click.

Early versus late binding

Before you can work with an external object, you must create an instance of the object. You can do so in two ways: early binding or late binding. *Binding* refers to matching the function calls written by the programmer to the actual code that implements the function.

Early binding

To use early binding, create a reference to the object library by choosing the Tools➜References command in Visual Basic Editor (VBE) to display the dialog box shown in Figure 18-4. Then put a check mark next to the object library you need to reference.

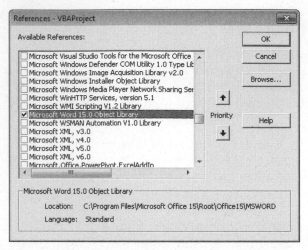

Figure 18-4: Adding a reference to an object library file.

After the reference to the object library is established, you can use Object Browser, shown in Figure 18-5, to view the object names, methods, and properties. To access Object Browser, press F2 in VBE.

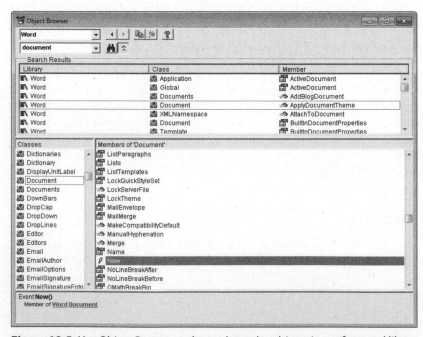

Figure 18-5: Use Object Browser to learn about the objects in a referenced library.

When you use early binding, you must establish a reference to a version-specific object library. For example, you can specify Microsoft Word 10.0 Object Library (for Word 2002), Microsoft Word 11.0 Object Library (for Word 2003), Microsoft Word 12.0 Object Library (for Word 2007), Microsoft Word

14.0 Object Library (for Word 2010), or Microsoft Word 15.0 Object Library (for Word 2013). Then you use a statement like the following to create the object:

```
Dim WordApp As New Word.Application
```

Using early binding to create the object by setting a reference to the object library is usually more efficient and also often yields better performance. Early binding is an option, however, only if the object that you're controlling has a separate type library or object library file. You also need to ensure that the user of the application actually has a copy of the specific library installed.

Another advantage of early binding is that you can use constants that are defined in the object library. For example, Word (like Excel) contains many predefined constants that you can use in your VBA code. If you use early binding, you can use the constants in your code. If you use late binding, you'll need to use the actual value rather than the constant.

Still another benefit of using early binding is that you can take advantage of the VBE Object Browser and Auto List Members option to make it easier to access properties and methods; this feature doesn't work when you use late binding because the type of the object is known only at runtime.

Late binding

At runtime, you use either the CreateObject function to create the object or the GetObject function to obtain a saved instance of the object. Such an object is declared as a generic Object type, and its object reference is resolved at runtime.

You can use late binding even when you don't know which version of the application is installed on the user's system. For example, the following code, which works with Word 97 and later, creates a Word object:

```
Dim WordApp As Object
Set WordApp = CreateObject("Word.Application")
```

If multiple versions of Word are installed, you can create an object for a specific version. The following statement, for example, uses Word 2010:

```
Set WordApp = CreateObject("Word.Application.14")
```

The Registry key for Word's automation object and the reference to the Application object in VBA just happen to be the same: Word.Application. They do not, however, refer to the same thing. When you declare an object As Word.Application or As New Word.Application, the term refers to the Application object in the Word library. But when you invoke the function CreateObject("Word.Application"), the term refers to the moniker by which the latest version of Word is known in the Windows System Registry. This isn't the case for all automation objects, although it is true for the main Office 2013 components. If the user replaces Word 2010 with Word 2013, CreateObject("Word.Application") will continue to work properly, referring to the new application. if Word 2013 is removed, however,

CreateObject("Word.Application.15"), which uses the alternate version-specific name for Word 2013, will fail to work.

The CreateObject function used on an automation object such as Word.Application or Excel.Application always creates a new *instance* of that automation object. That is, it starts a new and separate copy of the automation part of the program. Even if an instance of the automation object is already running, a new instance is started, and then an object of the specified type is created.

To use the current instance or to start the application and have it load a file, use the GetObject function.

Note

If you need to automate an Office application use early binding and reference the earliest version of the product that you expect could be installed on your client's system. For example, if you need to be able to automate Word 2007, Word 2010, and Word 2013, you should use the type library for Word 2007 to maintain compatibility with all three versions. With this approach, you can't use features found only in the later version of Word.

A simple example of late binding

The following example demonstrates how to create a Word object by using late binding. This procedure creates the object, displays the version number, closes the Word application, and then destroys the object (thus freeing the memory that it used):

```
Sub GetWordVersion()
    Dim WordApp As Object
    Set WordApp = CreateObject("Word.Application")
    MsgBox WordApp.Version
    WordApp.Quit
    Set WordApp = Nothing
End Sub
```

Note

The Word object that's created in this procedure is invisible. If you'd like to see the object's window while it's being manipulated, set its Visible property to True, as follows:

```
WordApp.Visible = True
```

This example can be programmed also using early binding. Before doing so, choose Tools→ References to set a reference to the Word object library. Then you can use the following code:

```
Sub GetWordVersion()
    Dim WordApp As New Word.Application
    MsgBox WordApp.Version
    WordApp.Quit
    Set WordApp = Nothing
End Sub
```

GetObject versus CreateObject

The VBA GetObject and CreateObject functions both return a reference to an object but work in different ways.

The CreateObject function creates an interface to a new instance of an application. Use this function when the application isn't running. If an instance of the application is already running, a new instance is started. For example, the following statement starts Excel, and the object returned in XLApp is a reference to the Excel.Application object that it created:

```
Set XLApp = CreateObject("Excel.Application")
```

The GetObject function is used either with an application that's already running or to start an application with a file already loaded. The following statement, for example, starts Excel with the file Myfile.xls already loaded. The object returned in XLBook is a reference to the Workbook object (the Myfile.xlsx file):

```
Set XLBook = GetObject("C:\Myfile.xlsx")
```

Figure 18-6 shows how Auto List Members works with early binding. When using late binding, you get no assistance when writing code.

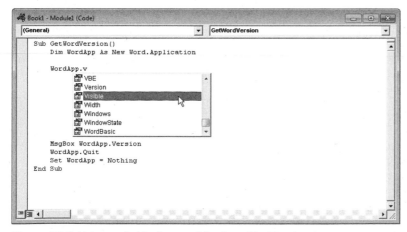

Figure 18-6: Using early binding enables Auto List Members.

Controlling Word from Excel

The example in this section demonstrates automation by using Word. The MakeMemos procedure creates three customized memos in Word and then saves each document to a file. The information used to create the memos is stored in a worksheet, as shown in Figure 18-7.

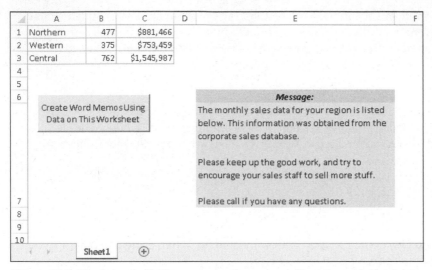

Figure 18-7: Word automatically generates three memos based on this Excel data.

The MakeMemos procedure starts by creating an object called WordApp. The routine cycles through the three rows of data in Sheet1 and uses Word's properties and methods to create each memo and save it to disk. A range named Message (in cell E6) contains the text used in the memo. All the action occurs behind the scenes — that is, Word isn't visible.

```
Sub MakeMemos()
'    Creates memos in word using Automation
    Dim WordApp As Object
    Dim Data As Range, message As String
    Dim Records As Integer, i As Integer
    Dim Region As String, SalesAmt As String, SalesNum As String
    Dim SaveAsName As String

'    Start Word and create an object (late binding)
    Set WordApp = CreateObject("Word.Application")

'    Information from worksheet
    Set Data = Sheets("Sheet1").Range("A1")
    Message = Sheets("Sheet1").Range("Message")

'    Cycle through all records in Sheet1
    Records = Application.CountA(Sheets("Sheet1").Range("A:A"))
    For i = 1 To Records
```

```vba
'       Update status bar progress message
        Application.StatusBar = "Processing Record " & i

'       Assign current data to variables
        Region = Data.Cells(i, 1).Value
        SalesNum = Data.Cells(i, 2).Value
        SalesAmt = Format(Data.Cells(i, 3).Value, "#,000")

'       Determine the filename
        SaveAsName = Application.DefaultFilePath & _
            "\" & Region & ".docx"

'       Send commands to Word
        With WordApp
            .Documents.Add
            With .Selection
                .Font.Size = 14
                .Font.Bold = True
                .ParagraphFormat.Alignment = 1
                .TypeText Text:="M E M O R A N D U M"
                .TypeParagraph
                .TypeParagraph
                .Font.Size = 12
                .ParagraphFormat.Alignment = 0
                .Font.Bold = False
                .TypeText Text:="Date:" & vbTab & _
                    Format(Date, "mmmm d, yyyy")
                .TypeParagraph
                .TypeText Text:="To:" & vbTab & Region & _
                 " Manager"
                .TypeParagraph
                .TypeText Text:="From:" & vbTab & _
                    Application.UserName
                .TypeParagraph
                .TypeParagraph
                .TypeText Message
                .TypeParagraph
                .TypeParagraph
                .TypeText Text:="Units Sold:" & vbTab & _
                 SalesNum
                .TypeParagraph
                .TypeText Text:="Amount:" & vbTab & _
                    Format(SalesAmt, "$#,##0")
            End With
                .ActiveDocument.SaveAs FileName:=SaveAsName
        End With
    Next i

'   Kill the object
    WordApp.Quit
```

```
      Set WordApp = Nothing

'      Reset status bar
       Application.StatusBar = ""
       MsgBox Records & " memos were created and saved in " & _
         Application.DefaultFilePath
End Sub
```

Figure 18-8 shows one of the documents created by the MakeMemos procedure.

Figure 18-8: an Excel procedure created this Word document.

On the Web   **This workbook, named make memos.xlsm, is available on the book's website.**

Creating this macro involved several steps. I started by recording my actions in Word while creating a new document, adding and formatting some text, and saving the file. That Word macro provided the information that I needed about the appropriate properties and methods. I then copied the macro to an

Excel module. Note that I used With-End With, adding a dot before each instruction between With and End With. For example, the original Word macro contained (among others) the following instruction:

```
Documents.Add
```

I modified the macro as follows:

```
With WordApp
    .Documents.Add
'   more instructions here
End With
```

The macro that I recorded in Word used a few built-in constants. Because this example uses late binding, I had to substitute actual values for those constants. I was able to learn the values by using the Immediate window in Word's VBE.

Controlling Excel from another application

You can also control Excel from another application (such as another programming language or a Word VBA procedure). For example, you may want to perform some calculations in Excel and return the result to a Word document.

You can create any of the following Excel objects with the adjacent functions:

➤ Application object: CreateObject("Excel.Application")

➤ Workbook object: CreateObject("Excel.Sheet")

➤ Chart object: CreateObject("Excel.Chart")

The code that follows is a procedure in a VBA module in a Word 2013 document. This procedure creates an Excel Worksheet object (whose moniker is "Excel.Sheet") from an existing workbook and pastes it into the Word file.

```
Sub MakeLoanTable()
    Dim XLSheet As Object
    Dim LoanAmt
    Dim Wbook As String
```

```vba
'    Prompt for values
    LoanAmt = InputBox("Loan Amount?")
    If LoanAmt = "" Then Exit Sub

'    Clear the document
    ThisDocument.Content.Delete

'    Create Sheet object
    Wbook = ThisDocument.Path & "\mortgagecalcs.xlsx"
    Set XLSheet = GetObject(Wbook, "Excel.Sheet").ActiveSheet

'    Put values in sheet
    XLSheet.Range("LoanAmount") = LoanAmt
    XLSheet.Calculate

'    Insert page heading
    Selection.Style = "Title"
    Selection.TypeText "Loan Amount: " & _
      Format(LoanAmt, "$#,##0")
    Selection.TypeParagraph
    Selection.TypeParagraph

'    Copy data from sheet & paste to document
    XLSheet.Range("DataTable").Copy
    Selection.Paste

    Selection.TypeParagraph
    Selection.TypeParagraph

'    Copy chart and paste to document
    XLSheet.ChartObjects(1).Copy
    Selection.PasteSpecial _
        Link:=False, _
        DataType:=wdPasteMetafilePicture, _
        Placement:=wdInLine

'    Kill the object
    Set XLSheet = Nothing
End Sub
```

On the Web

This example is available on the book's website. The Word document is named auto-mate excel.docm, and the Excel workbook is named mortgagecalcs.xlsx. When you open the Word file, execute the MakeLoanTable macro by choosing Insert➜Mortgage➜Get Mortgage Amount.

The Excel worksheet used by this Word procedure is shown in Figure 18-9. The MakeLoanTable procedure prompts the user for a loan amount and inserts the value into cell C7 (named LoanAmount).

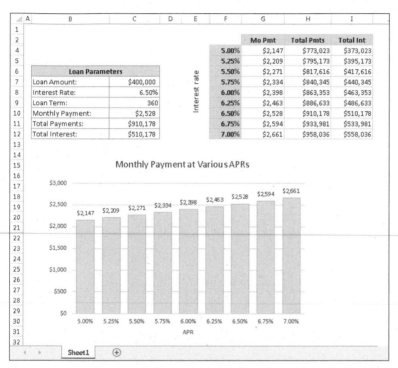

Figure 18-9: a VBA procedure in Word uses this worksheet.

Recalculating the worksheet updates a data table in range F2:I12 (named DataTable) and also updates the chart. The DataTable range and the chart are then copied from the Excel object and pasted into the Word document. The result is shown in Figure 18-10.

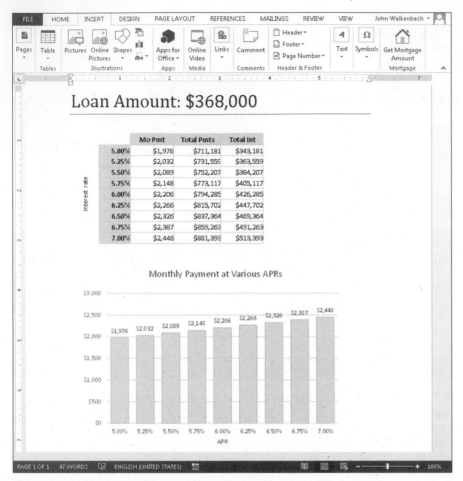

Figure 18-10: The Word VBA procedure uses Excel to create this document.

Sending Personalized E-Mail via Outlook

The example in this section demonstrates automation with Microsoft Outlook.

Figure 18-11 shows a worksheet that contains data used in the e-mail messages: name, e-mail address, and bonus amount. The SendMail procedure loops through the rows in the worksheet, retrieves the data, and creates an individualized message (stored in the Msg variable).

	A	B	C	D
1	**Name**	**Email**	**Bonus**	
2	John Jones	jjones@zx-prrtgfw.com	$4,000	
3	Bob Smith	bsmith@zx-prrtgfw.com	$5,000	
4	Fred Simpson	fsimpson@zx-prrtgfw.com	$6,500	
5	Ann Hutton	ahutton@zx-prrtgfw.com	$7,500	
6				
7				

Sheet1

Figure 18-11: This information is used in the Outlook e-mail messages.

```
Sub SendEmail()
  'Uses early binding
  'Requires a reference to the Outlook Object Library
  Dim OutlookApp As Outlook.Application
  Dim MItem As Outlook.MailItem
  Dim cell As Range
  Dim Subj As String,  EmailAddr As String,  Recipient As String
  Dim Bonus As String, Msg As String

  'Create Outlook object
  Set OutlookApp = New Outlook.Application

  'Loop through the rows
  For Each cell In Columns("B").Cells.SpecialCells(xlCellTypeConstants)
    If cell.Value Like "*@*" Then
      'Get the data
      Subj = "Your Annual Bonus"
      Recipient = cell.Offset(0, -1).Value
      EmailAddr = cell.Value
      Bonus = Format(cell.Offset(0, 1).Value, "$0,000.")

     'Compose message
      Msg = "Dear " & Recipient & vbCrLf & vbCrLf
      Msg = Msg & "I am pleased to inform you that your annual bonus is "
      Msg = Msg & Bonus & vbCrLf & vbCrLf
      Msg = Msg & "William Rose" & vbCrLf
      Msg = Msg & "President"

      'Create Mail Item and send it
      Set MItem = OutlookApp.CreateItem(olMailItem)
      With MItem
        .To = EmailAddr
        .Subject = Subj
        .Body = Msg
        .Save
      End With
    End If
  Next
End Sub
```

Figure 18-12 shows one of the e-mail messages displayed in Outlook.

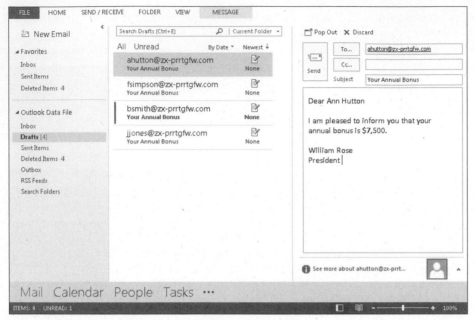

Figure 18-12: An Outlook e-mail message created by Excel.

This example uses early binding, so it requires a reference to the Outlook Object Library. Note that two objects are involved: an Outlook object and a MailItem object. The Outlook object is created with this statement:

```
Set OutlookApp = New Outlook.Application
```

The MailItem object is created with this statement:

```
Set MItem = OutlookApp.CreateItem(olMailItem)
```

The code sets the To, Subject, and Body properties and then uses the Send method to send each message.

Tip   The example uses the Save method, which places the messages in Outlook's Draft folder. To send the messages immediately, use the Send method. Using the Save method is particularly useful while you're testing and debugging the code.

On the Web   This example, named personalized email - outlook.xlsm, is available on the book's website. You must have Microsoft Outlook installed. A slightly modified version that uses late binding is also available in personalized email - outlook (late binding).xlsm.

Sending E-Mail Attachments from Excel

As you probably know, Excel can send a workbook by e-mail as an attachment. And, of course, you can use VBA to automate this type of task. The following procedure uses the SendMail method to send the active workbook (as an attachment) to joeblow@zx-prrtgfw.com, using the default e-mail client (if any). The e-mail message has the subject *My Workbook*.

```
Sub SendWorkbook()
    ActiveWorkbook.SendMail "joeblow@zx-prrtgfw.com", "My Workbook"
End Sub
```

The SendMail method uses the default e-mail client.

Note

If you'd like to e-mail only a single sheet from a workbook, you need to copy the sheet to a new (temporary) workbook, send that workbook as an attachment, and then close the temporary file. Here's an example that sends Sheet1 from the active workbook, attached to an e-mail with the subject *My Workbook*. Note that the copied sheet becomes the active workbook.

```
Sub Sendasheet()
    ActiveWorkbook.Worksheets("sheet1").Copy
    ActiveWorkbook.SendMail "joeblow@zx-prrtgfw.com", "My Workbook"
    ActiveWorkbook.Close False
End Sub
```

In the preceding example, the file will have the default workbook name (for example, Book2.xlsx). If you'd like to give the single-sheet workbook attachment a more meaningful name, you need to save the temporary workbook and then delete it after it's sent. The following procedure saves Sheet1 to a file named my file.xlsx. After sending this temporary workbook as an e-mail attachment, the code uses the VBA Kill statement to delete the file.

```
Sub SendOneSheet()
    Dim Filename As String
    Filename = "my file.xlsx"
    ActiveWorkbook.Worksheets("sheet1").Copy
    ActiveWorkbook.SaveAs Filename
    ActiveWorkbook.SendMail "joeblow@zx-prrtgfw.com", "My Workbook"
    ActiveWorkbook.Close False
    Kill Filename
End Sub
```

Note

Unfortunately, Excel doesn't provide a way to automate saving a workbook as a PDF file and sending it as an attachment. You can, however, automate part of the process. The following SendSheetAsPDF procedure saves the active sheet as a PDF file and then displays the compose message window from your default e-mail client (with the PDF file attached) so that you can fill in the recipient's name and click Send:

```
Sub SendSheetAsPDF()
    CommandBars.ExecuteMso "FileEmailAsPdfEmailAttachment"
End Sub
```

When Excel is lacking powers, it's time to call on Outlook. The procedure that follows saves the active workbook as a PDF file and automates Outlook to create an e-mail message with the PDF file as an attachment:

```
Sub SendAsPDF()
'   Uses early binding
'   Requires a reference to the Outlook Object Library
    Dim OutlookApp As Outlook.Application
    Dim MItem As Object
    Dim Recipient As String, Subj As String
    Dim Msg As String, Fname As String

'   Message details
    Recipient = "myboss@xrediyh.com"
    Subj = "Sales figures"
    Msg = "Hey boss, here's the PDF file you wanted."
    Msg = Msg & vbNewLine & vbNewLine & "-Frank"
    Fname = Application.DefaultFilePath & "\" & _
      ActiveWorkbook.Name & ".pdf"

'   Create the attachment
    ActiveSheet.ExportAsFixedFormat _
        Type:=xlTypePDF, _
        Filename:=Fname

'   Create Outlook object
    Set OutlookApp = New Outlook.Application

'   Create Mail Item and send it
    Set MItem = OutlookApp.CreateItem(olMailItem)
    With MItem
      .To = Recipient
      .Subject = Subj
      .Body = Msg
      .Attachments.Add Fname
```

```
        .Save 'to Drafts folder
        '.Send
    End With
    Set OutlookApp = Nothing

'   Delete the file
    Kill Fname
End Sub
```

This example, named send pdf via outlook.xlsm, is available on the book's website.

Creating and Using Add-Ins

In This Chapter

- Understanding the concept of add-ins

- Exploring Excel's Add-In Manager

- Creating an add-in

- Comparing XLAM add-in files to XLSM files

- Viewing VBA code that manipulates add-ins

- Detecting whether an add-in is installed properly

What Is an Add-In?

One of Excel's most useful features for developers is the capability to create add-ins. Creating add-ins adds a professional touch to your work, and add-ins offer several key advantages over standard workbook files.

Generally speaking, a *spreadsheet add-in* is something added to a spreadsheet to give it additional functionality. Excel ships with several add-ins. Examples include *Analysis ToolPak,* (which adds statistical and analysis capabilities) and *Solver* (which performs advanced optimization calculations).

Some add-ins also provide new worksheet functions that you can use in formulas. With a well-designed add-in, the new features blend in well with the original interface, so they appear to be part of Excel.

Comparing an add-in with a standard workbook

Any knowledgeable Excel user can create an add-in from an Excel workbook file; no additional software or programming tools are required. You can convert any workbook file to an add-in, but not every workbook is appropriate for an add-in. An Excel add-in is basically a normal XLSM workbook with the following differences:

➤ The IsAddin property of the ThisWorkbook object is True. By default, this property is False.

➤ The workbook window is hidden in such a way that it can't be unhidden by choosing the View➜Window➜Unhide command. This means that you can't display worksheets or chart sheets contained in an add-in unless you write code to copy the sheet to a standard workbook.

➤ An add-in isn't a member of the Workbooks collection. Rather, it's a member of the AddIns collection. However, you *can* access an add-in through the Workbooks collection (see "XLAM file VBA collection membership," later in this chapter).

➤ You install and uninstall add-ins by using the Add-Ins dialog box. When an add-in is installed, it remains installed across Excel sessions.

➤ The Macro dialog box (invoked by choosing Developer➜Code➜Macros or View➜Macros➜ Macros) doesn't display the names of the macros contained in an add-in.

➤ When you write formulas, you can use a custom worksheet function stored in an add-in without having to precede the function's name with the source workbook's filename.

Note

In the past, Excel allowed you to use any extension for an add-in. Beginning with Excel 2007, you can still use any extension for an add-in, but if the extension is not XLA or XLAM, you see the warning shown in Figure 19-1. This prompt occurs even if the add-in is an installed add-in that opens automatically when Excel starts, and even if the file is in a trusted location. Microsoft calls this security feature extension hardening.

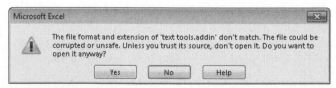

Figure 19-1: Excel warns you if an add-in uses a nonstandard file extension.

Why create add-ins?

You might decide to convert your Excel application into an add-in for any of the following reasons:

➤ **To restrict access to your code and worksheets:** When you distribute an application as an add-in and you protect its VBA project with a password, users can't view or modify the sheets or the VBA code in the workbook. Therefore, if you use proprietary techniques in your application, you can prevent anyone from copying the code — or at least make it more difficult to do so.

➤ **To avoid confusion:** If a user loads your application as an add-in, the file isn't visible and is, therefore, less likely to confuse novice users or get in the way. Unlike a hidden workbook, an add-in can't be unhidden.

➤ **To simplify access to worksheet functions:** Custom worksheet functions stored in an add-in don't require the workbook name qualifier. For example, if you store a custom function named MOVAVG in a workbook named Newfuncs.xlsm, you must use syntax like the following to use this function in a formula that's in a different workbook:

```
=Newfuncs.xlsm!MOVAVG(A1:A50)
```

But if this function is stored in an add-in file that's open, you can use much simpler syntax because you don't need to include the file reference:

```
=MOVAVG(A1:A50)
```

➤ **To provide easier access for users:** After you identify the location of your add-in, it appears in the Add-Ins dialog box with a friendly name and a description of what it does.

➤ **To gain better control over loading:** Add-ins can be opened automatically when Excel starts, regardless of the directory in which they are stored.

➤ **To avoid displaying prompts when unloading:** When an add-in is closed, the user never sees the Do you want to save change? prompt.

Note

The capability to use add-ins is determined by the user's security settings in the Add-Ins tab of the Trust Center dialog box (see Figure 19-2). To display this dialog box, choose Developer➜Code➜Macro Security. Or, if the Developer tab isn't displayed, choose Office➜Excel Options➜Trust Center, and then click the Trust Center Settings button.

About COM add-ins

Excel also supports COM (Component Object Model) add-ins. These files have a .dll or .exe file extension. A COM add-in can be written so that it works with all Office applications that support add-ins. An additional advantage is that the code is compiled, so the original source isn't viewable. Unlike XLAM add-ins, a COM add-in can't contain Excel sheets or charts. COM add-ins are developed in Visual Basic .NET. Discussion of creating COM add-in procedures is well beyond the scope of this book.

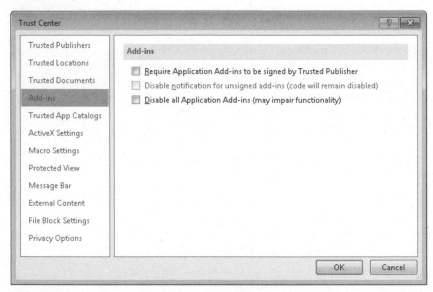

Figure 19-2: These settings affect whether add-ins can be used.

Understanding Excel's Add-In Manager

The most efficient way to load and unload add-ins is with Excel's Add-Ins dialog box, which you access by using either of these methods:

➤ Choose File➜Options➜Add-Ins. Then, in the Excel Options dialog box, choose Excel Add-Ins from the Manage drop-down box and click Go.

➤ Choose Developer➜Add-Ins➜Add-Ins. Note that, by default, the Developer tab is not visible.

➤ Press Alt+TI, a shortcut key sequence used in earlier versions of Excel that still works.

Figure 19-3 shows the Add-Ins dialog box. The list contains the names of all add-ins that Excel knows about, and check marks identify installed add-ins. You can open (install) and close (uninstall) add-ins from this dialog box by selecting or deselecting the check boxes. When you uninstall an add-in, it is not removed from your system. It remains in the list in case you want to install it later. Use the Browse button to locate additional add-ins and add them to the list.

Figure 19-3: The Add-Ins dialog box.

Caution

You can open most add-in files also by choosing the File➜Open command. Because an add-in is never the active workbook, however, you can't close an add-in by choosing File➜Close. You can remove the add-in only by exiting and restarting Excel or by executing VBA code to close the add-in. For example:

```
Workbooks("myaddin.xlam").Close
```

Opening an add-in with the File➜Open command opens the file but does not officially install the add-in.

When you open an add-in, you might notice something different about Excel. In almost every case, the user interface changes in some way: Excel displays either a new command on the Ribbon or new menu items on a shortcut menu. For example, when the Analysis ToolPak add-in is installed, it gives you a new command: Data➜Analysis➜Data Analysis. When you install Excel's Euro Currency Tools add-in, you get a new group in the Formulas tab: Solutions.

If the add-in contains only custom worksheet functions, the new functions appear in the Insert Function dialog box.

Note

If you open an add-in created in a version before Excel 2007, any user interface modifications made by the add-in won't appear as they were intended to appear. Rather, you must access the user interface items (menus and toolbars) by choosing Add-Ins→Menu Commands or Add-Ins→Custom Toolbars.

Creating an Add-in

You can convert any workbook to an add-in, but not all workbooks are appropriate candidates for add-ins. First, an add-in must contain macros. (Otherwise, it's useless.)

Generally, a workbook that benefits most from being converted to an add-in is one that contains general-purpose macro procedures. A workbook that consists only of worksheets would be inaccessible as an add-in because worksheets within add-ins are hidden from the user. You can, however, write code that copies all or part of a sheet from your add-in to a visible workbook.

Creating an add-in from a workbook is simple. The following steps describe the general procedure for creating an add-in from a normal workbook file:

1. Develop your application and make sure that everything works properly.

2. Include a way to execute the macro or macros in the add-in.

   See Chapters 20 and 21 for more information about modifying Excel's user interface.

3. Activate Visual Basic Editor (VBE) and select the workbook in the Project window.

4. Choose Tools→*xxx* Properties (where *xxx* represents the name of the project), click the Protection tab, and select the Lock Project for Viewing check box. Then enter a password (twice), and click OK.

   This step is necessary only if you want to prevent others from viewing or modifying your macros or UserForms.

5. Reactivate Excel and choose Developer→Modify→Document Panel to display the Document Properties panel.

6. Enter a brief descriptive title in the Title field and a longer description in the Comments field.

   This step isn't required, but it makes the add-in easier to use by displaying descriptive text in the Add-Ins dialog box.

7. Choose File→Save As to display the Save As dialog box.

8. In the Save As dialog box, select Excel Add-In (*.xlam) from the Save as Type drop-down list.

    Excel proposes the standard add-ins directory, but you can save the add-in to any location.

9. Click Save.

    A copy of the workbook is saved (with an .xlam extension), and the original workbook remains open.

10. Close the original workbook, and then install the add-in version.

11. Test the add-in to make sure it works correctly.

    If your add-in doesn't work, make changes to your code. And don't forget to save your changes. Because an add-in doesn't appear in an Excel window, you must save it from VBE.

Caution

A workbook being converted to an add-in must have at least one worksheet, and a worksheet must be the active sheet when you create the add-in. If a chart sheet is active, the option to save the workbook as an add-in does not appear in the Save As dialog box.

An Add-In Example

In this section, I discuss the steps involved in creating a useful add-in. The example uses a utility I created that exports charts to separate graphic files. The utility adds a new group (Export Charts) to the Home tab (and can be accessed also by pressing Ctrl+Shift+E). Figure 19-4 shows the main dialog box for this utility. This is a fairly complicated utility, and you might want to take some time to see how it works.

On the Web

The XLSM version of the Export Charts utility (named export charts.xlsm) is available on the book's website. You can use this file to create the described add-in.

A few words about passwords

Microsoft has never promoted Excel as a product that creates applications in which the source code is secure. The password feature provided in Excel is sufficient to prevent casual users from accessing parts of your application that you'd like to keep hidden. However, if you must be absolutely sure that no one ever sees your code or formulas, Excel isn't your best choice as a development platform.

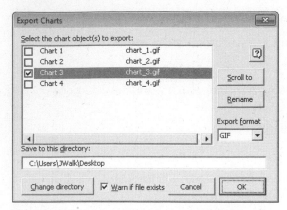

Figure 19-4: The Export Charts workbook will make a useful add-in.

In this example, you'll be working with an application that has already been developed and debugged. The workbook consists of the following items:

➤ **A worksheet named Sheet1:** This sheet is not used, but it must be present because every add-in must have at least one worksheet.

➤ **A UserForm named UserForm1:** This dialog box serves as the primary user interface. The code module for this UserForm contains several event-handler procedures.

➤ **A UserForm named UserForm2:** This dialog box is displayed when the user clicks the Rename button to change the filename of a chart to be exported.

➤ **A UserForm named UserForm3:** This dialog box is displayed when the workbook is opened. It briefly describes how to access the Export Charts utility and also contains a Don't Show This Message Again check box.

➤ **A VBA module named Module1:** This module contains several procedures, including the main procedure (named StartExportCharts), which displays the UserForm1 dialog box.

➤ **ThisWorkbook code module:** This module contains a Workbook_Open procedure that reads the saved settings and displays a start-up message.

➤ **XML code to customize the Ribbon:** This customization was done outside Excel. See Chapter 20 for more information about customizing the Ribbon by using RibbonX.

Adding descriptive information for the example add-in

To enter a title and description for your add-in, choose Developer➔Modify➔Document Panel, which displays the Document Properties panel below the Ribbon.

Enter a title for the add-in in the Title field. This text will appear in the list in the Add-Ins dialog box. In the Comments field, enter a description of the add-in. This information will appear at the bottom of the Add-Ins dialog box when the add-in is selected.

Adding a title and description for the add-in is optional but highly recommended.

Creating an add-in

To create an add-in, do the following:

1. Activate VBE and select the future add-in workbook in the Project window.

2. Choose Debug➜Compile.

   This step forces a compilation of the VBA code and also identifies any syntax errors so that you can correct them. When you save a workbook as an add-in, Excel creates the add-in even if it contains syntax errors.

3. Choose Tools➜*xxx* Properties (where *xxx* represents the name of the project) to display the Project Properties dialog box, click the General tab, and enter a new name for the project.

   By default, all VB projects are named *VBProject*. In this example, the project name is changed to *ExpCharts*. This step is optional but recommended.

4. Save the workbook one last time using its *.XLSM name.

   Strictly speaking, this step isn't necessary, but it gives you an XLSM backup (with no password) of your XLAM add-in file.

5. With the Project Properties dialog box still displayed, click the Protection tab, select the Lock Project for Viewing check box, and enter a password (twice). Click OK.

   The code will remain viewable, and the password protection will take effect the next time the file is opened. If you don't need to protect the project, you can skip this step.

6. In Excel, choose File➜Save As.

   Excel displays its Save As dialog box.

7. In the Save as Type drop-down list, select Excel Add-In (*.xlam).

8. Click Save.

   A new add-in file is created, and the original XLSM version remains open.

When you create an add-in, Excel proposes the standard add-ins directory, but add-ins can be located in any directory.

About Excel's Add-In Manager

You install and uninstall add-ins by using Excel's Add-Ins dialog box. This dialog box lists the names of all available add-ins. those with check marks are open.

In VBA terms, the Add-In dialog box lists the Title property of each AddIn object in the AddIns collection. Each add-in that appears with a check mark has its Installed property set to True.

You can install an add-in by selecting its check box, and you can uninstall an installed add-in by removing the check mark. To add an add-in to the list, use the Browse button to locate its file. By default, the Add-In dialog box lists files of the following types:

- **XLAM:** An Excel 2007 or later add-in created from an XLSM file
- **XLA:** A pre–Excel 2007 add-in created from an XLS file
- **XLL:** A stand-alone compiled DLL file

If you click the Automation button, you can browse for COM add-ins. Note that the Automation Servers dialog box will probably list many files, including COM add-ins that don't work with Excel.

You can enroll an add-in file into the AddIns collection with the Add method of the VBA AddIns collection, but you can't remove one by using VBA. You can also open an add-in from within VBA code by setting the AddIn object's Installed property to True. Setting it to False closes the add-in.

Add-In Manager stores the installed status of the add-ins in the Windows Registry when you exit Excel. Therefore, all add-ins that are installed when you close Excel are automatically opened the next time you start Excel.

Installing an add-in

To avoid confusion, close the XLSM workbook before installing the add-in created from that workbook.

To install an add-in, do the following:

1. Choose File➜Options, and click the Add-Ins tab.
2. Choose Excel Add-Ins from the Manage drop-down list, and then click Go (or press Alt+TI).

   Excel displays the Add-Ins dialog box.
3. Click the Browse button and locate and double-click the add-in that you just created.

   After you find your new add-in, the Add-Ins dialog box displays the add-in in its list. As shown in Figure 19-5, the Add-Ins dialog box also displays the descriptive information that you provided in the Document Properties panel.
4. Click OK to close the dialog box and open the add-in.

Figure 19-5: The Add-Ins dialog box with the new add-in selected.

When the Export Charts add-in is opened, the Home tab displays a new group, Export Charts, with two controls. One control displays the Export Charts dialog box; the other displays the Help file.

You can use the add-in also by pressing its shortcut key combination: Ctrl+Shift+E.

Testing the add-in

After installing the add-in, it's a good idea to perform some additional testing. For this example, open a new workbook and create some charts to try out the various features in the Export Charts utility. Do everything you can think of to try to make the add-in fail. Better yet, seek the assistance of someone unfamiliar with the application to give it a crash test.

If you discover any errors, you can correct the code in the add-in (the original file is not required). After making changes, save the file by choosing File➜Save in VBE.

Distributing an add-in

You can distribute this add-in to other Excel users simply by giving them a copy of the XLAM file (they don't need the XLSM version) along with instructions on how to install it. If you locked the file with a password, your macro code cannot be viewed or modified by others unless they know the password.

Modifying an add-in

If you need to modify an add-in, first open it and then unlock the VB project if you applied a password. To unlock it, activate VBE and then double-click its project's name in the Project window. You'll be prompted for the password. Make your changes, and then save the file from VBE (choose File➜Save).

If you create an add-in that stores its information in a worksheet, you must set its IsAddIn property to False before you can view that workbook in Excel. You do this in the Properties window shown in Figure 19-6 when the ThisWorkbook object is selected. After you make your changes, set the IsAddIn property back to True before you save the file. If you leave the IsAddIn property set to False, Excel won't let you save the file with the XLAM extension.

 Creating an add-in: A checklist

Before you release your add-in to the world, take a few minutes to run through this checklist:

- Did you test your add-in with all supported platforms and Excel versions?

- Did you give your VB project a new name? By default, every project is named *VBProject*. It's a good idea to give your project a more meaningful name.

- Does your add-in make any assumptions about the user's directory structure or directory names?

- When you use the Add-Ins dialog box to load your add-in, are its name and description correct and appropriate?

- If your add-in uses VBA functions that aren't designed to be used in a worksheet, have you declared the functions as Private? If not, these functions will appear in the Insert Function dialog box.

- Did you remember to remove all Debug.Print statements from your code?

- Did you force a recompile of your add-in to ensure that it contains no syntax errors?

- Did you account for any international issues?

- Is your add-in file optimized for speed? See "Optimizing the Performance of Add-Ins" later in this chapter.

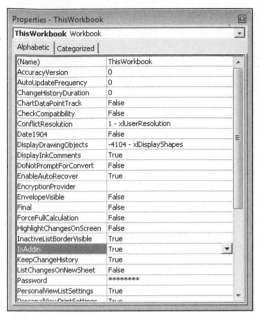

Figure 19-6: Making an add-in not an add-in.

Comparing XLAM and XLSM Files

This section begins by comparing an XLAM add-in file with its XLSM source file. Later in this chapter, I discuss methods that you can use to optimize the performance of your add-in.

For starters, an add-in based on an XLSM source file is the same size as the original. The VBA code in XLAM files isn't optimized, so faster performance isn't among the benefits of using an add-in.

XLAM file VBA collection membership

An add-in is a member of the AddIns collection but isn't an official member of the Workbooks collection. However, you *can* refer to an add-in by using the Workbooks method of the Application object and supplying the add-in's filename as its index. The following instruction creates an object variable that represents an add-in named myaddin.xlam:

```
Dim TestAddin As Workbook
Set TestAddin = Workbooks("myaddin.xlam")
```

Add-ins cannot be referenced by an index number in the Workbooks collection. If you use the following code to loop through the Workbooks collection, the myaddin.xlam workbook isn't displayed:

```
Dim w as Workbook
For Each w in Application.Workbooks
    MsgBox w.Name
Next w
```

The following For-Next loop, on the other hand, displays myaddin.xlam — assuming that Excel "knows" about it — in the Add-Ins dialog box:

```
Dim a as Addin
For Each a in Application.AddIns
    MsgBox a.Name
Next a
```

Visibility of XLSM and XLAM files

Ordinary workbooks are displayed in one or more windows. For example, the following statement displays the number of windows for the active workbook:

```
MsgBox ActiveWorkbook.Windows.Count
```

You can manipulate the visibility of each window for a workbook by choosing the View➜Window➜ Hide command (in Excel) or by changing the Visible property using VBA. The following code hides all windows for the active workbook:

```
Dim Win As Window
For Each Win In ActiveWorkbook.Windows
    Win.Visible = False
Next Win
```

Add-in files are never visible, and they don't officially have windows, even though they have unseen worksheets. Consequently, add-ins don't appear in the windows list when you choose the View➜ Window➜Switch Windows command. If myaddin.xlam is open, the following statement returns 0:

```
MsgBox Workbooks("myaddin.xlam").Windows.Count
```

Worksheets and chart sheets in XLSM and XLAM files

Add-in files, like normal workbook files, can have any number of worksheets or chart sheets. But, as I note earlier in this chapter, to convert an XLSM file to an add-in, the file must have at least one worksheet. In many cases, this worksheet will be empty.

When an add-in is open, your VBA code can access its sheets as if they were in an ordinary workbook. Because add-in files aren't part of the Workbooks collection, however, you must always reference an add-in by its name and not by an index number. The following example displays the value in cell A1 of the first worksheet in myaddin.xla, which is assumed to be open:

```
MsgBox Workbooks("myaddin.xlam").Worksheets(1).Range("A1").Value
```

If your add-in contains a worksheet that you'd like the user to see, you can either copy the sheet to an open workbook or create a new workbook from the sheet.

The following code, for example, copies the first worksheet from an add-in and places it in the active workbook (as the last sheet):

```
Sub CopySheetFromAddin()
    Dim AddinSheet As Worksheet
    Dim NumSheets As Long
    Set AddinSheet = Workbooks("myaddin.xlam").Sheets(1)
    NumSheets = ActiveWorkbook.Sheets.Count
    AddinSheet.Copy After:=ActiveWorkbook.Sheets(NumSheets)
End Sub
```

Note that this procedure works even if the VBA project for the add-in is protected with a password.

Creating a new workbook from a sheet within an add-in is even simpler:

```
Sub CreateNewWorkbook()
    Workbooks("myaddin.xlam").Sheets(1).Copy
End Sub
```

Note

The previous examples assume that the code is in a file other than the add-in file. VBA code within an add-in should always use ThisWorkbook to qualify references to sheets or ranges within the add-in. For example, the following statement is assumed to be in a VBA module in an add-in file. This statement displays the value in cell A1 on Sheet 1:

```
MsgBox ThisWorkbook.Sheets("Sheet1").Range("A1").Value
```

Accessing VBA procedures in an add-in

Accessing the VBA procedures in an add-in is a bit different from accessing procedures in a normal XLSM workbook. First of all, when you choose the View➜Macros➜Macros command, the Macro dialog box doesn't display the names of macros that are in open add-ins. It's almost as if Excel were trying to prevent you from accessing them.

 Tip

If you know the name of the procedure in the add-in, you can enter it directly in the Macro dialog box and click Run to execute it. The Sub procedure must be in a general VBA module and not in a code module for an object.

Because procedures contained in an add-in aren't listed in the Macro dialog box, you must provide other means to access them. Your choices include direct methods (such as shortcut keys and Ribbon commands) as well as indirect methods (such as event handlers). One such candidate, for example, may be the OnTime method, which executes a procedure at a specific time of day.

You can use the Run method of the Application object to execute a procedure in an add-in. For example:

```
Application.Run "myaddin.xlam!DisplayNames"
```

Another option is to use the Tools➜References command in VBE to enable a reference to the add-in. Then you can refer directly to one of its procedures in your VBA code without the filename qualifier. In fact, you don't need to use the Run method; you can call the procedure directly as long as it's not declared as Private. The following statement executes a procedure named DisplayNames in an add-in that has been added as a reference:

```
Call DisplayNames
```

 Note

Even when a reference to the add-in has been established, its macro names don't appear in the Macro dialog box.

Function procedures defined in an add-in work just like those defined in an XLSM workbook. They're easy to access because Excel displays their names in the Insert Function dialog box under the User Defined category (by default). The only exception is if the Function procedure was declared with the Private keyword; then the function doesn't appear there. That's why it's a good idea to declare custom functions as Private if they will be used only by other VBA procedures and aren't designed to be used in worksheet formulas.

You can use worksheet functions contained in add-ins without the workbook name qualifier. For example, if you have a custom function named MOVAVG stored in the file newfuncs.xlsm, you'd use the following instruction to address the function from a worksheet in a different workbook:

```
=newfuncs.xlsm!MOVAVG(A1:A50)
```

But if this function is stored in an add-in file that's open, you can omit the file reference and write the following instead:

```
=MOVAVG(A1:A50)
```

Keep in mind that a workbook that uses a function defined in an add-in will have a link to that add-in. Therefore, the add-in must be available whenever that workbook is used.

Sleuthing a protected add-in

The Macro dialog box doesn't display the names of procedures contained in add-ins. But what if you'd like to run such a procedure? You can't run a procedure if you don't know it's name, but you can find its name by using Object Browser.

To illustrate, install the Euro Currency Tools add-in. This add-in is distributed with Excel and is password-protected, so you can't view the code. When installed, the add-in creates a new group, called Solutions, on the Formulas tab of the Ribbon. When you click the Euro Conversion button, the Euro Conversion dialog box is displayed. This dialog box lets you convert a range that contains currencies.

To determine the name of the procedure that displays this dialog box, follow these steps:

1. Activate VBE, and then select the EUROTOOL.XLAM project in the Project window.
2. Press F2 to activate Object Browser.
3. In the Libraries drop-down list, select EuroTool, which displays all the classes in the EUROTOOL.XLAM add-in, as depicted in the following figure.
4. Select various items in the Classes list to see what class they are and the members that they contain.

You see that this add-in has quite a few worksheets. Excel allows you to copy sheets from protected add-ins, so if you'd like to take a look at one of the worksheets, use the Immediate window and copy the worksheet to a new workbook using a statement like this:

```
Workbooks("eurotool.xlam").Sheets(1).Copy
```

Or to examine all the worksheets, execute this statement, which converts the add-in to a standard workbook:

```
Workbooks("eurotool.xlam").IsAddin = False
```

continued

continued

The following figure shows a portion of the workbook. This sheet (and the others) contain information used to localize the add-in for different languages.

That's interesting, but it doesn't help identify the procedure name we're seeking.

This add-in has many procedures; I tried executing several likely candidates, but none of them displayed the dialog box. Then I looked at the members listed in the ThisWorkbook code module and noticed a procedure called EuroConversionWizard. I tried to execute it, but I got an error. Then I tried another command:

```
Application.Run "eurotool.xlam!ThisWorkbook.EuroConversionWizard"
```

Success! Executing this statement displays the Euro Conversion dialog box.

Armed with this information, you can write VBA code to display the Euro Conversion dialog box — assuming, of course, that you can think of a reason to do so.

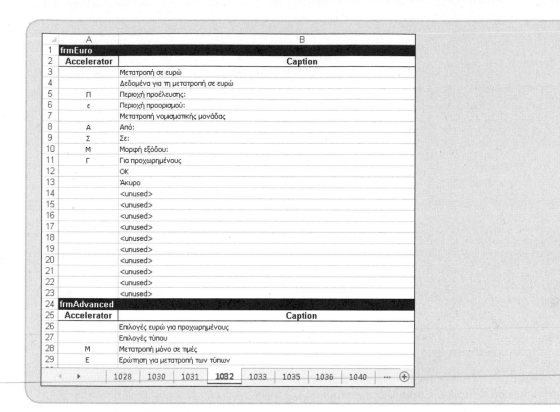

	A	B
1	**frmEuro**	
2	**Accelerator**	**Caption**
3		Μετατροπή σε ευρώ
4		Δεδομένα για τη μετατροπή σε ευρώ
5	Π	Περιοχή προέλευσης:
6	ε	Περιοχή προορισμού:
7		Μετατροπή νομισματικής μονάδας
8	Α	Από:
9	Σ	Σε:
10	Μ	Μορφή εξόδου:
11	Γ	Για προχωρημένους
12		OK
13		Άκυρο
14		<unused>
15		<unused>
16		<unused>
17		<unused>
18		<unused>
19		<unused>
20		<unused>
21		<unused>
22		<unused>
23		<unused>
24	**frmAdvanced**	
25	**Accelerator**	**Caption**
26		Επιλογές ευρώ για προχωρημένους
27		Επιλογές τύπου
28	Μ	Μετατροπή μόνο σε τιμές
29	Ε	Ερώτηση για μετατροπή των τύπων

1028 | 1030 | 1031 | **1032** | 1033 | 1035 | 1036 | 1040 | ⋯ | ⊕

Manipulating Add-Ins with VBA

In this section, I present information that can help you write VBA procedures that manipulate add-ins.

The AddIns collection consists of all add-ins that Excel knows about. These add-ins can be either installed or not. The Add-Ins dialog box lists all members of the AddIns collection. Those entries accompanied by a check mark are installed.

Note

Beginning with Excel 2010, an additional collection is available: AddIns2. This collection is the same as the AddIns collection but also includes add-ins that were opened using the File➔Open command. In the past, accessing these add-ins required an XLM macro.

Adding an item to the AddIns collection

The add-in files that make up the AddIns collection can be stored anywhere. Excel maintains a partial list of these files and their locations in the Windows Registry. For Excel 2013, this list is stored at

```
HKEY_CURRENT_USER\Software\Microsoft\Office\15.0\Excel\Add-in Manager
```

You can use the Windows Registry Editor (regedit.exe) to view this Registry key. Note that the standard add-ins shipped with Excel do not appear in this Registry key. In addition, add-in files stored in the following directory also appear in the list but aren't listed in the Registry:

```
C:\Program Files (x86)\Microsoft Office\Office15\Library
```

You can add a new AddIn object to the AddIns collection either manually or programmatically. To add a new add-in to the collection manually, display the Add-Ins dialog box, click the Browse button, and locate the add-in.

To add a new member to the AddIns collection with VBA, use the collection's Add method. Here's an example:

```
Application.AddIns.Add "c:\files\newaddin.xlam"
```

After the preceding instruction is executed, the AddIns collection has a new member, and the Add-Ins dialog box shows a new item in its list. If the add-in already exists in the collection, nothing happens and an error isn't generated.

If the add-in is on removable media (for example, a CD-ROM), you can also copy the file to Excel's library directory with the Add method. The following example copies myaddin.xlam from drive E and adds it to the AddIns collection. The second argument (True, in this case) specifies whether the add-in should be copied. If the add-in resides on a hard drive, the second argument can be ignored.

```
Application.AddIns.Add "e:\myaddin.xla", True
```

Note

Adding a new file to the AddIns collection does not install it. To install the add-in, set its Installed property to True.

Caution

The Windows Registry doesn't get updated until Excel closes normally. Therefore, if Excel ends abnormally (that is, if it crashes), the add-in's name won't get added to the Registry and the add-in won't be part of the AddIns collection when Excel restarts.

Removing an item from the AddIns collection

Oddly, there is no direct way to remove an add-in from the AddIns collection. The AddIns collection doesn't have a Delete or Remove method. One way to remove an add-in from the Add-Ins dialog box is to edit the Windows Registry database (using regedit.exe). After you do this, the add-in won't appear in the Add-Ins dialog box the next time that you start Excel. Note that this method isn't guaranteed to work with all add-in files.

Another way to remove an add-in from the AddIns collection is to delete, move, or rename its XLAM (or XLA) file. You'll get a warning like the one in Figure 19-7 the next time you try to install or uninstall the add-in, along with an opportunity to remove it from the AddIns collection.

Figure 19-7: One way to remove a member of the AddIns collection.

AddIn object properties

An AddIn object is a single member of the AddIns collection. For example, to display the filename of the first member of the AddIns collection, use the following:

```
Msgbox AddIns(1).Name
```

An AddIn object has 14 properties, which you can read about in the Help system. Of these properties, 5 are hidden. Some of the terminology is a bit confusing, so I discuss a few of the more important properties in the sections that follow.

The Name property of an AddIn object

The Name property holds the filename of the add-in. Name is a read-only property, so you can't change the name of the file by changing the Name property.

The Path property of an AddIn object

The Path property holds the drive and path where the add-in file is stored. It doesn't include a final backslash or the filename.

The FullName property of an AddIn object

The FullName property holds the add-in's drive, path, and filename. This property is redundant because this information is also available from the Name and Path properties. The following instructions produce the same message:

```
MsgBox AddIns(1).Path & "\" & AddIns(1).Name
MsgBox AddIns(1).FullName
```

The Title property of an AddIn object

The Title property is a hidden property that holds a descriptive name for the add-in. The Title property is what appears in the Add-Ins dialog box. This property is read-only, and the only way to add or change the Title property of an add-in is to use the Document Properties panel (choose the Developer➜Modify➜Document command). You must use this menu command with the XLSM version of the file before converting it to an add-in. Another option is to right-click the add-in file in Windows Explorer and choose Properties from the shortcut menu. Then click the Details tab and make the change. This method won't work if the file is open in Excel.

Typically, a member of a collection is addressed by way of its Name property setting. The AddIns collection is different; it uses the Title property instead. The following example displays the filename for the Analysis ToolPak add-in (that is, analys32.xll), whose Title property is "Analysis ToolPak".

```
Sub ShowName()
    MsgBox AddIns("Analysis Toolpak").Name
End Sub
```

You can also reference a particular add-in with its index number if you happen to know it. But in the vast majority of cases, you will want to refer to an add-in by using its Name property.

The Comments property of an AddIn object

The Comments property stores text that is displayed in the Add-Ins dialog box when a particular add-in is selected. Comments is a read-only property. To change it, use the Document Properties panel before you convert the workbook to an add-in. Or use Windows Explorer, as described earlier for the Title property. Comments can be as long as 255 characters, but the Add-Ins dialog box can display only about 100 characters.

If your code attempts to read the Comments property of an add-in that has no comments, you get an error.

The Installed property of an AddIn object

The Installed property is True if the add-in is currently installed — that is, if it has a check mark in the Add-Ins dialog box. Setting the Installed property to True opens the add-in. Setting it to False unloads it. Here's an example of how to install (that is, open) the Analysis ToolPak add-in with VBA:

```
Sub InstallATP()
    AddIns("Analysis ToolPak").Installed = True
End Sub
```

After this procedure is executed, the Add-Ins dialog box displays a check mark next to Analysis ToolPak. If the add-in is already installed, setting its Installed property to True has no effect. To remove this add-in (uninstall it), simply set the Installed property to False.

Caution

If an add-in was opened with the File➜Open command, it isn't considered to be officially installed. Consequently, its Installed property is False. An add-in is installed only if it appears in the Add-Ins dialog box, with a check mark next to its name.

The ListAllAddIns procedure that follows creates a table that lists all members of the AddIns collection and displays the following properties: Name, Title, Installed, Comments, and Path.

```
Sub ListAllAddins()
    Dim ai As AddIn
    Dim Row As Long
    Dim Table1 As ListObject
    Cells.Clear
    Range("A1:E1") = Array("Name", "Title", "Installed", _
      "Comments", "Path")
    Row = 2
    On Error Resume Next
    For Each ai In Application.AddIns
        Cells(Row, 1) = ai.Name
        Cells(Row, 2) = ai.Title
        Cells(Row, 3) = ai.Installed
        Cells(Row, 4) = ai.Comments
        Cells(Row, 5) = ai.Path
        Row = Row + 1
    Next ai
    On Error GoTo 0
    Range("A1").Select
    ActiveSheet.ListObjects.Add
    ActiveSheet.ListObjects(1).TableStyle = _
      "TableStyleMedium2"
End Sub
```

Figure 19-8 shows the result of executing this procedure. If you modify the code to use the AddIns2 collection, the table will also include add-ins that were opened using the File➜Open command (if any). The AddIns2 collection is available only in Excel 2010 and later.

Name	Title	Installed	Comments	Path
ANALYS32.XLL	Analysis ToolPak	FALSE		C:\Program Files (x86)\Microsoft Office\Office15\Library\Analysis
ATPVBAEN.XLAM	Analysis ToolPak - VBA	FALSE		C:\Program Files (x86)\Microsoft Office\Office15\Library\Analysis
custom functions.xlam	Custom Functions	FALSE		C:\Users\JWalk\Desktop
EUROTOOL.XLAM	Euro Currency Tools	FALSE		C:\Program Files (x86)\Microsoft Office\Office15\Library
export charts.xlam	Export Charts	FALSE		C:\Users\JWalk\Desktop
mscoree.dll	Inquire.InteractiveDiagnostics	FALSE		C:\Windows\SysWOW64
pup6.xla	Power Utility Pak v6	FALSE	Add-In Tools For Excel - Licensed ©1999-2006 J-Walk && Associates.	C:\Users\JWalk\Documents\Excel\PUP 6 DEVELOPMENT\pup6
pup7.xlam	Power Utility Pak v7.1	TRUE	Add-In Tools For Excel 2007-2010 (Licensed) Copyright 1999-2010 J-Walk && Associates	C:\Program Files (x86)\pup7
SOLVER.XLAM	Solver Add-in	FALSE		C:\Program Files (x86)\Microsoft Office\Office15\Library\SOLVER

Figure 19-8: A table that lists information about all members of the AddIns collection.

On the Web

This procedure is available on the book's website in the list add-in information.xlsm file.

Note

You can determine whether a particular workbook is an add-in by accessing its IsAddIn property. This property isn't read-only, so you can also convert a workbook to an add-in by setting the IsAddIn property to True.

And, conversely, you can convert an add-in to a workbook by setting the IsAddIn property to False. After doing so, the add-in's worksheets will be visible in Excel — even if the add-in's VBA project is protected. By using this technique, I learned that most of the dialog boxes in SOLVER.XLAM are old Excel 5/95 dialog sheets, not UserForms. Also, SOLVER.XLAM contains more than 500 named ranges.

Accessing an add-in as a workbook

You can open an XLAM add-in file by using the Add-Ins dialog box or by choosing the File➜Open command. The former method is the preferred method for the following reason: When you open an add-in with the File➜Open command, its Installed property is *not* set to True. Therefore, you can't close the file by using the Add-Ins dialog box. In fact, the only way to close such an add-in is with a VBA statement such as the following:

```
Workbooks("myaddin.xlam").Close
```

Caution   Using the Close method on an installed add-in removes the add-in from memory but does not set its Installed property to False. Therefore, the Add-Ins dialog box still lists the add-in as installed, which can be confusing. The proper way to remove an installed add-in is to set its Installed property to False.

As you may have surmised, Excel's add-in capability is quirky. This component (except for the addition of the AddIns2 collection) hasn't been improved in many years. Therefore, as a developer, you need to pay particular attention to issues involving installing and uninstalling add-ins.

AddIn object events

An AddIn object has two events: AddInInstall (occurs when the add-in is installed) and AddInUninstall (occurs when it is uninstalled). You can write event-handler procedures for these events in the ThisWorkbook code module for the add-in.

The following example is displayed as a message when the add-in is installed:

```
Private Sub Workbook_AddInInstall()
    MsgBox ThisWorkbook.Name & _" add-in has been installed."
End Sub
```

Caution   Don't confuse the AddInInstall event with the Open event. The AddInInstall event occurs only when the add-in is first installed — not every time it is opened. If you need to execute code every time the add-in is opened, use a Workbook_Open procedure.

Cross-Ref   For additional information about events, see Chapter 17.

Optimizing the Performance of Add-ins

If you ask a dozen Excel programmers to automate a particular task, chances are that you'll get a dozen different approaches. Most likely, not all these approaches will perform equally well.

Following are a few tips that you can use to ensure that your code runs as quickly as possible. These tips apply to all VBA code, not just the code in add-ins.

➤ **Set the Application.ScreenUpdating property to False** when writing data to a worksheet or performing any other actions that cause changes to the display.

➤ **Declare the data type for all variables used and avoid variants whenever possible.** Use an Option Explicit statement at the top of each module to force yourself to declare all variables.

➤ **Create object variables to avoid lengthy object references.** For example, if you're working with a Series object for a chart, create an object variable by using code like this:

```
Dim S1 As Series
Set S1 = ActiveWorkbook.Sheets(1).ChartObjects(1). _
    Chart.SeriesCollection(1)
```

➤ **Whenever possible, declare object variables as a specific object type** — not As Object.

➤ **Use the With-End With construct,** when appropriate, to set multiple properties or call multiple methods for a single object.

➤ **Remove all extraneous code.** This tip is especially important if you've used the macro recorder to create procedures.

➤ **Manipulate data with VBA arrays rather than worksheet ranges,** if possible. Reading and writing to a worksheet usually take much longer than manipulating data in memory. However, for best results, test both options.

➤ **Consider setting the calculation mode to Manual** if your code writes lots of data to worksheets. Doing so may increase the speed significantly. Here's a statement that changes the calculation mode:

```
Application.Calculation = xlCalculationManual
```

➤ **Avoid linking UserForm controls to worksheet cells.** Doing so may trigger a recalculation whenever the user changes the UserForm control.

➤ **Compile your code before creating the add-in.** Doing so may increase the file size slightly, but it eliminates the need for Excel to compile the code before executing the procedures.

Special Problems with Add-Ins

Add-ins are great, but you should realize by now that there's no free lunch. Add-ins present their share of problems — or should I say *challenges?* In this section, I discuss some issues that you need to know about if you'll be developing add-ins for widespread user distribution.

Ensuring that an add-in is installed

In some cases, you may need to ensure that your add-in is installed properly — that is, opened using the Add-Ins dialog box and not the File➔Open command. This section describes a technique that determines how an add-in was opened and gives the user an opportunity to install the add-in if it is not properly installed.

If the add-in isn't properly installed, the code displays a message (see Figure 19-9). Clicking Yes installs the add-in. Clicking No leaves the file open but doesn't install it. Clicking Cancel closes the file.

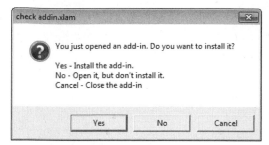

Figure 19-9: When attempting to open the add-in incorrectly, the user sees this message.

The code that follows is the code module for the add-in's ThisWorkbook object. This technique relies on the fact that the AddInInstall event occurs before the Open event for the workbook.

```vba
Dim InstalledProperly As Boolean

Private Sub Workbook_AddinInstall()
    InstalledProperly = True
End Sub

Private Sub Workbook_Open()
    Dim ai As AddIn, NewAi As AddIn
    Dim M As String
    Dim Ans As Integer
    'Was just installed using the Add-Ins dialog box?
    If InstalledProperly Then Exit Sub

    'Is it in the AddIns collection?
    For Each ai In AddIns
        If ai.Name = ThisWorkbook.Name Then
            If ai.Installed Then
                MsgBox "This add-in is properly installed.", _
                    vbInformation, ThisWorkbook.Name
                Exit Sub
            End If
        End If
    Next ai

    'It's not in AddIns collection, prompt user.
    M = "You just opened an add-in. Do you want to install it?"
    M = M & vbNewLine
    M = M & vbNewLine & "Yes - Install the add-in. "
```

continued

continued

```
    M = M & vbNewLine & "No - Open it, but don't install it."
    M = M & vbNewLine & "Cancel - Close the add-in"
    Ans = MsgBox(M, vbQuestion + vbYesNoCancel, _
      ThisWorkbook.Name)
    Select Case Ans
        Case vbYes
            ' Add it to the AddIns collection and install it.
            Set NewAi = _
              Application.AddIns.Add(ThisWorkbook.FullName)
            NewAi.Installed = True
        Case vbNo
            'no action, leave it open
        Case vbCancel
            ThisWorkbook.Close
    End Select
End Sub
```

The procedure covers the following possibilities:

➤ The add-in was opened automatically because it's an installed add-in listed (and displaying a check mark) in the Add-Ins dialog box. The user doesn't see a message.

➤ The user uses the Add-Ins dialog box to install the add-in. The user doesn't see a message.

➤ The add-in was opened manually (by using File➜Open) and is not a member of the AddIns collection. The user sees the message and must take one of the three actions.

➤ The add-in was opened manually, is a member of the AddIns collection, but is not installed (not displayed with a check mark). The user sees the message and must take one of the three actions.

By the way, you can also use this code as a way to simplify the installation of an add-in that you give to someone. Just tell them to double-click the add-in's filename (which opens it in Excel) and respond Yes to the prompt. Better yet, modify the code so that the add-in is installed without a prompt.

On the Web

This add-in, named check addin.xlam, is available on the book's website. Try opening it using both methods (with the Add-Ins dialog box and by choosing File➜Open).

Referencing other files from an add-in

If your add-in uses other files, you need to be especially careful when distributing the application. You can't assume anything about the storage structure of the system on which users will run the application. The easiest approach is to insist that all files for the application be copied to a single directory. Then you can use the Path property of your application's workbook to build path references to all other files.

For example, if your application uses a custom help file, be sure that the help file is copied to the same directory as the application itself. Then you can use a procedure like the following to make sure that the help file can be located:

```
Sub GetHelp()
    Application.Help ThisWorkbook.Path & "\userhelp.chm"
End Sub
```

If your application uses Application Programming Interface (API) calls to standard Windows DLLs, you can assume that these can be found by Windows. But if you use custom DLLs, the best practice is to make sure that they're installed in the Windows\System directory (which might or might not be named Windows\System). You'll need to use the GetSystemDirectory Windows API function to determine the exact path of the System directory.

Detecting the proper Excel version for your add-in

As you may know, those who use an earlier version of Excel can open Excel 2007 (and later) files if they've installed Microsoft's Compatibility Pak. If your add-in uses any features unique to Excel 2007 or later, you'll want to warn users who attempt to open the add-in with an earlier version. The following code does the trick:

```
Sub CheckVersion()
    If Val(Application.Version) < 12 Then
        MsgBox "This works only with Excel 2007 or later"
        ThisWorkbook.Close
    End If
End Sub
```

The Version property of the Application object returns a string. For example, this might return 12.0a. This procedure uses VBA's Val function, which ignores everything beginning with the first non-numeric character.

 Cross-Ref   **See Chapter 24 for additional information about compatibility.**

PART **V**

Developing Applications

Chapter 20
Working with the Ribbon

Chapter 21
Working with Shortcut Menus

Chapter 22
Providing Help for Your Applications

Chapter 23
Developing User-Oriented Applications

Working with the Ribbon

In This Chapter

- Looking at the Excel Ribbon UI from a user's perspective

- Using VBA to work with the Ribbon

- Customizing the Ribbon with RibbonX code

- Looking at examples of workbooks that modify the Ribbon

- Using boilerplate code for creating an old-style toolbar

Ribbon Basics

Beginning with Microsoft Office 2007, the time-honored menus-and-toolbars user interface was scrapped and replaced with a new *tabs-and-Ribbon* interface. Although the new interface kind of resembles the old-fashioned menus-and-toolbars interface, you'll find that it's radically different.

Long-time Excel users probably noticed that the menu system had become increasingly complicated with each new version. In addition, the number of toolbars had become almost overwhelming. After all, every new feature must be accessible. In the past, this access meant adding more items to the menus and building new toolbars. The Microsoft designers set out to solve this overcrowding problem, and the Ribbon interface was their solution.

Reactions to the Office Ribbon interface can best be described as mixed. As with anything new, some people love it, and others hate it. Count me among the former group. I find it painful to go back to the confusing menu system in Excel 2003.

Many experienced Excel users suffered from a mild case of bewilderment when they realized that many of their familiar command sequences no longer worked. Beginning users, on the other hand, are usually able to get up to speed much more quickly because they aren't overwhelmed with irrelevant menus and toolbars.

For the benefit of Ribbon newcomers, I provide some additional user-oriented information in the sections that follow.

The commands available in the Ribbon vary, depending on which tab is selected. The Ribbon is arranged into groups of related commands. Here's a quick overview of Excel's tabs:

➤ **Home:** You'll probably spend most of your time on the Home tab. This tab contains the basic Clipboard commands, formatting commands, style commands, commands to insert and delete rows and columns, plus an assortment of worksheet-editing commands.

➤ **Insert:** Select this tab when you need to insert something in a worksheet — a table, a diagram, a chart, a symbol, and so on.

➤ **Page Layout:** This tab contains commands that affect the overall appearance of your worksheet, including settings that deal with printing.

➤ **Formulas:** Use this tab to insert a formula, name a range, access the formula-auditing tools, or control how Excel performs calculations.

➤ **Data:** Excel's data-related commands are on this tab.

➤ **Review:** This tab contains tools to check spelling, translate words, add comments, and protect sheets.

➤ **View:** The View tab contains commands that control various aspects of how a sheet is viewed. Some commands on this tab are also available on the status bar.

➤ **Developer:** This tab isn't visible by default. It contains commands that are useful for programmers. To display the Developer tab, right-click the Ribbon and choose Customize the Ribbon. In the Customize Ribbon tab of the Excel Options dialog box, place a check mark next to Developer.

➤ **Add-Ins:** This tab is visible only if you've loaded a workbook or add-in that customizes the menu or toolbars (by using the CommandBars object). Because menus and toolbars are no longer available, these customizations appear in the Add-Ins tab.

The appearance of the commands on the Ribbon varies, depending on the width of the Excel window. When the window is too narrow to display everything, the commands may seem to be missing but are still available. Figure 20-1 shows three views of the Home tab of the Ribbon. In the top image, all controls are fully visible. In the middle image, Excel's window is made narrower. Note that some of the descriptive text is gone, and some of the icons are smaller. The bottom image shows the extreme case in which the window is very narrow. Some groups display a single icon. However, if you click the icon, all the group commands are available to you.

Tip

If you'd like to hide the Ribbon to increase your worksheet view, just double-click any tab. The Ribbon goes away (but the tabs remain), and you're able to see about five additional rows of your worksheet. When you need to use the Ribbon again, just click a tab, and the Ribbon comes back temporarily. To permanently restore the Ribbon, double-click a tab. You can also press Ctrl+F1 to toggle the Ribbon display on and off, or use the ^ icon (next to the Help icon in the Excel title bar).

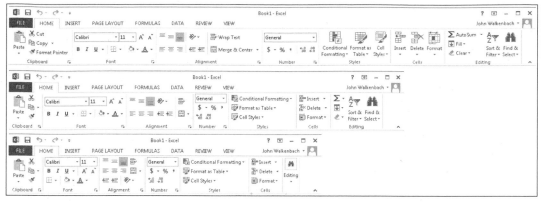

Figure 20-1: The Home tab of the Ribbon, with varying widths of the Excel window.

 # The CommandBar Object in Excel 2013

Excel 97 introduced a new way of handling toolbars and menus. These UI (user interface) elements are CommandBar objects. What's commonly called a toolbar is actually one of three types of command bars:

- **Toolbar:** This command bar has one or more clickable controls.
- **Menu bar:** The two built-in menu bars are the Worksheet menu bar and the Chart menu bar.
- **Shortcut menu:** A shortcut menu appears when you right-click an object.

For compatibility, Excel 2013 still supports the CommandBar object — but its functionality has been significantly deprecated. An end user can no longer create a custom toolbar. However, a VBA programmer can still create and work with CommandBar objects (see "Creating an Old-Style Toolbar," later in this chapter). The problem, however, is that many CommandBar properties and methods are ignored in Excel 2007 and later. For example, every toolbar or customized menu appears in the Add-Ins tab of the Ribbon. Properties that control a toolbar's dimensions and position no longer work. In addition, floating toolbars are no longer possible.

The accompanying figures show a customized menu and toolbar in Excel 2003, and the same menu and toolbar in Excel 2013. Although these UI elements are still functional in Excel 2013, it's clearly not what the developer (me!) had in mind. Needless to say, many VBA developers will want to redo the UI for their older applications.

Later in this chapter, I present a simple example of creating a custom toolbar by using the CommandBar object (see "Creating an Old-Style Toolbar"). For complete details on creating custom menus and toolbars with the CommandBar object, consult the Excel 2003 edition of this book.

Customizing shortcut menus by using the CommandBar object is still supported in Excel 2013, but the new single document interface makes this feature virtually useless for many applications. In many cases, using RibbonX to modify shortcut menus is a better solution. I cover the topic of shortcut menus in Chapter 21.

continued

continued

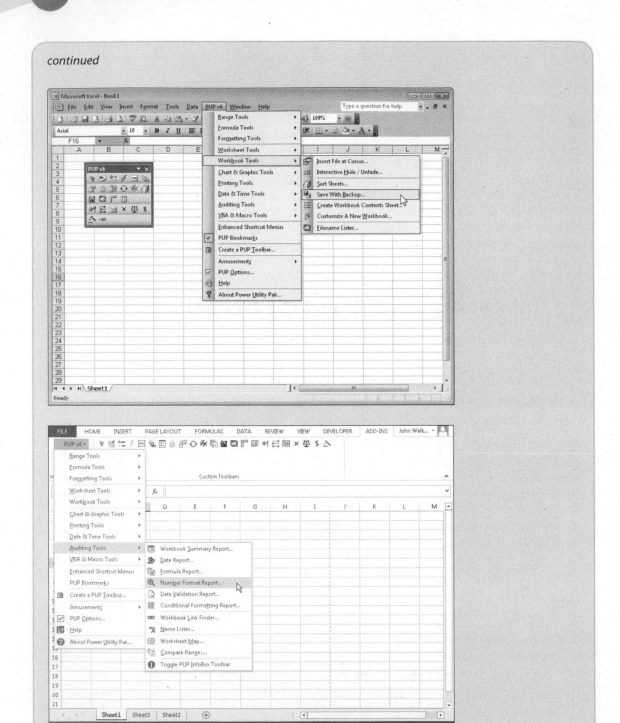

Using VBA with the Ribbon

Now, the big question: What can a VBA programmer do with the Ribbon? The simple answer: not much.

Following is a list of what you can do with the Ribbon using VBA:

➤ Determine whether a particular control is enabled.

➤ Determine whether a particular control is visible.

➤ Determine whether a particular control is pressed (for toggle buttons and check boxes).

➤ Get a control's label, screen tip, or supertip (a more detailed description of the control).

➤ Display the image associated with a control.

➤ Execute the command associated with a particular control.

Following is a list of things that you might like to do with the Ribbon but can't:

➤ Determine which tab is currently selected.

➤ Activate a particular tab.

➤ Add a new tab.

➤ Add a new group to a tab.

➤ Add a new control.

➤ Remove a control.

➤ Disable a control.

➤ Hide a control.

 Note Beginning with Excel 2010, the user can make modifications to the Ribbon by using the Customize Ribbon tab of the Excel Options dialog box. Unfortunately, you can't use VBA to make these changes.

Accessing a Ribbon control

All told, Excel has more than 1,700 Ribbon controls. Every Ribbon control has a name, and you use that name when you work with the control using VBA.

For example, the statement that follows displays a message box that shows the Enabled status of the ViewCustomViews control. (This control is located in the View➜Workbook Views group.)

```
MsgBox Application.CommandBars.GetEnabledMso("ViewCustomViews")
```

Normally, this control is enabled. But (inexplicably), if the workbook contains a table (created by choosing Insert➜Tables➜Table), the ViewCustomViews control is disabled. In other words, a workbook can use either the Custom Views feature or the Tables feature — but not both.

Determining the name of a particular control is a manual task. First, display the Customize Ribbon tab of the Excel Options dialog box. Locate the control in the list box on the left and then hover the mouse pointer over the item. The control's name appears in a pop-up screen tip, in parentheses (see Figure 20-2).

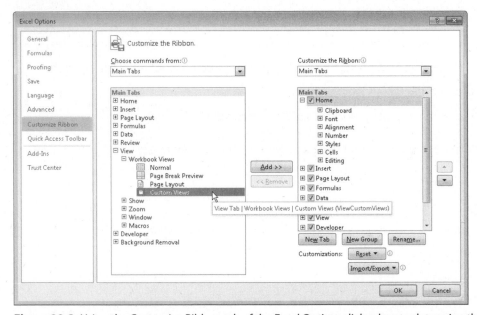

Figure 20-2: Using the Customize Ribbon tab of the Excel Options dialog box to determine the name of a control.

Unfortunately, it's not possible to write VBA code to loop through all the controls on the Ribbon and display a list of their names.

On the Web

The book's website contains a workbook with the names of all Excel controls for Excel 2013 and Excel 2010. Figure 20-3 shows a portion of this file, which is named ribbon control names.xlsx.

	A	B	C	D	E	F	G
1	idMso	Exists in Office Excel 2013	Type in Office Excel 2013	Label in Office Excel 2013	Exists in Office Excel 2010	Type in Office Excel 2010	Label in Office Excel 2010
55	AlignCenter	TRUE	toggleButton	Center	TRUE	toggleButton	Center
56	AlignDistributeHorizontallyClassic	TRUE	button	Distribute Horizont:	TRUE	button	Distribute Horizonta
57	AlignDistributeVerticallyClassic	TRUE	button	Distribute Vertically	TRUE	button	Distribute Vertically
58	AlignJustify	TRUE	toggleButton	Justify	TRUE	toggleButton	Justify
59	AlignLeft	TRUE	toggleButton	Align Left	TRUE	toggleButton	Align Left
60	AlignLeftToRightMenu	TRUE	splitButton	Left-to-Right	TRUE	splitButton	Left-to-Right
61	AlignMiddleExcel	TRUE	toggleButton	Middle Align	TRUE	toggleButton	Middle Align
62	AlignRight	TRUE	toggleButton	Align Right	TRUE	toggleButton	Align Right
63	AlignTopExcel	TRUE	toggleButton	Top Align	TRUE	toggleButton	Top Align
64	AllowPersonallyIdentifiableInformation	TRUE	control		FALSE		
65	AlternativeText	TRUE	button	Size and Properties	FALSE		
66	ApplicationOptionsDialog	TRUE	button	Options	TRUE	button	Options
67	AppShare	TRUE	task	Present	FALSE		
68	ArrowsMore	TRUE	button	More Arrows	TRUE	button	More Arrows
69	ArrowStyleGallery	TRUE	gallery	Arrows	TRUE	gallery	Arrows
70	ArtisticEffectsDialog	TRUE	button	Artistic Effects Opti:	TRUE	button	Artistic Effects Optic
71	AsppRelationships	TRUE	button	Relationships	FALSE		
72	AutoCorrect	TRUE	button	AutoCorrect Option	FALSE		
73	AutoFilterClassic	TRUE	button	AutoFilter	TRUE	button	AutoFilter
74	AutoFormatDialog	TRUE	button	AutoFormat	TRUE	button	AutoFormat

Sheet1

Figure 20-3: A workbook that displays information about each Ribbon control.

Working with the Ribbon

In the preceding section I provided an example of using the GetEnabledMso method of the CommandBars object. Following is a list of all methods relevant to working with the Ribbon via the CommandBars object. All these methods take one argument: idMso, which is a String data type and represents the name of the command. You must know the name — using index numbers is not possible.

➤ ExecuteMso: Executes a control

➤ GetEnabledMso: Returns True if the specified control is enabled

➤ GetImageMso: Returns the image for a control

➤ GetLabelMso: Returns the label for a control

➤ GetPressedMso: Returns True if the specified control is pressed (applies to check box and toggle button controls)

➤ GetScreentipMso: Returns the screen tip for a control (the text that appears in the control)

➤ GetSupertipMso: Returns the supertip for a control (the description of the control that appears when you hover the mouse pointer over the control)

Some of these methods are useless. Why would a VBA programmer need to determine the screen tip for a control? I can't think of a reason.

The VBA statement that follows toggles the Selection task pane (a feature introduced in Excel 2007 that facilitates selecting objects on a worksheet):

```
Application.CommandBars.ExecuteMso "SelectionPane"
```

The following statement displays the Paste Special dialog box (and will display an error message if the Windows Clipboard is empty):

```
Application.CommandBars.ExecuteMso "PasteSpecialDialog"
```

Here's a command that tells you whether the formula bar is visible (it corresponds to the state of the Formula Bar control in the View➜Show group):

```
MsgBox Application.CommandBars.GetPressedMso "ViewFormulaBar"
```

To toggle the formula bar, use this statement:

```
Application.CommandBars.ExecuteMso "ViewFormulaBar"
```

To make sure the formula bar is visible, use this code:

```
With Application.CommandBars
  If Not .GetPressedMso("ViewFormulaBar") Then .ExecuteMso "ViewFormulaBar"
End With
```

To make sure the formula bar is not visible, use this code:

```
With Application.CommandBars
  If .GetPressedMso("ViewFormulaBar") Then .ExecuteMso "ViewFormulaBar"
End With
```

Or don't bother with the Ribbon and set the DisplayFormulaBar property of the Application object to either True or False. This statement displays the formula bar (or has no effect if the formula bar is already visible):

```
Application.DisplayFormulaBar = True
```

The statement that follows displays True if the Merge & Center control is enabled. (This control is disabled if the sheet is protected or if the active cell is in a table.)

```
MsgBox Application.CommandBars.GetEnabledMso("MergeCenter")
```

The following VBA code adds an ActiveX Image control to the active worksheet and uses the GetImageMso method to display the binoculars icon from the Find & Select control in the Home➔ Editing group:

```
Sub ImageOnSheet()
    Dim MyImage As OLEObject
    Set MyImage = ActiveSheet.OLEObjects.Add _
      (ClassType:="Forms.Image.1", _
       Left:=50, _
       Top:=50)
    With MyImage.Object
        .AutoSize = True
        .BorderStyle = 0
        .Picture = Application.CommandBars. _
          GetImageMso("FindDialog", 32, 32)
    End With
End Sub
```

To display the Ribbon icon in an Image control (named Image1) on a UserForm, use this procedure:

```
Private Sub UserForm_Initialize()
    With Image1
        .Picture = Application.CommandBars.GetImageMso _
            ("FindDialog", 32, 32)
        .AutoSize = True
    End With
End Sub
```

Activating a tab

Microsoft provides no direct way to activate a Ribbon tab from VBA. But if you really need to do so, using SendKeys is your only option. The SendKeys method simulates keystrokes. The keystrokes required to activate the Home tab are Alt+H. These keystrokes display the keytips in the Ribbon. To hide the keytips, press F6. Using this information, the following statement sends the keystrokes required to activate the Home tab:

```
Application.SendKeys "%h{F6}"
```

To avoid the display of keytips, turn off screen updating:

```
Application.ScreenUpdating = False
Application.SendKeys "%h{F6}"
Application.ScreenUpdateing=True
```

The SendKeys arguments for the other tabs are

- ➤ **Insert:** "%n{F6}"
- ➤ **Page Layout:** "%p{F6}"
- ➤ **Formulas:** "%m{F6}"
- ➤ **Data:** "%a{F6}"
- ➤ **Review:** "%r{F6}"
- ➤ **View:** "%w{F6}"
- ➤ **Developer:** "%l{F6}"
- ➤ **Add-Ins:** "%x{F6}"

Caution As always, use SendKeys as a last resort. And then understand that SendKeys may not be perfectly reliable. For example, if you execute the previous example while a UserForm is displayed, the keystrokes will be sent to the UserForm, not to the Ribbon.

 # Storing UI changes

Beginning with Excel 2010, a user can easily make changes to the Ribbon and the Quick Access tool-bar. How does Excel keep track of these changes?

Quick Access toolbar and Ribbon modifications are stored in a file named Excel.officeUI. The location of this file varies. On my system, it's here:

```
C:\Users\<username>\AppData\Local\Microsoft\Office
```

I provide more information about the Excel.officeUI file in Chapter 3.

Customizing the Ribbon

You can't perform any Ribbon modifications using VBA. Rather, you must write RibbonX code and insert the code into the workbook file — outside Excel. You can, however, create VBA callback procedures. A *callback procedure* is a VBA macro that is executed when a custom Ribbon control is activated.

RibbonX code is XML markup that describes the controls, where on the Ribbon they're displayed, what they look like, and what happens when they're activated. This book does not cover RibbonX — the topic is complex enough to be the subject of an entire book. I do, however, provide a few simple examples so that you can understand what's involved in modifying the Excel UI and decide whether it's something you'd like to learn.

Cross-Ref

For information about Excel's file structure, refer to "Inside an Excel File" in Chapter 3. That section describes how to view the information inside an XLSX workbook file.

A simple RibbonX example

This section contains a step-by-step walkthrough that will give you a feel for what it takes to modify Excel's Ribbon. This example creates a new Ribbon group (named Custom) on the Data tab. It also creates two buttons in the new Ribbon group, labeled Hello World and Goodbye World. Clicking either of these buttons executes a VBA macro.

Note

The instructions that follow are tedious and error-prone. In reality, most developers don't use this method. Rather, they use software designed to make the process much easier.

 See your errors

Before you do any work with Ribbon customization, you should enable the display of RibbonX errors. Access the Excel Options dialog box (File➜Options) and click the Advanced tab. Scroll down to the General section and select Show Add-in User Interface Errors.

When this setting is enabled, RibbonX errors (if any) are displayed when the workbook opens — which is helpful for debugging.

Follow these steps to create a workbook that contains RibbonX code that modifies the Ribbon:

1. Create a new Excel workbook, insert a VBA module, and enter the two callback procedures that follow:

```
Sub HelloWorld(control As IRibbonControl)
    MsgBox "Hello World!"
End Sub


Sub GoodbyeWorld(control As IRibbonControl)
    ThisWorkbook.Close
End Sub
```

These procedures execute when the buttons are clicked.

2. Save the workbook and name it ribbon modification.xlsm.

3. Close the workbook.

4. Locate the folder that contains the ribbon modification.xlsm file and create a folder named customUI.

5. Inside the customUI folder, use a text editor (such as Windows Notepad) to create a text file named customUI.xml with the following RibbonX XML code (XML is case-sensitive):

```
<customUI xmlns="http://schemas.microsoft.com/office/2006/01/
   customui">
<ribbon>
<tabs>
<tab idMso="TabData">
  <group  id="Group1" label="Custom">
    <button id="Button1"
        label="Hello World"
        size="normal"
        onAction="HelloWorld"
        imageMso="HappyFace" />
    <button id="Button2"
        label="Goodbye World"
        size="normal"
        onAction="GoodbyeWorld"
        imageMso="DeclineInvitation" />
    </group>
</tab>
</tabs>
</ribbon>
</customUI>
```

Note

If your system is set up to hide extensions of known file types, you should turn off that option so that you always see file extensions. In Windows Explorer, use Tools➜Folder Options, and select the View tab in the Folder Options dialog box. Remove the check mark from Hide Extensions for Known File Types.

6. Using Windows Explorer, add a .zip extension to the ribbon modification.xlsm file in Windows Explorer.

   The filename should now be ribbon modification.xlsm.zip.

7. Drag the customUI folder you created in Step 4 into the ribbon modification.xlsm.zip file.

   Windows treats Zip files as if they were folders, so drag-and-drop operations are allowed.

8. Double-click the ribbon modification.xlsm.zip file to open it.

   Figure 20-4 shows the contents of the Zip file. As you see, the file contains several folders.

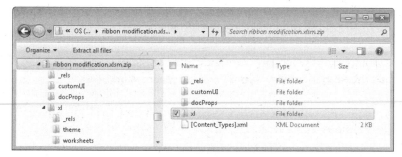

Figure 20-4: An Excel workbook, displayed as a Zip file.

9. In the Zip file, double-click the _rels folder.

   This folder contains one file, named .rels.

10. Drag the .rels file to a location outside the Zip file (to your desktop, for example).

11. Open the .rels file (which is an XML file) with a text editor, such as Notepad.

12. Add the following line to the .rels file, before the </Relationships> tag:

```
<Relationship Type="http://schemas.microsoft.com/office/2006/
   relationships/ui/extensibility" Target="/customUI/customUI.xml"
   Id="12345" />
```

13. Save the .rels file and drag it back into the Zip file, overwriting the original version.

14. Remove the .zip extension so that the file is back to its original name: ribbon modification.xlsm.

Open the workbook in Excel. If all went well, you should see a new group with two buttons in the Data tab, as shown in Figure 20-5.

Figure 20-5: RibbonX code created a new group with two buttons.

On the Web

This workbook, named ribbon modification.xlsm, is available on the book's website.

It's important to understand that the Ribbon modification is document-specific. In other words, the new Ribbon group is displayed only when the workbook that contains the RibbonX code is the active workbook. This is a major departure from how UI modifications worked in versions before Excel 2007.

Tip

To display Ribbon customizations when any workbook is active, convert the workbook to an add-in file or add the RibbonX code to your Personal Macro Workbook.

If you've concluded that modifying Excel's Ribbon isn't worth the effort, don't despair. Tools are available that make the process much less tedious than I've described.

A simple Ribbon example, take 2

This section provides step-by-step instructions for making the same Ribbon modification described in the preceding section. In this example, I use Custom UI Editor for Microsoft Office. This program still requires that you create the RibbonX code manually, but it will validate the code for you. It also eliminates all the tedious manual file manipulations. And finally, it can generate the VBA callback procedure declarations, which you can copy and paste to your VBA module.

On the Web

You can download a free copy of Custom UI Editor for Microsoft Office by searching the web for office custom ui editor. (I don't list the download URL because it changes from time to time.)

To add the new group and buttons (as described in the preceding section) using Custom UI Editor:

1. In Excel, create a new workbook and save it as a macro-enabled XLSM file.

2. Close the workbook.

3. Launch Custom UI Editor for Microsoft Office.

4. Choose File➜Open and locate the workbook you saved in Step 1.

5. Choose Insert→Office 2007 Custom UI Part.

   Choosing this option will make the file compatible with both Excel 2007 and later versions.

6. Enter the RibbonX code shown in Figure 20-6.

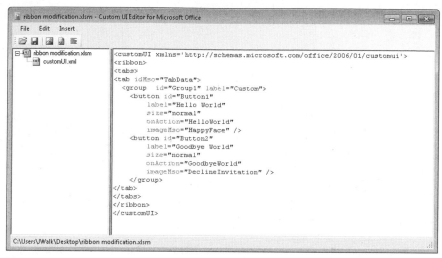

Figure 20-6: Custom UI Editor for Microsoft Office.

7. Click the Validate button to check for errors.

8. Click the Generate Callbacks button and copy the code that appears.

   Custom UI Editor generates two VBA callback procedures (see Figure 20-7). Select and copy this code; you will later paste it into a VBA module in the workbook.

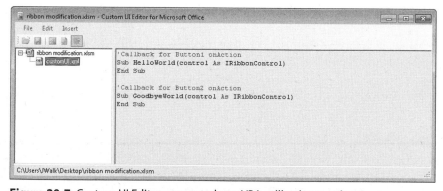

Figure 20-7: Custom UI Editor generated two VBA callback procedures.

9. In the tree diagram on the left, click the customUI.xml node.

10. Choose File→Save, and then choose File→Close.

11. Activate Excel and open the workbook.

12. Press Alt+11 to activate VB Editor.

13. Insert a VBA module and paste the code you copied in Step 8.

14. Add a MsgBox statement to each of the two procedures so that you can verify that they're being executed.

As you can see, working with Custom UI Editor is much easier than manipulating a file manually.

The CUSTOM UI part

In Step 5 of the preceding instructions, you inserted a customUI part for Office 2007. This choice makes the workbook compatible with Excel 2007 and later. The other option on the Insert menu is Office 2010 Custom UI Part. If you put the RibbonX code in an Office 2010 Custom UI part, the workbook won't be compatible with Excel 2007.

Note   **As I was writing this chapter, Custom UI Editor for Microsoft Office did not yet have an option to insert an Office 2013 customUI part.**

If your application doesn't use commands unique to Excel 2010 or later, using the Office 2007 custom UI part is the best solution. Also, keep in mind that a single file can have an Office 2007 part, an Office 2010 part, and an Office 2013 part. You use multiple parts if you want to load version-specific RibbonX code for the UI.

Note that the first statement in the RibbonX code must be changed for an Office 2010 Custom UI part. The code must refer to this namespace:

```
<customUI xmlns='http://schemas.microsoft.com/office/2009/07/customui'>
```

Note   **The namespace for an Office 2013 Custom UI part was not known when I wrote this chapter.**

If you use the wrong customUI tag, Custom UI Editor will let you know when you validate the code.

VBA callback procedures

Recall that the workbook contains two VBA procedures, HelloWorld and GoodbyeWorld. These procedure names correspond to the onAction parameters in the RibbonX code. The onAction parameter is one way to link the RibbonX code to your VBA code.

Both VBA procedures contain an argument named control, which is an IRibbonControl object. This object has three properties, which you can access in your VBA code:

➤ Context: A handle to the active window containing the Ribbon that triggered the callback. For example, use the following expression to get the name of the workbook that contains the RibbonX code:

```
control.Context.Caption
```

➤ Id: Contains the name of the control, specified as its Id parameter.

➤ Tag: Contains any arbitrary text associated with the control.

The VBA callback procedures can be as complex as necessary.

The .rels file

Inserting the file that contains the RibbonX code has no effect unless you specify a relationship between the document file and the customization file. These relationships, written in XML, are stored in the .rels file, which is in the _rels folder. Here's the relationship for the example presented in the preceding section:

```
<Relationship Type="http://schemas.microsoft.com/office/2006/
  relationships/ui/extensibility" Target="/customUI/customUI.xml"
  Id="12345" />
```

The Target parameter points to the customUI.xml file that contains the RibbonX code. The Id parameter contains an arbitrary text string. The string can contain anything, as long as it's unique to the file (that is, as long as no other <Relationship> tag uses the same Id).

If you use Custom UI Editor, you need not be concerned with the .rels file. Changes to this file are made automatically.

The RibbonX code

And now the tricky part. Writing the XML code that defines your UI modification is no easy task. As I've noted, this is not the book that will teach you how to write RibbonX code. You'll find a few simple examples here, but you'll need to consult other sources for the fine points.

When you're starting out, it's best to use examples that work (search the web) and then make small modifications, testing frequently along the way. It can be frustrating to spend an hour working on code that appears to be perfect in every way — and then realize that XML is case-sensitive. For example, *ID* is not the same as *Id*.

Note

You may be curious about the imageMso parameter, which determines which icon is displayed next to the control. Microsoft Office includes more than 1,000 icons that you can use with Ribbon controls. Each is accessed by its name. For more information, see the sidebar "Using imageMso images."

Using imageMso images

Microsoft Office provides more than 1,000 named images that are associated with various commands. You can specify any of these images for your custom Ribbon controls — if you know the image's name.

The accompanying figure shows a workbook that contains the names of all the imageMso images for various versions of Office. Scroll through the image names, and you see 50 images at a time (in small or large size), beginning with the image name in the active cell. This workbook, named mso image browser.xlsm, is available on the book's website.

You can also use these images in an Image control placed on a UserForm. The following statement assigns the imageMso image named ReviewAcceptChanges to the Picture property of a UserForm Image control named Image1. The size of the image is specified as 32 x 32 pixels.

```
Image1.Picture = Application.CommandBars. _
  GetImageMso("ReviewAcceptChange", 32, 32)
```

Another RibbonX example

This section contains another example of using RibbonX to modify the UI. This workbook creates a new group on the Page Layout tab and adds a check box control that toggles the display of page breaks.

Note

Although Excel has more than 1,700 commands, it doesn't have a command that toggles the page break display. After printing or previewing a worksheet, the only way to hide the page break display is to use the Excel Options dialog box. Therefore, the example in this section has some practical value.

This example is a bit tricky because it requires that the new Ribbon control be in synch with the active sheet. For example, if you activate a worksheet that doesn't display page breaks, the check box control should be in its deselected state. If you activate a worksheet that displays page breaks, the control should be selected. Furthermore, page breaks aren't relevant for a chart sheet, so the control should be disabled if you activate a chart sheet.

The RibbonX Code

The RibbonX code that adds a new group (with a CheckBox control) to the Page Layout tab follows:

```
<customUI
  xmlns="http://schemas.microsoft.com/office/2006/01/customui"
  onLoad="Initialize">
<ribbon>
<tabs>
<tab idMso="TabPageLayoutExcel">
  <group id="Group1" label="Custom">
    <checkBox id="Checkbox1"
        label="Page Breaks"
        onAction="TogglePageBreakDisplay"
        getPressed="GetPressed"
        getEnabled="GetEnabled"/>
    </group>
</tab>
</tabs>
</ribbon>
</customUI>
```

This RibbonX code references four VBA callback procedures (each of which is described later):

➤ Initialize: Executed when the workbook is opened

➤ TogglePageBreakDisplay: Executed when the user clicks the check box control

➤ GetPressed: Executed when the control is invalidated (the user activates a different sheet)

➤ GetEnabled: Executed when the control is invalidated (the user activates a different sheet)

Figure 20-8 shows the new control, placed in a group named Custom.

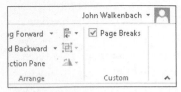

Figure 20-8: This check box control is always in synch with the page break display of the active sheet.

The VBA Code

The CustomUI tag includes an onLoad parameter, which specifies the Initialize VBA callback procedure, as follows (this code is in a standard VBA module):

```
Public MyRibbon As IRibbonUI

Sub Initialize(Ribbon As IRibbonUI)
'    Executed when the workbook loads
    Set MyRibbon = Ribbon
End Sub
```

The Initialize procedure creates an IRibbonUI object named MyRibbon. Note that MyRibbon is a Public variable, so it's accessible from other procedures in the module.

I created a simple event procedure that is executed whenever a worksheet is activated. This procedure, which is located in the ThisWorkbook code module, calls the CheckPageBreakDisplay procedure:

```
Private Sub Workbook_SheetActivate(ByVal Sh As Object)
    Call CheckPageBreakDisplay
End Sub
```

The CheckPageBreakDisplay procedure *invalidates* the check box control. In other words, it destroys any data associated with that control.

```
Sub CheckPageBreakDisplay()
'    Executed when a sheet is activated
    MyRibbon.InvalidateControl ("Checkbox1")
End Sub
```

When a control is invalidated, the GetPressed and GetEnabled procedures are called:

```
Sub GetPressed(control As IRibbonControl, ByRef returnedVal)
'    Executed when the control is invalidated
     On Error Resume Next
     returnedVal = ActiveSheet.DisplayPageBreaks
End Sub

Sub GetEnabled(control As IRibbonControl, ByRef returnedVal)
'    Executed when the control is invalidated
     returnedVal = TypeName(ActiveSheet) = "Worksheet"
End Sub
```

Note that the returnedVal argument is passed ByRef. This means your code is able to change the value — and that's exactly what happens. In the GetPressed procedure, the returnedVal variable is set to the status of the DisplayPageBreaks property of the active sheet. The result is that the control's Pressed parameter is True if page breaks are displayed (and the control is selected). Otherwise, the control isn't selected.

In the GetEnabled procedure, the returnedVal variable is set to True if the active sheet is a worksheet (as opposed to a chart sheet). Therefore, the control is enabled only when the active sheet is a worksheet.

The only other VBA procedure is the onAction procedure, TogglePageBreakDisplay, which is executed when the user selects or deselects the check box:

```
Sub TogglePageBreakDisplay(control As IRibbonControl, pressed As Boolean)
'    Executed when check box is clicked
     On Error Resume Next
     ActiveSheet.DisplayPageBreaks = pressed
End Sub
```

This pressed argument is True if the user selects the check box and False if the user deselects the check box. The code sets the DisplayPageBreaks property accordingly.

On the Web This workbook, named page break display.xlsm, is available on the book's website. The site also contains an add-in version of this workbook (named page break display add-in. xlam), which makes the new UI command available for all workbooks. The add-in version uses a class module to monitor sheet activation events for all workbooks. Refer to Chapter 17 for more information about events and Chapter 27 for more information about class modules.

Ribbon controls demo

Figure 20-9 shows a custom Ribbon tab (My Stuff) with four groups of controls. In this section, I briefly describe the RibbonX code and the VBA callback procedures.

Figure 20-9: A new Ribbon tab with four groups of controls.

On the Web

This workbook, named ribbon controls demo.xlsm, is available on the book's website.

Creating a new tab

The RibbonX code that creates the new tab is

```
<ribbon>
  <tabs>
    <tab id="CustomTab" label="My Stuff">
    </tab>
  </tabs>
</ribbon>
```

Tip

If you'd like to create a minimal UI, the ribbon tag has a startFromScratch attribute. If set to True, all the built-in tabs are hidden.

```
<ribbon startFromScratch="true" >
```

Creating a Ribbon group

The code in the ribbon controls demo.xlsm example creates four groups on the My Stuff tab. Here's the code that creates the four groups:

```
<group  id="Group1" label="Stuff">
</group>

<group  id="Group2" label="More Stuff">
</group>

<group  id="Group3" label="Built In Stuff">
```

```
    </group>

    <group  id="Group4" label="Galleries">
    </group>
```

These pairs of <group> and </group> tags are located between the <tab> and </tab> tags that create the new tab.

Creating controls

Following is the RibbonX code that creates the controls in the first group (Stuff). Figure 20-10 shows these controls on the Ribbon.

Figure 20-10: A Ribbon group with four controls.

```
<group id="Group1" label="Stuff">
    <labelControl id="Label1" getLabel="getLabel1" />
    <labelControl id="Label2" getLabel="getLabel2" />

    <editBox id="EditBox1"
        showLabel="true"
        label="Number:"
        onChange="EditBox1_Change"/>

    <button id="Button1"
        label="Calculator"
        size="large"
        onAction="ShowCalculator"
        imageMso="Calculator" />
</group>
```

Two label controls each have an associated VBA callback procedure (named getLabel1 and getLabel2). These procedures are:

```
Sub getLabel1(control As IRibbonControl, ByRef returnedVal)
    returnedVal = "Hello " & Application.UserName
End Sub

Sub getLabel2(control As IRibbonControl, ByRef returnedVal)
    returnedVal = "Today is " & Date
End Sub
```

When the RibbonX code is loaded, these two procedures are executed, and the captions of the label controls are dynamically updated with the username and the date.

The editBox control has an onChange callback procedure named EditBox1_Change, which displays the square root of the number entered (or an error message if the square root can't be calculated). The EditBox1_Change procedure is

```
Sub EditBox1_Change(control As IRibbonControl, text As String)
    Dim squareRoot As Double
    On Error Resume Next
    squareRoot = Sqr(text)
    If Err.Number = 0 Then
        MsgBox "The square root of " & text & " is: " & squareRoot
    Else
        MsgBox "Enter a positive number.", vbCritical
    End If
End Sub
```

The last control in the Stuff group is a simple button. Its onAction parameter executes a VBA procedure named ShowCalculator — which uses the VBA Shell function to display the Windows calculator:

```
Sub ShowCalculator(control As IRibbonControl)
    On Error Resume Next
    Shell "calc.exe", vbNormalFocus
    If Err.Number <> 0 Then MsgBox "Can't start calc.exe"
End Sub
```

Figure 20-11 shows the controls in the second group, labeled More Stuff.

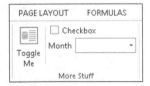

Figure 20-11: Three controls in a custom Ribbon group.

The RibbonX code for the second group is as follows:

```
<group  id="Group2" label="More Stuff">
  <toggleButton id="ToggleButton1"
      size="large"
      imageMso="FileManageMenu"
      label="Toggle Me"
      onAction="ToggleButton1_Click" />
```

```
    <separator id="sep1" />

    <checkBox id="Checkbox1"
        label="Checkbox"
        onAction="Checkbox1_Change"/>

    <comboBox id="Combo1"
        label="Month"
        onChange="Combo1_Change">
      <item id="Month1" label="January" />
      <item id="Month2" label="February"/>
      <item id="Month3" label="March"/>
      <item id="Month4" label="April"/>
      <item id="Month5" label="May"/>
      <item id="Month6" label="June"/>
      <item id="Month7" label="July"/>
      <item id="Month8" label="August"/>
      <item id="Month9" label="September"/>
      <item id="Month10" label="October"/>
      <item id="Month11" label="November"/>
      <item id="Month12" label="December"/>
    </comboBox>
  </group>
```

The group contains a toggleButton, a separator, a checkBox, and a comboBox control. These controls are straightforward. Except for the separator control (which inserts a vertical line), each has an associated callback procedure that simply displays the status of the control:

```
Sub ToggleButton1_Click(control As IRibbonControl, ByRef returnedVal)
    MsgBox "Toggle value: " & returnedVal
End Sub

Sub Checkbox1_Change(control As IRibbonControl, pressed As Boolean)
    MsgBox "Checkbox value: " & pressed
End Sub

Sub Combo1_Change(control As IRibbonControl, text As String)
    MsgBox text
End Sub
```

Note
The comboBox control also accepts user-entered text. If you would like to limit the choices to those that you provide, use a dropDown control.

The controls in the third group consist of built-in controls, as shown in Figure 20-12. To include a built-in control in a custom group, you just need to know its name (the idMso parameter).

Figure 20-12: This group contains built-in controls.

The RibbonX code is

```
<group id="Group3" label="Built In Stuff">
   <control idMso="Copy" label="Copy" />
   <control idMso="Paste" label="Paste" enabled="true" />
   <control idMso="WindowSwitchWindowsMenuExcel"
      label="Switch Window" />
   <control idMso="Italic" />
   <control idMso="Bold" />
   <control idMso="FileOpen" />
</group>
```

These controls don't have callback procedures because they perform the standard action.

Figure 20-13 shows the final group of controls, which consists of two galleries.

Figure 20-13: This Ribbon group contains two galleries.

The RibbonX code for these two gallery controls is

```
<group id="Group4" label="Galleries">
  <gallery id="Gallery1"
     imageMso="ViewAppointmentInCalendar"
     label="Pick a Month:"
     columns="2" rows="6"
     onAction="MonthSelected" >
   <item id="January" label="January" imageMso="QuerySelectQueryType"/>
   <item id="February" label="February" imageMso="QuerySelectQueryType"/>
   <item id="March" label="March" imageMso="QuerySelectQueryType"/>
   <item id="April" label="April" imageMso="QuerySelectQueryType"/>
   <item id="May" label="May" imageMso="QuerySelectQueryType"/>
   <item id="June" label="June" imageMso="QuerySelectQueryType"/>
   <item id="July" label="July" imageMso="QuerySelectQueryType"/>
   <item id="August" label="August" imageMso="QuerySelectQueryType"/>
```

```
    <item id="September" label="September" imageMso="QuerySelectQueryT
ype"/>
    <item id="October" label="October" imageMso="QuerySelectQueryType"/>
    <item id="November" label="November" imageMso="QuerySelectQueryType"/>
    <item id="December" label="December" imageMso="QuerySelectQueryType"/>
    <button id="Today"
        label="Today..."
        imageMso="ViewAppointmentInCalendar"
        onAction="ShowToday"/>
  </gallery>

<gallery id="Gallery2"
    label="Shapes"
    size="large"
    columns="4"
    itemWidth="60" itemHeight="65"
    imageMso=    "Camera"
    onAction="OnAction">
  <item id="bp01" image="bp01" />
  <item id="bp02" image="bp02" />
  <item id="bp03" image="bp03" />
  <item id="bp04" image="bp04" />
  <item id="bp05" image="bp05" />
  <item id="bp06" image="bp06" />
  <item id="bp07" image="bp07" />
  <item id="bp08" image="bp08" />
  <item id="bp09" image="bp09" />
  <item id="bp10" image="bp10" />
  <item id="bp11" image="bp11" />
  <item id="bp12" image="bp12" />
  <item id="bp13" image="bp13" />
  <item id="bp14" image="bp14" />
  <item id="bp15" image="bp15" />
  </gallery>
</group>
```

Figure 20-14 shows the first gallery, a list of month names in two columns.

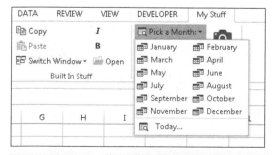

Figure 20-14: A gallery that displays month names, plus a button.

The onAction parameter executes the MonthSelected callback procedure, which displays the selected month (which is stored as the id parameter):

```
Sub MonthSelected(control As IRibbonControl, _
    id As String, index As Integer)
    MsgBox "You selected " & id
End Sub
```

The Pick a Month gallery also contains a button control with its own callback procedure (labeled Today) at the bottom:

```
Sub ShowToday(control As IRibbonControl)
    MsgBox "Today is " & Date
End Sub
```

The second gallery, shown in Figure 20-15, displays 15 images, saved as PNG images.

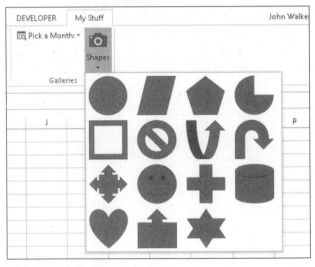

Figure 20-15: A gallery of images.

These images are stored in the workbook file, in a folder named images, within the customUI folder. Adding images also requires a _rels folder, with a list of relationships. To see how this works, add a .zip extension to the workbook and then examine its contents.

A dynamicMenu Control Example

One of the most interesting Ribbon controls is the dynamicMenu control. This control lets your VBA code feed XML data into the control — which provides the basis for menus that change based on context.

Setting up a dynamicMenu control isn't a simple task, but this control probably offers the most flexibility in terms of using VBA to modify the Ribbon dynamically.

I created a simple dynamicMenu control demo that displays a different menu for each of the three worksheets in a workbook. Figure 20-16 shows the menu that appears when Sheet1 is active. When a sheet is activated, a VBA procedure sends XML code specific to the sheet. For this demo, I stored the XML code directly in the worksheets to make it easier to read. Alternatively, the XML markup can be stored as a string variable in your code.

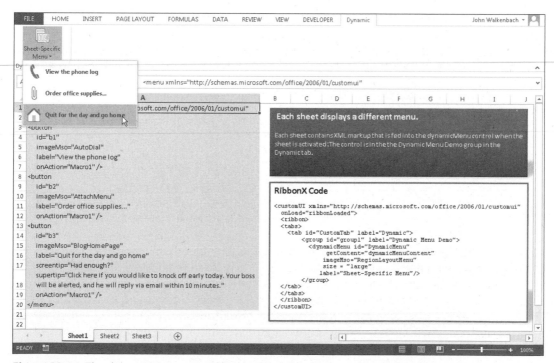

Figure 20-16: The dynamicMenu control lets you create a menu that varies depending on the context.

The RibbonX code that creates the new tab, the new group, and the dynamicMenu control follows:

```
<customUI xmlns="http://schemas.microsoft.com/office/2006/01/customui"
  onLoad="ribbonLoaded">
  <ribbon>
  <tabs>
    <tab id="CustomTab" label="Dynamic">
        <group id="group1" label="Dynamic Menu Demo">
          <dynamicMenu id="DynamicMenu"
              getContent="dynamicMenuContent"
              imageMso="RegionLayoutMenu"
              size = "large"
              label="Sheet-Specific Menu"/>
        </group>
  </tab>
  </tabs>
  </ribbon>
</customUI>
```

This example needs a way to invalidate the Ribbon whenever the user activates a new sheet. I use the same method I used for the page break display example earlier in this chapter (see "Another RibbonX example"): I declared a Public variable, MyRibbon, of type IRibbonUI. I used a Workbook_SheetActivate procedure that called the UpdateDynamicRibbon procedure whenever a new sheet is activated:

```
Sub UpdateDynamicRibbon()
'   Invalidate the Ribbon to force a call to dynamicMenuContent
    On Error Resume Next
    MyRibbon.Invalidate
    If Err.Number <> 0 Then
        MsgBox "Lost the Ribbon object. Save and reload."
    End If
End Sub
```

The UpdateDynamicRibbon procedure invalidates the MyRibbon object, which forces a call to the VBA callback procedure named dynamicMenuContent (a procedure referenced by the getContent parameter in the RibbonX code). Note the error-handling code. Some edits to your VBA code destroy the MyRibbon object, which is created when the workbook is opened. Attempting to invalidate an object that doesn't exist causes an error, and the message box informs the user that the workbook must be saved and reopened. Unfortunately, reopening the workbook is the only way to re-create the MyRibbon object.

The dynamicMenuContent procedure follows. This procedure loops through the cells in column A of the active sheet, reads the XML code, and stores it in a variable named XMLcode. When all the XML has been appended, it's passed to the returnedVal argument. The net effect is that the dynamicMenu control has new code, so it displays a different set of menu options.

```
Sub dynamicMenuContent(control As IRibbonControl, _
    ByRef returnedVal)
    Dim r As Long
    Dim XMLcode As String
'   Read the XML markup from the active sheet
    For r = 1 To Application.CountA(Range("A:A"))
        XMLcode = XMLcode & ActiveSheet.Cells(r, 1) & " "
    Next r
    returnedVal = XMLcode
End Sub
```

On the Web

The workbook that contains this example is available on the book's website in the dynamicmenu.xlsm file.

More on Ribbon customization

I conclude this section with some additional points to keep in mind as you explore the wonderful world of Excel Ribbon customization:

➤ When you're working with the Ribbon, make sure that you turn on the display of error messages. Refer to the "See your errors" sidebar, earlier in this chapter.

➤ Remember that RibbonX code is case-sensitive.

➤ All the named control IDs are in English, and they're the same across all language versions of Excel. Therefore, Ribbon modifications work regardless of what language version of Excel is used.

➤ Ribbon modifications appear only when the workbook that contains the RibbonX code is active. To make Ribbon modifications appear for all workbooks, the RibbonX code must be in an add-in.

➤ The built-in controls scale themselves when the Excel window is resized. Custom controls do not scale in Excel 2007, but they do in Excel 2010 and later.

➤ You cannot add or remove controls from a built-in Ribbon group.

➤ You can, however, hide tabs. The RibbonX code that follows hides three tabs:

```
<customUI xmlns="http://schemas.microsoft.com/office/2006/01/
    customui">
<ribbon>
  <tabs>
    <tab idMso="TabPageLayoutExcel" visible="false" />
    <tab idMso="TabData" visible="false" />
    <tab idMso="TabReview" visible="false" />
  </tabs>
</ribbon>
</customUI>
```

➤ You can also hide groups within a tab. Here's RibbonX code that hides four groups on the Insert tab (leaving only the Charts group):

```
<customUI xmlns="http://schemas.microsoft.com/office/2006/01/
  customui">
<ribbon>
  <tabs>
    <tab idMso="TabInsert">
     <group idMso="GroupInsertTablesExcel" visible="false" />
     <group idMso="GroupInsertIllustrations" visible="false" />
     <group idMso="GroupInsertLinks" visible="false" />
     <group idMso="GroupInsertText" visible="false" />
    </tab>
  </tabs>
</ribbon>
</customUI>
```

➤ You can assign your own macro to a built-in control. This is known as *repurposing the control.* The RibbonX code that follows intercepts three built-in commands:

```
<customUI xmlns="http://schemas.microsoft.com/office/2006/01/
  customui">
<commands>
  <command idMso="FileSave" onAction="mySave"/>
  <command idMso="FilePrint" onAction="myPrint"/>
  <command idMso="FilePrintQuick" onAction="myPrint"/>
</commands>
</customUI>
```

➤ You can also write RibbonX code to disable one or more built-in controls. The code that follows disables the Insert ClipArt command:

```
<customUI xmlns="http://schemas.microsoft.com/office/2006/01/
  customui">
<commands>
  <command idMso="ClipArtInsert" enabled="false"/>
</commands>
</customUI>
```

➤ If you have two or more workbooks (or add-ins) that add controls to the same custom Ribbon group, you must make sure that they both use the same namespace. Do this in the <CustomUI> tag at the top of the RibbonX code.

Creating an Old-Style Toolbar

If you find that customizing the Ribbon is just too much work, you may be content to create a simple custom toolbar using the pre–Excel 2007 CommandBar object. This technique is perfectly suitable for any workbook that only you will be using and is an easy way to provide quick access to a number of macros.

In this section, I provide boilerplate code that you can adapt as needed. I don't offer much in the way of explanation. For more information about CommandBar objects, search the web or consult the Excel 2003 edition of this book. CommandBar objects can be much more powerful than the example presented here.

Limitations of old-style toolbars in Excel 2007 and later

If you decide to create a toolbar for use in Excel 2007 or later, be aware of the following limitations:

> ➤ The toolbar can't be free-floating.

> ➤ The toolbar will always appear in the Add-Ins➔Custom Toolbars group (along with any other toolbars).

> ➤ Excel ignores some CommandBar properties and methods.

Code to create a toolbar

The code in this section assumes that you have a workbook with two macros (named Macro1 and Macro2). It also assumes that you want the toolbar to be created when the workbook is opened and deleted when the workbook is closed.

Note If you use Excel 2007 or Excel 2010, custom toolbars are visible regardless of which workbook is active. With Excel 2013, however, a custom toolbar is visible only in the workbook in which it was created — and also in new workbooks created while the original workbook is active.

In the ThisWorkbook code module, enter the following procedures. The first one calls the procedure that creates the toolbar when the workbook is opened. The second calls the procedure to delete the toolbar when the workbook is closed:

```
Private Sub Workbook_Open()
    Call CreateToolbar
End Sub

Private Sub Workbook_BeforeClose(Cancel As Boolean)
    Call DeleteToolbar
End Sub
```

Cross-Ref

In Chapter 17, I describe a potentially serious problem with the Workbook_BeforeClose event. Excel's "Do you want to save . . ." prompt is displayed after the Workbook_ BeforeClose event handler runs. So if the user clicks Cancel, the workbook remains open but the custom menu items have already been deleted. In Chapter 17, I also present a way to get around this problem.

The CreateToolbar procedure follows:

```vba
Const TOOLBARNAME As String = "MyToolbar"

Sub CreateToolbar()
    Dim TBar As CommandBar
    Dim Btn As CommandBarButton

'   Delete existing toolbar (if it exists)
    On Error Resume Next
    CommandBars(TOOLBARNAME).Delete
    On Error GoTo 0

'   Create toolbar
    Set TBar = CommandBars.Add
    With TBar
        .Name = TOOLBARNAME
        .Visible = True
    End With

'   Add a button
    Set Btn = TBar.Controls.Add(Type:=msoControlButton)
    With Btn
        .FaceId = 300
        .OnAction = "Macro1"
        .Caption = "Macro1 Tooltip goes here"
    End With

'   Add another button
    Set Btn = TBar.Controls.Add(Type:=msoControlButton)
    With Btn
        .FaceId = 25
        .OnAction = "Macro2"
        .Caption = "Macro2 Tooltip goes here"
    End With
End Sub
```

On the Web

A workbook that contains this code is available on the book's website in the old-style toolbar.xlsm file.

Figure 20-17 shows the two-button toolbar.

Figure 20-17: An old-style toolbar, located in the Custom Toolbars group of the Add-Ins tab.

I use a module-level constant, TOOLBAR, which stores the toolbar's name. This name is used also in the DeleteToolbar procedure, so using a constant ensures that both procedures work with the same name.

The procedure starts by deleting the existing toolbar that has the same name (if such a toolbar exists). Including this statement is useful during development and also eliminates the error you get if you attempt to create a toolbar using a duplicate name.

The toolbar is created by using the Add method of the CommandBars object. The two buttons are added by using the Add method of the Controls object. Each button has three properties:

➤ FaceID: A number that determines the image displayed on the button. Chapter 21 contains more information about FaceID images.

➤ OnAction: The macro executed when the button is clicked.

➤ Caption: The screen tip that appears when you hover the mouse pointer over the button.

> **Tip**
>
> **Rather than set the FaceID property, you can set the Picture property using any of the imageMso images. For example, the following statement displays a green check mark:**
>
> ```
> .Picture = Application.CommandBars.GetImageMso _
>     ("AcceptInvitation", 16, 16)
> ```
>
> **For more information about imageMso images, see the sidebar, "Using imageMso images."**

When the workbook is closed, the Workbook_BeforeClose event procedure fires, which calls DeleteToolbar:

```
Sub DeleteToolbar()
    On Error Resume Next
    CommandBars(TOOLBARNAME).Delete
    On Error GoTo 0
End Sub
```

Note that the toolbar is *not* deleted from workbook windows that were opened after the toolbar was created.

Working with Shortcut Menus

In This Chapter

- Identifying shortcut menus
- Customizing the shortcut menus
- Disabling shortcut menus
- Using events with shortcut menus
- Creating a new shortcut menu

CommandBar Overview

A CommandBar object is used for three Excel user interface elements:

➤ Custom toolbars

➤ Custom menus

➤ Customs shortcut (right-click) menus

Beginning with Excel 2007, the CommandBar object is in an odd position. If you write VBA code to customize a menu or a toolbar, Excel intercepts that code and ignores many of your commands. As I describe in Chapter 20, menu and toolbar customizations performed with the CommandBar object appear in the Add-Ins➔Menu Commands group or the Add-Ins➔Custom Toolbars group. So, for all practical purposes, the CommandBar object in Excel is now limited to shortcut menu operations.

New Feature

The new single-document interface for Excel 2013 affects custom shortcut menus. VBA code that creates custom shortcut menus may not work correctly in Excel 2013. I discuss this topic later in this chapter (see " What's different in Excel 2013").

In this section, I provide some background information about CommandBars.

CommandBar types

Excel supports three types of CommandBars, differentiated by their Type property. The Type property can be any of these three values:

➤ msoBarTypeNormal: A toolbar (Type = 0)

➤ msoBarTypeMenuBar: A menu bar (Type = 1)

➤ msoBarTypePopUp: A shortcut menu (Type = 2)

Even though toolbars and menu bars aren't used in Excel 2007 and later, these UI elements are still included in the object model for compatibility with older applications. However, attempting to display a CommandBar of Type 0 or 1 has no effect in Excel versions after Excel 2003. In Excel 2003, for example, the following statement displays the Standard toolbar:

```
CommandBars("Standard").Visible = True
```

In later versions of Excel, that statement is ignored.

This chapter focuses exclusively on Type 2 CommandBars (shortcut menus).

Listing shortcut menus

Excel 2013 has 67 shortcut menus. How do I know that? I ran the ShowShortcutMenuNames procedure that follows, which loops through all CommandBars. If the Type property is msoBarTypePopUp (a built-in constant that has a value of 2), it displays the shortcut menu's index, name, and the number of menu items it contains.

```
Sub ShowShortcutMenuNames()
    Dim Row As Long
    Dim cbar As CommandBar
    Row = 1
    For Each cbar In CommandBars
        If cbar.Type = msoBarTypePopUp Then
            Cells(Row, 1) = cbar.Index
            Cells(Row, 2) = cbar.Name
            Cells(Row, 3) = cbar.Controls.Count
            Row = Row + 1
        End If
    Next cbar
End Sub
```

Figure 21-1 shows part of the output from this procedure. The shortcut menu index values range from 10 to 156. Also, note that not all the names are unique. For example, CommandBar 10 and

CommandBar 39 both have a Name of Cell because right-clicking a cell gives a different shortcut menu when the worksheet is in page break preview mode.

◢	A	B	C	D
1	10	Cell	27	
2	24	PivotChart Menu	6	
3	36	Workbook tabs	16	
4	37	Column	13	
5	38	Row	13	
6	39	Cell	21	
7	40	Column	19	
8	41	Row	19	
9	42	Ply	11	
10	43	XLM Cell	15	
11	44	Document	9	
12	45	Desktop	5	
13	46	Nondefault Drag and Drop	11	
14	47	AutoFill	12	
15	48	Button	12	
16	49	Dialog	4	
17	50	Series	5	
18	51	Plot Area	8	
19	52	Floor and Walls	3	
20	53	Trendline	2	
21	54	Chart	2	

Sheet1 ⊕

Figure 21-1: A simple macro generates a list of all shortcut menus.

On the Web

This example is available on the book's website in the show shortcut menu names.xlsm file.

Referring to CommandBars

You can reference a particular CommandBar object by its Index or Name property. For example, the expressions that follow both refer to the shortcut menu that is displayed when you right-click a column letter in Excel 2013:

```
Application.CommandBars (37)
Application.CommandBars("Column")
```

The CommandBars collection is a member of the Application object. When you reference this collection in a regular VBA module or in a module for a sheet, you can omit the reference to the Application object. For example, the following statement (contained in a standard VBA module) displays the name of the object in the CommandBars collection that has an index of 42:

```
MsgBox CommandBars(42).Name
```

When you reference the CommandBars collection from a code module for a ThisWorkbook object, you must precede it with a reference to the Application object, like this:

```
MsgBox Application.CommandBars(42).Name
```

Caution

Unfortunately, the Index numbers for CommandBars have not always remained constant across the different Excel versions. For example, In Excel 2010, CommandBar 36 has the Name of Cell. In Excel 2013, CommandBar 36 has the Name of Workbook tabs. Therefore, using names rather than index numbers is more reliable.

Referring to controls in a CommandBar

A CommandBar object contains Control objects, which are buttons or menus. You can refer to a control by its Index property or by its Caption property. Here's a simple procedure that displays the caption of the first menu item on the Cell shortcut menu:

```
Sub ShowCaption()
    MsgBox CommandBars("Cell").Controls(1).Caption
End Sub
```

The following procedure displays the Caption property for each control in the shortcut menu that appears when you right-click a sheet tab (that shortcut menu is named Ply):

```
Sub ShowCaptions()
    Dim txt As String
    Dim ctl As CommandBarControl
    For Each ctl In CommandBars("Ply").Controls
        txt = txt & ctl.Caption & vbNewLine
    Next ctl
    MsgBox txt
End Sub
```

When you execute this procedure, you see the message box shown in Figure 21-2. The ampersand is used to indicate the underlined letter in the text — the keystroke that will execute the menu item.

In some cases, Control objects on a shortcut menu contain other Control objects. For example, the Filter control on the Cell right-click menu contains other controls. The Filter control is a submenu, and the additional items are submenu items.

The statement that follows displays the first submenu item in the Filter submenu:

```
MsgBox CommandBars("Cell").Controls("Filter").Controls(1).Caption
```

Figure 21-2: Displaying the Caption property for controls.

Finding a control

If you're writing code that will be used by a different language version of Excel, avoid using the Caption property to access a particular shortcut menu item. The Caption property is language-specific, so your code will fail if the user has a different language version of Excel.

Instead, use the FindControl method with the ID of the control (which is language-independent). For example, assume that you want to disable the Cut menu on the shortcut menu that appears when you right-click a column letter. If your workbook will be used only by people who have the English version of Excel, this statement will do the job:

```
CommandBars("Column").Controls("Cut").Enabled = False
```

To ensure that the command will work with non-English versions, you need to know the ID of the control. The following statement will tell you that the ID is 21:

```
MsgBox CommandBars("Column").Controls("Cut").ID
```

Then, to disable that control, use this statement:

```
CommandBars("Column").FindControl(ID:=21).Enabled = False
```

The CommandBar names are not internationalized, so a reference to CommandBars("Column") will always work. If two more command bars have the same name, the first one is used.

Properties of CommandBar controls

CommandBar controls have a number of properties that determine how the controls look and work. This list contains some of the more useful properties for CommandBar controls:

➤ Caption: The text displayed for the control. If the control shows only an image, the Caption appears when you move the mouse pointer over the control.

➤ ID: A unique numeric identifier for the control.

➤ FaceID: A number that represents a built-in graphic image displayed next to the control's text.

➤ Type: A value that determines whether a control is a button (msoControlButton) or a submenu (msoControlPopup).

➤ Picture: A graphics image displayed next to the control's text. This property is useful if you want to display a graphic from the Ribbon.

➤ BeginGroup: True if a separator bar appears before the control.

➤ OnAction: The name of a VBA macro that executes when the user clicks the control.

➤ BuiltIn: True if the control is an Excel built-in control.

➤ Enabled: True if the control can be clicked.

➤ Visible: True if the control is visible. Many of the shortcut menus contain hidden controls.

➤ ToolTipText: Text that appears when the user moves the mouse pointer over the control. (Not applicable for shortcut menus.)

Displaying all shortcut menu items

The ShowShortcutMenuItems procedure that follows creates a table that lists all the first-level controls on every shortcut menu. For each control, the table includes the shortcut menu's Index and Name, plus the ID, Caption , Type, Enabled, and Visible property values.

```
Sub ShowShortcutMenuItems()
  Dim Row As Long
  Dim Cbar As CommandBar
  Dim ctl As CommandBarControl
  Range("A1:G1") = Array("Index", "Name", "ID", "Caption", _
    "Type", "Enabled", "Visible")
  Row = 2
  Application.ScreenUpdating = False
  For Each Cbar In Application.CommandBars
    If Cbar.Type = 2 Then
      For Each ctl In Cbar.Controls
          Cells(Row, 1) = Cbar.Index
          Cells(Row, 2) = Cbar.Name
```

```
        Cells(Row, 3) = ctl.ID
        Cells(Row, 4) = ctl.Caption
        If ctl.Type = 1 Then
            Cells(Row, 5) = "Button"
        Else
            Cells(Row, 5) = "Submenu"
        End If
        Cells(Row, 6) = ctl.Enabled
        Cells(Row, 7) = ctl.Visible
        Row = Row + 1
    Next ctl
  End If
  Next Cbar
  ActiveSheet.ListObjects.Add(xlSrcRange, _
    Range("A1").CurrentRegion, , xlYes).Name = "Table1"
End Sub
```

Figure 21-3 shows a portion of the output.

	A	B	C	D	E	F	G
1	Index	Name	ID	Caption	Type	Enabled	Visible
2	10	Cell	21	Cu&t	Button	TRUE	TRUE
3	10	Cell	19	&Copy	Button	TRUE	TRUE
4	10	Cell	22	&Paste	Button	TRUE	TRUE
5	10	Cell	21437	Paste &Special...	Button	TRUE	TRUE
6	10	Cell	3624	&Paste Table	Button	TRUE	TRUE
7	10	Cell	3181	&Insert...	Button	TRUE	TRUE
8	10	Cell	292	&Delete...	Button	TRUE	TRUE
9	10	Cell	3125	Clear Co&ntents	Button	TRUE	TRUE
10	10	Cell	24508	&Quick Analysis	Button	FALSE	TRUE
11	10	Cell	31623	Sp&arklines	Submenu	TRUE	FALSE
12	10	Cell	31402	Filt&er	Submenu	TRUE	TRUE
13	10	Cell	31435	S&ort	Submenu	TRUE	TRUE
14	10	Cell	2031	Insert Co&mment	Button	TRUE	TRUE
15	10	Cell	1592	Delete Co&mment	Button	FALSE	FALSE
16	10	Cell	1593	Sh&ow/Hide Comments	Button	FALSE	FALSE
17	10	Cell	855	&Format Cells...	Button	TRUE	TRUE
18	10	Cell	1966	Pic&k From Drop-down List...	Button	TRUE	TRUE
19	10	Cell	1614	&Show Phonetic Field	Button	TRUE	FALSE
20	10	Cell	13380	Define N&ame...	Button	TRUE	TRUE
21	10	Cell	1576	&Hyperlink...	Button	TRUE	TRUE
22	10	Cell	1577	Edit &Hyperlink...	Button	FALSE	FALSE
23	10	Cell	1015	&Open Hyperlink	Button	FALSE	FALSE
24	10	Cell	3626	&Remove Hyperlink	Button	FALSE	FALSE
25	10	Cell	11299	E&xpand to detail	Button	FALSE	FALSE
26	10	Cell	31595	Additional Act&ions	Submenu	FALSE	FALSE
27	10	Cell	178	F&ull Screen	Button	TRUE	FALSE
28	10	Cell	22577	&Additional Actions	Button	TRUE	TRUE
29	24	PivotChart Menu	460	Field Setti&ngs	Button	TRUE	TRUE
30	24	PivotChart Menu	1604	&Options...	Button	FALSE	TRUE
31	24	PivotChart Menu	459	&Refresh Data	Button	TRUE	TRUE
32	24	PivotChart Menu	3956	&Hide PivotChart Field Buttons	Button	FALSE	TRUE
33	24	PivotChart Menu	30254	For&mulas	Submenu	TRUE	TRUE
34	24	PivotChart Menu	5416	Remo&ve Field	Button	FALSE	TRUE
35	36	Workbook tabs	957	Sheet1	Button	TRUE	TRUE
36	36	Workbook tabs	957	&Sheet List	Button	TRUE	FALSE
37	36	Workbook tabs	957	&Sheet List	Button	TRUE	FALSE

Sheet1 ⊕

Figure 21-3: Listing the items in all shortcut menus.

Displaying Excel 2003 menus

One of the built-in shortcut menus is named Built-In Menus, and it contains the menu items used in Excel 2003 (the final pre-Ribbon version of Excel). This shortcut menu isn't attached to an object, but you can display it using this VBA command:

```
Application.CommandBars("Built-in Menus").ShowPopup
```

This book's website has an example (named make xl 2003 menus.xlsm) that contains code to copy those shortcut menus to a toolbar. The toolbar is displayed on the Ribbon when the Add-Ins tab is active. As a result, you can use the Excel 2003 menus with Excel 2013.

The accompanying figure shows how the Excel 2003 menu looks in Excel 2013.

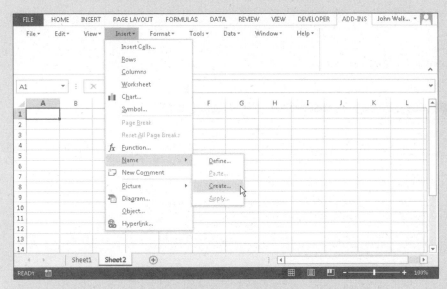

Some commands no longer function and (of course) newer features are not in the menus, so displaying Excel 2003 menus is more of a curiosity than a useful tool.

On the Web   This example, named show shortcut menu items.xlsm, is available on the book's website.

Using VBA to Customize Shortcut Menus

In this section, I present some practical examples of VBA code that manipulates Excel's shortcut menus. These examples, which can be modified to suit your needs, will give you an idea of the types of things you can do with shortcut menus.

What's different in Excel 2013

If you've used VBA to work with shortcut menus in previous versions of Excel, you need to be aware of a significant change in Excel 2013.

In the past, if your code modified a shortcut menu, that modification was in effect for all workbooks. For example, if you added a new item to the Cell right-click menu, that new item would appear when you right-clicked a cell in *any* workbook (and other workbooks that you open). In other words, shortcut menu modifications were at the *application* level.

Customizing shortcut menus with RibbonX code

You can also use RibbonX code to customize shortcut menus. When a workbook is opened that contains such code, the shortcut menus changes affect only that workbook. To make shortcut menu modifications in all workbooks, place the RibbonX code in an add-in.

Here's a simple example of RibbonX code that modifies the Cell right-click menu. As shown in the accompanying figure, the code adds a shortcut menu item after the Hyperlink menu item.

```
<customUI xmlns="http://schemas.microsoft.com/office/2009/07/customui">
   <contextMenus>
      <contextMenu idMso="ContextMenuCell">
         <button id="MyMenuItem"
     label="Run My Macro..."
            insertAfterMso="HyperlinkInsert"
            onAction="MyMacro"
            imageMso="AdvancedFileProperties"/>
      </contextMenu>
   </contextMenus>
</customUI>
```

Using RibbonX to modify shortcut menus was introduced in Excel 2010, so this technique doesn't work with Excel 2007.

As I explain in Chapter 20, you need to use a separate program to add RibbonX code.

Excel 2013 uses a single-document interface, which affects shortcut menus. Changes that you make to shortcut menus affect only the active workbook window. When you execute the code that modifies the shortcut menu, the shortcut menu for windows other than the active window will not be changed. This behavior is a radical departure from how things worked in previous versions of Excel.

And another twist: If the user opens a workbook (or creates a new workbook) when the active window displays the modified shortcut menu, the new workbook will also display the modified shortcut menu. In other words, new windows display the same shortcut menus as the window that was active when the new window was opened. If you write code to delete the shortcut menus, they are deleted only in the original workbook.

Even if a shortcut menu modification is intended to be used only in a single workbook, there's still a potential problem: If the user opens a new workbook, that new workbook will display the customized shortcut menus. Therefore, you might need to modify your code so the macros executed by the shortcut menus work only in the workbook for which they were designed.

If you want to use a custom shortcut menu as a way to execute a macro in an add-in, that menu item will be available only in workbooks that are opened *after* the add-in is opened.

Bottom line: In the past, if you opened a workbook or add-in that modified shortcut menus, you could be assured that the modified shortcut menus would be available in all workbooks. With Excel 2013, you no longer have that assurance.

Resetting a shortcut menu

The Reset method restores a shortcut menu to its original, default condition. The following procedure resets the Cell shortcut menu to its normal state:

```
Sub ResetCellMenu()
    CommandBars("Cell").Reset
End Sub
```

In Excel 2013, the Reset method affects the Cell shortcut menu only in the active window.

As I noted previously, Excel has two shortcut menus named Cell. The preceding code resets only the first one (index of 10). To reset the second Cell shortcut menu, you can use its index number (39) instead of its name. But remember, the index numbers aren't consistent across Excel versions. Here's a better procedure to reset both instances of the Cell shortcut menu in the active window:

```
Sub ResetCellMenu()
    Dim cbar As CommandBar
    For Each cbar In Application.CommandBars
        If cbar.Name = "Cell" Then cbar.Enabled = False
    Next cbar
End Sub
```

The following procedure resets all built-in shortcut menus to their original states:

```
Sub ResetAllShortcutMenus()
    Dim cbar As CommandBar
    For Each cbar In Application.CommandBars
        If cbar.Type = msoBarTypePopup Then
            cbar.Reset
            cbar.Enabled = True
        End If
    Next cbar
End Sub
```

In Excel 2013, the ResetAllShortcutMenus procedure works only with the active window. To reset the shortcut menus in all open windows, the code gets a bit more complex:

```
Sub ResetAllShortcutMenus2()
'   Works with all windows
    Dim cbar As CommandBar
    Dim activeWin As Window
    Dim win As Window
'   Remember current active window
    Set activeWin = ActiveWindow
'   Loop through each visible window
    Application.ScreenUpdating = False
    For Each win In Windows
        If win.Visible Then
            win.Activate
            For Each cbar In Application.CommandBars
                If cbar.Type = msoBarTypePopup Then
                    cbar.Reset
                    cbar.Enabled = True
                End If
            Next cbar
        End If
    Next win
'   Activate original window
    activeWin.Activate
    Application.ScreenUpdating = True
End Sub
```

The code starts by keeping track of the active window and storing it as an object variable (activeWin). The code then loops through all open windows and activates each one — but skips hidden windows because activating a hidden window makes it visible. For each active window, it loops through each CommandBar and resets those that are shortcut menus. Finally, the code reactivates the original window.

Disabling a shortcut menu

The Enabled property lets you disable an entire shortcut menu. For example, you can set this property so that right-clicking a cell does not display the normal shortcut menu. The following statement disables the Cell shortcut menu for the workbook in the active window:

```
Application.CommandBars("Cell").Enabled = False
```

To reenable the shortcut menu, set its Enabled property to True. Resetting a shortcut menu does not enable it.

If you want to disable *all* shortcut menus in the active window, use the following procedure:

```
Sub DisableAllShortcutMenus()
    Dim cb As CommandBar
    For Each cb In CommandBars
        If cb.Type = msoBarTypePopup Then _
          cb.Enabled = False
    Next cb
End Sub
```

Disabling shortcut menu items

You may want to disable one or more items on certain shortcut menus while your application is running. When an item is disabled, its text appears in light gray, and clicking it has no effect. The following procedure disables the Hide menu item from the Row and Column shortcut menus in the active window:

```
Sub DisableHideMenuItems()
    CommandBars("Column").Controls("Hide").Enabled = False
    CommandBars("Row").Controls("Hide").Enabled = False
End Sub
```

This procedure doesn't prevent a user from using other methods to hide rows or columns, such as the Format command in the Home➔Cells group.

Adding a new item to the Cell shortcut menu

The AddToShortcut procedure that follows adds a new menu item to the Cell shortcut menu: Toggle Wrap Text. Recall that Excel has two Cell shortcut menus. This procedure modifies the normal right-click menu but not the right-click menu that appears in page break preview mode.

```
Sub AddToShortCut()
'    Adds a menu item to the Cell shortcut menu
    Dim Bar As CommandBar
    Dim NewControl As CommandBarButton
    DeleteFromShortcut
    Set Bar = CommandBars("Cell")
    Set NewControl = Bar.Controls.Add _
        (Type:=msoControlButton)
    With NewControl
        .Caption = "Toggle &Wrap Text"
        .OnAction = "ToggleWrapText"
        .Picture = Application.CommandBars.GetImageMso _
            ("WrapText", 16, 16)
        .Style = msoButtonIconAndCaption
    End With
End Sub
```

Figure 21-4 shows the new menu item displayed after right-clicking a cell.

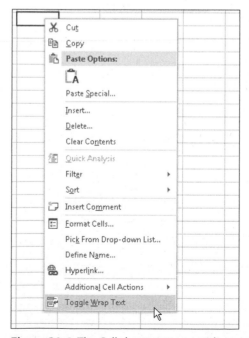

Figure 21-4: The Cell shortcut menu with a custom menu item.

The first command, after the declaration of a couple of variables, calls the DeleteFromShortcut procedure (listed later in this section). This statement ensures that only one Toggle Wrap Text menu item appears on the shortcut Cell menu. Note that the underlined hot key for this menu item is W, not T, because T is already used by the Cut menu item.

The Picture property is set by referencing the image used on the Ribbon for the Wrap Text command. Refer to Chapter 20 for more information about images used in Ribbon commands.

The macro executed when the menu item is selected is specified by the OnAction property. In this case, the macro is named ToggleWrapText:

```
Sub ToggleWrapText()
    On Error Resume Next
    CommandBars.ExecuteMso ("WrapText")
    If Err.Number <> 0 Then MsgBox "Could not toggle Wrap Text"
End Sub
```

This procedure simply executes the WrapText Ribbon command. If an error occurs (for example, the worksheet is protected), the user gets a message.

The DeleteFromShortcut procedure removes the new menu item from the Cell shortcut menu:

```
Sub DeleteFromShortcut()
    On Error Resume Next
    CommandBars("Cell").Controls ("Toggle &Wrap Text").Delete
End Sub
```

In most cases, you want to add and remove the shortcut menu additions automatically: Add the shortcut menu item when the workbook is opened and delete the menu item when the workbook is closed. Just add these two event procedures to the ThisWorkbook code module:

```
Private Sub Workbook_Open()
    Call AddToShortCut
End Sub

Private Sub Workbook_BeforeClose(Cancel As Boolean)
    Call DeleteFromShortcut
End Sub
```

The Workbook_Open procedure is executed when the workbook is opened, and the Workbook_BeforeClose procedure is executed before the workbook is closed. Just what the doctor ordered.

By the way, if shortcut menus are used only in Excel 2013, you don't need to remove them when the workbook closes because the shortcut menu modifications are applied only to the active workbook window.

On the Web

The workbook described in this section is available on the book's website in the add to cell shortcut.xlsm file. The file also includes a version of the macro that adds the new shortcut menu item to all open windows.

Adding a submenu to a shortcut menu

The example in this section adds a submenu with three options to the Cells shortcut menu of the active window. Figure 21-5 shows the worksheet after right-clicking a row. Each submenu item executes a macro that changes the case of text in the selected cells.

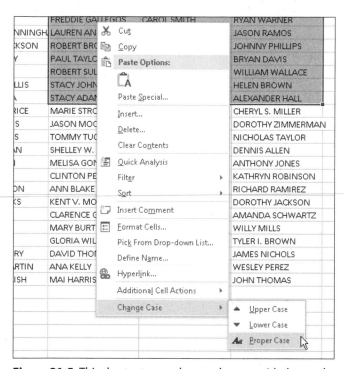

Figure 21-5: This shortcut menu has a submenu with three submenu items.

The code that creates the submenu and submenu items is as follows:

```
Sub AddSubmenu()
'    Adds a submenu to the six shortcut menus
     Dim Bar As CommandBar
     Dim NewMenu As CommandBarControl
     Dim NewSubmenu As CommandBarButton

     DeleteSubmenu
     Set Bar = CommandBars("Cell")
```

```
'    Add submenu
     Set NewMenu = Bar.Controls.Add _
        (Type:=msoControlPopup)
     NewMenu.Caption = "Ch&ange Case"
     NewMenu.BeginGroup = True
'    Add first submenu item
     Set NewSubmenu = NewMenu.Controls.Add _
        (Type:=msoControlButton)
     With NewSubmenu
        .FaceId = 38
        .Caption = "&Upper Case"
        .OnAction = "MakeUpperCase"
     End With
'    Add second submenu item
     Set NewSubmenu = NewMenu.Controls.Add _
        (Type:=msoControlButton)
     With NewSubmenu
        .FaceId = 40
        .Caption = "&Lower Case"
        .OnAction = "MakeLowerCase"
     End With
'    Add third submenu item
     Set NewSubmenu = NewMenu.Controls.Add _
        (Type:=msoControlButton)
     With NewSubmenu
        .FaceId = 476
        .Caption = "&Proper Case"
        .OnAction = "MakeProperCase"
     End With
End Sub
```

The submenu is added first, and its Type property is msoControlPopup. Then the three submenu items are added, and each has a different OnAction property.

The code to delete the submenu is much simpler:

```
Sub DeleteSubmenu()
    On Error Resume Next
    CommandBars("Cell").Controls("Cha&nge Case").Delete
End Sub
```

On the Web

The workbook described in this section is available on the book's website in the short-cut with submenu.xlsm file.

Finding FaceID images

The icon that's displayed on a shortcut menu item is determined by one of two property settings:

- Picture: This option lets you use an imageMso from the Ribbon. For an example, see "Adding a new item to the Cell shortcut menu," earlier in this chapter.

- FaceID: This option is the easiest because the FaceID property is just a numeric value that represents one of hundreds of images.

But how do you find out which number corresponds to a particular FaceID image? Excel doesn't provide a way, so I created an application the lets you enter beginning and ending FaceID numbers. Click a button, and the images are displayed in the worksheet. Each image has a name that corresponds to its FaceID value. See the accompanying figure, which shows FaceID values from 1 to 500. This workbook, named show faceids.xlsm, is available on the book's website.

Limiting a shortcut menu to a single workbook

As I've noted, in Excel 2013, shortcut menu modifications are applied only to the active workbook window (workbook A). For example, you might add a new item to the Cell right-click menu in workbook A. But if the user opens a new workbook when workbook A is active, the new workbook will also display the modified shortcut menu. If you want the shortcut menu to work only when workbook A is active, you can add some code to the macro that's executed by the shortcut menu.

Assume that you wrote code that adds a shortcut menu that, when clicked, executes the MyMacro procedure. To limit this procedure to only the workbook in which it's defined, use code like this:

```
Sub MyMacro()
    If Not ActiveWorkbook Is ThisWorkbook Then
        MsgBox "This shortcut menu doesn't work here."
    Else
'        [Macro code goes here]
    End If
End Sub
```

Shortcut Menus and Events

The examples in this section demonstrate various shortcut-menu programming techniques used with events.

 I discuss event programming in Chapter 17.
Cross-Ref

Adding and deleting menus automatically

If you need to modify a shortcut menu when a workbook is opened, use the Workbook_Open event. The following code, stored in the code module for the ThisWorkbook object, executes the ModifyShortcut procedure (not shown here):

```
Private Sub Workbook_Open()
    Call ModifyShortcut
End Sub
```

To return the shortcut back to its state before the modification, use a procedure such as the following. This procedure, which is executed before the workbook closes, calls the RestoreShortcut procedure (not shown here):

```
Private Sub Workbook_BeforeClose(Cancel As Boolean)
    Call RestoreShortcut
End Sub
```

If this code is used exclusively in Excel 2013, it's not necessary to restore the shortcut menus when the workbook is closed because the modifications are applied only to the active workbook and disappear when the workbook is closed.

Disabling or hiding shortcut menu items

When a shortcut menu item is disabled, its text appears in a faint shade of gray, and clicking it has no effect. When a menu item is hidden, it doesn't appear on the shortcut menu. You can, of course, write VBA code to enable or disable shortcut menu items. Similarly, you can write code to hide shortcut menu items. The key is tapping into the correct event.

The following code, for example, disables the Change Case shortcut menu item (which was added to the Cells menu) when Sheet2 is activated. This procedure is located in the code module for Sheet2:

```
Private Sub Worksheet_Activate()
    CommandBars("Cell").Controls("Change Case").Enabled = False
End Sub
```

To enable the menu item when Sheet2 is deactivated, add the following procedure. The net effect is that the Change Case menu item is available at all times except when Sheet2 is active.

```
Private Sub Worksheet_Deactivate()
    CommandBars("Cell").Controls("Change Case").Enabled = True
End Sub
```

To hide the menu item rather than disable it, simply access the Visible property instead of the Enabled property.

Creating a context-sensitive shortcut menu

You can create a new shortcut menu and display it in response to a particular event. The code that follows creates a shortcut menu named MyShortcut and adds six menu items to it. These menu items have their OnAction property set to execute a simple procedure that displays one of the tabs in the Format Cells dialog box (see Figure 21-6).

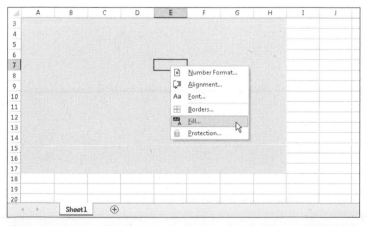

Figure 21-6: A new shortcut menu appears only when the user right-clicks a cell in the shaded area of the worksheet.

```
Sub CreateShortcut()
    Set myBar = CommandBars.Add _
      (Name:="MyShortcut", Position:=msoBarPopup)

'   Add a menu item
    Set myItem = myBar.Controls.Add(Type:=msoControlButton)
    With myItem
        .Caption = "&Number Format..."
        .OnAction = "ShowFormatNumber"
        .FaceId = 1554
    End With

'   Add a menu item
    Set myItem = myBar.Controls.Add(Type:=msoControlButton)
    With myItem
        .Caption = "&Alignment..."
        .OnAction = "ShowFormatAlignment"
        .FaceId = 217
    End With

'   Add a menu item
    Set myItem = myBar.Controls.Add(Type:=msoControlButton)
    With myItem
        .Caption = "&Font..."
        .OnAction = "ShowFormatFont"
        .FaceId = 291
    End With

'   Add a menu item
    Set myItem = myBar.Controls.Add(Type:=msoControlButton)
    With myItem
        .Caption = "&Borders..."
        .OnAction = "ShowFormatBorder"
        .FaceId = 149
        .BeginGroup = True
    End With

'   Add a menu item
    Set myItem = myBar.Controls.Add(Type:=msoControlButton)
    With myItem
        .Caption = "&Patterns..."
        .OnAction = "ShowFormatPatterns"
        .FaceId = 1550
    End With

'   Add a menu item
    Set myItem = myBar.Controls.Add(Type:=msoControlButton)
    With myItem
        .Caption = "Pr&otection..."
        .OnAction = "ShowFormatProtection"
```

```
        .FaceId = 2654
    End With
End Sub
```

After the shortcut menu is created, you can display it by using the ShowPopup method. The following procedure, located in the code module for a Worksheet object, is executed when the user right-clicks a cell:

```
Private Sub Worksheet_BeforeRightClick _
   (ByVal Target As Excel.Range, Cancel As Boolean)
    If Union(Target.Range("A1"), Range("data")).Address = _
      Range("data").Address Then
        CommandBars("MyShortcut").ShowPopup
        Cancel = True
    End If
End Sub
```

If the active cell is within a range named data when the user right-clicks, the MyShortcut menu appears. Setting the Cancel argument to True ensures that the normal shortcut menu isn't displayed. Note that the mini toolbar isn't displayed.

You can also display this shortcut menu without even using the mouse. Create a simple procedure and assign a shortcut key by using the Options button in the Macro dialog box.

```
Sub ShowMyShortcutMenu()
'   Ctrl+Shift+M shortcut key
    CommandBars("MyShortcut").ShowPopup
End Sub
```

On the Web

The book's website contains an example (named context-sensitive shortcut menu.xlsm) that creates a new shortcut menu and displays it in place of the normal Cell shortcut menu.

Providing Help for Your Applications

In This Chapter

- Providing user help for your applications
- Using only the components supplied with Excel to provide help
- Displaying help files created with the HTML Help system
- Associating a help file with your application
- Displaying HTML Help in other ways

Help for Your Excel Applications

If you develop a nontrivial application in Excel, you may want to consider building in some sort of help for end users. Doing so makes the users feel more comfortable with the application and could eliminate many of those time-wasting phone calls from users with basic questions. Another advantage is that help is always available: That is, the instructions for using your application can't be misplaced or buried under a pile of books.

 Online help?

In the past, I've referred to Excel's on-screen assistance as *online help*. In fact, that's the common name for this type of assistance. But in recent years, the term *online* has come to refer to information available through the Internet. Some people were confused by the expression *online help* because the help information is actually stored on their local drives.

About the examples in this chapter

Many of the examples in this chapter use a common workbook application to demonstrate various ways of providing help. The application uses data stored in a worksheet to generate and print form letters.

As you can see in the following figure, cells display the total number of records in the database (C2, calculated by a formula), the current record number (C3), the first record to print (C4), and the last record to print (C5). To display a particular record, the user enters a value in cell C3. To print a series of form letters, the user specifies the first and last record numbers in cells C4 and C5.

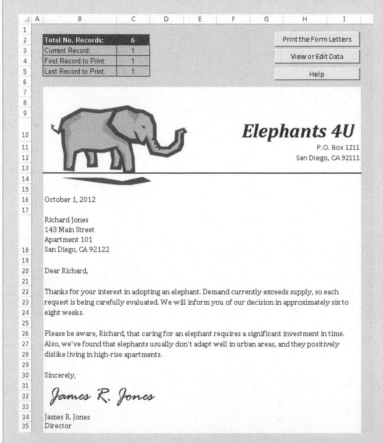

The application is simple but does consist of several discrete components. I use this example to demonstrate various ways of displaying context-sensitive help.

The form letter workbook consists of the following components:

- Form: A worksheet that contains the text of the form letter.
- Data: A worksheet that contains a seven-field table of customer information.

- HelpSheet: A worksheet that's present only in the examples that store help text on a worksheet.
- PrintMod: A VBA module that contains macros to print the form letters.
- HelpMod: A VBA module that contains macros that control the help display. The content of this module varies depending on the type of help being demonstrated.
- UserForm1: Present only if the help technique involves a UserForm.

Therefore, I now use the expression *Help system* to refer to assistance provided by an application. But beginning with Excel 2003, things have come full circle. The Help system for Excel 2003 and later is (optionally) truly online. You can view locally stored help information or (with an Internet connection) search for more up-to-date information at the Microsoft website. An exception is the VBA Help system for Excel 2013, which is online only and requires an Internet connection.

You can provide help for your Excel applications in a number of ways, ranging from simple to complex. The method that you choose depends on your application's scope and complexity and how much effort you're willing to put into this phase of development. Some applications might require only a brief set of instructions on how to start them. Others may benefit from a full-blown searchable Help system. Most often, applications need something in between.

This chapter classifies user help into two categories:

➤ **Unofficial Help system:** This method of displaying help uses standard Excel components (such as a UserForm). Or you can simply display the support information in a text file, a Word document, or a PDF file.

➤ **Official Help system:** This Help system uses a compiled CHM file produced by Microsoft's HTML Help Workshop.

Creating a compiled help file isn't a trivial task, but it is worth the effort if your application is complex or if it will be used by a large number of people.

Note

Beginning with Microsoft Office 2007, Microsoft abandoned CHM help files in their Office product and used a different (and more complicated) Help system called MS Help 2. This Help system isn't covered in this book.

On the Web

All the examples in this chapter are available on the book's website. Because most examples consist of multiple files, each example is in a separate directory.

Help Systems That Use Excel Components

Perhaps the most straightforward method of providing help to your users is to use the features in Excel itself. The primary advantage of this method is that you don't need to learn how to create HTML help files — which can be a major undertaking and might take longer to develop than your application.

In this section, I provide an overview of some help techniques that use the following built-in Excel components:

➤ **Cell comments:** Using comments is about as simple as it gets.

➤ **A text box control:** A short macro is all it takes to toggle the display of a text box that shows help information.

➤ **A worksheet:** An easy way to add help is to insert a worksheet, enter your help information, and name its tab *Help*. When the user clicks the tab, the worksheet is activated.

➤ **A custom UserForm:** a number of techniques involve displaying help text in a UserForm.

Using cell comments for help

Perhaps the simplest way to provide user help is to use cell comments. This technique is most appropriate for describing the type of input that's expected in a cell. When the user moves the mouse pointer over a cell that contains a comment, the comment appears in a small window, like a tooltip (see Figure 22-1). Another advantage is that this technique doesn't require macros.

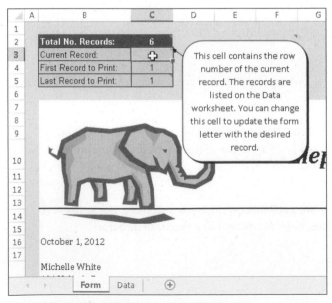

Figure 22-1: Using cell comments to display help.

The automatic display of cell comments is an option. The following VBA instruction, which can be placed in a Workbook_Open procedure, ensures that cell comment indicators are displayed for cells that contain comments:

```
Application.DisplayCommentIndicator = xlCommentIndicatorOnly
```

On the Web

A workbook that demonstrates the use of cell comments is available on the book's website in the cell comments\formletter.xlsm file.

Tip

Most users don't realize it, but a comment can also display an image. Right-click the comment's border and choose Format Comment from the shortcut menu. In the Format Comment dialog box, select the Colors and Lines tab. Click the Color drop-down list and select Fill Effects. In the Fill Effects dialog box, click the Picture tab and then click the Select Picture button to choose the image file.

As an alternative to cell comments, you can use Excel's Data➜Data Tools➜Data Validation command, which displays a dialog box that lets you specify validation criteria for a cell or range. You can just ignore the data validation aspect and use the Input Message tab of the Data Validation dialog box to specify a message that's displayed when the cell is activated. This text is limited to approximately 250 characters.

Using a text box for help

Using a text box to display help information is also easy to implement. Simply create a text box by choosing Insert➜Text➜Text Box, enter the help text, and format it to your liking.

Tip

In lieu of a text box, you can use a different shape and add text to it. Choose Insert➜Illustrations➜Shapes and choose a shape. Then just starting typing the text.

Figure 22-2 shows an example of a shape set up to display help information. I added a shadow effect to make the object appear to float above the worksheet.

Most of the time, you won't want the text box to be visible. Therefore, you can add a button to your application to execute a macro that toggles the Visible property of the text box. An example of such a macro follows. In this case, the TextBox is named HelpText.

```
Sub ToggleHelp()
    ActiveSheet.TextBoxes("HelpText").Visible = _
        Not ActiveSheet.TextBoxes("HelpText").Visible
End Sub
```

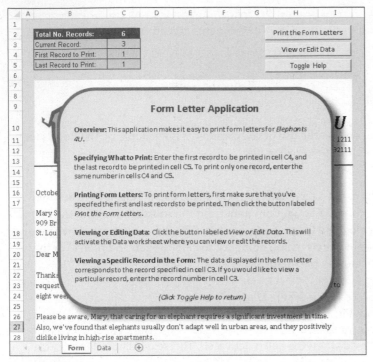

Figure 22-2: Using a shape object with text to display help for the user.

A workbook that demonstrates using a text box for help is available on the book's website in the textbox\formletter.xlsm file.

Using a worksheet to display help text

Another easy way to add help to your application is to create a macro that activates a separate worksheet that holds the help information. Just attach the macro to a button control and — voilà! — quick-and-dirty help.

Figure 22-3 shows a sample help worksheet. I designed the range that contains the help text to simulate a page from a yellow notebook pad — a touch that you may or may not like.

To keep the user from scrolling around the HelpSheet worksheet, the macro sets the ScrollArea property of the worksheet. Because this property isn't stored with the workbook, it must be set when the worksheet is activated.

```
Sub ShowHelp()
'   Activate help sheet
    Worksheets("HelpSheet").Activate
    ActiveSheet.ScrollArea = "A1:C35"
    Range("A1").Select
End Sub
```

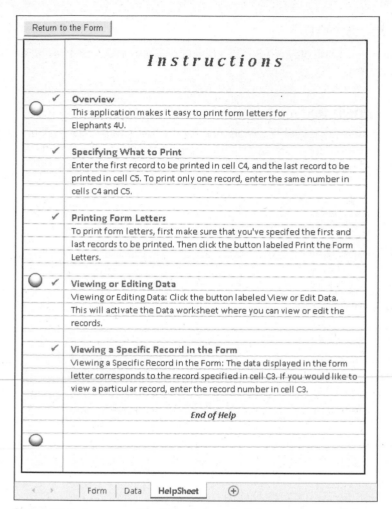

Figure 22-3: An easy method is to put user help in a separate worksheet.

I also protected the worksheet to prevent the user from changing the text and selecting cells, and I froze the first row so that the Return to the Form button is always visible, regardless of how far down the sheet the user scrolls.

The main disadvantage of using this technique is that the help text isn't visible along with the main work area. One possible solution is to write a macro that opens a new window to display the sheet.

On the Web

This book's website contains a workbook named worksheet\formletter.xlsm that demonstrates using a worksheet for help.

Displaying help in a UserForm

Another way to provide help to the user is to display the text in a UserForm. In this section, I describe several techniques that involve UserForms.

Using Label controls to display help text

Figure 22-4 shows a UserForm that contains two Label controls: one for the title and one for the help text. A SpinButton control enables the user to navigate among the topics. The text itself is stored in a worksheet, with topics in column A and text in column B. A macro transfers the text from the worksheet to the Label controls.

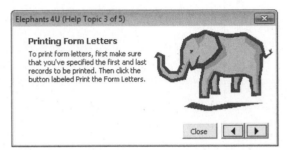

Figure 22-4: Clicking one of the arrows on the SpinButton changes the text displayed in the Labels.

Clicking the SpinButton control executes the following procedure. This procedure sets the Caption property of the two Label controls to the text in the appropriate row of the worksheet (named HelpSheet).

```
Private Sub SpinButton1_Change()
    HelpTopic = SpinButton1.Value
    LabelTopic.Caption = Sheets("HelpSheet").Cells(HelpTopic, 1)
    LabelText.Caption = Sheets("HelpSheet").Cells(HelpTopic, 2)
    Me.Caption = APPNAME & " (Help Topic " & HelpTopic & " of " _
      & SpinButton1.Max & ")"
End Sub
```

Here, APPNAME is a global constant that contains the application's name.

On the Web

A workbook that demonstrates this technique is available on the book's website in the userform1\formletter.xlsm file.

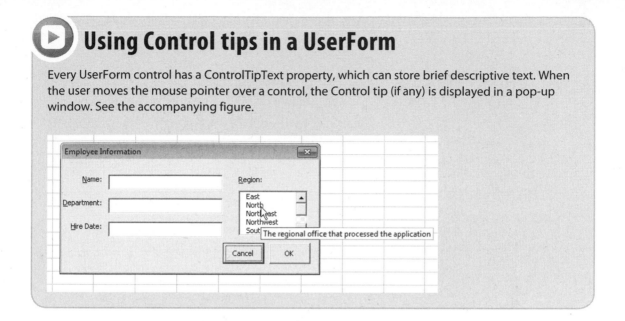

Using Control tips in a UserForm

Every UserForm control has a ControlTipText property, which can store brief descriptive text. When the user moves the mouse pointer over a control, the Control tip (if any) is displayed in a pop-up window. See the accompanying figure.

Using a scrolling Label to display help text

The next technique displays help text in a single Label control. Because a Label control can't contain a vertical scroll bar, the Label is placed inside a Frame control, which *can* contain a scroll bar. Figure 22-5 shows an example of a UserForm set up in this manner. The user can scroll through the text by using the Frame's scroll bar.

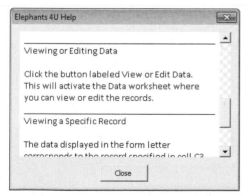

Figure 22-5: Inserting a Label control inside a Frame control adds scrolling to the Label.

The text displayed in the Label is read from a worksheet named HelpSheet when the UserForm is initialized. Here's the UserForm_Initialize procedure for this worksheet:

```
Private Sub UserForm_Initialize()
    Dim LastRow As Long
    Dim r As Long
    Dim txt As String
    Me.Caption = APPNAME & " Help"
    LastRow = Sheets("HelpSheet").Cells(Rows.Count, 1).End(xlUp).Row
    txt = ""
    For r = 1 To LastRow
      txt = txt & Sheets("HelpSheet").Cells(r, 1) _
        .Text & vbCrLf
    Next r
    With Label1
        .Top = 0
        .Caption = txt
        .Width = 260
        .AutoSize = True
    End With
    With Frame1
        .ScrollHeight = Label1.Height
        .ScrollTop = 0
    End With
End Sub
```

Note that the code adjusts the Frame's ScrollHeight property to ensure that the scrolling covers the complete height of the Label. Again, APPNAME is a global constant that contains the application's name.

Because a Label can't display formatted text, I used underscore characters in the HelpSheet worksheet to delineate the help topic titles.

On the Web

A workbook that demonstrates this technique is available on the book's website in a file named userform2\formletter.xlsm.

Using a ComboBox control to select a help topic

The example in this section improves upon the preceding example. Figure 22-6 shows a UserForm that contains a ComboBox control and a Label control. The user can select a topic from the drop-down ComboBox or view the topics sequentially by clicking the Previous or Next button.

This example is a bit more complex than the example in the preceding section, but it's also much more flexible. It uses the label-within-a-scrolling-frame technique (described previously) to support help text of any length.

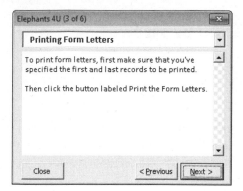

Figure 22-6: Using a drop-down list control to select a help topic.

The help text is stored in a worksheet named HelpSheet in two columns (A and B). The first column contains the topic headings, and the second column contains the text. The ComboBox items are added in the UserForm_Initialize procedure. The CurrentTopic variable is a module-level variable that stores an integer that represents the help topic.

```
Private Sub UpdateForm()
    ComboBoxTopics.ListIndex = CurrentTopic - 1
    Me.Caption = HelpFormCaption & _
      " (" & CurrentTopic & " of " & TopicCount & ")"

    With LabelText
        .Caption = HelpSheet.Cells(CurrentTopic, 2)
        .AutoSize = False
        .Width = 212
        .AutoSize = True
    End With
    With Frame1
        .ScrollHeight = LabelText.Height + 5
        .ScrollTop = 1
    End With

    If CurrentTopic = 1 Then
        NextButton.SetFocus
    ElseIf CurrentTopic = TopicCount Then
        PreviousButton.SetFocus
    End If
    PreviousButton.Enabled = CurrentTopic <> 1
    NextButton.Enabled = CurrentTopic <> TopicCount
End Sub
```

On the Web

A workbook that demonstrates this technique is available on the book's website in the userform3\formletter.xlsm file.

Displaying Help in a Web Browser

This section describes two ways to display user help in a web browser.

Using HTML files

Yet another way to display help for an Excel application is to create one or more HTML files and provide a hyperlink that displays the file in the default web browser. The HTML files can be stored locally or on your corporate intranet. You can create the hyperlink to the help file in a cell (macros not required). Figure 22-7 shows an example of help in a browser.

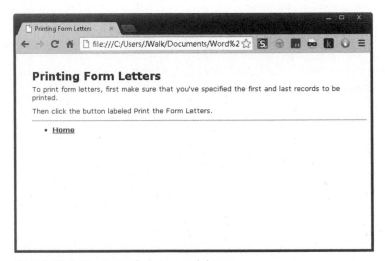

Figure 22-7: Displaying help in a web browser.

Easy-to-use HTML editors are readily available, and your HTML-based Help system can be as simple or as complex as necessary. A disadvantage is that you may need to distribute a large number of HTML files. One solution to this problem is to use an MHTML file, which I describe next.

On the Web

A workbook that demonstrates this technique is available on the book's website in the web browser\formletter.xlsm file.

Using an MHTML file

MHTML, which stands for MIME Hypertext Markup Language, is a web archive format. MHTML files can be displayed by Microsoft Internet Explorer (and a few other browsers).

The nice thing about using an MHTML file for an Excel Help system is that you can create these files in Excel. Just create your help text using any number of worksheets. Then choose File➔Save As, click the Save As Type drop-down list, and select Single File Web Page (*.mht; *.mhtml). VBA macros aren't saved in this format.

In Excel, you can create a hyperlink to display the MHTML file.

Figure 22-8 shows an MHTML file displayed in Internet Explorer. Note that the bottom of the file contains tabs that link to the help topics. These tabs correspond to the worksheet tabs in the Excel workbook used to create the MHTML file.

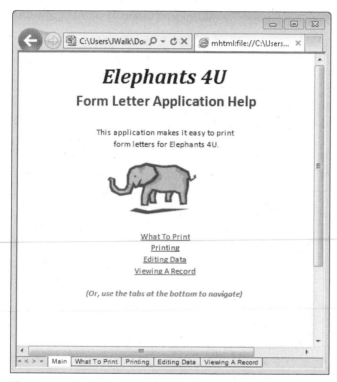

Figure 22-8: Displaying an MHTML file in a web browser.

On the Web

A workbook that demonstrates this technique is available on the book's website in the mhtml_file\formletter.xlsm file. Also included is the workbook used to create the MHTML file (helpsource.xlsx). Apparently, some versions of Internet Explorer won't display an MHTML file that's hyperlinked from a Microsoft Office file if the filename or path includes space characters. The example on the book's website uses a Windows API function (ShellExecute) to display the MHTML file if the hyperlink fails.

Note

If you save a multisheet Excel workbook as an MHTML file, the file will contain JavaScript code — which may generate a security warning when the file is opened.

Using the HTML Help System

One of the most common Help systems used in Windows applications is HTML Help, which creates CHM files. This system replaces the old Windows Help system (WinHelp), which used Hlp files. Both Help systems enable the developer to associate a context ID with a particular help topic, which makes it possible to display context-sensitive help topics.

Office XP was the last version of Microsoft Office to use HTML Help. Each subsequent version of Office has used a different Help system. Although HTML Help can't duplicate the look and feel of Microsoft Office Help, it is still useful because it's easy to work with — at least for simple Help systems.

In this section I briefly describe the HTML help-authoring system. Details on creating such Help systems are well beyond the scope of this book. However, you'll find lots of information and examples online.

Note

If you plan to develop a large-scale Help system, I strongly recommend that you purchase a help-authoring software product. Help-authoring software makes it much easier to develop help files because the software takes care of lots of the tedious details for you. Many products are available, including freeware, shareware, and commercial offerings.

A compiled HTML Help system transforms a series of HTML files into a compact Help system. Additionally, you can create a combined table of contents and index as well as use keywords for advanced hyperlinking capability. HTML Help can also use additional tools such as graphics files, ActiveX controls, scripting, and DHTML (Dynamic HTML). Figure 22-9 shows an example of a simple HTML help system.

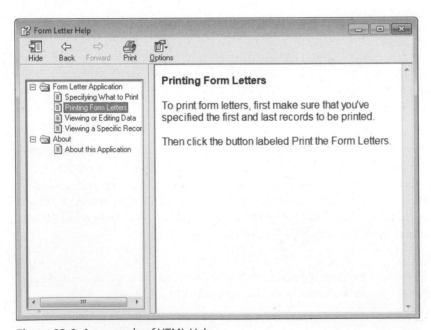

Figure 22-9: An example of HTML Help.

On the Web

A workbook that demonstrates this technique is available on the book's website in the html help\formletter.xlsm file.

HTML Help is displayed by HTML Help Viewer, which uses the layout engine of Internet Explorer. The information is displayed in a window, and the table of contents, index, and search tools are displayed in a separate pane. In addition, the help text can contain standard hyperlinks that display another topic or even a document on the Internet. It's also important that HTML Help can access files stored on a website, so that you can direct users to more up-to-date information.

You need a special compiler (HTML Help Workshop) to create an HTML Help system. HTML Help Workshop, along with lots of additional information, is available free from Microsoft's MSDN website. Navigate to this address and search for *HTML Help Workshop:* `http://msdn.microsoft.com`.

Figure 22-10 shows HTML Help Workshop with the project file that created the Help system shown in Figure 22-9.

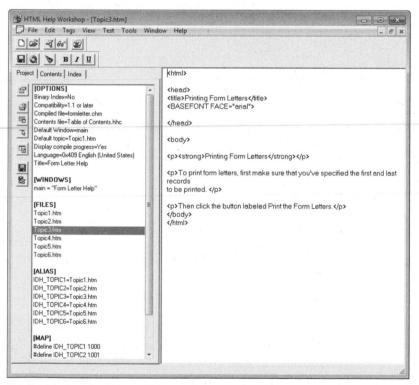

Figure 22-10: Using HTML Help Workshop to create a help file.

Displaying an Excel help topic

In some situations, you may want your VBA code to display a particular topic from Excel's Help system. Every help topic has a topic ID, but identifying the topic ID is tricky in Excel 2013. For example, assume that you'd like to give the user the option to view Help information about the AGGREGATE function.

Start by searching for this topic in the Excel Help system. In the search results, highlight the appropriate link and press Ctrl+C to copy the link. Then activate a blank cell and press Ctrl+V to paste the link. Press Ctrl+K to display the Edit Hyperlink dialog box, which displays the address of the hyperlink. You'll find, for example, that the address for the AGGREGATE function help topic is

```
ms-help://MS.EXCEL.15.1033/EXCEL/content/HA102753246.htm
```

The topic ID is the filename without the HTM extension. In this example, the topic ID is HA102753246. Use this topic ID as the argument in a VBA statement that uses the ShowHelp method of the Assistance object. For this example, the statement is

```
Application.Assistance.ShowHelp "HA102753246"
```

When this statement is executed, Excel's Help system displays information about the AGGREGATE function.

Another option for displaying Excel help is to use the SearchHelp method. Just supply a search term, and the user will see a list of matching help topics. Here's an example:

```
Application.Assistance.SearchHelp "AGGREGATE function"
```

Using the Help method to display HTML Help

Use the Help method of the Application object to display a help file — either a WinHelp HLP file or an HTML Help CHM file. This method works even if the help file doesn't have context IDs defined.

The syntax for the Help method is as follows:

```
Application.Help(helpFile, helpContextID)
```

Both arguments are optional. If the name of the help file is omitted, Excel's help file is displayed. If the context ID argument is omitted, the specified help file is displayed with the default topic.

The following example displays the default topic of myapp.chm, which is assumed to be in the same directory as the workbook from which it's called. Note that the second argument is omitted.

```
Sub ShowHelpContents()
    Application.Help ThisWorkbook.Path & "\myapp.chm"
End Sub
```

The following instruction displays the help topic with a context ID of 1002 from an HTML help file named myapp.chm:

```
Application.Help ThisWorkbook.Path & "\myapp.chm", 1002
```

Associating a help file with your application

You can associate a particular HTML help file with your Excel application in one of two ways: by using the Project Properties dialog box or by writing VBA code.

In Visual Basic Editor (VBE), choose Tools➜*xxx* Properties (where *xxx* corresponds to your project's name). In the Project Properties dialog box, click the General tab and specify a compiled HTML help file for the project. This file should have a .chm extension.

The statement that follows demonstrates how to associate a help file with your application by using a VBA statement. The following instruction sets up an association to myfuncs.chm, which is assumed to be in the same directory as the workbook:

```
ThisWorkbook.VBProject.HelpFile = ThisWorkbook.Path & "\myfuncs.chm"
```

Note

If this statement generates an error, you must enable programmatic access to VBA projects. In Excel, choose Developer➜Code➜Macro Security to display the Trust Center dialog box. Then deselect the option labeled Trust Access to the VBA Project Object Model.

When a help file is associated with your application, you can call up a particular help topic in the following situations:

> ➤ When the user presses F1 while a custom worksheet function is selected in the Insert Function dialog box.

> ➤ When the user presses F1 while a UserForm is displayed. The help topic associated with the control that has the focus is displayed.

Associating a help topic with a VBA function

If you create custom worksheet functions with VBA, you might want to associate a help file and context ID with each function. After these items are assigned to a function, the help topic can be displayed from the Insert Function dialog box by pressing F1.

To specify a context ID for a custom worksheet function, follow these steps:

1. Create the function as usual.

2. Make sure that your project has an associated help file (refer to the preceding section).

3. In VBE, press F2 to activate Object Browser.

4. Select your project from the Project/Library drop-down list.

5. In the Classes window, select the module that contains your function.

6. In the Members Of window, select the function.

7. Right-click the function and then select Properties from the shortcut menu.

The Member Options dialog box is displayed, as shown in Figure 22-11.

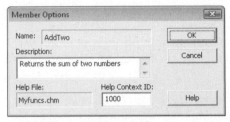

Figure 22-11: Specify a context ID for a custom function.

8. Enter the context ID of the help topic for the function.

You can also enter a description of the function.

Note

The Member Options dialog box doesn't let you specify the help file. It always uses the help file associated with the project.

You may prefer to write VBA code that sets up the context ID and help file for your custom functions. You can do this by using the MacroOptions method.

The following procedure uses the MacroOptions method to specify a description, help file, and context ID for two custom functions (AddTwo and Squared). You need to execute this macro only one time.

```
Sub SetOptions()
'    Set options for the AddTwo function
    Application.MacroOptions Macro:="AddTwo", _
        Description:="Returns the sum of two numbers", _
        HelpFile:=ThisWorkbook.Path & "\myfuncs.chm", _
        HelpContextID:=1000, _
        ArgumentDescriptions:=Array("The first number to add", _
          "The second number to add")

'    Set options for the Squared function
```

```
    Application.MacroOptions Macro:="Squared", _
        Description:="Returns the square of an argument", _
        HelpFile:=ThisWorkbook.Path & "\myfuncs.chm", _
        HelpContextID:=2000, _
        ArgumentDescriptions:=Array("The number to be squared")
End Sub
```

After executing these procedures, the user can get help directly from the Insert Function dialog box by clicking the Help on This Function hyperlink.

On the Web

A workbook that demonstrates this technique is available on the book's website in the function help\myfuncs.xlsm file.

Developing User-Oriented Applications

In This Chapter

- Describing a user-oriented application
- Looking at the Loan Amortization Wizard, which generates a worksheet with an amortization schedule for a fixed-rate loan
- Demonstrating application development concepts and techniques used by the Loan Amortization Wizard
- Reviewing an application development checklist

What Is a User-Oriented Application?

I use the term *user-oriented application* for an Excel application that someone with minimal training can use. These applications produce useful results even for users who know virtually nothing about Excel.

The Loan Amortization Wizard discussed in this chapter qualifies as a user-oriented application because anyone can use it without knowing the intimate details of Excel. Replying to a few simple prompts produces a useful and flexible worksheet complete with formulas.

The Loan Amortization Wizard

The Loan Amortization Wizard generates a worksheet that contains an amortization schedule for a fixed-rate loan. An amortization schedule projects month-by-month details for a loan. The details include the monthly payment amount, the amount of the payment that goes toward interest, the amount that goes toward reducing the principal, and the new loan balance.

An alternative to creating an amortization schedule using a wizard is to create a template file. As you'll see, this wizard approach offers several advantages.

Figure 23-1 shows an amortization schedule generated by the Loan Amortization Wizard.

	A	B	C	D	E	F	G
1	**Amortization Schedule**						
2	**Prepared by Amanda Richards**						
3	*Generated Tuesday, December 02, 2012*						
4							
5	Purchase Price:		$389,000.00				
6	Down Pmt Pct:		20.0%				
7	Down Pmt:		$77,800.00				
8	Loan Amount:		$311,200.00				
9	Term (Months):		360				
10	Interest Rate:		5.80%				
11	First Payment:		1/1/2013				
12							
13	Pmt No.	Year	Month	Payment	Interest	Principal	Balance
14	1	2013	1	$1,825.98	$1,504.13	$321.84	$310,878.16
15	2	2013	2	$1,825.98	$1,502.58	$323.40	$310,554.76
16	3	2013	3	$1,825.98	$1,501.01	$324.96	$310,229.80
17	4	2013	4	$1,825.98	$1,499.44	$326.53	$309,903.27
18	5	2013	5	$1,825.98	$1,497.87	$328.11	$309,575.16
19	6	2013	6	$1,825.98	$1,496.28	$329.70	$309,245.46
20	7	2013	7	$1,825.98	$1,494.69	$331.29	$308,914.17
21	8	2013	8	$1,825.98	$1,493.09	$332.89	$308,581.28
22	9	2013	9	$1,825.98	$1,491.48	$334.50	$308,246.78
23	10	2013	10	$1,825.98	$1,489.86	$336.12	$307,910.67
24	11	2013	11	$1,825.98	$1,488.23	$337.74	$307,572.93
25	12	2013	12	$1,825.98	$1,486.60	$339.37	$307,233.55
26	*2013 Total*			*$21,911.71*	*$17,945.26*	*$3,966.45*	*$307,233.55*
27	13	2014	1	$1,825.98	$1,484.96	$341.01	$306,892.54
28	14	2014	2	$1,825.98	$1,483.31	$342.66	$306,549.88
29	15	2014	3	$1,825.98	$1,481.66	$344.32	$306,205.56
30	16	2014	4	$1,825.98	$1,479.99	$345.98	$305,859.58
31	17	2014	5	$1,825.98	$1,478.32	$347.65	$305,511.93

Sheet1

Figure 23-1: This amortization schedule shows details for a 30-year mortgage.

On the Web

The Loan Amortization Wizard is available on the book's website in an unprotected add-in named **loan amortization wizard.xlam.**

Using the Loan Amortization Wizard

The Loan Amortization Wizard consists of a five-step dialog box sequence that collects information from the user. Typical of a wizard, this application enables the user to go forward and backward through the steps. Clicking the Finish button creates the new worksheet. If all the steps haven't been completed when the user clicks Finish, default values are used. Clicking the Cancel button closes the UserForm, and no action is taken.

The Loan Amortization Wizard uses a single UserForm with a MultiPage control to display the five steps, shown in Figure 23-2.

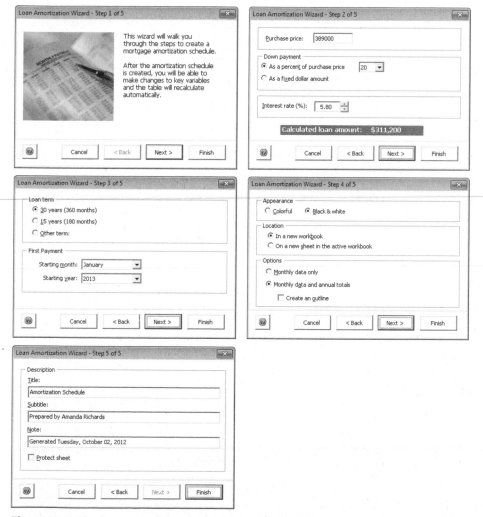

Figure 23-2: The five steps of the Loan Amortization Wizard.

The Loan Amortization Wizard workbook structure

The Loan Amortization Wizard consists of the following components:

➤ FormMain: A UserForm that serves as the primary user interface.

➤ FormHelp: A UserForm that displays online help.

➤ FormMessage: A UserForm that displays a message when the add-in is opened. The user can disable this display.

➤ HelpSheet: A worksheet that contains the text used in the online help.

➤ ModMain: A VBA module that contains a procedure that displays the main UserForm.

➤ ThisWorkbook: The code module that contains the Workbook_Open event-handler procedure.

In addition, the workbook file contains some simple RibbonX XML code that creates the Loan Amortization Wizard button in the Insert tab on the Ribbon. This code is not visible in Excel.

How the Loan Amortization Wizard works

The Loan Amortization Wizard is an add-in, so you should install it by using the Add-Ins dialog box. To display this dialog box, choose File➜Options➜Add-Ins. Then, in the Excel Options dialog box, choose Excel Add-Ins from the Manage drop-down list and click Go. Use the Browse button to locate the add-in file. After it's installed, an add-in remains installed across Excel sessions. The add-in works perfectly well, however, if it's opened with the File➜Open command.

 ## Creating the Loan Amortization Wizard

The Loan Amortization Wizard application started out as a simple concept and evolved into a relatively complex project. My primary goal was to demonstrate as many development concepts as possible and still have a useful end product. I would like to say that I clearly envisioned the end result before I began developing the application, but I'd be lying.

My basic idea was much less ambitious. I simply wanted to create an application that gathered user input and created a worksheet. But after I got started, I began thinking of ways to enhance my simple program. I eventually stumbled down several blind alleys. Some folks would consider my wanderings a waste of time, but those false starts became a vital part of the development process.

I completed the entire project in one (long) day, and I spent a few more hours fine-tuning and testing it. I added a few more cosmetic accoutrements for the version included in this edition of the book.

Modifying the user interface

Every add-in needs a way to allow the user to access the procedures. I added some RibbonX code to the file that adds a button to a new group in the Insert tab (see Figure 23-3). Clicking this button executes the StartAmortizationWizard procedure, which displays the FormMain UserForm.

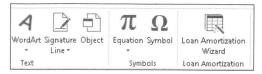

Figure 23-3: A new group on the Insert tab contains one control.

The RibbonX code that creates the Ribbon control is

```
<customUI xmlns="http://schemas.microsoft.com/office/2006/01/customui">
  <ribbon>
    <tabs>
      <tab idMso="TabInsert">
        <group id="gpUtils" label="Loan Amortization">
          <button id="b1"
            size="large"
            imageMso="CreateQueryFromWizard"
            label="Loan Amortization Wizard"
            supertip="Click here to create an amortization schedule."
            onAction="StartAmortizationWizard"/>
        </group>
      </tab>
    </tabs>
  </ribbon>
</customUI>
```

Cross-Ref

Refer to Chapter 20 for information about modifying the Ribbon.

Displaying an initial message

I've installed many Excel add-ins over the years, and I've found that many of them don't provide a clue as to how to access the add-in. To make this application as user-friendly as possible, I added a UserForm that is displayed when the workbook is opened. This form tells the user how to start the wizard. Figure 23-4 shows the UserForm.

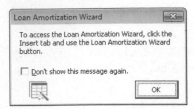

Figure 23-4: This form is displayed when the Loan Amortization Wizard is opened.

To prevent the UserForm from become annoying, I included an option to turn off the message in the future.

Following is the Workbook_Open procedure that displays the dialog box:

```
Private Sub Workbook_Open()
    If GetSetting(APPNAME, "Defaults", "ShowMessage", "Yes") = "Yes" Then
        FormMessage.Show
    End If
End Sub
```

The user's choice regarding the future display of the UserForm is stored in the Windows Registry. The Registry key is specified by the application's name (a global constant, APPNAME). The default value is "Yes," so the UserForm will display at least one time.

Following is the code that is executed when the user clicks the OK button:

```
Private Sub OKButton_Click()
    If cbMessage Then
        SaveSetting APPNAME, "Defaults", "ShowMessage", "No"
    Else
        SaveSetting APPNAME, "Defaults", "ShowMessage", "Yes"
    End If
    Unload Me
End Sub
```

If the user checks the check box control (named cbMessage), the Registry setting is set to "No," and the UserForm won't be displayed again.

Initializing FormMain for the wizard

The UserForm_Initialize procedure for FormMain does quite a bit of work:

➤ It sets the MultiPage control's Style property to fmTabStyleNone. The tabs are present in Visual Basic Editor to make the UserForm easier to edit.

➤ It sets the MultiPage control's Value property to 0. This ensures that the UserForm displays the first page, regardless of its value when the workbook was last saved.

➤ It adds items to three ComboBox controls used on the form.

➤ It calls the GetDefaults procedure, which retrieves the most recently used setting from the Windows Registry (see the upcoming section "Saving and retrieving default settings").

➤ It checks whether a workbook is active. If no workbook is active, the code disables the OptionButton that enables the user to create the new worksheet in the active workbook. In Excel 2013, a workbook will always be active because of the single-document interface. I left the code in place because it's necessary for previous versions of Excel.

➤ If a workbook is active, an additional check determines whether the workbook's structure is protected. If so, the procedure disables the OptionButton that enables the user to create the worksheet in the active workbook.

Processing events while the UserForm is displayed

The code module for the FormMain UserForm contains several event-handler procedures that respond to the Click and Change events for the controls on the UserForm.

Cross-Ref

Clicking the Back and Next buttons determines which page of the MultiPage control is displayed. The MultiPage1_Change procedure adjusts the UserForm's caption and enables and disables the Back and Next buttons as appropriate. See Chapter 13 for more information about programming a wizard.

Displaying help in the wizard

You have several options when it comes to displaying help. I chose a technique that displays help text (which is stored in a worksheet) in the UserForm shown in Figure 23-5. You'll notice that this help is context-sensitive. When the user clicks the Help button, the Help topic displayed is relevant to the current page of the MultiPage control.

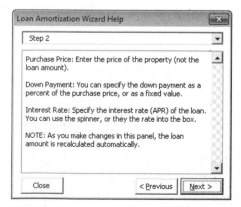

Figure 23-5: User help is presented in a UserForm that copies text stored in a worksheet.

Worksheets in an add-in aren't visible. To view the worksheet that contains the help text for this add-in, you need to temporarily set the workbook's IsAddin property to False. One way to accomplish this is to select the project in the Project window and execute this statement in the Immediate window:

```
ThisWorkbook.IsAddin = False
```

Cross-Ref

For more information about the technique of transferring worksheet text to a UserForm, refer to Chapter 22.

Creating the new worksheet

When the user clicks the Finish button, the action begins. The Click event-handler procedure for this button performs the following actions:

> ➤ It calls a function named DataIsValid, which checks the user's input to ensure that it's valid. If all the entries are valid, the function returns True and the procedure continues. If an invalid entry is encountered, DataIsValid sets the focus to the control that needs to be corrected and returns a descriptive error message (see Figure 23-6).

Figure 23-6: If an invalid entry is made, the focus is set back to the control that contains the error.

> ➤ If the user's responses are valid, the procedure creates a new worksheet either in the active workbook or in a new workbook, per the user's request.

> ➤ The loan parameters (purchase price, down payment information, loan amount, term, and interest rate) are written to the worksheet. I used some If statements because the down payment can be expressed as a percentage of the purchase price or as a fixed amount.

> ➤ The column headers are written to the worksheet.

> ➤ The first row of formulas is written below the column headers. The first row is different from the remaining rows because its formulas refer to data in the loan parameters section. The other formulas all refer to the preceding row. Note that I use named ranges in the formulas. These names are sheet-level names, so the user can store more than one amortization schedule in the same workbook.

➤ For unnamed references, I use row number and column number notation, which is much easier than trying to determine actual cell addresses.

➤ The second row of formulas is written to the worksheet and then copied down one row for each month.

➤ If the user requested annual totals as opposed to simply monthly data, the procedure uses the Subtotal method to create subtotals. This, by the way, is an example of how using a native feature in Excel can save *lots* of coding.

➤ Because subtotaling the Balance column isn't appropriate, the procedure replaces formulas in the Balance column with a formula that returns the year-end balance.

➤ When Excel adds subtotals, it also creates an outline. If the user didn't request an outline, the procedure uses the ClearOutline method to remove it. If an outline was requested, the procedure hides the outline symbols.

➤ The code then applies the appropriate number formatting to the cells.

➤ The amortization schedule is then converted to a table, and a style is applied based on the user's choice of black-and-white or color.

➤ The procedure then adjusts the column widths, freezes the titles just below the header row, and protects the formulas and a few other key cells that shouldn't be changed.

➤ If the Protect Sheet option is specified in Step 5, the sheet is protected (but not with a password).

➤ Finally, the SaveDefaults procedure writes the current values of the UserForm's controls to the Windows registry. These values will be the new default settings the next time the user creates an amortization schedule. (See the following section.)

Saving and retrieving default settings

If you run this application, you'll note that the FormMain UserForm always displays the setting that you most recently used. In other words, it remembers your last choices and uses them as the new default values. This step makes it easy to generate multiple *what-if* amortization schedules that vary in only a single parameter. The code remembers the user input by storing the values in the Windows Registry and then retrieving them when the UserForm is initialized. When the application is used for the first time, the Registry doesn't have any values, so it uses the default values stored in the UserForm controls.

The following GetDefaults procedure loops through each control on the UserForm. If the control is a TextBox, ComboBox, OptionButton, CheckBox, or SpinButton, it calls the VBA GetSetting function and reads the value to the Registry. Note that the third argument for GetSetting is the value to use if the setting isn't found. In this case, it uses the value of the control specified at design time. APPNAME is a global constant that contains the name of the application.

```
Sub GetDefaults()
'   Reads default settings from the registry
    Dim ctl As Control
    Dim CtrlType As String

    For Each ctl In Me.Controls
        CtrlType = TypeName(ctl)
        If CtrlType = "TextBox" Or _
            CtrlType = "ComboBox" Or _
            CtrlType = "OptionButton" Or _
            CtrlType = "CheckBox" Or _
            CtrlType = "SpinButton" Then
            ctl.Value = GetSetting _
               (APPNAME, "Defaults", ctl.Name, ctl.Value)
        End If
    Next ctl
End Sub
```

Figure 23-7 shows how these values appear in the Registry, as displayed by the Windows Registry Editor program.

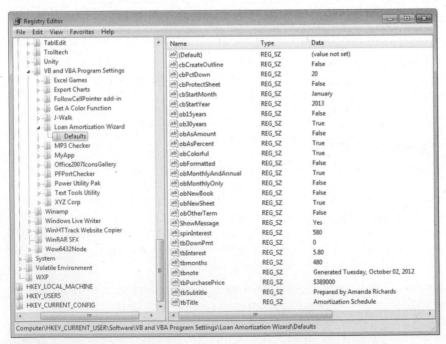

Figure 23-7: The Windows Registry stores the default values for the wizard.

The following SaveDefaults procedure is similar to the GetDefaults procedure. It uses the VBA SaveSetting statement to write the current values to the Registry:

```
Sub SaveDefaults()
'    Writes current settings to the registry
    Dim ctl As Control
    Dim CtrlType As String

    For Each ctl In Me.Controls
        CtrlType = TypeName(ctl)
        If CtrlType = "TextBox" Or _
            CtrlType = "ComboBox" Or _
            CtrlType = "OptionButton" Or _
            CtrlType = "CheckBox" Or _
            CtrlType = "SpinButton" Then
            SaveSetting APPNAME, "Defaults", ctl.Name, CStr(ctl.Value)
        End If
    Next ctl
End Sub
```

Note that the code uses the CStr function to convert each setting to a string. This function helps avoid problems for those who use non-English regional settings. Without the string conversion, True and False are translated to the user's language before they're stored in the Registry. But they're *not* translated back to English when the setting is retrieved — which causes an error.

The SaveSetting statement and the GetSetting function always use the following Registry key:

```
HKEY_CURRENT_USER\Software\VB and VBA Program Settings\
```

Potential enhancements for the Loan Amortization Wizard

It's been said that you never finish writing an application — you just stop working on it. Without even thinking too much about it, I can come up with several enhancements for the Loan Amortization Wizard:

➤ An option to display cumulative totals for interest and principal

➤ An option to work with adjustable-rate loans and make projections based on certain interest rate scenarios

➤ More formatting options (for example, no decimal places, no dollar signs, and so on)

➤ Options to enable the user to specify page headers or footers

Application Development Concepts

Following the logic in an application developed by someone other than yourself is often difficult. To help you understand my work, I included lots of comments in the code and described the general program flow in the preceding sections. But if you really want to understand this application, I suggest that you use the Debugger to step through the code.

 ## Application development checklist

When developing user-oriented applications, you need to keep in mind many things. Let the following checklist serve as a reminder:

- **Do the dialog boxes all work from the keyboard?** Don't forget to add hot keys and check the tab order carefully.

- **Did you make any assumptions about directories?** If your application reads or writes files, you can't assume that a particular directory exists or that it's the current directory.

- **Did you make provisions for canceling all dialog boxes?** You can't assume that the user will end a dialog box by clicking the OK button.

- **Did you assume that no other worksheets are open?** If your application is the only workbook open during testing, you could overlook something that happens when other workbooks are open.

- **Did you assume that a workbook is visible?** It's possible to use pre–Excel 2013 versions with no workbooks visible.

- **Did you attempt to optimize the speed of your application?** For example, you often can speed up your application by declaring variable types and defining object variables.

- **Are your procedures adequately documented?** Will you understand your code if you revisit it in six months?

- **Did you include appropriate end-user documentation?** Doing so often eliminates (or at least reduces) the number of follow-up questions.

- **Did you allow time to revise your application?** Chances are the application won't be perfect the first time out. Build in some time to fix it.

At the very least, the Loan Amortization Wizard demonstrates some useful techniques and concepts that are important for Excel developers:

➤ Modifying the Ribbon

➤ Using a wizard-like UserForm to gather information

➤ Setting the Enabled property of a control dynamically

➤ Linking a TextBox control and a SpinButton control

➤ Displaying context-sensitive help to a user

➤ Naming cells with VBA

➤ Writing and copying formulas with VBA

➤ Creating a table with VBA

➤ Reading from and writing to the Windows Registry

Developing user-oriented applications in Excel isn't easy. You must be keenly aware of how people will use (and abuse) the application in real life. Although I tried to make this application bulletproof, I did not do extensive real-world testing, so I wouldn't be surprised if it fails under some conditions.

PART **VI**

Other Topics

Compatibility Issues

In This Chapter

- Increasing the probability that your Excel 2013 applications will also work with previous versions of Excel

- Declaring API functions that work with 32-bit Excel 2013, 64-bit Excel 2013, and earlier versions of Excel

- Being aware of issues when you're developing Excel applications for international use

What Is Compatibility?

Compatibility is an often-used term among computer people. In general, it refers to how well software performs under various conditions. These conditions might be defined in terms of hardware, software, or a combination of the two. For example, software written for Windows will not run directly on other operating systems, such as Mac OS X or Linux.

In this chapter, I discuss a more specific compatibility issue involving how your Excel 2013 applications will work with earlier versions of Excel for Windows and Excel for Mac. The fact that two versions of Excel might use the same file format isn't always enough to ensure complete compatibility between the contents of their files. For example, Excel 97, Excel 2000, Excel 2002, Excel 2003, and Excel 2008 for Mac all use the same file format, but compatibility problems are rampant. Just because a particular version of Excel can open a worksheet file or an add-in doesn't guarantee that that version of Excel can carry out the VBA macro instructions contained in it. Another example: Excel 2013 and Excel 2007 both use the same file format. If your application uses features that were introduced in Excel 2010 or Excel 2013, you can't expect that Excel 2007 users will magically have access to these new features.

Microsoft Office Compatibility Pack

If you plan to share your Excel 2013 application with others who use an Excel version before Excel 2007, you have two choices:

- Always save your files in the older XLS file format.
- Make sure the recipients of your files have installed Microsoft Office Compatibility Pack.

Microsoft Office Compatibility Pack is a free download available at www.microsoft.com. When installed, Office XP and Office 2003 users can open, edit, and save documents, workbooks, and presentations in the new file formats for Word, Excel, and PowerPoint.

Keep in mind that this compatibility pack doesn't endow earlier versions of Excel with any of the new features in Excel 2007 and later versions. It simply allows those users to open and save files in the new file format.

New Feature

And now that Microsoft Office is available on the web and for Windows RT devices such as tablets and phones, I expect compatibility issues to get even more complicated. These non-desktop versions of Office 2013 do not support VBA, add-ins, or features that rely on ActiveX controls.

Excel is a moving target, and you can't guarantee complete compatibility. In most cases, you must do quite a bit of additional work to achieve compatibility.

Types of Compatibility Problems

You need to be aware of several categories of potential compatibility problems. These issues are listed here and discussed further in this chapter:

➤ **File format issues:** You can save workbooks in several different Excel file formats. Earlier versions of Excel might not be able to open workbooks that were saved in a later version's file format. For more information about sharing Excel 2007 through Excel 2013 files, see the sidebar, "The Microsoft Office Compatibility Pack."

➤ **New feature issues:** It should be obvious that you can't use a feature introduced in a particular version of Excel in previous versions of Excel.

➤ **Microsoft issues:** Microsoft itself is responsible for some types of compatibility issues. For example, as I note in Chapter 21, index numbers for shortcut menus haven't remained consistent across Excel versions.

➤ **Windows versus Mac issues:** If your application must work on both platforms, plan to spend lots of time ironing out various compatibility problems. Also, note that VBA was removed in Excel 2008 for Mac but then came back in Excel 2011 for Mac.

➤ **Bit issues:** Excel 2010 was the first version of Excel that's available in both 32-bit and 64-bit editions. If your VBA code uses API functions, you'll need to be aware of some potential problems if the code must run in both 32-bit and 64-bit Excel, as well as other versions of Excel.

➤ **International issues:** If your application will be used by those who use a different language version of Excel, you must address a number of additional issues.

After reading this chapter, it should be clear that you can ensure compatibility in only one way: Test your application on every target platform and with every target version of Excel.

Note

If you're reading this chapter in search of a complete list of specific compatibility issues among the various versions of Excel, you will be disappointed. As far as I know, no such list exists, and it would be virtually impossible to compile one because these types of issues are too numerous and complex.

Tip

A good source for information about potential compatibility problems is Microsoft's support site. The URL is www.support.microsoft.com. **Information at this site can often help you identify bugs that appear in a particular version of Excel.**

Avoid Using New Features

If your application must work with both Excel 2013 and earlier versions, you need to avoid any features that were added after the earliest Excel version that you will support. Another alternative is to incorporate the new features selectively. In other words, your code can determine which version of Excel is being used and then take advantage of the new features or not.

 ## Determining Excel's version number

The Version property of the Application object returns the version of Excel. The returned value is a string, so you might need to convert it to a value. Use the VBA Val function to make the conversion. The following function, for example, returns True if the user is running Excel 2007 or later:

```
Function XL12OrLater()
    XL12OrLater = Val(Application.Version) >= 12
End Function
```

Excel 2007 is version 12, Excel 2010 is version 14, and Excel 2013 is version 15. No version 13 exists, presumably because some people think it's an unlucky number.

VBA programmers must be careful not to use any objects, properties, or methods that aren't available in earlier versions. In general, the safest approach is to develop your application for the lowest version number. For compatibility with Excel 2003 and later, you should use Excel 2003 for development; then test thoroughly by using later versions.

A useful feature introduced in Excel 2007 is Compatibility Checker, shown in Figure 24-1. Display this dialog box by choosing File➜Info➜Check for Issues➜Check Compatibility. Compatibility Checker identifies any compatibility issues that might cause a problem if the file is opened using an earlier version of Excel.

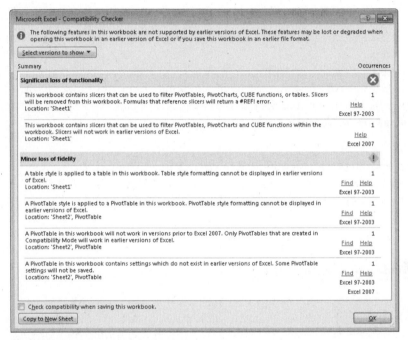

Figure 24-1: Compatibility Checker.

Unfortunately, Compatibility Checker doesn't even look at the VBA code — which is a prime candidate for compatibility problems. However, you can download Microsoft Office Code Compatibility Inspector (search for it at www.microsoft.com). This tool installs as an add-in and adds new commands to the Developer tab. It may help you locate potential compatibility problems in your VBA code. Inspector adds comments to your code to identify potential problems and also creates a report. As I write this book, Microsoft Office Code Compatibility Inspector hadn't been updated for Excel 2013 (but it still installs). I've used this tool a few times and found it marginally useful. Figure 24-2 shows a summary report.

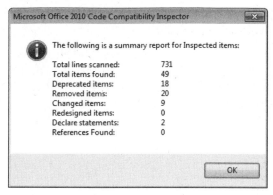

Figure 24-2: A summary report from Microsoft Office Code Compatibility Inspector.

But Will It Work on a Mac?

A common problem that I hear about is Mac compatibility. Excel for Mac represents a small propor-
tion of the total Excel market, and many developers choose simply to ignore it. The good news is that
the file format is compatible across both platforms. The bad news is that the features supported
aren't identical, and VBA macro compatibility is far from perfect. And, as I noted, Excel 2008 for Mac
had no support for VBA.

You can write VBA code to determine which platform your application is running. The following function accesses the OperatingSystem property of the Application object and returns True if the operating system is any version of Windows (that is, if the returned string contains the text "Win"):

```
Function WindowsOS() As Boolean
    If Application.OperatingSystem Like "*Win*" Then
        WindowsOS = True
    Else
        WindowsOS = False
    End If
End Function
```

Subtle (and not so subtle) differences exist between the Windows versions and the Mac versions of
Excel. Many of these differences are cosmetic (for example, different default fonts), but others are
more serious. For example, Excel for Mac doesn't include ActiveX controls. Also, some Mac versions
use the 1904 date system as the default but Excel for Windows uses the 1900 date system by default,
so workbooks that use dates could be off by four years.

Another limitation concerns Windows API functions: They won't work with Excel for Mac. If your application depends on such functions, you need to develop a workaround.

Here's an example of a potential compatibility problem. If your code deals with paths and filenames, you need to construct your path with the appropriate path separator (a colon for the Mac, a backslash for Windows). A better approach is to avoid hard-coding the path separator character and use VBA to determine it. The following statement assigns the path separator character to a variable named PathSep:

```
PathSep = Application.PathSeparator
```

After this statement is executed, your code can use the PathSep variable in place of a hard-coded colon or backslash.

Rather than try to make a single file compatible with both platforms, most developers choose to develop on one platform and then modify the application so that it works on the other platform. In some situations, you'll probably need to maintain two separate versions of your application.

You can make sure that your application is compatible with a particular Mac version of Excel in only one way: Test it thoroughly on a Mac — and be prepared to develop some workarounds for procedures that don't work correctly.

On the Web

Ron de Bruin, a Microsoft Excel MPV in the Netherlands, created a web page with many examples relevant to VBA compatibility between Excel 2011 for Mac and Excel for Windows. The URL for the web page is `http://www.rondebruin.nl/mac.htm`.

Dealing with 64-bit Excel

You can install Excel 2010 and Excel 2013 as a 32-bit application or as a 64-bit application. The latter works only if you're running a 64-bit version of Windows. The 64-bit version can handle much larger workbooks because it takes advantage of the larger address space in 64-bit Windows.

Most users don't need the 64-bit version of Excel because they don't work with massive amounts of data in a workbook. And remember, the 64-bit version offers no performance boost. Some operations may actually be slower in the 64-bit version.

In general, workbooks and add-ins created using the 32-bit version will work fine in the 64-bit version. Note, however, that ActiveX controls will not work in the 64-bit version. Also, if the workbook contains VBA code that uses Windows API functions, the 32-bit API function declarations won't compile in the 64-bit version.

For example, the following declaration works with 32-bit Excel versions but causes a compile error with 64-bit Excel 2010 or 64-bit Excel 2013:

```
Declare Function GetWindowsDirectoryA Lib "kernel32" _
   (ByVal lpBuffer As String, ByVal nSize As Long) As Long
```

The following declaration works with Excel 2010 and Excel 2013 (both 32-bit and 64-bit), but causes a compile error in previous versions of Excel:

```
Declare PtrSafe Function GetWindowsDirectoryA Lib "kernel32" _
   (ByVal lpBuffer As String, ByVal nSize As Long) As Long
```

To use this API function in both 32-bit and 64-bit Excel, you must declare two versions of the function by using two conditional compiler directives:

➤ VBA7 returns True if your code is using Version 7 of VBA (which is included in Office 2010 and later).

➤ Win64 returns True if the code is running in 64-bit Excel.

Here's an example of how to use these directives to declare an API function that's compatible with 32-bit and 64-bit Excel:

```
#If VBA7 And Win64 Then
   Declare PtrSafe Function GetWindowsDirectoryA Lib "kernel32" _
   (ByVal lpBuffer As String, ByVal nSize As Long) As Long
#Else
   Declare Function GetWindowsDirectoryA Lib "kernel32" _
   (ByVal lpBuffer As String, ByVal nSize As Long) As Long
#End If
```

The first Declare statement is used when VBA7 and Wind64 are both True — which is the case only for 64-Bit Excel 2010 or Excel 2013. In all other versions, the second Declare statement is used.

Creating an International Application

The final compatibility concern deals with language issues and international settings. Excel is available in many different language versions. The following statement displays the country code for the version of Excel:

```
MsgBox Application.International(xlCountryCode)
```

The United States/English version of Excel has a country code of 1. Other country codes are listed in Table 24-1.

Table 24-1: Excel Country Codes

Country Code	Country/Region	Language
1	United States	English
7	Russian Federation	Russian
30	Greece	Greek
31	The Netherlands	Dutch
33	France	French
34	Spain	Spanish
36	Hungary	Hungarian
39	Italy	Italian
42	Czech Republic	Czech
45	Denmark	Danish
46	Sweden	Swedish
47	Norway	Norwegian
48	Poland	Polish
49	Germany	German
55	Brazil	Portuguese
66	Thailand	Thai
81	Japan	Japanese
82	Korea	Korean
84	Vietnam	Vietnamese
86	People's Republic of China	Simplified Chinese
90	Turkey	Turkish
91	India	Indian
92	Pakistan	Urdu
351	Portugal	Portuguese
358	Finland	Finnish
886	Taiwan	Traditional Chinese
966	Saudi Arabia	Arabic
972	Israel	Hebrew
982	Iran	Farsi

Excel also supports language packs, so a single copy of Excel can display any number of different languages. The language comes into play in two areas: the user interface and the execution mode.

You can determine the current language used by the user interface by using a statement such as:

```
Msgbox  Application.LanguageSettings.LanguageID(msoLanguageIDUI)
```

The language ID for English U.S. is 1033.

If your application will be used by those who speak another language, you need to ensure that the proper language is used in your dialog boxes. Also, you need to identify the user's decimal and thousands separator characters. In the United States, these are almost always a period and a comma, respectively. However, users in other countries might have their systems set up to use other characters. Yet another issue is date and time formatting: The United States is one of the few countries that use the (illogical) month/day/year format.

If you're developing an application that will be used only by people within your company, you probably won't need to be concerned with international compatibility. But if your company has offices throughout the world or you plan to distribute your application outside your country, you need to address a number of issues to ensure that your application will work properly. I discuss these issues in the following sections.

Multilanguage applications

An obvious consideration involves the language used in your application. For example, if you use one or more dialog boxes, you probably want the text to appear in the language of the user. Fortunately, changing the language isn't too difficult (assuming, of course, that you or someone you know can translate your text).

On the Web The book's website contains an example that demonstrates how to allow the user to choose from three languages in a dialog box: English, Spanish, or German. The example is in the multilingual wizard.xlsm file.

The first step of the multilingual wizard contains three OptionButtons that enable the user to select a language. The text for the three languages is stored in a worksheet.

The UserForm_Initialize procedure contains code that attempts to guess the user's language by checking the International property:

```
Select Case Application.International(xlCountryCode)
    Case 34 'Spanish
        UserLanguage = 2
    Case 49 'German
        UserLanguage = 3
    Case Else 'default to English
        UserLanguage = 1 'default
End Select
```

Figure 24-3 shows the UserForm displaying text in all three languages.

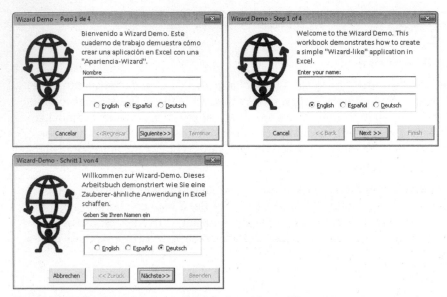

Figure 24-3: The Wizard Demo in English, Spanish, and German.

VBA language considerations

In general, you need not be concerned with the language in which you write your VBA code. Excel uses two object libraries: the Excel object library and the VBA object library. When you install Excel, it registers the English language version of these object libraries as the default libraries (regardless of the language version of Excel).

Using local properties

If your code will display worksheet information, such as a formula or a range address, you probably want to use the local language. For example, the following statement displays the formula in cell A1:

```
MsgBox Range("A1").Formula
```

For international applications, a better approach is to use the FormulaLocal property rather than the Formula property:

```
MsgBox Range("A1").FormulaLocal
```

Several other properties also have local versions. These are shown in Table 24-2 (refer to the Help system for specific details).

Table 24-2: Properties That Have Local Versions

Property	Local Version	Return Contents
Address	AddressLocal	Address
Category	CategoryLocal	Function category (XLM macros only)
Formula	FormulaLocal	Formula
FormulaR1C1	FormulaR1C1Local	Formula, using R1C1 notation
Name	NameLocal	Name
NumberFormat	NumberFormatLocal	Number format
RefersTo	RefersToLocal	Reference
RefersToR1C1	RefersToR1C1Local	Reference, using R1C1 notation

Identifying system settings

Generally, you can't assume that the end user's system is set up like the system on which you develop your application. For international applications, you need to be aware of the following settings:

➤ **Decimal separator:** The character used to separate the decimal portion of a value

➤ **Thousands separator:** The character used to delineate every three digits in a value

➤ **List separator:** The character used to separate items in a list

You can determine the current separator settings by accessing the International property of the Application object. For example, the following statement displays the decimal separator, which won't always be a period:

```
MsgBox Application.International(xlDecimalSeparator)
```

The 45 international settings that you can access with the International property are listed in Table 24-3.

Table 24-3: Constants for the International Property

Constant	What It Returns
xlCountryCode	Country version of Microsoft Excel
xlCountrySetting	Current country setting in the Windows Control Panel
xlDecimalSeparator	Decimal separator
xlThousandsSeparator	Thousands separator
xlListSeparator	List separator
xlUpperCaseRowLetter	Uppercase row letter (for R1C1-style references)
xlUpperCaseColumnLetter	Uppercase column letter
xlLowerCaseRowLetter	Lowercase row letter
xlLowerCaseColumnLetter	Lowercase column letter
xlLeftBracket	Character used instead of the left bracket ([) in R1C1-style relative references
xlRightBracket	Character used instead of the right bracket (]) in R1C1-style references
xlLeftBrace	Character used instead of the left brace ({) in array literals
xlRightBrace	Character used instead of the right brace (}) in array literals
xlColumnSeparator	Character used to separate columns in array literals
xlRowSeparator	Character used to separate rows in array literals
xlAlternateArraySeparator	Alternate array item separator to be used if the current array separator is the same as the decimal separator
xlDateSeparator	Date separator (/)
xlTimeSeparator	Time separator (:)
xlYearCode	Year symbol in number formats (y)
xlMonthCode	Month symbol (m)
xlDayCode	Day symbol (d)
xlHourCode	Hour symbol (h)
xlMinuteCode	Minute symbol (m)
xlSecondCode	Second symbol (s)
xlCurrencyCode	Currency symbol
xlGeneralFormatName	Name of the General number format
xlCurrencyDigits	Number of decimal digits to be used in currency formats
xlCurrencyNegative	A value that represents the currency format for negative currency values
xlNoncurrencyDigits	Number of decimal digits to be used in noncurrency formats
xlMonthNameChars	Always returns three characters for backward-compatibility; abbreviated month names are read from Microsoft Windows and can be any length
xlWeekdayNameChars	Always returns three characters for backward-compatibility; abbreviated weekday names are read from Microsoft Windows and can be any length

Constant	What It Returns
xlDateOrder	An integer that represents the order of date elements
xl24HourClock	True if the system is using 24-hour time; False if the system is using 12-hour time
xlNonEnglishFunctions	True if the system isn't displaying functions in English
xlMetric	True if the system is using the metric system; False if the system is using the English measurement system
xlCurrencySpaceBefore	True if a space is added before the currency symbol
xlCurrencyBefore	True if the currency symbol precedes the currency values; False if it follows them
xlCurrencyMinusSign	True if the system is using a minus sign for negative numbers; False if the system is using parentheses
xlCurrencyTrailingZeros	True if trailing zeros are displayed for zero currency values
xlCurrencyLeadingZeros	True if leading zeros are displayed for zero currency values
xlMonthLeadingZero	True if a leading zero is displayed in months (when months are displayed as numbers)
xlDayLeadingZero	True if a leading zero is displayed in days
xl4DigitYears	True if the system is using four-digit years; False if the system is using two-digit years
xlMDY	True if the date order is month-day-year for dates displayed in the long form; False if the date order is day/month/year
xlTimeLeadingZero	True if a leading zero is displayed in times

Date and time settings

If your application writes formatted dates and will be used in other countries, you might want to make sure that the date is in a format familiar to the user. The best approach is to specify a date by using the VBA DateSerial function and let Excel take care of the formatting details. (It will use the user's short date format.)

The following procedure uses the DateSerial function to assign a date to the StartDate variable. This date is then written to cell A1 with the local short date format.

```
Sub WriteDate()
    Dim StartDate As Date
    StartDate = DateSerial(2013, 4, 15)
    Range("A1") = StartDate
End Sub
```

If you need to do any other formatting for the date, you can write code to do so after the date has been entered in the cell. Excel provides several named date and time formats, plus quite a few named number formats. The Help system describes all these formats (search for *named date/time formats* or *named numeric formats*).

Manipulating Files with VBA

In This Chapter

- Getting a basic overview of VBA text file manipulation features
- Performing common file operations
- Opening a text file
- Displaying extended file information, such as details for media files
- Reading and writing a text file with VBA
- Exporting a range to HTML and XML format
- Zipping and unzipping files
- Using ActiveX Data Objects to import data

Performing Common File Operations

Many applications that you develop for Excel require working with external files. For example, you might need to get a listing of files in a directory, delete files, or rename files. Excel can import and export several types of text files. In many cases, however, Excel's built-in text file handling isn't sufficient. For example, you might want to paste a list of filenames into a range or export a range of cells to a simple HyperText Markup Language (HTML) file.

In this chapter, I describe how to use Visual Basic for Applications (VBA) to perform common (and not so common) file operations and work directly with text files.

Excel provides two ways to perform common file operations:

> ➤ **Use traditional VBA statements and functions:** This method works for all versions of Excel.

> ➤ **Use the FileSystemObject object, which uses the Microsoft Scripting Library:** This method works for Excel 2000 and later.

Caution Some earlier versions of Excel also supported the use of the FileSearch object. That feature was removed, beginning with Excel 2007. If you execute an old macro that uses the FileSearch object, the macro will fail.

In the sections that follow, I discuss these two methods and present examples.

Using VBA file-related statements

The VBA statements that you can use to work with files are summarized in Table 25-1. Most of these statements are straightforward, and all are described in the Help system.

Table 25-1: VBA File-Related Statements

Command	What It Does
ChDir	Changes the current directory
ChDrive	Changes the current drive
Dir	Returns a filename or directory that matches a specified pattern or file attribute
FileCopy	Copies a file
FileDateTime	Returns the date and time when a file was last modified
FileLen	Returns the size of a file, in bytes
GetAttr	Returns a value that represents an attribute of a file
Kill	Deletes a file
MkDir	Creates a new directory
Name	Renames a file or directory
RmDir	Removes an empty directory
SetAttr	Changes an attribute for a file

The remainder of this section consists of examples that demonstrate some of the file manipulation commands.

A VBA function to determine whether a file exists

The following function returns True if a particular file exists and False if it doesn't exist. If the Dir function returns an empty string, the file couldn't be found, so the function returns False.

```
Function FileExists(fname) As Boolean
    FileExists = Dir(fname) <> ""
End Function
```

The argument for the FileExists function consists of a full path and filename. The function can be used in a worksheet or called from a VBA procedure. Here's an example:

```
MyFile = "c:\budgeting\2013 budget notes.docx"
Msgbox FileExists(MyFile)
```

A VBA function to determine whether a path exists

The following function returns True if a specified path exists and False otherwise:

```
Function PathExists(pname) As Boolean
'   Returns TRUE if the path exists
    On Error Resume Next
    PathExists = (GetAttr(pname) And vbDirectory) = vbDirectory
End Function
```

The pname argument is a string that contains a directory (without a filename). The trailing backslash in the pathname is optional. Here's an example of calling the function:

```
MyFolder = "c:\users\john\desktop\downloads\"
MsgBox PathExists(MyFolder)
```

On the Web

The FileExists and PathExists functions are available on the book's website in the file functions.xlsm file.

A VBA procedure to display a list of files in a directory

The following procedure displays (in the active worksheet) a list of files in a particular directory, along with the file size and date:

```
Sub ListFiles()
    Dim Directory As String
    Dim r As Long
    Dim f As String
    Dim FileSize As Double
    Directory = "f:\excelfiles\budgeting\"
    r = 1
'   Insert headers
    Cells(r, 1) = "FileName"
    Cells(r, 2) = "Size"
    Cells(r, 3) = "Date/Time"
    Range("A1:C1").Font.Bold = True
'   Get first file
    f = Dir(Directory, vbReadOnly + vbHidden + vbSystem)
    Do While f <> ""
        r = r + 1
        Cells(r, 1) = f
        'Adjust for filesize > 2 gigabytes
        FileSize = FileLen(Directory & f)
        If FileSize < 0 Then FileSize = FileSize + 4294967296#
        Cells(r, 2) = FileSize

        Cells(r, 3) = FileDateTime(Directory & f)
'       Get next file
        f = Dir()
    Loop
End Sub
```

Figure 25-1 shows an example of the output of the ListFiles procedure.

	A	B	C	D
1	**Files in E:\MUSIC\Folk Male\Bob Dylan\Tempest**	**Size**	**Date/Time**	
2	01 - Duquesne Whistle.mp3	10,773,674	9/11/2012 6:11	
3	02 - Soon After Midnight.mp3	6,279,217	9/11/2012 6:11	
4	03 - Narrow Way.mp3	13,786,524	9/11/2012 6:11	
5	04 - Long and Wasted Years.mp3	7,144,927	9/11/2012 6:11	
6	05 - Pay In Blood.mp3	9,593,360	9/11/2012 6:11	
7	06 - Scarlet Town.mp3	13,191,125	9/11/2012 6:11	
8	07 - Early Roman Kings.mp3	9,900,481	9/11/2012 6:11	
9	08 - Tin Angel.mp3	17,383,326	9/11/2012 6:12	
10	09 - Tempest.mp3	26,235,664	9/11/2012 6:12	
11	10 - Roll On John.mp3	13,659,781	9/11/2012 6:12	
12	cover.jpg	55,912	9/11/2012 6:13	
13				

Sheet1 (+)

Figure 25-1: Output from the ListFiles procedure.

The VBA FileLen function uses the Long data type. Consequently, it will return an incorrect size (a negative number) for files larger than about 2GB. The code checks for a negative value from the FileLen function and makes an adjustment if necessary.

Note

Note that the procedure uses the Dir function twice. The first time (used with an argument), it retrieves the first matching filename found. Subsequent calls (without an argument) retrieve additional matching filenames. When no more files are found, the Dir function returns an empty string.

The book's website contains a version of this procedure that allows you to select a directory from a dialog box. The filename is create file list.xlsm.

On the Web

The Dir function also accepts wildcard file specifications in its first argument. To get a list of Excel files, for example, you could use a statement such as this:

```
f = Dir(Directory & "*.xl??", vbReadOnly + vbHidden + vbSystem)
```

This statement retrieves the name of the first *.xl?? file in the specified directory. The wildcard specification returns a four-character extension that begins with XL. For example, the extension could be .xlsx, .xltx, or .xlam. The second argument for the Dir function lets you specify the attributes of the files (in terms of built-in constants). In this example, the Dir function retrieves filenames that have no attributes, read-only files, hidden files, and system files.

To also retrieve Excel files in an earlier format (for example, .xls and .xla files), use the following wildcard specification:

```
*.xl*
```

Table 25-2 lists the built-in constants for the Dir function.

Table 25-2: File Attribute Constants for the Dir Function

Constant	Value	Description
vbNormal	0	Files with no attributes. This is the default setting and is always in effect.
vbReadOnly	1	Read-only files.
vbHidden	2	Hidden files.
vbSystem	4	System files.
vbVolume	8	Volume label. If any other attribute is specified, this attribute is ignored.
vbDirectory	16	Directories. This attribute doesn't work. Calling the Dir function with the vbDirectory attribute doesn't continually return subdirectories.

Caution

If you use the Dir function to loop through files and call another procedure to process the files, make sure that the other procedure doesn't use the Dir function. Only one "set" of Dir calls can be active at any time.

A recursive VBA procedure to display a list of files in nested directories

The example in this section creates a list of files in a specified directory, including its subdirectories. This procedure is unusual because it calls itself — a concept known as *recursion*.

```
Public Sub RecursiveDir(ByVal CurrDir As String, Optional ByVal Level As Long)
    Dim Dirs() As String
    Dim NumDirs As Long
    Dim FileName As String
    Dim PathAndName As String
    Dim i As Long
    Dim Filesize As Double

'   Make sure path ends in backslash
    If Right(CurrDir, 1) <> "\" Then CurrDir = CurrDir & "\"

'   Put column headings on active sheet
    Cells(1, 1) = "Path"
    Cells(1, 2) = "Filename"
    Cells(1, 3) = "Size"
    Cells(1, 4) = "Date/Time"
    Range("A1:D1").Font.Bold = True

'   Get files
    FileName = Dir(CurrDir & "*.*", vbDirectory)
    Do While Len(FileName) <> 0
      If Left(FileName, 1) <> "." Then 'Current dir
        PathAndName = CurrDir & FileName
        If (GetAttr(PathAndName) And vbDirectory) = vbDirectory Then
          'store found directories
          ReDim Preserve Dirs(0 To NumDirs) As String
          Dirs(NumDirs) = PathAndName
          NumDirs = NumDirs + 1
        Else
          'Write the path and file to the sheet
          Cells(WorksheetFunction.CountA(Range("A:A")) + 1, 1) = _
            CurrDir
          Cells(WorksheetFunction.CountA(Range("B:B")) + 1, 2) = _
            FileName
          'adjust for filesize > 2 gigabytes
          Filesize = FileLen(PathAndName)
          If Filesize < 0 Then Filesize = Filesize + 4294967296#
```

```
            Cells(WorksheetFunction.CountA(Range("C:C")) + 1, 3) = Filesize
            Cells(WorksheetFunction.CountA(Range("D:D")) + 1, 4) = _
                FileDateTime(PathAndName)
        End If
    End If
        FileName = Dir()
    Loop
    ' Process the found directories, recursively
    For i = 0 To NumDirs - 1
        RecursiveDir Dirs(i), Level + 2
    Next i
End Sub
```

The procedure takes one argument, CurrDir, which is the directory being examined. Information for each file is displayed in the active worksheet. As the procedure loops through the files, it stores the subdirectory names in an array named Dirs. When no more files are found, the procedure calls itself using an entry in the Dirs array for its argument. When all directories in the Dirs array have been processed, the procedure ends.

Because the RecursiveDir procedure uses an argument, it must be executed from another procedure by using a statement like this:

```
Call RecursiveDir("c:\directory\")
```

On the Web

The book's website contains a version of this procedure that allows you to select a directory from a dialog box. The filename is recursive file list.xlsm.

Using the FileSystemObject object

The FileSystemObject object is a member of Windows Scripting Host and provides access to a computer's file system. This object is often used in script-oriented web pages (for example, VBScript and JavaScript) and can be used with Excel 2000 and later versions.

Caution

Windows Scripting Host can potentially be used to spread computer viruses and other malware, so it may be disabled on some systems. In addition, some antivirus software products have been known to interfere with Windows Scripting Host. Therefore, use caution if you're designing an application that will be used on many different systems.

The name FileSystemObject is a bit misleading because it includes a number of objects, each designed for a specific purpose:

- ➤ **Drive:** A drive or a collection of drives
- ➤ **File:** A file or a collection of files
- ➤ **Folder:** A folder or a collection of folders
- ➤ **TextStream:** A stream of text that is read from, written to, or appended to a text file

The first step in using the FileSystemObject object is to create an instance of the object. You can do this task in two ways: early binding or late binding.

The late binding method uses two statements, like this:

```
Dim FileSys As Object
Set FileSys = CreateObject("Scripting.FileSystemObject")
```

Note that the FileSys object variable is declared as a generic Object rather than as an actual object type. The object type is resolved at runtime.

The early binding method of creating the object requires that you set up a reference to Windows Script Host Object Model. You do this by using Tools➜References in VBE (see Figure 25-2). After you've established the reference, create the object by using statements like these:

```
Dim FileSys As FileSystemObject
Set FileSys = CreateObject("Scripting.FileSystemObject")
```

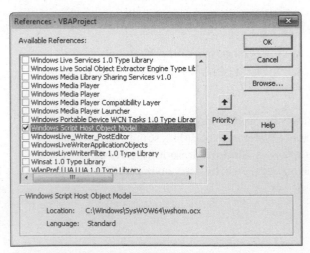

Figure 25-2: Creating a reference to the Windows Script Host Object Model.

Using the early binding method enables you to take advantage of the VBE Auto List Members feature to help you identify properties and methods as you type. In addition, you can use Object Browser (by pressing F2) to learn more about the object model.

The examples that follow demonstrate various tasks using the FileSystemObject object.

Using FileSystemObject to determine whether a file exists

The Function procedure that follows accepts one argument (the path and filename) and returns True if the file exists:

```
Function FileExists3(fname) As Boolean
    Dim FileSys As Object 'FileSystemObject
    Set FileSys = CreateObject("Scripting.FileSystemObject")
    FileExists3 = FileSys.FileExists(fname)
End Function
```

The function creates a new FileSystemObject object named FileSys and then accesses the FileExists property for that object.

Using FileSystemObject to determine whether a path exists

The Function procedure that follows accepts one argument (the path) and returns True if the path exists:

```
Function PathExists2(path) As Boolean
    Dim FileSys As Object 'FileSystemObject
    Set FileSys = CreateObject("Scripting.FileSystemObject")
    PathExists2 = FileSys.FolderExists(path)
End Function
```

Using FileSystemObject to list information about all available disk drives

The example in this section uses FileSystemObject to retrieve and display information about all disk drives. The procedure loops through the Drives collection and writes various property values to a worksheet.

Figure 25-3 shows the results when the procedure is executed on a system with six drives. The data shown is the drive letter, whether the drive is ready, the drive type, the volume name, the total size, and the available space.

Drive	Ready	Type	Vol. Name	Size	Available
C	TRUE	Fixed	OS	6.30506E+11	4.2626E+11
D	TRUE	CD-ROM	The_Fifth_String	3367841792	0
E	TRUE	Fixed	Backup 1	1.00017E+12	3.9281E+11
F	TRUE	Removable		3956801536	3533471744
G	FALSE	Removable			
L	TRUE	Removable		31902400512	2.9959E+10

Figure 25-3: Output from the ShowDriveInfo procedure.

On the Web

This workbook, named show drive info.xlsm, is available on the book's website.

```
Sub ShowDriveInfo()
    Dim FileSys As FileSystemObject
    Dim Drv As Drive
    Dim Row As Long
    Set FileSys = CreateObject("Scripting.FileSystemObject")
    Cells.ClearContents
    Row = 1
'   Column headers
    Range("A1:F1") = Array("Drive", "Ready", "Type", "Vol. Name", _
      "Size", "Available")
    On Error Resume Next
'   Loop through the drives
    For Each Drv In FileSys.Drives
        Row = Row + 1
        Cells(Row, 1) = Drv.DriveLetter
        Cells(Row, 2) = Drv.IsReady
        Select Case Drv.DriveType
            Case 0: Cells(Row, 3) = "Unknown"
            Case 1: Cells(Row, 3) = "Removable"
            Case 2: Cells(Row, 3) = "Fixed"
            Case 3: Cells(Row, 3) = "Network"
            Case 4: Cells(Row, 3) = "CD-ROM"
            Case 5: Cells(Row, 3) = "RAM Disk"
        End Select
        Cells(Row, 4) = Drv.VolumeName
        Cells(Row, 5) = Drv.TotalSize
        Cells(Row, 6) = Drv.AvailableSpace
    Next Drv
    'Make a table
    ActiveSheet.ListObjects.Add xlSrcRange, _
      Range("A1").CurrentRegion, , xlYes
End Sub
```

Cross-Ref   Chapter 9 describes another method of getting drive information by using Windows API functions.

Displaying Extended File Information

The example in this section displays extended file properties for all files in a specified directory. The available information depends on the file type. For example, image files have properties such as Camera Model and Dimensions; audio files have properties such as Artist, Title, and Duration.

The available properties depend on the version of Windows. Windows Vista supports 267 properties and Windows 7 supports even more. Here's a procedure that creates a list of file properties in the active worksheet:

```vba
Sub ListFileProperties()
    Dim i As Long
    Dim objShell As Object 'IShellDispatch4
    Dim objFolder As Object 'Folder3

'   Create the object
    Set objShell = CreateObject("Shell.Application")

'   Specify any folder
    Set objFolder = objShell.Namespace("C:\")

'   List the properties
    For i = 0 To 500
        Cells(i + 1, 1) = _
            objFolder.GetDetailsOf(objFolder.Items, i)
    Next i
End Sub
```

Caution   Unfortunately, property values aren't consistent across Windows versions. For example, the Title property is stored as number 11 in Windows 2000, 10 in Windows XP, 21 in Windows Vista, and 22 in Windows 7.

The FileInfo procedure, which uses the Windows Shell.Application object, follows. This procedure prompts for a directory using the GetDirectory function (not shown here) and then lists the first 41 properties of each file in the directory.

```
Sub FileInfo()
    Dim c As Long, r As Long, i As Long
    Dim FileName As Object 'FolderItem2
    Dim objShell As Object 'IShellDispatch4
    Dim objFolder As Object 'Folder3

'   Create the object
    Set objShell = CreateObject("Shell.Application")

'   Prompt for the folder
    Set objFolder = objShell.Namespace(GetDirectory)

'   Insert headers on active sheet
    Worksheets.Add
    c = 0
    For i = 0 To 40
        c = c + 1
        Cells(1, c) = objFolder.GetDetailsOf(objFolder.Items, i)
    Next i

'   Loop through the files
    r = 1
    For Each FileName In objFolder.Items
        c = 0
        r = r + 1
        For i = 0 To 40
            c = c + 1
            Cells(r, c) = objFolder.GetDetailsOf(FileName, i)
        Next i
    Next FileName
'   Make it a table
    ActiveSheet.ListObjects.Add xlSrcRange, Range("A1").CurrentRegion
End Sub
```

Figure 25-4 shows the seven columns of output from this procedure, with Windows 7 as the operating system.

This example uses late binding to create a Shell.Application object, so the objects are declared generically. To use early binding, use the VBE Tools→References command and create a reference to Microsoft Shell Controls and Automation.

On the Web

This example, named file information.xlsm, is available on the book's website.

Name	Size	Item type	Date modified	Date created	Date accessed	Attributes
01 - Maybelle Rag.mp3	5.52 MB	MPEG Layer 3 Audio File	8/27/2012 16:28	8/27/2012 16:29	8/27/2012 16:29	A
02 - Say Darling Say.mp3	5.63 MB	MPEG Layer 3 Audio File	8/27/2012 16:28	8/27/2012 16:29	8/27/2012 16:29	A
03 - Durang's Hornpipe_Forked Deer.mp3	7.96 MB	MPEG Layer 3 Audio File	9/3/2012 13:38	8/27/2012 16:29	9/3/2012 13:38	A
04 - Dolly.mp3	3.55 MB	MPEG Layer 3 Audio File	8/27/2012 16:28	8/27/2012 16:29	8/27/2012 16:29	A
05 - Tempie_Dance Boatman Dance.mp3	4.48 MB	MPEG Layer 3 Audio File	8/27/2012 16:29	8/27/2012 16:29	8/27/2012 16:29	A
06 - Rockingham Cindy.mp3	4.51 MB	MPEG Layer 3 Audio File	8/27/2012 16:28	8/27/2012 16:29	8/27/2012 16:29	A
07 - Cumberland Gap.mp3	7.11 MB	MPEG Layer 3 Audio File	8/27/2012 16:28	8/27/2012 16:29	8/27/2012 16:29	A
08 - Old Blue Sow.mp3	6.05 MB	MPEG Layer 3 Audio File	8/27/2012 16:28	8/27/2012 16:29	8/27/2012 16:29	A
09 - Corrinne.mp3	3.99 MB	MPEG Layer 3 Audio File	8/27/2012 16:28	8/27/2012 16:29	8/27/2012 16:29	A
10 - Christmas Eve.mp3	4.91 MB	MPEG Layer 3 Audio File	8/27/2012 16:28	8/27/2012 16:29	8/27/2012 16:29	A
11 - John Sharp Medley.mp3	4.58 MB	MPEG Layer 3 Audio File	8/27/2012 16:28	8/27/2012 16:29	8/27/2012 16:29	A
12 - L&N Rag.mp3	6.70 MB	MPEG Layer 3 Audio File	8/27/2012 16:28	8/27/2012 16:29	8/27/2012 16:29	A
13 - Altamont.mp3	4.48 MB	MPEG Layer 3 Audio File	8/27/2012 16:28	8/27/2012 16:29	8/27/2012 16:29	A
14 - Take Me As I Am.mp3	4.83 MB	MPEG Layer 3 Audio File	8/27/2012 16:29	8/27/2012 16:29	8/27/2012 16:29	A
cover.jpg	46.8 KB	IrfanView JPG File	8/27/2012 16:30	8/27/2012 16:30	8/27/2012 16:30	A

Figure 25-4: A table of information about the files in a directory.

Working with Text Files

VBA contains a number of statements that allow low-level manipulation of files. These input/output (I/O) statements give you much more control over files than Excel's normal text file import and export options.

You can access a file in any of three ways:

> **Sequential access:** By far the most common method. This type allows reading and writing individual characters or entire lines of data.

> **Random access:** Used only if you're programming a database application, which is not often done using VBA.

> **Binary access:** Used to read or write to any byte position in a file, such as when storing or displaying a bitmap image. This access method is rarely used in VBA.

Because random and binary access files are rarely used with VBA, this chapter focuses on sequential access files. In sequential access, your code starts reading from the beginning of the file and reads each line sequentially. For output, your code writes data to the end of the file.

Note   The method of reading and writing text files discussed in this book is the traditional data-channel approach. Another option is to use the object approach. The FileSystemObject object contains a TextStream object that can be used to read and write text files. The FileSystemObject object is part of Windows Scripting Host, which is disabled on some systems because of the malware potential.

Opening a text file

The VBA Open statement (not to be confused with the Open method of the Workbooks object) opens a file for reading or writing. Before you can read from or write to a file, you must open it.

The Open statement is versatile and has a complex syntax:

```
Open pathname For mode [Access access] [lock]  _
  As [#]filenumber [Len=reclength]
```

> pathname: Required. The pathname part of the Open statement is straightforward. It simply contains the name and path (optional) of the file to be opened.

> mode: Required. The file mode must be one of the following:

  - Append: A sequential access mode that either allows the file to be read or allows data to be appended to the end of the file.

  - Input: A sequential access mode that allows the file to be read but not written to.

  - Output: A sequential access mode that allows the file to be read or written to. In this mode, a new file is always created. (An existing file with the same name is deleted.)

  - Binary: A random access mode that allows data to be read or written to on a byte-by-byte basis.

  - Random: A random access mode that allows data to be read or written in units determined by the reclength argument of the Open statement.

> access: Optional. The access argument determines what can be done with the file. It can be Read, Write, or Read Write.

> lock: Optional. The lock argument is useful for multiuser situations. The options are Shared, Lock Read, Lock Write, and Lock Read Write.

> filenumber: Required. A file number ranging from 1 to 511. You can use the FreeFile function to get the next available file number. (Read about FreeFile in the upcoming section, "Getting a file number.")

> reclength: Optional. The record length (for random access files) or the buffer size (for sequential access files).

Reading a text file

The basic procedure for reading a text file with VBA consists of the following steps:

1. Open the file by using the Open statement.
2. Specify the position in the file by using the Seek function (optional).
3. Read data from the file (by using the Input, Input #, or Line Input # statements).
4. Close the file by using the Close statement.

Writing a text file

The basic procedure for writing a text file is as follows:

1. Open or create the file by using the Open statement.
2. Optional. Specify the position in the file by using the Seek function.
3. Write data to the file by using the Write # or Print # statement.
4. Close the file by using the Close statement.

Getting a file number

Most VBA programmers simply designate a file number in their Open statement. For example:

```
Open "myfile.txt" For Input As #1
```

Then you can refer to the file in subsequent statements as #1.

If a second file is opened while the first is still open, you'd designate the second file as #2:

```
Open "another.txt" For Input As #2
```

Another approach is to use the VBA FreeFile function to get a file handle. Then you can refer to the file by using a variable. Here's an example:

```
FileHandle = FreeFile
Open "myfile.txt" For Input As FileHandle
```

Excel's text file import and export features

Excel can directly read and write three types of text files:

- **CSV (comma-separated value) files:** Columns of data are separated by a comma, and each row of data ends in a carriage return character. For some non-English versions of Excel, a semicolon rather than a comma is used.

- **PRN:** Columns of data are aligned by character position, and each row of data ends in a carriage return. These files are also known as *fixed-width files*.

- **TXT (Tab-delimited) files:** Columns of data are separated by tab characters, and each row of data ends in a carriage return.

When you attempt to open a text file with the File➜Open command, the Text Import Wizard might appear to help you delineate the columns. If the text file is tab-delimited or comma-delimited, Excel usually opens the file without displaying the Text Import Wizard. If the data isn't interpreted correctly, close the file and try renaming it to use a .txt extension.

The Text to Columns Wizard (accessed by choosing Data➜Data Tools➜Text to Columns) is identical to the Text Import Wizard but works with data stored in a single worksheet column.

Determining or setting the file position

For sequential file access, you rarely need to know the current location in the file. If for some reason you need to know this information, you can use the Seek function.

Statements for reading and writing

VBA provides several statements to read and write data to a file.

Three statements are used for reading data from a sequential access file:

➤ Input: Reads a specified number of characters from a file.

➤ Input #: Reads data as a series of variables, with variables separated by a comma.

➤ Line Input #: Reads a complete line of data (delineated by a carriage return character, or a linefeed character, or both).

Two statements are used for writing data to a sequential access file:

➤ Write #: Writes a series of values, with each value separated by a comma and enclosed in quotes. If you end the statement with a semicolon, a carriage return/linefeed sequence is not inserted after each value. Data written with Write # is usually read from a file with an Input # statement.

➤ Print #: Writes a series of values, with each value separated by a tab character. If you end the statement with a semicolon, a carriage return/linefeed sequence isn't inserted after each value. Data written with Print # is usually read from a file with a Line Input # or an Input statement.

Text File Manipulation Examples

This section contains a number of examples that demonstrate various techniques that manipulate text files.

Importing data in a text file

The code in the following example reads a text file and then places each line of data in a single cell (beginning with the active cell):

```
Sub ImportData()
    Open "c:\data\textfile.txt" For Input As #1
    r = 0
    Do Until EOF(1)
        Line Input #1, data
        ActiveCell.Offset(r, 0) = data
        r = r + 1
    Loop
    Close #1
End Sub
```

In most cases, this procedure won't be very useful because each line of data is simply dumped into a single cell. It would be easier to just open the text file directly by using File➜Open.

When Excel parses your data incorrectly

Have you ever imported a CSV file, or pasted data into a worksheet, only to find that Excel split your data incorrectly? If so, the culprit is probably the Text To Columns feature. Here's Step 2 of the wizard that's used to split a single column of delimited data into multiple columns.

In this case, three delimiters are specified: tab, comma, and colon.

Splitting text into separate columns is a useful feature. The problem, however, is that Excel tries to be helpful by remembering these settings for subsequent CSV imports and paste operations. Sometimes remembering these settings is helpful, but often it's not. To clear these delimiters, you must display this dialog box, clear the settings, and click Cancel.

If you're importing or pasting via a macro, your macro cannot check or reset these settings directly. The solution is to fake a text-to-columns operation. The following procedure does that, with the effect of clearing all the settings from the Text to Columns dialog box (and making no changes to your workbook).

```
Sub ClearTextToColumns()
    On Error Resume Next
    If IsEmpty(Range("A1")) Then Range("A1") = "XYZZY"
    Range("A1").TextToColumns Destination:=Range("A1"), _
        DataType:=xlDelimited, _
        TextQualifier:=xlDoubleQuote, _
        ConsecutiveDelimiter:=False, _
        Tab:=False, _
        Semicolon:=False, _
        Comma:=False, _
        Space:=False, _
```

```
        Other:=False, _
        OtherChar:=""
    If Range("A1") = "XYZZY" Then Range("A1") = ""
    If Err.Number <> 0 Then MsgBox Err.Description
End Sub
```

This macro assumes that a worksheet is active and is not protected. Note that the contents of cell A1 won't be modified because no operations are specified for the TextToColumns method. If cell A1 is empty, the code inserts a temporary string (because the TextToColumns method will fail if the cell is empty). Before ending, the procedure deletes the temporary string.

Exporting a range to a text file

The example in this section writes the data in a selected worksheet range to a CSV text file. Although Excel can export data to a CSV file, it exports the entire worksheet. This macro works with a specified range of cells.

```
Sub ExportRange()
    Dim Filename As String
    Dim NumRows As Long, NumCols As Integer
    Dim r As Long, c As Integer
    Dim Data
    Dim ExpRng As Range
    Set ExpRng = Selection
    NumCols = ExpRng.Columns.Count
    NumRows = ExpRng.Rows.Count
    Filename = Application.DefaultFilePath & "\textfile.csv"
    Open Filename For Output As #1
        For r = 1 To NumRows
            For c = 1 To NumCols
                Data = ExpRng.Cells(r, c).Value
                If IsNumeric(Data) Then Data = Val(Data)
                If IsEmpty(ExpRng.Cells(r, c)) Then Data = ""
                If c <> NumCols Then
                    Write #1, Data;
                Else
                    Write #1, Data
                End If
            Next c
        Next r
    Close #1
End Sub
```

Note that the procedure uses two Write # statements. The first statement ends with a semicolon, so a return/linefeed sequence isn't written. For the last cell in a row, however, the second Write # statement doesn't use a semicolon, which causes the next output to appear on a new line.

I used a variable named Data to store the contents of each cell. If the cell is numeric, the variable is converted to a value. This step ensures that numeric data won't be stored with quotation marks. If a cell is empty, its Value property returns 0. Therefore, the code also checks for a blank cell (by using the IsEmpty function) and substitutes an empty string instead of a 0.

Figure 25-5 shows the contents of the resulting file, viewed in Windows Notepad.

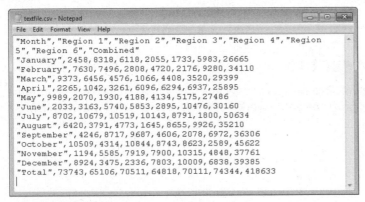

Figure 25-5: VBA generated this text file.

This example and the example in the next section are available on the book's website in the export and import csv.xlsm file.

Importing a text file to a range

The example in this section reads the CSV file created in the preceding example and then stores the values beginning at the active cell in the active worksheet. The code reads each character and essentially parses the line of data, ignoring quote characters and looking for commas to delineate the columns.

```
Sub ImportRange()
    Dim ImpRng As Range
    Dim Filename As String
    Dim r As Long, c As Integer
    Dim txt As String, Char As String * 1
    Dim Data
    Dim i As Integer

    Set ImpRng = ActiveCell
    On Error Resume Next
```

```
      Filename = Application.DefaultFilePath & "\textfile.csv"
      Open Filename For Input As #1
      If Err <> 0 Then
          MsgBox "Not found: " & Filename, vbCritical, "ERROR"
          Exit Sub
      End If
      r = 0
      c = 0
      txt = ""
      Application.ScreenUpdating = False
      Do Until EOF(1)
          Line Input #1, Data
          For i = 1 To Len(Data)
              Char = Mid(Data, i, 1)
              If Char = "," Then 'comma
                  ActiveCell.Offset(r, c) = txt
                  c = c + 1
                  txt = ""
              ElseIf i = Len(Data) Then 'end of line
                  If Char <> Chr(34) Then txt = txt & Char
                  ActiveCell.Offset(r, c) = txt
                  txt = ""
              ElseIf Char <> Chr(34) Then
                  txt = txt & Char
              End If
          Next i
          c = 0
          r = r + 1
      Loop
      Close #1
      Application.ScreenUpdating = True
  End Sub
```

Note

The preceding procedure works with most data, but it has a flaw: It doesn't handle data that contains a comma or a quote character. But commas resulting from formatting are handled correctly (they're ignored). In addition, an imported date will be surrounded by number signs: for example, #2013-05-12#.

Logging Excel usage

The example in this section writes data to a text file every time Excel is opened and closed. For this example to work reliably, the procedure must be located in a workbook that's opened every time you start Excel. Storing the macro in your Personal Macro Workbook is an excellent choice.

The following procedure, stored in the code module for the ThisWorkbook object, is executed when the file is opened:

```
Private Sub Workbook_Open()
    Open Application.DefaultFilePath & "\excelusage.txt" For Append As #1
    Print #1, "Started " & Now
    Close #1
End Sub
```

The procedure appends a new line to a file named excelusage.txt. The new line contains the current date and time and might look something like this:

```
Started 11/16/2013 9:27:43 PM
```

The following procedure is executed before the workbook is closed. It appends a new line that contains the word *Stopped* along with the current date and time.

```
Private Sub Workbook_BeforeClose(Cancel As Boolean)
    Open Application.DefaultFilePath & "\excelusage.txt" _
      For Append As #1
    Print #1, "Stopped " & Now
    Close #1
End Sub
```

On the Web

A workbook that contains these procedures is available on the book's website in the excel usage log.xlsm file.

Cross-Ref

Refer to Chapter 17 for more information about event-handler procedures such as Workbook_Open and Workbook_BeforeClose.

Filtering a text file

The example in this section demonstrates how to work with two text files at once. The FilterFile procedure that follows reads a text file (infile.txt) and copies only the rows that contain a specific text string ("January") to a second text file (output.txt):

```
Sub FilterFile()
    Open ThisWorkbook.Path & "\infile.txt" For Input As #1
    Open Application.DefaultFilePath & "\output.txt" For Output As #2
    TextToFind = "January"
```

```
     Do Until EOF(1)
         Line Input #1, data
         If InStr(1, data, TextToFind) Then
             Print #2, data
         End If
     Loop
     Close 'Close all files
End Sub
```

On the Web   **This example, named filter text file.xlsm, is available on the book's website.**

Exporting a range to HTML format

The example in this section demonstrates how to export a range of cells to an HTML file. An *HTML file*, as you might know, is simply a text file that contains special formatting tags that describe how the information will be presented in a web browser.

Why not use Excel's File➜Save As command and choose the Web Page file type? The procedure listed here has a distinct advantage: It doesn't produce bloated HTML code. For example, I used the ExportToHTML procedure to export a range of 70 cells. The file size was 2.6KB. Then I used Excel's File➜Save as Web Page command to export the sheet. The result was 15.8KB — more than six times larger.

On the other hand, the only formatting information that the ExportToHTML procedure maintains is bold, italic, and horizontal alignment. However, the procedure is good enough for many situations and serves as the basis for additional enhancements.

```
Sub ExportToHTML()
    Dim Filename As Variant
    Dim TDOpenTag As String, TDCloseTag As String
    Dim CellContents As String
    Dim Rng As Range
    Dim r As Long, c As Integer

'   Use the selected range of cells
    Set Rng = Application.Intersect(ActiveSheet.UsedRange, Selection)
    If Rng Is Nothing Then
        MsgBox "Nothing to export.", vbCritical
        Exit Sub
    End If

'   Get a file name
    Filename = Application.GetSaveAsFilename( _
```

continued

```
            InitialFileName:="myrange.htm", _
            fileFilter:="HTML Files(*.htm), *.htm")
    If Filename = False Then Exit Sub

'   Open the text file
    Open Filename For Output As #1

'   Write the tags
    Print #1, "<HTML>"
    Print #1, "<TABLE BORDER=0 CELLPADDING=3>"

'   Loop through the cells
    For r = 1 To Rng.Rows.Count
        Print #1, "<TR>"
        For c = 1 To Rng.Columns.Count
            Select Case Rng.Cells(r, c).HorizontalAlignment
                Case xlHAlignLeft
                    TDOpenTag = "<TD ALIGN=LEFT>"
                Case xlHAlignCenter
                    TDOpenTag = "<TD ALIGN=CENTER>"
                Case xlHAlignGeneral
                    If IsNumeric(Rng.Cells(r, c)) Then
                        TDOpenTag = "<TD ALIGN=RIGHT>"
                    Else
                        TDOpenTag = "<TD ALIGN=LEFT>"
                    End If
                Case xlHAlignRight
                    TDOpenTag = "<TD ALIGN=RIGHT>"
            End Select

            TDCloseTag = "</TD>"
            If Rng.Cells(r, c).Font.Bold Then
                TDOpenTag = TDOpenTag & "<B>"
                TDCloseTag = "</B>" & TDCloseTag
            End If
            If Rng.Cells(r, c).Font.Italic Then
                TDOpenTag = TDOpenTag & "<I>"
                TDCloseTag = "</I>" & TDCloseTag
            End If
            CellContents = Rng.Cells(r, c).Text
            Print #1, TDOpenTag & CellContents & TDCloseTag
        Next c
        Print #1, "</TR>"
    Next r
'   Close the table
```

```
    Print #1, "</TABLE>"
    Print #1, "</HTML>"

'   Close the file
    Close #1

'   Tell the user
    MsgBox Rng.Count & " cells were exported to " & Filename
End Sub
```

The procedure starts by determining the range to export, based on the intersection of the selected range and the used area of the worksheet. This step ensures that entire rows or columns aren't processed. Next, the user is prompted for a filename, and the text file is opened. The bulk of the work is done in two For-Next loops. The code generates the appropriate HTML tags and writes the information to the text file. The only complicated part is determining the cell's horizontal alignment because Excel doesn't report this information directly. Finally, the file is closed, and the user sees a summary message.

Figure 25-6 shows a range in a worksheet, and Figure 25-7 shows how the range looks in a web browser after being converted to HTML.

	A	B	C	D	E	F
1		New York	Los Angeles	Chicago	Total	
2	January	$11,249.09	$11,423.69	$4,936.33	$5,438.79	
3	February	$9,265.44	$10,778.64	$10,519.65	$5,044.97	
4	March	$11,606.05	$8,306.11	$11,055.09	$8,388.56	
5	April	$7,956.91	$11,509.05	$6,951.02	$8,965.71	
6	May	$7,850.21	$9,937.65	$9,346.92	$10,907.65	
7	June	$8,399.23	$6,456.32	$8,669.86	$4,898.50	
8	July	$6,298.21	$6,530.04	$8,403.11	$8,848.34	
9	August	$5,013.93	$7,690.16	$9,527.34	$7,327.38	
10	September	$8,986.08	$11,600.23	$5,740.46	$11,394.59	
11	October	$5,574.59	$5,011.99	$9,417.73	$10,519.65	
12	November	$10,320.80	$9,994.88	$7,996.68	$7,659.12	
13	December	$11,436.30	$6,500.94	$10,557.48	$10,421.68	
14	Total	$103,956.84	$105,739.70	$103,121.67	$312,818.21	
15						

Sheet1 ⊕

Figure 25-6: A worksheet range, ready to be converted to HTML.

On the Web

This example, named **export to HTML.xlsm, is available on the book's website.**

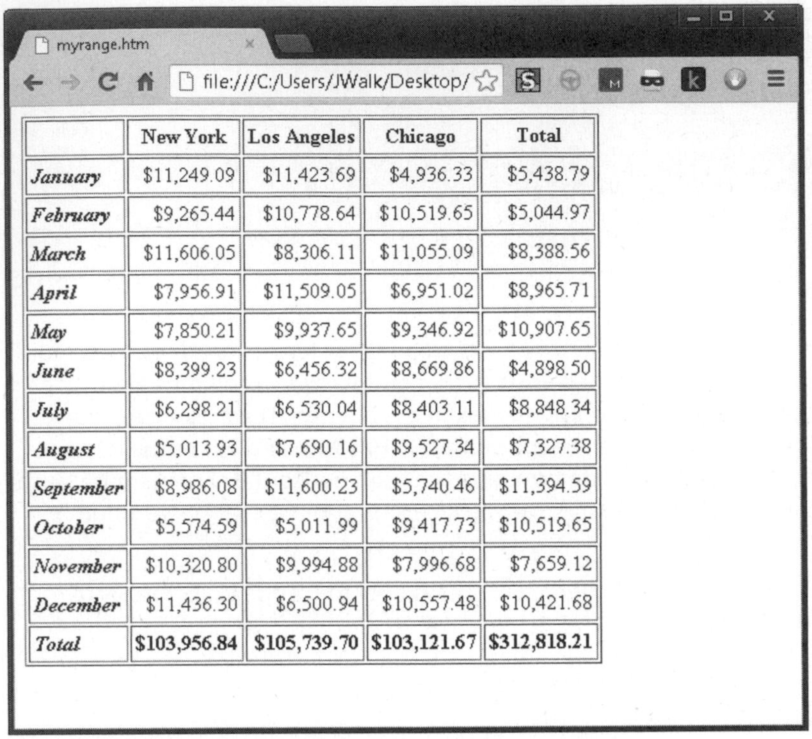

Figure 25-7: The worksheet data after being converted to HTML.

Exporting a range to an XML file

The next example exports an Excel range to a simple XML data file. As you might know, an XML file uses tags to wrap each data item. The procedure in this section uses the labels in the first row as the XML tags. Figure 25-8 shows the range in a worksheet table, and Figure 25-9 shows the XML file displayed in a web browser.

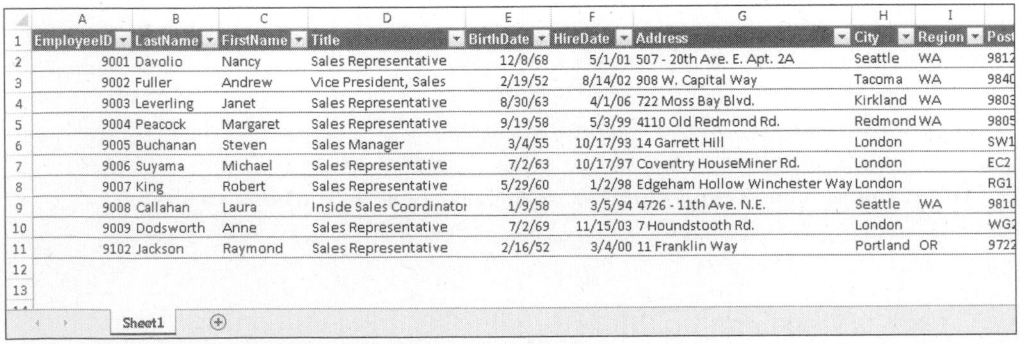

Figure 25-8: The data in this range will be converted to XML.

Note

Although Excel 2003 introduced improved support for XML files, even Excel 2013 can't create an XML file from an arbitrary range of data unless you have a map file (schema) for the data.

Figure 25-9: The worksheet data after being converted to XML.

The ExportToXML procedure follows. You'll notice that it has quite a bit in common with the ExportToHTML procedure, in the preceding section.

```
Sub ExportToXML()
    Dim Filename As Variant
    Dim Rng As Range
    Dim r As Long, c As Long

'   Set the range
    Set Rng = Range("Table1[#All]")

'   Get a file name
    Filename = Application.GetSaveAsFilename( _
        InitialFileName:="myrange.xml", _
        fileFilter:="XML Files(*.xml), *.xml")
    If Filename = False Then Exit Sub
```

continued

```
'   Open the text file
    Open Filename For Output As #1

'   Write the <xml> tags
    Print #1, "<?xml version=""1.0"" encoding=""UTF-8"" standalone=""yes""?>"
    Print #1, "<EmployeeList xmlns:xsi=""http://www.w3.org/2001/XMLSchema-
    instance"">"

'   Loop through the cells
    For r = 2 To Rng.Rows.Count
        Print #1, "<Employee>"
        For c = 1 To Rng.Columns.Count
            Print #1, "<" & Rng.Cells(1, c) & ">";
            If IsDate(Rng.Cells(r, c)) Then
                Print #1, Format(Rng.Cells(r, c), "yyyy-mm-dd");
            Else
                Print #1, Rng.Cells(r, c).Text;
            End If
            Print #1, "</" & Rng.Cells(1, c) & ">"
        Next c
        Print #1, "</Employee>"
    Next r
'   Close the table
    Print #1, "</EmployeeList>"

'   Close the file
    Close #1

'   Tell the user
    MsgBox Rng.Rows.Count - 1 & " records were exported to " & Filename
End Sub
```

On the Web   **This example, named export to XML.xlsm, is available on the book's website.**

You can open the exported XML file with Excel. When opening an XML file, you'll see the dialog box shown in Figure 25-10. If you choose the As an XML Table option, the file will be displayed as a table. Keep in mind that any formulas in the original table aren't preserved.

Figure 25-10: When opening an XML file, Excel offers three options.

Zipping and Unzipping Files

Perhaps the most commonly used type of file compression is the Zip format. Even Excel 2007 (and later) files are stored in the Zip format (although they don't use the .zip extension). A Zip file can contain any number of files, and even complete directory structures. The content of the files determines the degree of compression. For example, JPG image files and MP3 audio files are already compressed, so zipping these file types has little effect on the file size. Text files, on the other hand, usually shrink quite a bit when compressed.

On the Web The examples in this section are available on the book's website in files named zip files. xlsm and unzip a file.xlsm.

Zipping files

The example in this section demonstrates how to create a Zip file from a group of user-selected files. The ZipFiles procedure displays a dialog box so that the user can select the files. It then creates a Zip file named compressed.zip in Excel's default directory.

```
Sub ZipFiles()
    Dim ShellApp As Object
    Dim FileNameZip As Variant
    Dim FileNames As Variant
    Dim i As Long, FileCount As Long

'   Get the file names
    FileNames = Application.GetOpenFilename _
        (FileFilter:="All Files (*.*),*.*", _
        FilterIndex:=1, _
        Title:="Select the files to ZIP", _
        MultiSelect:=True)

'   Exit if dialog box canceled
    If Not IsArray(FileNames) Then Exit Sub

    FileCount = UBound(FileNames)
    FileNameZip = Application.DefaultFilePath & "\compressed.zip"

    'Create empty Zip File with zip header
    Open FileNameZip For Output As #1
    Print #1, Chr$(80) & Chr$(75) & Chr$(5) & Chr$(6) & String(18, 0)
    Close #1

    Set ShellApp = CreateObject("Shell.Application")
    'Copy the files to the compressed folder
```

continued

```
For i = LBound(FileNames) To UBound(FileNames)
    ShellApp.Namespace(FileNameZip).CopyHere FileNames(i)
    'Keep script waiting until Compressing is done
    On Error Resume Next
    Do Until ShellApp.Namespace(FileNameZip).items.Count =  i
        Application.Wait (Now + TimeValue("0:00:01"))
    Loop
Next i



If MsgBox(FileCount & " files were zipped to:" & _
    vbNewLine & FileNameZip & vbNewLine & vbNewLine & _
    "View the zip file?", vbQuestion + vbYesNo) = vbYes Then _
    Shell "Explorer.exe /e," & FileNameZip, vbNormalFocus
End Sub
```

Figure 25-11 shows the file selection dialog box generated by using the GetOpenFilename method of the Application object (see Chapter 10 for more information). This dialog box allows the user to select multiple files from a single directory.

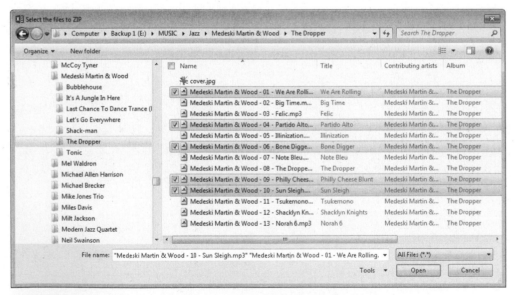

Figure 25-11: This dialog box lets the user select the files to be zipped.

The ZipFiles procedure creates a file named compressed.zip and writes a string of characters, which identify it as a Zip file. Next, a Shell.Application object is created, and the code uses its CopyHere method to copy the files to the Zip archive. The next section of the code is a Do Until loop, which checks the number of files in the Zip archive every second. This step is necessary because copying the files could take some time, and if the procedure ends before the files are copied, the Zip file will be incomplete (and probably corrupt). This loop slows the procedure considerably, but I haven't been able to figure out an alternative.

When the number of files in the Zip archive matches the number that should be there, the loop ends and the user is presented with a message like the one shown in Figure 25-12. Clicking the Yes button opens a Windows Explorer window that shows the zipped files.

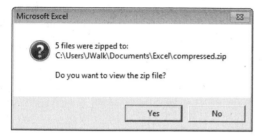

Figure 25-12: The user is informed when the Zip file is complete.

Caution   The ZipFiles procedure presented here was kept simple to make it easy to understand. The code does no error checking and is not flexible. For example, there is no option to choose the Zip filename or location, and the current compressed.zip file is always over-written without warning. It's certainly no replacement for the zipping tools built into Windows, but it's an interesting demonstration of what you can do with VBA.

Unzipping a file

The example in this section performs the opposite function of the preceding example. It asks the user for a ZIP filename and then unzips the files and puts them in a directory named Unzipped, located in Excel's default file directory.

```
Sub UnzipAFile()
    Dim ShellApp As Object
    Dim TargetFile
    Dim ZipFolder

'   Target file & temp dir
    TargetFile = Application.GetOpenFilename _
```

continued

```
            (FileFilter:="Zip Files (*.zip), *.zip")
    If TargetFile = False Then Exit Sub

    ZipFolder = Application.DefaultFilePath & "\Unzipped\"

'   Create a temp folder
    On Error Resume Next
    RmDir ZipFolder
    MkDir ZipFolder
    On Error GoTo 0

'   Copy the zipped files to the newly created folder
    Set ShellApp = CreateObject("Shell.Application")
    ShellApp.Namespace(ZipFolder).CopyHere _
        ShellApp.Namespace(TargetFile).items

    If MsgBox("The files was unzipped to:" & _
        vbNewLine & ZipFolder & vbNewLine & vbNewLine & _
        "View the folder?", vbQuestion + vbYesNo) = vbYes Then _
        Shell "Explorer.exe /e," & ZipFolder, vbNormalFocus
End Sub
```

The UnzipAFile procedure uses the GetOpenFilename method to get the Zip file. It then creates the new folder and uses the Shell.Application object to copy the contents of the Zip file to the new folder. Finally, the user can choose to display the new directory.

Working with ADO

ADO (ActiveX Data Objects) is an object model that enables you to access data stored in a variety of formats (including common database formats and even text files). Importantly, this methodology allows you to use a single object model for all your data sources. ADO is currently the preferred data access methodology and shouldn't be confused with DAO (Data Access Objects).

This section presents a simple example that uses ADO to retrieve data from an Access database.

 Note ADO programming is a complex topic. If you need to access external data in your Excel application, you'll probably want to invest in one or more books that cover this topic in detail.

The ADO_Demo example retrieves data from an Access database named budget data.accdb. This database contains one table (named Budget). The example retrieves the data in which the Item field contains the text *Lease,* the Division field contains the text *N. America,* and the Year field contains *2008.* The qualifying data is stored in a Recordset object, and the data is then transferred to a worksheet (see Figure 25-13).

	A	B	C	D	E	F	G	H	I	J	K
1	ID	SORT	DIVISION	DEPARTMENT	CATEGORY	ITEM	YEAR	MONTH	BUDGET	ACTUAL	VARIANCE
2	10	10	N. America	Data Processing	Facility	Lease	2008	Jan	3450	2631	819
3	34	34	N. America	Human Resources	Facility	Lease	2008	Jan	4353	3875	478
4	58	58	N. America	Accounting	Facility	Lease	2008	Jan	3898	2979	919
5	82	82	N. America	Training	Facility	Lease	2008	Jan	3185	3545	-360
6	106	106	N. America	Security	Facility	Lease	2008	Jan	3368	4120	-752
7	130	130	N. America	R&D	Facility	Lease	2008	Jan	3926	3432	494
8	154	154	N. America	Operations	Facility	Lease	2008	Jan	3329	3715	-386
9	178	178	N. America	Shipping	Facility	Lease	2008	Jan	4095	2892	1203
10	202	202	N. America	Sales	Facility	Lease	2008	Jan	3242	2687	555
11	226	226	N. America	Advertising	Facility	Lease	2008	Jan	3933	3580	353
12	250	250	N. America	Public Relations	Facility	Lease	2008	Jan	4316	4328	-12
13	1330	1330	N. America	Data Processing	Facility	Lease	2008	Feb	4440	4357	83
14	1354	1354	N. America	Human Resources	Facility	Lease	2008	Feb	4210	3196	1014
15	1378	1378	N. America	Accounting	Facility	Lease	2008	Feb	2860	3658	-798
16	1402	1402	N. America	Training	Facility	Lease	2008	Feb	4468	3759	709
17	1426	1426	N. America	Security	Facility	Lease	2008	Feb	3499	3568	-69
18	1450	1450	N. America	R&D	Facility	Lease	2008	Feb	3394	4196	-802
19	1474	1474	N. America	Operations	Facility	Lease	2008	Feb	4187	3074	1113
20	1498	1498	N. America	Shipping	Facility	Lease	2008	Feb	2870	3751	-881
21	1522	1522	N. America	Sales	Facility	Lease	2008	Feb	4046	4013	33
22	1546	1546	N. America	Advertising	Facility	Lease	2008	Feb	3131	3864	-733
23	1570	1570	N. America	Public Relations	Facility	Lease	2008	Feb	4153	3980	173
24	2650	2650	N. America	Data Processing	Facility	Lease	2008	Mar	4166	3673	493
25	2674	2674	N. America	Human Resources	Facility	Lease	2008	Mar	3739	3884	-145
26	2698	2698	N. America	Accounting	Facility	Lease	2008	Mar	3796	4406	-610
27	2722	2722	N. America	Training	Facility	Lease	2008	Mar	2587	3605	-1018

Sheet1 | Description

Figure 25-13: This data was retrieved from an Access database.

```
Sub ADO_Demo()
'   This demo requires a reference to
'   the Microsoft ActiveX Data Objects 2.x Library

    Dim DBFullName As String
    Dim Cnct As String, Src As String
    Dim Connection As ADODB.Connection
    Dim Recordset As ADODB.Recordset
    Dim Col As Integer

    Cells.Clear

'   Database information
    DBFullName = ThisWorkbook.Path & "\budget data.accdb"

'   Open the connection
    Set Connection = New ADODB.Connection
    Cnct = "Provider=Microsoft.ACE.OLEDB.12.0;"
    Cnct = Cnct & "Data Source=" & DBFullName & ";"
    Connection.Open ConnectionString:=Cnct

'   Create RecordSet
    Set Recordset = New ADODB.Recordset
    With Recordset
```

continued

```
'       Filter
        Src = "SELECT * FROM Budget WHERE Item = 'Lease' "
        Src = Src & "and Division = 'N. America' "
        Src = Src & "and Year = '2008'"
        .Open Source:=Src, ActiveConnection:=Connection

'       Write the field names
        For Col = 0 To Recordset.Fields.Count - 1
            Range("A1").Offset(0, Col).Value = _
                Recordset.Fields(Col).Name
        Next

'       Write the recordset
        Range("A1").Offset(1, 0).CopyFromRecordset Recordset
      End With
    Set Recordset = Nothing
    Connection.Close
    Set Connection = Nothing
End Sub
```

On the Web

This example (named simple ado example.xlsm), along with the Access database file (named budget data.accdb), is available on the book's website. An additional example, simple ado example2.xlsm, uses ADO to query a CSV text file named music_list.csv.

Manipulating Visual Basic Components

In This Chapter

- Getting an overview of VBA Integrated Development Environment (IDE) and its object model
- Using VBA to add and remove modules from a project
- Writing VBA code that creates more VBA code
- Using VBA to help create UserForms
- Creating a UserForm on the fly

Introducing IDE

This chapter covers a topic that some readers might find extremely useful: writing VBA code that manipulates components in a VBA project. VBA Integrated Development Environment (IDE) contains an object model that exposes key elements of your VBA projects, including Visual Basic Editor (VBE) itself. This object model enables you to write VBA code that adds or removes modules, generates other VBA code, or even creates UserForms on the fly.

IDE is essentially an Object Linking and Embedding (OLE) automation interface for Visual Basic Editor. After you establish a reference to the object, you have access to all VBE objects, properties, and methods, and you can also declare objects from IDE member classes.

Use the VBE Tools➜References command to display the References dialog box, where you can add a reference to Microsoft Visual Basic for Applications Extensibility Library (see Figure 26-1). This gives you access to an object called VBIDE. Creating a reference to VBIDE enables you to declare object variables contained in VBIDE and also gives you access to a number of predefined constants that relate to IDE. Actually, you can access the objects in IDE *without* creating a reference, but you won't be able to use the constants in your code, nor will you be able to declare specific objects that refer to IDE components.

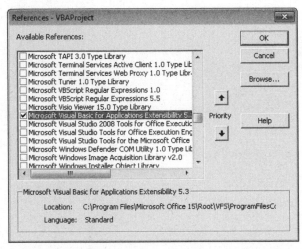

Figure 26-1: Adding a reference to Microsoft Visual Basic for Applications Extensibility Library.

After you understand how the IDE object model works, you can write code to perform a variety of operations, including the following:

➤ Adding and removing VBA modules

➤ Inserting VBA code

➤ Creating UserForms

➤ Adding controls to a UserForm

An important security note

If you're using Excel to develop applications for others to use, be aware that the procedures in this chapter may not work. Because of the threat of macro viruses, Microsoft (beginning with Excel 2002) made it much more difficult for a VBA macro to modify components in a VBA project. If you attempt to execute any of the procedures in this chapter, you may see an error message.

Whether you see this error message depends on a setting in Excel's Trust Center dialog box. To view this setting:

1. Choose File➔Options.
2. In the Excel options dialog box, click the Trust Center tab.
3. In the Trust Center Tab, click the Trust Center Settings button.
4. In the Trust Center dialog box, click the Macro Settings tab.

Or you can use the Developer➔Code➔Macro Security command to go directly to the Trust Center dialog box.

You'll find a check box labeled Trust Access to the VBA Project Object Model.

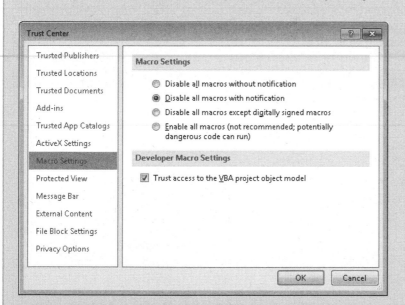

This setting is turned off by default. Even if the user chooses to trust the *macros* contained in the workbook, the macros can't modify the VBA project if this setting is turned off. Note that this setting applies to all workbooks and can't be changed for only a particular workbook.

continued

continued

You can't directly determine the value of this particular setting by using VBA. The only way to detect this setting is to attempt to access the VBProject object and then check for an error, as follows:

```
On Error Resume Next
Set x = ActiveWorkbook.VBProject
If Err <> 0 Then
  MsgBox "Your security settings do not allow this macro to run."
  Exit Sub
End If
```

The book's website contains a workbook that demonstrates how to check the Trust Access to the VBA Project Object Model setting and how to instruct the user to change the setting. The file is named check security.xlsm.

Not all the examples in this chapter are intended to be used by end users. Many of them are designed to help developers create projects. For these projects, you'll need to enable the Trust Access to the VBA Project Object Model setting.

The IDE Object Model

Programming the IDE requires an understanding of its object model. The top object in the object hierarchy is VBE (Visual Basic Environment). As with Excel's object model, VBE contains other objects. A simplified version of the IDE object hierarchy follows:

```
VBE
    VBProject
      VBComponent
          CodeModule
          Designer
          Property
      Reference
    Window
    CommandBar
```

Note

This chapter ignores the Extensibility Library Windows collection and CommandBars collection, which aren't useful for Excel developers. Rather, the chapter focuses on the VBProject object, which can be very useful for developers — but make sure that you read the "An important security note" sidebar.

The VBProjects collection

Every open workbook or add-in is represented by a VBProject object. To access the VBProject object for a workbook using early binding, make sure that you've established a reference to Microsoft Visual Basic for Applications Extensibility Library (see the section "Introducing the IDE," earlier in this chapter).

The VBProject property of the Workbook object returns a VBProject object. The following instructions, for example, create an object variable that represents the VBProject object for the active workbook:

```
Dim VBP As VBProject
Set VBP = ActiveWorkbook.VBProject
```

 Note   **If you get an error message when VBA encounters the Dim statement, make sure that you've added a reference to Microsoft Visual Basic for Applications Extensibility Library.**

Each VBProject object contains a collection of the VBA component objects in the project (UserForms, modules, class modules, and document modules). Not surprisingly, this collection is called VBComponents. A VBProject object also contains a References collection for the project, representing the libraries being referenced currently by the project.

You can't add a new member to the VBProjects collection directly. Rather, you do so indirectly by opening or creating a new workbook in Excel. Doing so automatically adds a new member to the VBProjects collection. Similarly, you can't remove a VBProject object directly; closing a workbook removes the VBProject object from the collection.

The VBComponents collection

To access a member of the VBComponents collection, use the VBComponents property with an index number or name as its argument. The following instructions demonstrate the two ways to access a VBA component and create an object variable:

```
Set VBC = ThisWorkbook.VBProject.VBComponents(1)
Set VBC = ThisWorkbook.VBProject.VBComponents("Module1")
```

The References collection

Every VBA project in Excel contains a number of references. You can view, add, or delete the references for a project by choosing the Tools➡References command. (Refer to Figure 26-1 to see the References dialog box.) Every project contains some references (such as VBA itself, Excel, OLE Automation, and the Office object library), and you can add more references to a project as needed.

You can also manipulate the references for a project by using VBA. The References collection contains Reference objects, and these objects have properties and methods. The following procedure, for example, displays a message box that lists the Name, Description, and FullPath property for each Reference object in the active workbook's project:

```
Sub ListReferences()
    Dim Ref As Reference
    Msg = ""
    For Each Ref In ActiveWorkbook.VBProject.References
        Msg = Msg & Ref.Name & vbNewLine
        Msg = Msg & Ref.Description & vbNewLine
        Msg = Msg & Ref.FullPath & vbNewLine & vbNewLine
    Next Ref
    MsgBox Msg
End Sub
```

Figure 26-2 shows the result of running this procedure when a workbook that contains six references is active.

Figure 26-2: This message box displays information about the references for a project.

Note

Because it declares an object variable of type Reference, the ListReferences procedure requires a reference to VBA Extensibility Library. If you declare Ref as a generic Object, the VBA Extensibility Library reference is not needed.

You can also add a reference programmatically by using either of two methods of the Reference class. The AddFromFile method adds a reference if you know its filename and path. AddFromGuid adds a reference if you know the reference's *globally unique identifier,* or GUID. Refer to the Help system for more information.

Displaying All Components in a VBA Project

The ShowComponents procedure, which follows, loops through each VBA component in the active workbook and writes the following information to a worksheet:

➤ The component's name

➤ The component's type

➤ The number of lines of code in the code module for the component

```
Sub ShowComponents()
    Dim VBP As VBIDE.VBProject
    Dim VBC As VBComponent
    Dim row As Long

    Set VBP = ActiveWorkbook.VBProject

'   Write headers
    Cells.ClearContents
    Range("A1:C1") = Array("Name", "Type", "Code Lines")
    Range("A1:C1").Font.Bold = True
    row = 1

'   Loop through the VB Components
    For Each VBC In VBP.VBComponents
        row = row + 1
'       Name
        Cells(row, 1) = VBC.Name
'       Type
        Select Case VBC.Type
```

continued

```
            Case vbext_ct_StdModule
                Cells(row, 2) = "Module"
            Case vbext_ct_ClassModule
                Cells(row, 2) = "Class Module"
            Case vbext_ct_MSForm
                Cells(row, 2) = "UserForm"
            Case vbext_ct_Document
                Cells(row, 2) = "Document Module"
        End Select
        ' Lines of code
        Cells(row, 3) = VBC.CodeModule.CountOfLines
    Next VBC
End Sub
```

Note that I used built-in constants (for example, vbext_ct_StdModule) to determine the component type. These constants aren't defined unless you've established a reference to Microsoft Visual Basic for Applications Extensibility Library.

Figure 26-3 shows the result of running the ShowComponents procedure. In this case, the VBA project contained six components, and only one of them had an empty code module.

	A	B	C	D
1	**Name**	**Type**	**Code Lines**	
2	ThisWorkbook	Document Module	49	
3	Sheet1	Document Module	0	
4	Module1	Module	171	
5	FormAbout	UserForm	159	
6	Utilities	Module	118	
7	Bookmarks	Module	196	
8				
9				
10				
11				

Sheet1   (+)

Figure 26-3: The result of executing the ShowComponents procedure.

On the Web

This code is available on the book's website in a workbook named list VB components. xlsm. The workbook includes an enhancement that lets you choose a project from all open VB projects.

Listing All VBA Procedures in a Workbook

The ListProcedures macro in this section creates a list (in a message box) of all VBA procedures in the active workbook:

```
Sub ListProcedures()
    Dim VBP As VBIDE.VBProject
    Dim VBC As VBComponent
    Dim CM As CodeModule
    Dim StartLine As Long
    Dim Msg As String
    Dim ProcName As String

'   Use the active workbook
    Set VBP = ActiveWorkbook.VBProject

'   Loop through the VB components
    For Each VBC In VBP.VBComponents
        Set CM = VBC.CodeModule
        Msg = Msg & vbNewLine
        StartLine = CM.CountOfDeclarationLines + 1
        Do Until StartLine >= CM.CountOfLines
            Msg = Msg & VBC.Name & ": " & _
              CM.ProcOfLine(StartLine, vbext_pk_Proc) & vbNewLine
            StartLine = StartLine + CM.ProcCountLines _
              (CM.ProcOfLine(StartLine, vbext_pk_Proc), _
               vbext_pk_Proc)
        Loop
    Next VBC
    MsgBox Msg
End Sub
```

Figure 26-4 shows the result for a workbook that has nine procedures.

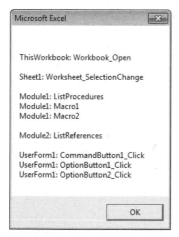

Figure 26-4: The message box lists all procedures in the active workbook.

This example, named list all procedures.xlsm, is available on the book's website.

Replacing a Module with an Updated Version

The example in this section demonstrates how to replace a VBA module with a different VBA module. Besides demonstrating three VBComponent methods (Export, Remove, and Import), the procedure also has a practical use. For example, you might distribute a workbook to a group of users and then later discover that a macro contains an error or needs to be updated. Because the users could have added data to the workbook, replacing the entire workbook isn't practical. The solution is to distribute another workbook that contains a macro that replaces the VBA module with an updated version stored in a file.

This example consists of two workbooks:

➤ UserBook.xlsm: Contains a module (Module1) that needs to be replaced.

➤ UpdateUserBook.xlsm: Contains VBA procedures to replace Module1 in UserBook.xlsm with a later version of Module1 (which is stored in UpdateUserBook.xlsm).

The BeginUpdate procedure follows. This macro is contained in the UpdateUserBook.xlsm workbook, which would be distributed to users of UserBook.xlsm. This procedure ensures that UserBook.xlsm is open. It then displays the message shown in Figure 26-5 to inform the user of what is about to happen.

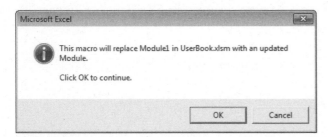

Figure 26-5: This message box informs the user that a module will be replaced.

```
Sub BeginUpdate()
    Dim Filename As String
    Dim Msg As String
    Filename = "UserBook.xlsm"

'   Activate workbook
    On Error Resume Next
    Workbooks(Filename).Activate
    If Err <> 0 Then
        MsgBox Filename & " must be open.", vbCritical
```

```
        Exit Sub
    End If


    Msg = "This macro will replace Module1 in UserBook.xlsm "
    Msg = Msg & "with an updated Module." & vbCrLf & vbCrLf
    Msg = Msg & "Click OK to continue."
    If MsgBox(Msg, vbInformation + vbOKCancel) = vbOK Then
        Call ReplaceModule
    Else
        MsgBox "Module not replaced,", vbCritical
    End If
End Sub
```

When the user clicks OK to confirm the replacement, the ReplaceModule procedure is called. This procedure replaces Module1 in the UserBook.xlsm with the copy of Module1 in the UpdateUserBook.xlsm file:

```
Sub ReplaceModule()
    Dim ModuleFile As String
    Dim VBP As VBIDE.VBProject

'   Export Module1 from this workbook
    ModuleFile = Application.DefaultFilePath & "\tempmodxxx.bas"
    ThisWorkbook.VBProject.VBComponents("Module1") _
      .Export ModuleFile

'   Replace Module1 in UserBook
    Set VBP = Workbooks("UserBook.xlsm").VBProject
    On Error GoTo ErrHandle
    With VBP.VBComponents
        .Remove VBP.VBComponents("Module1")
        .Import ModuleFile
    End With

'   Delete the temporary module file
    Kill ModuleFile
    MsgBox "The module has been replaced.", vbInformation
    Exit Sub

ErrHandle:
'   Did an error occur?
    MsgBox "ERROR. The module may not have been replaced.", _
      vbCritical
End Sub
```

This procedure performs the following actions:

1. Exports Module1 (the updated module) to a file.

   The file has an unusual name to reduce the likelihood of overwriting an existing file.

2. Removes Module1 (the old module) from UserBook.xlsm, using the Remove method of the VBComponents collection.

3. Imports the module (saved in Step 1) to UserBook.xlsm.

4. Deletes the file saved in Step 1.

5. Reports the action to the user.

   General error handling is used to inform the user that an error occurred.

On the Web

This example is available on the book's website. The demo uses two workbooks: UserBook.xlsm and UpdateUserBook.xlsm.

Using VBA to Write VBA Code

The example in this section demonstrates how you can write VBA code that writes more VBA code. The AddButtonAndCode procedure does the following:

1. Inserts a new worksheet.

2. Adds an ActiveX CommandButton control to the worksheet.

3. Adjusts the position, size, and caption of the CommandButton.

4. Activates Sheet1 by inserting an event-handler procedure for the CommandButton named CommandButton1_Click in the sheet's code module.

The AddButtonAndCode procedure follows.

```
Sub AddButtonAndCode()
    Dim NewSheet As Worksheet
    Dim NewButton As OLEObject

'   Add the sheet
    Set NewSheet = Sheets.Add

'   Add a CommandButton
    Set NewButton = NewSheet.OLEObjects.Add _
      ("Forms.CommandButton.1")
```

```
    With NewButton
        .Left = 4
        .Top = 4
        .Width = 100
        .Height = 24
        .Object.Caption = "Return to Sheet1"
    End With

'   Add the event handler code
    Code = "Sub CommandButton1_Click()" & vbCrLf
    Code = Code & "    On Error Resume Next" & vbCrLf
    Code = Code & "    Sheets(""Sheet1"").Activate" & vbCrLf
    Code = Code & "    If Err <> 0 Then" & vbCrLf
    Code = Code & "        MsgBox ""Cannot activate Sheet1.""" _
    & vbCrLf
    Code = Code & "    End If" & vbCrLf
    Code = Code & "End Sub"

    With ActiveWorkbook.VBProject. _
      VBComponents(NewSheet.Name).CodeModule
        NextLine = .CountOfLines + 1
        .InsertLines NextLine, Code
    End With
End Sub
```

Figure 26-6 shows the worksheet and the CommandButton control that were added by the AddButtonAndCode procedure.

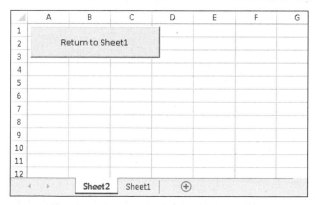

Figure 26-6: This sheet, the CommandButton, and its event handler were added by using VBA.

On the Web

This example is available on the book's website in the add button and code.xlsm file.

The tricky part of this procedure is inserting the VBA code in the code module for the new worksheet. The code is stored in a String variable named Code, with each instruction separated by a return and linefeed sequence. The InsertLines method adds the code to the code module for the inserted worksheet.

The NextLine variable stores the number of existing lines in the module incremented by 1. This ensures that the procedure is added to the end of the module. If you simply insert the code beginning at line 1, it causes an error if the user's system is set up to add an Option Explicit statement to each module automatically.

Figure 26-7 shows the procedure created by the AddButtonAndCode procedure in its new home in the code window.

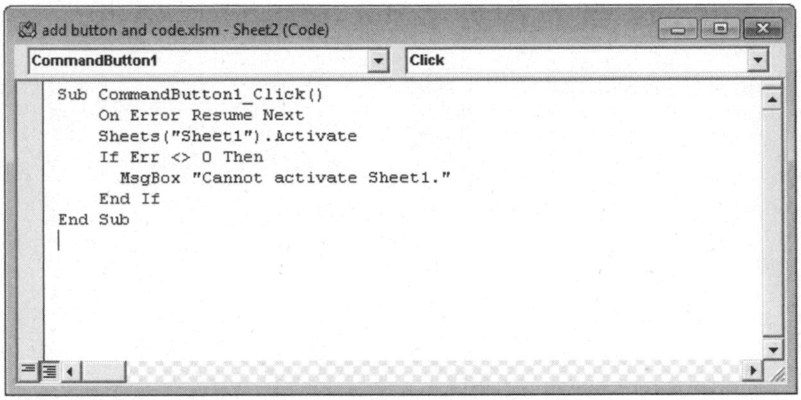
add button and code.xlsm - Sheet2 (Code)
CommandButton1
Click
Sub CommandButton1_Click()
On Error Resume Next
Sheets("Sheet1").Activate
If Err <> 0 Then
MsgBox "Cannot activate Sheet1."
End If
End Sub

Figure 26-7: VBA generated this event-handler procedure.

Adding Controls to a UserForm at Design Time

If you've spent any time developing UserForms, you probably know that adding and adjusting the controls so that they're aligned and sized consistently can be tedious. Even if you take full advantage of the VBE formatting commands, getting the controls to look just right can take a long time.

The UserForm shown in Figure 26-8 contains 100 CommandButtons, all of which are identical in size and positioned precisely on the form. Furthermore, each CommandButton has its own event-handler procedure. Adding these buttons manually and creating their event handlers would take lots of time. Adding them automatically at design time by using a VBA procedure takes less than a second.

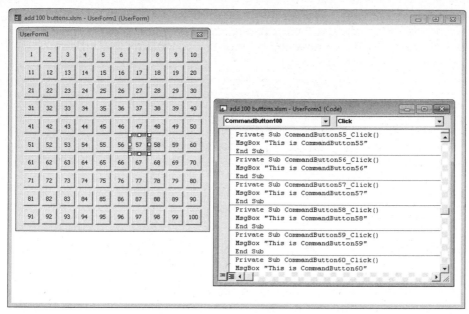

Figure 26-8: A VBA procedure adds the CommandButtons on this UserForm and writes the event-handler procedures.

Design-time versus runtime UserForm manipulations

It's important to understand the distinction between manipulating UserForms or controls at design time and manipulating these objects at runtime. Runtime manipulations are apparent when the UserForm is shown, but the changes made aren't permanent. For example, you might write code that changes the Caption property of the UserForm before the form is displayed. The new caption appears when the UserForm is shown, but when you return to VBE, the UserForm displays its original caption. Runtime manipulation is common, and Part III contains many code examples that perform runtime manipulation of UserForms and controls.

Design-time manipulations, on the other hand, *are* permanent — just as if you made the changes manually by using the tools in VBE. Normally, you perform design-time manipulations to automate the tedious chores in designing a UserForm. to make design-time manipulations, you access the Designer object for the UserForm.

To demonstrate the difference between design-time and runtime manipulations, I developed two simple procedures that add a CommandButton to a UserForm. One procedure adds the button at runtime; the other adds it at design time.

The following RunTimeButton procedure is straightforward. When used in a general (non-UserForm) module, it adds a CommandButton to the UserForm, changes a few of the CommandButton's properties, and then displays the UserForm. The CommandButton appears on the form when the form is shown but isn't there when you view the form in VBE.

```
Sub RunTimeButton()
'    Adds a button at runtime
    Dim Butn As CommandButton
    Set Butn = UserForm1.Controls.Add("Forms.CommandButton.1")
    With Butn
        .Caption = "Added at runtime"
        .Width = 100
        .Top = 10
    End With
    UserForm1.Show
End Sub
```

Following is the DesignTimeButton procedure. Unlike the preceding example, this procedure uses the Designer object, which is contained in the VBComponent object. Specifically, it uses the Add method to add the CommandButton control. Because the Designer object was used, the CommandButton is added to the UserForm just as if you did it manually in VBE.

```
Sub DesignTimeButton()
'    Adds a button at design time
    Dim Butn As CommandButton
    Set Butn = ThisWorkbook.VBProject. _
      VBComponents("UserForm1") _
        .Designer.Controls.Add("Forms.CommandButton.1")
    With Butn
        .Caption = "Added at design time"
        .Width = 120
        .Top = 40
    End With
End Sub
```

Adding 100 CommandButtons at design time

The example in this section demonstrates how to take advantage of the Designer object to help you design a UserForm. In this case, the code adds 100 CommandButtons (perfectly spaced and aligned), sets the Caption property for each CommandButton, and also creates 100 event-handler procedures (one for each CommandButton).

```vba
Sub Add100Buttons()
  Dim UFvbc As VBComponent
  Dim CMod As CodeModule
  Dim ctl As Control
  Dim cb As CommandButton
  Dim n As Long, c As Long, r As Long
  Dim code As String

  Set UFvbc = ThisWorkbook.VBProject.VBComponents("UserForm1")

' Delete all controls, if any
  For Each ctl In UFvbc.Designer.Controls
    UFvbc.Designer.Controls.Remove ctl.Name
  Next ctl

' Delete all VBA code
  UFvbc.CodeModule.DeleteLines 1, UFvbc.CodeModule.CountOfLines

' Add 100 CommandButtons
  n = 1
  For r = 1 To 10
    For c = 1 To 10
      Set cb = UFvbc.Designer. _
        Controls.Add("Forms.CommandButton.1")
      With cb
        .Width = 22
        .Height = 22
        .Left = (c * 26) - 16
        .Top = (r * 26) - 16
        .Caption = n
      End With

'     Add the event handler code
      With UFvbc.CodeModule
        code = ""
        code = code & "Private Sub CommandButton" & n & _
         "_Click" & vbCr
        code = code & "Msgbox ""This is CommandButton" & n & _
          """" & vbCr
        code = code & "End Sub"
        .InsertLines .CountOfLines + 1, code
      End With
      n = n + 1
    Next c
  Next r
End Sub
```

On the Web   **This example is available on the book's website in the add 100 buttons.xlsm file.**

The Add100Buttons procedure requires a UserForm named UserForm1. You'll need to make the UserForm a bit larger than its default size so that the buttons will fit. The procedure starts by deleting all controls on the form by using the Remove method of the Controls collection and then deleting all code in the code module by using the DeleteLines method of the CodeModule object. Next, the CommandButtons are added, and the event-handler procedures are created in two For-Next loops. These event handlers are simple. Here's an example of such a procedure for CommandButton1:

```
Private Sub CommandButton1_Click()
  MsgBox "This is CommandButton1"
End Sub
```

If you'd like to show the form after adding the controls at design time, you need to add the following instruction right before the End Sub statement:

```
VBA.UserForms.Add("UserForm1").Show
```

It took me quite a while to figure out how to display the UserForm. When VBA generates the 100-button UserForm, it indeed exists in VBA's memory, but it isn't officially part of the project. You need the Add method to formally enroll UserForm1 into the collection of userForms. The return value of this method is a reference to the form itself, which is why the Show method can be appended to the Add method. So, as a rule, the UserForm must be added to the UserForms collection before it can be used.

Creating UserForms Programmatically

The final topic in this chapter demonstrates how to use VBA code to create UserForms at runtime. I present two examples. One is relatively simple, and the other is more complex.

A simple runtime UserForm example

The example in this section demonstrates some useful concepts. The MakeForm procedure performs several tasks:

1. Creates a temporary UserForm in the active workbook by using the Add method of the VBComponents collection.

2. Adds a CommandButton control to the UserForm by using the Designer object.

3. Adds an event-handler procedure to the UserForm's code module (CommandButton1_Click). This procedure, when executed, simply displays a message box and then unloads the form.

4. Displays the UserForm.

5. Deletes the UserForm.

The net result is a UserForm that's created on the fly, put to use, and then deleted. This example and the one in the next section both blur the distinction between modifying forms at design time and modifying forms at runtime. The form is created by using design-time techniques, but creating the form happens at runtime.

The following shows the MakeForm procedure:

```
Sub MakeForm()
    Dim TempForm As Object
    Dim NewButton As Msforms.CommandButton
    Dim Line As Integer

    Application.VBE.MainWindow.Visible = False

'   Create the UserForm
    Set TempForm = ThisWorkbook.VBProject. _
      VBComponents.Add(3) 'vbext_ct_MSForm
    With TempForm
        .Properties("Caption") = "Temporary Form"
        .Properties("Width") = 200
        .Properties("Height") = 100
    End With

'   Add a CommandButton
    Set NewButton = TempForm.Designer.Controls _
      .Add("Forms.CommandButton.1")
    With NewButton
        .Caption = "Click Me"
        .Left = 60
        .Top = 40
    End With

'   Add an event-hander sub for the CommandButton
    With TempForm.CodeModule
        Line = .CountOfLines
        .InsertLines Line + 1, "Sub CommandButton1_Click()"
        .InsertLines Line + 2, "  MsgBox ""Hello!"""
        .InsertLines Line + 3, "  Unload Me"
        .InsertLines Line + 4, "End Sub"
```

continued

```
    End With

'   Show the form
    VBA.UserForms.Add(TempForm.Name).Show
'
'   Delete the form
    ThisWorkbook.VBProject.VBComponents.Remove TempForm
End Sub
```

On the Web

This example, named create userform on the fly.xlsm, is available on the book's website.

The MakeForm procedure creates and displays the simple UserForm shown in Figure 26-9.

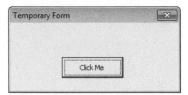

Figure 26-9: This UserForm and its underlying code were generated on the fly.

Note

The workbook that contains the MakeForm procedure doesn't need a reference to VBA Extensibility Library because it declares TempForm as a generic Object (not specifically as a VBComponent object). Moreover, it doesn't use any built-in constants.

Note that one of the first instructions hides the VBE window by setting its Visible property to False. This eliminates the on-screen flashing that might occur while the form and code are being generated.

A useful (but not simple) dynamic UserForm example

The example in this section is both instructive and useful. It consists of a function named GetOption that displays a UserForm. Within this UserForm are a number of OptionButtons whose captions are specified as arguments to the function. The function returns a value that corresponds to the OptionButton selected by the user.

On the Web

The example in this section is available on the book's website in the getoption function. xlsm file.

The GetOption function procedure follows.

```
Function GetOption(OpArray, Default, Title)
    Dim TempForm As Object
    Dim NewOptionButton As Msforms.OptionButton
    Dim NewCommandButton1 As Msforms.CommandButton
    Dim NewCommandButton2 As Msforms.CommandButton
    Dim i As Integer, TopPos As Integer
    Dim MaxWidth As Long
    Dim Code As String

'   Hide VBE window to prevent screen flashing
    Application.VBE.MainWindow.Visible = False

'   Create the UserForm
    Set TempForm = _
      ThisWorkbook.VBProject.VBComponents.Add(3)
    TempForm.Properties("Width") = 800

'   Add the OptionButtons
    TopPos = 4
    MaxWidth = 0 'Stores width of widest OptionButton
    For i = LBound(OpArray) To UBound(OpArray)
        Set NewOptionButton = TempForm.Designer.Controls. _
          Add("Forms.OptionButton.1")
        With NewOptionButton
            .Width = 800
            .Caption = OpArray(i)
            .Height = 15
            .Accelerator = Left(.Caption, 1)
            .Left = 8
            .Top = TopPos
            .Tag = i
            .AutoSize = True
            If Default = i Then .Value = True
            If .Width > MaxWidth Then MaxWidth = .Width
        End With
        TopPos = TopPos + 15
    Next i

'   Add the Cancel button
    Set NewCommandButton1 = TempForm.Designer.Controls. _
      Add("Forms.CommandButton.1")
    With NewCommandButton1
        .Caption = "Cancel"
        .Cancel = True
        .Height = 18
```

continued

```
        .Width = 44
        .Left = MaxWidth + 12
        .Top = 6
    End With

'   Add the OK button
    Set NewCommandButton2 = TempForm.Designer.Controls. _
        Add("Forms.CommandButton.1")
    With NewCommandButton2
        .Caption = "OK"
        .Default = True
        .Height = 18
        .Width = 44
        .Left = MaxWidth + 12
        .Top = 28
    End With

'   Add event-hander subs for the CommandButtons
    Code = ""
    Code = Code & "Sub CommandButton1_Click()" & vbCrLf
    Code = Code & "  GETOPTION_RET_VAL=False" & vbCrLf
    Code = Code & "  Unload Me" & vbCrLf
    Code = Code & "End Sub" & vbCrLf
    Code = Code & "Sub CommandButton2_Click()" & vbCrLf
    Code = Code & "  Dim ctl" & vbCrLf
    Code = Code & "  GETOPTION_RET_VAL = False" & vbCrLf
    Code = Code & "  For Each ctl In Me.Controls" & vbCrLf
    Code = Code & "    If TypeName(ctl) = ""OptionButton""" _
        & " Then" & vbCrLf
    Code = Code & "      If ctl Then GETOPTION_RET_VAL = " _
        & "ctl.Tag" & vbCrLf
    Code = Code & "    End If" & vbCrLf
    Code = Code & "  Next ctl" & vbCrLf
    Code = Code & "  Unload Me" & vbCrLf
    Code = Code & "End Sub"

    With TempForm.CodeModule
        .InsertLines .CountOfLines + 1, Code
    End With

'   Adjust the form
    With TempForm
        .Properties("Caption") = Title
        .Properties("Width") = NewCommandButton1.Left + _
            NewCommandButton1.Width + 10
        If .Properties("Width") < 160 Then
            .Properties("Width") = 160
            NewCommandButton1.Left = 106
            NewCommandButton2.Left = 106
```

```
        End If
        .Properties("Height") = TopPos + 24
    End With

'   Show the form
    VBA.UserForms.Add(TempForm.Name).Show

'   Delete the form
    ThisWorkbook.VBProject.VBComponents.Remove VBComponent:=TempForm

'   Pass the selected option back to the calling procedure
    GetOption = GETOPTION_RET_VAL
End Function
```

The GetOption function is remarkably fast, considering all that's going on behind the scenes. On my system, the form appears instantaneously, just like a preconstructed UserForm. The UserForm is deleted after it has served its purpose.

Using the GetOption function

The GetOption function takes three arguments:

➤ OpArray: A string array that holds the items to be displayed in the form as OptionButtons.

➤ Default: An integer that specifies the default OptionButton selected when the UserForm is displayed. If 0, no OptionButton is selected.

➤ Title: The text to be displayed in the title bar of the UserForm.

How GetOption works

The GetOption function performs the following operations:

1. Hides the VBE window to prevent any flashing that could occur when the UserForm is created or the code is added.

2. Creates a UserForm and assigns it to an object variable named TempForm.

3. Adds the OptionButton controls by using the array passed to the function via the OpArray argument.

   It uses the Tag property of the control to store the index number. The Tag setting of the chosen option is the value that's eventually returned by the function.

4. Adds two CommandButton controls: the OK button and the Cancel button.

5. Creates an event-handler procedure for each CommandButton.

6. Does some final cleanup work.

   It adjusts the position of the CommandButtons as well as the overall size of the UserForm.

7. Displays the UserForm.

   When the user clicks OK, the CommandButton1_Click procedure is executed. This procedure determines which OptionButton is selected and also assigns a number to the GETOPTION_RET_VAL variable (a Public variable).

8. Deletes the UserForm after it's dismissed.

9. Returns the value of GETOPTION_RET_VAL as the function's result.

Note **A significant advantage of creating the UserForm on the fly is that the function is self-contained in a single module and doesn't even require a reference to VBA Extensibility Library. Therefore, you can export this module (which is named modOptionsForm) and then import it into any workbook, thus giving you access to the GetOption function.**

The following procedure demonstrates how to use the GetOption function. In this case, the UserForm presents five options (contained in the Ops array).

```
Sub TestGetOption()
    Dim Ops(1 To 5)
    Dim UserOption
    Ops(1) = "North"
    Ops(2) = "South"
    Ops(3) = "West"
    Ops(4) = "East"
    Ops(5) = "All Regions"
    UserOption = GetOption(Ops, 5, "Select a region")
    MsgBox Ops(UserOption)
End Sub
```

The UserOption variable contains the index number of the option selected by the user. If the user clicks Cancel (or presses Escape), the UserOption variable is set to False.

Note that the Accelerator property is set to the first character of each option's caption, so the user can use an Alt+letter combination to make a choice. I made no attempt to avoid duplicate Accelerator keys, so the user may need to press the key combination multiple times to make a selection. However, it's certainly possible to write code that attempts to eliminate duplicate Accelerator keys.

Figure 26-10 shows the UserForm that this function generates.

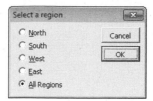

Figure 26-10: The GetOption function generated this UserForm.

Note

The UserForm adjusts its size to accommodate the number of elements in the array passed to it. Theoretically, the UserOption function can accept an array of any size. Practically speaking, however, you'll want to limit the number of options to keep the UserForm at a reasonable size. Figure 26-11 shows how the form looks when the options contain more text.

Figure 26-11: The UserForm adjusts its height and width to accommodate the number of options and the length of the text.

GetOption event-handler code

Following are the event-handler procedures for the two CommandButtons. This code is generated in the GetOption function and placed in the code module for the temporary UserForm.

```
Sub CommandButton1_Click()
  GETOPTION_RET_VAL = False
  Unload Me
End Sub

Sub CommandButton2_Click()
  Dim ctl
  GETOPTION_RET_VAL = False
```

continued

```
   For Each ctl In Me.Controls
     If TypeName(ctl) = "OptionButton" Then
       If ctl Then GETOPTION_RET_VAL = ctl.Tag
     End If
   Next ctl
   Unload Me
End Sub
```

Note

Because the UserForm is deleted after it's used, you can't see what it looks like in VBE. If you'd like to view the UserForm, convert the following instruction to a comment by typing an apostrophe (') in front of it:

```
ThisWorkbook.VBProject.VBComponents.Remove _
  VBComponent:=TempForm
```

Understanding Class Modules

In This Chapter

- Introducing class modules

- Exploring some typical uses for class modules

- Seeing examples that demonstrate some key concepts related to class modules

What Is a Class Module?

For many VBA programmers, the concept of a class module is a mystery. This feature can be confusing, but the examples in this chapter may help to make it less mysterious.

A *class module* is a special type of VBA module that you can insert in a VBA project. Basically, a class module enables the programmer (you) to create a new object class. As you should know by now, programming Excel really boils down to manipulating objects. A class module allows you to create new objects, along with corresponding properties, methods, and events.

Cross-Ref

Examples in previous chapters in this book use class modules. See Chapters 13, 16, and 17.

At this point, you might be asking, "Do I really need to create new objects?" The answer is no. You don't *need* to, but you might want to after you understand some of the benefits of doing so. In many cases, a class module simply serves as a substitute for functions or procedures, but it could be a more convenient and manageable alternative. In other cases, however, you'll find that a class module is the only way to accomplish a particular task.

Following is a list of some typical uses for class modules:

➤ **To handle events associated with embedded charts.** (see Chapter 16 for an example.)

➤ **To monitor application-level events,** such as activating any worksheet. (See Chapter 17 for examples.)

➤ **To encapsulate a Windows Application Programming Interface (API) function to make it easier to use in your code.** For example, you can create a class that makes it easy to detect or set the state of the Num Lock or Caps Lock key. Or you can create a class that simplifies access to the Windows Registry.

➤ **To enable multiple objects in a UserForm to execute a single procedure.** Normally, each object has its own event handler. The example in Chapter 13 demonstrates how to use a class module so that multiple CommandButtons have a single Click event-handler procedure.

➤ **To create reusable components that can be imported into other projects.** After you create a general-purpose class module, you can import it into other projects to reduce your development time.

Example: Creating a NumLock Class

In this section, I provide step-by-step instructions for creating a useful, albeit simple, class module. This class module creates a NumLock class that has one property (Value) and one method (Toggle).

Detecting or changing the state of the Num Lock key requires several Windows API functions and is fairly complicated. The purpose of this class module is to simplify things. All the API declarations and code are in a class module (not in a normal VBA module). The benefits? Your code will be much easier to work with, and you can reuse this class module in your other projects.

After the class is created, your VBA code can determine the current state of the Num Lock key by using an instruction such as the following, which displays the Value property:

```
MsgBox NumLock.Value
```

Or your code can change the state of the Num Lock key by changing the Value property. The following instruction, for example, turns on the Num Lock key:

```
NumLock.Value = True
```

In addition, your code can toggle the Num Lock key by using the Toggle method:

```
NumLock.Toggle
```

It's important to understand that a class module contains the code that *defines* the object, including its properties and methods. You can then create an instance of this object in your VBA general code modules and manipulate its properties and methods.

To better understand the process of creating a class module, you might want to follow the instructions in the next sections. Start with an empty workbook.

Inserting a class module

Activate Visual Basic Editor (VBE) and choose Insert➜Class Module. This step adds an empty class module named Class1. If the Properties window isn't displayed, press F4 to display it. Then change the name of the class module to NumLockClass (see Figure 27-1).

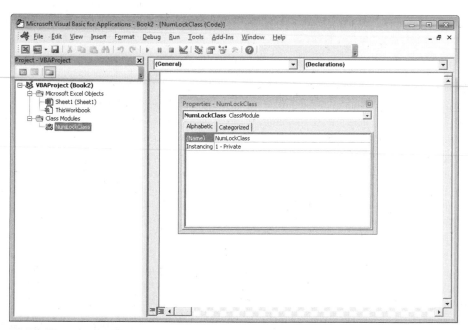

Figure 27-1: An empty class module named NumLockClass.

Adding VBA code to the class module

In the next step, you create the code for the Value property. to detect or change the state of the Num Lock key, the class module needs the Windows API declarations that detect and set the Num Lock key. That code follows.

Note

The VBA code for this example was adapted from an example at the Microsoft website. The code shown here works only for Excel 2010 and later. The version on this book's website is compatible with previous versions of Excel.

```
' Type declaration
Private Type OSVERSIONINFO
    dwOSVersionInfoSize As Long
    dwMajorVersion As Long
    dwMinorVersion As Long
    dwBuildNumber As Long
    dwPlatformId As Long
    szCSDVersion As String * 128
End Type

' API declarations
Private Declare PtrSafe Function GetVersionEx Lib "Kernel32" _
    Alias "GetVersionExA" _
    (lpVersionInformation As OSVERSIONINFO) As Long

Private Declare PtrSafe Sub keybd_event Lib "user32" _
    (ByVal bVk As Byte, _
    ByVal bScan As Byte, _
    ByVal dwflags As Long, ByVal dwExtraInfo As Long)

Private Declare PtrSafe Function GetKeyboardState Lib "user32" _
    (pbKeyState As Byte) As Long

Private Declare PtrSafe Function SetKeyboardState Lib "user32" _
    (lppbKeyState As Byte) As Long

'Constant declarations
Const VK_NUMLOCK = &H90
Const VK_SCROLL = &H91
Const VK_CAPITAL = &H14
Const KEYEVENTF_EXTENDEDKEY = &H1
Const KEYEVENTF_KEYUP = &H2
```

Next, you need a procedure that retrieves the current state of the Num Lock key. I called this the Value property of the object, but you can use any name for the property. To retrieve the state, insert the following Property Get procedure:

```
Property Get Value() As Boolean
'   Get the current state
    Dim keys(0 To 255) As Byte
    GetKeyboardState keys(0)
    Value = keys(VK_NUMLOCK)
End Property
```

Cross-Ref
The details of Property procedures are described later in this chapter, in the "Programming properties of objects" section.

This procedure, which uses the GetKeyboardState Windows API function to determine the current state of the Num Lock key, is called whenever VBA code reads the Value property of the object. For example, after the object is created, a VBA statement such as this executes the Property Get procedure:

```
MsgBox NumLock.Value
```

You now need a procedure that sets the Num Lock key to a particular state: either on or off. You can do this with the following Property Let procedure:

```
Property Let Value(boolVal As Boolean)
    Dim o As OSVERSIONINFO
    Dim keys(0 To 255) As Byte
    o.dwOSVersionInfoSize = Len(o)
    GetVersionEx o
    GetKeyboardState keys(0)
'   Is it already in that state?
    If boolVal = True And keys(VK_NUMLOCK) = 1 Then Exit Property
    If boolVal = False And keys(VK_NUMLOCK) = 0 Then Exit Property
'   Toggle it
    'Simulate Key Press
    keybd_event VK_NUMLOCK, &H45, KEYEVENTF_EXTENDEDKEY Or 0, 0
    'Simulate Key Release
    keybd_event VK_NUMLOCK, &H45, KEYEVENTF_EXTENDEDKEY Or _
      KEYEVENTF_KEYUP, 0
End Property
```

The Property Let procedure accepts one argument, which is either True or False. A VBA statement such as the following sets the Value property of the NumLock object to True by executing the Property Let procedure:

```
NumLock.Value = True
```

Finally, you need a procedure to toggle the NumLock state. I called this procedure the Toggle method.

```
Sub Toggle()
'    Toggles the state
    Dim o As OSVERSIONINFO
    o.dwOSVersionInfoSize = Len(o)
    GetVersionEx o
    Dim keys(0 To 255) As Byte
    GetKeyboardState keys(0)
    'Simulate Key Press
    keybd_event VK_NUMLOCK, &H45, KEYEVENTF_EXTENDEDKEY Or 0, 0
    'Simulate Key Release
    keybd_event VK_NUMLOCK, &H45, KEYEVENTF_EXTENDEDKEY Or _
      KEYEVENTF_KEYUP, 0
End Sub
```

Note that Toggle is a standard Sub procedure (not a Property Let or Property Get procedure). A VBA statement such as the following one toggles the state of the NumLock object by executing the Toggle procedure:

```
NumLock.Toggle
```

Using the NumLockClass class

Before you can use the NumLockClass class module, you must create an instance of the object. The following statement, which resides in a regular VBA module (not the class module), does just that:

```
Dim NumLock As New NumLockClass
```

Note that the object type is NumLockClass (that is, the name of the class module). The object variable can have any name, but NumLock certainly seems like a logical name for this.

The following procedure sets the Value property of the NumLock object to True, which turns on the Num Lock key:

```
Sub NumLockOn()
    Dim NumLock As New NumLockClass
    NumLock.Value = True
End Sub
```

The next procedure displays a message box that indicates the current state of the Num Lock key (True is on; False is off):

```
Sub GetNumLockState()
    Dim NumLock As New NumLockClass
    MsgBox NumLock.Value
End Sub
```

The following procedure toggles the Num Lock key:

```
Sub ToggleNumLock()
    Dim NumLock As New NumLockClass
    NumLock.Toggle
End Sub
```

Note that you can also toggle the Num Lock key without using the Toggle method:

```
Sub ToggleNumLock2()
    Dim NumLock As New NumLockClass
    NumLock.Value = Not NumLock.Value
End Sub
```

Using the NumLock class is much simpler than dealing directly with the API functions. After you create a class module, you can reuse it in any other project simply by importing the class module.

On the Web

The completed class module for this example is available on the book's website. The workbook, named keyboard classes.xlsm, also contains class modules to detect and set the state of the Caps Lock key and the Scroll Lock key.

More about Class Modules

The example in the preceding section demonstrates how to create a new object class with a single read/write property named Value and a single method named Toggle. An object class can contain any number of properties, methods, and events.

The name that you use for the class module in which you define the object class is also the name of the object class. By default, class modules are named Class1, Class2, and so on. Usually, you'll want to provide a more meaningful name for your object class.

Programming properties of objects

Most objects have at least one property, and you can give them as many as you need. After a property is defined and the object is created, you can use it in your code using the standard dot syntax:

```
object.property
```

The VBE Auto List Members option works with objects defined in a class module, which makes it easier to select properties or methods when writing code.

Properties for the object that you define can be read-only, write-only, or read/write. You define a read-only property with a single procedure — using the Property Get keyword. Here's an example of a Property Get procedure:

```
Property Get FileNameOnly() As String
    Dim Sep As String, LastSep As Long
    Sep = Application.PathSeparator
    LastSep = InStrRev(FullName, Sep)
    FileNameOnly = Right(FullName, Len(FullName) - LastSep)
End Property
```

You may have noticed that a Property Get procedure works like a Function procedure. The code performs calculations and then returns a property value that corresponds to the procedure's name. In this example, the procedure's name is FileNameOnly. The property value returned is the filename part of a path string (contained in a Public variable named FullName). For example, if FullName is c:\data\myfile.txt, the procedure returns a property value of myfile.txt. The FileNameOnly procedure is called when VBA code references the object and property.

For read/write properties, you create two procedures: a Property Get procedure (which reads a property value) and a Property Let procedure (which writes a property value). The value being assigned to the property is treated as the final argument (or the only argument) of a Property Get procedure.

Two example procedures follow:

```
Dim XLFile As Boolean

Property Get SaveAsExcelFile() As Boolean
    SaveAsExcelFile = XLFile
End Property

Property Let SaveAsExcelFile(boolVal As Boolean)
    XLFile = boolVal
End Property
```

Note   **Use Property Set in place of Property Let when the property is an object data type.**

A Public variable in a class module can also be used as a property of the object. In the preceding example, the Property Get and Property Let procedures could be eliminated and replaced with this module-level declaration:

```
Public SaveAsExcelFile As Boolean
```

In the unlikely event that you need to create a write-only property, you create a single Property Let procedure with no corresponding Property Get procedure.

The previous examples use a Boolean module-level variable named XLFile. The Property Get procedure simply returns the value of this variable as the property value. If the object were named FileSys, for example, the following statement would display the current value of the SaveAsExcelFile property:

```
MsgBox FileSys.SaveAsExcelFile
```

The Property Let statement, on the other hand, accepts an argument and uses the argument to change the value of a property. For example, you could write a statement such as the following to set the SaveAsExcelFile property to True:

```
FileSys.SaveAsExcelFile = True
```

In this case, the value True is passed to the Property Let statement, thus changing the property's value.

You'll need to create a variable that represents the value for each property that you define within your class module.

Note

Normal procedure-naming rules apply to property procedures, and you'll find that VBA won't let you use some names if they are reserved words. If you get a syntax error when creating a property procedure, try changing the name of the procedure.

Programming methods for objects

A method for an object class is programmed by using a standard Sub or Function procedure placed in the class module. An object might or might not use methods. Your code executes a method by using standard notation:

```
object.method
```

Like any other VBA method, a method that you write for an object class will perform some type of action. The following procedure is an example of a method that saves a workbook in one of two file formats, depending on the value of the XLFile variable. As you can see, nothing about this procedure is special.

```
Sub SaveFile()
    If XLFile Then
        ActiveWorkbook.SaveAs FileName:=FName, _
          FileFormat:=xlWorkbookNormal
    Else
        ActiveWorkbook.SaveAs FileName:=FName, _
          FileFormat:=xlCSV
    End If
End Sub
```

The CSVFileClass example in the next section should clarify the concepts of properties and methods for object classes defined in a class module.

Class module events

Every class module has two events: Initialize and Terminate. The Initialize event occurs when a new instance of the object is created; the Terminate event occurs when the object is destroyed. You might want to use the Initialize event to set default property values.

The frameworks for these event-handler procedures are as follows:

```
Private Sub Class_Initialize()
'    Initialization code goes here
End Sub

Private Sub Class_Terminate()
'    Termination code goes here
End Sub
```

An object is *destroyed* (and the memory it uses is freed) when the procedure or module in which it is declared finishes executing. You can destroy an object at any time by setting it to Nothing. The following statement, for example, destroys the object named MyObject:

```
Set MyObject = Nothing
```

Example: A CSV File Class

The example presented in this section defines an object class called CSVFileClass. This class has two properties and two methods:

➤ **Properties:**

- ExportRange: (Read/write) A worksheet range to be exported as a CSV file

- ImportRange: (Read/write) The range into which a CSV file will be imported

➤ **Methods:**

- Import: Imports the CSV file represented by the CSVFileName argument into the range represented by the ImportRange property

- Export: Exports the range represented by the ExportRange property to a CSV file represented by the CSVFileName argument

On the Web

The example in this section is available on the book's website in the csv class.xlsm file.

Class module–level variables for the CSVFileClass

A class module must maintain its own private variables that mirror the property settings for the class. The CSVFileClass class module uses two variables to keep track of the two property settings. These variables are declared at the top of the class module:

```
Private RangeToExport As Range
Private ImportToCell As Range
```

RangeToExport is a Range object that represents the range to be exported. ImportToCell is a Range object that represents the upper-left cell of the range into which the file will be imported. These variables are assigned values by the Property Get and Property Let procedures listed in the next section.

Property procedures for the CSVFileClass

The property procedures for the CSVFileClass class module follow. The Property Get procedures return the value of a variable, and the Property Let procedures set the value of a variable.

```
Property Get ExportRange() As Range
    Set ExportRange = RangeToExport
End Property

Property Let ExportRange(rng As Range)
    Set RangeToExport = rng
End Property

Property Get ImportRange() As Range
    Set ImportRange = ImportToCell
End Property

Property Let ImportRange(rng As Range)
    Set ImportToCell = rng
End Property
```

Method procedures for the CSVFileClass

The CSVFileClass class module contains two procedures that represent the two methods. These are listed and discussed in the sections that follow.

The Export procedure

The Export procedure is called when the Export method is executed. It takes one argument: the full name of the file receiving the exported range. The procedure provides some basic error handling. For example, it ensures that the ExportRange property has been set by checking the RangeToExport variable. The procedure sets up an error handler to trap other errors.

```vba
Sub Export(CSVFileName)
'    Exports a range to CSV file
    If RangeToExport Is Nothing Then
        MsgBox "ExportRange not specified"
        Exit Sub
    End If

    On Error GoTo ErrHandle
    Application.ScreenUpdating = False
    Set ExpBook = Workbooks.Add(xlWorksheet)
    RangeToExport.Copy
    Application.DisplayAlerts = False

    With ExpBook
        .Sheets(1).Paste
        .SaveAs FileName:=CSVFileName, FileFormat:=xlCSV
        .Close SaveChanges:=False
    End With
    Application.CutCopyMode = False
    Application.ScreenUpdating = True
    Application.DisplayAlerts = True
    Exit Sub
ErrHandle:
    ExpBook.Close SaveChanges:=False
    Application.CutCopyMode = False
    Application.ScreenUpdating = True
    Application.DisplayAlerts = True
    MsgBox "Error " & Err & vbCrLf & vbCrLf & Error(Err), _
        vbCritical, "Export Method Error"
End Sub
```

The Export procedure works by copying the range specified by the RangeToExport variable to a new temporary workbook, saving the workbook as a CSV text file, and closing the file. Because screen updating is turned off, the user doesn't see this happening. If an error occurs — for example, an invalid filename is specified — the procedure jumps to the ErrHandle section and displays a message box that contains the error number and description.

The Import procedure

The Import procedure imports a CSV file specified by the CSVFileName argument and copies its contents to a range specified by the ImportToCell variable, which maintains the ImportRange property. The file is then closed. Again, screen updating is turned off, so the user doesn't see the file being opened. Like the Export procedure, the Import procedure incorporates some basic error handling.

```
Sub Import(CSVFileName)
'   Imports a CSV file to a range
    If ImportToCell Is Nothing Then
        MsgBox "ImportRange not specified"
        Exit Sub
    End If

    If CSVFileName = "" Then
        MsgBox "Import FileName not specified"
        Exit Sub
    End If

    On Error GoTo ErrHandle
    Application.ScreenUpdating = False
    Application.DisplayAlerts = False
    Workbooks.Open CSVFileName
    Set CSVFile = ActiveWorkbook
    ActiveSheet.UsedRange.Copy Destination:=ImportToCell
    CSVFile.Close SaveChanges:=False
    Application.ScreenUpdating = True
    Application.DisplayAlerts = True
    Exit Sub
ErrHandle:
    CSVFile.Close SaveChanges:=False
    Application.ScreenUpdating = True
    Application.DisplayAlerts = True
    MsgBox "Error " & Err & vbCrLf & vbCrLf & Error(Err), _
        vbCritical, "Import Method Error"
End Sub
```

Using the CSVFileClass object

To create an instance of a CSVFileClass object in your code, start by declaring a variable as type CSVFileClass in a standard VBA module. Here's an example:

```
Dim CSVFile As New CSVFileClass
```

You might prefer to declare the object variable first and then create the object when needed. This requires a Dim statement and a Set statement:

```
Dim CSVFile As CSVFileClass
' other code may go here
Set CSVFile = New CSVFileClass
```

The advantage of using both a Dim statement and a Set statement is that the object isn't actually created until the Set statement is executed. You might want to use this technique to save memory by not creating an object if it's not needed. For example, your code might contain logic that determines whether the object is actually created. In addition, using the Set command enables you to create multiple instances of an object.

After creating an instance of the object, you can write other instructions to access the properties and methods defined in the class module.

As you can see in Figure 27-2, the VBE Auto List Members feature works just like any other object. After you type the variable name and a dot, you see a list of properties and methods for the object.

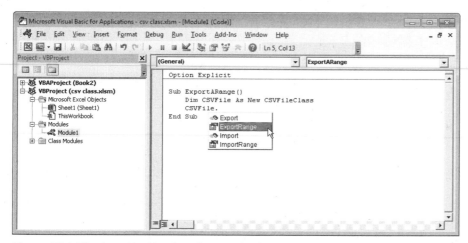

Figure 27-2: The Auto List Members feature displays the available properties and methods.

The following procedure demonstrates how to save the current range selection to a CSV file named temp.csv, which is stored in the same directory as the current workbook:

```
Sub ExportARange()
    Dim CSVFile As New CSVFileClass
    With CSVFile
        .ExportRange = ActiveWindow.RangeSelection
        .Export CSVFileName:=ThisWorkbook.Path & "\temp.csv"
    End With
End Sub
```

Using the With-End With structure isn't mandatory. For example, the procedure could be written as follows:

```
Sub ExportARange()
    Dim CSVFile As New CSVFileClass
    CSVFile.ExportRange = ActiveWindow.RangeSelection
    CSVFile.Export CSVFileName:=ThisWorkbook.Path & "\temp.csv"
End Sub
```

The following procedure demonstrates how to import a CSV file, beginning at the active cell:

```
Sub ImportAFile()
    Dim CSVFile As New CSVFileClass
    With CSVFile
    On Error Resume Next
        .ImportRange = ActiveCell
        .Import CSVFileName:=ThisWorkbook.Path & "\temp.csv"
    End With
    If Err <> 0 Then _
      MsgBox "Cannot import " & ThisWorkbook.Path & "\temp.csv"
End Sub
```

Your code can work with more than one instance of an object. The following code, for example, creates an array of three CSVFileClass objects:

```
Sub Export3Files()
    Dim CSVFile(1 To 3) As New CSVFileClass
    CSVFile(1).ExportRange = Range("A1:A20")
    CSVFile(2).ExportRange = Range("B1:B20")
    CSVFile(3).ExportRange = Range("C1:C20")

    For i = 1 To 3
        CSVFile(i).Export CSVFileName:="File" & i & ".csv"
    Next i
End Sub
```

Working with Colors

Specifying Colors

Dealing with color in Excel can be complicated. And often, recording a macro while you change the color of a cell or an object only adds to the confusion.

One of the most significant changes introduced in Excel 2007 was the abandonment of the old 56-color workbook palette. Back in the pre–Excel 2007 days, a workbook stored a palette of 56 colors. These colors were the only ones available for cell backgrounds, cell text, and charts. You could modify those colors, but you couldn't exceed the 56-color limit for a workbook.

The situation changed in Excel 2007, which provided access to a virtually unlimited number of colors in a workbook. (The limit is 16,777,216 colors, which I think qualifies as virtually unlimited.)

In VBA, you can specify a color as a decimal color value between 0 and 16,777,215. For example, the VBA statement that follows changes the background color of the active cell to a dark maroon:

```
ActiveCell.Interior.Color = 5911168
```

In addition, VBA has predefined constants for some common colors. For example, vbRed has a value of 255 (the decimal value for pure red), and vbGreen has a value of 65,280.

No one can keep track of nearly 17 million colors, and the predefined constants are limited. A better way to change a color is to specify the color in terms of its red, green, and blue components — the RGB color system.

The RGB color system

The RGB color system combines various levels of three colors: red, green, and blue. Each color value can range from 0 to 255. Therefore, the total number of possible colors is 256 x 256 x 256 = 16,777,216. When all three color components are 0, the color is pure black. When all three components are 255, the color is pure white. When all three are 128 (the halfway point), the color is middle gray. The remaining 16,777,213 possible combinations of these three values represent other colors.

To specify a color using the RGB system in VBA, use the RGB function. This function accepts three arguments that represent the red, blue, and green components of a color. The function returns a decimal color value.

The statement that follows uses the RGB function to assign a color that's the same as the one assigned in the preceding section (that dark maroon, 5911168):

```
ActiveCell.Interior.Color = RGB(128, 50, 90)
```

Table 28-1 shows the RGB values and the decimal color code of some common colors.

Table 28-1: Color Examples

Name	Red Component	Green Component	Blue Component	Color Value
Black	0	0	0	0
White	255	255	255	16777215
Red	255	0	0	255
Green	0	255	0	65280
Blue	0	0	255	16711680
Yellow	255	255	0	65535
Pink	255	0	255	16711935

Name	Red Component	Green Component	Blue Component	Color Value
Turquoise	0	255	255	16776960
Brown	153	51	0	13209
Indigo	51	51	153	10040115
80% Gray	51	51	51	3355443

The HSL color system

If you select the More Colors option when choosing a color in Excel, you see the Colors dialog box. Click the Custom tab, and you can choose from two color models to specify your color: RGB and HSL. Figure 28-1 shows the Colors dialog box with the HSL color model selected.

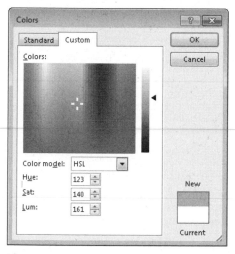

Figure 28-1: Choosing a color using the HSL color system.

In the HSL color system, colors are specified using three parameters: Hue, Saturation, and Luminance. As with RGB colors, each parameter can range from 0 to 255. Each RGB color has an equivalent HSL color, and each HSL color has an equivalent decimal color value. In other words, you can specify any of the 16,777,216 colors by using any of the three color systems: RGB, HSL, or decimal.

The Colors dialog box is the *only* area in which Excel supports the HSL color model. For example, when you specify a color using VBA, it must be a decimal color value. You can use the RGB function to return a decimal color value. However, VBA doesn't have a function that allows you to specify a color in terms of hue, saturation, and luminance.

A function that returns a color value

If you need to let the user select a color, check out the following useful function. The GetAColor function displays the Colors dialog box (refer to Figure 28-1) and returns a decimal color value (or False, if the dialog box is canceled).

```
Function GetAColor() As Variant
    Dim OldColor As Double
    OldColor = ActiveWorkbook.Colors(1)
    If Application.Dialogs(xlDialogEditColor).Show(1) = True Then
        GetAColor = ActiveWorkbook.Colors(1)
    Else
        GetAColor = False
    End If
    ActiveWorkbook.Colors(1) = OldColor
End Function
```

The function takes advantage of the old 56-color palette. It's the same dialog box that would appear if the user were replacing the first color in the palette. However, the palette doesn't get changed, and the function returns the value of the color selected.

This example is available on the book's website in the get a color function.xlsm file.

Converting colors

If you know a color's red, green, and blue component values, converting the color to a decimal color is easy. Just use the VBA RGB function. Assume three variables (r, g, and b), each of which represents a color component value between 0 and 255. To calculate the equivalent decimal color value, use a statement like this:

```
DecimalColor = RGB(r, g, b)
```

To perform this conversion in a worksheet formula, create this simple VBA wrapper function:

```
Function RGB2DECIMAL(R, G, B) As Long
'   Converts from RGB to decimal color
    RGB2DECIMAL = RGB(R, G, B)
End Function
```

The following example worksheet formula assumes that the three color values are in A1:C1:

```
=RGB2DECIMAL(A1,B1,C1)
```

Converting a decimal color to its red, green, and blue components is more complicated. Here's a function that returns a three-element array:

```
Function DECIMAL2RGB(ColorVal) As Variant
'    Converts a color value to an RGB triplet
'    Returns a 3-element variant array
     DECIMAL2RGB = Array(ColorVal \ 256 ^ 0 And 255, _
       ColorVal \ 256 ^ 1 And 255, ColorVal \ 256 ^ 2 And 255)
End Function
```

To use the DECIMAL2RGB function in a worksheet formula, the formula must be entered as a three-cell array formula. For example, assume that cell A1 contains a decimal color value. To convert that color value to its RGB components, select a three-cell horizontal range and then enter the following formula. Press Ctrl+Shift+Enter to make it an array formula and don't enter the braces.

```
{=DECIMAL2RGB(A1)}
```

If the three-cell range is vertical, you need to transpose the array, as follows:

```
{=TRANSPOSE(DECIMAL2RGB(A1))}
```

Figure 28-2 shows the DECIMAL2RGB and DECIMAL2HSL functions in use in a worksheet.

On the Web **The book's website contains a workbook with the following color conversion functions: DECIMAL2RGB, DECIMAL2HSL, HSL2RGB, RGB2DECIMAL, RGB2HSL, and HSL2DECIMAL. The file is named color conversion functions.xlsm.**

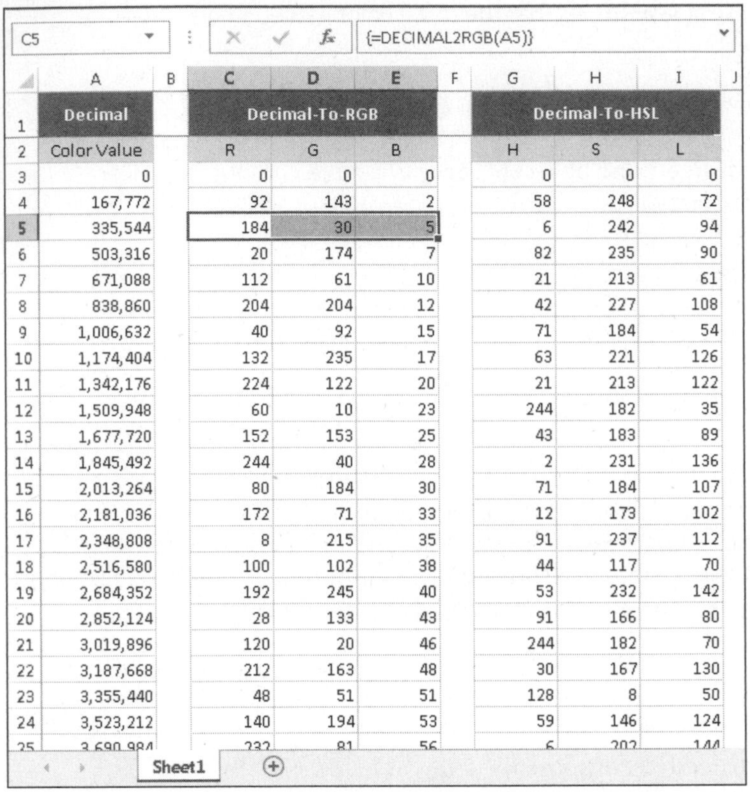

	A	B	C	D	E	F	G	H	I
1	Decimal		Decimal-To-RGB				Decimal-To-HSL		
2	Color Value		R	G	B		H	S	L
3	0		0	0	0		0	0	0
4	167,772		92	143	2		58	248	72
5	335,544		184	30	5		6	242	94
6	503,316		20	174	7		82	235	90
7	671,088		112	61	10		21	213	61
8	838,860		204	204	12		42	227	108
9	1,006,632		40	92	15		71	184	54
10	1,174,404		132	235	17		63	221	126
11	1,342,176		224	122	20		21	213	122
12	1,509,948		60	10	23		244	182	35
13	1,677,720		152	153	25		43	183	89
14	1,845,492		244	40	28		2	231	136
15	2,013,264		80	184	30		71	184	107
16	2,181,036		172	71	33		12	173	102
17	2,348,808		8	215	35		91	237	112
18	2,516,580		100	102	38		44	117	70
19	2,684,352		192	245	40		53	232	142
20	2,852,124		28	133	43		91	166	80
21	3,019,896		120	20	46		244	182	70
22	3,187,668		212	163	48		30	167	130
23	3,355,440		48	51	51		128	8	50
24	3,523,212		140	194	53		59	146	124
25	3,690,984		232	81	56		6	202	144

Figure 28-2: A worksheet that uses the DECIMAL2RGB and DECIMAL2HSL functions.

More about decimal color values

You may be curious about how the 16,777,216 decimal color values are arranged. Color 0 is black and color 16,777,216 is white, but what about all the colors in between?

It might help to think of the decimal color values as being generated by nested For-Next loops, as shown in the following code:

```
Sub GenerateColorValues()
    Dim Red As Long, Blue As Long, Green As Long
    Dim AllColors(0 To 16777215) As Long
    Dim ColorNum As Long
    ColorNum = 0
```

```
       For Blue = 0 To 255
           For Green = 0 To 255
               For Red = 0 To 255
                   AllColors(ColorNum) = RGB(Red, Blue, Green)
                   ColorNum = ColorNum + 1
               Next Red
           Next Green
       Next Blue

End Sub
```

After this procedure runs, the values in the AllColors array correspond to the decimal color values used by Excel.

Understanding Grayscale

When you create worksheets and charts that are intended to be printed, it's important to remember that not everyone has a color printer. And even if your chart is printed on a color printer, it's possible that it may be photocopied or faxed, or viewed by someone who is color-blind (a condition that affects about 8 percent of the male population).

When content is printed on a noncolor device, colors are converted to grayscale. Sometimes you'll be lucky, and your colors will display nicely when converted to grayscale. Other times, you won't be so lucky. For example, the columns in a chart may be indistinguishable when the colors are converted.

Every grayscale color has an equal component of red, green, and blue. Pure black is RGB(0, 0, 0). Pure white is RGB(255, 255, 255). Neutral gray is RGB(128, 128, 128). Using this color system produces 256 shades of gray.

To create a 256-color grayscale in a range of cells, execute the procedure that follows. It colors the background of cells in the range A1:A256, starting with black and ending with white. The result is a smooth gradient. You might want to zoom out on the worksheet to see the entire range.

```
Sub GenerateGrayScale()
    Dim r As Long
    For r = 0 To 255
        Cells(r + 1, 1).Interior.Color = RGB(r, r, r)
    Next r
End Sub
```

Figure 28-3 shows the result, after decreasing the row heights and making column A wider.

Figure 28-3: Cells displaying 256 shades of gray.

Converting colors to gray

One approach to grayscale conversion is to simply average the red, green, and blue components of a color and use that single value for the red, green, and blue components of its grayscale equivalent. That method, however, doesn't take into account the fact that different colors are perceived as varying levels of brightness. For example, green is perceived to be brighter than red, and red is perceived to be brighter than blue.

Perceptual experiments have arrived at the following recipe to convert an RGB color value to an approximate grayscale value:

➤ 29.9 percent of the red component

➤ 58.7 percent of the green component

➤ 11.4 percent of the blue component

For example, consider color value 16751001, a shade of violet that corresponds to RGB(153, 153, 255). Applying the factors listed previously, the RGB values (rounded) are

➤ **Red:** 29.9 percent $\times$ 153 = 46

➤ **Green:** 58.7 percent $\times$ 153 = 90

➤ **Blue:** 11.4 percent $\times$ 255 = 29

The sum of these values is 165. Therefore, the corresponding grayscale RGB value for color value 16751001 is RGB(165, 165, 165).

Following is a VBA function that accepts a decimal color value as its argument and returns the corresponding grayscale decimal value:

```
Function Grayscale(color) As Long
    Dim r As Long, g As Long, b As Long
    r = (color \ 256 ^ 0 And 255) * 0.299
    g = (color \ 256 ^ 1 And 255) * 0.587
    b = (color \ 256 ^ 2 And 255) * 0.114
    Grayscale = RGB(r + g + b, r + g + b, r + g + b)
End Function
```

Experimenting with Colors

Figure 28-4 shows a workbook that I created that deals with colors. If you're at all confused about how the RGB color model works, spend some time with this color demo workbook.

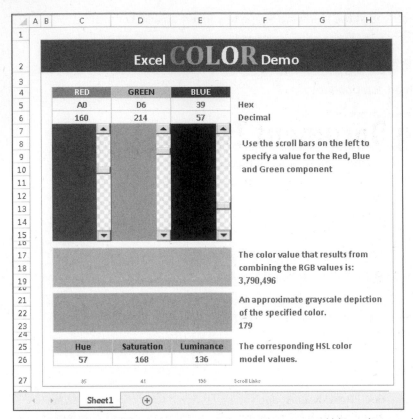

Figure 28-4: This workbook demonstrates how red, green, and blue colors combine.

On the Web

This workbook, named RGB color demo.xlsm, is available on the book's website.

This workbook contains three vertical scroll bars, each of which controls the background color of a range. Use these scroll bars to specify the red, green, and blue components for a color to values between 0 and 255. Moving the scroll bars changes several areas of the worksheet:

➤ The cells above the scroll bars display the color components in hexadecimal (00–FF) and in decimal (0–255). Hexadecimal RGB color values are often used in specifying colors for HTML documents.

➤ The ranges next to each scroll bar change intensity, corresponding to the scroll bar's position (that is, the value of the color component).

➤ A range below the scroll bars depicts the combined color, determined by the RGB values you specify.

➤ A cell displays the decimal color value.

➤ Another range depicts the color's approximate appearance when it's converted to grayscale.

➤ A range of cells shows the corresponding HSL color values.

Understanding Document Themes

A significant feature introduced in Excel 2007 was document themes. With a single mouse click, the user can change the entire look of a document. A document theme consists of three components: colors, fonts, and effects (for graphic objects). The rationale for using themes is that they may help users produce better-looking and more consistent documents. A theme applies to the entire work-book, not just the active worksheet.

About document themes

Microsoft Office 2013 ships with many document themes, and you can also download or create addi-tional themes. The Ribbon includes several style galleries (for example, the Chart Styles gallery). The styles available in these galleries vary depending on which theme is assigned to the document. If you apply a different theme to the document, the document changes to reflect the new theme's colors, fonts, and effects.

On the Web

If you haven't explored document themes, open the workbook named document theme demo.xlsx found on the book's website. This workbook contains a range that shows each theme color, two shapes, text (using the headings and body fonts), and a chart. Choose Page Layout➔Themes➔Themes Gallery to see how the worksheet changes with each theme.

Users can also mix and match theme elements. For example, you can use the colors from one theme, the fonts from another theme, and the effects from yet a different theme. In addition, the user can create a new color set or a new font set. You can save these customized themes and then apply them to other workbooks.

Note

The concept of document themes is based on the notion that users will apply little, if any, non-theme formatting to the document. If the user applies colors or fonts that aren't part of the current theme, this formatting will not be modified if a new theme is applied to the document. Therefore, it's still easy to create an ugly document with mis-matched colors and too many different fonts.

Understanding document theme colors

When a user applies a color to a cell or an object, the color is selected from a control like the one shown in Figure 28-5. The control displays the 60 theme colors (10 columns by 6 rows) plus 10 additional standard colors. Clicking the More Colors option displays the Color dialog box, in which the user can specify any of the 16,777,216 available colors.

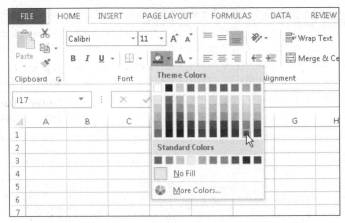

Figure 28-5: A color selection control.

Note

Excel objects (such as ranges, shapes, and chart elements) can be colored in two ways: by applying a theme color or by applying a standard color. When you use a color selection control, you apply a theme color by clicking a color in the Theme Colors section. If you choose a color from the Standard Colors section (or if you click More Colors), the color is not a theme color and will not change if you change the document theme.

The 60 theme colors are identified by pop-up tooltips. For example, the color in the second row of the sixth column is known as "Accent 2, Lighter 80%." The tooltip also displays a color name, which varies depending on the theme.

The first row in each column of colors contains the pure color. Below each pure color are six tint and shade variations. Table 28-2 shows the color descriptions for the color picker controls.

Table 28-2: Theme Color Names

Row/Column	1	2	3	4	5	6	7	8	9	10
1	Background 1	Text 1	Background 2	Text 2	Accent 1	Accent 2	Accent 3	Accent 4	Accent 5	Accent 6
2	Darker 5%	Lighter 50%	Darker 10%	Lighter 80%	Lighter 80%	Lighter 80%	Lighter 80%	Lighter 80%	Lighter 80%	Lighter 80%
3	Darker 15%	Lighter 35%	Darker 25%	Lighter 80%	Lighter 60%	Lighter 60%	Lighter 60%	Lighter 60%	Lighter 60%	Lighter 60%
4	Darker 25%	Lighter 25%	Darker 50%	Lighter 80%	Lighter 40%	Lighter 40%	Lighter 40%	Lighter 40%	Lighter 40%	Lighter 40%
5	Darker 35%	Lighter 15%	Darker 75%	Darker 25%	Darker 25%	Darker 25%	Darker 25%	Darker 25%	Darker 25%	Darker 25%
6	Darker50%	Lighter 5%	Darker 90%	Darker 50%	Darker 50%	Darker 50%	Darker 50%	Darker 50%	Darker 50%	Darker 50%

Keep in mind that these color names remain the same, even if a different document theme is applied. The document theme colors consist of the ten colors displayed in the top row (four text/background colors and six accent colors), and each of these ten colors has five tint/shade variations. If you select Page Layout➞Themes➞Colors➞Create New Theme Colors, you'll see that a theme has two additional colors: Hyperlink and Followed Hyperlink. These are the colors applied when a hyperlink is created, and they are not shown in the color selection control.

You may find it enlightening to record a macro while you change the fill color and text color of a range. Following is a macro that I recorded when a range was selected. For the fill color, I chose "Accent 2, Darker 25%," and for the text color, I chose "Text 2, Lighter 80%."

```
Sub ChangeColors()
    With Selection.Interior
        .Pattern = xlSolid
        .PatternColorIndex = xlAutomatic
        .ThemeColor = xlThemeColorAccent2
        .TintAndShade = -0.249977111117893
        .PatternTintAndShade = 0
    End With
    With Selection.Font
        .ThemeColor = xlThemeColorLight2
        .TintAndShade = 0.799981688894314
    End With
End Sub
```

You can safely ignore the three pattern-related properties (Pattern, PatternColorIndex, and PatternTintAndShade). These properties refer to the ugly, old-fashioned (but still supported) cell patterns, which you can specify in the Fill tab of the Format Cells dialog box. These statements are included to maintain any pattern that may exist in the range.

The recorded macro, after I deleted the three pattern-related properties and added comments, is

```
Sub ChangeColors()
    With Selection.Interior
        '(Accent 2, Darker 25%)
        .ThemeColor = xlThemeColorAccent2
        .TintAndShade = -0.249977111117893
    End With
    With Selection.Font
        '(Text 2, Lighter 80%)
        .ThemeColor = xlThemeColorLight2
        .TintAndShade = 0.799981688894314
    End With
End Sub
```

As you can see, each color is specified in terms of a ThemeColor property and a TintAndShade property. The ThemeColor property is easy enough to decipher. Property values are assigned using built-in constants, and these values correspond to the column number of the 10 x 6 theme color table. For example, xlThemColorAccent2 has a value of 6. But what about the TintAndShade property?

The TintAndShade property can have a value between –1 and +1. A value of –1 results in black, and a value of +1 results in white. A TintAndShade property value of 0 gives the *pure* color. In other words, as the TintAndShade value goes negative, the color gets increasingly darker until it's pure black. As the TintAndShade value goes positive, the color gets increasingly lighter until it's pure white. The TintAndShade value corresponds to the color name displayed in the color selection controls.

If the color variation is expressed as "Darker," the TintAndShade property value is negative. If the color variation is expressed as "Lighter," the TintAndShade property value is positive.

Note that the actual colors are not specified. The colors applied depend on the document theme.

Note

I don't know why the TintAndShade values have such a high level of precision in recorded macros. It's certainly not necessary. For example, a TintAndShade property value of –0.249977111117893 produces the same visual result as a TintAndShade property value of –0.25.

On the Web

For a demonstration of how the TintAndShade property changes a color, open the tintandshade demo.xlsm workbook on the book's website (see Figure 28-6). Specify a starting color, and the macro displays that color with 50 levels of the TintAndShade property values, ranging from –1 to +1. It also displays the decimal color value and the red, green, and blue components of the color (which are displayed in a chart).

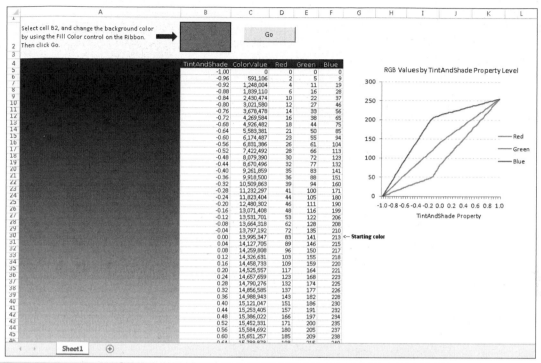

Figure 28-6: This workbook demonstrates how the TintAndShade property affects a color.

Displaying all theme colors

I wrote a macro that displays all 60 theme color variations in a range of cells. These are the 60 colors that appear in the color selection controls.

```
Sub ShowThemeColors()
  Dim r As Long, c As Long
  For r = 1 To 6
    For c = 1 To 10
        With Cells(r, c).Interior
        .ThemeColor = c
        Select Case c
          Case 1 'Text/Background 1
            Select Case r
              Case 1: .TintAndShade = 0
              Case 2: .TintAndShade = -0.05
              Case 3: .TintAndShade = -0.15
              Case 4: .TintAndShade = -0.25
              Case 5: .TintAndShade = -0.35
              Case 6: .TintAndShade = -0.5
            End Select
```

continued

```
          Case 2 'Text/Background 2
              Select Case r
                  Case 1: .TintAndShade = 0
                  Case 2: .TintAndShade = 0.5
                  Case 3: .TintAndShade = 0.35
                  Case 4: .TintAndShade = 0.25
                  Case 5: .TintAndShade = 0.15
                  Case 6: .TintAndShade = 0.05
              End Select
          Case 3 'Text/Background 3
              Select Case r
                  Case 1: .TintAndShade = 0
                  Case 2: .TintAndShade = -0.1
                  Case 3: .TintAndShade = -0.25
                  Case 4: .TintAndShade = -0.5
                  Case 5: .TintAndShade = -0.75
                  Case 6: .TintAndShade = -0.9
              End Select
          Case Else  'Text/Background 4, and Accent 1-6
              Select Case r
                  Case 1: .TintAndShade = 0
                  Case 2: .TintAndShade = 0.8
                  Case 3: .TintAndShade = 0.6
                  Case 4: .TintAndShade = 0.4
                  Case 5: .TintAndShade = -0.25
                  Case 6: .TintAndShade = -0.5
              End Select
          End Select
        Cells(r, c) = .TintAndShade
          End With
      Next c
    Next r
End Sub
```

Figure 28-7 shows the result of executing the ShowThemeColors procedure. (It looks better in color.) If you switch to a different document theme, the colors will be updated to reflect those in the new theme.

On the Web

This example, named generate theme colors.xlsm, is available on the book's website.

Earlier in this chapter, I described how to change the fill color of a range by setting the Color property of the Interior object. As I noted, using the VBA RGB function makes this task easier. The following two statements demonstrate how to change the fill color of a range (they both have the same result):

```
Range("A1:F24").Interior.Color = 5913728
Range("A1:F24").Interior.Color = RGB(128, 60, 90)
```

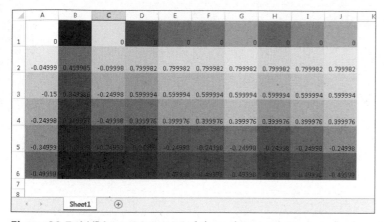

Figure 28-7: A VBA macro generated these theme colors.

It's important to understand that assigning a color in this way doesn't make it a theme color. In other words, if the user switches to a new document theme, range A1:F24 won't change colors. To change cell colors in a way that is consistent with themes, you must use the ThemeColor property and (optionally) the TintAndShade property.

Working with Shape Objects

So far, this chapter has focused exclusively on modifying the color of a range. This section provides examples of changing colors in Shape objects. In Excel, use the Insert➤Illustrations➤Shapes group to add a shape to a worksheet.

Figure 28-8 shows a shape inserted in a worksheet. This object's default name is Right Arrow 1. The number in the name varies, depending on how many shapes you have inserted. For example, if you had previously inserted two other shapes (of any style), the name would be Right Arrow 3.

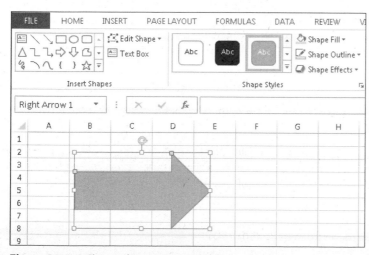

Figure 28-8: A Shape object on a worksheet.

A shape's background color

The background color of a Shape object is determined by the RGB property. So, to get the decimal color value of this shape, use a statement like this:

```
MsgBox ActiveSheet.Shapes("Right Arrow 1").Fill.ForeColor.RGB
```

This statement may be a bit confusing, so I'll break it down. The Fill property of the Shape object returns a FillFormat object. The ForeColor property of the FillFormat object returns a ColorFormat object. So the RGB property actually applies to the ColorFormat object, and this property contains the decimal color value.

Note If you're confused about the use of the ForeColor property in this example, you're not alone. Most people, myself included, would expect to use the BackColor property of the FillFormat object to change the background color of an object. As it turns out, the BackColor property is used for the second color if the object is shaded or filled with a pattern. For an unfilled Shape with no pattern, the ForeColor property controls the background color.

When working with Shape objects, you almost always want your code to perform multiple actions. Therefore, it's efficient to create an object variable. The code that follows creates an object variable named Shp:

```
Dim Shp As Shape
Set Shp = ActiveSheet.Shapes("Right Arrow 1")
MsgBox Shp.Fill.ForeColor.RGB
```

Tip An additional advantage to creating an object variable is that you can take advantage of the VBE Auto List Members feature, which displays the possible properties and objects as you type (see Figure 28-9). This feature is particularly helpful in the case of Shape objects because some actions you take with Shapes are recorded by Excel's macro recorder.

If you'll be working only with the shape's colors, you can create an object variable for the shape's ColorFormat object, like this:

```
Dim ShpCF As ColorFormat
Set ShpCF = ActiveSheet.Shapes("Right Arrow 1").Fill.ForeColor
MsgBox ShpCF.RGB
```

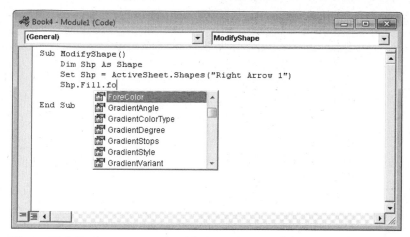

Figure 28-9: Typing a statement with the assistance of the Auto List Members feature.

The RGB property of the ColorFormat object controls the color of the shape. Following are some additional properties. If you're not familiar with document theme colors, see the section "Understanding document theme colors," earlier in this chapter.

➤ Brightness: A number between −1 and +1 that represents the luminosity of the color. A value of −1 makes the color black, and a value of +1 makes the color white.

➤ ObjectThemeColor: A number between 1 and 15 that represents the theme color.

➤ SchemeColor: A number that ranges from 0 to 80 that represents the color as an index in the current color scheme. These are colors from the old 56-color palette, and I don't see any need to use the SchemeColor property.

➤ TintAndShade: A number between −1 and +1 that represents the darkness or lightness of the theme color.

➤ Type: A number that represents the ColorFormat object type. As far as I can tell, this read-only property is always 1, which represents the RGB color system.

Changing the background color of a shape doesn't affect the shape's outline color. To modify the color of a shape's outline, access the ColorFormat object of the shape's LineFormat object. The following statements set a Shape's background color and outline to red:

```
Dim Shp As Shape
Set Shp = ActiveSheet.Shapes("Right Arrow 1")
Shp.Fill.ForeColor.RGB = RGB(255, 0, 0)
Shp.Line.ForeColor.RGB = RGB(255, 0, 0)
```

Here's an alternative way to accomplish the same effect, using object variables:

```
Dim Shp As Shape
Dim FillCF As ColorFormat
Dim LineCF As ColorFormat
Set Shp = ActiveSheet.Shapes("Right Arrow 1")
Set FillCF = Shp.Fill.ForeColor
Set LineCF = Shp.Line.ForeColor
FillCF.RGB = RGB(255, 0, 0)
LineCF.RGB = RGB(255, 0, 0)
```

Keep in mind that the preceding code does *not* produce colors that are compatible with document themes. To specify theme-compatible colors, you must use the ObjectThemeColor property and (optionally) the TintAndShade property.

Shapes and theme colors

To apply theme colors to a shape, you use the ObjectThemeColor, TintAndShade and Brightness properties of the shape's Forecolor object. I recorded a macro while setting a shape's color to "Accent 4, Lighter 40%." It produced this code:

```
ActiveSheet.Shapes.Range(Array("Right Arrow 1")).Select
With Selection.ShapeRange.Fill
    .Visible = msoTrue
    .ForeColor.ObjectThemeColor = msoThemeColorAccent4
    .ForeColor.TintAndShade = 0
    .ForeColor.Brightness = 0.400000006
    .Transparency = 0
    .Solid
End With
```

Note that the macro adjusts the Brightness property, not the TintAndShade property. I discovered that the Brightness property for a shape corresponds to the TintAndShade property for a cell. The Brightness property was introduced in Excel 2010, so using this property will generate an error in Excel 2007.

Unfortunately, Microsoft's implementation of document themes is seriously flawed. For example, cell theme colors don't always match up with shape theme colors. Cell theme colors range from 1 to 12, and theme colors for objects range from 1 to 15. The first four numbers don't match.

I wrote a macro that makes a shape the same color as cell A1, but the macro is not as simple as it should be.

```
Sub ColorShapeLikeCell()
'   Make a shape's color match cell A1's color
    Dim Cell As Interior
    Dim Shape As ColorFormat
    Set Cell = Range("A1").Interior
    Set Shape = ActiveSheet.Shapes(1).Fill.ForeColor

    If Cell.ThemeColor = 0 Then
        Shape.RGB = Cell.Color
    Else
        Select Case Cell.ThemeColor
            Case 1: Shape.ObjectThemeColor = 2
            Case 2: Shape.ObjectThemeColor = 1
            Case 3: Shape.ObjectThemeColor = 4
            Case 4: Shape.ObjectThemeColor = 3
            Case Else
                Shape.ObjectThemeColor = Cell.ThemeColor
        End Select
        Shape.Brightness = Cell.TintAndShade
    End If
End Sub
```

If the ThemeColor property is 0, the cell's color is not a theme color. In such a case, the shape gets the same color. If the cell uses a theme color, the code needs to adjust if the theme color is 1, 2, 3, or 4. Also, the shape's Brightness property is set to the cell's TintAndShade value.

And here's the complementary macro, ColorCellLikeShape. This macro makes cell A1 the same color as a shape.

```
Sub ColorCellLikeShape()
'   Make cell A1 color match a shape's color
    Dim Cell As Interior
    Dim Shape As ColorFormat
    Set Cell = Range("A1").Interior
    Set Shape = ActiveSheet.Shapes(1).Fill.ForeColor

    If Shape.ObjectThemeColor = 0 Then
        Cell.Color = Shape.RGB
    Else
        Select Case Shape.ObjectThemeColor
            Case 1: Cell.ThemeColor = 2
            Case 2: Cell.ThemeColor = 1
```

continued

```
        Case 3: Cell.ThemeColor = 4
        Case 4: Cell.ThemeColor = 3
        Case Else
            Cell.ThemeColor = Shape.ObjectThemeColor
    End Select
    Cell.TintAndShade = Shape.Brightness
    End If
End Sub
```

On the Web

A workbook that contains these two procedures is available on the book's website in the matching colors.xlsm file.

Modifying Chart Colors

This section describes how to change colors in a chart. The most important point is to identify the specific chart element that you want to modify. In other words, you need to identify the object and then set the appropriate properties.

Figure 28-10 shows a simple column chart named Chart 1. This chart has two data series, a legend, and a chart title.

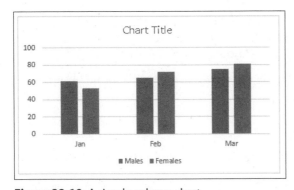

Figure 28-10: A simple column chart.

Following is a VBA statement that changes the color of the first data series to red:

```
ActiveSheet.ChartObjects("Chart 1").Chart. _
    SeriesCollection(1).Format.Fill.ForeColor.RGB = vbRed
```

To the uninitiated, this statement is probably confusing because so many objects are involved. The object hierarchy is as follows.

The active sheet contains a ChartObjects collection. One object in that collection is the ChartObject named Chart 1. The Chart property of the ChartObject object returns a Chart object. The Chart object has a SeriesCollection collection, and one Series object in the collection has an index number of 1. The Format property of the Series object returns a ChartFormat object. The Fill property of the ChartFormat object returns a FillFormat object. The ForeColor property of the FillFormat object returns a ColorFormat object. The RGB property of the ColorFormat object is set to red.

 Refer to Chapter 16 for more information about using VBA to work with charts.
Cross-Ref

Another way of writing the preceding statement, using object variables to identify the individual objects (and, perhaps, clarify the objects' relationships), is

```
Sub ChangeSeries1Color
    Dim MyChartObject As ChartObject
    Dim MyChart As Chart
    Dim MySeries As Series
    Dim MyChartFormat As ChartFormat
    Dim MyFillFormat As FillFormat
    Dim MyColorFormat As ColorFormat

'   Create the objects
    Set MyChartObject = ActiveSheet.ChartObjects("Chart 1")
    Set MyChart = MyChartObject.Chart
    Set MySeries = MyChart.SeriesCollection(1)
    Set MyChartFormat = MySeries.Format
    Set MyFillFormat = MyChartFormat.Fill
    Set MyColorFormat = MyFillFormat.ForeColor

'   Change the color
    MyColorFormat.RGB = vbRed
End Sub
```

The RGB property accepts a decimal color value, which I specified using a built-in VBA constant.

Other color-related properties of the ColorFormat object are the same as for shapes (described earlier in this chapter). The following properties are relevant to document theme colors:

➤ Brightness: A number between –1 and +1 that represents the luminosity of the color. A value of –1 makes the color black, and a value of +1 makes the color white.

➤ ObjectThemeColor: A number between 1 and 15 that represents the theme color.

➤ TintAndShade: A number between –1 and +1 that represents the darkness or lightness of the theme color.

On the Web

The examples in this section are available on the book's website in the chart colors.xlsm file.

Caution

If you use VBA to set a theme color for any element of a chart, the color will be applied but will not change if the user switches to a different document theme. When your code sets the ObjectThemeColor property value, it always reverts to zero — which means that the color is not controlled by document themes. This long-standing bug has not been corrected in Excel 2013.

You can also specify color gradients. Here's an example that applies a preset gradient to the second data series in a chart. Note that the gradient is set using the FillFormat object:

```
Sub AddPresetGradient()
    Dim MyChart As Chart
    Set MyChart = ActiveSheet.ChartObjects("Chart 1").Chart
    With MyChart.SeriesCollection(1).Format.Fill
        .PresetGradient _
            Style:=msoGradientHorizontal, _
            Variant:=1, _
            PresetGradientType:=msoGradientFire
    End With
End Sub
```

Working with other chart elements is similar. The procedure that follows changes the colors of the chart's chart area and plot area, using colors from the current document theme:

```
Sub RecolorChartAndPlotArea()
    Dim MyChart As Chart
    Set MyChart = ActiveSheet.ChartObjects("Chart 1").Chart
    With MyChart
        .ChartArea.Format.Fill.ForeColor.ObjectThemeColor = _
            msoThemeColorAccent6
        .ChartArea.Format.Fill.ForeColor.TintAndShade = 0.9
        .PlotArea.Format.Fill.ForeColor.ObjectThemeColor = _
            msoThemeColorAccent6
        .PlotArea.Format.Fill.ForeColor.TintAndShade = 0.5
    End With
End Sub
```

The final example in this section applies a random color to each chart element. Using this macro virtually guarantees an ugly chart. However, this code demonstrates how to change the color for other chart elements. The UseRandomColors procedure uses a simple function, RandomColor, to determine the color used.

```
Sub UseRandomColors()
    Dim MyChart As Chart
    Set MyChart = ActiveSheet.ChartObjects("Chart 4").Chart
    With MyChart
        .ChartArea.Format.Fill.ForeColor.RGB = RandomColor
        .PlotArea.Format.Fill.ForeColor.RGB = RandomColor
        .SeriesCollection(1).Format.Fill.ForeColor.RGB = RandomColor
        .SeriesCollection(2).Format.Fill.ForeColor.RGB = RandomColor
        .Legend.Font.Color = RandomColor
        .ChartTitle.Font.Color = RandomColor
        .Axes(xlValue).MajorGridlines.Border.Color = RandomColor
        .Axes(xlValue).TickLabels.Font.Color = RandomColor
        .Axes(xlValue).Border.Color = RandomColor
        .Axes(xlCategory).TickLabels.Font.Color = RandomColor
        .Axes(xlCategory).Border.Color = RandomColor
    End With
End Sub

Function RandomColor()
    RandomColor = Application.RandBetween(0, RGB(255, 255, 255))
End Function
```

Frequently Asked Questions about Excel Programming

In This Chapter

- Understanding Excel quirks
- Exploring FAQs about Excel programming
- Getting VBE help

Getting the Scoop on FAQs

People tend to ask the same questions about Excel programming (and related topics), so I put together a list of frequently asked questions (FAQs).

Although this FAQ list won't answer all your questions, it covers many common questions and might set you straight about a thing or two.

I organized this list of questions by assigning each question to one of these categories:

➤ General Excel questions

➤ Visual Basic Editor (VBE)

➤ Sub procedures

➤ Function procedures

➤ Objects, properties, methods, and events

➤ Security-related issues

➤ UserForms

➤ Add-ins

➤ Excel user interface modification

In some cases, my classifications are arbitrary; a question could justifiably be assigned to other categories. Moreover, questions within each category are listed in no particular order.

By the way, most of the information in this chapter is discussed in greater detail in other chapters in this book.

General Excel Questions

How do I record a macro?

Click the little square icon in the left side of the status bar, at the bottom of Excel's window.

How do I run a macro?

Choose View➜Macros➜Macros (or press Alt+F8). Or choose Developer➜Code➜Macros. The Macros dialog box will display a list of all available macros.

What do I do if I don't have a Developer tab?

Right-click anywhere in the Ribbon and choose Customize the Ribbon. In the Customize Ribbon tab of the Excel Options dialog box, place a check mark next to Developer (which is in the list labeled Main tabs).

I recorded a macro and saved my workbook. When I reopened it, the macro was gone! Where did it go?

Excel proposes that you destroy your macros when you first save a new workbook. When you save the file, read Excel's warning carefully and don't accept the default Yes button. If your workbook contains macros, you must save it as an XLSM file, not an XLSX file.

 ## What if my question isn't answered here?

If this chapter doesn't provide an answer to your question, start by checking the index. This book includes lots of information that doesn't qualify as a frequently asked question. If you still come up empty-handed, try an Internet search.

How do I hide the Ribbon so that it doesn't take up so much space?

One way is to use the Ribbon Display Options control, in the Excel title bar. This control gives you three Ribbon display options.

Or just double-click a tab to hide the Ribbon. When you click a tab, the Ribbon redisplays. Double-click a tab to revert to normal.

Yet another option is to press Ctrl+F1. This key combination toggles the visibility of the Ribbon.

By using an XLM macro, you can remove the Ribbon completely:

```
ExecuteExcel4Macro "SHOW.TOOLBAR(""Ribbon"",False)"
```

When this statement is executed, the user can't make the Ribbon visible. The only way to display the Ribbon again is to rerun the XLM code, with the last argument set to True.

Where are my old custom toolbars?

If the toolbars are set to display automatically, click the Add-Ins tab, and you'll see them in the Custom Toolbars group.

Can I make my old custom toolbars float?

No, you can't. The old custom toolbars are fixed in place in the Add-Ins➜Custom Toolbars group.

How can I hide the status bar?

You must use VBA to hide the status bar. The following statement will do the job:

```
Application.DisplayStatusBar = False
```

Is there a utility that will convert my Excel application into a stand-alone .exe file?

No.

Why doesn't Ctrl+A select all the cells in my worksheet?

The cell pointer is probably inside a table. When the active cell is in a table, you must press Ctrl+A three times to select all worksheet cells. The first keypress selects the data cells, the second keypress selects the data cells and header row, and the third keypress selects all cells in the worksheet.

If the active cell is in a block of cells, Ctrl+A selects the entire range. Pressing Ctrl+A again selects all cells in the worksheet.

Why is the Custom Views command disabled?

Your workbook probably contains a table. Convert the table to a range, and then you can use Views➜Workbook Views➜Custom Views. Nobody (except Microsoft) knows why that command is disabled when the workbook contains a table.

How can I add a drop-down list to a cell so the user can choose a value from the list?

This technique doesn't require any macros. Type the list of valid entries in a single column. You can hide this column from the user if you want. Select the cell or cells that will display the list of entries, choose Data➜Data Tools➜Data Validation, and then click the Settings tab in the Data Validation dialog box. From the Allow drop-down list, select List. In the Source box, enter a range address or a reference to the single-column list on your sheet. Make sure the In-Cell Dropdown check box is selected. If the list is short, you can simply type the items, each separated by a comma.

I use Application.Calculation to set the calculation mode to manual. However, this seems to affect all workbooks and not just the active workbook.

The Calculation property is a member of the Application object. Therefore, the calculation mode affects all workbooks. You can't set the calculation mode for only one workbook. Excel 2000 and later versions provide a new Worksheet object property called EnableCalculation. When this property is False, the worksheet will not be calculated, even if the user requests a calculation. Setting the property to True will cause the sheet to be calculated.

What happened to the ability to "speak" the cell contents?

To use those commands, you must customize your Quick Access toolbar or customize the Ribbon. Perform these tasks in the Excel Options dialog box. The speech commands are listed in the Commands Not in the Ribbon category (they all begin with the word *Speak*).

I opened a workbook, and it has only 65,546 rows. What happened?

By default, worksheet in Excel 2007 and later contain 1,048,576 rows and 16,384 columns. If you're not seeing this many rows and columns, the workbook is in compatibility mode. When Excel opens a workbook that was saved in a previous version's file format, it doesn't automatically convert it to an Excel 2007 workbook. You need to do the conversion manually: Save the workbook in the newer format (*.xlsx or *.xlsm), close it, and then reopen it. You'll then see the additional rows and columns.

How do I get my old workbook to use the new fonts?

Beginning with Excel 2007, the default font is much easier to read because it is not as cramped-looking as in previous versions. To force an old workbook to use these new fonts, press Ctrl+N to create a blank workbook. Activate your old workbook and choose the Home tab. Click the very bottom of the vertical scroll bar in the Styles gallery and choose Merge Styles. In the Merge Styles dialog box, double-click the new workbook you created with Ctrl+N, and the old styles will be replaced with the new styles. But this technique works only with cells that haven't been formatted with other font attributes. For example, bold cells retain their old fonts. For these cells, you must update the styles manually.

How do I get a print preview?

Print preview occurs automatically when you choose File➜Print. Another option is to use the Page Layout view (the icon on the right side of the status bar).

To get the old-style print preview, you need to use VBA. The following statement displays a print preview for the active sheet:

```
ActiveSheet.PrintPreview
```

When I switch to a new document theme, my worksheet no longer fits on a single page. Why?

The new theme probably uses different fonts. After applying the theme, use the Page Layout➜ Themes➜Fonts control to select your original fonts to use with the new theme. Or modify the font size for the Normal style. If page fitting is critical, you should choose the theme before you do much work on the document.

How do I get rid of the annoying dotted-line page break display in Normal view mode?

Open the Excel Options dialog box, click the Advanced tab, scroll down to the Display Options for This Worksheet section, and remove the check mark from Show Page Breaks.

Can I add that Show Page Breaks option to my Quick Access toolbar or to the Ribbon?

No. For some reason, this useful command can't be added to the Quick Access toolbar or Ribbon. You can turn off the page break display by using this VBA statement:

```
ActiveSheet.DisplayPageBreaks = False
```

I'm trying to apply a table style to a table, but it has no visible effect. What can I do?

The table cells were probably formatted manually. Select the cells and set the fill color to No Fill and the font color to Automatic. You can then apply a table style.

Can I change the color of the sheet tabs?

Right-click the sheet tab and select Tab Color. Tab colors will change if you apply a different document theme.

Can I write VBA macros that play sounds?

Yes, you can play WAV and MIDI files, but it requires Windows Application Programming Interface (API) functions. You might prefer to take advantage of the Speech object. The following statement, when executed, greets the user by name:

```
Application.Speech.Speak ("Hello" & Application.UserName)
```

When I open a workbook, Excel asks whether I want to update the links. I've searched all my formulas and can't find any links in this workbook. Is this a bug?

Probably not. Try using the Edit Links dialog box (choose Data➜Connections➜Edit Links). In the Edit Links dialog box, click Break Link. Keep in mind that links can occur in places other than formulas. If you have a chart in your workbook, click each data series in the chart and examine the SERIES formula in the formula bar. If the formula refers to another workbook, you've identified the link. To eliminate it, move the chart's data into the current workbook and re-create your chart.

If your workbook contains any Excel 5/95 dialog sheets, select each object in each dialog box and examine the formula bar. If any object contains a reference to another workbook, edit or delete that reference.

Choose Formulas➜Defined Names➜Name Manager. Scroll down the list in the Name Manager dialog box and examine the Refers To column. Delete names that refer to another workbook or that contain an erroneous reference (such as #REF!). This is the most common cause of phantom links.

Where can I find examples of VBA code?

The Internet has thousands of VBA examples. A good starting point is my website at `http://spreadsheetpage.com`. Or do a search at `http://google.com`.

Visual Basic Editor

Can I use the VBA macro recorder to record all my macros?

No. Recording is useful for simple macros only. Macros that use variables, looping, or any other type of program-flow changes can't be recorded. In addition, you can't record Function procedures. you can, however, often take advantage of the macro recorder to write some parts of your code or to discover relevant properties or methods.

I have some general macros that I would like to have available all the time. What's the best way to do this?

Consider storing those general-purpose macros in your Personal Macro Workbook, a (normally) hidden workbook that is loaded automatically by Excel. When you record a macro, you have the option of recording it to your Personal Macro Workbook. The file, Personal.xlsb, is stored in your \XLStart directory.

I can't find my Personal Macro Workbook. Where is it?

The Personal.xlsb file doesn't exist until you record a macro to it and then close Excel.

When I insert a new module, it always starts with an Option Explicit line. What does this mean?

If Option Explicit is included at the top of a module, it means that you must declare every variable before you use it in a procedure (which is a good idea). If you don't want this line to appear in new modules, activate VB Editor, choose Tools➜Options, click the Editor tab, and clear the Require Variable Declaration check box. Then you can either declare your variables or let VBA handle the data typing automatically.

Why does my VBA code appear in different colors? Can I change these colors?

VBA uses color to differentiate various types of text: comments, keywords, identifiers, statements with a syntax error, and so on. You can adjust these colors and the font used by choosing the Tools➜Options command (Editor Format tab) in VBE.

Can I delete a VBA module by using VBA code?

Yes. The following code deletes Module1 from the active workbook:

```
With ActiveWorkbook.VBProject
    .VBComponents.Remove .VBComponents("Module1")
End With
```

This might not work, though. See the next question.

I wrote a macro that adds VBA code to the VB project. When my colleague tries to run it, he gets an error message. What's wrong?

Excel has a setting that determines whether VBA code can modify a VB Project: Trust Access to Visual Basic Project. By default, this setting is turned off. To change it, choose File➜Options➜Trust Center. Click the Trust Center Settings button to display the Trust Center dialog box. Click the Macro Settings tab and place a check mark next to Trust Access to the VBA Project Object Model.

How can I write a macro to change the user's macro security setting? I want to avoid the security message when my application is opened.

The ability to change the security level using VBA would render the entire macro security system worthless. Think about it.

How does the UserInterfaceOnly option work when protecting a worksheet?

When protecting a worksheet using VBA code, you can use a statement such as

```
ActiveSheet.Protect UserInterfaceOnly:=True
```

This causes the sheet to be protected, but your macros can still make changes to the sheet. It's important to understand that this setting isn't saved with the workbook. When the workbook is reopened, you'll need to re-execute the statement to reapply the UserInterfaceOnly protection.

How can I tell whether a workbook has a macro virus?

In VB Editor, activate the project that corresponds to the workbook. Examine all the code modules (including the ThisWorkbook code module) and look for unfamiliar VBA code. Usually, virus code won't be formatted well and will contain many unusual variable names. Another option is to use a commercial virus-scanning program.

Why do I get an error message when I try to concatenate two strings with the concatenation operator (&) in VBA?

VBA is probably interpreting the ampersand as a type-declaration character. Make sure that you insert a space before and after the concatenation operator.

I can't seem to get the VBA line continuation sequence (underscore) to work.

The line continuation sequence is actually two characters: a space followed by an underscore. If you omit the space, it won't work.

I distributed an Excel application to many users. On some machines, my VBA error-handling procedures don't work. Why not?

The error-handling procedures won't work if the user has the Break on All Errors option set. This option is available in the General tab of the Options dialog box in VB Editor (choose Tools➔Options). You can't change this setting with VBA.

Another possibility is that the user has installed Microsoft's Euro Currency Tools add-in. Older versions of that add-in are known to cause problems with other add-ins.

Procedures

What's the difference between a VBA procedure and a macro?

Nothing, really. The term *macro* is a carry-over from the old days of spreadsheets. These terms are now used interchangeably.

What's a procedure?

A *procedure* is a grouping of VBA instructions that can be called by name. If these instructions are to give an explicit result (such as a value) back to the instruction that called them, they most likely belong to a Function procedure. Otherwise, they probably belong to a Sub procedure.

What is a variant data type?

Variables that aren't specifically declared are assigned the Variant type by default, and VBA automatically converts the data to the proper type when it's used. This behavior is particularly useful for retrieving values from a worksheet cell when you don't know in advance what the cell contains. Generally, it's a good idea to specifically declare your variables with the Dim, Public, or Private statement because using variants is slower and is an inefficient use of memory.

What's the difference between a variant array and an array of variants?

A *variant* is a unit of memory with a special data type that can contain any kind of data: a single value or an array of values (that is, a variant array). The following code creates a variant that contains a three-element array:

```
Dim X As Variant
X = Array(30, 40, 50)
```

A normal array can contain items of a specified data type, including nontyped variants. The following statement creates an array that consists of three variants:

```
Dim X (0 To 2) As Variant
```

Although a variant containing an array is conceptually different from an array whose elements are of type Variant, the array elements are accessed in the same way.

What's a type-definition character?

VBA lets you append a character to a variable's name to indicate the data type. For example, you can declare the MyVar variable as an integer by tacking % onto the name, as follows:

```
Dim MyVar%
```

VBA supports these type-declaration characters:

➤ Integer: %

➤ Long: &

➤ Single: !

➤ Double: #

➤ Currency: @

➤ String: $

Type-definition characters are included primarily for compatibility. Declaring variables by using words is the standard approach.

I would like to create a procedure that automatically changes the formatting of a cell based on the data that I enter. For example, if I enter a value greater than 0, the cell's background color should be red. Is this possible?

It's certainly possible, and you don't need any programming. Use Excel's Conditional Formatting feature, accessed with the Home➡Styles➡Conditional Formatting command.

The Conditional Formatting feature is useful, but can I perform other types of operations when data is entered into a cell?

You can take advantage of the Change event for a worksheet object. Whenever a cell is changed, the Change event is triggered. If the code module for the Sheet object contains a procedure named Worksheet_Change, this procedure will be executed automatically.

What other types of events can be monitored?

Lots! Search the Help system for events to get a complete listing.

I tried entering an event procedure (Sub Workbook_Open), but the procedure isn't executed when the workbook is opened. What's wrong?

You probably put the procedure in the wrong place. Workbook event procedures must be in the code module for the ThisWorkbook object. Worksheet event procedures must be in the code module for the appropriate Sheet object, as shown in the VB Editor Project window.

Another possibility is that macros are disabled. Check your settings in the Trust Center dialog box (accessible from the Excel Options dialog box).

I can write an event procedure for a particular workbook, but can I write an event procedure that will work for any workbook that's open?

Yes, but you need to use a class module. Details are in Chapter 17.

I'm familiar with creating formulas in Excel. Does VBA use the same mathematical and logical operators?

Yes. And VBA includes the following additional operators that aren't valid in worksheet formulas:

Operator	Function
\	Division with an integer result
Eqv	Returns True if both expressions are true or both are false
Imp	A bitwise logical implication on two expressions (rarely used)
Is	Compares two object variables
Like	Compares two strings by using wildcard characters
Xor	Returns True if only one expression is true

How can I execute a procedure that's in a different workbook?

Use the Run method of the Application object. The following instruction executes a procedure named Macro1 located in the Personal.xlsb workbook:

```
Run "Personal.xlsb!Macro1"
```

Another option is to add a reference to the workbook. Do this by choosing the Tools➜References command in VBE. After you've added a reference, you can then run the procedures in the referenced workbook without including the name of the workbook.

I've used VBA to create several custom functions. I like to use these functions in my worksheet formulas, but I find it inconvenient to precede the function name with the workbook name. Is there any way around this?

Yes. Convert the workbook that holds the function definitions to an XLAM add-in. When the add-in is open, you can use the functions in any other worksheet without referencing the function's filename.

In addition, if you set up a reference to the workbook that contains the custom functions, you can use the function without preceding it with the workbook name. To create a reference, choose the Tools➜References command in VB Editor.

I would like a particular workbook to be loaded every time I start Excel. I would also like a macro in this workbook to execute automatically. Am I asking too much?

Not at all. To open the workbook automatically, just store it in your \XLStart directory. To have the macro execute automatically, create a Workbook_Open macro in the code module for the workbook's ThisWorkbook object.

I have a workbook that uses a Workbook_Open procedure. Is there a way to prevent this from executing when I open the workbook?

Yes. Hold down Shift when you open the file. To prevent a Workbook_BeforeClose procedure from executing, press Shift when you close the workbook. Using the Shift key won't prevent these procedures from executing when you're opening an add-in.

Can a VBA procedure access a cell's value in a workbook that isn't open?

VBA can't do it, but Excel's old XLM language can. Fortunately, you can execute XLM from VBA. Here's a simple example that retrieves the value from cell A1 on Sheet1 in a workbook named myfile.xlsx in the c:\files directory:

```
MsgBox ExecuteExcel4Macro("'c:\files\[myfile.xlsx]Sheet1'!R1C1")
```

Note that the cell address must be in R1C1 notation.

Unless the file is very large, it may be simpler to just open the workbook, retrieve the values, and then close the workbook. If you turn off screen updating, the user won't even notice that a workbook was opened and closed.

How can I prevent the "save file" prompt from being displayed when I close a workbook from VBA?

You can use this statement:

```
ActiveWorkbook.Close SaveChanges:=False
```

Or you can set the workbook's Saved property to True by using a statement like this:

```
ActiveWorkbook.Saved = True
```

This statement, when executed, doesn't actually save the file, so any unsaved changes will be lost when the workbook is closed.

A more general solution to avoid Excel prompts is to insert the following instruction:

```
Application.DisplayAlerts = False
```

Normally, you'll want to set the DisplayAlerts property back to True after the file is closed.

How can I run a particular macro once every hour?

You need to use the OnTime method of the Application object. This enables you to specify a procedure to execute at a particular time of day. When the procedure ends, use the OnTime method again to schedule another event in one hour.

How do I prevent the display of a macro in the macro list?

To prevent the macro from being listed in the Macro dialog box (displayed by using View➜Macros➜Macro), declare the procedure by using the Private keyword:

```
Private Sub MyMacro()
```

Or you can add a dummy optional argument, declared as a specific data type:

```
Sub MyMacro (Optional FakeArg as Long)
```

Can I save a chart as a .gif file?

Yes. The following code saves the first embedded chart on Sheet1 as a .gif file named Mychart.gif:

```
Set CurrentChart = Sheets("Sheet1").ChartObjects(1).Chart
Fname = ThisWorkbook.Path & "\Mychart.gif"
CurrentChart.Export Filename:=Fname, FilterName:="GIF"
```

Are variables in a VBA procedure available to other VBA procedures?

You're referring to a variable's scope. The scope of a variable can be any of three levels: local, module, and public. Local variables have the narrowest scope and are declared within a procedure. A local variable is visible only to the procedure in which it was declared. Module-level variables are declared at the top of a module, before the first procedure. Module-level variables are visible to all procedures in the module. Public variables have the broadest scope, and they're declared by using the Public keyword.

Functions

I created a VBA function for use in worksheet formulas. However, it always returns #NAME?. What went wrong?

You probably put the function in the code module for a Sheet (for example, Sheet1) or in the ThisWorkbook module. Custom worksheet functions must reside in standard VBA modules.

I wrote a VBA function that works perfectly when I call it from another procedure but doesn't work when I use it in a worksheet formula. What's wrong?

VBA functions called from a worksheet formula have some limitations. In general, they must be strictly passive. That is, they can't change the active cell, apply formatting, open workbooks, or change the active sheet. If the function attempts to do any of these things, the formula will return an error.

When I access a custom worksheet function with the Insert Function dialog box, it reads "No help available." How can I get the Insert Function dialog box to display a description of my function?

To add a description for your custom function, activate the workbook that contains the Function procedure. Then choose View➜Macros➜Macros to display the Macro dialog box. Your function won't be listed, so you must type it in the Macro Name box. After typing the function's name, click Options to display the Macro Options dialog box. Enter the descriptive text in the Description box.

Can I also display help for the arguments for my custom function in the Insert Function dialog box?

Yes. Excel 2010 added a new argument to the MacroOptions method. You can write a macro to assign descriptions to your function arguments. See Chapter 8 for details.

My custom worksheet function appears in the User Defined category in the Insert Function dialog box. How can I make my function appear in a different function category?

You need to use VBA to do this. The following instruction assigns the function named MyFunc to Category 1 (Financial):

```
Application.MacroOptions Macro:="MyFunc", Category:=1
```

See Chapter 8 for a list of category numbers and names.

How can I create a new function category?

Specify a text string for the Category argument in the MacroOptions method. Here's an example:

```
Application.MacroOptions Macro:="MyFunc", Category:="XYZ Corp Functions"
```

I have a custom function that will be used in a worksheet formula. If the user enters inappropriate arguments, how can I make the function return a true error value (#VALUE!)?

If your function is named MyFunction, you can use the following instruction to return an error value to the cell that contains the function:

```
MyFunction = CVErr(xlErrValue)
```

In this example, xlErrValue is a predefined constant. Constants for the other error values are listed in the Help system.

I use a Windows API function in my code, and it works perfectly. I gave the workbook to a colleague, and he gets a compile error. What's the problem?

Most likely, your colleague uses a 64-bit version of Excel. API declarations must be designated as "PtrSafe" to work with 64-bit Excel. For example, the following declaration works with 32-bit Excel versions but causes a compile error with 64-bit Excel 2010 or 64-bit Excel 2013:

```
Declare Function GetWindowsDirectoryA Lib "kernel32" _
  (ByVal lpBuffer As String, ByVal nSize As Long) As Long
```

In many cases, making the declaration compatible with 64-bit Excel is as simple as adding PtrSafe after the Declare keyword. Adding the PtrSafe keyword works for most commonly used API functions, but some functions might require that you change the data types for the arguments.

The following declaration is compatible with both 32-bit and 64-bit versions of Excel 2010 and Excel 2013:

```
Declare PtrSafe Function GetWindowsDirectoryA Lib "kernel32" _
  (ByVal lpBuffer As String, ByVal nSize As Long) As Long
```

However, the code will fail in Excel 2007 (and earlier versions) because the PtrSafe keyword isn't recognized. Here's an example of how to use compiler directives to declare an API function that's compatible with 32-bit Excel (including versions prior to Excel 2010) and 64-bit Excel:

```
#If VBA7 And Win64 Then
  Declare PtrSafe Function GetWindowsDirectoryA Lib "kernel32" _
  (ByVal lpBuffer As String, ByVal nSize As Long) As Long
#Else
  Declare Function GetWindowsDirectoryA Lib "kernel32" _
  (ByVal lpBuffer As String, ByVal nSize As Long) As Long
#End If
```

The first Declare statement is used when VBA7 and Wind64 are both True — which is the case only for 64-Bit Excel. In all other versions, the second Declare statement is used.

How can I force a recalculation of formulas that use my custom worksheet function?

To force a single formula to be recalculated, select the cell, press F2, and then press Enter. To force all formulas and functions to be recalculated, press Ctrl+Alt+F9.

Can I use Excel's built-in worksheet functions in my VBA code?

In most cases, yes. You access Excel's worksheet functions via the WorksheetFunction method of the Application object. For example, you could access the SUM worksheet function with a statement such as the following:

```
Ans = Application.WorksheetFunction.Sum(Range("A1:A3"))
```

This example assigns the sum of the values in A1:A3 (on the active sheet) to the Ans variable.

Generally, if VBA includes an equivalent function, you can't use Excel's worksheet version. For example, because VBA has a function to compute square roots (Sqr), you can't use the SQRT worksheet function in your VBA code.

Can I force a line break in the text of a message box?

Use a carriage return or a linefeed character to force a new line. The following statement displays the message box text on two lines (vbNewLine is a built-in constant that represents a carriage return):

```
MsgBox "Hello" & vbNewLine & Application.UserName
```

Objects, Properties, Methods, and Events

Is there a listing of the Excel objects I can use?

Yes. The Help system has that information.

I'm overwhelmed with all the properties and methods available. How can I find out which methods and properties are available for a particular object?

You can use the Object Browser available in VBE. Press F2 to access Object Browser and then choose Excel from the Libraries/Workbooks drop-down list. The Classes list (on the left) shows all the Excel objects. When you select an object, its corresponding properties and methods appear in the Member Of list on the right.

You can also get a list of properties and methods as you type. For example, enter the following:

```
Range("A1").
```

When you type the dot, you'll see a list of all properties and methods for a Range object. If the list doesn't appear, choose Tools➔Options (in VBE), click the Editor tab, and place a check mark next to Auto List Members. Unfortunately, Auto List Members doesn't work for all objects. For example, you won't see a list of properties and methods when you type this statement:

```
ActiveSheet.Shapes(1).
```

But if you declare an object variable, Auto List Members will work. Here's an example of declaring an object variable:

```
Dim S as Shapes
```

And, of course, the Help system for VBA is extensive; it lists the properties and methods available for most objects of importance. The easiest way to access these lists is to type the object name into the Immediate window at the bottom of VBE and move the cursor anywhere in the object name. Then press F1, and you'll get the help topic appropriate for the object.

What's the story with collections? Is a collection an object?

A collection, which is an object that contains a group of related objects, is designated by a plural noun. For example, the Worksheets collection is an object that contains all the Worksheet objects in a workbook. You can think of this as an array (although a collection is not an array): Worksheets(1) refers to the first Worksheet object in the Workbook. Rather than use index numbers, you can also use the actual worksheet name, such as Worksheets("Sheet1"). The concept of a collection makes it easy to work with all related objects at once and to loop through all objects in a collection by using the For Each-Next construct.

When I refer to a worksheet in my VBA code, I get a "subscript out of range" error. I'm not using any subscripts. What gives?

This error occurs when you attempt to access an element in a collection that doesn't exist. For example, the following instruction generates the error if the active workbook doesn't contain a worksheet named MySheet:

```
Set X = ActiveWorkbook.Worksheets("MySheet")
```

How can I prevent the user from scrolling around the worksheet?

You can either hide the unused rows and columns or use a VBA instruction to set the scroll area for the worksheet. The following instruction, for example, sets the scroll area on Sheet1 so that the user can't activate any cells outside of B2:D50:

```
Worksheets("Sheet1").ScrollArea = "B2:D50"
```

To set scrolling back to normal, use a statement like this:

```
Worksheets("Sheet1").ScrollArea = ""
```

Keep in mind that the ScrollArea setting is not saved with the workbook. Therefore, you need to execute the ScrollArea assignment instruction whenever the workbook is opened. This instruction can
go in the Workbook_Open event-handler procedure.

What's the difference between using Select and Application.Goto?

The Select method of the Range object selects a range on the active worksheet only. Use
Application.Goto to select a range on any worksheet in a workbook. Application.Goto might or might
not make another sheet the active sheet. The Goto method also lets you scroll the sheet so that the
range is in the upper-left corner.

What's the difference between activating a range and selecting a range?

In some cases, the Activate method and the Select method have exactly the same effect. But in other
cases, they produce different results. Assume that range A1:C3 is selected. The following statement
activates cell C3. The original range remains selected, but C3 becomes the active cell — that is, the
cell that contains the cell pointer.

```
Range("C3").Activate
```

Again, assuming that range A1:C3 is selected, the following statement selects a single cell, which also
becomes the active cell:

```
Range("C3").Select
```

Can I quickly delete all values from a worksheet yet keep the formulas intact?

Yes. The following code works on the active sheet and deletes all nonformula cells. (The cell formatting isn't affected.)

```
On Error Resume Next
Cells.SpecialCells(xlCellTypeConstants, 23).ClearContents
```

The second argument, 23, is the sum of the values of the following built-in constants: xlErrors (16),
xlLogical (4), xlNumbers (1), and xlTextValues (2).

Using On Error Resume Next prevents the error message that occurs if no cells qualify.

I know how to write a VBA instruction to select a range by using a cell address, but how can I write one to select a range if I know only its row and column numbers?

Use the Cells method. The following instruction, for example, selects the cell in the 5th row and the 12th column (that is, cell L5):

```
Cells(5, 12).Select
```

How can I turn off screen updating while a macro is running?

The following instruction turns off screen updating and speeds up macros that modify the display:

```
Application.ScreenUpdating = False
```

When your procedure ends, the ScreenUpdating property is set back to True. However, you can resume screen updating at any time by executing this statement:

```
Application.ScreenUpdating = True
```

I wrote a macro that uses a loop to animate a chart, but I don't see any animation.

Try inserting the following statement inside your loop:

```
DoEvents
```

What's the easiest way to create a range name in VBA?

If you turn on the macro recorder while you name a range, you get code something like this:

```
Range("D14:G20").Select
ActiveWorkbook.Names.Add Name:="InputArea", _
    RefersToR1C1:="=Sheet1!R14C4:R20C7"
```

A much simpler method is to use a statement like this:

```
Sheets("Sheet1").Range("D14:G20").Name = "InputArea"
```

How can I determine whether a particular cell or range has a name?

You need to check the Name property of the Name object contained in the Range object. The following function accepts a range as an argument and returns the name of the range (if it has one). If the range has no name, the function returns False.

```
Function RangeName(rng) As Variant
    On Error Resume Next
    RangeName = rng.Name.Name
    If Err <> 0 Then RangeName = False
End Function
```

I have a lengthy macro, and it would be nice to display its progress in the status bar. Can I display messages in the status bar while a macro is running?

Yes. Assign the text to the StatusBar property of the Application object. Here's an example:

```
Application.StatusBar = "Now processing File " & FileNum
```

Before your routine finishes, return the status bar back to normal with either of the following instructions:

```
Application.StatusBar = False
Application.StatusBar = ""
```

I recorded a VBA macro that copies a range and pastes it to another area. The macro uses the Select method. Is there a more efficient way to copy and paste?

Yes. Although the macro recorder generally selects cells before doing anything with them, selecting is not necessary and can slow down your macro. Recording a simple copy-and-paste operation generates four lines of VBA code, two of which use the Select method. Here's an example:

```
Range("A1").Select
Selection.Copy
Range("B1").Select
ActiveSheet.Paste
```

These four lines can be replaced with a single instruction, such as the following:

```
Range("A1").Copy Range("B1")
```

Note that this instruction doesn't use the Select method.

I have not been able to find a method to sort a VBA array. Does this mean that I have to copy the values to a worksheet and then use the Range.Sort method?

There is no built-in way to sort an array in VBA. Copying the array to a worksheet is one method, but you can also write your own sorting procedure. Many sorting algorithms are available, and some are easy to code in VBA. This book contains VBA code for several sorting techniques.

My macro works with the selected cells, but it fails if something else (such as a chart) is selected. How can I make sure that a range is selected?

You can use the VBA TypeName function to check the Selection object. Here's an example:

```
If TypeName(Selection) <> "Range" Then
    MsgBox "Select a range!"
    Exit Sub
End If
```

Another approach is to use the RangeSelection property, which returns a Range object that represents the selected cells on the worksheet in the specified window, even if a graphic object is active or selected. This property applies to a Window object — not a Workbook object. The following instruction, for example, displays the address of the selected range:

```
MsgBox ActiveWindow.RangeSelection.Address
```

How can I determine if a chart is activated?

Use a block of code like this:

```
If ActiveChart Is Nothing Then
  MsgBox "Select a chart"
  Exit Sub
End If
```

The message box will be displayed only if a chart isn't activated. (This includes embedded charts and charts on a chart sheet.)

My VBA macro needs to count the number of rows selected by the user. Using Selection.Rows. Count doesn't work when nonadjacent rows are selected. Is this a bug?

Actually, this is the way it's supposed to work. The Count method returns the number of elements in only the first area of the selection (a noncontiguous selection has multiple areas). To get an accurate row count, your VBA code must first determine the number of areas in the selection and then count the number of rows in each area. Use Selection.Areas.Count to count the number of areas. Here's an example that stores the total number of selected rows in the NumRows variable:

```
NumRows = 0
For Each area In Selection.Areas
    NumRows = NumRows + area.Rows.Count
Next area
```

By the way, this process is also relevant to counting selected columns and cells.

I use Excel to create invoices. Can I generate a unique invoice number?

One way to do this is to use the Windows Registry. The following code demonstrates:

```
Counter = GetSetting("XYZ Corp", "InvoiceNum", "Count", 0)
Counter = Counter + 1
SaveSetting "XYZ Corp", "InvoiceNum", "Count", Counter
```

When these statements are executed, the current value is retrieved from the Registry, incremented by 1, and assigned to the Counter variable. Then this updated value is stored back to the Registry. You can use the value of Counter as your unique invoice number.

You can adapt this technique for other purposes. For example, you can keep track of the number of times a workbook has been opened by including similar code in a Workbook_Open procedure.

Is there a workbook property that forces an Excel workbook to always remain visible so it won't be hidden by another application's window?

No.

Is there a VBA instruction to select the last entry in a column or row? Normally, I can use Ctrl+Shift+↓ or Ctrl+Shift+→ to do this, but how can I do it with a macro?

The VBA equivalent for Ctrl+Shift+↓ is the following:

```
Selection.End(xlDown).Select
```

The constants used for the other directions are xlToLeft, xlToRight, and xlUp.

How can I determine the last nonempty cell in a particular column?

The following instruction displays the address of the last nonempty cell in column A:

```
MsgBox ActiveSheet.Cells(Rows.Count, 1).End(xlUp).Address
```

But that instruction won't work if the last cell in the column is not empty. To handle that unlikely occurrence, use this code:

```
With ActiveSheet.Cells(Rows.Count, 1)
    If IsEmpty(.Value) Then
        MsgBox .End(xlUp).Address
    Else
        MsgBox .Address
    End If
End With
```

VBA references can be lengthy, especially when I need to fully qualify an object by referencing its sheet and workbook. Can I reduce the length of these references?

Yes. use the Set statement to create an object variable. Here's an example:

```
Dim MyRange as Range
Set MyRange = ThisWorkbook.Worksheets("Sheet1").Range("A1")
```

After the Set statement is executed, you can refer to this single-cell Range object simply as MyRange. For example, you can assign a value to the cell with the following:

```
MyRange.Value = 10
```

Besides making it easier to refer to objects, using object variables can also help your code execute more quickly.

Can I declare an array if I don't know how many elements it will have?

Yes. You can declare a dynamic array with the Dim statement by using empty parentheses; then allocate storage for that array later with the ReDim statement when you know how many elements the array should have. Use ReDim Preserve if you don't want to lose the current array's contents when reallocating it.

How can I undo previous actions when I execute a macro?

You can't. Unfortunately, running a macro in Excel destroys the Undo stack.

Can I let the user undo my macro?

In some cases, yes — but undoing a macro can't be done automatically. And it does not restore the Undo stack.

To enable the user to undo the effects of your macro, your VBA code module must keep track of what was changed by the macro and then be capable of restoring the original state if the user chooses Undo.

To enable the Undo command, use the OnUndo method as the last action in your macro. This method enables you to specify text that will appear on the Undo menu item and also to specify a procedure to run if the user chooses Undo. Here's an example:

```
Application.OnUndo "The Last Macro", "MyUndoMacro"
```

See Chapter 14 for more information about undoing a macro.

Can I pause a macro so the user can enter data into a certain cell?

You can use Excel's InputBox statement to get a value from a user and place it in a particular cell. The first instruction that follows, for example, displays an input box. When the user enters a value, that value is placed in cell A1.

```
UserVal = Application.InputBox(prompt:="Value?", Type:=1)
If TypeName(UserVal)<>"Boolean" Then Range("A1") = UserVal
```

VBA has an InputBox function as well as an InputBox method for the Application object. Are these the same?

No. Excel's InputBox method is more versatile because it allows a user to select a range. In addition, Excel's InputBox method allows validation of the user's entry. The preceding example uses 1 (which represents a numeric value) for the Type argument of the InputBox method. This ensures that the user enters a value into the input box.

I'm trying to write a VBA instruction that creates a formula. To do so, I need to insert a quote character (") within quoted text. How can I do that?

Assume that you want to enter the following formula into cell B1 with VBA:

```
=IF(A1="Yes",TRUE,FALSE)
```

The following instruction generates a syntax error because of the embedded quote characters:

```
Range("B1").Formula = "=IF(A1="Yes",TRUE,FALSE)"    'erroneous
```

The solution is to use two double quotes side by side. When two quotes are embedded within another set of quotes, Excel interprets the double quote characters as a single quote. The following instruction produces the desired result:

```
Range("B1").Formula = "=IF(A1=""Yes"",TRUE,FALSE)"
```

Another approach is to use the VBA Chr function with an argument of 34, which returns a quotation mark. The following example demonstrates:

```
Range("B1").Formula = _
  "=IF(A1=" & Chr(34) & "Yes" & Chr(34) & ",TRUE,FALSE)"
```

Yet another technique is to compose your formula using apostrophes in place of the quote marks. Then use the VBA Replace function to replace the apostrophes with quote characters:

```
MyFormula = "=IF(A1='Yes',TRUE,FALSE)"
Range("B1").Formula = Replace(MyFormula, "'", Chr(34))
```

I created an array, but the first element in that array is being treated as the second element. What's wrong?

Unless you tell it otherwise, VBA uses 0 as the first index number for an array. If you want all your arrays to always start with 1, insert the following statement at the top of your VBA module:

```
Option Base 1
```

Or you can specify the upper and lower bounds of an array when you declare it. Here's an example:

```
Dim Months(1 To 12) As String
```

I would like my VBA code to run as quickly as possible. Any suggestions?

Here are a few general tips:

➤ Make sure that you declare all your variables. Use Option Explicit at the top of your modules to force yourself to do this.

➤ If you reference an Excel object more than once, create an object variable for it.

➤ Use the With-End With construct whenever possible.

➤ If your macro writes information to a worksheet, turn off screen updating by using Application.ScreenUpdating = False.

➤ If your application enters data into cells that are referenced by one or more formulas, set the calculation mode to manual to avoid unnecessary calculations.

Security-Related Issues

When I open a file, why does Excel indicate that macros have been disabled when the workbook has no macros?

You will see this warning even if a workbook contains an empty VBA module. Remove the empty module and you won't see the message.

How can I ensure that everyone who opens my workbook enables macros?

There's no way to ensure that, but one approach is to make the workbook useless if macros are not enabled. For example, you can hide critical worksheets, and unhide them via a macro. But this method isn't foolproof.

How do I protect the code in my add-in from being viewed by others?

Activate VBE and choose Tools➜*xxxx* Properties (where *xxxx* is the name of your project). Click the Protection tab, select Lock Project for Viewing, and enter a password. Then save the file.

Are my add-ins safe? In other words, if I distribute an XLAM file, can I be assured that no one else will be able to view my code?

Protect your add-in by locking it with a password. This prevents most users from being able to access your code. Recent versions of Excel have improved security features, but the password still might be broken by using any of a number of utilities. Bottom line? Don't think of an XLAM as being a secure file.

I locked my VBA project with a password, and I forget what it was. Is there any way to unlock it?

Several third-party password-cracking products exist. Use a web search engine to search for *Excel password*. The existence of these products should tell you that Excel passwords aren't very secure.

How can I write a macro to change the password of my project?

You can't. The protection elements of a VBA project aren't exposed in the object model. Most likely, this was done to make it more difficult for password-cracking software.

I wrote a macro that creates other macros. It works great on my system, but it doesn't work for others.

Most likely, the other users haven't enabled the setting called Trust Access to the VBA Project Object Model. This setting is available in the Macro Settings tab of the Trust Center dialog box. See Chapter 26 for more information.

UserForms

My macro needs to get just a few pieces of information from the user, and a UserForm seems like overkill. Are there any alternatives?

Yes, check out the VBA MsgBox function and its InputBox function. Alternatively, you might want to use the Excel InputBox method. See Chapter 10 for examples that use these functions.

I have 12 CommandButtons on a UserForm. How can I assign a single macro to be executed when any of the buttons are clicked?

You can't do this easily because each CommandButton has its own Click event procedure. One solution is to call another procedure from each of the CommandButton_Click procedures. Another solution is to use a class module to create a new class. This technique is described in Chapter 13.

How can I display a chart in a UserForm?

You can't display a chart in a UserForm directly. One solution is to write a macro that saves the chart to a GIF file and then loads the GIF file into an Image control on the UserForm. You'll find an example in Chapter 13.

How can I remove the X from the title bar of my UserForm? I don't want the user to click that button to close the form.

Removing the close button on a UserForm's title bar requires some complex API functions. A simpler approach is to intercept all attempts to close the UserForm by using a UserForm_QueryClose event procedure in the code module for the UserForm. The following example doesn't allow the user to close the form by clicking the close button:

```
Private Sub UserForm_QueryClose _
   (Cancel As Integer, CloseMode As Integer)
     If CloseMode = vbFormControlMenu Then
         MsgBox "You can't close the form like that."
         Cancel = True
     End If
End Sub
```

I created a UserForm with controls that are linked to cells on the worksheet with the ControlSource property. Is this the best way to do this?

Probably not. In some cases, using links to worksheet cells can slow your application because the worksheet is recalculated every time a control changes the cell. In addition, if your UserForm has a Cancel button, the cells might have already been changed when the user clicks Cancel.

Can I create a control array for a UserForm? It's possible with Visual Basic, but I can't figure out how to do it with Excel VBA.

You can't create a control array, but you can create an array of Control objects. The following code creates an array consisting of all CommandButton controls:

```
Private Sub UserForm_Initialize()
    Dim Buttons() As CommandButton
    Cnt = 0
    For Each Ctl In UserForm1.Controls
        If TypeName(Ctl) = "CommandButton" Then
            Cnt = Cnt + 1
            ReDim Preserve Buttons(1 To Cnt)
            Set Buttons(Cnt) = Ctl
        End If
    Next Ctl
End Sub
```

Is there any difference between hiding a UserForm and unloading a UserForm?

Yes. The Hide method keeps the UserForm in memory but makes it invisible. The Unload statement unloads the UserForm, beginning the termination process (invoking the Terminate event for the UserForm) and removing the UserForm from memory.

How can I make my UserForm stay open while I do other things?

By default, each UserForm is modal, which means that it must be dismissed before you can do anything else. However, you can make a UserForm modeless by using vbModeless as the argument for the Show method. Here's an example:

```
UserForm1.Show vbModeless
```

I need to display a progress indicator like those you see when you're installing software and a lengthy process is being executed. How can I do this?

You can display a progress indicator with a UserForm. Chapter 13 describes several different techniques, including one in which the code gradually stretches a shape inside a frame while the lengthy macro is running.

How can I use Excel's shapes on my UserForm?

You can't use the shapes directly with a UserForm, but you can do so indirectly. Start by adding a shape to a worksheet. Then select the shape and press Ctrl+C to copy it. Activate your UserForm and insert an Image object. Press F4 to display the Properties window. Select the Picture property and press Ctrl+V to paste the Clipboard contents to the Image control. You might also need to set the AutoSize property to True.

How can I generate a list of files and directories in my UserForm so the user can select a file from the list?

There's no need to do that. Use the VBA GetOpenFilename method. This method displays an Open dialog box in which the user can select a drive, directory, and file. This method doesn't open the selected file, so you need to write additional code.

I need to concatenate strings and display them in a ListBox control. But when I do so, they aren't aligned properly. How can I get them to display equal spacing between strings?

You can use a monospaced font such as Courier New for the ListBox. A better approach, however, is to set up your ListBox to use two or more columns. (See Chapter 12 for details.)

Is there an easy way to fill a ListBox or ComboBox control with items?

Yes. You can use an array. The statement that follows adds three items to ListBox1:

```
ListBox1.List = Array("Jan", "Feb", "Mar")
```

Can I display a built-in Excel dialog box from VBA?

Many of Excel's dialog boxes can be displayed by using the Application.Dialogs method. For example, the following instruction displays the dialog box that enables you to format numbers in cells:

```
Application.Dialogs(xlDialogFormatNumber).Show
```

However, this method isn't reliable, and not all of Excel's dialog boxes are available.

A better option is to execute Ribbon commands (including those that display a dialog box) by using the ExecuteMso method along with the control name. The statement that follows, for example, displays the dialog box that enables you to format numbers in a cell:

```
Application.CommandBars.ExecuteMso("NumberFormatsDialog")
```

See Chapter 20 for more information.

I tried the technique described in the preceding question and received an error message. Why is that?

The ExecuteMso method will fail if the context isn't appropriate. For example, the following statement displays the Insert Cells dialog box. But if you execute this statement when a chart is selected or the worksheet is protected, you'll get an error message.

```
Application.CommandBars.ExecuteMso "CellsInsertDialog"
```

Every time I create a UserForm, I go through the steps of adding an OK button and a Cancel button. Can I get these controls to appear automatically?

Yes. Set up a UserForm with the controls that you use most often. Then choose File➜Export File to save the UserForm. When you want to add a new form to another project, choose File➜Import File.

Can I create a UserForm without a title bar?

Yes, but it requires some complex API functions. See Chapter 13 for an example.

When I click a button on my UserForm, nothing happens. What am I doing wrong?

Controls added to a UserForm do nothing unless you write event-handler procedures for them. These procedures must be located in the code module for the UserForm, and they must have the correct name.

Can I create a UserForm whose size is always the same, regardless of the video display resolution?

You can, but it's probably not worth the effort. You can write code to determine the video resolution and then use the Zoom property of a UserForm to change its size. The normal way to deal with this matter is simply to design your UserForm for the lowest resolution that will be used.

Can I create a UserForm box that lets the user select a range in a worksheet by pointing?

Yes. Use the RefEdit control for this. See Chapter 12 for an example.

Can I change the startup position of a UserForm?

Yes. You can set the UserForm's Left and Top properties, but you also need to set the UserForm's StartUpPosition property to 0.

I use a system with two monitors, and UserForms don't display in the center of Excel's window. Can I force the UserForm to be centered?

Yes. Use the following code to display your UserForm:

```
With UserForm1
  .StartUpPosition = 0
  .Left = Application.Left + (0.5 * Application.Width) - (0.5 * .Width)
  .Top = Application.Top + (0.5 * Application.Height) - (0.5 * .Height)
  .Show 0
End With
```

Can I make a UserForm that's resizable by the user?

Yes. See Chapter 13 for an example.

Add-Ins

Where can I get Excel add-ins?

You can get Excel add-ins from a number of places:

> ➤ Excel includes several add-ins that you can use whenever you need them. Use the Add-Ins dialog box to install them.

> ➤ You can download more add-ins from the Microsoft Office Update website.

> ➤ Third-party developers distribute and sell add-ins for special purposes.

> ➤ Many developers create free add-ins and distribute them through their Internet sites.

> ➤ You can create your own add-ins.

How do I install an add-in?

The most common way to install an add-in is by using the Add-Ins dialog box. Choose File➜Options. In the Excel Options dialog box, select the Add-Ins tab. Then select Excel Add-ins from the Manage drop-down control and click Go. A quicker method to display the Add-Ins dialog box is to press Alt+TI. Or, if the Developer tab is displayed, choose Developer➜Add-Ins➜Add-Ins.

You can also open an add-in by using the File➜Open command, but using the Add-Ins dialog box is the preferred method. An add-in opened with File➜Open can't be closed without using VBA.

When I install my add-in from Excel's Add-Ins dialog box, it shows up without a name or description. How can I give my add-in a description?

Before creating the add-in, use the File➜Info➜Properties➜Advanced Properties command to display the Properties dialog box. Click the Summary tab. In the Title field, enter the text that you want to appear in the Add-Ins dialog box. In the Comments field, enter the description for the add-in. Then create the add-in as usual.

I have several add-ins that I no longer use, but I can't figure out how to remove them from the Add-Ins Available list in the Add-Ins dialog box. What's the story?

Oddly, you cannot remove unwanted add-ins from the list directly from Excel. One way to remove an add-in from the list is to move or delete the add-in file. Then, when you attempt to open the add-in from the Add-Ins dialog box, Excel will ask whether you want to remove the add-in from the list. Answer yes.

How do I create an add-in?

Activate any worksheet and then choose File➜Save As. Then select Excel Add-in (*.xlam) from the Save as Type drop-down list. The add-in is created, and the original workbook remains open.

I try to create an add-in, but the Save as Type drop-down box doesn't provide Add-in as an option.

The most likely reason is that the active sheet isn't a worksheet. An add-in must have at least one worksheet, and a worksheet must be the active sheet when you save the file as an add-in.

If I create an add-in, will it work with the Excel Web App (the online version of Excel)?

No, the Excel Web App doesn't support add-ins or even macros.

Will my add-ins work with the version of Excel that runs on Windows RT ARM-based devices?

No, these devices don't support add-ins or macros.

Should I convert all my essential workbooks to add-ins?

No! Although you can create an add-in from any workbook, not all workbooks are suitable. When a workbook is converted to an add-in, it's essentially invisible. For most workbooks, being invisible isn't a good thing.

Do I need to keep two copies of my workbook: the XLSM version and the XLAM version?

No, you can edit an add-in and even convert an add-in back to a normal workbook.

How do I modify an add-in after it has been created?

If you need to modify only the VBA code, no special action is required; you can access the code from VB Editor and then save your changes in VBE. If you need to modify information on a worksheet, activate VB Editor (press Alt+F11) and then set the IsAddIn property of the ThisWorkbook object to False. Make your changes to the worksheet, set the IsAddIn property to True, and resave the file.

What's the difference between an XLSM file and an XLAM file created from an XLSM file? Is the XLAM version compiled? Does it run faster?

There isn't a great deal of difference between the files, and you generally won't notice any speed differences. VBA code is always compiled before it's executed, whether it's in an XLSM file or an XLAM file. However, XLAM files still contain the actual VBA code — not some special optimized code that runs faster. Another difference is that the workbook is never visible in an XLAM file.

User Interface

How do I use VBA to add a button to the Ribbon?

You can't. You must write special XML code (known as RibbonX code) and insert the XML document into a workbook file by using third-party tools. Or, if you're a glutton for punishment (and know what you're doing), you can unzip the document and make the edits manually.

What are my options for modifying the user interface to make it easy for a user to run my macros?

In Excel 2010 and later, you have these choices:

> ➤ Modify the Ribbon by adding RibbonX code (not an easy task).

> ➤ Add a new item to a right-click shortcut menu by using RibbonX code (not an easy task).

> ➤ Add your macro to the Quick Access toolbar (a manual task that's not possible to perform using VBA).

> ➤ Add your macro to the Ribbon (a manual task that's not possible to perform using VBA).

> ➤ Assign a shortcut key to the macro.

> ➤ Use VBA to add a new menu item to a right-click shortcut menu. In Excel 2013, this method has some limitations.

> ➤ Use VBA to create an old-style toolbar or menu, which will display in the Add-Ins tab.

How do I add a macro to the Quick Access toolbar?

It must be done manually. Right-click the Quick Access toolbar and choose Customize Quick Access Toolbar from the shortcut menu. In the Quick Access Toolbar tab of the Excel Options dialog box, choose Macros from the drop-down list on the left. Select your macro and click Add. To change the icon or text displayed, click the Modify button.

How do I add a macro to the Ribbon?

It must be done manually. Right-click the Ribbon and choose Customize the Ribbon from the shortcut menu. In the Customize Ribbon tab of the Excel Options dialog box, choose Macros from the drop-down list on the left. Select your macro and click Add. Note that you can't add a macro to an existing group. You must first add a new group to a tab by using the New Group button.

How do I use VBA to activate a particular tab on the Ribbon?

SendKeys is your only choice. Press the Alt key to find out the keystroke(s) required. For example, to switch to the Page Layout tab, use this:

```
Application.SendKeys "%p{F6}"
```

This statement works only when Excel is the active window. For example, you can't execute this statement directly from VBE.

My custom shortcut menus aren't working correctly in Excel 2013. What's wrong?

Excel 2013 uses a single document interface — each workbook has its own window. Because of this, custom shortcut menus work very differently. When your code customizes a shortcut menu, the customization occurs only in the active workbook. So if you want your customized shortcut menus to work in all workbooks, you need to write additional code that loops through all workbooks. And even then, you can't be certain that the shortcut menu modification is available to all workbooks.

Does this mean that using customized shortcut menus to execute macros in an add-in is no longer a viable option in Excel 2013?

Shortcut menus are still viable, but they must be modified by using RibbonX code, not VBA.

Appendixes

VBA Statements and Functions Reference

This appendix contains a complete listing of all Visual Basic for Applications (VBA) statements (Table A-1) and built-in functions (Table A-2). For details, consult Excel's online help.

Note Excel 2013 has no new VBA statements.

Table A-1: Summary of VBA Statements

Statement	Action
AppActivate	Activates an application window
Beep	Sounds a tone through the computer's speaker
Call	Transfers control to another procedure
ChDir	Changes the current directory
ChDrive	Changes the current drive
Close	Closes a text file
Const	Declares a constant value
Date	Sets the current system date
Declare	Declares a reference to an external procedure in a Dynamic Link Library (DLL)
DefBool	Sets the default data type to Boolean for variables that begin with specified letters
DefByte	Sets the default data type to Byte for variables that begin with specified letters
DefCur	Sets the default data type to Currency for variables that begin with specified letters

continued

Table A-1: Summary of VBA Statements *(continued)*

Statement	Action
DefDate	Sets the default data type to Date for variables that begin with specified letters
DefDec	Sets the default data type to Decimal for variables that begin with specified letters
DefDbl	Sets the default data type to Double for variables that begin with specified letters
DefInt	Sets the default data type to Integer for variables that begin with specified letters
DefLng	Sets the default data type to Long for variables that begin with specified letters
DefObj	Sets the default data type to Object for variables that begin with specified letters
DefSng	Sets the default data type to Single for variables that begin with specified letters
DefStr	Sets the default data type to String for variables that begin with specified letters
DefVar	Sets the default data type to Variant for variables that begin with specified letters
DeleteSetting	Deletes a section or key setting from an application's entry in the Windows Registry
Dim	Declares variables and (optionally) their data types
Do-Loop	Loops through a set of instructions
End	Used by itself, exits the program; also used to end a block of statements that begin with If, With, Sub, Function, Property, Type, or Select
Enum	Declares a type for enumeration
Erase	Reinitializes an array
Error	Simulates a specific error condition
Event	Declares a user-defined event
Exit Do	Exits a block of Do-Loop code
Exit For	Exits a block of For-Next code
Exit Function	Exits a Function procedure
Exit Property	Exits a property procedure
Exit Sub	Exits a subroutine procedure
FileCopy	Copies a file
For Each-Next	Loops through a set of instructions for each member of a series
For-Next	Loops through a set of instructions a specific number of times

Statement	Action
Function	Declares the name and arguments for a Function procedure
Get	Reads data from a text file
GoSub...Return	Branches to and returns from a procedure
GoTo	Branches to a specified statement within a procedure
If-Then-Else	Processes statements conditionally
Implements	Specifies an interface or class that will be implemented in a class module
Input #	Reads data from a sequential text file
Kill	Deletes a file from a disk
Let	Assigns the value of an expression to a variable or property
Line Input #	Reads a line of data from a sequential text file
Load	Loads an object but doesn't show it
Lock...Unlock	Controls access to a text file
Lset	Left-aligns a string within a string variable
Mid	Replaces characters in a string with other characters
MkDir	Creates a new directory
Name	Renames a file or directory
On Error	Gives specific instructions for what to do in the case of an error
On...GoSub	Branches, based on a condition
On...GoTo	Branches, based on a condition
Open	Opens a text file
Option Base	Changes the default lower limit for arrays
Option Compare	Declares the default comparison mode when comparing strings
Option Explicit	Forces declaration of all variables in a module
Option Private	Indicates that an entire module is Private
Print #	Writes data to a sequential file
Private	Declares a local array or variable
Property Get	Declares the name and arguments of a Property Get procedure
Property Let	Declares the name and arguments of a Property Let procedure
Property Set	Declares the name and arguments of a Property Set procedure
Public	Declares a public array or variable
Put	Writes a variable to a text file
RaiseEvent	Fires a user-defined event
Randomize	Initializes the random number generator

continued

Table A-1: Summary of VBA Statements *(continued)*

Statement	Action
ReDim	Changes the dimensions of an array
Rem	Specifies a line of comments (same as an apostrophe ['])
Reset	Closes all open text files
Resume	Resumes execution when an error-handling routine finishes
RmDir	Removes an empty directory
RSet	Right-aligns a string within a string variable
SaveSetting	Saves or creates an application entry in the Windows Registry
Seek	Sets the position for the next access in a text file
Select Case	Processes statements conditionally
SendKeys	Sends keystrokes to the active window
Set	Assigns an object reference to a variable or property
SetAttr	Changes attribute information for a file
Static	Declares variables at the procedure level so that the variables retain their values as long as the code is running
Stop	Pauses the program
Sub	Declares the name and arguments of a Sub procedure
Time	Sets the system time
Type	Defines a custom data type
Unload	Removes an object from memory
While...Wend	Loops through a set of instructions as long as a certain condition remains true
Width #	Sets the output line width of a text file
With	Sets a series of properties for an object
Write #	Writes data to a sequential text file

Invoking Excel functions in VBA instructions

If a VBA function that's equivalent to one you use in Excel isn't available, you can use Excel's worksheet functions directly in your VBA code. Just precede the function with a reference to the WorksheetFunction object. For example, VBA doesn't have a function to convert radians to degrees, but Excel has a worksheet function for this procedure, so you can use a VBA instruction such as the following:

```
Deg = Application.WorksheetFunction.Degrees(3.14)
```

Note

Excel 2013 has no new VBA functions.

Table A-2: Summary of VBA Functions

Function	Action
Abs	Returns the absolute value of a number
Array	Returns a variant containing an array
Asc	Converts the first character of a string to its ASCII value
Atn	Returns the arctangent of a number
CallByName	Executes a method, or sets or returns a property of an object
CBool	Converts an expression to a Boolean data type
CByte	Converts an expression to a Byte data type
CCur	Converts an expression to a Currency data type
CDate	Converts an expression to a Date data type
CDbl	Converts an expression to a Double data type
CDec	Converts an expression to a Decimal data type
Choose	Selects and returns a value from a list of arguments
Chr	Converts a character code to a string
CInt	Converts an expression to an Integer data type
CLng	Converts an expression to a Long data type
Cos	Returns the cosine of a number
CreateObject	Creates an Object Linking and Embedding (OLE) Automation object
CSng	Converts an expression to a Single data type
CStr	Converts an expression to a String data type
CurDir	Returns the current path
CVar	Converts an expression to a variant data type
CVDate	Converts an expression to a Date data type (for compatibility, not recommended)
CVErr	Returns a user-defined error value that corresponds to an error number
Date	Returns the current system date
DateAdd	Adds a time interval to a date
DateDiff	Returns the time interval between two dates
DatePart	Returns a specified part of a date
DateSerial	Converts a date to a serial number
DateValue	Converts a string to a date
Day	Returns the day of the month of a date

continued

Table A-2: Summary of VBA Functions *(continued)*

Function	Action
DDB	Returns the depreciation of an asset
Dir	Returns the name of a file or directory that matches a pattern
DoEvents	Yields execution so the operating system can process other events
Environ	Returns an operating environment string
EOF	Returns True if the end of a text file has been reached
Error	Returns the error message that corresponds to an error number
Exp	Returns the base of natural logarithms (*e*) raised to a power
FileAttr	Returns the file mode for a text file
FileDateTime	Returns the date and time when a file was last modified
FileLen	Returns the number of bytes in a file
Filter	Returns a subset of a string array, filtered
Fix	Returns the integer portion of a number
Format	Displays an expression in a particular format
FormatCurrency	Returns an expression formatted with the system currency symbol
FormatDateTime	Returns an expression formatted as a date or time
FormatNumber	Returns an expression formatted as a number
FormatPercent	Returns an expression formatted as a percentage
FreeFile	Returns the next available file number when working with text files
FV	Returns the future value of an annuity
GetAllSettings	Returns a list of settings and values from the Windows Registry
GetAttr	Returns a code representing a file attribute
GetObject	Retrieves an OLE Automation object from a file
GetSetting	Returns a specific setting from the application's entry in the Windows Registry
Hex	Converts from decimal to hexadecimal
Hour	Returns the hour of a time
IIf	Evaluates an expression and returns one of two parts
Input	Returns characters from a sequential text file
InputBox	Displays a box to prompt a user for input
InStr	Returns the position of a string within another string
InStrRev	Returns the position of a string within another string from the end of the string
Int	Returns the integer portion of a number
IPmt	Returns the interest payment for a given period of an annuity

Function	Action
IRR	Returns the internal rate of return for a series of cash flows
IsArray	Returns True if a variable is an array
IsDate	Returns True if a variable is a date
IsEmpty	Returns True if a variable has not been initialized
IsError	Returns True if an expression is an error value
IsMissing	Returns True if an optional argument was not passed to a procedure
IsNull	Returns True if an expression contains a Null value
IsNumeric	Returns True if an expression can be evaluated as a number
IsObject	Returns True if an expression references an OLE Automation object
Join	Combines strings contained in an array
LBound	Returns the smallest subscript for a dimension of an array
LCase	Returns a string converted to lowercase
Left	Returns a specified number of characters from the left of a string
Len	Returns the number of characters in a string
Loc	Returns the current read or write position of a text file
LOF	Returns the number of bytes in an open text file
Log	Returns the natural logarithm of a number
LTrim	Returns a copy of a string with no leading spaces
Mid	Returns a specified number of characters from a string
Minute	Returns the minute of a time
MIRR	Returns the modified internal rate of return for a series of periodic cash flows
Month	Returns the month of a date as a number
MonthName	Returns the month of a date as a string
MsgBox	Displays a modal message box
Now	Returns the current system date and time
NPer	Returns the number of periods for an annuity
NPV	Returns the net present value of an investment
Oct	Converts from decimal to octal
Partition	Returns a string representing a range in which a value falls
Pmt	Returns a payment amount for an annuity
Ppmt	Returns the principal payment amount for an annuity
PV	Returns the present value of an annuity
QBColor	Returns a red/green/blue (RGB) color code

continued

Table A-2: Summary of VBA Functions *(continued)*

Function	Action
Rate	Returns the interest rate per period for an annuity
Replace	Returns a string in which a substring is replaced with another string
RGB	Returns a number representing an RGB color value
Right	Returns a specified number of characters from the right of a string
Rnd	Returns a random number between 0 and 1
Round	Returns a rounded number
RTrim	Returns a copy of a string with no trailing spaces
Second	Returns the seconds portion of a specified time
Seek	Returns the current position in a text file
Sgn	Returns an integer that indicates the sign of a number
Shell	Runs an executable program
Sin	Returns the sine of a number
SLN	Returns the straight-line depreciation for an asset for a period
Space	Returns a string with a specified number of spaces
Spc	Positions output when printing to a file
Split	Returns a one-dimensional array containing a number of substrings
Sqr	Returns the square root of a number
Str	Returns a string representation of a number
StrComp	Returns a value indicating the result of a string comparison
StrConv	Returns a converted string
String	Returns a repeating character or string
StrReverse	Returns a string, reversed
Switch	Evaluates a list of Boolean expressions and returns a value associated with the first True expression
SYD	Returns the sum-of-years' digits depreciation of an asset for a period
Tab	Positions output when printing to a file
Tan	Returns the tangent of a number
Time	Returns the current system time
Timer	Returns the number of seconds since midnight
TimeSerial	Returns the time for a specified hour, minute, and second
TimeValue	Converts a string to a time serial number
Trim	Returns a string without leading spaces and/or trailing spaces
TypeName	Returns a string that describes the data type of a variable

Function	Action
UBound	Returns the largest available subscript for a dimension of an array
UCase	Converts a string to uppercase
Val	Returns the number formed from any initial numeric characters of a string
VarType	Returns a value indicating the subtype of a variable
Weekday	Returns a number indicating a day of the week
WeekdayName	Returns a string indicating a day of the week
Year	Returns the year of a date

VBA Error Codes

This appendix contains a complete listing of the error codes for all trappable errors in Visual Basic for Applications (VBA). This information is useful for error trapping. For complete details, consult Excel's Help system.

Error Code	Message
3	Return without GoSub.
5	Invalid procedure call or argument.
6	Overflow (for example, value too large for an integer).
7	Out of memory. This error rarely refers to the amount of physical memory installed on your system. Rather, it usually refers to a fixed-size area of memory used by Excel or Windows (for example, the area used for graphics or custom formats).
9	Subscript out of range. You will also get this error message if a named item is not found in a collection of objects. For example, if your code refers to Sheets("Sheet2"), and Sheet2 does not exist.
10	This array is fixed or temporarily locked.
11	Division by zero.
13	Type mismatch.
14	Out of string space.
16	Expression too complex.
17	Can't perform requested operation.
18	User interrupt occurred. This error occurs if the user interrupts a macro by pressing the Cancel key.
20	Resume without error. This error probably indicates that you forgot the Exit Sub statement before your error handler code.
28	Out of stack space.
35	Sub or Function not defined.
47	Too many Dynamic Link Library (DLL) application clients.
48	Error in loading DLL.

continued

Error Code	Message
49	Bad DLL calling convention.
51	Internal error.
52	Bad filename or number.
53	File not found.
54	Bad file mode.
55	File already open.
57	Device Input/Output (I/O) error.
58	File already exists.
59	Bad record length.
61	Disk full.
62	Input past end of file.
63	Bad record number.
67	Too many files.
68	Device unavailable.
70	Permission denied.
71	Disk not ready.
74	Can't rename with different drive.
75	Path/File access error.
76	Path not found.
91	Object variable or With block variable not set. This error occurs if you don't use Set at the beginning of a statement that creates an object variable or you refer to a worksheet object (such as ActiveCell) when a chart sheet is active.
92	For loop not initialized.
93	Invalid pattern string.
94	Invalid use of Null.
96	Unable to sink events of object because the object is already firing events to the maximum number of event receivers that it supports.
97	Cannot call friend function on object that is not an instance of defining class.
98	A property or method call can't include a reference to a private object, either as an argument or as a return value.
321	Invalid file format.
322	Can't create necessary temporary file.
325	Invalid format in resource file.
380	Invalid property value.
381	Invalid property array index.

Error Code	Message
382	Set not supported at runtime.
383	Set not supported (read-only property).
385	Need property array index.
387	Set not permitted.
393	Get not supported at runtime.
394	Get not supported (write-only property).
422	Property not found.
423	Property or method not found.
424	Object required. This error occurs if text preceding a dot is not recognized as an object.
429	ActiveX component can't create object (might be a registration problem with a library that you've referenced).
430	Class doesn't support Automation or doesn't support expected interface.
432	Filename or class name not found during Automation operation.
438	Object doesn't support this property or method.
440	Automation error.
442	Connection to type library or object library for remote process has been lost.
443	Automation object doesn't have a default value.
445	Object doesn't support this action.
446	Object doesn't support named arguments.
447	Object doesn't support current locale setting.
448	Named argument not found.
449	Argument not optional.
450	Wrong number of arguments or invalid property assignment.
451	Property Let procedure not defined, and Property Get procedure did not return an object.
452	Invalid ordinal.
453	Specified DLL function not found.
454	Code resource not found.
455	Code resource lock error.
457	Key is already associated with an element of this collection.
458	Variable uses an Automation type not supported in Visual Basic.
459	Object or class doesn't support the set of events.
460	Invalid Clipboard format.
461	Method or data member not found.
462	Remote server machine doesn't exist or is unavailable.

continued

Error Code	Message
463	Class not registered on local machine.
481	Invalid picture.
482	Printer error.
735	Can't save file to TEMP.
744	Search text not found.
746	Replacements too long.
1004	Application-defined or object-defined error. This is a common catch-all error message. This error occurs when an error doesn't correspond to an error defined by VBA. In other words, the error is defined by Excel (or some other object) and is propagated back to VBA.

This Book's Website

This appendix describes the files that were created to accompany this book. To download these files, use your browser to navigate to this URL: www.wiley.com/go/Excel2013PowerProgramming.

The book's website contains more than 300 files used as examples in the book. The files are organized by chapter. With a few exceptions, the files are all Excel 2013 files that have one of the following extensions:

> .xlsx: Excel workbook file

> .xlsm: Excel workbook file that contains VBA macros

> .xlam: Excel add-in file that contains VBA macros

When you open an XLSM file, Excel may display a security warning that tells you that macros have been disabled. To enable macros, click the Options button in the security warning panel and then select Enable This Content.

Because the files are from a trusted source, you may want to copy the files to your hard drive and then designate the top-level folder as a trusted location. To do so, follow these steps:

1. Start Excel and choose File➜Options to display the Excel Options dialog box.

2. In the Excel Options dialog box, click the Trust Center tab.

3. Click the Trust Center Settings button.

4. In the Trust Center dialog box, click the Trusted Locations tab.

5. Click the Add New Location button to display the Microsoft Office Trusted Location dialog box.

6. In the Microsoft Office Trusted Location dialog box, click the Browse button and locate the folder that contains the files.

7. Make sure you select the option labeled Subfolders of This Location Are Also Trusted.

After performing these steps, when you open XLSM files from this location, the macros are enabled and you don't see the security warning.

Following is a list of the sample files, along with a brief description of each. Examples that use multiple files are contained in a separate subfolder.

Note **Some chapters don't use any sample files.**

Chapter 2

➤ array formula examples.xlsx: A workbook that contains various examples of array formulas

➤ basic lookup examples.xlsx: A workbook that contains examples of common lookup formulas

➤ counting and summing examples.xlsx: A workbook that contains examples of counting and summing formulas

➤ megaformula.xlsm: A workbook that demonstrates intermediate formulas, a megaformula, and a VBA function

➤ named formulas.xlsx: A workbook that contains several examples of named formulas

➤ specialized lookup examples.xlsx: A workbook that contains examples of specialized lookup formulas

➤ yearly calendar.xlsx: A workbook that contains a yearly calendar, generated using array formulas

Chapter 3

➤ sample.xlsm: A sample file used to demonstrate the file structure of an Excel workbook

Chapter 4

➤ worksheet controls.xlsx: A workbook that demonstrates the use of ActiveX controls on a worksheet (with no macros)

Chapter 5

➤ comment object.xlsm: A workbook that demonstrates some ways to manipulate Comment objects using VBA

Chapter 6

➤ timing test.xlsm: A workbook that demonstrates the speed advantage of declaring variables as a specific data type

Chapter 7

➤ sheet sorter.xlsm: A macro that sorts worksheets in a workbook

Chapter 8

➤ array argument.xlsm: A workbook that contains an example of a function that uses an array argument

➤ commission functions.xlsm: A workbook that contains an example of a function that uses an argument

➤ draw.xlsm: A workbook that contains a function that selects a cell randomly

➤ extended date functions.xlsm: A workbook that demonstrates functions to work with pre-1900 dates

➤ extended date functions help.pdf: A PDF file that describes the extended data functions

➤ key press.xlsm: A workbook that uses an API function to determine if the Ctrl, Shift, or Alt key is pressed

➤ month names.xlsm: A workbook that demonstrates returning an array from a function

➤ mysum function.xlsm: A workbook that contains a function that simulates the Excel SUM function

➤ no argument.xlsm: A workbook that contains functions that don't use an argument

➤ remove vowels.xlsm: A workbook that contains a function that removes the vowels from its argument

➤ upper case.xlsm: A workbook that contains a function that converts text to uppercase

➤ windows directory.xlsm: A workbook that uses an API function to determine the Windows folder

Chapter 9

➤ \batch processing: A folder that contains files used by the batch processing example

➤ \value from closed workbook: A folder that includes files to demonstrate how to use a function to retrieve a value from a closed workbook

➤ about range selection.xlsm: A workbook that contains a macro that describes the current range selection

➤ celltype function.xlsm: A workbook that contains a function that describes the data type of its single-cell argument

➤ copy multiple selection.xlsm: A workbook that contains a macro that copies a noncontiguous range selection

➤ create hyperlinks.xlsm: A workbook that contains a macro to create a hyperlink table of contents for a workbook

➤ date and time.xlsm: A workbook that contains a macro that displays the current date and time

➤ delete empty rows.xlsm: A workbook that contains a macro that deletes all empty rows in a workbook

➤ drive information.xlsm: A workbook that uses API functions to list information about all disk drives

➤ duplicate rows.xlsm: A workbook that contains a macro that duplicates rows, based on the contents of a cell

➤ efficient looping.xlsm: A workbook that demonstrates an efficient way to loop through a range

➤ file association.xlsm: A workbook that contains an API function that returns the application associated with a particular file

➤ friendly time.xlsm: A workbook that contains a function that returns a description of a time difference

➤ hide rows and columns.xlsm: A workbook that contains a macro that hides all rows and columns outside the current range selection

➤ inputbox demo.xlsm: A workbook that contains a macro that demonstrates how to prompt for a value

➤ inrange function.xlsm: A workbook that contains a function that determines whether a range is contained in another range

➤ list fonts.xlsm: A workbook that contains a macro that lists all installed fonts

➤ loop vs array fill range.xlsm: A workbook that contains macros that demonstrate ways to fill a range of cells

➤ next empty cell.xlsm: A workbook that contains a macro that determines the next empty cell in a column

➤ printer info.xlsm: A workbook that contains an API function that returns information about the active printer

➤ prompt for a range.xlsm: A workbook that contains a macro that demonstrates how to prompt for a user-selected range

➤ range selections.xlsm: A workbook that contains macros that perform various types of range selections

➤ select by value.xlsm: A workbook that contains a macro that demonstrates how to select cells based on their values

➤ sorting demo.xlsm: A workbook that contains macros that demonstrate four ways to sort an array

➤ spelldollars function.xlsm: A workbook that contains a function that returns a value, as words

➤ synchronize sheets.xlsm: A workbook that contains a macro that synchronizes worksheets

➤ variant transfer.xlsm: A workbook that contains a macro that transfers a range to a variant array

➤ vba utility functions.xlsm: A workbook that contains several useful functions for use in your VBA code

➤ video mode.xlsm: A workbook that contains an API function that determines the current video mode

➤ windows registry.xlsm: A workbook that contains macros that read from and write to the Windows Registry

➤ worksheet functions.xlsm: A workbook that contains some useful worksheet functions created using VBA

Chapter 10

➤ data form example.xlsm: A workbook that contains a macro that displays Excel's built-in data form

➤ get directory.xlsm: A workbook that contains macros that demonstrate two ways to prompt a user for a folder

➤ inputbox method.xlsm: A workbook that contains macros that demonstrate the use of the Excel InputBox method

➤ message box examples.xlsm: A workbook that contains examples of the MsgBox function

➤ prompt for file.xlsm: A workbook that demonstrates how to prompt for one or more filenames

➤ VBA inputbox.xlsm: A workbook that contains macros that demonstrate the use of the VBA InputBox function

Chapter 11

➤ activex worksheet controls.xlsx: A workbook that demonstrates the use of ActiveX controls on a worksheet (with no macros)

➤ all userform controls.xlsm: A workbook that contains a UserForm that uses all available controls

➤ get name and sex.xlsm: A workbook that contains a simple UserForm example

➤ newcontrols.pag: A file that contains customized controls that can be imported into your UserForm Toolbox as a new page

➤ spinbutton and textbox.xlsm: A workbook that demonstrates the use of a paired SpinButton control and TextBox control in a UserForm

➤ spinbutton events.xlsm: A workbook that demonstrates SpinButton events

➤ userform events.xlsm: A workbook that demonstrates UserForm events

Chapter 12

➤ \mediaplayer: A folder that contains mediaplayer.xlsm (a workbook that demonstrates the Media Player control), plus several MP3 audio files

➤ change userform size.xlsm: A workbook that demonstrates how to use VBA to change the size of a UserForm

➤ date and time picker.xlsm: A workbook that demonstrates the use of the Date and Time Picker control

➤ listbox activate sheet.xlsm: A workbook that demonstrates how to allow a user to select a sheet by using a ListBox control

➤ listbox fill.xlsm: A workbook that demonstrates how to fill a ListBox control in a UserForm

➤ listbox item transfer.xlsm: A workbook that demonstrates how to transfer items between two ListBox controls

➤ listbox move items.xlsm: A workbook that demonstrates how to allow the user to change the order of items in a ListBox control

➤ listbox multicolumn1.xlsm: A workbook that demonstrates a range-based multicolumn ListBox control

➤ listbox multicolumn2.xlsm: A workbook that demonstrates an array-based multicolumn ListBox control

➤ listbox multiple lists.xlsm: A workbook that demonstrates how to display multiple lists in a single ListBox control

➤ listbox select rows.xlsm: A workbook that demonstrates how to allow a user to select worksheet rows by using a ListBox control

➤ listbox selected items.xlsm: A workbook that demonstrates how to identify the selected item(s) in a ListBox

➤ listbox unique items1.xlsm: A workbook that demonstrates how to fill a ListBox control with unduplicated items

➤ listbox unique items2.xlsm: A variation of the listbox unique items1.xlsm example that also sorts the items

➤ multipage control demo.xlsm: A workbook that demonstrates the MultiPage control in a UserForm

➤ queryclose demo.xlsm: A workbook that demonstrates how to prevent a user from closing a UserForm by clicking its Close button in the title bar

➤ random number generator.xlsm: A workbook that demonstrates how to program simple animation in a UserForm

➤ range selection demo.xlsm: A workbook that demonstrates the RefEdit control in a UserForm

➤ splash screen.xlsm: A workbook that demonstrates how to use a UserForm as a splash screen that displays when a workbook is opened

➤ userform menus.xlsm: A workbook that demonstrates how to use a UserForm to display a menu of macros

➤ zoom and scroll sheet.xlsm: A workbook that demonstrates how to zoom and scroll a worksheet while a UserForm is displayed

➤ zoom userform.xlsm: A workbook that demonstrates how to allow the user to change the size of a UserForm

Chapter 13

➤ \dataform: A folder that contains the Enhanced Data Form add-in created by the author

➤ chart in userform.xlsm: A workbook that demonstrates how to display a chart in a UserForm

➤ emulate task pane.xlsm: A workbook that demonstrates how to make a UserForm resemble an Excel 2013 task pane

➤ excel light-box.xlsm: A workbook that demonstrates how to darken the Excel window while a UserForm is displayed

➤ getacolor function.xlsm: A workbook that contains a function that allows the user to select a color by using controls on a UserForm

➤ modeless SDI.xlsm: A workbook that demonstrates how to display a modeless userform that stays on top of the active window

➤ modeless userform1.xlsm: A workbook that demonstrates how to display a modeless UserForm to display information about the active cell

➤ modeless userform2.xlsm: A more sophisticated version of modeless userform1.xlsm

➤ move controls.xlsm: A workbook that demonstrates how to allow the user to move controls on a UserForm

➤ msgbox emulation.xlsm: A workbook that contains macros that simulate the VBA MsgBox function

➤ multiple buttons.xlsm: A workbook that demonstrates how to use a class module to allow a single procedure to handle events for multiple controls on a UserForm

➤ no title bar.xlsm: A workbook that uses API functions to display a UserForm without a title bar

➤ progress indicator1.xlsm: A workbook that displays a progress indicator in a UserForm

➤ progress indicator2.xlsm: A workbook that uses a MultiPage control to display a progress indicator in a UserForm

➤ progress indicator3.xlsm: A workbook that displays a progress indicator in a UserForm by changing the size of the UserForm

➤ resizable userform.xlsm: A workbook that demonstrates a UserForm that's resizable by the user

➤ semitransparent userform.xlsm: A workbook that demonstrates how to display a semitransparent UserForm

➤ simulated toolbar.xlsm: A workbook that uses a UserForm to simulate a toolbar

➤ sliding tile puzzle.xlsm: A workbook that contains a UserForm with a sliding tile puzzle

➤ splash screen2.xlsm: The splash screen.xlsm example from Chapter 12, with a UserForm that doesn't have a title bar

➤ video poker.xlsm: A workbook that displays a video poker game in a UserForm

➤ wizard demo.xlsm: A workbook that uses a MultiPage control to display a simple wizard UserForm

Chapter 14

➤ \text tools help source: A folder that contains the source files used to create the texttools.chm help file

➤ simple undo demo.xlsm: A workbook that demonstrates a method to undo the effects of a VBA macro

➤ text tools.xlam: An add-in that adds text manipulation features to Excel

➤ text tools.chm: The help file for text tools.xlam

Chapter 15

➤ budget pivot table.xlsm: A workbook that contains data suitable for a pivot table

➤ normalized data.xlsx: A workbook that shows the difference between normalized data and summarized data

➤ reverse pivot table.xlsm: A workbook that contains a macro that converts a summary table into a three-column data table

➤ simple pivot table.xlsm: A workbook that contains data suitable for a pivot table

➤ survey data pivot tables.xlsm: A workbook that contains a macro to generate 28 pivot tables from a range of data

Chapter 16

➤ animated charts.xlsm: A workbook that demonstrates how to use VBA to animate charts

➤ chart active cell.xlsm: A workbook that contains a macro that displays a chart that uses data based on the active cell position

➤ chart image map.xlsm: A workbook that uses chart events to create a simple clickable image map

➤ chart in userform.xlsm: A workbook that displays a chart in a UserForm, using the data based on the active cell position

➤ climate data.xlsx: An interactive chart application that uses no macros

➤ data labels.xlsm: A workbook that contains a macro that applies chart data labels that are stored in a range

➤ events - chart sheet.xlsm: A workbook that demonstrates events for a chart on a chart sheet

➤ events - embedded chart.xlsm: A workbook that demonstrates events for an embedded chart

➤ export all graphics.xlsm: A workbook that contains a macro that exports all graphic objects in a workbook

➤ format all charts.xlsm: A workbook that contains a macro that changes the formatting of all charts on a worksheet

➤ get series ranges.xlsm: A workbook that contains functions that identify the ranges used in a chart

➤ hide and unhide series.xlsm: A workbook that contains check boxes that allow a user to indicate which chart series to display

➤ hypocycloid - animated.xlsm: A workbook that includes macros to display an animated hypocycloid chart

➤ mouseover event - chart sheet.xlsm: A workbook that demonstrates the MouseOver event for a chart sheet

➤ mouseover event - embedded.xlsm: A workbook that demonstrates the MouseOver event for an embedded chart

➤ PUP chart data labeler.xlsm: The chart data labeling utility from the author's Power Utility Pak add-in

➤ scrolling chart.xlsm: A workbook that demonstrates how to create an animated scrolling chart

➤ size and align charts.xlsm: A workbook that contains a macro that sizes and aligns all charts on a worksheet

➤ sparkline report.xlsm: A workbook that generates a report that describes Sparkline graphics on a worksheet

➤ unlinked chart.xlsm: A workbook that contains macros that demonstrate two ways to unlink a chart from its source data

➤ vba clock chart.xlsm: A workbook that displays a chart that resembles an analog clock

Chapter 17

- ➤ application event tracker.xlsm: A workbook that demonstrates how to monitor application-level events

- ➤ hide columns before printing.xlsm: A workbook that uses an event both to hide columns before printing and to unhide the columns after printing

- ➤ log workbook open.xlsm: A workbook that demonstrates how to keep track of every workbook that is opened by using a class module

- ➤ make formulas bold.xlsm: A workbook that demonstrates the Worksheet Change event

- ➤ no shortcut menus.xlsm: A workbook that uses the Workbook_Open event to disable shortcut keys and the Workbook_BeforeClose event to re-enable shortcut keys

- ➤ onkey event demo.xlsm: A workbook that demonstrates the OnKey event

- ➤ ontime event demo.xlsm: A workbook that demonstrates the OnTime event

- ➤ shade active row and column.xlsm: A workbook that uses the Worksheet SelectionChange event to apply shading to the row and column of the active cell

- ➤ validate entry1.xlsm: A workbook that demonstrates how to validate data entered into a cell by using VBA (uses the EnableEvents property)

- ➤ validate entry2.xlsm: A workbook that demonstrates how to validate data entered into a cell by using VBA (uses a static variable)

- ➤ validate entry3.xlsm: A workbook that demonstrates how to validate data by using Excel's data validation feature — and ensuring that the data validation conditions do not get erased

- ➤ workbook_beforeclose workaround.xlsm: A workbook that demonstrates how to overcome a problem with the Workbook BeforeClose event

Chapter 18

- ➤ \automate excel: A folder that contains a Word document with macros that automate Excel

- ➤ \shellexecute: A folder that contains a workbook that demonstrates the ShellExecute API function (shellexecute examples.xlsm), plus a few ancillary files

- ➤ control panel dialogs.xlsm: A workbook that contains macros that display Windows Control Panel dialog boxes

- ➤ make memos.xlsm: A workbook that automates Word and creates a customized memo

- ➤ personalized email - outlook.xlsm: A workbook that contains a macro to send personalized e-mail via Outlook (using early binding)

➤ personalized email - outlook (late binding).xlsm: A workbook that contains a macro to send personalized e-mail via Outlook (using late binding)

➤ send pdf via outlook.xlsm: A workbook that contains a macro that sends e-mail with a PDF file attachment using Outlook

➤ start calculator.xlsm: A workbook that contains a macro that launches the Calculator application

Chapter 19

➤ \export charts help source: A folder that contains the source files that were used to create the export charts.chm help file

➤ check addin.xlam: A workbook that contains code to ensure that an add-in is installed properly

➤ export charts.chm: The help file for the export charts.xlsm workbook

➤ export charts.xlsm: The Export Charts Utility workbook, which can be converted to an add-in

➤ list add-in information.xlsm: A workbook that contains a macro that lists information about all add-ins

Chapter 20

➤ dynamicmenu.xlsm: A workbook that demonstrates the dynamicMenu control

➤ mso image browser.xlsm: A workbook that contains a macro that displays the images associated with Ribbon commands

➤ old-style toolbar.xlsm: A workbook that demonstrates how to create a toolbar, used in previous versions of Excel

➤ page break display.xlsm: The workbook file used to create the page break display add-in.xlam add-in

➤ page break display add-in.xlam: An add-in that adds a useful control to Excel's Ribbon

➤ ribbon control names.xlsx: A workbook that contains the names of all Excel 2010 and Excel 2013 Ribbon controls

➤ ribbon controls demo.xlsm: A workbook that demonstrates several types of Ribbon controls

➤ ribbon modification.xlsm: A workbook that contains a simple example that modifies Excel's Ribbon

Chapter 21

➤ add to cell shortcut.xlsm: A workbook that contains a macro that adds a new menu item to a shortcut menu

➤ context-sensitive shortcut menu.xlsm: A workbook that contains a macro that creates a new shortcut menu that's context-sensitive

➤ make xl 2003 menus.xlsm: A workbook that contains a macro that adds a toolbar that mimics the Excel 2003 menu

➤ reset all shortcut menus.xlsm: A workbook that contains a macro to reset all shortcut menus

➤ shortcut with submenu.xlsm: A workbook that contains a macro that adds new menu and submenu items to a shortcut menu

➤ show faceids.xlsm: A workbook that contains a macro that displays FaceId images

➤ show shortcut menu items.xlsm: A workbook that contains a macro that lists all menu items on all shortcut menus

➤ show shortcut menu names.xlsm: A workbook that contains a macro that lists the names of all shortcut menus

Chapter 22

➤ \cell comments: A folder that contains a workbook that demonstrates using cell comments to display help information

➤ \function help: A folder that contains a workbook that demonstrates how to display help for custom VBA worksheet functions

➤ \html help: A folder that contains files that demonstrate using compiled HTML help

➤ \mhtml file: A folder that contains files that demonstrate using an MHTML file to display help information in Internet Explorer

➤ \textbox: A folder that contains a workbook that demonstrates using a text box to display help information

➤ \userform1: A folder that contains a workbook that demonstrates using a UserForm with a SpinButton control to display help information

➤ \userform2: A folder that contains a workbook that demonstrates using a UserForm with a scrolling Label control to display help information

➤ \userform3: A folder that contains a workbook that demonstrates using a UserForm with a ComboBox control to display help information

➤ \web browser: A folder that contains files that demonstrate using a UserForm to display help information

➤ \worksheet: A folder that contains a file that demonstrates using a worksheet to display help information

Chapter 23

➤ loan amortization wizard.xlam: An add-in used for the Loan Amortization Wizard example

Chapter 24

➤ multilingual wizard.xlsm: A workbook used for the Multilingual Wizard example

Chapter 25

➤ \filter text file: A folder that contains files used to import selected information from a text file

➤ \simple ADO 1: A folder that contains an example of using ADO to query an Access file

➤ \simple ADO 2: A folder that contains an example of using ADO to query a CSV text file

➤ create file list.xlsm: A workbook that contains a macro that creates a list of files contained in a folder

➤ excel usage log.xlsm: A workbook that contains event-handler macros to store the times files are opened and closed

➤ export and import csv.xlsm: A workbook that contains macros that export and import a CSV file

➤ export to HTML.xlsm: A workbook that contains a macro that exports worksheet data to an HTML file

➤ export to XML.xlsm: A workbook that contains a macro that exports worksheet data to an XML file

➤ file functions.xlsm: A workbook that contains the FileExists and PathExists functions

➤ file information.xlsm: A workbook that contains a macro that creates a list of files and extended file information

➤ recursive file list.xlsm: A workbook that contains a macro that creates a list of files contained in a folder, including all subfolders

➤ show drive info.xlsm: A workbook that contains a macro that displays information about all disk drives

➤ unzip a file.xlsm: A workbook that contains a macro that unzips a file

➤ zip files.xlsm: A workbook that contains a macro that zips files

Chapter 26

➤ \update user workbook: A folder that contains a workbook that demonstrates a macro that replaces a VBA module with a new module

➤ add 100 buttons.xlsm: A workbook that contains a macro that adds 100 CommandButton controls and code to a UserForm at design time

➤ add button and code.xlsm: A workbook that contains both a macro that adds a button to a worksheet and VBA code that is executed when the button is clicked

➤ check security.xlsm: A workbook that contains a macro that informs the user if access to the VBA project object model is allowed

➤ create userform on the fly.xlsm: A workbook that contains a macro that creates a UserForm

➤ getoption function.xlsm: A workbook that contains a function that creates a UserForm (with OptionButton controls) on the fly and returns a value that corresponds to the user's choice

➤ list all procedures.xlsm: A workbook that contains a macro that lists all VBA procedures in a workbook

➤ list VB components.xlsm: A workbook that contains a macro that lists all VB components in a workbook

Chapter 27

➤ csv class.xlsm: A workbook that makes it easy to import and export a CSV file

➤ keyboard class.xlsm: A workbook that contains a class module that defines a NumLock, a CapsLock, and a ScrollLock class

Chapter 28

➤ chart colors.xlsm: A workbook that contains macros that work with chart colors

➤ color conversion functions.xlsm: A workbook that contains functions that convert between various color systems

➤ document theme demo.xlsx: A workbook that contains various elements that demonstrate the effects of applying a different theme

➤ generate theme colors.xlsm: A workbook that contains a macro that demonstrates theme colors

➤ get a color function.xlsm: A workbook that demonstrates an easy way to let a user choose a color

➤ matching colors.xlsm: A workbook that contains macros to match a cell's color to a shape and vice versa

➤ rgb color demo.xlsm: A workbook that contains an interactive demonstration of the RGB color system

➤ tintandshade demo.xlsm: A workbook that demonstrates how the TintAndShade property works

▶ Index

More great Excel guides from Mr. Spreadsheet!

Need to know more about Excel? John Walkenbach has it covered.

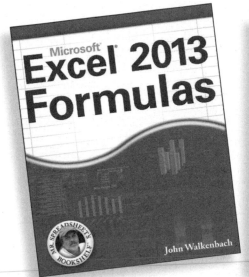

978-1-118-49044-0

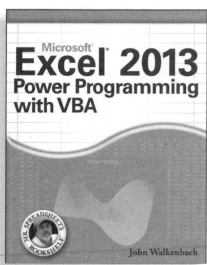

978-1-118-49039-6

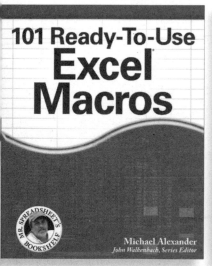

978-1-118-28121-5

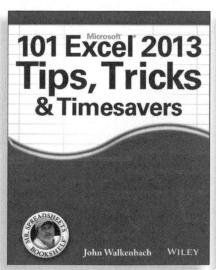

978-1-118-64218-4

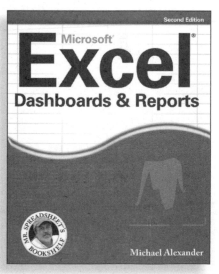

978-1-118-49042-6

 Available in print and e-book formats.

WILEY

Special Offer: Save $30.00!

Power Utility Pak v7

"The Excel tools Microsoft forgot"

A $40.00 value — yours for only $10.00

Pro-Quality Tools

PUP v7 is a handy collection of 60 general-purpose Excel utilities, plus 50 new worksheet functions. Download a trial version from the URL at the bottom of this page. If you like it, use this coupon to save $30 on the licensed version.

VBA Source Code Is Available

You can also get the complete VBA source files for only $20 more. Learn how the utilities and functions were written, and pick up useful tips and programming techniques in the process. These files are a must-have for all VBA programmers.

YES, I want Power Utility Pak v7

Name: _____

Company: _____

Address: _____

City: _____ State: _____ Zip: _____

Check one:

☐ PUP v7 Licensed Version $10.00

☐ Developer's Pak: Licensed version ($10) + VBA Source ($20.00) $30.00

Upon receipt of this coupon, you will receive download instructions via e-mail. Please make your e-mail address legible.

E-mail: _____

Credit Card: _____ Expires:_____

Make check or money order (U.S. funds only) payable to:

JWalk & Associates Inc.
P.O. Box 68797
Tucson, AZ 85737 (USA)

Download a free 30-day trial version of PUP from:

`http://spreadsheetpage.com`

PUP v7 is compatible *only* with Excel 2007 and later. For earlier versions of Excel, use PUP v6.